AMERICAN ERAS

THE
COLONIAL ERA
1 6 0 0 - 1 7 5 4

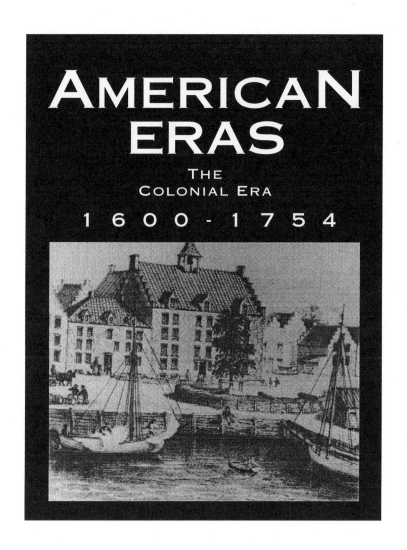

AMERICAN
ERAS

THE
COLONIAL ERA
1 6 0 0 - 1 7 5 4

EDITED BY
JESSICA KROSS

A MANLY, INC. BOOK

AMERICAN ERAS

1600-1754

Matthew J. Bruccoli and Richard Layman, Editorial Directors
Karen L. Rood, Senior Editor

ADVISORY BOARD

LIBRARY OF CONGRESS CATALOGING-IN-PUBLICATION DATA

American eras, 1600–1754: the colonial era / edited by Jessica Kross.
        p. cm.
    ISBN 0–7876–1479–3 (alk. paper)
    1. United States—Civilization—To 1783. I. Kross, Jessica.
E162.A5144 1997   97–31404
973.2—dc21   CIP

CONTENTS

INTRODUCTION

Old World Background. The Europeans and Africans who came to the New World brought with them ideas and attitudes about religion, society, gender, race, and power. Europeans self-consciously tried to model their new societies after what they had known before, attempting to re-create the Old World as faithfully as possible while simultaneously trying to avoid what they considered to be the evils they had left behind. Europeans also brought with them an international context—a relationship between nations—that structured how they felt about one another and what their attitudes and behaviors would be once they got there. Rivalries among the Spanish, Dutch, French, and English that embroiled them in competitive trade and outright warfare in Europe played themselves out in America as well. Major conflicts after 1689 had American theaters that often involved Native Americans on both sides. Wars were not the only institutions that entwined the fates of those on both sides of the Atlantic. While it is tempting to think that the colonies severed all ties with their mother countries, such was not the case, nor would the settlers have found such a scenario appealing. As European nations evolved in the seventeenth and eighteenth centuries through increased trade and Enlightenment thought, so did their overseas settlements. Increasing economic ties with Britain made English colonists feel like they were a part of the mother country and strengthened their sense of themselves as "Englishmen," entitled to all the rights and privileges that such an identity conveyed. Africans shared a different experience. Brought to America in small groups or as isolated individuals, they had a much more difficult time re-creating Old World ways. The antipathy of whites and the demands of slave labor left blacks with few resources. What they were able to salvage was their religious beliefs as well as forms of music and dance.

Native Americans. Aggressive European colonization made America as much a new world for Native Americans as it was for Europeans and Africans. But while America proved to be a land of opportunity for many Europeans, it became a much more difficult and problematic place for Indians. The earliest Europeans enslaved many of the Native Americans whom they first encountered in the West Indies and Latin America. European diseases decimated many native populations, leading to the overthrow of the great civilizations of Mexico and Peru and the disruption of life in most places along the eastern seaboard. Once-independent groups found themselves with too few members to continue and either died out entirely or joined with others in similar circumstances to produce hybrid societies such as the Delaware and the Catawba. European demands for Indian trade goods introduced new products such as wool blankets, guns, and alcohol into traditional cultures, undermining the basic social structure in areas ranging from relationships with nature to the selection of political leaders. European demand for furs and deerskins caused overhunting, which changed the ecology of coastal regions and brought about warfare between the Indians along the coast and those further inland who still had access to animals. European desire for land either pushed native groups from their home territories or marginalized those who stayed behind. European conflicts brought Native American warriors into battles not only with each other but also with Europeans, changing both the underlying meaning of warfare (from a rite of passage or a means of relieving internal tensions to an impersonal slaughter) and its practice (from raids, in which the goal was to capture a few of the enemy while sustaining no losses, to full-scale destruction of enemy villages with major casualties).

Diversity of Motives. Europeans who came to the New World did so for a variety of reasons. The Spanish ostensibly traveled to America for "God, glory, and gold." Ordinary Spaniards who migrated to the borderlands—the Southwest and Florida—sought financial rewards. The same can be said for the French in Illinois or Louisiana. Neither Spaniards nor Frenchmen came to America in any great number, and those intrepid colonists who ended up in the borderlands often came from either Mexico, in the case of the Spanish, or Canada, in the case of the French. These early colonists were often entrepreneurs, and at some point all the nationalities in America used private companies as the vehicle to establish colonies. None found that it worked. New Netherland was planted by the Dutch West India Company in the hope of monopolizing the fur trade. Those they enticed to America came from all over northern Europe. But the settlers had no loyalty to the company and became farmers and often part-time fur traders, especially around Fort Orange (Albany). They came to better their lives. The first English colonies were also underwritten by joint-stock companies. Virginia was settled by indentured servants who hoped one day to become small-time landowners. Others had more-ideological motives. Plymouth drew religious dissidents whose main goal was freedom of worship for themselves (but not others) and an economic sufficiency that they could pass on to their children. Religious and economic motives were not antithetical—both existed at the same time in the same people. Religious toleration drew Quakers, Germans, and even some Roman Catholics and Jews. Economic opportunity made coming to America a viable choice.

Labor Needs. The New World offered an abundance of land but limited labor, the opposite of conditions in Europe. The question, then, was how to exploit the land. Initially Europeans tried using Native Americans, but for various reasons this solution did not work. By the early 1500s the Spaniards were bringing in African slaves to work plantations in the West Indies. Those regions which offered a tropical or semitropical climate lent themselves to plantation-style agriculture. In British North America the first colony, Virginia, fit this description, and the Virginia Company quickly found a staple crop in tobacco. Initially Virginia attracted young, white, male indentured servants from England and a few female servants to serve as domestics. Unfortunately mismanagement and then disease plagued Virginia and its sister colony, Maryland, and as economic conditions improved in England and the Chesapeake's reputation as a death trap spread, white labor became increasingly difficult to find. After the Restoration of Charles II in 1660 more colonial settlements gave European settlers greater choice, further narrowing the pool of white laborers willing to come to the Chesapeake. At the same time, African laborers became more available and cheaper as the slave trade grew. Blacks first appeared in Virginia in 1619, but slavery as an institution did not take shape until after midcentury. Africans were unwilling migrants to the New World, kidnapped or captured from their homes in West Africa and shipped to America as part of an international business. The discovery of rice as a profitable crop in the Carolinas and African immunity to malaria ensured that slavery would spread south along the eastern seaboard. Georgia modeled its economy after that of South Carolina's.

North. Labor needs in the North were different. In New England most labor was provided by the sons and daughters of the settlers. Such a native-born labor supply was possible because New England as a whole was healthier than the South, and both parents and children lived longer. Relying on local labor was a necessity since there was little immigration into New England after 1640. The Middle Colonies had more immigrants and slaves, but labor there also centered on family farms and urban occupations. Immigrants from Europe found the Middle Colonies welcoming, Pennsylvania especially, and settled in ethnic enclaves where they grew crops for themselves and for export. There were no plantations north of southern Delaware.

Political Stability. During the seventeenth century there occurred experimentation in the ways that colonies were administered. The joint-stock companies tried to get by with minimal political representation but found that colonies were difficult to govern when their adult males were excluded from the political process. In 1619 the Virginia Company created the House of Burgesses, the first representative assembly in North America. In New England the authorities quickly found that they had to broaden the base of those who voted and those who held office. Colonies such as Maryland, New York, the Carolinas, and Pennsylvania all experimented with more-centralized authority in the hands of proprietors. All in the end had to admit defeat as locals refused to register land, pay rent, or raise taxes. The principle of "no taxation without representation" was part of an Englishman's rights going back to the Magna Carta in the thirteenth century. It did not originate on the eve of the American Revolution. As joint-stock companies or proprietorships declined, the Crown took over their colonies. Royal colonies came to have similar governmental structures: a Crown-appointed governor and council and an elected assembly. The proprietary colonies that survived also had governors and elected assemblies. By 1700 the worst of the political strife within most of the colonies had ended. The factionalism in the Carolinas, however, did not stop until royal control in 1729. What emerged was an overall political stability in which the assemblies developed ways both to work with councils and governors and to prevent infighting. Their control over revenue bills gave them the ability to negotiate with royal officials on terms that favored the colonies.

Religion. Religious toleration in the colonies resulted from both ethical and economic considerations. Maryland was founded as a haven for Roman Catholics, and its 1649 Act of Toleration was passed to protect them from the Protestant majority. Roger Williams opened up Rhode Island to people of many faiths because he did not believe in state religions. He believed state interference would inhibit spiritual growth. Quaker investors in western New Jersey were looking for a place where Quakers could practice their religion in peace. So was William Penn when he petitioned the Crown for land in exchange for a debt due his family. Others had more worldly motives. The need for capital or labor brought about a toleration of others that might not have happened without it. Peter Stuyvesant was forced to admit Jews to New Amsterdam because the Dutch West India Company had Jewish investors. The duke of York in New York and New Jersey and the Carolina proprietors understood that by opening their lands to people of many persuasions they could attract the settlers who made profits possible. Massachusetts was forced to abandon its narrow religious policies on an edict from the Crown once it lost its charter and became a royal colony in the 1680s. England itself was becoming more accepting of religious diversity. Many of those who came to America, such as the French Huguenots, Jews, and some German Pietist sects, escaped first to England, where many of their members stayed. The Enlightenment, which opened up people's thinking about science and the world, brought a generosity of spirit not only to Europe but also to parts of America. Religious toleration made ethical, economic, and philosophic sense to many people.

Ethnic Diversity. The need for labor not only fostered religious diversity but also created an acceptance of ethnic pluralism. The colonists in New Netherland were really a mixture of peoples from the Netherlands and from various German states, Belgium, Sweden, Norway, France, England, and even Croatia. There were also African slaves from several places along the West African coast and Madagascar. New England and the early Chesapeake drew their populations mainly from England. After 1660 the Chesapeake began bringing in Africans from the whole African coast—Senegambia to the Congo. The conquest of New Netherland opened the region to those from England and Scotland. William Penn advertised his new colony in Germany and other parts of Europe, including Wales. In the eighteenth century Pennsylvania would attract Germans, Scots, and Scotch-Irish. As colonists pushed west and then south down the Shenandoah Valley, Germans, Scots, and Scotch-Irish settled in western Maryland and North and South Carolina. Georgia drew Germans and Swiss. The Carolinas and Georgia eventually also brought in large numbers of Africans—South Carolina had a black majority in the first decade of the 1700s and never lost it during the colonial period.

Emotion and Rationality. It is tempting to think of the colonists as isolated, emotionally deprived, and pragmatic, but to do so would be to ignore the richness of their inner lives. Religion played a large part in the way seventeenth- and eighteenth-century people thought about themselves and the world. Puritan belief in predestination and a righteous God sent them to their Bibles, which in turn fostered literacy. It suggested to them ways of ordering their societies and their families, which stressed control but also allowed them emotional attachments to their spouses and families. Anglicans were more at ease with themselves and the Deity. In their eyes God did not prejudge and allowed humans to do good work in this life and enjoy heaven in the next. Quakers believed that God dwelt in all humans if they could only see him. The great religious upheavals of the eighteenth century that united America with the British Isles opened people to their own emotional natures. The revivals known collectively as the Great Awakening brought people face to face with their longing for union with God. In the process they split their old churches and challenged author-

ity. Coincident with an international outpouring of emotion were the ideas emanating from Europe and England known as the Enlightenment. Rationality was the key to understanding the universe and the meaning of life, according to many thinkers who embraced the science of Sir Isaac Newton and the psychology of John Locke. Both camps came to realize that literacy and education were important. Both were proud to be part of an international community (including women) that spoke a common language and shared common goals. Far from being cut off, the colonists became more integrated into a world of both religious and secular ideas.

Anglicization. While Europeans and Africans of various nationalities settled in British America, the dominant culture was British. The first colonists had no reason to question their nationality or their ties to the mother country, but as the founding generation passed they were replaced not only by new immigrants but also by those born in America. Many second-, third-, and fourth-generation Americans had never been to England even though they considered themselves English. Several forces came together in the eighteenth century to bring Americans culturally closer to England and to reinforce their sense of British identity. English governors and bureaucrats, army officers, and educated immigrants provided models from the old country. Rising incomes in the cities, in the hinterlands that supplied the grains and cattle exported to the West Indies and southern Europe, and on Southern plantations created surpluses available to fuel demand for consumer goods and services. Newspapers, which began publishing in the eighteenth century, publicized what the latest styles were and where to purchase them. Packet boats made regularly scheduled trips between Northern port cities and England, facilitating correspondence and the exchange of both religious and secular ideas. Books on architecture and furniture gave wealthy colonists models for their mansions. Merchants imported the "latest fashions" in rugs, wallpapers, mirrors, glassware, ceramics, and silverware. By the 1740s a best-selling London novel was available to a colonial audience within a few months. Theater troupes found an increasingly sophisticated clientele, as did music, dancing, painting, and even fencing masters. By 1754, just before the start of the French and Indian War, which changed the colonists' relationship to England, free white Americans were relatively pleased with themselves. Most were well fed, moderately comfortable by eighteenth-century standards, lightly taxed by their own representatives, literate, and able to enjoy at least a few of the better things in life. Slaves, Native Americans, and the really poor were not privy to this bounty. For some life would get worse after 1754. The French and Indian War deprived Native Americans of an ally once the French were defeated and left North America. The depression following the conflict increased the number of poor, especially in the cities, which also began to look, just a little, like their European counterparts.

ACKNOWLEDGMENTS

This book was produced by Manly, Inc. Anthony J. Scotti and Karen L. Rood were the in-house editors.

Production manager is Samuel W. Bruce.

Office manager is Kathy Lawler Merlette.

Administrative support was provided by Ann M. Cheschi and Brenda A. Gillie. Bookkeeper is Joyce Fowler.

Copyediting supervisor is Jeff Miller. The copyediting staff includes Phyllis A. Avant, Patricia Coate, Christine Copeland, Thom Harman, and William L. Thomas Jr.

Editorial associates are L. Kay Webster and Mark McEwan.

Layout and graphics supervisor is Janet E. Hill.

Photography editors are Margaret Meriwether and Paul Talbot. Photographic copy work was performed by Joseph M. Bruccoli.

Systems manager is Marie L. Parker.

Typesetting supervisor is Kathleen M. Flanagan. The typesetting staff includes Pamela D. Norton and Patricia Flanagan Salisbury.

Walter W. Ross, Steven Gross, and Ron Aiken did library research. They were assisted by the following librarians at the Thomas Cooper Library of the University of South Carolina: Linda Holderfield and the interlibrary-loan staff; reference-department head Virginia Weathers; reference librarians Marilee Birchfield, Stefanie Buck, Stefanie DuBose, Rebecca Feind, Karen Joseph, Donna Lehman, Charlene Loope, Anthony McKissick, Jean Rhyne, Kwamine Simpson, and Virginia Weathers; circulation-department head Caroline Taylor; and acquisitions-searching supervisor David Haggard.

AMERICAN ERAS

THE
COLONIAL ERA
1 6 0 0 - 1 7 5 4

WORLD EVENTS:

SELECTED OCCURRENCES OUTSIDE NORTH AMERICA

MAJOR POWERS AND LEADERS

China—Wan-li (1572–1620), T'ai-ch'ang (1620), T'ien-ch'i (1620–27), Ch'ung-chen (1627–44), Shun Chih (1644–61), K'ang-hsi (1661–1722), Yung Cheng (1723–35), Ch'ien Lung (1735–96).

England—Elizabeth I (1558–1603); James I (1603–25); Charles I (1625–49); The Commonwealth (1649–60), Lords Protector: Oliver Cromwell (1653–58), Richard Cromwell (1658–59); Charles II (1660–85); James II (1685–88); The Interregnum (1688); William III (1689–1702) and Mary II (1689–94); Anne (1702–14); George I (1714–27); George II (1727–60).

France—Henry IV (1580–1610), Louis XIII (1610–43), Louis XIV (1643–1715), Louis XV (1715–74).

Holland—Maurice (1584–1625); Frederick Henry (1625–47); William II (1647–50); States-General (1652–72); William III (1672–1702), who was also William III of England (1689–1702); States-General (1702–47); William IV (1748–51); William V (1751–95).

Holy Roman Empire—Rudolf II (1576–1612); Matthias (1612–19); Ferdinand II (1619–37); Ferdinand III (1637–57); Leopold I (1658–1705); Joseph I (1705–11); Charles VI (1711–40); two claimants: Maria Theresa (1740–45) and Charles VII (1742–45), Francis I (1745–65).

Japan—Tokugawa Ieyasu (1603–05), Tokugawa Hidetada (1605–23), Tokugawa Iemitsu (1623–51), Tokugawa Ietsuna (1651–80), Tokugawa Tsunayoshi (1680–1709), Tokugawa Ineobu (1709–12), Tokugawa Ietsugu (1712), Yoshimune (1716–45), Tokugawa Ieshige (1745–60).

Ottoman Empire—Mohammed III (1595–1603), Ahmed I (1603–17), Mustafa I (1617–18, 1622–23), Osman II (1618–22), Murad IV (1623–40), Ibrahim I (1640–48), Mohammed IV (1648–87), Suleiman II (1687–91), Ahmed II (1691–95), Mustapha II (1695–1703), Ahmed III (1703–30), Mahmud II (1730–54).

Poland—Sigismund III (1587–1632), Wladyslaw (1632–48), John II Casimir (1648–68), Michael Wisniowiecki (1669–73), John III Sobieski (1674–96), Augustus II (1697–1704, 1709–33), Stanislas Leszczynski (1704–09), Augustus III (1734–63).

Portugal—Philip II (1598–1621), who was also Philip III of Spain (1598–1621); Philip III (1621–40), who was also Philip IV of Spain (1621–65); John IV (1640–56); Afonso VI (1656–67); Peter II (1667–1706); John V (1706–50); José (1750–77).

Prussia—Frederick I (1701–03), Frederick William I (1713–40), Frederick II (1740–86).

Russia—Boris Godunov (1598–1605), Theodore II (1605), Basil Shuisky (1606–10), Michael (1613–45), Alexis I (1645–76), Theodore III (1676–82), Ivan V (1682–89) and Peter I (1682–1725), Catherine I (1725–27), Peter II (1727–30), Anna (1730–40), Ivan VI (1740–41), Elizabeth (1741–62).

Spain—Philip III (1598–1621), who was also Philip II of Portugal (1598–1621); Philip IV (1621–65), who as also Philip III of Portugal (1621–40); Charles II (1665–1700); Philip V (1700–24, 1725–46); Louis I (1724–25); Ferdinand VI (1746–59).

Sweden—Sigismund (1592–1604), Charles IX (1604–11), Gustavus II Adolphus (1611–32), Christina (1632–54), Charles X Gustavus (1654–60), Charles XI (1660–97), Charles XII (1697–1718), Ulrica Eleanora (1718–20), Frederick (1720–51), Adolphus Frederick (1751–71).

MAJOR CONFLICTS

1618–1648—Thirty Years' War
1642–1646—First English Civil War
1648— Second English Civil War
1652–1654—First Anglo-Dutch War
1664–1667—Second Anglo-Dutch War
1667–1668—War of Devolution
1676–1681—First Russo-Turkish War
1688–1697—War of the League of Augsburg
1695–1696—Second Russo-Turkish War
1700–1721—Great Northern War
1701–1713—War of the Spanish Succession
1710–1711—Third Russo-Turkish War
1733–1738—War of the Polish Succession
1736–1739—Fourth Russo-Turkish War
1740–1748—War of the Austrian Succession

1600

- Merchants in London found the English East India Company to challenge the Dutch spice trade in the East Indies.

- Having been granted a monopoly on the North American fur trade, Frenchmen Pierre Chauvin; François Gravé, Sieur de Pontgravé; and Pierre du Guast, Sieur de Monts, try unsuccessfully to establish a colony at Tadoussac on the lower Saint Lawrence River at the mouth of the Saguenay River.

- *Cynthia's Revels,* a play by Ben Jonson, is performed in London.

- William Gilbert, an English physician and physicist, writes *De Magnete, Magneticisique Corporibus,* a pioneering treatise on electricity.

- The popular New World plant tobacco sells in London for a price equal to its weight in silver shillings.

- At about this time Dutch lens grinders begin making the refracting telescope and the compound microscope.

17 Feb. Italian philosopher Giordano Bruno is burned at the stake in Rome for advocating the Copernican theory that the planets revolve around the sun and for suggesting that there may be other worlds with other absolute deities.

1601

- *Twelfth Night,* a play by William Shakespeare, is performed in London.

- The English Act for the Relief of the Poor makes local parishes responsible for levying local taxes to provide for the needy and establishes residence requirements to prevent poor people from flocking to wealthy parishes.

- English adventurer John Smith is captured by the Turks and sold into slavery.

25 Feb. Robert Devereux, second Earl of Essex, a onetime favorite of Elizabeth I, is executed for plotting against the queen.

1602

- An English East India Company fleet commanded by James Lancaster defeats a large Portuguese treasure galleon and loots its valuable cargo, trading some for pepper from Dutch merchants in Java.

- The Dutch East India Company doubles or nearly triples European pepper prices.

1603

- Elizabeth I of England dies. James VI of Scotland succeeds her as James I of England.

- Sir Walter Raleigh is imprisoned in the Tower of London for his alleged part in a plot to depose James I in favor of his cousin Arabella Stuart.

- England makes an alliance with France.

- John Smith escapes from slavery in the Near East and returns to England.

- John Mildenhall of the English East India Company reaches India and presents himself to the Great Mogul Akbar seeking trade privileges for England.

- James Lancaster's English East India Company fleet returns to Great Britain with more than a million pounds of pepper.
- Johann Bayer compiles the first celestial atlas that uses Greek letters to indicate the brightest stars in the constellations.

1604

- *Othello*, a play by William Shakespeare, is performed in London.
- As part of a long-term attempt to regain control over the Netherlands, Spanish forces seize Ostend from the Dutch after a siege of three and one-half years.
- England signs a peace treaty with Spain.
- Samuel de Champlain establishes a French colony in Nova Scotia. It is abandoned in 1607.

Jan.   James I presides over the Hampton Court Conference between the Anglican bishops and the Puritans, who fail in their attempts to institute reforms in the Church of England. The king issues the Act of Uniformity requiring strict adherence to the tenets of the Anglican Church, banishes all Jesuits and Roman Catholic seminary priests from England, and appoints a commission headed by Lancelot Andrewes to make a new English translation of the Bible.

Spring   Part one of *The Honest Whore*, a play by Thomas Dekker and Thomas Middleton, is performed in London.

1605

Jan.   *The Masque of Blackness*, by Ben Jonson, is performed at Whitehall Palace in Westminster.

4 Nov.   Guy Fawkes is arrested during preparations to blow up the houses of Parliament while James I is presiding over the opening of Parliament on 5 November. The plot was originated by Robert Catesby, John Wright, and Thomas Winter in 1604 and eventually included many other English Catholics who were unhappy about renewed enforcement of laws requiring them to attend Anglican church services and placing severe penalties on saying Mass or assisting at it.

1606

- *Macbeth*, a play by William Shakespeare, is performed in London.
- James I of England grants the Virginia Charter, establishing the Plymouth Company and the London Company to found separate settlements in the New World.

Feb.–Mar.   *Volpone*, a play by Ben Jonson, is performed in London.

1607

- English peasants revolt against the enclosure of common grazing lands and other abuses by the landed gentry. The rebellion is suppressed by the forces of James I.
- Jesuits establish a settlement in Paraguay.

	Members of the Plymouth Company attempt to establish a settlement in Maine but abandon it after a harsh winter.
14 May	Members of the London Company found Jamestown, Virginia.

1608

- The *Hector* becomes the first English East India Company ship to land in India.
- Frederick IV, Elector Palatine of the Rhine, organizes the Protestant Union.
- English separatists, who later become known as the Pilgrims, leave England for religious freedom in Holland.

1609

- *Cymbeline,* a play by William Shakespeare, is performed in London.
- The Twelve Years' Truce ends fighting between the Spanish and Dutch, and Philip III of Spain recognizes the independence of the northern provinces of the Low Countries (Holland).
- Duke Maximilian of Bavaria organizes the Catholic League to oppose the Protestant Union.
- In his *Astronomia nova* Johannes Kepler explains his first two laws of planetary motion: that the planets move in elliptical paths around the sun and that the planets do not travel at uniform rates of speed.
- Galileo Galilei uses a telescope to view the Milky Way.
- Dutch merchants found a post in western Japan, ending the Portuguese monopoly on trade with that country.
- The city of Amsterdam founds a bank and issues coins made from South American silver. Its practice of weighing coins initiates the principle of public regulation of money, and the bank soon begins lending money at interest.

1610

- *An Anatomy of the World,* an elegy by English poet John Donne, is published in London.
- *The Alchemist,* a play by Ben Jonson, is performed in London.
- Galileo discovers the moons of Jupiter and publishes *Siderius nuncius,* arguing the validity of Copernicus's theory that the planets orbit the sun.
- Marie de Médicis removes from office Maximilien de Béthune, Duc de Sully, who has instituted reforms in taxation and improvements in agriculture and frontier defenses. Concino Concini, Marquis d'Ancre, increases his influence at court.

14 May	Henry IV is assassinated in Paris. He is succeeded by his nine-year-old son, Louis XIII, whose mother, Marie de Médicis, becomes his regent.

1611

- Lancelot Andrewes and fellow translators complete the King James, or Authorized, version of the Bible.

- After the failure of an uprising against England, Hugh O'Neill, Earl of Tyrone, flees to Rome, and the Plantation of Ulster in Northern Ireland is forfeited to the Crown.

- The University of Rome is founded.

- The University of Santo Tomas is founded at Manila in the Philippines.

9 Feb. James I of England dissolves Parliament.

15 May *The Winter's Tale,* a play by William Shakespeare, is performed in London.

30 Oct. Charles IX of Sweden dies. His sixteen-year-old son, who begins a twenty-one-year reign as Gustavus II Adolphus, signs a charter giving the council and estates a voice in legislation and veto power in matters of war and peace.

1 Nov. *The Tempest,* a play by Shakespeare, is performed in London.

1612

- *The Second Anniuersarie,* by English poet John Donne, is published in London.

- An enlarged edition of *Essays,* by English philosopher Francis Bacon, is published in London (first edition, 1597).

- After two English East India Company ships defeat four Portuguese galleons off the coast of India, Emperor Jahangir is impressed with their military skills and grants the British trading rights at Surat.

- The British establish a colony at Bermuda.

1613

- The English East India Company establishes its first trading post in India.

- The Dutch establish a fur-trading post at the southern tip of Manhattan Island.

22 July Michael Romanov becomes Russian emperor, establishing the Romanov dynasty.

1614

- *The Duchess of Malfi,* a play by John Webster, is published in London.

- Louis XIII is declared of age, but his mother continues to exert strong influence on the government of France.

- Armand Jean du Plessis, Duc de Richelieu, is elected to the Estates-General of France and engineers its dissolution. It does not meet again until 1789.

- Sweden takes Novgorod from the Russians.

- Scotsman John Napier introduces the system of arithmetical calculation that is the basis for the slide rule.

- Designed by the late Andrea Palladio, the Church of San Giorgio Maggiore is completed in Venice after fifty-five years of construction.

1615

5 Apr.　James I calls Parliament into session. After it argues with him over his finances, the king dissolves Parliament on 7 June. It becomes known as the "Addled Parliament" because it has passed no enactments.

- In the East Indies, Dutch forces take the Moluccas from the Portuguese, and a British fleet defeats a Portuguese armada off the coast of Bombay.

- Chocolate paste is imported from the Spanish colonies in the New World to Spain, Italy, and Flanders, introducing the practice of drinking chocolate.

1616

- The Vatican orders Galileo to stop defending the "heretical" notion that the planets orbit the sun.

- The English East India Company begins trade with Persia.

- James I of England begins selling peerages to replenish the royal treasury.

Nov.–Dec.　*The Devil Is an Ass,* a play by Ben Jonson, is performed in London.

1617

- Released from the Tower of London in 1616, Sir Walter Raleigh sails for the Orinoco in South America in an unsuccessful attempt to find a gold mine. Though he has agreed not to disturb Spanish settlements there, one of his men leads an expedition that attacks a Spanish town.

- Prime Minister Concino Concini of France, a favorite of Marie de Médicis, is arrested and assassinated.

1618

23 May　Angry over the closing of one of their churches and the destruction of another and upset because seven of the ten governors appointed to administer Bohemia are Catholic, the Protestant Count Matthias von Thurn leads a rebellion. Two of the governors are thrown from a window in the Palace of Prague into a ditch below, escaping with their lives. This "Defenestration of Prague" precipitates the Thirty Years' War. Fought mainly on German soil, it begins as a dispute between the German Protestant states and the Catholic forces of the Holy Roman Empire (Germany, Austria, Bohemia, Moravia, parts of northern Italy, present-day Belgium, the Netherlands, and Switzerland), but virtually all the states of Europe become involved in this long war of shifting alliances.

29 Oct.　As reparation to Spain for the attack in the Orinoco, Raleigh is executed in London.

1619

20 Mar.　Holy Roman Emperor Matthias dies and is succeeded by Ferdinand II, who has been deposed as king of Bohemia, where the Protestant Frederick V is now king.

1620

- In *Novum Organum* Sir Francis Bacon proposes inductive logic as a means of interpreting nature rather than the deductive method put forth by Aristotle. In his insistence that observation and experience are the sole source of knowledge, Bacon inaugurates the modern scientific method.

8 Nov. The forces of Frederick V are defeated at the Battle of the White Mountain. He flees to Holland. The leading rebels are executed, and Protestantism is wiped out in Bohemia. After the battle the Protestant Union is dissolved, and the seat of the war is moved to the Palatinate states of Germany.

11 Nov. The *Mayflower* arrives off the coast of Cape Cod, bearing the first group of Pilgrims. Discovering that Cape Cod is outside the jurisdiction of the London Company, which has granted them their charter, they decide to establish a settlement in Plymouth, Massachusetts.

1621

- *The Anatomy of Melancholy,* by English clergyman Robert Burton, is published in Oxford.

- The States-General of the Netherlands charters the Dutch West India Company.

- Pembroke College is founded at Oxford.

30 Jan. In need of funds to support British military efforts in the Thirty Years' War, James I of England calls the third Parliament of his reign, which impeaches Sir Francis Bacon, who has been lord chancellor since 1618, on charges of taking bribes. Bacon is found guilty, fined, and banned from holding future offices, but he is pardoned by James I, who also remits Bacon's fine.

31 Mar. Philip III of Spain dies and is succeeded by fifteen-year-old Philip IV, who allows his prime minister, Gaspar de Guzmán, Duque de Olivares, to conduct affairs of state. Olivares resumes the war with Holland that ended with the Twelve Years' Truce of 1609.

18 Dec. After James I rebukes the House of Commons for meddling in foreign affairs by protesting the proposed marriage of the Prince of Wales to a Spanish princess, Parliament issues the Great Protestation, declaring "That the liberties, franchises, privileges, and jurisdictions of parliament are the ancient and undoubted birthright and inheritance of the subjects of England, and that the arduous and urgent affairs concerning the king, state, and defense of the realm . . . Are proper subjects and the matter of council in debate in parliament."

1622

- Designed by architect Inigo Jones, the banqueting hall at Whitehall in London is completed.

8 Feb. James I tears the Great Protestation from the journal of the House of Commons and dissolves Parliament.

1623

- The first collected edition of William Shakespeare's plays (the First Folio) is published in London.

- After the failure of negotiations to arrange the marriage of Charles, Prince of Wales, and Maria, sister of Philip IV of Spain, Charles and Charles Villiers, first Duke of Buckingham, return to England in anger.

- The Dutch drive colonists of the English East India Company from the Spice Islands.

- The Dutch grant a formal charter to New Netherland, and some thirty families establish a permanent settlement on Manhattan Island.

Aug.   *The Bellman of Paris,* a play by Thomas Dekker and John Day, is performed in London.

1624

- Designed by Jacques Lemercier, the earliest section of the Louvre in Paris is completed as a palace for Louis XIII. The Palais de Luxembourg in Paris, designed by Salomon de Brosse, is completed as a residence for his mother, Marie de Médicis.

- A cardinal since 1622, Richelieu becomes the chief minister of Louis XIII and continues to dominate French government until his death in 1642.

- France and England agree to the marriage of Charles, Prince of Wales, and Henrietta Maria, sister of Louis XIII of France.

- England goes to war against Spain.

1625

- French settlers colonize the Caribbean island of St. Kitts.

- The British found the first colony on Barbados.

5 Mar.   James I of England dies and is succeeded by Charles I.

1 May   Charles I marries Henrietta Maria of France by proxy and receives her at Canterbury on 13 June.

18 June   Charles I calls the first Parliament of his reign.

12 Aug.   After Parliament limits appropriations for the war with Spain, in part because of anger over sending English troops to help Louis XIII put down a rebellion of Huguenots (Protestants) in France, Charles I dissolves Parliament.

8 Sept.   The English and Dutch sign the Treaty of Southampton, forming an alliance against Spain.

1626

6 Feb.   Charles I calls a second Parliament, which impeaches Buckingham for the embarrassing failure of his expedition against Cádiz in Spain in 1625.

15 June   Charles I dissolves Parliament to prevent the trial of his favorite Buckingham.

1627

- Cardinal Richelieu of France founds a company to colonize New France.

- Inigo Jones completes Queen's Chapel in St. James's Palace at Westminster.

- Louis XIII commissions Jacques Lemercier to design a château at Versailles.

- The French Huguenots rise again, and Richelieu personally supervises the Siege of La Rochelle, the Protestants' center of power.

1628

- English physician William Harvey publishes a treatise establishing that the heart is a muscle whose regular contractions cause the circulation of blood.

17 Mar. Charles I calls his third Parliament, which passes the Petition of Rights, prohibiting all forms of taxation without the consent of Parliament, the billeting of soldiers in private homes, the declaration of martial law in peacetime, and the imprisonment of an individual without a specific charge. The king agrees to the petition on 7 June.

23 Aug. After leading one unsuccessful mission to help the Huguenots at La Rochelle, Buckingham is assassinated on the eve of embarking on another expedition.

28 Oct. Despite the aid of three English fleets, La Rochelle falls, resulting in the complete subjugation of the French Huguenots.

1629

- The Massachusetts Bay Company is chartered in England.

- The Dutch West India Company grants Kiliaen van Rensselaer lands near Albany, New York.

- Pope Urban VIII appoints Giovanni Lorenzo Bernini to complete Saint Peter's Cathedral in Rome.

10 Mar. Charles I dissolves Parliament after members of the House of Commons oppose the king's continued levying of taxes without the consent of Parliament. Charles rules without Parliament until 1640.

1630

- Faced with the growing influence of Bishop William Laud, a favorite of Charles I and an absolutist in his advocacy of enforcing strict adherence to the Anglican Church, Puritans begin settling in New England in what becomes known as the "Great Migration."

- Having heard of atrocities committed by Gen. Albrecht von Wallenstein and his Catholic troops, Emperor Ferdinand II of the Holy Roman Empire consents to a decree dismissing Wallenstein and much of his army.

Apr. England and France make peace.

July Gustavus II Adolphus of Sweden sends troops to aid German Protestants in Pomerania.

Nov. England makes peace with Spain.

1631

- Richelieu subsidizes Gustavus and Bernhard, Duke of Saxony, bringing France into the Thirty Years' War.

22 Feb. *Chloridia,* a play by Ben Jonson, is performed in London.

20 May Forces under Johann Tserclaes, Graf von Tilly, commander-in-chief of Catholic League armies, sack and burn Magdeburg, massacring the citizens.

17 Sept. An army of Swedish troops led by Gustavus II Adolphus and the troops of John George, Elector of Saxony, defeat Tilly's forces at the Battle of Breitenfeld (or Leipzig).

1632

- Charles I of England grants Maryland to Lord Baltimore.

- Galileo repeats his support for Copernicus's theory that the planets orbit the sun.

30 Apr. Tilly dies after receiving a mortal wound in the defeat of his forces by Gustavus's troops at the confluence of the Lenz and Danube Rivers.

16 Nov. The Swedes defeat Catholic forces at Lutzen, but Gustavus is killed in battle. He is succeeded by his six-year-old daughter, Christina. Until she ascends the throne on her eighteenth birthday, in December 1644, Sweden is governed by a chancellorship.

1633

- *Poems by J. D.,* by the late English poet John Donne, is published in London.

- William Laud becomes archbishop of Canterbury.

12 Apr. The Catholic Church in Rome tries Galileo for heresy because he has refused to retract his support for the Copernican view of the universe. Threatened with torture on the rack, he recants and is confined to his villa outside Florence for the remaining nine years of his life.

1634

- *Love's Mistress,* a play by Thomas Heywood, is performed in London.

- Tulip mania in Holland reaches a high point, as speculators pay enormously inflated prices for single bulbs.

18 Feb. Recalled to duty in 1632, Gen. Albrecht von Wallenstein is formally deposed amid accusations that he intended to seize the crown of Bohemia or even the throne of the Holy Roman Empire for himself.

25 Feb. Wallenstein is assassinated by an Irish officer.

1635

- The Academie Française is founded to establish French grammar and usage rules and cleanse the language of "impurities."

30 May   The Treaty of Prague ends hostilities between John George of Saxony and Emperor Ferdinand II. The Thirty Years' War becomes largely a battle between French and Swedish troops and the forces of the Holy Roman Empire and Spain.

1637

- *Comus,* a masque by English poet John Milton, is published in London.

- Hundreds of Dutch tulip speculators are ruined as the bottom falls out of the tulip market.

- In *La géometrie* René Descartes applies algebra to geometry, creating analytic geometry and establishing the basis for modern mathematics.

15 Feb.   Ferdinand II dies and is succeeded as Holy Roman Emperor by his twenty-eight-year-old son, Ferdinand III.

23 June   Riots erupt in Edinburgh after Charles I orders the Anglican liturgy read in Scottish churches—the decree is part of Archbishop Laud's campaign to root out Calvinism in England and Presbyterianism in Scotland.

1638

28 Feb.   Scots Presbyterians sign the Solemn League and Covenant in defense of their religion.

Nov.   The Scottish "Covenanters" hold a general assembly in Glasgow, abolishing the episcopacy of the Anglican Church and adopting the liturgy and canons of the Scottish Kirk (Church).

1639

- The First Bishops' War begins as Scots seize Edinburgh Castle and raise an army.

18 June   The Scots meet the forces of Charles I near Berwick. Negotiations result in peace without bloodshed after Charles promises that differences can be resolved by a new general assembly and a new Scottish parliament after the armies have disbanded.

1640

- *Love's Masterpiece,* a play by Thomas Heywood, is performed in London.

- Supported by the French, who recognize its independence, Catalonia begins a revolt against Spain that continues until 1659.

- Portugal declares its independence from Spain, which the Spanish do not recognize until 1668.

13 Apr.   In financial distress and still in trouble with the Scots, Charles I calls his fourth Parliament.

5 May   Because it refuses to grant any money until he solves Scottish grievances, Charles dissolves Parliament, which thus becomes known as the "Short Parliament." In response to the king's actions rioters attack Archbishop Laud's palace.

28 Aug.	A Scottish army defeats the troops of Charles I in a skirmish at Newburn on the Tyne as the Second Bishops' War erupts over the unresolved dispute between the Presbyterians and the Anglican Church.
26 Oct.	In the Treaty of Ripon, which ends the Second Bishops' War, Charles I agrees to pay the Scottish army £850 a day until all disputes are resolved.
3 Nov.	In need of money to pay the Scots, Charles I is forced to call his fifth Parliament, which becomes known as the "Long Parliament."
11 Nov.	Because Charles I cannot dissolve it until it gives him the money he needs, Parliament takes advantage of its unusual hold over the king and impeaches the king's chief adviser, Thomas Wentworth, first Earl of Strafford, who had urged invasion of Scotland in the Second Bishops' War. He is sent to the Tower of London on 25 November.
18 Dec.	Parliament impeaches Archbishop William Laud for treason, blaming him for causing the difficulties that resulted in the Bishops' Wars. He is committed to the Tower of London in March 1641, but his trial does not occur until 1644.

1641

•	Dutch forces take Malacca, beginning their domination of the East Indies.
Mar.	Strafford goes on trial for treason. He is found guilty and executed on 12 May.
May	Parliament passes the Triennial Act, requiring that Parliament meet every three years even if not called by the Crown. This act was followed by a bill preventing Parliament from being dissolved without its own consent.
	The moderate Puritans in Parliament split from the more-radical Presbyterians when they propose the Root and Branch Bill, which calls for doing away with the office of bishop.
July	Parliament abolishes the constitutionally established courts of Star Chamber and High Commission, which Laud has used in his efforts to destroy Calvinism and Presbyterianism in England. This radical move has been interpreted as a sign that Parliament intends to bring about a revolution.
Aug.	England and Scotland sign a treaty, and both armies are paid with the revenues from a special poll tax voted by Parliament.
Oct.	Charles I is implicated in a plot by James Graham, Marquis of Montrose, to seize Presbyterian leader Archibald Campbell, second Duke of Argyll. As a result Charles is forced to give virtually all control over Scotland to Argyll and the Presbyterians.
21 Oct.	Irish Catholics rise up against their mostly English landlords and slaughter thirty thousand Protestants in Ulster.
1 Dec.	Parliament gives Charles I the Grand Remonstrance, listing all their grievances against him since the beginning of his reign. They order it printed on 14 December.

1642

•	French settlers found Montreal.
•	Dutch explorer Abel Tasman discovers Tasmania and New Zealand.

3 Jan.	Charles I orders the impeachment of Edward Montagu, Lord Kimbolton, and three members of Parliament on allegations of treason during the recent troubles in Scotland. The House of Commons refuses to order their arrest, and when the king sends troops to seize them, they go into hiding. After Charles leaves London on 10 January, the five members of the Commons return in triumph to Parliament.
Mar.	From York, Charles I sends word to the House of Commons that he will not sign bills excluding bishops from the House of Lords. Thirty-two members of the Lords and sixty-five members of Commons join the king in York. Because he has the Great Seal, Parliament in London begins passing ordinances without the seal or the king's signature.
2 June	Parliament makes a final attempt to resolve its differences with the king, sending him the Nineteen Propositions, which include the requests that he sign a bill giving control of the militia to Parliament and that Parliament be allowed to reform church liturgy and government as it chooses. The king rejects the propositions.
July	Parliament appoints a committee of public safety and puts Robert Devereux, third Earl of Essex, at the head of a parliamentarian army.
22 Aug.	Charles I raises his royal standard at Nottingham, signaling the beginning of the military phase of the English Civil War, pitting parliamentarians and Puritans (Roundheads) against royalists (Cavaliers).
12 Nov.	Essex turns back royalist troops at Brentford, ending their march on London. After Oliver Cromwell distinguishes himself in this battle, the associate counties of Norfolk, Suffolk, Essex, Cambridge, Hertford, and Huntington put him in charge of their combined force, which becomes the best in the war and earns the nickname "the Ironsides."
4 Dec.	Cardinal Richelieu of France dies.

1643

•	Italian mathematician Evangelista Torricelli invents the barometer.
May	Louis XIII of France dies and is succeeded by his five-year-old son, Louis XIV. The government is dominated by Cardinal Jules Mazarin.
19 May	The French defeat the Spanish at the Battle of Rocroi, marking the end of Spanish military supremacy.
1 July	The Westminster Assembly convenes to discuss religious differences. It meets until 1649.
25 Sept.	The Solemn League and Covenant is signed by 25 members of the House of Lords and 288 members of the Commons, agreeing to make the religions of England, Ireland, and Scotland as similar as possible and to reform them "according to . . . The examples of the best reformed churches." As a result the Scots Presbyterians agree to help the parliamentarians in the war effort. At the same time Charles alienates many of his English allies by enlisting the aid of the Irish Catholics, with whom he has just reached a peace agreement.

1644

•	*Areopagitica*, an essay in favor of freedom of the press by English poet John Milton, is published in London.

- The last Ming emperor of China dies and is succeeded by the first Manchu emperor of the Ch'ing dynasty, which rules China until 1912.

- Charles I convenes a rival parliament at Oxford.

12 Mar. Archbishop Laud goes on trial for treason. He is found guilty and beheaded on 10 January 1645.

2 July Oliver Cromwell defeats royalist forces at Marston Moor, a decisive battle that gives the north to Parliament.

Aug. Montrose slips into Scotland from abroad and raises an army of Highlanders to support the royalist cause.

1645

Jan.–Feb. A truce in the English Civil War ends after Charles I once again rejects Parliament's proposals.

14 June The defeat of royalist troops at the Battle of Naseby spells the ruin of Charles's cause.

12 July Czar Michael Romanov of Russia dies and is succeeded by his son Alexis I.

13 Sept. After several victories Montrose's Highland army is decisively beaten at Philiphaugh.

1646

26 Mar. Royalists are defeated at Stowe-on-the-Wold, the final battle of the English Civil War.

5 May Charles I surrenders himself to the Scots.

July Parliament submits the Newcastle Proposals to Charles I, demanding that it control the militia for twenty years and that the king take the Covenant and support the Presbyterian establishment. Foreseeing a split between the radical Presbyterians in Parliament and the more moderate Independents in the army, Charles rejects the proposals.

1647

30 Jan. The Scots surrender Charles I to Parliament as the rift widens between it and the army, which refuses an order to disband.

11 Nov. After several months of disputes between Parliament and the army, Charles I flees to the Isle of Wight, where the governor of Carisbrooke Castle takes him into custody.

24 Dec. Parliament sends Charles I the Four Bills, including one allowing it to determine the time of its own adjournment.

26 Dec. Charles I signs a secret agreement with the Scots, who disapprove of the increasing religious toleration in England and agree to restore him to the throne by military action.

28 Dec. Charles I rejects the Four Bills.

1648

15 Jan.	Parliament renounces allegiance to the king, setting in motion the Second English Civil War, pitting England against Scotland, Roundheads against royalists, and Independents against Presbyterians.
17–20 Aug.	Cromwell's forces defeat the Scottish army at Preston, the final battle of the Second English Civil War.
24 Oct.	The Treaties of Westphalia end the Thirty Years' War and recognize the independence of the Dutch Republic of the United Provinces. The treaty does not apply to the war between France and Spain, which continues for eleven more years.
6–7 Dec.	Ninety-six Presbyterians are excluded by force from Parliament, creating a sixty-member body known as the "Rump Parliament."
13 Dec.	The Rump Parliament votes to bring Charles I to trial.

1649

20–27 Jan.	Charles I is tried for treason and sentenced to death by a court appointed by the House of Commons. He is beheaded on 30 January. The monarchy and House of Lords are abolished. England is governed by Parliament and a council of state, but power rests mainly with the army.
5 Feb.	Scots in Edinburgh proclaim Charles II, son of Charles I, king.
Sept.	Cromwell suppresses royalist forces in Scotland.

1650

27 Apr.	Montrose, who has returned to Scotland to lead a royalist army, is defeated at Corbiesdale. He is captured and executed at Edinburgh on 21 May.
24 June	Landing in Scotland, Charles II takes the Covenant and is again proclaimed king.
3 Sept.	The Scots are utterly defeated by Cromwell at the Battle of Worcester. Charles II escapes to France.

1651

•	*Leviathan,* by English philosopher Thomas Hobbes, is published in London.
9 Oct.	Parliament passes the first of several Navigation Acts. The first, aimed at Dutch shippers, prohibits importing goods to England except in British ships or in vessels from the countries where the goods have been made.

1652

8 July	The First Anglo-Dutch War breaks out over the Navigation Act of 1651. The conflict continues until 1654.

1653

•	*The Compleat Angler,* a book on fishing by English clergyman Izaak Walton, is published in London.

•	Cardinal Mazarin of France crushes a three-year rebellion of nobles opposed to the king.
20 Apr.	Cromwell dismisses the Rump Parliament and abolishes the council of state.
4 July	Cromwell establishes a new council of state and a 140-member appointed Parliament, which becomes known as the "Barebones' Parliament."
16 Dec.	After his supporters in Parliament surrender their powers to him, Cromwell sets up the Protectorate, with himself as lord protector, and a 460-member Parliament that will meet every three years and cannot be dissolved for five months after it is summoned.

1654

•	Christina of Sweden abdicates her throne and is succeeded by her cousin Charles X Gustavus.
•	Russia and Poland begin a thirteen-year war over the Ukraine.
5 Apr.	Under the Treaty of Westminster, which ends the First Anglo-Dutch War, the Dutch and English establish a defensive league.
12 Sept.	After a quarrel with Parliament, Cromwell orders the exclusion of some members.

1655

22 Jan.	Cromwell dissolves Parliament after it votes to make the office of lord protector elective rather than hereditary.
May	Catholic priests are ordered to leave England, and Anglican clergymen are prohibited from preaching or teaching.

1656

•	Charles X Gustavus of Sweden invades Poland.
May	England seizes Jamaica in the West Indies, provoking a war with Spain.
17 Sept.	Cromwell calls his third Parliament, which lasts until 4 February 1658. During its tenure it establishes a second house, deprives the lord protector of the power to exclude members, and establishes toleration for all Christians except Anglicans and Catholics.

1657

•	The first London chocolate shop opens in Bishopsgate Street.
•	Charles X Gustavus of Sweden is driven out of Poland and then goes to war with Denmark, trying to expand his territories on the southern coast of the Baltic. The Dutch intervene to protect their fishing rights. The war continues until 1660.
•	The Dutch begin a four-year war with the Portuguese over their conflicting interests in Brazil.
2 Apr.	Holy Roman Emperor Ferdinand III dies and is succeeded by his sixteen-year-old son, Leopold I.

1658

- Charles X Gustavus of Sweden twice invades Denmark but fails to capture Copenhagen.

4 June — England and France defeat Spain at the Battle of the Dunes; the English take Dunkirk.

3 Sept. — Oliver Cromwell dies and is succeeded as lord protector by his son Richard.

1659

22 Apr. — Richard Cromwell dissolves Parliament, which has been meeting since 27 January, after a dispute over the army.

7 May — The Rump Parliament comes together and convinces Cromwell to resign.

Oct. — The army expels the Rump Parliament but, after public outcry, restores it on 26 December.

7 Nov. — The Treaty of the Pyrenees gives Flanders, Luxembourg, and other Spanish possessions in the Low Countries to France; gives Dunkirk to England; and arranges the marriage of Louis XIV of France to Maria Teresa, eldest daughter of Philip IV of Spain.

1660

- Parliament passes a second Navigation Act, listing articles that the colonies can ship only to England. The list includes tobacco, sugar, wool, indigo, and apples. (Molasses and rice are added later.) Tobacco prices in Virginia drop sharply.

- The Lords of Trade are given authority to oversee the American colonies under the authority of the King's Privy Council.

3 Feb. — Gen. George Monk leads an army from Scotland to London and reestablishes the Long Parliament, which is finally dissolved on 16 March.

12 Feb. — Charles X Gustavus of Sweden dies and is succeeded by his four-year-old son, Charles XI. The Treaty of Copenhagen ends the war between Sweden and Denmark.

14 Apr. — Charles II issues the Declaration of Breda, promising amnesty to his opponents and freedom of conscience to all.

3 May — The Treaty of Oliva ends the war between Sweden and Poland.

8 May — A Convention Parliament, chosen in April without restriction, proclaims Charles II king. He restores the Anglican bishops to their sees and to the House of Lords, grants amnesty to all but the judges who condemned Charles I, and declares in force all the acts of the Long Parliament to which he assented.

29 Dec. — The Convention Parliament is dissolved.

1661

- Cardinal Mazarin of France dies.

- The royalist Scottish Parliament abolishes the Covenant.

8 May — Charles II calls his first Parliament, which becomes known as the "Cavalier Parliament," in part because it repeals the Puritans' bans on theater, gaming, and dancing.

	20 Nov.	Parliament passes the Corporation Act, which includes a provision requiring all magistrates to be Anglicans. This act is the first of four repressive measures that become known as the Clarendon Code.

1662

- The Royal Society for the Promotion of Natural Knowledge is founded in London.
- England sells Dunkirk to France.
- Holland and France form an alliance against attack by England.

20 May Charles II marries Catherine Braganza, daughter of John IV of Portugal.

24 Aug. The second act of the Clarendon Code, the Act of Uniformity, requires all clergymen, college fellows, and teachers to accept everything in the Anglican Book of Common Prayer. Those who refuse become known as Nonconformists.

1663

- Part one of *Hudibras,* a long satiric poem by Englishman Samuel Butler, is published in London. Part two is published in 1664, and part three appears in 1678.
- The Black Death (bubonic plague) kills some ten thousand people in Amsterdam.

1664

- *The Rival Ladies,* a play by English poet John Dryden, is published in London.

May The third act of the Clarendon Code, the Conventicle Act, forbids Nonconformist meetings of more than five people, except in private homes.

27 Aug. The English take New Amsterdam from the Dutch. Charles II grants New Netherland to his brother, James, Duke of York, who in turn gives part of it to John Berkeley, first Baron Berkeley, and Sir George Carteret.

1665

Apr. The Black Death strikes London, killing at least 68,596 people as some two-thirds of the 460,000 inhabitants flee to the countryside.

3 June In the Second Anglo-Dutch War the English fleet defeats the Dutch off Lowestoft.

17 Sept. Philip IV of Spain dies and is succeeded by his four-year-old son, Charles II.

Oct. The Five Mile Act, the fourth act in the Clarendon Code, requires Nonconformists to swear nonresistance toward the established church and state and forbids those who refuse to sign to be within five miles of any incorporated town.

1666

- Sir Isaac Newton invents calculus and establishes the laws of gravity.
- Louis XIV founds the French Academy of Science in Paris.

	France enters the Second Anglo-Dutch War on the side of Holland.
2 Sept.	The Great Fire of London destroys four-fifths of the city within the walls and sixty-three acres outside them. The Gothic Cathedral of Saint Paul's, eighty-six other churches, the Guildhall, the Custom House, the Royal Exchange, and many other buildings, including more than thirteen thousand houses, are destroyed. In part because many of the old buildings that harbored rats have been burned, deaths from the plague are reduced to two thousand.
28 Nov.	Scottish Covenanters revolting against the restrictions of the Clarendon Code are crushed in the Battle of Portland Hills.

1667

	Paradise Lost, an epic poem by English poet John Milton, is published in London.
	Though there are no formal political parties in the English Parliament, it is beginning to split into court and country factions that later evolve into the Tories (court) and Whigs (country).
	Louis XIV of France claims the Spanish possessions in the Belgian provinces on the grounds that on the death of his father-in-law, Philip IV of Spain, these lands passed by right to Louis's wife. France invades the Spanish Netherlands, taking Flanders and Hainault.
20 Jan.	The Treaty of Andrussovo ends the thirteen-year war between Russia and Poland, which cedes Kiev, Smolensk, and the eastern Ukraine to Russia.
21 July	The Treaties of Breda end the Second Anglo-Dutch War. England gets Antigua, Montserrat, and St. Kitts from France and is allowed to keep New Netherland. France gets Acadia (Nova Scotia), and Holland gets Surinam in South America.

1668

23 Jan.	England, Holland, and Spain form a Triple Alliance as a check on Louis XIV of France.
2 May	The Treaty of Aix-la-Chapelle ends the war between France and Spain. France gets twelve fortified towns on the border of the Spanish Netherlands.

1670

	Without the knowledge of Parliament Charles II signs the Treaty of Dover with Louis XIV. In secret provisions he and James, Duke of York, agree to become Catholics and to support France against Spain and Holland. James openly declares his Catholicism immediately.

1671

	Paradise Regain'd, an epic poem by English poet John Milton, is published in London.
	Parliament passes the Test Act, requiring all officeholders to take oaths of allegiance and supremacy and to take the sacrament in the Church of England.

1672

- Sir Isaac Newton publishes his "New Theory about Light and Colors," demonstrating that white light can be broken down into a spectrum of colors.

- England and France go to war against Holland. Sweden enters the war on the side of England and France. Spain enters on the side of Holland.

1673

- *Marriage a-La-Mode,* a play by English poet John Dryden, is published in London.

- The Dutch retake New York and Delaware from England.

21 Nov.   James, Duke of York, takes as his second wife, the Catholic Maria d'Este of Modena.

1674

9 Feb.   The Treaty of Westminster ends the war between England and Holland. The Dutch return New York and Delaware to England.

1675

- Dutch scientist Antoni van Leeuwenhoek discovers microorganisms.

1676

8 Feb.   Czar Alexis of Russia dies and is succeeded by his son Fedor III.

21 June   Architect Sir Christopher Wren lays the cornerstone on the new Saint Paul's Cathedral in London, one of many churches he designs to replace those destroyed in the Great Fire of 1666.

1677

4 Nov.   Mary (daughter of the duke of York by his first wife, Anne Hyde) marries the Dutch prince William of Orange.

1678

10 Aug.   A series of treaties signed between this date and 26 September 1679 ends the war between Holland and France and their allies. All its territory is returned to Holland on the condition that it remain neutral.

Sept.   Titus Oakes alleges a "popish plot" in which Catholics have planned to massacre Protestants, burn London, and kill Charles II. As a result several Catholics are executed, including the confessor of Maria, Duchess of York, and Parliament passes an act excluding Catholics from both its houses.

1679

24 Jan.   The Cavalier Parliament is dissolved.

1680

6 Mar.   Charles II calls his third Parliament, which unsuccessfully attempts to exclude the Catholic duke of York from the line of succession the the throne. After much controversy with the king, this Parliament is dissolved on 27 May 1680.

1 June   The Covenanters of Scotland rise up again and are put down at the Battle of Bothwell Brigg on 22 June.

21 Oct.   Charles II calls his fourth Parliament. The bill to exclude the duke of York passes in the Commons but fails in the House of Lords. This Parliament is dissolved on 18 January 1681.

1681

•   *Absalom and Achitophel,* an allegorical poem on the exclusion crisis written by English poet John Dryden, is published in London.

21 Mar.   Charles II calls his fifth Parliament but dissolves it on 28 March, after the exclusion bill is introduced again.

1682

•   Robert Cavelier, Sieur de La Salle, claims the Mississippi River valley for France.

27 Apr.   Czar Fedor III of Russia dies and is succeeded by his nine-year-old brother Peter, but after a palace revolt Fedor's fifteen-year-old physically and mentally defective brother, Ivan, becomes an associate ruler, beginning a seven-year reign in which his sister Sophia is his regent and holds all real power.

1683

•   France invades the Spanish Netherlands. Carlos II of Spain forms the League of the Hague with Emperor Leopold of the Holy Roman Empire, joining a Dutch-Swedish alliance against Louis XIV.

June   Two separate conspiracies to kill Charles II are uncovered in London.

1684

•   The English East India Company builds a trading station in Canton, China.

•   French architect Jules Hardouin-Mansart completes the Hall of Mirrors at Versailles.

•   France takes Lorraine. Louis XIV signs a twenty-year truce at Regensburg, which gives France Strasbourg and Lorraine.

1685

•   Elector Charles of the Palatine dies with no male heir. His lands are claimed by Louis XIV, whose brother is married to the elector's sister.

6 Feb.	Charles II dies and is succeeded by the duke of York as James II. He alienates both Tories and Whigs by his attempts to secure freedom of worship for his fellow Catholics.
19 May	The Parliament of James II convenes. It is dissolved on 2 July 1687.
6 July	Another Scottish uprising ends with their defeat at the Battle of Sedgemoor.
18 Oct.	France revokes the Edict of Nantes (1598), which gave French Huguenots (Protestants) equal political rights with French Catholics. Forbidden to practice their religion and required to educate their children in the Catholic faith, many Huguenots immigrate to Holland, England, Brandenburg, British North America, and South Africa.

1686

•	France annexes Madagascar.
9 July	The Holy Roman Empire, Spain, Sweden, Bavaria, Saxony, and the Palatine form the League of Augsburg in opposition to France.

1687

•	Sir Isaac Newton's *Philosophiae naturalis principia mathematica (Principles of Natural Philosophy)* is published.
•	The University of Bologna is founded.
Apr.	James II issues his first Declaration of Liberty of Conscience, granting freedom of worship to all denominations in England and Scotland.

1688

Apr.	The archbishop of Canterbury and six other bishops are sent to the Tower of London for asking the king to excuse them from the requirement that his Declaration of Liberty of Conscience be read in all churches. They are tried on 29–30 June for seditious libel and acquitted.
30 June	After the birth of a son and heir to James II on 10 June, seven eminent Englishmen invite William of Orange, James's son-in-law, to save England from Catholicism. Hoping for English help for Holland against France, William accepts their offer in late September.
Oct.	France invades the Palatine, beginning the War of the League of Augsburg. In North America it becomes known as King William's War.
5 Nov.	William of Orange lands in England, setting in motion the so-called Glorious Revolution.
11 Dec.	James II flees London, is captured and brought back, but on 22 December he escapes to France, where Louis XIV sets the exiled Stuarts at the Court of St. Germaine.
12 Dec.	Amid rioting in London, the peers set up the Interregnum, or provisional government.
19 Dec.	William of Orange enters London.

1689

•	Regent and Czarina Sophia is deposed, and her brother Peter becomes sole ruler of Russia. He becomes known as Peter the Great.
22 Jan.	On the advice of the peers a Convention Parliament is called. It is dissolved on 27 January 1690, after transforming itself into a regular Parliament on 22 February 1689.
28 Jan.	Parliament declares that James II is no longer king and offers the throne to William of Orange. He refuses the crown but then agrees to rule jointly with his wife, Mary, daughter of James II.
13 Feb.	William III and Mary II are proclaimed the rulers of England, with chief responsibility for administering the government going to William.
•	Parliament issues the Declaration of Rights, asserting its powers to govern, along with free elections, freedom of debate, the right to trial by jury, and other rights of British subjects.
22 Feb.	Parliament and the clergy take the Oaths of Allegiance and Supremacy to the new monarchs. Six bishops and some four hundred clergymen, who become known as Nonjurors, refuse and establish a separate and private Church of England, which continues to exist until the nineteenth century.
14 Mar.	James II lands in Ireland and besieges Protestant Londonderry on 20 April. The siege is lifted by British troops on 30 July.
7 May	Scots Highlanders rise up in support of James II, but after victory at the Battle of Killiecankie on 17 July, the rebels gradually lose force.
12 May	England and Holland enter the War of the League of Augsburg against France. The primary focus of the war shifts to the Netherlands.
16 Dec.	The English Bill of Rights, a parliamentary enactment of the Declaration of Rights, is passed.

1690

•	*An Essay Concerning Human Understanding,* by English philosopher John Locke, is published in London.
20 Mar.	William III's second Parliament convenes. It is dissolved on 3 May 1695.
30 June	The French defeat the English fleet in the Battle of Beachy Head.
1 July	William III defeats James II at the Battle of the Boyne in Ireland, and James flees to France.
12 July	The English defeat Irish and French forces at the Battle of Aughrim in Ireland.
3 Oct.	An English victory over Irish and French troops at Limerick results in the Pacification of Limerick, ending James II's military attempt to regain the English throne.

1692

19 May	The English achieve a naval victory over the French at Cap de la Hogue, but William III's land campaigns on the Continent are unsuccessful.

1694

27 July	The Bank of England is chartered after its founders lend to government £1.2 million to help cover its soaring war debts.

	22 Dec.	The Triennial Bill, requiring Parliament to meet every three years, becomes law.
	28 Dec.	Mary II of England dies.
1695	22 Nov.	William III's third Parliament, the First Triennial Parliament, convenes. It is dissolved on 5 July 1698.
1696	•	Parliament passes the Trials for Treason Act, requiring two witnesses to prove the commission of treason.
	•	A plot to kill William III is uncovered.
	•	The Board of Trade replaces the Lords of Trade as overseers of the colonies.
	10 Apr.	Parliament passes a Navigation Act prohibiting the American colonies from exporting goods directly to Scotland or Ireland.
1697	•	Peter I (Peter the Great) of Russia visits Holland, France, and England incognito to learn about Western civilization. He returns home determined to modernize Russia.
	•	The Board of Trade establishes Vice-Admiralty Courts whose jurisdiction covers colonial maritime cases. These courts have no juries.
	5 Apr.	Charles XI of Sweden dies and is succeeded by his fourteen-year-old son, Charles XII.
	20 Sept.	The Treaty of Ryswick among France, England, Spain, and Holland ends the War of the League of Augsburg and acknowledges William III as king of England and Anne of Denmark, the second daughter of James II, as his successor. Louis XIV of France agrees not to help James II and his son, James Edward, who are in exile in France. Spain cedes the western third of the Caribbean island of Hispaniola (Haiti) to France.
	30 Oct.	In a separate treaty with the Holy Roman Empire, France is allowed to keep Alsace and Strasbourg, but it gives up Lorraine.
	2 Dec.	Saint Paul's Cathedral is completed in London.
1698	•	The first modern stock exchange is formed in London.
	•	Parliament opens the slave trade to British merchants, allowing their ships to carry sugar and molasses from the West Indies to New England rum distilleries, rum from New England to African slave traders, and slaves from Africa to the West Indies.
	•	In London a fire destroys all of Whitehall Palace except for the Banqueting Hall built by Inigo Jones in 1622.

	6 Dec.	The fourth Parliament of William III convenes, passing further anti–Catholic measures. It is dissolved on 11 April 1700.
1699	•	Parliament passes the Woolen Act, forbidding the American colonies from exporting wool, wool yarn, and wool cloth.
1700	•	The Great Northern War, a state of general warfare that lasts twenty-one years, erupts as Russia, Poland, and Denmark oppose Swedish attempts to maintain and extend its supremacy in the Baltic region.
	1 Nov.	The last Hapsburg monarch of Spain, Charles II dies, having just named Philip of Anjou, grandson of Louis XIV of France, as his heir, Philip V.
1701	•	The Anglican Church creates a missionary arm, the Society for the Propagation of the Gospel in Foreign Parts (S.P.G.), sending ministers to the English colonies.
	•	The War of the Spanish Succession (Queen Anne's War in North America) breaks out, as other Hapsburg rulers claim precedence and territory. Holy Roman Emperor Leopold I, a German Hapsburg, moves to take over Spain's possessions in the Low Countries and Italy.
	7 Sept.	Great Britain and Holland, fearing that France will ally itself with Spain, join in a Grand Alliance with Leopold I and Eugene, Prince of Savoy. Eugene invades Italy.
	16 Sept.	James II dies in exile in France, where Louis XIV proclaims James's son James Edward king of England and Ireland. He becomes known as the Old Pretender.
1702	8 Mar.	William III of England dies. He is succeeded by his sister-in-law Anne, second daughter of James II and wife of Prince George of Denmark.
	14 May	The Grand Alliance declares war on France.
	14 Dec.	After Gen. John Churchill, Earl of Marlborough's major victories in the Spanish Netherlands, Queen Anne makes him duke of Marlborough.
1703	•	The Grand Alliance proclaims Archduke Charles of Austria king of Spain. He invades Catalonia and establishes himself as Charles III.
1704	•	The Southern Department replaces the Board of Trade as the body that appoints governors to British Crown colonies.

	4 Aug.	The English take Gibraltar from Spain.
	13 Aug.	Marlborough achieves a major victory over troops of the French and their Bavarian and Prussian allies at the Battle of Blenheim.
1705	•	Queen Anne commissions architect John Vanbrugh to build Blenhiem Palace in Oxfordshire for the duke of Marlborough.
	5 May	Leopold I dies and is succeeded as Holy Roman emperor by his twenty-six-year-old son, Josef I.
1706	23 May	Marlborough's triumph at the Battle of Ramilles is followed by the surrender of Antwerp, Ghent, Ostend, and other major cities in the Spanish Netherlands.
	June	With the help of Portuguese forces Leszczynska takes Madrid but holds it only briefly.
1707	1 May	Great Britain is established through the union of the kingdoms of England and Scotland. The Scottish parliament is abolished, with Scotland sending sixteen elected peers and forty-five members of commons to Parliament in England. The Union Jack, combining the English cross of Saint George and the Scottish cross of Saint Andrew, becomes the new national flag.
1708	Mar.	James Edward (the Old Pretender) lands in Scotland but soon returns to France after the French fleet sent to support him is beaten by the British.
	11 July	The victory of Marlborough and Eugene of Savoy at Ooudenarde results in unsuccessful peace negotiations. The War of the Spanish Succession continues.
1709	9 Apr.	Joseph Addison and Richard Steele begin publishing their magazine *The Tatler* in London. It continues until 2 January 1711.
1710	•	*A Treatise Concerning the Principles of Human Knowledge,* by Irish philosopher George Berkeley, is published in Dublin.

1711

- Parliament passes the Landed Property Qualification Act, an attempt by Tory landowners to keep merchants, financiers, and industrialists out of the House of Commons. It also passes the Occasional Conformity Bill, aimed at dissenters who regularly attend Nonconformist religious services but qualify to hold office because they have once taken communion in an Anglican Church.

- Parliament charters the South Sea Company for investment in overseas enterprises and allows it to take over part of the national debt, issuing £1 worth of stock for every £1 of debt it assumes.

1 Mar.   Joseph Addison and Richard Steele begin publishing their magazine *The Spectator* in London, continuing until 6 December 1712.

17 Apr.   Holy Roman Emperor Joseph I dies and is succeeded by his brother Charles VI, claimant to the Spanish throne as Charles III.

1713

- Joseph Addison's tragedy *Cato* is published in London.

11 Apr.   The Treaty of Utrecht recognizes Philip V as king of Spain. Great Britain gets Newfoundland, Acadia (Nova Scotia), and the Hudson Bay territory from France and Gibraltar and Minorca from Spain. The Spanish Netherlands are turned over to the Republic of Holland with the agreement that they will be given to Austria in a separate treaty. Savoy gets Sicily. Charles VI and the Holy Roman Empire continue the war.

1714

- German physicist Gabriel Daniel Fahrenheit introduces the Fahrenheit mercury thermometer.

- The Treaty of Rastatt and Baden gives the Spanish Netherlands to Austria, ending the War of the Spanish Succession, but the Holy Roman Empire refuses to recognize Philip V and his heirs as the rulers of Spain.

- Anne of England dies. She is succeeded by a great-grandson of James I, Prince George Louis of Hanover, who becomes George I of England. His sympathy to the Whigs results in a shift in power from the Tories to the Whigs.

18 June   Joseph Addison revives *The Spectator* in London, publishing it until 20 December 1714.

1715

- *Gil Blas,* a picaresque novel by Alain René Lesage, is published in Paris.

- Jacobites, supporters of James Edward, pretender to the British throne, riot in London.

Sept.   A Jacobite uprising begins in Scotland.

1 Sept.   Louis XIV of France dies and is succeeded by his five-year-old grandson, Louis XV. Philippe, Duc d'Orléans, serves as regent.

Dec.   Calling himself James III, James Edward arrives in Scotland from France.

1716

Feb.   The Jacobite uprising in Scotland is suppressed, and James Edward returns to France.

1717

•   Spain seizes Sardinia.

4 Jan.   Britain, Holland, and France form a Triple Alliance, forcing James Edward, who has been intriguing with Charles XII and the prime minister of Spain, to leave France.

1718

Jan.   Parliament repeals the Occasional Conformity Act.

July   Spain takes Sicily.

2 Aug.   The Holy Roman Empire joins the Triple Alliance, making it the Quadruple Alliance.

11 Dec.   Charles XII of Sweden is killed during a military expedition in Norway. He is succeeded by his sister, Ulrika Eleanora, who attempts to end the Great Northern War.

1719

•   *Robinson Crusoe,* the first novel by Englishman Daniel Defoe, is published in London.

•   Spain launches an abortive mission to Scotland in support of the pretender.

20 Nov.   The Treaty of Stockholm ends hostilities between England and Sweden.

1720

•   Ulrika Eleanora of Sweden abdicates in favor of her husband, Frederick I. The Treaties of Stockholm, signed in 1720 and 1721, end the Great Northern War, restoring the status quo, as before the war, among Sweden, Saxony, and Poland. Denmark restores all its conquests.

Jan.   The "South Sea Bubble" bursts in London as the collapse of the South Sea Company causes a financial panic.

17 Feb.   In the Treaty of the Hague Philip V gives up his claims in Italy, and Emperor Charles VI renounces his claims on the Spanish throne. Austria gets Sicily, and Savoy gets Sardinia.

June   Spain makes peace with Great Britain and joins in an alliance with Britain and France.

1721

•   *Moll Flanders,* a novel by Daniel Defoe, is published in London.

•   *Lettres persanes* (Persian Letters), a satire of life in Paris by French philosopher Charles-Louis de Secondat, Baron de Montesquieu, is published in Paris.

- Chancellor of the Exchequer John Aislabie is sent to the Tower of London on charges of fraud connected to the collapse of the South Sea Company.

Apr. Sir Robert Walpole, who has profited in South Sea Company speculation, becomes prime minister and chancellor of the exchequer, encouraging trade by reducing import and export duties and avoiding further panic by amalgamating stock in the South Sea Company with the stock of the Bank of England. He also slackens enforcement of the Navigation Acts.

30 Aug. In the Treaty of Nystadt Sweden cedes Livonia, Estonia, Ingermanland, and several islands to Russia, which restores Finland to Sweden. As a result of this treaty Russia emerges as an important European power, and Sweden loses its dominance in the Baltic region.

1722

- Peter the Great takes the Bosporus and the Dardanelles from Constantinople, giving Russia an outlet to the Mediterranean.

1723

- Great Britain and Prussia sign the Treaty of Charlottenburg, agreeing that George I's grandson will marry a Prussian princess and Prince Frederick of Prussia will marry the daughter of the Prince of Wales.

- Great Britain exiles Bishop Francis Atterbury for his involvement in a Jacobite plot.

1725

- Louis XV of France marries Marie Leszczynska, daughter of Stanislas Leszczynski, who was deposed from the throne of Poland in 1709.
- Peter the Great establishes the Russian Academy of Sciences.

28 Jan. Peter the Great of Russia dies and is succeeded by his consort, Catherine I.

3 Sept. Britain, France, and Prussia sign the Treaty of Hanover.

1727

- Spain lays siege to Gibraltar, beginning a war with England. France enters on the side of Britain.

16 May Catherine I of Russia dies and is succeeded by her twelve-year-old son, Peter II.

10 June George I of Great Britain dies and is succeeded by his forty-four-year-old son, George II. Prime Minister Walpole remains in office.

1728

- *The Christian Poet,* a collection of verse by Joseph Addison, is published in London.

1729

9 Nov.   The Treaty of Seville ends the war between Spain and the allied nations of Great Britain and France.

1730

30 Jan.   Peter II of Russia dies. On 8 March his cousin Anna Ivanovna and her supporters overthrow the supreme privy council, making her czarina.

1731

•   English mathematician John Hadley invents a reflecting quadrant, which allows mariners to determine longitude at night.

16 Mar.   England and the Holy Roman Empire sign the Treaty of Vienna, in which Emperor Charles VI agrees to dissolve the Ostend East India Company set up by the Empire to rival the Dutch and English East India Companies.

1732

•   English agriculturalist Jethro Tull publishes *New Horse-Hoeing Husbandry*, which calls for using a plow to keep lands fertile.

1733

•   Englishman John Kay patents the flying shuttle, the first of several inventions that transform the textile industry and usher in the Industrial Revolution.

1 Feb.   Augustus II of Poland dies. Austria and Russia want the throne to go to Augustus's only legitimate son, Frederick Augustus, Elector of Saxony. Louis XV of France, however, wants to reinstate his father-in-law, Stanislas Leszczynski, thus beginning the War of the Polish Succession, involving Russia and the Holy Roman Empire against France, Spain, and Sardinia.

1734

•   In his *Lettres philosophiques* Voltaire (François-Marie Arouet) praises the Quakers and English government, philosophy, science, and literature. Sensing the implied criticism of authoritarianism in France, the French government orders the burning of the book.

1735

•   *A Defence of Free-Thinking in Mathematics,* by Irish philosopher George Berkeley, is published in Dublin.

•   Hostilities end in the War of the Polish Succession, but no treaty is signed until 1738.

•   Swedish botanist Carolus Linnaeus publishes his system for classifying plants.

1736

- British inventor John Harrison introduces the ship's chronometer, an improved means of determining longitude.

1738

18 Nov. The Treaty of Vienna formally ends the War of the Polish Succession. Stanislas Leszczynski renounces the Polish throne in return for the duchies of Lorraine and Bar, which will go to France on his death. Austria cedes Naples, Sicily, and Elba to Spain.

1739

Oct. After learning that a Spanish captain cut off one of British seaman Robert Jenkins's ears in Havana in 1731, Parliament decides to make an issue of Spain's alleged mistreatment of British mariners and orders British naval squadrons to intercept Spanish galleons, beginning the War of Jenkins' Ear between Britain and Spain, which continues until 1748.

1740

31 May Frederick William I dies, having made Prussia a formidable military power. He is succeeded by his twenty-eight-year-old son, Frederick II (Frederick the Great), who occupies part of Silesia, claiming it belongs to Prussia, thus bringing about a drawn conflict with Austria. The First Silesian War lasts until 1742.

17 Oct. Czarina Anna Ivanovna of Russia dies and is succeeded by her infant nephew Ivan VI.

20 Oct. Holy Roman Emperor Charles VI dies, having named his daughter Maria Theresa, Queen of Hungary and Bohemia, as his successor. Charles Albert, Elector of Bavaria; Augustus III of Saxony; and Philip V of Spain each claim the throne and challenge Maria Theresa's right to it, starting the War of the Austrian Succession, which continues until 1748.

1741

May France, Bavaria, and Spain conclude a secret alliance against Austria, which is supported by Great Britain. Saxony and Prussia later join the alliance against Austria.

1742

- *Joseph Andrews,* a novel by Englishman Henry Fielding, is published in London.

June–July In the Treaties of Breslau and Berlin, Prussia agrees to withdraw from the alliance against Maria Theresa in return for a large portion of Silesia. Austria proceeds to drive the allies out of Bohemia.

1743

- Austria drives the allies out of Bavaria.

- The Whigs retain control of Parliament after the fall of Walpole's government in February 1742. Whig Henry Pelham becomes prime minister, but his party is breaking up into rival factions.

27 June An army of British, Hanoverian, and Hessian troops led by George II of England defeats the French at the Battle of Dettingen. After this success Holland joins Britain in support of Maria Theresa, who makes an alliance with Saxony.

7 Aug. In the Treaty of Abo, ending a war between Sweden and Russia that began in 1741, Sweden cedes part of Finland to Russia.

1744

- Anxious about the increasing power of Austria, Frederick the Great of Prussia concludes another alliance with France and starts the Second Silesian War, marching through Saxony, invading Bohemia, and reaching Prague before Maria Theresa's forces drive him back to Saxony. The war ends in 1745.

- King George's War breaks out in North America as an offshoot of the War of the Austrian Succession.

- The anthem "God Save the King" is published in London.

1745

- Dutch scientist Pieter van Musschenbroek invents the Leyden Jar, which artificially generates an electric current.

- Charles Albert of Bavaria withdraws his claim to be Holy Roman Emperor and promises to support Maria Theresa's husband, Francis Stephen, who becomes Emperor Francis I.

11 May The French begin their conquest of the Austrian Netherlands.

25 July Charles Edward Stuart ("Bonnie Prince Charlie," or the Young Pretender) lands in the Hebrides to lead Scottish Highlanders in a Jacobite rebellion, proclaiming his father James Edward (the Old Pretender) James VIII of Scotland and James III of England.

Sept. The Jacobites enter Edinburgh on the eleventh and win the Battle of Prestonpans on the twenty-first.

4 Dec. The Jacobites reach Derby in England.

1746

- The French complete their conquest of the Austrian Netherlands.

16 Apr. The defeat of the Jacobites at the Battle of Culloden Moor ends efforts to restore the Stuarts to the British throne.

29 June "Bonnie Prince Charlie" escapes to the Isle of Skye disguised as a woman and remains hidden there until he is able to get away to France in September. As a result of this uprising Scotsmen are forbidden by law to wear any tartan. The ban is not lifted until 1782.

9 July Philip V of Spain dies and is succeeded by his thirty-three-year-old son, Ferdinand VI.

1747

- After severe defeats by the French in European land battles, the British achieve major naval victories against them in the Caribbean.

1748

- *De l'Esprit des lois* (The Spirit of Laws), Montesquieu's essay about the relationship between human and natural law, is published in Paris.

- The Treaty of Aix-la-Chapelle ends the War of the Austrian Succession, affirming the election of Francis I as Holy Roman Emperor and the succession of George II and his descendants (the House of Hanover) in Great Britain and their German states and giving Silesia to Frederick the Great. France gets Louisburg in Nova Scotia from Great Britain but returns the Austrian Netherlands to Austria. Prussia emerges as a world power. Great Britain comes away a defeated nation, except in North America.

1749

- *Tom Jones,* a novel by Englishman Henry Fielding, is published in London.

1750

- In his *Discours sur les sciences et les arts* (Discourse on the Sciences and the Arts) French philosopher Jean-Jacques Rousseau charges that so-called progress in the arts and sciences have corrupted humankind.

- Parliament passes the Iron Act, prohibiting the North American colonies from making iron products. Colonists are permitted to smelt iron ore into bar iron and pig iron and ship it to England, exchanging it for manufactured items. The Iron Act is generally ignored in America.

- The Westminster Bridge is completed in London. It is the first new bridge across the Thames since the London Bridge opened in the tenth century.

- French writer Denis Diderot publishes the first volume of his *Encyclopedia.* The final, twenty-eighth, volume appears in 1771.

- Frederick I of Sweden dies and is succeeded by Adophus Frederick of Oldenberg-Holstein-Gottorp, brother-in-law of Frederick the Great of Prussia.

1752

- Great Britain and her colonies adopt the modern, or Gregorian, calendar that has been in use on the Continent for some time. Because the difference between this calendar and the old, Julian calendar has grown to eleven days, 2–14 September are omitted from the 1752 British calendar.

1753

- The library and collections of the late Sir Hans Sloane form the basis for the foundation of the British Museum.

1754

● In his *Discours sur l'origine et les fondements de l'inégalité parmi les hommes* (Discourse on the Origin and Bases of Inequality among Men) Rousseau celebrates the "natural man" and calls private property and politics causes of inequality and oppression.

Mar. Prime Minister Henry Pelham dies. He is succeeded by his brother Thomas Pelham-Holles, first Duke of Newcastle.

EUROPE in the 17th CENTURY

Spanish Hapsburg Lands
Austrian Hapsburg Lands
Holy Roman Empire

THE ARTS

by KAREN L. ROOD and TIMOTHY D. HALL

CONTENTS

Sidebars and tables are listed in italics.

1603   Literature   Samuel de Champlain, *Des Sauvages.*

1605   Literature   Inca Garcilaso de la Vega, *La Florida del Inca: O historia de Adelantado Hernando de Soto.*

1608   Literature   John Smith, *A True Relation of Such Occurences and Accidents of Noate as Hath Hapned in Virginia since the First Planting of That Collony.*

1609   •   Spanish settlers begin construction on the Governor's Palace in Santa Fe, New Mexico.

1610   Literature   Gaspar Pérez de Villagrá, *Historia de la Nuevo-Mexico.*

1616   Literature   John Smith, *A Description of New England.*

1632   Literature   Samuel de Champlain, *Les Voyages de la Nouvelle-France occidentale dicte Canada.*

1634   Literature   William Wood, *New Englands Prospect.*

1637   Literature   Thomas Morton, *New English Canaan or New Canaan.*

1638   •   Construction begins on the wood-frame house of Jonathan Fairbanks in Dedham, Massachusetts. It is the earliest New England house to survive into the late twentieth century.

1640   Literature   *The Whole Booke of Psalmes (The Bay Psalm Book).*

1644

- The mission church of San Estéban in Ácoma, New Mexico, is completed by this year.

1647

Literature — Nathaniel Ward, *The Simple Cobbler of Aggawam in America;* John Winthrop, *A Declaration of the Former Passages and Proceedings betwixt the English and the Narrowgansets.*

Music — John Cotton, *Singing of Psalmes a Gospel-Ordinance.*

1650

Literature — Anne Bradstreet, *The Tenth Muse Lately Sprung Up in America.*

1654

Literature — Edward Johnson, *Wonder-working Providence of Sions Saviour in New-England.*

1655

Literature — John Hammond, *Leah and Rachel, or The two fruitfull sisters Virginia and Maryland.*

1657

Literature — John Wilson, *A Copy of Verses made by that Reverend Man of God Mr. John Wilson, pastor of the first Church in Boston: on the sudden Death of Mr. Joseph Brisco.*

1661

Literature — John Eliot, *The New Testament of our Lord and Saviour Jesus Christ. Translated into the Indian Language.*

1662

Literature — Michael Wigglesworth, *The Day of Doom.*

1663

Literature — John Eliot, *The Holy Bible: Containing the Old Testament and the New. Translated into the Indian Language.*

1664

- The first dated portraits are painted in New England: *Elizabeth Eggington,* by an unknown artist, and *Dr. John Clark,* possibly by Augustine Clement (or Clemens) of Boston.

1666

Literature   George Alsop, *A Character of the Province of Mary-land*; Michael Wigglesworth, *The Day of Doom*, second edition.

1668

Literature   Philip Pain, *Daily Meditations*.

• The Turner House is built in Salem, Massachusetts. It later becomes the setting for Nathaniel Hawthorne's novel *The House of Seven Gables* (1851).

1669

Literature   Nathaniel Morton, *New-Englands Memoriall*.

1670

Literature   Daniel Denton, *A Brief Description of New-York: Formerly Called New-Netherlands*; Michael Wigglesworth, *Meat Out of the Eater*.

• An anonymous New England artist paints *Alice Mason* and a larger painting of three other Mason children. Portraits of the three Gibbs children, also painted in 1670, may be by the same artist, possibly Samuel Clement of Boston, son of Augustine Clement.

• Retired sea captain Thomas Smith begins painting portraits in New England.

• Boston printer John Foster engraves a portrait of Reverend Richard Mather.

1672

Literature   John Josselyn, *New-Englands Rarities Discovered*.

• Spanish settlers begin construction of the Castillo de San Marcos in Saint Augustine, Florida.

1674

• An anonymous New England artist, possibly the same man who executed portraits of the Mason and Gibbs children in 1670, paints *Mrs Elizabeth Freake and Baby Mary* and *Mr John Freake*.

1676

Literature   Increase Mather, *A Brief History of the Warr with the Indians of New-England*; Benjamin Tompson, *New-Englands Tears for Her Present Miseries*.

1677

Literature   William Hubbard, *A Narrative of the Troubles with the Indians in New-England*; Increase Mather, *A Relation of the Troubles which Have Hapned in New-England, by Reason of the Indians there, from the year 1614 to the year 1675*; Urian Oakes, *An Elegie upon the Death of the Reverend Mr. Thomas Shepard*.

1678

Literature   Anne Bradstreet, *Several Poems Compiled with Great Variety of Wit and Learning.*

1681

Literature   William Penn, *Some Account of the Province of Pennsilvania.*

•   Samuel Green of Boston prints the first American edition of John Bunyan's *Pilgrim's Progress,* first published in London in 1678.

1682

Literature   Cotton Mather, *A Poem Dedicated to the Memory of the Reverend and Excellent Mr. Urian Oakes;* Mary Rowlandson, *The Soveraignty & Goodness of God.*

1683

Literature   Michael Wigglesworth, *The Day of Doom,* fourth edition.

1684

Literature   Increase Mather, *An Essay for the Recording of Illustrious Providences;* Richard Steere, *A Monumental Memorial of Marine Mercy.*

1685

Literature   Thomas Budd, *Good Order Established in Pennsilvania & New Jersey;* Cotton Mather, *An Elegy on the Much-to-Be-Deplored Death of that Never-to-Be-Forgotten Person, the Reverend Mr. Nathanael Collins;* William Penn, *A Further Account of the Province of Pennsylvania.*

1688

Literature   Juan Laiors and Fernando del Bosque, *Autos de la conquista de la Provincia de Coahuila;* Increase Mather, *A Narrative of the Miseries of New-England.*

1689

Literature   Cotton Mather, *Memorable Providences, Relating to Witchcrafts and Possessions;* Michael Wigglesworth, *Meat Out of the Eater,* fourth edition.

1692

Literature   Increase Mather, *Cases of Conscience Concerning evil Spirits Personating Men, Witchcraft, infallible Proofs of Guilt in such as are accused with that Crime;* Samuel Willard, *Some Miscellany Observations on our Present Debates Respecting Witchcrafts.*

1693

Literature   Cotton Mather, *The Wonders of the Invisible World.*

1697

Literature   John Danforth, *Kneeling to God, at Parting with Friends.*

1698

Literature   Cotton Mather, *The Boston Ebenezer. Some Historical Remarks, on the State of Boston.*

1701

Literature   Michael Wigglesworth, *The Day of Doom*, fifth edition.

1702

Literature   Cotton Mather, *Magnalia Christi Americana: or, The Ecclesiastical History of New-England.*

1704

•   English organ maker Christopher Witt arrives in the British colonies.

1705

Literature   Robert Beverley, *The History and Present State of Virginia.*

•   Artist Henrietta Johnston establishes herself as a portrait painter in Charleston, South Carolina.

1707

Literature   Benjamin Colman, *A Poem on Elijah's Translation*; Michael Wigglesworth, *Meat Out of the Eater*, fourth edition; John Williams, *The Redeemed Captive, Returning to Zion.*

1708

Literature   Ebenezer Cook, *The Sot-Weed Factor*; Benjamin Tompson, *The Grammarian's Funeral.*

•   German artist Justus Engelhardt Kühn establishes himself as a portrait painter in Annapolis, Maryland.

1710

Literature   Cotton Mather, *Bonifacius*; Benjamin Tompson, *A Neighbour's Tears.*

1711

•   Swedish artist Gustavus Hesselius arrives in America and settles in Philadelphia where he becomes the leading portrait painter.

•   Thomas Brattle of Boston installs an organ in his home. It is the first such instrument in New England and only the second in all the British colonies.

1713

Literature   Richard Steere, *The Daniel Catcher;* Nathaniel Ward, *The Simple Cobbler of Agawam in America,* first American edition.

1714

Literature   John Danforth, *A Poem, Upon the Much Honoured and Very Exemplarily Gracious Mrs. Maria Mather;* Robert Hunter, *Androboros.*

- Scottish artist John Watson settles in Perth Amboy, New Jersey.

- Thomas Brattle buys an organ for King's Chapel in Boston.

- Musicians are paid to perform in New York City at a parade and ball celebrating the coronation of George I.

- The first known advertisement for an American psalm-singing school is published in Boston.

1715

Literature   Michael Wigglesworth, *The Day of Doom,* sixth edition.

- English musician Edward Enstone arrives in Boston to become organist at King's Chapel. He soon opens a singing and dancing school and begins sponsoring public balls.

1717

Literature   Samuel Phillips, *An Elegy Upon the Deaths of Those Excellent and Learned Divines the Reverend Nicholas Noyes, A.M. and the Reverend George Curwin, A.M.;* Michael Wigglesworth, *Meat Out of the Eater,* fifth edition.

1718

Literature   Cotton Mather, *Psalterum Americanum. The Book of Psalms, In a Translation Exactly Conforming to the Original.*

1719

- *Divine Songs Attempted in Easy Language, For the Use of Children,* the first American publication of hymns by Isaac Watts, is printed in Boston.

1720

Literature   Cotton Mather, *The Christian Philosopher;* Mary Rowlandson, *The Soveraignty and Goodness of God,* second edition.

Music   Thomas Symmes, *The Reasonableness of Regular Singing by Note.*

- Henrietta Johnston paints a pastel portrait of Anne Broughton.

- Moravian composer Johann Beissel arrives in North America.

- The first known singing societies are founded in New England.

1721

Literature   Michael Wigglesworth, *Meat Out of the Eater*, sixth edition.

Music   Cotton Mather, *The Accomplished Singer*; John Tufts, *A Very Plain and Easy Introduction to the Art of Singing Psalm Tunes*; Thomas Walter, *The Grounds and Rules of Musick Explained.*

1722

Music   Thomas Walter, *The Sweet Psalmist of Israel. A Sermon Preach'd at the Lecture Held in Boston, by the Society for Promoting Regular & Good Singing, and for Reforming the Depravations and Debasements Our Psalmody Labours Under.*

1724

Literature   Hugh Jones, *The Present State of Virginia.*

- Work begins on the first Saint Louis parish church in New Orleans.

- The Dutch Reformed Church in New York installs the first known organ in that city.

1725

Literature   Benjamin Franklin, *A Dissertation on Liberty and Necessity, Pleasure and Pain*; Roger Wolcott, *Poetical Meditations.*

Music   Josiah Dwight, *An Essay to Silence the Outcry That Has Been Made in Some Places Against Regular Singing.*

1727

Literature   Mather Byles, *A Poem on the Death of His Late Majesty King George*; Cadwallader Colden, *The History of the Five Indian Nations Depending on the Province of New York.*

- Peter Pelham, an English engraver of mezzotint portraits, settles in Boston.

- Construction begins on the first Ursuline convent in New Orleans.

1728

Literature   Mather Byles, *A Poem Presented to His Excellency William Burnet, Esq.*

Music   Nathaniel Chauncey, *Regular Singing Defended, and Proved to Be the Only Way of Singing the Songs of the Lord.*

- Pipe organs are installed in Christ Church, Philadelphia, and Saint Philip's Church, Charleston.

1729

- John Smibert settles in Boston and paints portraits of notable Bostonians such as Judges Samuel Sewall and Nathaniel Byfield.

•	The first American edition of John Bunyan's spiritual autobiography, *Grace Abounding to the Chief of Sinners*, is printed for bookseller Nicholas Boone of Boston. The book was published first in London in 1666.
18 Feb.	The first known public concert in the thirteen colonies is held at Edward Enstone's school in Boston.

1730

Literature	Mather Byles, "To Mr. Smibert on the sight of his Pictures"; Ebenezer Cook, *Sotweed Redivivus*.
•	The French build a prison in New Orleans, the first brick building in the city.
•	The Men's Musical Society of Boston performs a concert to honor Saint Cecilia, the patron saint of music.

1731

Literature	Ebenezer Cook, *The Maryland Muse;* Richard Lewis, "A Journey from Patapsco to Annapolis" and "Food for Critics."

1732

Literature	Joseph Green, "A Parody on a Hymn by Mather Byles"; Richard Lewis, *A Rhapsody.*

1733

•	German organ builder Johann Gottlob Klemm settles in Philadelphia.
•	The first documented American singing recital takes place in Charleston, South Carolina.
•	A pipe organ is installed at Trinity Church in Newport, Rhode Island.

1734

Literature	Richard Lewis, "Upon Prince Madoc's Expedition to the Country now called America in the 12th Century."

1735

•	Artist Charles Bridges begins painting portraits of the Virginia gentry.
•	Charleston musicians give a public concert honoring Saint Cecilia.

1736

Literature	Thomas Prince, *A Chronological History of New-England.*
•	The first known American fiddling contest is held in Hanover County, Virginia.

21 Jan.		Charles T. Pachelbel gives a concert of vocal and instrumental music with harpsichord, flute, and violin in New York City.

1737

- French settlers build a house at Cahokia, Illinois, which becomes the courthouse and jail in 1793 and survives to become the oldest French house in the United States.

- The first edition of John and Charles Wesley's *A Collection of Psalms and Hymns* is printed by Lewis Timothy of Charleston, South Carolina, while the Wesley brothers are serving as missionaries in the colonies. The first British edition of their hymns is published in 1738.

- Charles T. Pachelbel becomes organist at Saint Philip's Church in Charleston.

1738

Literature   Mather Byles, *On the Death of the Queen. A Poem.*

1739

Music   *Zionitischer Weyrauchs-Hügel Oder* (the first American collection of Moravian hymns).

- Swiss artist Jeremiah Theüs settles in Charleston, South Carolina, where he becomes a successful portrait painter.

1741

Literature   Jonathan Edwards, *Sinners in the Hands of an Angry God.*

- Johann Gottlob Klemm installs his first American-made organ in Trinity Church, New York City.

1743

- Work begins on the mission church of Nuestra Señora de la Purisima Concepción de Acuna, near San Antonio, Texas.

- Peter Pelham III becomes organist at Trinity Church in Boston.

1744

Literature   Mather Byles, *Poems on Several Occasions;* James Logan, trans., *M. T. Cicero's Cato Major, or His Discourse of Old-Age;* Pierre François Xavier de Charlevoix, *Histoire et description de la Nouvelle France avec la Journal d'un voyage fait par ordre du Roi dans l'Amerique Septentrionale;* Patrick Tailfer, Hugh Anderson, David Douglas, and others, *A True and Historical Narrative of the Colony of Georgia.*

- Construction begins on the church at the mission of San Antonio de Valero (the Alamo), near San Antonio, Texas.

- Benjamin Franklin of Philadelphia publishes the first American edition of Samuel Richardson's popular novel *Pamela*, first published in England in 1740–1741.

- The Collegium Musicum is founded in Bethlehem, Pennsylvania.

1745

- Work begins on the second Ursuline convent in New Orleans.

1746

- Edward Bromfield of Boston becomes the first American-born craftsman to build a pipe organ in New England.

1747

Literature · William Douglass, *A Summary, Historical and Political, of the First Planting, Progressive Improvements, and Present State of the British Settlements in North America*, volume 1, nos. 1–16; William Livingston, *Philosophic Solitude*; William Stith, *The History of the First Discovery and Settlement of Virginia*.

Music · *Das Gesaeng der Einsamen und Verlassenen Turtel-Taube Nemlich der Christlichen Kirche* [the first collection of hymns published by the Ephrata religious colony in Pennsylvania].

- William Bradford of Philadelphia prints the first American edition of Alexander Pope's *An Essay on Man*, first published in England in 1732–1734.

1748

Literature · William Douglass, *A Summary, Historical and Political, of the First Planting, Progressive Improvements, and Present State of the British Settlements in North America*, volume 1, nos. 17–28.

1749

Literature · William Douglass, *A Summary, Historical and Political, of the First Planting, Progressive Improvements, and Present State of the British Settlements in North America*, volume 1, nos. 29–36.

- The chapel at the Presidio la Bahía in Goliad, Texas, is built.

- Charles T. Pachelbel opens a singing school in Charleston, South Carolina.

1750

Literature · William Douglass, *A Summary, Historical and Political, of the First Planting, Progressive Improvements, and Present State of the British Settlements in North America*, volume 2, nos. 1–14; Joseph Green, *Entertainment for a Winter's Evening*.

- French settlers build Parlange on a plantation in Point Coupée Parish, Louisiana.

- Thomas Fleet of Boston prints the first American edition of Joseph Addison's *Cato: A Tragedy*, first produced in London in 1713.

1751

Literature   Benjamin Church, *A Poem Occasioned by the Death of the honorable Jonathan Law, Esq., Late Governor of Connecticut;* William Douglass, *A Summary, Historical and Political, of the First Planting, Progressive Improvements, and Present State of the British Settlements in North America,* volume 2, nos. 15–23; Michael Wigglesworth, *The Day of Doom,* seventh edition.

- James Parker of New York prints the first American edition of John Gay's *The Beggar's Opera,* first performed in London in 1728.

1752

Literature   William Douglass, *A Summary, Historical and Political, of the First Planting, Progressive Improvements, and Present State of the British Settlements in North America,* volume 2; James Sterling, *An Epistle to the Hon. Arthur Dobbs, Esq.*

- Thomas Johnston establishes himself as an organ builder and restorer in Boston.

- The first documented use of an orchestra in an opera performance takes place in Upper Marlborough, Maryland.

1753

- Hugh Gaines of New York prints the first American edition of Hugh Blair's long poem *The Grave,* first published in England in 1743.

- English singer-composer William Tuckey begins giving private singing lessons in New York City.

1754

Literature   Thomas Cradock, *A Poetical Translation of the Psalms of David;* George Washington, *The Journal of Major George Washington.*

Music   Johann Conrad Beissel, *Paradisisches Wunder-Spiel.*

OVERVIEW

The Limits of Taste in Seventeenth-Century British America. The homeland of the first English colonists boasted a culture of high artistic achievement. William Shakespeare was still writing plays as the settlers at Jamestown, Virginia, struggled to survive. English painters produced vibrant, lifelike works on canvas, and the music of English composers enlivened the banquets and balls of the gentry, nobility, and court. Yet for a variety of reasons the first American colonists seldom enjoyed the artistic achievements of seventeenth-century England. The fine arts required significant money, time, and talent to sustain them, and most of the early colonists' energies and resources were committed to establishing livable settlements. Most of these settlers came from the middle ranks of society, which found the luxuries of fine arts beyond their means, and thus rarely cultivated artistic taste. Puritan colonists consciously rejected fine arts such as the theater and some forms of painting and sculpture. They thought such pursuits wasteful of time and money at best and immoral at worst. Puritans considered sacred art to be idolatry and the use of instrumental music in worship to be one of the "popish" rituals of Roman Catholicism. Puritan meetinghouses were austere and unadorned. Their worship was simple, making Scripture central in unaccompanied psalm singing and preaching. Yet Puritan New England was a highly literate culture, and an emphasis on the written word gave rise to accomplished poets such as Anne Bradstreet and Edward Taylor. In New England and elsewhere in seventeenth-century America, the demands of survival and colony building restricted most artistic expression to useful objects produced by artisans. A cabinetmaker might adorn a clock or chest with fancy carvings; a carpenter might decorate the facade of a house with carved trim; a stonecutter might cut a skull or other designs on a tombstone; and a seamstress might embroider a floral design on a handkerchief.

The Artistic Heritage of the Continent. Settlers from the great colonial powers of continental Europe brought with them the heritage of their homelands. The Protestant Netherlands boasted some of the highest artistic achievements of the seventeenth century, particularly in painting. Dutch colonists brought some of these paintings with them to adorn their New World homes, and several Dutch painters came to the colonies to paint landscapes and portraits. Over time, however, Dutch colonial art declined. The ceremonial requirements of Roman Catholicism stimulated artistic achievement in New France and the Spanish Borderlands. Though the earliest church interiors in the Spanish Southwest date from the end of the eighteenth century, it is known that colonial sculptors and painters adorned them with sacred statues and paintings far earlier. Catholic missionaries perpetuated Old World traditions of sacred music. Ceremony and festival accompanied important life passages such as weddings and funerals. In Spanish colonies a rich tradition of folk song and festival sprang up to take a place alongside religious ceremonies or to replace them in the absence of priests. French settlers perpetuated old folk traditions in New France. French and Spanish colonial officials likewise sought to reproduce the grandeur of courtly entertainment they had known in Europe, staging concerts and plays and adorning public buildings with imported sculptures and paintings.

The Rise of Genteel Sensibilities in British America. Near the end of the seventeenth century a prosperous colonial gentry who had satisfied what Benjamin Franklin termed "the first cares and necessaries of life" began surrounding themselves with the "embellishments" of decor, entertainments, and leisure pursuits enjoyed by the English gentry. Contemporaries termed these fineries "genteel" or "polite" to signify a level of polish, refinement, elegance, or intellectual attainment appropriate to English and colonial elites. Stately Georgian mansions began to appear along the streets of bustling port cities or on the banks of busy waterways. Their owners began adorning their walls with handsome tapestries and family portraits, covering the floors with rich Turkish rugs, lining shelves with fashionable English books, displaying fancy tea sets or an occasional sculpture on elegant cherry-wood tables, and filling the halls with polite English music. While skilled colonial artisans often produced furniture for these homes, much of the artwork, and most of the fancy tableware, books, and music were imported from England. Colonial musicians learned to play popular European dance numbers. Wealthy patrons placed organs in Anglican and Lutheran churches so that European sacred music could enhance worship. In some cities the gentry were also able to encourage public entertainments such as the theater. In the field of portraiture Gustavus Hesselius of Philadelphia and John Smibert of Boston set new standards and led the way for the emergence of the first great native-born painters, Benjamin West, Charles Willson Peale, and John Singleton Copley in the late 1750s and early 1760s. They achieved international fame, however, by imitating the very best in European cultural achievements of the period.

Literature. The first Anglo-American printing press was set up in Cambridge, Massachusetts, in 1640 to provide Puritan colonists with copies of religious books and to print books for Harvard College, and by 1720 there were presses in ten other colonial cities. The first full-length book printed in Cambridge was *The Whole Booke of Psalmes* (1640), also called *The Bay Psalm Book.* Most colonial readers also wanted to buy almanacs, cheap "chapbooks" of poems or stories, and reprints of popular English literature. Colonial printers did their best to meet these demands, sometimes risking trouble from religious leaders to do so. Yet they lacked the resources to print many longer books, which were usually imported from England. John Bunyan's *Pilgrim's Progress* became a best-seller in America within a few years of its first publication in England in 1678, and Samuel Green of Boston printed the first American edition in 1681. The novels of English writers such as Daniel Defoe, Henry Fielding, and Samuel Richardson found an avid eighteenth-century American readership. Eighteenth-century American gentlemen's clubs such as the Junto, established by Benjamin Franklin in 1727, provided the literate gentry with opportunities to read and discuss the latest European works of literature, philosophy, political theory, and science. These clubs also provided budding American writers a readership for manuscripts of their own works. Many were never printed. Authors and their friends produced multiple copies by hand and circulated them among gentlemen's clubs throughout the colonies. One distinctly American form of popular literature did emerge in the colonial period: captivity narratives, harrowing tales of wartime capture by Native Americans. These narratives usually shared a standard theme: how God enabled the captive to survive the ordeal, escape or be ransomed, and return home.

Sacred Music. Americans rarely think of their colonial forebears as having been musically inclined, but much surviving evidence indicates that music making was a popular colonial pastime. Singing versifications of the Psalms was a common form of worship throughout colonial America. Congregationalist, Presbyterian, and Dutch and German Reformed churches all discouraged composition of sacred lyrics to prevent errors in doctrine, often prohibited instrumental accom-

paniment of sacred singing to guard against empty ritualism, and frowned on the singing of parts or harmonizing to keep good singers from becoming vain. In the early eighteenth century, however, controversy broke out in Boston as ministers such as Benjamin Colman and Cotton Mather encouraged musical education to improve the singing in their congregations. The Great Awakening of the 1740s and after brought with it a new wave of popular hymn singing throughout the colonies, as the compositions of Isaac Watts and John and Charles Wesley antagonized an older generation of strict "psalm singers."

Secular Music. Ordinary colonists brought a rich repertoire of popular folk music and dance from Europe and eventually adapted it to American situations. They enjoyed this music and dance in taverns and at popular gatherings such as weddings, feasts, and other celebrations. African Americans often became accomplished players of European music and musical instruments, providing accompaniment at such gatherings. Over time they introduced selected African forms into Anglo-American music and dance as well as incorporating European forms into their own musical traditions. Cultured European music also made its way into eighteenth-century port cities, often introduced by immigrant musicians such as professional organists, hired to play the new organs that were beginning to appear in churches. These musicians could rarely support themselves by performance alone, living mainly on income from teaching music and dance and selling printed music and musical instruments. The first known public concert in America was given in Boston in 1729 by an ensemble of a few professional musicians and a larger number of amateurs. Until the 1750s such performances were usually confined to port cities and colonial capitals, and most were available by private subscription only.

Theater. American theater performances were prohibited by religious and secular authorities in some colonies, including Massachusetts and Connecticut. Productions were staged in Williamsburg as early as 1716, in Charleston and New York by the 1730s, and in Philadelphia by the late 1740s, but the market was too small for many acting companies to become self-supporting. Eighteenth-century gentlemen's clubs provided the most common venue for amateur musical concerts and theater, and they often supplied most of the performers as well.

Colonial Portraiture. Wealthy colonial gentry commissioned portraits of family members to signify their importance in society and impose a sense of duty on generations to come. Public figures commissioned portraits to commemorate accomplishments such as the assumption of governorships or the winning of military campaigns. Successful portrait painters such as Smibert might sustain a brisk business by completing a new commission every two weeks, but even the best found it necessary to supplement their incomes by selling imported artistic prints and supplies. Many other portrait painters made their livings on the road, traveling from town to town in search of families who wanted to preserve their likenesses for future generations. These itinerant portrait makers created hundreds of family portraits that survive to the present, providing historians with rich insights into eighteenth-century American tastes, values, dress, family life, and patterns of consumption.

Sources:

Richard L. Bushman, *The Refinement of America: Persons, Houses, Cities* (New York: Knopf, 1992);

Cary Carson, Ronald Hoffman, and Peter J. Albert, eds., *Of Consuming Interests: The Style of Life in the Eighteenth Century* (Charlottesville: University Press of Virginia, 1994);

Diana Fane, ed., *Converging Cultures: Art and Identity in Spanish America* (New York: Abrams, 1996).

TOPICS IN THE NEWS

ARCHITECTURE

Spanish Influences. The most lasting contribution of Spanish colonists to American culture is in the field of architecture. Though the early architecture of Florida differs from that of the Southwest and California, both are derived from the tastes of the seventeenth-century Spanish court, as they were transmitted to the New World by Catholic missionary-priests.

Florida. The earliest surviving buildings in Florida date from around the middle of the seventeenth century. Of these the most notable is the Castillo de San Marcos in Saint Augustine, begun in 1672 and often called the finest structure of its kind in the United States. Built around a one-hundred-square-foot central courtyard, this castle has spear-shaped bastions at its four corners, massive walls made of coquina (a form of limestone), and a forty-foot moat. Comparing favorably to fortresses constructed in Europe at the same time, the Castillo was successfully defended during attacks from English forces in 1702, 1728, and 1740.

The Southwest and Texas. In the Southwest, where the Spanish adapted the building practices of the Pueblo Indians, Native American builders created the only examples of American architecture in which the traditions of the indigenous culture significantly altered European tradition. An important example of this style is the Governor's Palace in Santa Fe, New Mexico, built in 1609–1614 and rebuilt in 1680 and at several later dates. Constructed from adobe and featuring a long covered porch, it is believed to be the oldest surviving structure built for white people in the United States. The earliest of the many Spanish mission churches still in existence in the United States is San Estéban in Ácoma, New Mexico, completed before 1644. The earliest surviving examples of murals in Southwestern Spanish missions, which date from the late eighteenth century, reveal a distinctive local style that combines imagery from Native American mythology with Christian symbolism—a style that probably developed earlier. Texas has three mission churches that were started in the 1740s and completed during the second half of the century: Nuestra Señora de la Purisima Concepción de Acuna, begun by 1743 and dedicated by 1755; the church at the mission of San Antonio de Valero (the Alamo), started in 1744 and completed after 1777; and the chapel at the Presidio la Bahía in Goliad, established in 1749. The missions of California were constructed between 1769 and 1823.

French Influences. After René-Robert Cavelier, Sieur de La Salle, explored the region in 1682, the French began establishing trading posts at strategic locations in the Mississippi River valley from Canada all the way south to the Gulf of Mexico. The original seventeenth-century structures built at these settlements have been destroyed by fire or flood. The oldest surviving French house is the so-called Courthouse in Cahokia, Illinois, built as a private residence around 1737 and converted to a courthouse and jail in 1793. This and other early French buildings were built of upright logs set in the ground or on stone foundations. The logs were hewn flat on the sides that faced the interior and exterior of the structure, and the spaces between them were filled with stones, bricks, or clay mixed with binding materials such as moss, grass, or hair. Often the outside was covered with lime plaster to retard erosion by wind and rain. Like later French houses in the New World, Cahokia Courthouse has a high, double-pitched roof to accommodate a covered *galerie*, or veranda, around all four sides of the house. Especially adapted to hot climates, this style was employed in the larger, often two-story plantation houses built in Louisiana later in the eighteenth century. The earliest of these houses, Parlange, was built around 1750 in Pointe Coupée Parish.

The Governor's Palace in Santa Fe, New Mexico (top), erected by the Spanish in 1609–1614, and the Courthouse in Cahokia, Illinois (bottom), built by French settlers as a private residence around 1737

New Orleans. In New Orleans, settled by the French in 1718, the earliest buildings were constructed according to a medieval technique called *briqueté entre poteaux*, which employed massive wooden vertical posts with brick infilling between them. These walls were often covered with boards or plaster, but in and around New Orleans they were sometimes left exposed and consequently suffered deterioration from the weather. Many of the early-eighteenth-century buildings in New Orleans were destroyed by fires that devastated the city in 1788 and 1794. Among these was the first parish church of Saint Louis, designed in 1724–1727 by Adrien de Pauger. Built of plastered *briqueté entre poteaux*, the church had a cruciform (cross-shaped) floor plan typical of European churches, a pedimented facade, and a circular window over the arched doorway. In 1727 François Broutin designed another *briqueté entre poteaux* building to serve as the first Ursuline convent. The first major brick building in the city was the prison (1730), designed in Louis XV style by Pierre Baron. The only surviving public building in New Orleans that dates from before the city was ceded to Spain in 1764 is the second Ursuline convent, a brick structure designed by Broutin in 1745 to replace the first convent, whose wooden timbers had not held up well in the humid climate of the city.

New Netherland. Dutch and Flemish settlers brought to New Netherland a rich tradition of brickwork that is still evident in the Low Countries of Europe. Though some bricks may at first have been imported from Europe as ballast on ships, kilns capable of producing good-quality bricks were established not long after the first settlers arrived in New Amsterdam in 1626. Before long the first settlement of thirty bark-covered houses and a palisaded blockhouse was replaced by a city that looked much like those of Holland. Most of the buildings were brick with steep tile roofs and stepped-up gable ends facing the street. These steps were useful to chimney sweeps, who would otherwise have had to climb on the perilously slippery roof tiles. Similar houses were built in Albany and other larger settlements. None of these early Dutch townhouses has survived. The earliest Dutch farmhouses were built in the same style, but they tended to have straight gables at the sides.

Dutch Farmhouses. Dutch farm settlements in the lower Hudson River valley, northern New Jersey, and western Long Island usually had houses of stone or wood, or the two combined. The still-popular Dutch colonial style with its double-hipped, or gambrel, roof had its origins in these settlements. Buildings in this style are not found in the Netherlands, and it may have been derived from a combination of Dutch and Flemish construction techniques adapted to suit the weather and available materials of the region.

Swedish and German Settlements. The major contribution of the first settlers of New Sweden, established in the Delaware River Valley in 1636, was the log cabin. Such houses constructed of round logs notched at corners and with projecting ends were unknown in England, Holland, and France. Some historians believe that the German settlers of Pennsylvania brought similar con-

A Dutch townhouse (left), built in Beverwyck (Albany, New York) in the mid seventeenth century, somewhat altered in 1805, and demolished during the 1870s; and a Dutch farmhouse (right), built in East Greenbush, New York, around 1722 and in ruins by the 1940s

Bacon's Castle, built in Surry County, Virginia, around 1655

struction traditions with them from the Old World, but others think the Germans may have learned cabin building from their Swedish neighbors. In either case the Swedes and Germans are responsible for teaching settlers of other nationalities how to build the housing that dominated western frontier settlements for all of the eighteenth century and well into the nineteenth as well. Later German farmers in Pennsylvania built beautiful, practical stone houses and barns. Though they were not unconcerned with aesthetics, even the most prosperous of the so-called Pennsylvania Dutch were antagonistic to the aristocratic pretensions that led eighteenth-century southern planters and merchant princes of the New England and mid-Atlantic colonies to build houses that rivaled those of the English gentry and lesser nobility.

The Dominance of British Architecture. While colonists of several nationalities contributed to American architecture, housing styles in the English colonies were predominantly based on British models. Yet architectural trends were slow to reach the New World and were often modified to meet the demands of colonial life, including extremes of temperature uncommon in England and a scarcity of craftsmen sufficiently skilled to fashion ornate architectural details. Colonists also modified plans to suit available construction materials. For exam-

ple, wood was far more plentiful in North America than in England or on the Continent, while the lack of a plentiful source for the lime used in mortar in New England and coastal areas of Virginia made brick buildings expensive in those regions.

The First English Settlements. The earliest settlers of Jamestown in 1607 and New England in the 1620s and 1630s built simple shelters in the primitive folk tradition of the English peasant class. Using tree branches to frame a small, one-room cabin or a "wigwam" of bent poles, they often made walls of woven wattle (willow rods or slender branches from other trees) and covered them with daub, or mud. Typically the thatched roof had a hole in it to let out the smoke from a stone hearth in the center of the earth floor. Occasionally such a structure had a mud-and-stick chimney. In Connecticut, Philadelphia, and eastern Long Island the earliest English colonists' shelters were dugouts in banks with roofs and walls formed of brush and sod. Some buildings, such as the church at Plymouth and houses in the English settlements of eastern New Jersey, were of palisade construction, sawn planks driven into the ground. The English most often used this construction technique for forts and churches.

Seventeenth-Century New England. The first full-scale houses in New England were built for ministers and important officials, such as Gov. John Winthrop of the Massachusetts Bay Colony soon after the colonists' arrival. These houses were modeled after the half-timbered, thatched-roof houses of England, with heavy hewn-oak frames filled with clay and straw, wattle, or sun-dried brick and covered with clay. This sort of house was warm enough and sturdy enough for the temperate climate of England, but not for the cold winters and harsh storms of New England. The colonists soon began covering the exteriors of such houses with weather boards and then adapted their methods to build timber-frame houses. The earliest surviving New England houses are of this type. Though some thatched roofs continued to be used until the end of the seventeenth century, wood shingles, which had become too expensive for general use in England, were the most common form of roofing throughout the English colonies well before that time. While most surviving New England houses are two stories high, historians point out that preservationists have nearly always concentrated their efforts on saving bigger houses. In fact most New Englanders of the seventeenth century probably lived in one-story or one-and-a-half-story wooden houses.

Saltboxes. Two rooms wide and one room deep, the surviving examples of New England houses from the seventeenth century typically have a second story that extends beyond the first in front, creating a slight overhang. The heavy ceiling beams are exposed while the spaces between the vertical timbers in the walls are filled with insulating materials such as clay and straw, wattle and straw, or unfired brick. The interior walls were then covered with plaster or wooden wainscot. Some larger houses have single-story lean-to rooms on the back. In cases where the roof line is continuous these dwellings came to be named after the wooden boxes in which the colonists kept their salt. This "saltbox" style became more common later in the seventeenth century, and lean-to rooms were also added to existing houses. Sometimes extra gables were added to create more space under the roof. For windows small, diamond-shaped panes of glass were held together with strips of lead. Because window glass was heavily taxed and imported from Europe until after the Revolution, windows were usually small. Most seventeenth-century windows did not open. Those that did open were hinged at one side. The earliest surviving New England house is probably the residence of Jonathan Fairbanks, begun in 1636 in Dedham, Massachusetts. Because the house has been altered by later renovations and additions, however, other, slightly later houses are better examples of seventeenth-century New England architecture. In Massachusetts such houses include the Whipple House (1640) at Ipswich, the "Scotch"-Boardman House (circa 1650) at Saugus, the Turner House (1668) at Salem (Nathaniel Hawthorne's "House of Seven Gables"), the Parson Capen House

(1683) at Topsfield, and the John Ward House (1684) at Salem. Among the notable seventeenth-century houses in Connecticut is the faithfully restored Stanley-Whitman House (circa 1660) in Farmington, one of the best-preserved and most-typical examples of the framed-overhang, saltbox houses in New England.

The Meetinghouse. The first public building in the New England village was the meetinghouse, which served as both church and town hall. The only surviving seventeenth-century building of this sort is the Old Ship Meeting House, built in 1681 in Hingham, Massachusetts, which got its name because its roof looks like a ship's hull turned upside down. The structure of its interior has been compared to the great halls of medieval Europe, but—in keeping with its builders' Puritan beliefs—its stark furnishings and simple exterior seem to have been modeled on churches in Protestant Holland, not on the Gothic-style Anglican churches of England. Other New England towns are known to have built similar meetinghouses during the seventeenth century.

Seventeenth-Century Southern Architecture. While early Virginians built wooden houses similar to those in New England, the only surviving seventeenth-century houses in Virginia, and most seventeenth-century houses found throughout the South, are brick. (One notable exception is Bond Castle, a wooden house built in Calvert County, Maryland, during the last quarter of the century.) In most areas throughout the southern colonies, settlers had adequate supplies of lime for mortar, and consequently brick construction was more common there than in New England. While documents from the period reveal that most colonial southerners lived in wooden houses, as in other parts of the country, the nicest houses have been those most likely to survive. Like New England houses of the same period, the earliest southern houses were only one room deep. While New Englanders usually put the chimney at the center of the house for maximum warmth, southerners tended to put them at either end, with a central passageway for ventilation during hot weather. This differentiation became more pronounced as time passed. In general Southern architecture of the seventeenth century was more varied than that of New England.

Bacon's Castle. One of the most unusual and interesting southern houses is Bacon's Castle in Surry County, Virginia. Built of brick around 1655 by Arthur Allen, it gets its name because followers of Nathaniel Bacon used it as a fortress during Bacon's Rebellion of 1676. With a style of shaped gable that came to England from the Low Countries just before 1600 and three diamond-shaped chimney stacks at either end, a style dating from earlier in the sixteenth century, Bacon's Castle resembles some houses that were built in England during the first forty years of the seventeenth century. This style of architecture is uncommon in North America, but in its cross-shaped layout the house does have some similarity to other southern buildings of the period, notably the

Stratford Hall (top), built in Westmoreland County, Virginia, around 1725–1730, and Drayton Hall (bottom), erected near Charleston, South Carolina, in 1738–1742

fourth Virginia statehouse, constructed at Jamestown in 1685 and destroyed by fire in 1698. Newport Parish Church (Saint Luke's), begun in 1632 at Smithfield, Virginia, also has architectural features similar to those of Bacon's Castle. This church, which also bears some resemblance to the ruined brick church built in 1647 at Jamestown, has been compared to the many rural churches built in England during the late-medieval period.

The Georgian Period. While folk tradition continued to influence colonial building practices in the early eighteenth century, there was a move toward the use of classical motifs in architecture and furniture, a style that came to the colonies from England and first became apparent in the homes of the wealthy, who created plans for their houses by consulting architectural illustrations in design books imported from England. An eighteenth-century colonial gentleman might have several such books in his library. Virginian William Byrd of Westover owned ten design books published before 1730, and by 1750 several other design books could be found in the colonies. Among the earliest and most influential were *Vitruvius Britannicus* (1715), examples of classical-style British architecture compiled by Scottish architect Colin Campbell, and *The Architecture of A. Palladio* (1715), by Venetian architect Giacomo Leoni. Leoni's book was called an English translation of *Quattro Libri dell' Architecttura* (1570), by Venetian Andrea Palladio, who is often credited with launching the revival of classical-style architecture on the Continent. In fact, Leoni altered Palladio's designs to suit his own tastes, and the English architects who wrote design books put their own stamps on the style, which is widely known as Georgian. (Some architectural historians, recognizing that the use of this style in England predates the ascension of George I to the throne in 1714, call it Anglo-Palladianism.)

New World Classicism. Owing in large part to the various Navigation Acts passed between 1650 and 1775, which restricted imports—including books and furniture—from countries other than Great Britain, wealthy colonists of the eighteenth century, regardless of their ethnic backgrounds, looked to British models when they built new homes to display their affluence and refined tastes. Some of these houses have classical design elements but are not truly Palladian. Stratford Hall in Westmoreland County, Virginia, built by the Lee family in 1725–1730, has the symmetrical floor plan favored by classicists but seems to owe more to an earlier English Baroque tradition. Westover, the circa 1730–1735 home of the Byrd family in Charles City County, Virginia, has an unbalanced floor plan and classical-looking door frames. It also has two features that appeared for the first time throughout the colonies in the eighteenth century: dormers and sash windows. The Ionic-style door frame at Whitehall, the Newport, Rhode Island, house remodeled for George Berkeley in 1728–1731, is possibly the first truly Palladian feature in America. The first com-pletely Georgian, or Anglo-Palladian, house in America is Drayton Hall, near Charleston, South Carolina, built by John Drayton in 1738–1742. This house seemed to signal the arrival of the new style that would dominate American architecture for the rest of the century, but at the same time the wealthy Hancock family of Boston built a mansion that hearkened back to an Anglo-Dutch style that had been popular in England during the previous century.

Church Architecture. The greatest influence on eighteenth-century colonial church architecture was Sir Christopher Wren, who designed fifty-one churches to replace those destroyed in 1666 during the Great Fire of London. Wren's steeples, which differed from earlier Gothic-style towers, were widely copied in the colonies and sometimes added to existing churches. The second Saint Philip's Church in Charleston, constructed in 1711–1723 and destroyed by fire in 1835, had a steeple that was a shorter version of the one Wren designed for the Church of Saint Magnus the Martyr in London. Christ Church, or Old North Church in Boston, designed by William Price and begun in 1723 with a spire added in 1741, was influenced by two Wren churches, Saint James's, Picadilly, and Saint Lawrence Jewery—as was Trinity Church in Newport, Rhode Island, designed and built by Richard Munday in 1725–1726 with its spire also added in 1741. In addition to these Anglican churches, the Congregationalist Old South Church of Boston, designed by Robert Twelves and built in 1729–1730, has a traditional, almost square New England–meetinghouse shape, but its external architectural elements are similar to those of the Old North Church and its spire resembles the one Wren designed for Saint Mary-le-Bow in London.

Sources:

Marcus Whiffen and Frederick Koeper, *American Architecture, 1607–1976* (Cambridge, Mass.: MIT Press, 1981);

Louis B. Wright, George B. Tatum, John W. McCoubrey, and Robert C. Smith, *The Arts in America: The Colonial Period* (New York: Scribners, 1966).

ART: PORTRAIT PAINTING

Dutch Artistic Traditions. The Dutch brought to the New World the tastes of the sophisticated art world of the Netherlands. Their homes were decorated with oil paintings and prints, including landscapes, still lifes, and religious subjects. Artists were active in New Netherland before painters are known to have begun creating portraits in New England, but only three seventeenth-century Dutch colonial works have survived: portraits of Gov. Peter Stuyvesant, Nicholas William Stuyvesant, and Jacobus Strycker, probably painted around 1661–1666. They are attributed to Huguenot Henri Couturier, who arrived in New Amsterdam in 1660. These paintings are more sophisticated than those produced in New York and New Jersey over the next century, as families of Dutch descent bought portraits painted by several generations of "limners" (that is, de-

Self-portrait by Gerrit Duyckinck, painted in 1695 (New-York Historical Society)

lineators, or artists who depicted their subjects by drawing). Usually earning their livings at other trades such as decorative painting of houses or making and decorating glass (glaziers), these artists were sometimes self-taught, and some were known to travel from place to place in search of commissions.

The Duyckincks. One of the earliest limners was Evert Duyckinck (1621–circa 1703). None of his paintings has survived, but coats of arms enameled on the windows of the Dutch Reformed Church at Albany in 1656 are known to be his work. Some ten portraits are attributed to his youngest son, Gerrit Duyckinck (1660–circa 1712), and Gerrit's son Gerardus Duyckinck (1695–circa 1746) painted *The Birth of the Virgin* (1713), the earliest dated and signed New York painting, and many other portraits and biblical works. Evert Duyckinck III (1677–circa 1725), son of nonartist Evert Duyckinck II, painted portraits in a style similar to that of his cousin Gerardus, whose eldest son, also named Gerardus, took over the family's art-supply business and may also have been an artist.

Later Dutch Artists. Dutch painters continued to arrive in New York and New Jersey during the early years of the eighteenth century. Pietr Vanderlyn painted portraits of leading Kingston and Albany families around

PRINTMAKING

As in England, the most popular art form in the British colonies during the seventeenth and eighteenth centuries was the print. The "pictures" listed in many seventeenth-century household inventories were usually small engravings, most often portraits of prominent people. The first known portrait print made in the British colonies—and the only one surviving from the seventeenth century—is a portrait of the Reverend Richard Mather, a woodcut made by Boston printer-engraver John Foster in 1670.

In the eighteenth century most prints were still imported from England, but Americans began making their own portrait prints for use in books and almanacs. Thomas Emmes's 1728 copperplate engraving of Reverend Increase Mather became a model for other frontispiece engravings of clergymen. Boston printer James Franklin studied printmaking in London and is believed to have done most or all of the illustrations for the books and almanacs he published, including the frontispiece portrait of the author in Hugh Peter's *A Dying Father's Last Legacy to an Only Child* (1717). Thomas Johnson's 1755 line engraving of *A Perspective Plan of the Battle fought Near Lake George on the 8ᵗʰ of September 1755* may be the first historical print published in the British colonies.

By 1710 colonial artists were making mezzotints, engraving images on copper or steel in a manner that allowed them to create images that appeared more three-dimensional than in simpler forms of engraving. The earliest may be John Simon's portraits of four Iroquois chieftains, published in 1710. William Burgis, who was active in Boston in 1716–1731, produced topographical mezzotints such as *A Northeast View of the Great Town of Boston* (circa 1723), *The Boston Lighthouse* (1729), and *View of Fort George* (1729–1731).

The best-known colonial mezzotint artist was Peter Pelham, who had been a printmaker in London before he set up shop in Boston in 1727. His best-known mezzotint is his portrait of Reverend Cotton Mather (1728), for which Pelham copied his own oil painting of the famous Puritan. After John Smibert arrived in Boston in 1729, Pelham based many of his mezzotints on Smibert's portraits of notable New Englanders. Pelham's 1747 portraits of Sir William Pepperrell and Gov. William Shirley, both based on paintings by Smibert, are considered Pelham's finest works. Pelham passed on his knowledge of printmaking to his stepson John Singleton Copley, who eventually surpassed both Pelham and Smibert as an artist.

Source: Jacob Ernest Cooke, ed., *Encyclopedia of the North American Colonies,* volume 3 (New York: Scribners, 1993).

Portrait of Margaret Gibbs painted by an unknown artist in the early 1670s and a self-portrait painted by Thomas Smith around 1690 (both paintings: Worcester Art Museum, Worcester, Massachusetts)

1730–1745. John Heaten, who married a Dutch woman and painted in the Dutch style, was active as a portrait painter in the upper Hudson Valley during the same time. He is also known for his landscapes and genre paintings. Yet by the eighteenth century even colonists of Dutch extraction, particularly those prosperous enough to buy artworks, had come to favor English styles of painting—as the tastes of the English aristocracy gradually prevailed over the traditions settlers of various nationalities brought with them from the Old World.

Puritanism and Practicality. The nonaristocratic origins of the colonists and the practical demands of everyday life in the new American colonies guaranteed that the idea of "art for art's sake" was slow in developing in the New World. In New England the Puritans' belief that religious images in particular and ornamentation in general smacked of popery and heresy reinforced the general emphasis on utility over artistry in early colonial history. Yet throughout the British colonies settlers tended to share a distrust of art that had been fostered in the mother country by several generations of religious reformers. Like their fellow Englishmen, however, even the Puritans approved of portrait painting, not as an art form but as a practical means of preserving the likeness of an esteemed political or religious leader or a beloved family member, and ironically mid-seventeenth-century New England, blessed with prosperity and political stability, was the first British colony to foster the arts of portraiture and decorative painting.

Seventeenth-Century New England. As in New Netherland, the first New England portrait painters of-ten made their livings as house painters or glaziers. Others were primarily sign painters. There are also records of early, anonymous portrait painters who traveled from town to town. Little is known about the work of the earliest portraitists. One of the most talented was Augustine Clement, a glassmaker from Reading who arrived in Boston in 1635. Unsigned portraits of Reverend Richard Mather, Dr. John Clark, and Gov. John Endicott are attributed to Clement. The portrait of Clark and an unsigned portrait of Elizabeth Eggington are both inscribed 1664, making them the first New England portraits that can be dated with certainty. Though these portraits share some traditional stylistic similarities, they were clearly painted by different artists. Seven unsigned portraits of parents and their children, all painted between 1670 and 1674, have sometimes been attributed to Clement's son Samuel. *Mr. John Freake, Mrs. Elizabeth Freake and Baby Mary, The Mason Children, Alice Mason,* and three individual portraits of children in the Gibbs family share a richness of color and a sympathetic attention to facial details. These portraits are painted in an Elizabethan style that had gone out of fashion in London but was still practiced in provincial England. Rather than creating the illusion of three dimensions through the use of perspective shading, the artist emphasized color, decorative pattern, and symbolic details (a bird as a symbol of the soul, for example). Another anonymous artist active in Boston during the 1670s painted portraits of John Wensley and Elizabeth Paddy Wensley that display more spatial sense than the Freake, Mason, and Gibbs portraits, but the figures are still rather flat, and the artist also concentrated his efforts on color and symbolism.

Portrait of Tishcohan (1735), by Gustavus Hesselius (Historical Society of Pennsylvania, Philadelphia)

Thomas Smith. In England artistic tastes had shifted to the realistic Dutch Baroque style brought to England by Sir Anthony Van Dyck in the 1620s and 1630s. The first British colonial artist to paint in this style was Capt. Thomas Smith, who seems to have learned something about painting in England or Holland and arrived in New England around 1650. Between 1670 and 1691 he painted several portraits of political and military leaders, including a self-portrait. The background includes a naval battle in which Smith was probably involved, and the foreground includes objects that express his Puritan religious convictions. More a gifted amateur than a professional artist, Smith attempted to use the latest painterly techniques to give his portraits a sense of space and three-dimensionality, but while he seems to have captured true likenesses of his subjects, his paintings remain rather flat and wooden in comparison to portraits by contemporaries in England.

The Eighteenth Century. By the 1680s in England Sir Godfrey Kneller had become official court painter in England, establishing the Anglo-Dutch style formulated by Van Dyck and others as the one preferred by the English aristocracy and all others with aspirations to become people of taste. In the early eighteenth century the prosperity of the colonies began to draw trained artists to growing port cities. Henrietta Johnston, a painter of miniatures, arrived in Charleston, South Carolina, in 1705 and remained active there until her death around 1728–1729. She was followed by Swiss artist Jeremiah Theüs, who established a practice that lasted until 1774. German painter Justus Engelhardt Kühn was active in Annapolis from 1708 until his death in 1717. Scots painter John Watson (1684–1762) settled in Perth Amboy, New Jersey, in 1714. British portrait engraver Peter Pelham began work in Boston in 1727. Though these artists' portraits came close to the style then current in England, they were generally beneath British standards. Charles Bridges, who arrived in Virginia in 1735 and spent the next several years traveling from plantation to plantation to paint portraits of the Virginia aristocracy, came close to capturing the sophisticated elegance of Kneller's aristocratic court portraits, but Bridge did not stay in the colonies long enough to have much influence on other artists.

Hesselius. Two men were largely responsible for the course of American painting for the rest of the eigh-

The Bermuda Group (1729–1731), by John Smibert: (standing) Smibert, Richard Dalton, John James, and George Berkeley; (seated) John Wainwright, Miss Hancock, and Anne Berkeley holding the Berkeleys' first child, Henry (Yale University Art Gallery, gift of Isaac Lothrop of Plymouth, Massachusetts)

teenth century: Gustavus Hesselius (1682–1755) and John Smibert (1688–1751). Born in Sweden and having had part of his artistic training in England, Hesselius lived in Philadelphia during the 1710s, spent the 1720s in Annapolis, and returned in 1734 to Philadelphia, where he lived and worked until his death. Also a painter of signs and other decorative work, as well as a builder of spinet pianos and pipe organs, Hesselius painted straightforward, unassuming, thoroughly realistic portraits. With his portraits of the Delawares Tishcohan and Lopowinsa, painted in 1735, Hesselius became the first artist of European origin to depict Native Americans objectively and sensitively. His *Last Supper,* painted around 1721–1722 for Saint Barnabas's Church in Queen Anne's Parish, Maryland, was the first painting commissioned for a public building in America. This religious painting and his later *Holy Family* are now lost. During the 1720s Hesselius also painted *Bacchus and Ariadne* and *Bacchanale,* two depictions of classical nudity that suggest the relative sophistication of Philadelphia in comparison to Boston. Hesselius taught painting to his son John, who briefly taught Charles Willson Peale, one of the great American artists who came into their own in the late 1750s and early 1760s.

Smibert. When he arrived in Boston in 1729 Smibert was already an established painter of portraits in the style of Kneller. One of the works he completed after his arrival was *The Bermuda Group* (1729–1731), depicting the future bishop Dean George Berkeley, members of his family, and others, including Smibert, who participated

in Berkeley's abortive plan to establish a college in Bermuda. In its unified organization and clear demarcation of the relative importance of the various individuals, the painting became a model for later American group portraits. Smibert's best work seems to have been behind him by 1730. His New World paintings have been called unspectacular, honest, and unflattering, but he pleased the citizens of Boston with portraits far more sophisticated and competent than those of his Boston contemporaries such as Nathaniel Emmons (1704–1740) and Joseph Badger (1708–1765).

Smibert's Legacy. Smibert also passed on the English court style to younger artists. Robert Feke, born in Oyster Bay, Long Island, around 1707, may have studied with Smibert and was certainly influenced by him. Feke's *Family of Isaac Royall,* painted in Boston in 1741, is similar to *The Bermuda Group* in composition and in the poses of two subjects. Active in Newport, Rhode Island, during the 1740s, Feke, who died in Barbados around 1752, is considered by some art historians to be a more imaginative painter than Smibert. Feke passed on the Smibert legacy to lesser painters of the 1740s and 1750s, including Badger, John Wollston, and John Greenwood, none of whom had the talent to rival Feke. Though the two men may never have met, Feke also influenced John Singleton Copley, whose earliest works are variously modeled on portraits by Feke and Smibert, and Greenwood. By 1754 American portrait painting was on the verge of a great leap forward with the emergence of Benjamin West, as well as Copley and Peale.

Gravestone of John Foster (died 1681), Dorchester, Massachusetts

Sources:

Jacob Ernest Cooke, ed., *Encyclopedia of the North American Colonies*, volume 3 (New York: Scribners, 1993);

Wayne Craven, *Colonial American Portraiture* (Cambridge, London & New York: Cambridge University Press, 1986);

John Wilmerding, *American Art* (Harmondsworth, U.K. & New York: Penguin, 1976);

Louis B. Wright, George B. Tatum, John W. McCoubrey, and Robert C. Smith, *The Arts in America: The Colonial Period* (New York: Scribners, 1966).

ART: SCULPTURE

The First American Sculptors. In the seventeenth century, struggling to eke out a meager livelihood in the New World, colonists had little time for the decorative arts and paid little heed to artistic trends in England or on the Continent. When they did embellish the utilitarian objects they created, they based their decorations on the folk traditions of their home countries. The first American sculptors were the stonecutters and carpenters who carved low-relief designs on gravestones and wooden objects such as trunks and Bible boxes.

Stonecutters. Early grave markers were made from several kinds of stone, some of which weather badly. Only a few markers from before 1660 are still in existence. The first decorations on gravestones, which began to appear in the mid seventeenth century, are simple geometric designs such as rosettes, pinwheels, and radiating suns. Such ornaments could be carved with simple tools by craftsmen with no artistic training.

Death's Heads and Skeletons. By the end of the century the winged skull had become the most widely used motif, and it continued to dominate graveyard art throughout the eighteenth century. One ambitious use of this motif appears on the stone of Joseph Tapping (died 1678) in the churchyard of King's Chapel, Boston. The stone also includes Gothic architectural elements, an hourglass resting on the winged skull, a skeleton carrying the dart of death while preparing to snuff out the flame of temporal life (a candle on a globe), and Father Time holding a second hourglass. The stone also bears two popular Latin inscriptions: "Memento mori" (Remember that you must die) and "Fugit Hora" (Time flies) to reinforce the message that time and death eventually destroy all life. The depiction of the skeleton and Father Time, which is derived from an engraving in Francis Quarles's *Hieroglyphikes of the Life of Man* (1638), was repeated with some variations on the gravestone of printer John Foster (died 1681) in Dorchester, Massachusetts. Tapping's stone is attributed to an artisan known to historians as the Charleston Carver, who was active in Boston at the time and may also be responsible for Foster's stone, on which the carving is deeper and more three-dimensional. A different variation appeared in 1745 on another stone in the King's Chapel burial ground.

Portrait Stones. By the early eighteenth century depictions of the deceased began to appear on gravestones, becoming the first American portrait sculptures. The earliest of these works may be the portrait signed "N.L." on the stone of Reverend Jonathan Pierpont (died 1709) in Wakefield, Massachusetts. By the 1740s such carvings could be found in graveyards throughout the colonies, including the Congregational churchyard in Charleston, South Carolina, where the stone of Mrs. Richard Owen (died 1749) shows a smiling woman in contemporary dress. Most of these portraits are rather primitive and two-dimensional, but others approach the realism of European sculpture. The burial ground of the Congregational Church in Charleston has two such gravestones: those of Mrs. Elizabeth Simmons (died 1740) and Solomon Milner (died 1757). Carved by Henry Eames of Boston, these portraits are noted for their realism and three-dimensional form. Other eighteenth-century motifs—including coats of arms, ships, and cherubs' heads with wings—also attest to the increased skills of colonial stone carvers.

Wood Carvers. Seventeenth-century colonial wood carvers were also untrained artisans working in the folk tradition. Their carvings were typically the sort of geometrical designs that could be made with simple carpenters' tools such as the chisel, gouge, and mallet. Examples of their work may be found on the boxes made to hold a family's Bible and writing materials and on various storage chests. One style of elaborately carved chest that has become particularly popular with twentieth-century collectors was made by various carpenters in the Con-

A carved wooden chest made in the Connecticut River Valley during the seventeenth century.
Its original owner was Polly Warner of Harwinton, Connecticut, whose initials are carved
in the front panel (The Henry Francis du Pont Winterthur Museum,
Winterthur, Delaware)

necticut River valley, including Peter Blin, who worked in Wethersfield, Connecticut, around 1675–1725 and John Allis and Samuel Belding, who were active in Hadley and Hatfield, Massachusetts, between 1675 and 1740.

The Refinement of Carving. During the second quarter of the seventeenth century, American carvers came under the influence of European design books illustrating the latest classical styles of furniture and architectural ornamentation. A new, refined classicism began to replace the medieval folk carving of the seventeenth century. Because they were frequently called on to produce figureheads for ships, wood carvers often set up shop in the wharf sections of port cities, but they also carved shop signs and ornaments for furniture. As early as 1717 there were professional wood carvers working in Philadelphia, and Henry Burnett was working in Charleston in 1750. Boston had many talented carvers, beginning with George Robinson the Younger (1680–1737) and Isaac Fowle (1648–1718), and including John Welch (1711–1789), who opened his Boston shop in 1733; William Codner, active around 1711; Moses Deshon, active in the 1740s; Francis Dewing, who arrived from London in 1716; Richard Hubbard, active in the 1730s; Samuel More, who was making figureheads as early as 1736; and Samuel Skillin Sr. (1716–1778), who set up his shop in 1740. Welch carved the "Sacred Cod" that now hangs in

the Old State House in Boston. Deshon carved the coat of arms for Faneuil Hall in 1742.

The "Little Admiral." Though little or none of his work survives, Samuel Skillin was a notable craftsman in his day, and some twentieth-century art historians believe that he may have carved the "Little Admiral," widely considered the earliest freestanding statue created in America. (In his 1844 short story "Drowne's Wooden Image" Nathaniel Hawthorne attributes it to Boston tinsmith Shem Drowne.) Though someone later painted the date "1770" on the base of this wooden figure, art historians believe that it was carved in the 1740s or 1750s. Because the figure once held an object such as a beer stein or nautical instrument, it is thought to have been made as a trade sign. In fact some scholars believe that it is the portrait of Adm. Edward Vernon (1684–1757) that was standing outside the Admiral Vernon Tavern in Boston in 1750. Another expert, however, says the "Little Admiral" is the portrait of a Captain Hunnewell that stood outside a nautical instruments shop.

Wax Modeling. Another form of sculpture was also popular in the colonies during the eighteenth century, but because wax melts so easily few examples of wax sculpture have survived. Working with wax was also popular with amateurs. Wax was plentiful and easy to mold. As early as 1731 the gentlewomen of New York City were offered classes in sculpting fruit, flowers, and

John Wilmerding, *American Art* (Harmondsworth, U.K. & New York: Penguin, 1976);

Louis B. Wright, George B. Tatum, John W. McCoubrey, and Robert C. Smith, *The Arts in America: The Colonial Period* (New York: Scribners, 1966).

LITERATURE

Colonial Readers. The first European settlers in North America depended on the Old World for reading matter, bringing with them or importing books from their mother countries. Even in New England, where a printing press was established at Cambridge, Massachusetts, in 1639, most books of any length came from England. Printers set up shop in Boston in 1675, Philadelphia in 1683, and New York in 1693. (A Dutch printer had been active in New Amsterdam during the 1650s.) By 1750 there were also printing presses in New London, Connecticut; Newport, Rhode Island; Annapolis, Maryland; Williamsburg, Virginia; Charleston, South Carolina; and at Germantown and Ephrata in Pennsylvania. Yet printing a long work required more type and equipment than most of them could muster, and until after the Revolution most books sold in America were imported. With some notable exceptions most colonial printers concentrated on government documents, almanacs, sermons, and other pamphlet-length works such as primers, political tracts, and writings on contemporary issues. Not everyone could read, though in New England by 1750 an estimated 90 percent of white males and 40 percent of white females were literate, and in the other British colonies literacy rates for white males ranged from about 35 percent to more than 50 percent. In many literate households, however, the only books might be a Bible, an almanac, and possibly a psalter. There were impressive private libraries in all the colonies, but the first libraries to which the general public had access were the subscription libraries that began springing up in the eighteenth century. The earliest were the Library Company of Philadelphia (1731); the Redwood Library in Newport, Rhode Island (1747); the Charleston Library Society (1748); and the New York Library Society (1754). Though some wealthy readers ordered books directly from England, by 1700 booksellers in the major colonial cities had sizable stocks of imported popular books.

The Native American Oral Tradition. When the first Europeans arrived in North America, they discovered that the various tribes of Native Americans had rich traditions of stories, poems, oratory, and religious utterances, which were passed on by storytellers from generation to generation. Much of this oral literature has been lost, in part because of the gradual acculturation of Native Americans and in part because most Europeans of the seventeenth and eighteenth centuries considered such narratives childlike and subliterate at best, and at worst the products of brutish agents of Satan. The Jesuits of New France were among the few Europeans in the New World to be impressed with the eloquence of the Native Americans they encountered, and their yearly re-

The "Little Admiral," probably carved during the 1740s or 1750s to stand outside a Boston tavern or shop (Old State House, Boston)

"other Wax-Works," and on 28 August 1749 the *New York Gazette* advertised an exhibit of wax effigies of members of European royalty. Artists were also beginning to make small portraits in wax, an art that became more widespread and further refined during the second half of the century.

Sources:
Wayne Craven, *Sculpture in America* (New York: Crowell, 1968);

ports to their French superiors include accounts of how Huron, Iroquois, and other tribes delivered speeches and narrated stories and poems. The Jesuits also translated some oral performances into French. In his report for 1645–1646 Jesuit missionary Paul Ragueneau described the storytelling at a meeting of elders who gathered to elect "a very celebrated Captain." They used the meeting to pass on tribal history by telling stories about their ancestors, "even those most remote." Another Frenchman, Louis Hennepin, included accounts of Native American creation mythology in his 1698 account of his explorations in North America. Pointing to parallels with the Old Testament creation story, he was one of many Europeans who attempted to prove that Native Americans were descendants of the lost tribes of Israel. The Puritans of New England occasionally summarized Native American stories, usually to illustrate that the Indians were deluded heathens acting as agents for the devil. Two such stories can be found in the 1736 memoir of John Gyles, commander of a garrison on the Saint George River. In one of these stories a large bird carries a boy to her nest as food for her babies, but when they refuse to eat the boy she takes him back to the place where she found him. Gyles claimed that he had been shown the site of her nest. Though some scholars have argued that all Native American oral literature ought to be viewed as poetry, others create a special category for those works that most closely resemble the European form lyric poetry. The language of these poems was highly musical, with the narrator conveying meaning not just through the words but also by how he said them. Because the beauty and meanings of these poems were so dependent on oral transmission, translation does not do them justice, especially when Europeans imposed their own conventions of rhyme and meter. European transcribers, such as Paul Le Jeune in 1634 and 1637 and Jacques Marquette in 1673, failed to capture the true quality of the poetry they had heard.

Spanish Colonial History. The earliest written New World literature came from sixteenth-century Spanish explorers who published accounts of their journeys after they returned to Spain. The first was Alvar Nuñez Cabeza de Vaca, whose account of his party's eight-year overland journey from Florida to the west coast of Mexico (1528–1535) was published in 1542. The exploration by Hernando de Soto and his men of the area that is now the southeastern United States (1539–1543) was the subject of Inca Garcilaso de la Vega's colorful and popular *La Florida del Inca: O historia de Adelantado Hernando de Soto* (The Florida of the Inca; Or, The History of Commander Hernando de Soto, 1605), based on firsthand accounts by expedition members. In the 1560s Pedro de Casteñeda wrote about his experiences as a member of Francisco Vasquez de Coronado's expedition in the American West (1540–1542).

A New Mexico Epic. Among several other histories of expeditions is an epic poem, *Historia de la Nuevo-México*

John Foster's 1670 engraving of one of the Puritan clergymen whose translations and paraphrases were published in the 1640 *Whole Booke of Psalmes* (American Antiquarian Society, Worcester, Massachusetts)

(History of New Mexico, 1610), by Gaspar Pérez de Villagrá, a member of the group of about six hundred colonists who had established the first Spanish settlement in the province of New Mexico in 1598. Like many other poets before and since, Villagrá tried to write a heroic poem that would rival the great epics of the ancients, consciously echoing the first line of Virgil's *Aeneid* with his opening salute to Juan de Oñate, the leader of the expedition: "I sing of arms and that heroic man." Beginning with a brief description of earlier Spanish expeditions, Villagrá wrote thirty-four cantos that include a detailed account of the events in which he took part. Although he did not succeed in creating a great epic, his poem is still consulted by historians.

The Oral Tradition of the Southwest. Much of the early literature of the Spanish colonies of the Southwest was passed on orally. Hoping to convert Native Americans as well as instruct colonists, missionaries often staged religious dramas, either versions of Spanish plays or new plays written in Mexico. Some of the songs and poems from these plays inspired traveling troubadours, who used the subjects and verse forms in original compositions of their own, sometimes religious but often secular verses about local people and events. Spanish settlers also passed on long romance poems, narratives that often had moral or religious messages. Another popular tradi-

In a society that condemned novels, plays, and many kinds of poetry, the Puritans found the captivity narrative a welcome relief from their typical reading matter—the Bible, sermons, and history. These exciting tales of warfare, capture, suffering, and ultimate freedom were acceptable to Puritan clergymen because they were true stories and because they could be read as sermons or as spiritual autobiographies—records of the individual soul's struggle with God and Satan, which many ministers encouraged their congregations to write. With the common belief that Native Americans were agents of Satan or God's means of punishing the Puritans for backsliding from performing his will, it was easy for Puritans to see the physical hardships of Indian captivity as allegorical representations of the soul's spiritual struggles.

The first and best known of these popular narratives, Mary Rowlandson's *The Soveraignty & Goodness of God* (1682), came out of the bloody King Philip's War (1675–1676). The wife of a Puritan clergyman, Mrs. Rowlandson was captured in February 1676 from the frontier village of Lancaster, Massachusetts, during a massacre in which many neighbors and members of her family were killed. Wounded in the raid, she was ransomed eleven weeks later, after witnessing the death of her six-year-old daughter during captivity and enduring near starvation and exhaustion from forced marches under difficult circumstances.

Instigated by the French, sporadic Indian raids continued after King Philip's War, especially in sparsely populated areas. "Quentin Stockwell's Relation of His Captivity and Redemption," first published in Increase Mather's *An Essay for the Re-cording of Illustrious Providences* (1684), reports on Stockwell's experiences during eight months as a prisoner taken captive during a raid on Deerfield, Massachusetts, in September 1677. A ten-year-old taken prisoner during another raid on a remote outpost, John Gyles was captured in Pemaquid, Maine, in 1689 and held for six years among Indians and nearly three by the French. He, or possibly a ghostwriter, told of his adventures years later in *Memoirs of Odd Adventures, Strange Deliverances, etc., in the Captivity of John Gyles, Esq.* (1736).

After five years of relative peace, the outbreak of Queen Anne's War with the French and their Native American allies in 1702 spelled fresh trouble for settlements on the New England frontier. During a raid on Deerfield in February 1704, many of the townsfolk were killed, including two sons of Reverend John Williams. In his popular narrative, *The Redeemed Captive, Returning to Zion* (1707), Williams recounted how he and the other survivors were forced to walk to Canada. During this long march his wife died. For nearly three years of captivity Williams struggled to win freedom for his children and his congregation while also trying to prevent them from giving in to French pressures to convert to Roman Catholicism. Despite efforts before and after his release, Williams failed to ransom his daughter Eunice, who was seven years old when they were captured. She not only became a Catholic but also married an Indian and lived for the rest of her life among Native Americans.

Source: Alden T. Vaughan and Edward W. Clark, eds., *Puritans Among Indians: Accounts of Captivity and Redemption, 1676–1724* (Cambridge, Mass. & London: Harvard University Press, 1981).

tion was the telling of *cuentos,* or prose tales. Many of these traditional stories had their origins in Spanish folktales but were modified over time in the New World, while others are similar in form to Old World stories but have their origin in the New. Juan B. Rael, who collected some five hundred *cuentos* during the 1930s, estimated that the large majority of them were more than three hundred years old.

French Colonial History. The earliest French colonial writings were also historical, including Marc Lescarbot's *Histoire de la Nouvelle-France* (History of New France, 1609–1618) and Samuel de Champlain's accounts of his explorations (1603–1632). The Jesuits' annual reports, *Jesuit Relations,* were begun by Paul Le Jeune in 1632 and continued through 1673. The most notable French colonial history to include Louisiana is Pierre François Xavier de Charlevoix's *Histoire et description de la Nouvelle France avec la Journal d'un voyage fait par ordre du Roi dans l'Amerique Septentrionale* (History and Description de la Nouvelle France, with the Journal of a Voyage Made by Order of the King in Northern America, 1744).

French Colonial Poetry. Mock-heroic poems, which were popular in France during the seventeenth century, were also written in New France. René-Louis Chartier de la Lotbinière wrote a verse epic about an expedition against the Mohawk led by Rémy de Courcelle in 1666. Probably not intended for publication, this comic picture of military life seems to have been circulated widely in New France and France. Louis-Armand de Lom d'Arce de Lahontan's *Nouveaux Voyages* (New Voyages) and *Dialogues,* both published in 1703, poetic accounts of his travels in the New World, are far more satirical than Chartier de la Lotbinière's poem in their views of the politics and society of New France. The first surviving poem written in Louisiana is Dumont de Montigny's "Poème en vers" (Poem in Verse), a history of the province from 1716 to 1746. Written in the 1740s, it remained unpublished until 1931. As in the Spanish colonies, there was an active oral tradition in New France. When folklorists began collecting these stories and songs in the nineteenth century, some were discovered to have origins in medieval France.

The African American Oral Tradition. The first Africans were brought to Virginia as early as 1619, bringing with them a rich heritage of orally transmitted stories and folktales, some of which eventually became part of mainstream American literature. Since most slaves were not taught to read and write English, they passed on Anglicized versions of African stories orally, maintaining a strong African American folk tradition. The first African Americans to write in the English literary tradition and have their work published were poets Jupiter Hammon, whose first published poem appeared in 1760, and Phillis Wheatley, whose first poem was published seven years later, when she was only thirteen. By about 1760 African Americans were also writing autobiographical slave narratives to describe their experiences and bear witness to the inhumanity of their condition.

The Literature of New Netherland. The Dutch colonists in North America included three notable poets. Jacob Steendam wrote "The Complaint of New Amsterdam" and "The Praise of New Netherland," poems promoting the colony as a place of abundance, minimizing hardships such as Indian attacks, characterizing New Englanders as envious swine. His promotional "Spurring-Verses" were published in Peter C. Plockhoy's *Kort en Klaer Ontwerp* (Short and Clear: Antwerp; 1662), written to encourage settlement in Delaware. According to Steendam New Netherland was an Edenic land of plenty, where "birds obscure the sky," the land is filled with wild animals, the waters are teeming with fish, and oysters "Are piled up, heap on heap, till islands they attain." Henricus Selyns, a Dutch Reform minister in New Netherland in 1660–1664 and 1682–1701, wrote marriage poems, epitaphs for prominent colonists such as Peter Stuyvesant, punning satires, and verses in Latin. Nicasius de Sille, who held important administrative posts in the colony, also wrote poems, including "The Earth Speaks to Its Cultivator," in which the main character is a New Adam, an image of the European in the New World that resonated throughout American literature well into the nineteenth century. The first histories by a Dutch colonist were written by lawyer Adriaen van der Donck and published in the Netherlands in 1649. His later work, *A Description of the New Netherland* (1655), was the first book published in New York.

Promoting the British Colonies. Though notable historians and poets were at work throughout the British

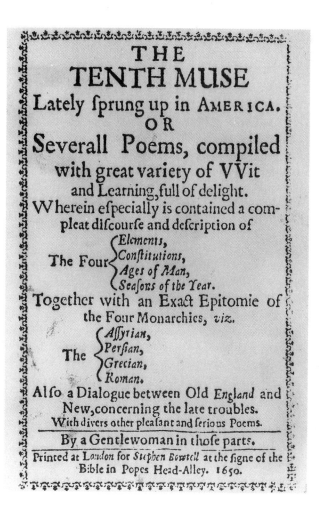

Title page for the first book by an American woman, a collection of poems by Massachusetts Puritan Anne Bradstreet

colonies, histories of their literature tend to be dominated by discussions of New England writers. Some of the earliest New World writings in English are works written to promote the colonies or record the exploits of colonial explorers. Capt. John Smith's *A True Relation of Such Occurences and Accidents of Noate as Hath Hapned in Virginia* (1608) is the first of several books he wrote about his experiences in Virginia and later New England, culminating in his self-congratulatory *The true Travels, Adventures, and Observations of Captaine John Smith* (1630). Some books were written expressly to promote colonization. *A Briefe and True Report of the New Found Land of Virginia* (1588), by Thomas Harriot, a surveyor with Sir Richard Grenville's 1585 expedition to Virginia, had been reprinted seventeen times by 1610. *New Englands Prospect* (1634), by William Wood, a member of a 1629 scouting party in Massachusetts, also aroused considerable interest in England. Other influential promotional tracts for southern colonies were John Hammond's *Leah and Rachel, or The two fruitfull sisters Virginia and Mary-land* (1655), George Alsop's witty *A Character of the Province of Mary-land* (1666), John Lawson's *A New Voyage to Carolina* (1708), Hugh Jones's *The Present State of Virginia* (1724), and William Stith's *The History of the First Discovery and Settlement of Virginia* (1747). Daniel

Denton's *A Briefe Description of New-York* (1670) attracted English settlers to the colony the Dutch had recently ceded to Great Britain, and William Penn lured settlers to his colony with *Some Account of the Province of Pennsilvania* (1681) and other pamphlets.

New England Historians. Early New England historians tended to focus less on events than on illustrating that God had chosen the Puritans as instruments of his will and fully supported their actions. This defense of the Puritan enterprise is apparent in seventeenth-century histories of the Massachusetts Bay Colony such as Edward Johnson's *Wonder-working Providence of Sions Saviour in New-England* (1654) and Nathaniel Morton's *New Englands Memoriall* (1669), as well as accounts of the Puritans' dealings and conflicts with Native Americans, including John Winthrop's *A Declaration of the Former Passages and Proceedings Betwixt the English and the Narrowgansets* (1645) and several books on the bloody King Philip's War with the Narragansetts (1675–1676): Increase Mather's *A Brief History of the Warr with the Indians of New England* (1676) and *A Relation of the Troubles which Have Hapned in New-England* (1677), William Hubbard's *A Narrative of the Troubles with the Indians in New-England* (1677), and Cotton Mather's *Duodecennium Luctuosum* (Two Decades Full of Sorrow, 1699).

Cotton Mather. Cotton Mather's major work, *Magnalia Christi Americana* (The Great Works of Christ in America, 1702), exhibits a similar slant, drawing biblical parallels in its biographies of more than sixty Puritan "saints." The son of Reverend Increase Mather and grandson of two first-generation New England men of God, John Cotton and Richard Mather, Cotton Mather had 444 works (mostly pamphlets) separately published during his lifetime, making him probably the most published American author of all time.

Documentary History. A generation after Mather, Thomas Prince, another clergyman who believed in the Puritans' providential mission in the New World, took a step toward modern historiography by basing *A Chronological History of New-England* (1736–1755) on a large collection of historical materials that he had amassed. Two of the most useful documents for modern historians of New England were not published during their authors' lifetimes: William Bradford's *Of Plimmoth Plantation*, written in 1630 and 1646–1650 and first published in 1856, and John Winthrop's journals, written in 1630–1649 and first published in part in 1790. Another New England Puritan, Daniel Gookin, who spent more than twenty years of his life as Indian Superintendent in the Massachusetts Bay Colony, attempted to counter the traditional Puritan view of Native Americans in his *Historical Collections of the Indians in New England*, which remained unpublished until 1792, more than one hundred years after Gookin's death. He also took the side of the Indians in another posthumously published work, *An Historical Account of the Doings and Suffering of the Christian Indians in New England in the Years 1657, 1676,* 1677 (1836), written in response to Increase Mather's and William Hubbard's accounts of King Philip's War.

Southern Historians. Historians in the middle and southern colonies were neither as prolific nor as unified in viewpoint as the New Englanders. In *The History and Present State of Virginia* (1705) Robert Beverley openly criticized several royal governors for infringing on Virginians' personal liberties, while finding much to praise in the simple lifestyle of Native Americans. His fellow Virginian William Byrd II made a valuable and humorous contribution to the knowledge of life in the Virginia backcountry in two posthumously published accounts of his experiences as part of a group of men charged in 1728 with establishing the boundary between Virginia and North Carolina: *The History of the Dividing Line Betwixt Virginia and North Carolina* (1841) and a shorter, saltier version, *The Secret History of the Line* (1929). Byrd's sometimes X-rated diaries, which he kept in a shorthand code he invented, were deciphered and published in the twentieth century, providing fascinating glimpses of the life of a colonial Virginia gentleman. *A True and Historical Narrative of the Colony of Georgia* (1741), by Patrick Tailfer, Hugh Anderson, David Douglas, and others, slides into satire and anecdotal "tall tales" as they criticize James Oglethorpe's administration, in particular for its denunciation of slavery and the rum trade.

Historians of the Middle Colonies. One early history, *Good Order Established in Pennsilvania & New-Jersey* (1685), was written by Thomas Budd, who successfully recommended comprehensive public education. Cadwallader Colden, who was motivated by his admiration of the Native Americans he had met and the belief that the Iroquois could play a powerful role in protecting New York against the French and their Indian allies to the north, wrote *The History of the Five Indian Nations Depending on the Province of New York* (1727). Sometimes called the first American historian to examine the thirteen colonies as a single unit, New Yorker William Douglass wrote his ambitious *A Summary, Historical and Political, of the First Planting, Progressive Improvements, and Present State of the British Settlements in North America* (1747–1752) to counter the "intolerably erroneous" work of Cotton Mather and other New England historians. Subsequent historians have called Douglass's own work sloppy and unreliable.

New England Poetry. In part because of the early establishment of printing in Cambridge, the published works of New England colonial poets far outnumber those by residents of the other British colonies. Many of the earliest New England poems are elegies written by Puritan clergymen (often for other clergymen) or brief verses about months and seasons in almanacs. Puritans were also fond of creating anagrams from people's names and then using them as the starting points for poems. For example, Reverend John Wilson turned Claudius Gilbert into "Tis Braul I Cudgel" and then wrote a poem about the "brawling" of the Quakers and other dissenters and how God "cudgeled" them with his holy word. Wilson was so fond of making anagrams that his good friend and fellow clergyman Nathaniel Ward of Agawam, Massachusetts, wrote a humorous poem about him:

> We poor Agawams
> are so stiff in the hams
> that we cannot make Anagrams,
> But Mr John Wilson
> the great Epigrammist
> Can let out an Anagram
> even as he list.

The Bay Psalm Book. The first book published in Cambridge, *The Whole Booke of Psalmes* (1640), or *The Bay Psalm Book*, includes some of the Puritans' earliest poetic efforts. With the help of other Puritan divines, clergymen Thomas Welde, John Eliot, and Richard Mather paraphrased the Psalms so that they could be sung to traditional hymn tunes. Disapproving of other paraphrases because they were not always accurate translations, they went back to the original Hebrew to produce a "plaine translation," aiming for "fidelity rather than poetry." Most modern readers believe they succeeded. For example, in their hands the opening lines of the Twenty-third Psalm—"The Lord is my Shepherd. I shall not want"—became "The Lord to mee a shepherd is, want therefore shall not I." Whatever its literary merits, *The Bay Psalm Book* could be found in many New England homes and went through twenty-five editions. By the mid eighteenth century it had been largely replaced by the more aesthetically pleasing hymns of Isaac Watts and John and Charles Wesley.

The Simple Cobbler. Not all Puritan pastors were humorless even when, like Nathaniel Ward, they were employing verse to forecast the imminent end of the world and to plead with their flocks to mend their ways. In *The Simple Cobbler of Aggawam in America* (1647) Ward used puns and coined new words in his pleas for English society in the Old World and the New to cease its divisive behavior and agree on mutual accommodation. He expressed his deepest distrust of theological debate, explaining that the devil "cannot sting the vitals of the Elect morally," but he can "fly-blow their Intellectuals miserably." Ward's singsong couplets can often be unintentionally laughable as well, but at their best they make his point in memorable style:

> The world's a well strung fiddle, mans tongue the quill,
> That fills the world with fumble for want of skill,
> When things and words in tune and tone doe meet,
> The universall song goes smooth and sweet.

The First American Woman Poet. Ward, who was a misogynist even by the standards of his own day, wrote a dedicatory poem for the first book by an American woman, Anne Bradstreet's anonymously published *The Tenth Muse Lately Sprung Up in America* (1650). Modern readers admire Bradstreet's love poems, including "To

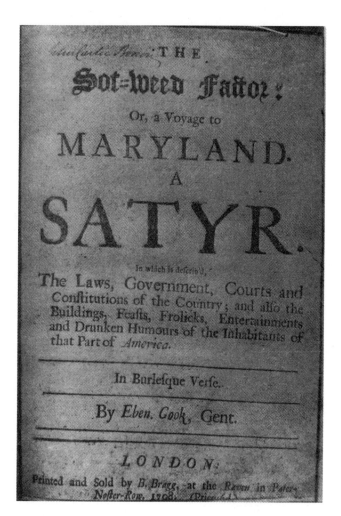

Title page for Ebenezer Cook's humorous poem about harsh living conditions and crude behavior in colonial Maryland

my Dear and Loving Husband," which begins with the memorable lines:

> If ever two were one, then surely we
> If ever man were lov'd by wife, then thee;
> If ever wife was happy in a man
> Compare with me ye women if you can.

Yet her contemporaries admired her philosophical and religious poems, marveling at the extent of her knowledge and the quality of her verse. Ward was not alone in his sentiments when he grudgingly wrote, "It half revives my chil frost-bitten blood, To see a Woman once, do ought that's good."

The First Best-Seller. Seventeenth-century New Englanders read Bradstreet's poetry, especially after her husband had an enlarged edition of her book published in Boston, again anonymously, in 1678. Yet the poet whose name was a household word in Puritan families was Michael Wigglesworth, a clergyman whose book *The Day of Doom* (1662) has been called the first American best-seller. *The Day of Doom* had gone through seven editions by 1751, and the sixth edition of his popular second book, *Meat Out of the Eater* (1670), was published in

1721. These books were so often read and reread that no copies of the first edition of either have survived. Wigglesworth's sermons in verse have not worn well with later generations, but his contemporaries admired and heeded his warnings about the hellfires that awaited "whining hypocrites," "Idolaters, false worshippers, / Prophaners of Gods Name," "Blasphemers lewd, and Swearers, shrewd, / Scoffers at Purity," "Sabbath-polluters, Saints persecuters, / Presumptuous men and proud"—and a whole array of other sinners bound for eternal damnation.

The Metaphysical Poet of New England. The only verses by Edward Taylor that appeared in print during his lifetime were two stanzas from his "Upon Wedlock and Death of Children" (written in 1682 or 1683), which Cotton Mather included in his *Right Thoughts in Sad Hours* (1689). While he is believed to have read a few of his poems to his congregation in Westfield, Massachusetts, Taylor was virtually unknown until scholars discovered the manuscripts for his poems and published them in the twentieth century. Yet today he is considered a major American poet, and his more than two hundred *Poetical Meditations* (written 1682–1725) have been called the most important poetic achievements of colonial America. The best of these poems, which Taylor wrote as preparations for administering the Lord's Supper (the Puritans' term for Communion), have been compared favorably to poems by the Metaphysical poets of England, including John Donne, George Herbert, and Richard Crashaw. While Taylor accepted the stern religious beliefs of his fellow Puritans, including Wigglesworth's convictions about eternal damnation, he often focused on God's grace and the experience of religious ecstasy:

> God is Gone up with a triumphant Shout
> The Lord with sounding Trumpets melodies.
>
> Sing Praise, sing Praise, sing Praise, sing Praises out,
> Unto our King sing praise seraphickwise.
> Lift up your Heads ye lasting Doore they sing
> And let the King of Glory Enter in.

Cosmopolitan Bostonians. By the eighteenth century literary tastes were becoming more secular throughout the colonies, as prosperity gave Americans the opportunity to learn about the latest cultural trends in London through imported books, magazines, and engravings. The change became apparent even in New England, where Boston clergyman Mather Byles, nephew of Cotton Mather, wrote sermons that are more notable for their polished prose than for their theological insights and poems that are known less for their content than for their stylistic imitations of Alexander Pope and other eighteenth-century British poets. Unlike his predecessor Wigglesworth's poetic efforts, "The Conflagration" (1729), Byles's description of the day of doom, seems unlikely to have inspired many sinners to repent. In his later years Byles became known as a wit. "Punning Byles invokes our smiles," wrote poet Thomas Morton Jones in 1774. Another eighteenth-century Boston poet, Joseph Green, wrote humorous verses that poked fun at prominent people and public events, including "A Parody on a Hymn by Mather Byles" (1733) and his most popular work, *Entertainment for a Winter's Evening* (1750), a satire on the Freemasons with references to actual people.

Poets of the Middle Colonies. Little verse by New Yorkers survives from the colonial period after the Dutch ceded New Netherland to the British. Jupiter Hammon and William Livingston emerged during the second half of the eighteenth century, but only Richard Steere, who is considered the first poet of Long Island, achieved any recognition for his poetic efforts before the Revolution. A Puritan who settled in Southold, on eastern Long Island, in 1710, Steere had fled to Boston in 1682–1683, after his anti-Tory verses angered British authorities, and then to Southold, after he ran afoul of Puritan authorities for voicing unorthodox religious views. The poems he collected in *The Daniel Catcher* (1713) include some of the earliest examples of American nature poetry and what is probably the first American poem in blank verse. In Philadelphia James Logan, secretary to William Penn, wrote original poems in Latin and Greek and two verse translations from the Latin, *Cato's Moral Distiches Englished in Couplets* (1735) and *M. T. Cicero's Cato Major* (1744).

Southern Poets. The first published poet to live in Virginia was George Sandys, who was established as a literary figure in England by the time he arrived in the New World in 1621. Before he left Virginia in 1625 he had completed the translation of Ovid's *Metamorphoses* that he published in London on his return. Sandys's time in Virginia was brief, and his poetry does not deal with his experiences there. Ebenezer Cook, a lawyer who wrote satiric verse on life in colonial Maryland, has been called the father of traditional Southern humor writing. Cook's best-known poem is *The Sot-Weed Factor* (1708), about an English tobacco merchant (or sot-weed factor) who is cheated of all his possessions by a series of Maryland colonists. Cook's burlesque of a land "where no Man's Faithful, nor a Woman Chast" also makes fun of Englishmen who expected to get rich fast in a New World Eden. Another Marylander, Richard Lewis, has been called the foremost American nature poet before Philip Freneau. In poems such as "A Journey from Patapsco to Annapolis" (1731) he wrote vivid descriptions based on careful observations, as in this description of a hummingbird:

> He takes with rapid Whirl his noisy Flight,
> His gemmy Plummage strikes the Gazer's Sight
> And as he moves his ever-flutt'ring Wings,
> Ten thousand Colours he around him flings.

Sources:

Jacob Ernest Cooke, ed., *Encyclopedia of the North American Colonies*, volume 3 (New York: Scribners, 1993);

Emory Elliott, ed., *American Colonial Writers, 1606–1734, Dictionary of Literary Biography,* volume 24 (Columbia, S.C.: Bruccoli Clark / Detroit: Gale Research, 1984);

Elliott, ed., *American Colonial Writers, 1735–1781, Dictionary of Literary Biography,* volume 31 (Columbia, S.C.: Bruccoli Clark / Detroit: Gale Research, 1984);

Harold S. Jantz, *The First Century of New England Verse* (Worcester, Mass.: American Antiquarian Society, 1944);

Kenneth Silverman, ed., *Colonial American Poetry* (New York & London: Hafner, 1968).

MUSIC

Old World Traditions. The European settlers of North America brought with them their own instruments, music, and musical traditions. Except in the Spanish Southwest, where there was some crossover in both directions, colonists were little influenced by the music of Native Americans. Little is known about the early music of the Louisiana Territory. In the British colonies, as with the other arts the prevailing trends in music came from England.

African American Music. While the music of African Americans eventually had a widespread and deep-seated impact on the evolution of American music, during the colonial period its influence seemed minimal. African Americans preserved their musical traditions in the slave quarters of the great plantations, singing and playing homemade African-style drums and reed and string instruments. One such instrument was a *banjer* or *banjar,* brought from West Africa as early as the seventeenth century. A gourd with an attached handle and four catgut strings, it was the precursor of the banjo, which American instrument manufacturers began making in the nineteenth century. The first European instruments played by African Americans—as early as the 1690s—were violins, or fiddles, sometimes homemade but other times given to them by white masters. Some slave owners also had their slaves taught to play European-style music for white audiences. Over time black musicians began to incorporate their own musical ideas into European music and eventually wrote music that integrated aspects of both musical traditions.

Religious Music in the Southwest. Spanish missionaries in the Southwest used music as a means of religious education and even encouraged Native Americans to compose music in the European tradition. Enthusiastic, Native American choirs learned not only formal liturgical music but also the folk carols and other traditional religious songs of the Spanish settlers. Franciscans also created Christian music and drama to go with or build on the traditional feasts and ceremonies of Native Americans. Though much of this music is lost, some evolved to become part of the folk tradition of the Southwest.

Religious Music in the British Colonies. Although they used different psalters, the various colonial churches all followed John Calvin's dictum that worship services should include singing versifications of the Old Testament Psalms. The Pilgrims and Puritans of seventeenth-century New England considered professional singers, the singing of parts, and any sort of musical accompaniment to be popish excesses, but even denominations that did not oppose these practices did not employ them. Organs and most other instruments were too expensive for early colonial churches, and few parishioners were trained singers.

Lining Out. When the typical congregation sang a hymn, a deacon or clerk announced which tune would be sung (usually from a choice of only four or five melodies) and then read out each line before it was sung. As memories of church music in England grew dimmer and fewer and fewer churchgoers could read the music printed in increasingly scarce music books, American music became dramatically different—and worse—in comparison to that of England. Especially among the rugged individualists of New England, everyone seemed to sing a different tune and sometimes slipped from one melody to another while paying no attention to tempo. The result, according to Reverend Thomas Walter, was a noise "so hideous and disorderly, as is bad beyond expression."

Reform. By the turn of the eighteenth century ministers throughout the colonies were calling for schools to instruct people in reading music and singing psalms. Anglican singing instruction began in Maryland as early as 1699; there were singing classes in Virginia in 1710–1711; and the first school for psalmody was advertised in Boston in 1714. Such schools were most popular in New England, where many were in operation from 1720 to about 1750, after clergymen such as Benjamin Colman, Thomas Symmes, Cotton Mather, and Thomas Walter spoke out in favor of singing reform. Once Congregationalists accepted singing reform, they began appointing "choristers" to sound the first note by voice or pitch pipe and then lead the singing. The use of the pitch pipe aroused controversy because some traditionalists considered it a violation of the rule forbidding musical instruments. Many of the same people were also opposed when some young singing-school graduates began to ask that they be allowed to sit together and perform some of the religious songs and anthems they had learned. The first New England church to agree to such a request was the West Church in Boston, which designated "singers' seats" in 1754. By the end of the 1760s twenty-three churches in New England had made similar provisions.

Church Organs. With Puritans debating the use of pitch pipes, it is no surprise that the first organ in a Congregational church was not installed until 1770 (in Providence, Rhode Island). Other denominations began to buy organs as soon as they could afford them. The Anglican King's Chapel in Boston installed an organ in 1714, and the other two Anglican churches in the city had them by 1744. Other Anglican churches that bought organs during the first half of the eighteenth century include Saint Philip's Church, Charleston, South Carolina (1728); Christ Church, Philadelphia (1728); Trinity Church, Newport, Rhode Island (1733); and Trinity Church, New York City (1737). Between 1737 and 1767 five Virginia churches also installed organs. The first known organ in New York City was installed at the Dutch Reformed Church in 1724.

American Religious Music. Until the second half of the eighteenth century little original music of any sort was composed in the colonies. The first piece of new music, secular or sacred, written in America may be "Southwell New Tune," a brief hymn published in Reverend Thomas Walter's *The Grounds and Rules of Musick Explained* (1721), a popular manual for would-be singers. The 1723 edition of John Tufts's *A Very Plain and Easy Introduction to the Art of Singing Psalm Tunes* (first published in 1721) includes another tune, "100 Psalm Tune New," that was probably written in America.

Secular Music. While colonists brought their own musical traditions with them, their music began to evolve over time. In the Southwest ancient romances of European wars gave way to ballads that reflected the everyday experiences of the settlers, who were making history of their own. In the British colonies new lyrics on contemporary topics were fitted to old ballad or hymn tunes, or—especially in the eighteenth century—to new music brought from England, such as marches or stage and opera music by composers such as Henry Purcell and George Frideric Handel. While poorer people continued to enjoy folk music and dancing in the eighteenth century, prosperous colonists wanted to learn the latest trends in music and dancing among aristocratic circles in England. They bought instruments, music, and dancing books and hired professional music and dancing masters. They also enjoyed listening to British and Continental performers.

Secular Music in New England. Despite modern beliefs to the contrary, music and dancing were popular forms of recreation among early Puritans. The authorities intervened only when they thought the revelry had become excessive. In the seventeenth century New Englanders sang traditional English ballads, and by the eighteenth century prosperous Bostonians were eager to hear new compositions by Handel and other composers in England. In fact Boston led the way in supporting musical culture in the colonies. Thomas Brattle, a wealthy Boston merchant, installed an organ in his home in 1711 and four years later donated another to King's Chapel. Edward Enstone, who arrived from England in 1715 to be organist there, started a music and dancing school and began holding public balls. By 1717 he had also opened a music store, where he sold and repaired musical instruments, as well as offering music and musical instruction books. In 1729 he sponsored the first documented public concert held in the colonies. The following year the Men's Musical Society of Boston sponsored a concert in honor of Saint Cecilia, patron saint of music.

The Middle Colonies. While settlers of the mid-Atlantic region brought diverse musical traditions, only a few survived the influx of British influence in the eighteenth century: English and Scottish settlers of remote areas in the Appalachians kept their ballads and tunes uncorrupted by new influences into the twentieth century. The similarly isolated French settlers of northern New England also maintained their musical traditions, as did some of the German musicians of Pennsylvania. The Moravian communities of Pennsylvania and North Carolina were well known in the eighteenth century for their vast repertoires of European sacred and secular music and for their expertise in performing and composing such music. An early documented private concert was held in 1710 in New York City, where in 1714 musicians were hired for a parade and ball celebrating the coronation of George I. The Philadelphia Assembly, a dancing club founded in 1748, also encouraged musical performance.

The Southern Colonies. By the eighteenth century secular music was exceptionally popular in the South, where people from outlying plantations often came together for only a few weeks or months of the year during

MORTON'S MAYPOLE AT MERRY MOUNT

Thomas Morton took an unorthodox view of the Puritan mission in his *New English Canaan* (1637), in which he described the Native Americans he met in Massachusetts as more "full of humanity" than his fellow Englishmen in nearby Plymouth. A non-Puritan, Morton established a trading post called Merry Mount in present-day Quincy, Massachusetts, in 1625 and invited local Indians to dance around a maypole he had erected. This revelry angered his Puritan neighbors and—along with charges that he was selling firearms to the Indians—resulted in his arrest and deportation to England for trial in 1628. He was acquitted and returned to Merry Mount the following year, but Gov. John Endicott, who had chopped down the maypole while Morton was gone, arrested him again in 1630, confiscating his property, burning down his house, and shipping him back to England once again. Morton took his revenge on the Puritans in *New English Canaan*, in which he also included a glowing description of the region. He returned in 1643, and after a series of run-ins with Massachusetts authorities, he settled in Maine. Nathaniel Hawthorne based his 1836 short story "The May-Pole of Merry Mount" on the events at Morton's trading post.

Source: Emory Elliott, ed., *American Colonial Writers, 1606–1734, Dictionary of Literary Biography,* volume 24 (Columbia, S.C.: Bruccoli Clark / Detroit: Gale Research, 1984).

sessions of the courts or legislatures. During that time they attended concerts, plays, and balls and took home the music they heard at those events. By 1735 musicians in Charleston, South Carolina, had begun giving public concerts honoring Saint Cecilia. There were also private music clubs, including the Saint Cecilia Society of Charleston, founded in 1762. An earlier group was the Tuesday Club of Annapolis, Maryland, which met from May 1745 until February 1756 and fostered its members' literary and musical interests. By 1752 the club included five string players, two flute players, a keyboardist, and perhaps a bassoonist. Songs written by several members for performance at club meetings may be the earliest secular music written in America.

Sources:

Gilbert Chase, *America's Music, from the Pilgrims to the Present,* third edition, revised (Urbana: University of Illinois Press, 1987);

Jacob Ernest Cooke, ed., *Encyclopedia of the North American Colonies,* volume 3 (New York: Scribners, 1993).

THEATER

Early Spanish and French Plays. According to Gaspar Pérez de Villagrá's *Historia de la Nuevo-México* (1610), the first European play produced within the modern boundaries of the United States was a *comedia* by Capt. Marcos Farfán de los Godos, staged on the banks of the Rio Grande in New Mexico on 30 April 1598. Villagrá described this lost play as a drama about the willing conversion to Christianity of huge numbers of Native Americans. He also mentioned a production of the medieval Spanish drama *Moros y Cristianos* (The Moors and the Christians) and a *comedia,* perhaps by Farfán, at San Juan de los Caballeros, near present-day El Paso, in September 1598. Throughout the Southwest Spanish priests made extensive use of ecclesiastical plays in their attempts to convert Native Americans to Christianity, and drama became part of the oral literary tradition of the region. The French also brought their theater traditions to the New World. Marc Lescarbot's *Le Théâtre de Neptune en Nouvelle-France,* performed in Port Royal, Acadia (later Annapolis Royal, Nova Scotia), on 14 November 1606, was the first play written and staged in French Canada, and from 1640 until 1699 plays were frequently performed in Quebec. Louisiana theater lagged behind that of northern French settlements. The first theatrical performance in New Orleans may be an amateur production staged in a private home during the 1760s.

British Models. American theater as it exists today evolved from English models, and until well into the nineteenth century Americans preferred British plays. (Scholars speculate that there may have been some amateur theatricals in New Netherland, but there are no records to support that theory.) A distinctly American drama was the last of all literary forms to develop in the United States. Hardworking colonists in the New World had little time for entertainments, and the Puritans of New England, as well as the Quakers of Pennsylvania,

Robert Hunter, author of *Androboros* (1714), the first play published in America (portrait attributed to Sir Godfrey Kneller; New-York Historical Society)

objected to theatrical performances on religious grounds. Even in the southern colonies, plays were suspected of provoking undesirable behavior in the lower classes.

Amateur Theatricals. The first known performance of a play in one of the thirteen original colonies was an amateur production in Accomac County, Virginia, of *Ye Bare and Ye Cubb,* by William Darby. There are no surviving copies of this play, which is known only through court records. After Darby and some friends performed the play on 27 August 1665, they were arrested for playacting but were eventually judged not guilty. There were other amateur play productions as well. In 1690 Harvard students earned the disapproval of local authorities by staging a play called *Gustavus Vasa.* Another recorded instance was the recitation of a "pastoral colloquy" by students at William and Mary College in 1702.

Roots of Professional Theater. Around 1699–1702 Richard Hunter petitioned the governor of New York for permission to stage plays in New York City. His request was granted, but there are no records of any performances. In 1703 British actor-playwright Anthony Aston arrived in Charleston, where by his account he made a living writing and performing in a play. He next went to New York City and spent a season "acting, writing, courting, and fighting" before returning in spring 1704 to Virginia and embarking for England later that year. By 1709 the province of New York had passed a ban on public playacting, along with cockfighting and other forms of entertainment considered immoral.

The First Published American Play. The following year, however, Robert Hunter, the new provincial governor of New York and New Jersey, wrote a play of his own, a satirical farce he titled *Androboros,* which translates as "man eater." Not intended for performance, the play appeared in print in 1714, becoming the first published American play. Hunter's play is an attempt to sway public opinion in his favor during a political dispute with the provincial assembly, the Anglican Church, and the ill-tempered royal commissioner of accounts, Gen. Francis Nicholson. Set in a lunatic asylum, the play features several thinly disguised characters, including the Keeper (Hunter) and Androboros (Nicholson). Although Hunter's play has been judged to have some literary merit, it is the work of an amateur.

The Rise of Public Theatricals. During the first half of the eighteenth century professional theater began to take hold in the southern and mid-Atlantic colonies. In 1716 or 1717 authorities in Williamsburg allowed a theater to be built, and amateur actors staged plays there for the next several years. In 1723, despite the antitheater sentiment of Philadelphia Quakers, strolling players performed outside the city limits. In Charleston and New York amateur acting groups built theaters during the 1730s.

Murray and Kean. Although battles between forces supporting and opposing theatrical productions continued throughout the century, by August 1749 Quaker opposition had eased sufficiently to allow a company headed by Walter Murray and Thomas Kean to stage Joseph Addison's tragedy *Cato* and other plays in a Philadelphia warehouse. From 5 March through 23 July 1750 Murray and Kean's company performed regularly in the large room of a New York building, meeting with such success that they presented fifteen more plays in a second season, which lasted from 13 September 1750 until 8 July 1751. The company then moved on to Williamsburg, where they opened in October in a recently constructed theater building.

The Company of Comedians. Usually considered the first fully professional theater company to perform in English-speaking North America, the Company of Comedians arrived in Williamsburg in September 1752, hoping to repair the financial woes that had beset it in London. With brothers William and Lewis Hallam as proprietor and actor-manager and Lewis's wife as one of the actors, the company remained in Williamsburg for eleven months, performing about twice a week. They then proceeded to New York, where they spent several months working to obtain permission to perform, finally opening with Sir Richard Steele's moral comedy *The Conscious Lovers* in September 1753. Meeting with great success, the company performed two or three times a week until 25 March 1754. The final stop of their North American tour was Philadelphia, where despite strenuous opposition from local Quakers they played for two months before sailing to Jamaica. Though the Hallams' tour was successful, it did not spur an upsurge of theatrical activity. Its plans interrupted by the death of Lewis Hallam, the newly organized Company of Comedians did not return to the colonies until 1758. Taking a new name, the American Company, after the passage of the Stamp Act (1765) spurred anti-British sentiments, this company had the distinction of staging the first professional production of a play by an American: Thomas Godfrey's *The Prince of Parthia,* which opened in Philadelphia on 24 April 1767.

Sources:

William Dunlap, *A History of the American Theatre* (New York: Printed and published by J. & J. Harper, 1832);

Bernard Hewitt, *Theatre U.S.A., 1668 to 1957* (New York, Toronto & London: McGraw-Hill, 1959);

Walter J. Meserve, *An Emerging Entertainment: The Drama of the American People to 1828* (Bloomington & London: Indiana University Press, 1977).

HEADLINE MAKERS

ANNE BRADSTREET

CIRCA 1612-1672
POET

A Major Poet. Anne Bradstreet's poetry is recognized as one of the greatest literary achievements of seventeenth-century New England and a valuable source of information on the Puritan woman's perspectives on her society. Her work remains a tribute to the power of her intellect, the depth of her passion, and her capacity for self-expression.

Early Life. Anne Dudley Bradstreet, like many early Puritans, sacrificed a comfortable life in England to settle in the wilderness of Massachusetts. She was born in Northampton, England, where her father, Thomas Dudley, was a clerk and a member of the gentry. When she was seven he became steward to Theophilus Clinton, Earl of Lincoln, and moved his family to the earl's estate at Sempringham. There she, her older brother, and four younger sisters grew up amid the amenities and refined social life of a great country manor. The earl's house was a center of Puritan learning and activism. Leading ministers of the day often preached and taught in the earl's chapel, and many of the Puritan gentry and nobility met there to discuss issues of the day. Anne heard some of the finest preaching in England; read Scripture, theology, philosophy, and literature in the earl's extensive library; listened to and participated in discussions on these subjects; and learned to appreciate the art and music of the day. When she was nine she met her future husband, Simon Bradstreet, a recent graduate of Cambridge University, who came to Sempringham as Thomas Dudley's assistant. Anne married Bradstreet in about 1628. At fifteen or sixteen she was rather young to be married by the standards of her time. The couple moved to the estate of the dowager countess of Warwick, where Simon had become steward.

Migration to Massachusetts. Anne and Simon Bradstreet did not remain in the countess's household for long. The religious situation had been worsening dramatically for the Puritans since Charles I had inherited the throne from his father, James I, in 1625. Charles fa-vored Bishop William Laud, who used his influence to exclude Puritans from church offices. Charles's efforts to limit the role of Parliament in government, culminating in his suspension of Parliament in 1629, forced the Puritans to recognize that they were losing influence at home. Puritan leaders responded with bold plans to influence England to reform by establishing a "Godly Commonwealth" in America. In 1630 the Bradstreets and Dudleys embarked for the Massachusetts Bay Colony. The harsh climate and rustic surroundings Bradstreet encountered when she arrived in America contrasted starkly with the privileged existence she had known in England. Yet "convinced it was the way of God," she "submitted to it."

Poet of New England. Anne Bradstreet and her family moved several times in the next twenty years. Her husband assumed a leading role in early Massachusetts society, holding various official posts including service as governor of the colony after her death. Anne devoted herself to domestic life, giving birth to eight children between 1633 and 1652, but she also found time to write. The earliest of her surviving poems dates from 1632, when she was ill and hovering near death while residing in New Towne (later renamed Cambridge), Massachusetts. Three years later the Bradstreets moved to the frontier town of Ipswich, Massachusetts, where they remained for ten years. Here Bradstreet began to write poetry in earnest. Her whole family took great pride in her work, encouraging her to continue writing. In 1645 the Bradstreets moved again, to the inland town of Andover, where Anne continued to find time to write amid a busy schedule of child rearing, domestic work, and entertaining.

The Tenth Muse. In 1647 her brother-in-law John Woodbridge carried to England a manuscript of her poems and prepared it for publication without her knowledge or consent. It appeared anonymously as *The Tenth Muse Lately Sprung Up in America* (1650), gaining her recognition on both sides of the Atlantic as a learned and expressive poet. The poems in this volume display her knowledge of history, philosophy, and current affairs in England and America and include elegies to Elizabeth I and Sir Philip Sidney.

Later Years. Bradstreet continued writing until her death in 1672. After she died her husband collected her corrected versions of the poems in *The Tenth Muse* and some of her later poems in *Several Poems Compiled with Great Variety of Wit and Learning, Full of Delight* (1678), the first book by a woman to be published in America. The later poems in this volume are far more candid than her earlier verse about Bradstreet's spiritual doubts—and far more personal. Many of these are the poems for which she is most admired by modern readers—including her poems about her love for her husband and family. While the poems in *The Tenth Muse* have been called brilliant but imitative and strained, the later poems are the work of a talented, original poet shaping the raw material of her life into art.

Sources:

Joseph R. McElrath Jr. and Allan P. Robb, *The Complete Works of Anne Bradstreet* (Boston: Twayne, 1981);

Rosamond Rosenmeier, *Anne Bradstreet Revisited* (Boston: Twayne, 1991);

Ann Stanford, *Anne Bradstreet: The Worldly Puritan* (New York: Burt Franklin, 1974).

JOHN SMIBERT

1688-1751

ARTIST

Influence on American Art. John Smibert, who arrived in America in January 1729 at the age of forty, exerted a profound influence on eighteenth-century American portrait painting. His training in the Dutch-influenced style of portraiture that was fashionable among the British aristocracy brought a new sophistication to the art of New England.

Early Life. Born in Edinburgh, Scotland, where he was raised as a Presbyterian, Smibert studied in 1713–1716 at the London artists' academy headed by Sir Godfrey Kneller, whose style influenced several generations of British portrait painters. After a few years as a professional portrait painter in Edinburgh, Smibert left for Italy in spring 1719 and spent the next three years studying and copying paintings in the great art collections in Florence and Rome and buying works for his own growing collection. On his return to Britain in summer 1722, he established a studio in London, where he achieved a modest reputation but no great distinction.

The Bermuda Group. His fortunes took a dramatic turn, however, when Irish philosopher and Anglican churchman Dean George Berkeley invited Smibert to teach painting, drawing, and architecture at a new college that Berkeley hoped to establish in Bermuda. Leav-

ing England in late 1728, Berkeley, his family, Smibert, and others involved in the plan went to Newport, Rhode Island, where they settled while waiting for funding from Parliament. Smibert commemorated the enterprise in his best-known painting, *The Bermuda Group* (1729–1731). The allotment was never approved, and Berkeley returned to England after a fruitless two-year wait. Even before his patron had left, however, Smibert had found his niche in America, settling in Boston to pursue a lucrative career as a portrait painter.

American Painter. Within a year of his arrival in Boston in spring 1729, Smibert gained wide recognition, attracting people to his studio with an exhibit of his own paintings, his copies of works by the old masters, and items from his personal collection. Poet Mather Byles welcomed Smibert to the city with a poem that proclaimed:

> Thy Fame, O *Smibert,* shall the Muse rehearse,
> And sing her Sister-Art in softer Verse.
> 'Tis yours, Great Master, in just lines to trace,
> The rising prospect or the lovely Face.

Within eight months the artist had completed twenty-six portraits—including paintings of Judges Samuel Sewell and Nathaniel Byfield. In July 1730 Smibert cemented his ties to the Boston elite when he married Mary Williams, daughter of Dr. Nathaniel Williams, the highly respected master of the Boston Latin School, and after five years in Boston Smibert had done more than one hundred portraits. Smibert's paintings might have been considered only average in London, but British Americans had never seen anything like them for their lifelike poses, elegant textures, and perceptive characterization. His eight-foot-by-five-foot painting *The Bermuda Group* hung in Smibert's studio to the end of his life, attracting local admirers as well as many travelers from other colonies.

Later Life. Smibert's reputation also brought him a wealth of paying customers to purchase art supplies and imported prints from the shop he kept on the side. There aspiring young Boston painters such as John Greenwood, a friend of John Singleton Copley's family, came for supplies and advice on portrait painting. Younger American artists incorporated many of Smibert's techniques in their own work, extending his influence far beyond Boston. He also dabbled in architecture, designing the original Faneuil Hall in Boston in 1742. Yet as he settled into a complacent, prosperous life, his portraits grew less and less imaginative.

Sources:

Frank W. Bayley, *Five Colonial Artists of New England* (Boston: Privately printed, 1929);

Richard H. Saunders, *John Smibert: Colonial America's First Portrait Painter* (New Haven & London: Yale University Press, 1995).

PUBLICATIONS

A Catalogue of Curious and Valuable Books, Belonging to the Late Reverend & Learned Mr. Ebenezer Pemberton, Consisting of Divinity, Philosophy, History, Poetry, & Generally Well Bound (Boston: Printed by B. Green, 1717)—the first catalogue for a book auction in the American colonies; this and other such catalogues are valuable tools for scholars of colonial literary tastes;

Joshua Gee, *Catalogus Librorum Bibliothecæ Collegij Harvardini Quad Est Cantabriglæ in Nova Anglia* (Boston: Printed by B. Green, 1723)—the first catalogue of a college library printed in America;

John Hancock, *Continuatio Supplementi Catalogi Librorum Bibliothecæ Collegij Harvardini, Quad Est Cantabriglæ in Nova Anglia* (Boston: Printed by B. Green, 1725)—the first supplement to the catalogue of the Harvard College Library printed in 1723;

The Library of the Late Reverend and learned Mr. Samuel Lee . . . Exposed . . . to Sale, by Duncan Campbell (Boston: Printed by Benjamin Harris for Duncan Campbell, 1693)—probably the first catalogue for the sale of an American library;

Increase Mather, *The Life and Death of the Reverend Man of Gos, Mr. Richard Mather, Teacher of the Church in Dorchester in New-England* (Cambridge, Mass.: Printed by S. G. & M. J., 1670)—a son's biography of one of the authors of *The Bay Psalm Book* and the founder of the Mather family in America; like most Purtian biographies, this one focuses more on its subject's spiritual development than on the events of his life.

Baccus and Ariadne (1720s), by Gustavus Hesselius (Detroit Institute of Arts)

BUSINESS AND COMMUNICATIONS

by ELIZABETH PRUDEN and TIMOTHY D. HALL

CONTENTS

Sidebars and tables are listed in italics.

1603
- The king of France grants a ten-year monopoly on the fur trade in eastern Canada to Pierre du Guast, Sieur de Monts.

1606
- King James I charters two profit-seeking Virginia companies.

1612
- John Rolfe plants his first successful crop of tobacco in Virginia.

1613
- Dutch fur traders first arrive on the island of Manhattan.

1617
- English convicts are sent to Virginia as indentured servants.

1619
- Virginia planters export tobacco, and it quickly becomes a medium of exchange in the colony.
- The first Africans arrive in Jamestown, Virginia.

1620
- A tobacco boom begins in the Chesapeake colonies.

1624
- Edward Winslow, later governor of Plymouth Colony, introduces cattle to New England by importing one bull and three heifers from Devon, England.
- The English Crown takes control of Virginia.

1626
- In exchange for goods worth sixty guilders (twenty-four dollars), the Dutchman Peter Minuit purchases Manhattan Island from local Indians.

1632
- Lord Baltimore receives a land grant for the first proprietary colony in British North America; he names it Maryland.

1640
- New England merchants enter the slave trade.

- The Five Nations of the Iroquois confederacy begin to wage war with neighboring tribes over control of the fur trade.

1641

- The first patent in the colonies is awarded to Samuel Winslow for a process used in manufacturing salt.

1642

- Joseph Jencks, a skilled English ironmaker, arrives in Lynn, Massachusetts, to establish an iron-and-brass works.

1643

- The first American textile factory, a small woolen mill, is established at Rowley, Massachusetts.

1644

- The first successful ironworks is founded on the Saugus River, near Lynn, Massachusetts.

1646

- Joseph Jencks receives a Massachusetts patent for a scythe-grinding machine.

1651

- Parliament begins to enact a series of navigation laws to regulate colonial commerce, industry, and shipping.

1654

- The Massachusetts General Court licenses Richard Thurley to build and maintain a toll bridge over the Newbury River at Rowley. It is the first of its kind in the colonies and charges two shillings for horses, cows, and oxen; one-half shilling for hogs, sheep, and goats; and no fee for humans.

1661

- A Maryland law makes slavery hereditary.

1662

- A Virginia law makes slavery hereditary.

1664

- King Charles II assigns his brother, James, Duke of York, the proprietor of the colony called New York.
- King Charles II awards New Jersey to Lord John Berkeley and Sir George Carteret.

1673

- The first mounted mail service is inaugurated between New York and Boston, and it takes three weeks for a rider to travel the route.

1675

- More than six hundred ships and four thousand New England sailors are engaged in the fishing industry.

1690

- German settlers in Pennsylvania establish the first paper mill.
- Large-scale whaling operations begin off of Nantucket, Massachusetts.
- Enslaved Africans begin to replace white indentured laborers in the Southern colonies.
- Benjamin Harris begins to publish the first newspaper in the British colonies, the Boston *Publick Occurrences*.

1696

- Parliament creates the Board of Trade and Plantations to counsel the king regarding his North American possessions.
- Rice cultivation is introduced in South Carolina.

1698

- Britain opens the slave trade to all its merchants.
- The Woolen Act prohibits the export of woolen goods from America or between the colonies.

1704

- John Campbell establishes the *Boston News-Letter*.

1712

- Whalers begin to hunt in deeper waters after Christopher Hussey becomes the first American to kill a sperm whale.

1713

- Capt. Andrew Robinson of Gloucester, Massachusetts, builds the first American schooner.

1715

- The volume of the slave trade doubles over the next fifteen years.

1716

- Probably the first lighthouse in the colonies is built on Little Brewster Island in Boston Harbor.

1719

- Scots-Irish immigrants begin to grow potatoes in Londonderry, New Hampshire.

1720

- Rice exports from South Carolina grow over the course of the next thirty years.

1728

- Benjamin Franklin begins to publish the *Pennsylvania Gazette.*

1731

- The Hat Act prevents the production of beaver and felt hats in the colonies.

1732

- A stagecoach line starts operations and connects Burlington with Amboy, New Jersey.

1733

- The Molasses Act imposes a six-pence tax on each gallon of molasses imported from the French and Dutch sugar islands.
- Trustees open Georgia to debtors with the intention that they will help defend the colony from Spanish Florida.

1737

- John Higley of Simsbury, Connecticut, mints the first copper coins in the colonies.

1739

- Caspar Wistar opens his glassworks at Allowaystown, New Jersey.

1740

- James Oglethorpe convinces Parliament to ban slavery in Georgia.
- Indigo is established as a successful staple crop in South Carolina.

1741

- Andrew Duché, a Huguenot residing in Savannah, Georgia, makes the first porcelain in British North America.

1750

- The Iron Act prohibits the expansion of finished iron and steel manufacturing in British North America.

1751

- The Currency Act prevents the colonies from establishing land banks and using public bills of credit to pay private debts.
- Sugarcane is introduced in Louisiana by Catholic missionaries; it is used to make taffia, a kind of rum.

1752

- Georgia trustees legalize slavery.

1753

- The first steam engine arrives in America; John Schuyler of North Arlington, New Jersey, uses it to pump water from his copper mine.
- There are approximately 140,000 African slaves in North America.

OVERVIEW

Early Exploration. English exploration and settlement of the Atlantic seaboard of North America began at the end of the sixteenth century. This development followed Spanish and French exploration during the sixteenth century into the area the English would call Carolina. Poor planning, natural disasters, and distance from more-populated settlements drove the Spanish and French back to the Caribbean. Frustrated in their attempts to find gold and silver and to establish staging areas for further exploration, the French and Spanish turned their attention to other parts of the world. However, the English commitment to settle North America resulted in a thriving economy that eventually compensated for the early risks.

English Immigrants. A variety of motives prompted 155,000 English immigrants to cross the Atlantic Ocean to settle the coast of North America during the seventeenth century. Social, political, religious, and economic factors influenced a wide variety of people to risk the experience of emigration during the seventeenth century. An expanding population and decreasing opportunity for employment drove many impoverished English men and women to seek their future in a new world. Because only firstborn sons could hope to inherit family lands, younger sons sought their fortunes in the colonies. Families who wanted to practice their trades far from the English Crown risked the journey to establish new communities. Promotional literature tempted Puritans, Cavaliers, Quakers, and Scots-Irish to settle in "one of the goodlyst, best and frutfullest cultures that ever was sene, and where nothing lacketh." The economic status and assorted intentions of settlers who responded to such advertisements often determined their destination, which in turn shaped colonial development.

Other Nationalities. Although the number of English immigrants surpassed all other groups, other Europeans found cause to journey to a foreign land to benefit from the favorable economic opportunities. French Huguenots who escaped persecution that resulted from the revocation of the Edict of Nantes in 1685 sailed to Massachusetts, New York, and South Carolina. Emigrants who had suffered the hardships of war, persecution, and famine left Germany and Switzerland for Pennsylvania in the seventeenth and eighteenth centuries. Ten percent of the American colonial population spoke German. The Dutch who traded furs in New York in the seventeenth century were followed by Dutch families who moved to Pennsylvania in the eighteenth century. Swedes made their way to Delaware. Each of these groups could have migrated to other parts of the world but chose instead the British colonies because of the promise of economic prosperity.

Virginia. Members of the English gentry sought quick wealth in the Virginia colony in 1607. Single men unaccustomed to working for a living joined the original venture. Poor planning and lack of discipline doomed 67 of the first 105 men to death within a year. The high mortality rate (four hundred out of five hundred men by 1609) prevented initial stability. Striving to identify a crop that would assure economic security and profit, John Rolfe developed a strain of tobacco that thrived in the Virginia soil.

Massachusetts Bay. In 1629 four hundred English Puritans traveled to the Massachusetts Bay Colony and were followed by seven hundred more settlers in 1630. These orderly families and servants hoped to establish a community that would offer a religious and economic alternative to the growing depravity of England. Communal support rather than individual profit led these families to cluster in communities under the leadership of their Puritan ministers.

Carolina. English proprietors intent on establishing a pseudofeudal colony gained the rights to settle Carolina. Settling first near present-day Charleston in 1670, English families accepted fifty acres per each family member and servant. Families from Barbados in the West Indies left the sugar island with their slaves to seek new opportunities. They received land for each slave they transported. In a climate different from both England and Barbados, Carolinian settlers sought a staple crop that would bring wealth. Within twenty years of arriving, planters identified rice as the crop most conducive to coastal lowlands. Defying the original model of a feudal fiefdom, these independent southern settlers spread out along the coast and forty miles inland into a colony of their own making.

Middle Colonies. The most diverse region was the mid-Atlantic, or Middle, Colonies. Dutch, French, Germans, and Scandinavians settled New Netherland before the English Crown claimed the area of New York in 1664. Further south along the Delaware River, Swedes settled a small colony. From 1638 until 1655, the Swedes traded for furs with nearby Lenni Lenape, or Delaware, Indians. For the next nine years the Swedes fell under Dutch control, until the English Crown claimed them as well. In 1682 William Penn led a group of Quakers to a colony that promised religious freedom. Within five years eight thousand more Quakers, Baptists, French Huguenots, Lutherans, and Catholics settled in Pennsylvania. With an industrious group of settlers who had the good fortune to reside on fertile land, the Middle Colonies would become the breadbasket of the British colonies.

Native Americans. The land the European settlers embraced was not virgin land. Indians had been burning, farming, and hunting this vast continent for twenty-five hundred years before the European explorers arrived. Southwest Indians irrigated their land to grow maize, beans, and squash. Eastern Woodland Indians burned forests and prairies to stimulate crop production and wild berry growth. They grew maize, potatoes, beans, squash, sunflowers, and tobacco. Pottery shards, baskets, stone weapons, and shells unearthed in archaeological digs reveal an elaborate trading system among the seven million to ten million Indians who inhabited North America. These productive enterprises were interrupted when the Europeans brought ravishing disease along with their intentions to subdue the land. The absence of antibodies meant the Indians were particularly vulnerable to diphtheria, influenza, measles, smallpox, and typhus. The deaths of 90 percent of the Indian population north of the Rio Grande left a widowed land that offered little resistance to European settlement. Indians who survived contributed to the economic development by offering food during the starving days, trading the first valuable commodity of skins and pelts, and teaching the art and science of growing crops in America.

Farming. Contrary to popular myth, the American colonial economy was not anchored by self-sufficient farmers. Individuals placed a high value on independence and sufficiency but recognized that the hardships of settlement and getting started required mutual support. Even farmers living in relatively remote areas needed to rely on distant neighbors. The household was the fundamental unit of production in American agriculture. Farmers produced crops for consumption and sale, and their families provided most of the laboò to achieve those ends. Servants, hired hands, and slaves assisted in those efforts. But even that combination of workers was not enough to sustain a colonial family. Neighbors depended on each other to build their homes and churches, harvest crops, break sod, cut timber, raise barns, build fences, establish livestock herds, and give birth to babies. On a daily basis neighbors exchanged soap, candles, butchered meat, spun thread, or woven fabric. One family could not consume an entire butchered sow before the meat would spoil. They could preserve some of the meat but would trade the rest for a knitted shirt or new shoes. A family might also trade the meat for a service, such as help in weaving a blanket or harvesting a crop. This barter economy allowed families to specialize in particular crafts or to maintain a minimum of tools. The ways in which they relied on each other reinforced agricultural practices and labor systems.

TOPICS IN THE NEWS

CAPITAL INVESTMENT

Personal Finances. Money was necessary for colonial development, and few of the migrants had enough of it to build a new country. They could, however, provide labor if someone else would contribute the funds. Capital, or the personal wealth used for business purposes and not for household consumption, was plentiful in the European cities the immigrants had left. Some immigrants were wealthy and had enough capital to finance their own endeavors. Other investors remained in England and provided the capital the settlers needed to develop the abundant natural resources of the American colonies. Eventually the economic success of settlers allowed them to establish local credit markets so that they could borrow money from neighbors. In the seventeenth century more capital was needed for agricultural development than for industry. The smaller farms of the northern colonies demanded far less investment capital than did the southern plantation economy. The rice market in particular was booming, and planters required extensive

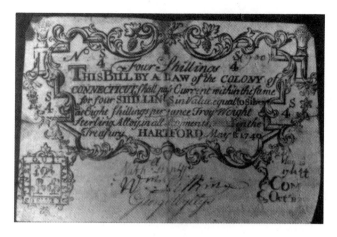

A four-shilling note issued by the New London Society United for Trade and Commerce in 1740 (Massachusetts Historical Society)

Currency in the British colonies took on various forms. Wampum, or woven belts of sea shells, were first available for trade between immigrants and Indians. When possible, colonists used the British sterling pound and shilling for European trade. This money was rare among colonists because they sent the money they had to England to pay for purchases of manufactured goods. Innovative colonists relied on other means to engage in trade. In the Chesapeake tobacco was the primary means of exchange. That meant that people could pay their taxes, duties, and court fees in tobacco. They even paid the salaries of their clergymen in tobacco. Some planters exchanged their tobacco at official storehouses, where they received receipts that they could use as money. Other colonists purchased items on credit with the promise that they would pay their debts with the commodities they harvested in their own region. Some colonies issued paper money that was based in some way on the British pound, but the rate of exchange varied from one colony to another. For example, seven South Carolina pounds were worth one British sterling pound. Crossing colonial borders meant using different forms of exchange. Land banks lent paper currency to farmers who were willing to mortgage their land.

Source: John J. McCusker and Russell R. Menard, *The Economy of British America, 1607–1789* (Chapel Hill: University of North Carolina Press, 1985).

capital to purchase land and more slaves to plant and harvest the profitable staple crop. Capital tended to flow from the city and mercantile fortunes toward the country and plantation development. As regions stabilized, interest rates declined slowly, but they remained higher than in Europe. For example, the legal interest rate in South Carolina was 10 percent until 1748 when it was lowered to 8 percent.

Bonds and Mortgages. The two primary instruments of capital formation in British North America were bonds and mortgages. Bonds were formal, legally recorded loan agreements between lender and borrower which involved a general obligation with no required collateral. The person taking out the loan was obliged to continue payment for the full term of the bond, commonly six months or one year. A mortgage was also a formal, legally recorded agreement, but it required collateral worth twice the value of the mortgage. Slaves and per-

Stivers (top) and guilders (bottom), the official coins of New Netherland. Twenty stivers equaled one guilder (Numismatic Society of America).

sonal goods were the most common forms of guarantee put up for such loans. The mortgage also had a limited term. Often lenders let the loan stay out past the termination date and continued to collect interest payments rather than the balance because it was a good long-term investment. Typically, the bonds and mortgages stipulated that the penalty for nonpayment of interest or principal was twice the value of the original loan.

Gender. English common law restricted the control and ownership of property by women. Only unmarried and widowed women could own property because once a woman married, everything she owned belonged to her husband. In spite of these restrictions women were involved in the capital market. Certainly more men with more money dominated the market, but widows lent money, lived off the interest, and participated in the growth of a new capital market between 1700 and 1750. Whereas some of these widows were extremely wealthy, other women with only meager holdings also invested, at times in nothing more substantial than a single bond extended to a neighbor. The majority of those women were not from prominent planter or merchant families with significant wealth. Most of these women had middling or meager estates. But even with only a small amount of capital, widows could invest money that would earn interest. For women who had only limited opportunities for earning money, the bond/mortgage market provided a good source of income.

Sources:

Peter A. Coclanis, *The Shadow of a Dream: Economic Life and Death in the South Carolina Low Country, 1670–1920* (New York: Oxford University Press, 1989);

Ralph Davies, *The Rise of the Atlantic Economies* (Ithaca, N.Y.: Cornell University Press, 1973);

Jack P. Greene and J. R. Pole, *Colonial British America: Essays in the New History of the Early Modern Era* (Baltimore: Johns Hopkins University Press, 1984);

Alice Hanson Jones, *Wealth of a Nation to Be: The American Colonies on the Eve of the Revolution* (New York: Columbia University Press, 1980);

John J. McCusker and Russell R. Menard, *The Economy of British America, 1607–1789* (Chapel Hill: University of North Carolina Press, 1985).

COMMUNICATIONS

The Need. Transatlantic migration and trade stimulated the development of a variety of communications throughout the colonial period. Investors in joint-stock companies often staked large sums of money on the success of early colonial ventures and were anxious for news of the settlements' progress. Family members who remained in Europe longed for word from loved ones separated by three thousand miles of ocean. Planters and traders in America needed reliable ways of exchanging information with European merchants concerning prices, crop yields, shipments, and supplies. Shippers, merchants, and insurers needed accurate information about piracy, outbreaks of conflict on the high seas, and important political developments so that they could calculate risks and make adjustments. Military officers needed to communicate with their superiors in Europe and with various colonial posts. This widespread need to know created an increasing demand for profitable new ways of delivering information. The growth of trade also aided communication as various forms of information accompanied goods throughout the Atlantic world and made their way inland from port cities like Quebec, Philadelphia, Charleston, and New Orleans.

Overlapping Networks. Seventeenth-century colonists kept abreast of personal and public affairs in a variety of ways. Ships arriving in the colonies with passengers and supplies also carried public communications and private letters from family or business associates. Special couriers and traveling government officials were entrusted with official correspondence and notices of royal edicts or recent acts of Parliament. Captains usually carried an official mailbag bearing correspondence. Private letters sometimes came by a trusted family member or friend who had taken passage across the ocean. Other times letters came by a more distant acquaintance who had embarked for the colonies or London and had agreed

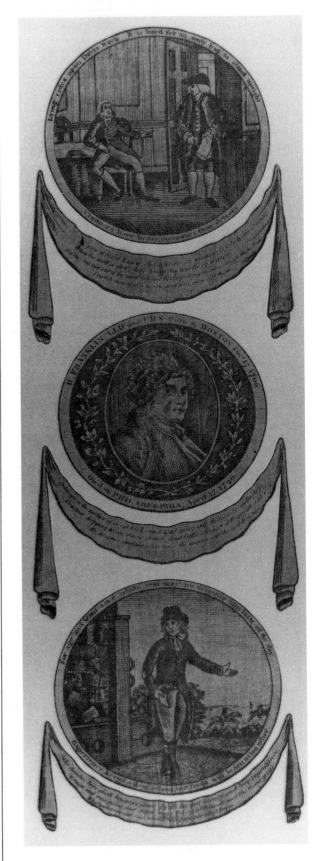

Part of a "Poor Richard's handkerchief." A portrait of Benjamin Franklin is in the center while the other two scenes depict maxims from *Poor Richard's Almanack.*

to carry them. Some information made its way around the Atlantic by word of mouth as persons on shipboard gleaned bits of news from port to port, hailed passing ships for news at sea, or witnessed or participated in hostile encounters with pirates or ships of foreign powers. Dockside taverns provided communications nodes where sailors could dispense such tidbits, and African Americans took special advantage of this method of communication as black sailors conveyed information among the slave communities of North America and the Caribbean. Information arriving at the coast moved inland in similar ways. Friends or acquaintances traveling to particular destinations carried letters with them, stopping at taverns along the way to dispense whatever news they had heard, to leave letters for pickup, and to catch up on the latest local happenings. Sunday gatherings at the church or meetinghouse provided another form of communication where people could exchange local news before or after worship, deliver letters to their recipients, or hand letters to a courier for delivery elsewhere. Ministers read royal proclamations or governor's edicts from the pulpit, made announcements of important public matters, and kept people abreast of important transatlantic religious concerns by summarizing or reading aloud correspondence from fellow ministers in the British Isles. People continued to use all these traditional forms of communication throughout the colonial period even as new forms began to arise.

Postal Service. A reliable postal service was well established in the British Isles by the end of the seventeenth century, but it took longer for such a service to arise in the colonies. Postal services usually followed the model begun in Massachusetts: in 1639 Boston officials designated the tavern kept by Richard Fairbanks as the official site for depositing and receiving ship letters. It took much longer to establish regular postal services to inland towns or even over land between important cities such as Boston and New York. Only in the 1690s did a regular overland postal route arise to link New York, Connecticut, and Massachusetts with riders that initially followed a monthly schedule and then increased to a weekly one as the volume of mail grew. Colonies followed the mother country in passing special postal acts that set rates and specified procedures for appointing postmasters and issuing patents that authorized private operators to set up services and hire carriers. Rates varied widely from colony to colony. Massachusetts, for example, set the charge for an overseas letter at two pence while New York set it at nine. A letter from Rhode Island to Boston at this time cost six pence, the equivalent of a half-day's pay for a sailor. In spite of their cost, however, postal routes played an important part in stimulating the economic growth along colonial coasts and rivers. Reliable postal service made it possible for artisans, shipbuilders, and merchants to establish themselves in smaller ports and market towns, where the cost of living and doing business was cheaper, without having to sacri-

fice regular communication with customers and suppliers in larger cities. As the eighteenth century wore on, the office of postmaster was frequently filled by prominent printers, such as Benjamin Franklin of Philadelphia, who often expanded postal routes to deliver their newspapers to ever-wider colonial audiences.

The Press. Between 1660 and 1695 newspapers were rare even in England. Their publication was tightly controlled by the Crown through legislation known as the Licensing Act because royal officials feared that the papers could be used to spread rebellious ideas throughout the realm. Consequently, when in 1690 the Boston printer Benjamin Harris published the first newspaper in America, *Publick Occurrences,* colonial officials quickly suppressed it. By 1695, however, such fears had diminished sufficiently that when the Licensing Act expired, neither the king nor Parliament attempted to renew it. English printers responded immediately by experimenting with a variety of new publications designed to make money from the demand for news. Many of these "publick prints," as they were called, made their way to the colonies. In 1704 the Boston postmaster and printer John Campbell borrowed freely from the format and news articles of these English newspapers to publish one of the first successful newspapers in America, the *Boston News-Letter.* Over the next three decades no fewer than seventeen additional English-language papers appeared in the colonies, along with one in German. Six of these appeared in Boston, where rival printers competed for readership by trying to outdo each other with interesting essays and features. They also took rival positions on various issues of the day, often lampooning each other's material as they carried on fierce debates between papers. The controversy helped publishers sell even more papers as people on each side bought the latest issues to see what debaters would say next. In Philadelphia young Benjamin Franklin purchased a struggling newspaper in 1728 from a former employer, renamed it the *Pennsylvania Gazette,* and built a fortune through witty writing, keen business sense, and shrewd competition with the rival Philadelphia paper, the *American Weekly Mercury.* Franklin diversified by printing books, government documents, and the popular *Poor Richard's Almanack.* He also built a network of publishers across the colonies, extending his own influence as a publisher as far away as Charleston, South Carolina, through partnership in Peter Timothy's *South Carolina Gazette.* Franklin's own paper benefited greatly because these contacts in other colonies gave him access to even more news. In Pennsylvania the large German population provided a market for the one non-English newspaper printed in the British mainland colonies, which ran from 1739 to 1746. The printer, Christopher Sauer, kept his German audiences abreast of events by translating some English news into German. He also published news from German lands, thus helping to maintain a vital transatlantic cultural link with the homeland of German immigrants.

A copy of the first continuing newspaper printed in the British North American colonies, founded in 1704

Culture of Newspapers. Early colonial newspapers initially targeted a well-to-do readership, merchants, planters, and government officials who needed to know what was happening in England and Europe that might affect trade or political affairs in the colonies. For this reason the papers usually focused on European news, often reprinting articles directly from London newspapers or publishing excerpts dealing with European affairs from private correspondence. European news was often two to three months old, yet in most cases it was still useful to persons who needed to plan for the next shipment of goods to Europe or who wanted to keep up with the latest English fashions and the latest gossip from the royal court in London. Colonial newspapers also provided an important forum for public debate, carrying essays and controversies on issues of the day. News from the colonies themselves rarely occupied much space, since business and politics depended more on happenings overseas and since word of mouth usually conveyed local news faster than weekly newspapers could circulate it. Yet newspapers quickly became an important tool for sellers to advertise their goods to buyers, for people to publish important notices, for owners to recover lost goods, and for masters to track down runaway servants or slaves. By 1740 at least two pages of an ordinary four-page newspaper were occupied with advertising a rapidly increasing range of imported British goods, colonial services, local real estate, printed material, public notices, and lost-and-found items.

Literary Community. With various methods of communication becoming more reliable, literature from Europe was more widely available. As more colonists read European books, pamphlets, and newspaper articles, they began to think of themselves as members of a vast community or "Republic of Letters" that extended across the Atlantic to incorporate both Europeans and Americans. For educated New England Puritans this literate community had existed since the early seventeenth century through correspondence and the exchange of books and ideas. The eighteenth-century religious revivals known as the Great Awakening brought many more people into the transatlantic religious community. Colonists who had experienced a revival in one colony began identifying in a new way with those who had enjoyed the same experience in other English colonies, as well as with similar people in the British Isles and the European Continent. Anglo-Americans also sought to participate in the great European scientific and philosophical discoveries known as the Enlightenment through reading the works of great figures such as the philosopher John Locke, the great physicist Isaac Newton, and the chemist Robert Boyle. Some wealthy merchants and planters, such as the Virginian William Byrd II, traveled to Europe for their education, studying law at prestigious English institutions and touring Continental Europe to gain firsthand exposure to Old World achievements, manners, tastes, learning, and company. Some Americans, such as the Puritan minister Cotton Mather, became members of the Royal Society, an English organization founded by Robert Boyle for the advancement of scientific learning, and regularly contributed scientific papers. Some American scientific papers, such as Benjamin Franklin's findings on electricity, were published by the Royal Society. These papers enhanced the reputations of their American writers in learned circles of Europe.

Sources:

Richard D. Brown, *Knowledge is Power: The Diffusion of Information in Early America* (New York: Oxford University Press, 1989);

Christopher Clark, *The Public Prints: The Newspaper in Anglo-American Culture, 1665–1740* (New York: Oxford University Press, 1994);

Ian K. Steele, *The English Atlantic, 1675–1740: An Exploration of Communication and Community* (New York: Oxford University Press, 1986);

Michael Warner, *The Letters of the Republic: Publication and the Public Sphere in Eighteenth-Century America* (Cambridge, Mass.: Harvard University Press, 1990).

GENDER

Working Together. Survival in the colonies required strenuous labor from both men and women. Often working side by side, they performed tasks conforming to the gender roles of preindustrial society. Typically, women's work was grounded in the family and men's work in the more public market economy. Yet women's work was not confined to the four walls of the home.

Family Economy. Women's responsibility for family

A spinner at work (illustration from Giles Firmin, *Some Proposals for the Imployment of the Poor,* 1681)

FEME SOLE/FEME COVERT

Traditional English common law made clear distinctions between single or widowed women and married women. Single and widowed women, or *feme sole*, had legal property rights similar to men. They could own property, retain wages, write wills, and file legal suits. Upon her wedding day a married woman, or *feme covert*, lost her separate legal identity and became one with her husband. Feme covert status restricted married women's legal rights. That status meant that women could not sue, be sued, own property, or give away property. Their property immediately belonged to their husbands. In some cases women could ask the courts for the status of feme sole if their husbands agreed. Women would make this request if they wanted to open a shop and be a trader. Such women could sell merchandise and collect debts without their husbands' daily involvement. A feme sole claimed the right to control her property and collect debts, but she removed herself from her husband's legal protection. In other words she exposed herself to legal suits by other people.

Source: Alice Kessler-Harris, *Women Have Always Worked: A Historical Overview* (Old Westbury, N.Y.: Feminist Press, 1981).

"housework" included baking, childcare, cleaning, nursing, sewing, and washing. The home's environs included the outdoors, where wives gardened, milked cows, and raised poultry and swine. Outdoor tasks included chipping ice from the well, chopping wood, and hauling water. Skills in butter churning, candle making, cheese making, knitting, and spinning provided her family with both necessities for daily use as well as commodities for exchange. In a barter economy women traded these manufactured goods for supplies that they could not produce. While men typically cleared the fields and cultivated their crops, women assisted during the harvest season. A critical role that some women pursued was that of nurse. They could treat burns, fevers, frostbite, and rashes as well as the daily ailments that families suffered. The more skilled practitioners could make ointments, salves, and syrups for the comfort of family and friends. Women learned the art and skills of housework and nursing from other women: mothers taught daughters; aunts taught nieces; and older women taught younger neighbors. The placement of young women in the homes of elder women increased the productivity of individual families and provided the training ground for continuous family economies.

Market Economy. Little written evidence of women's contribution to the market economy exists because their transactions were informal or made under the names of their husbands. Sporadic references in diaries, correspondence, and account records reveal routine and often crucial activity of women in the market economy. In 1709 the Reverend Gideon Johnston wrote, "Were it not for the Assistance my wife gives me by drawing of Pictures . . . I shou'd not have been able to live." The cash she earned for her portraits was essential to her family's survival. Just as Henrietta Johnston sold her artwork, other women sold the candles, soap, clothes, yarn, and cheese they produced, along with the milk, eggs, and vegetables they gathered. Women managed shops, sold millinery goods, and supervised inns and taverns. In an urban setting women could earn wages. In a Philadelphia hospital in 1762, women worked as nurses, clothes washers, chimney sweeps, potato diggers, cooks, maids, whitewashers, soap makers, and bakers. Women earned roughly half the wages of men, and if they were married, then those wages belonged legally to their husbands. Husbands could rely on their wives to replace them if they needed to be away for a short time. Women who served as "deputy husbands" admirably filled the place of their husbands but invariably returned to their primary position in the home. Women who outlived their husbands could continue the family business as blacksmith, silversmith, newspaper editor, butcher, cabinet maker, shoemaker, tanner, cooper, or planter. An important role unique to women was that of midwife. Whether earning wages or bartering with neighbors for goods and services for the delivery of babies, midwives blended women's roles by sustaining the family well-being and by augmenting the family economy.

Sources:

Carol Groneman and Mary Beth Norton, eds., *"To Toil the Livelong Day": America's Women at Work, 1780–1980* (Ithaca, N.Y.: Cornell University Press, 1987);

Alice Kessler-Harris, *Women Have Always Worked: A Historical Overview* (Old Westbury, N.Y.: Feminist Press, 1981);

Laurel Thatcher Ulrich, *Good Wives: Image and Reality in the Lives of Women in Northern New England, 1650–1750* (New York: Oxford University Press, 1983);

Nancy Woloch, *Women and the American Experience,* second edition (New York: McGraw-Hill, 1994).

INDIAN TRADING

Goods Exchanged. Deerskins and the pelts of other animals were the first lucrative commodity in New En-

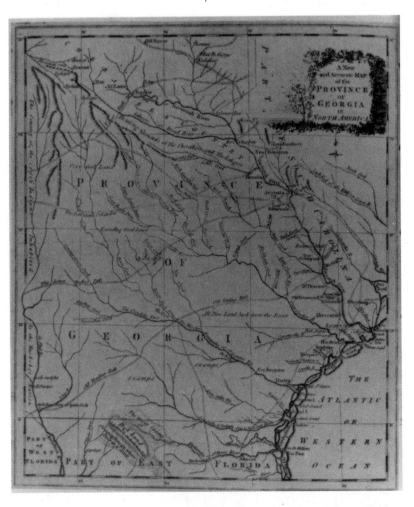

A map of Indian trading paths in Georgia, circa 1750 (Henry E. Huntington Library and Art Gallery, San Marino, California)

gland, New York, and South Carolina. There was a demand in Europe for the skins, and there was a ready supply in the colonies. Traders exchanged manufactured goods for bear, buffalo, deer, elk, beaver, fox, mink, muskrat, and raccoon furs from many Indian tribes. In return the Indians received awls, axes, beads, blankets, buttons, cloth, clothing, combs, guns, gunpowder and shot, hoes, mirrors, ribbon, rum, scissors, and thread. As early as 1717 the Superior Council of Louisiana prohibited the unauthorized sale of liquor to Indians. By 1721 the same Council established rates of exchange for trade on the lower Mississippi. One meter of cloth or one ax was worth four dressed skins. Two dressed skins would fetch one blanket or tomahawk. One dressed skin was worth two-thirds of a pound of gunpowder or twenty gun flints. Savvy Indians sought better deals by comparing the quality of French and English merchandise and bargaining for better exchange rates.

Systems. Trading skins and pelts was a tradition of many centuries among Native Americans. Inland Indians had routinely traveled to the coast to trade their furs and stone tools for fish and shells. Indians greeted European settlers with fish, corn, and pelts and began an extensive trading system. Iroquois hunters served as middlemen for New York Dutch traders, delivering furs to trading posts at Albany and Oswego. Pennsylvania traders went directly to Indian villages deep in the interior. Residents of Pennsylvania frontier towns furnished traders with supplies and maintained warehouses to store furs and skins until they could be shipped to the coast. Cherokees and Catawbas traded deerskins with South Carolinians well into the eighteenth century. As late as 1749 deerskins made up 18 percent of the Lower South's exports. Around the Great Lakes, the Hurons exchanged furs with French traders.

Effects. Although the trade in furs and skins proved an economic success for European settlers, it changed forever the way the Native Americans lived. They ceased to be self-sufficient as they ignored their crops in the effort to meet the demand for furs. They neglected the traditional production of clothing and household utensils because of the availability and quality of European merchandise. By focusing their energy on supplying a single export, the Indians became increasingly dependent on the European trader for manufactured goods. Finally, their migration further west, where they scouted for more skins, left their homeland vulnerable to European occupation.

Sources:

William Cronon, *Changes in the Land: Indians, Colonists, and the Ecology of New England* (New York: Hill & Wang, 1983);

Francis Jennings, *The Invasion of America: Indians, Colonialism, and the Cant of Conquest* (New York: Norton, 1975);

James H. Merrell, *The Indians' New World: Catawbas and Their Neighbors From European Contact Through The Era of Removal* (New York: Norton, 1989);

Daniel H. Usner Jr., *Indians, Settlers, and Slaves in a Frontier Exchange Economy: The Lower Mississippi Valley Before 1783* (Chapel Hill: University of North Carolina Press, 1992).

INDUSTRY

Limitations. Seventeenth-century manufacturing meant the production of articles or material by physical labor or mechanical labor. Industry during the seventeenth and early eighteenth centuries was limited. Low population, few urban markets, undeveloped inland transportation, scarce labor and capital, and the Navigation Acts prevented extensive development. Colonists

The forge and the rolling and slitting mill at the Saugus Ironworks Restoration in Massachusetts

Gray's Inn Creek Shipyard, Maryland, circa 1750 (painting from the mantelpiece of Spencer House, Kent County; Maryland Historical Society)

preferred to commit energy and capital to agricultural endeavors and downplayed consumerism. The manufacturing that did occur relied on simple tools in modest settings. Most colonial artisans toiled in workshops attached to their homes. The family was the primary unit of production, with the master craftsman assisted by his wife, children, and an occasional apprentice. These dispersed shops were located primarily in New England and Pennsylvania, where staple crops did not dominate the export economy. In contrast to the staple crops that were essential to the extended empire, colonial manufacturing was important to scattered local settlements.

Leader. Philadelphia was the leading manufacturing center during the colonial period, followed by New England. In spite of the focus on agriculture a range of small industries developed, especially in alcohol and leather. With increased access to West Indian molasses in 1717, sixty-three distilleries ran full-time in Massachusetts. Beer was the beverage of choice until the Scots-Irish introduced distilled spirits. As late as 1721 Pennsylvania shipped beer as far south as Charleston. Eventually the production of New England rum surpassed that of beer and cider. Nearly every farmer on the frontier had a still. Tanning proved a profitable venture, providing leather to shoemakers, saddlers, and harness makers in larger towns and villages. Pennsylvania, supplying most of the tanned leather and shoes for southern trade, was first among colonies in leather production.

Shipbuilding. The Navigation Act of 1651 limited colonial commerce to English and colonial vessels and stimulated colonial shipbuilding. As shipbuilding became the leading industry in Massachusetts in 1660, Edward Johnson noted, "Many a fair ship had her framing and finishing here, besides lesser vessels, barques, and ketches; many a Master, beside common Seamen, had their first learning in this colony." Pennsylvania also developed a thriving shipbuilding trade, and its ships earned a reputation for speed and beauty.

Textiles and Other Industries. By 1750 inhabitants of Pennsylvania were making nine-tenths of their own cloth from materials produced on their own farms. They produced mostly wool but also worked with flax to make linen. Their industry affected the larger economy by giving employment to dyers, fullers, cardmakers, combmak-

ers, spinners, and weavers. On a much smaller scale artisans produced bricks and tiles, pottery, clocks, silver, pewter, and gold artifacts.

Mills and Furnaces. Gristmills and sawmills emerged as the first industries that required a separate facility. They employed a larger workforce, required more substantial investment in plant and equipment, and depended in large part on water power. They supplied flour and lumber for both local and foreign trade. Other such structures housed ironworks, glassworks, paper mills, and powder mills. Small iron forges and furnaces multiplied in Pennsylvania because of abundant ore and water power. By 1750 Pennsylvania had taken first place in the manufacture of iron.

Fishing. The town of Marblehead, Massachusetts, protested against an export tax in 1669 because "Fish is the only great stapple which the Country produceth for forraine parts and is so benefitiall for making returns for what wee need." New England fishing fed the West Indies and Mediterranean countries. Codfish in those northern waters were unsurpassed for salting and drying. New Englanders produced three grades of fish for export. Dun fish, buried to dry and mellow, was the highest grade that merchants exported to Spain, Portugal, and France. The middling grade was easy to transport, keep, and prepare. It was the favorite winter food of colonial farmers. Merchants exported the third, and lowest, grade to the West Indies along with pickled mackerel and bass. The real profit was in distribution, not production. Merchants such as Thomas Hancock earned more money by distributing dried fish and other New England manufactured goods than by simply selling them at home. They split their exports roughly into thirds: foodstuffs, fish, and wood products.

Whaling. A resourceful Christopher Hussey fitted a vessel in 1715 to hunt sperm whales and tow them back to a Nantucket port. Ships sailing out of Cape Cod, Nantucket, and Martha's Vineyard sought whales that swam freely in the northern waters of the Atlantic. Whales were a valuable commodity that provided raw materials for the colonies to process and sell to domestic and overseas markets: ambergris for perfume, whalebone for stays and stiffeners, oil for lamps, and spermaceti for candles.

Sources:

Jack P. Greene and J. R. Pole, *Colonial British America: Essays in the New History of the Early Modern Era* (Baltimore: Johns Hopkins University Press, 1984);

Stephen Innes, ed., *Work and Labor in Early America* (Chapel Hill: University of North Carolina Press, 1988);

James T. Lemon, *The Best Poor Man's Country: A Geographical Study of Early Southeastern Pennsylvania* (Baltimore: Johns Hopkins University Press, 1972);

Marcus Rediker, *Between the Devil and the Deep Blue Sea: Merchant Seamen, Pirates, and the Anglo-American Maritime World, 1700-1750* (Cambridge: Cambridge University Press, 1987).

LABOR

Keen Observation. In 1657 one traveler in the New World wrote, "The lland is divided into three sorts of men; Masters, Servants, and slaves. The slaves and their posterity, being subject to their Masters for ever, are kept and preserv'd with greater care then the servants, who are theirs but for five years, according to the law of the lland."

Indentured Labor. An indenture contract obligated an immigrant to an agreed term of labor, usually for a period of four to seven years, in return for payment for passage across the Atlantic. Indentured servants received shelter, food, clothing, and a Sunday free of hard labor. Upon completion of the contract, bound servants typically received a suit of clothing or dress with some additional "assets." An asset might have been land in seventeenth-century Chesapeake or South Carolina. Often the "freedom dues" were distinguished by gender. A man would receive a horse, a gun, or tools, and a woman would receive a cow or spinning wheel. The high mortality rate in the Chesapeake meant that approximately 40 percent of the indentured servants died before they could reap the final benefits of their contract. Rural Pennsylvania farmers and Chesapeake planters relied the most on indentured labor to plant and harvest their crops. Three-quarters of the English migrants to the Chesapeake arrived as bound labor. It is estimated that one-half to two-thirds of the Europeans who traveled to British America were committed to some form of labor contract for their transatlantic passage. As many as fifty thousand convicts served out sentences of seven to fourteen years as indentured servants. Those servants who did not work on farms worked for bakers, blacksmiths, bricklayers, butchers, chairmakers, coopers, masons, plasterers, potters, tailors, weavers, or wheelwrights. In the seventeenth century indentured servants could capitalize on economic opportunities and advance in an upwardly mobile society. But the road to that success was not easy. Abusive conditions and harsh punishments plagued the lives of many servants. Contracts could be sold, obligating the servant to a different master for the rest of the term. A master could extend the contract if a servant ran away or became pregnant. By the eighteenth century opportunities for social and economic advancement decreased. As the urgency to escape England declined, so too did the willingness of people to commit

The sign that hung outside the shop of painter Thomas Child of Boston in 1701. The coat of arms is that of the Painters' Guild of London (Bostonian Society).

themselves to long contracts. Pennsylvania farmers turned to day laborers, and Chesapeake planters shifted to African slaves.

Ready to Work. Redemptioners were similar to indentured servants in that they agreed to work for a specific period in return for transatlantic passage. The difference was that they arranged a contract once they arrived in the British colonies rather than agreeing to terms for labor in England or Europe before beginning the trip. These bound laborers could not leave the ships until they found a colonist willing to pay for their voyage in return for labor. Whereas the indentured servants tended to be unmarried men and women from England, redemptioners were usually families from Germany. In some cases an entire family would commit to a labor contract. In other cases parents would obligate a child or children to a contract that would pay for the family's passage. These terms also were for from four to seven years.

Wage Labor. Wage laborers comprised the smallest group of workers in British America. In the seventeenth century they tended to be young men and women who were not yet married. Some wage laborers were former indentured servants who had completed a contract but were not yet self-sufficient. They were rare in the countryside because wages were high and land was cheap, so it did not take long to convert wages to land. Also, rural farmers tended to rely on family labor rather than pay wages to day laborers. As land became more scarce in the eighteenth century, the number of wage laborers in rural America increased. Such free, hired laborers were more common in urban centers, where the demand was higher and where more money was required to establish oneself.

For these workers wage labor was likely a lifelong condition. In 1762 a laborer would have needed fifty pounds a year for food, rent, fuel, and clothing for his family. That amount did not cover the additional expenses of soap, candles, taxes, or medical expenses. Even if he worked six days a week all year, which was unlikely due to seasonal demands and business cycles, a wage laborer could hope to bring home an annual wage of only sixty pounds. With the additional wages of a wife, who probably earned half of what he did, the wage earner faced an endless reality of bare subsistence. Injury or pregnancy could doom the family to dependence on the community.

Slaves. By 1750 slaves lived in all thirteen colonies, but their numbers were greatest in the Southern colonies where substantial staple exports required a large labor force. Slaves first arrived in Virginia in 1619 when a Dutch trader exchanged twenty slaves for provisions. Because slaves were wore expensive than indentured servants and bound labor was readily abundant, Chesapeake planters preferred short-term contracts with English servants. The transition to enslaved labor occurred in the Chesapeake at the beginning of the eighteenth century for a variety of reasons. Africans were less affected by the virulent diseases that killed whites. Living longer and better able to withstand the climate, Africans became a more profitable investment for white planters. The fact that the purchase price could mean a lifetime of servitude without the required freedom dues further influenced planters to develop a labor system based on enslaved labor. As the prices of the two groups of workers converged, planters recognized the profitability of shifting to enslaved labor. In 1670 a slave cost three times as much as an indentured servant. Twenty years later slaves were less than twice as expensive and were purchased for a lifetime rather than seven years. By 1660 the decreased availability of indentured servants increased the demand for enslaved Africans. By 1690 slaves outnumbered indentured servants in the Chesapeake. Slaves accompanied the first Barbadian settlers to South Carolina in 1670. The West Indians promoted the benefits of enslaved labor for the production of staple crops. Once rice was determined to be a profitable staple crop, the demand for enslaved Africans increased dramatically. By 1703 a majority of the labor force in South Carolina consisted of slaves. Enslaved blacks and Indians made up 47 percent of the entire population of South Carolina. Slaves in the Southern colonies typically worked in the fields although some worked as domestics or artisans. Subsistence agriculture in Northern colonies depended on family labor, so the need for large-scale enslaved labor never developed. Slaves in the Northern colonies more frequently worked as domestic servants and craft workers and less often on farms.

Frenchmen and Spaniards. West and north of British America, French and Spanish laborers pursued other endeavors. Because of their need to protect their empire and their intention to spread Catholicism, Spaniards split into two groups: military and religious. Ranging through the southwest to the western coast of North America, soldiers and officers built forts while priests and monks spread theology. Their interaction with the native inhabitants included organizing them into labor forces and imposing Catholicism. The French, who explored the Great Lakes and the Mississippi River, were as intent on spreading Catholicism but less preoccupied with military security. Jesuit missionaries traveled the same routes as coureurs de bois who found prosperity in fur trapping. French interaction with native inhabitants was based on commercial interests. Missionaries offered Catholicism as a complement to traditional religions rather than a replacement.

Sources:

David Galenson, *White Servitude in Colonial American: An Economic Analysis* (Cambridge: Cambridge University Press, 1981);

Carol Groneman and Mary Beth Norton, eds., *"To Toil the Livelong Day": America's Women at Work, 1780–1980* (Ithaca, N.Y.: Cornell University Press, 1987);

Stephen Innes, ed., *Work and Labor in Early America* (Chapel Hill: University of North Carolina Press, 1988);

Alice Kessler-Harris, *Women Have Always Worked: A Historical Overview* (Old Westbury, N.Y.: Feminist Press, 1981);

Sung Bok Kim, *Landlord and Tenant in Colonial New York: Manorial Society, 1664–1775* (Chapel Hill: University of North Carolina Press, 1978);

Peter Kolchin, *American Slavery, 1619–1877* (New York: Hill & Wang, 1995).

LAND GRANTS

Politics. The English Crown had a specific interest in wealthy investors creating a colonial empire. There were a variety of strategies to entice men to settle and develop the American colonies. The Crown could grant charters for land to individuals or groups, with political rights and privileges. King James I approved a joint-stock charter for Virginia in 1607 which would later include Plymouth Colony. Investors raised capital by selling stock in a company. This strategy shared profits and distributed economic risks of overseas business ventures. The Crown approved such ventures because they used private capital rather than royal funds. In 1629 the Massachusetts Bay Company received permission for its own charter, intending more to protect its utopian religious ideals than to secure a profit for investors. Expansion in the region resulted in individual Crown charters for Rhode Island (1644), Connecticut (1662), and New Hampshire (1681). Proprietary charters granted an individual or group of individuals outright ownership and control of large areas of land. This type of charter rewarded loyal subjects and promoted continued loyalty. The proprietor could then decide who settled the land and what terms would rule the colony. King Charles I awarded Lord Baltimore title to ten million acres in 1632, property he later named Maryland. In 1663 King Charles II awarded all of the land south of Virginia and north of Spanish territory to eight proprietors. They called the area Carolina. He then awarded the proprietary rights of New Netherland in 1664 to his brother, James, Duke of York. The Dutch originally settled New Netherland, but the English claimed the land and took it without a shot being fired. The smaller regions of Delaware and New Jersey received royal charters in 1665. Finally, William Penn received a proprietary charter for Pennsylvania in 1681 from King Charles II, who needed to settle a debt. The final form of charter was a trusteeship. In 1732 Parliament granted a charter to a group of trustees who agreed to establish Georgia as a colony that would serve as a military buffer against Spanish invasion from Florida. This protection was necessary to safeguard the lives and investments of the colonies to the north.

Headrights. Colonists who paid their own way received land from some of the colonies. Virginia awarded fifty acres and South Carolina granted fifty to one hundred acres to each person. An enterprising settler could increase a land allotment by paying the travel costs of other people, including extended family, indentured servants, and slaves. Ambitious migrants would collect and control the land allotted to their group. Margaret Brent, in the Chesapeake Bay region, took advantage of such an opportunity by sponsoring immigrants. The Dutch paid the costs of transportation of up to fifty immigrants who would agree to work the land as tenant farmers. They were obliged to pay rent in cash or with a share of the crops.

Availability. Land was relatively cheap in all the colonies in the seventeenth century. By offering land at reasonable rates, colonial governments hoped to stimulate settlement and development. The combination of cheap land and high wages in the seventeenth century meant laborers could establish themselves as independent farmers. Headrights were the first stage of land acquisition. Later, colonists could purchase varying amounts of land. Wealthy farmers could buy parcels of ten thousand acres of fertile soil in Pennsylvania. Indentured servants in the Chesapeake region in the seventeenth century could buy land cheaply at the end of their contract if they survived and did not receive land as dues for their service. Some squatters simply laid claims which were often honored once the area had been cleared and developed. New England communities divided communal land among themselves. Elite planters in New York rented rather than sold their property. By 1670 the best land in the Chesapeake was claimed, and the price of other land was going up. By the eighteenth century cheap, fertile regions lay to the west. Some colonists chose to cultivate marginal acres while others headed into the interior in search of land that would support their families.

Tenancy. Agreements to rent land for cash or a share of the crops prevailed in Maryland, Pennsylvania, New Jersey, and New York. These were areas where mixed crops to be sold at market were important. This arrange-

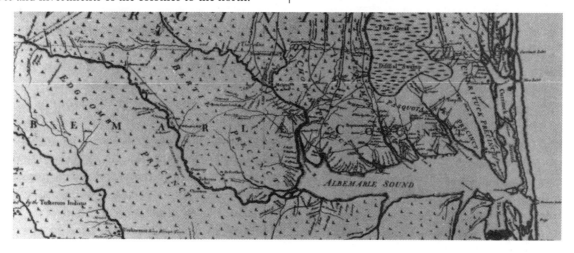

Edward Moseley's 1733 map of the boundary between Virginia and North Carolina as surveyed by William Byrd III and others (South Caroliniana Library, University of South Carolina)

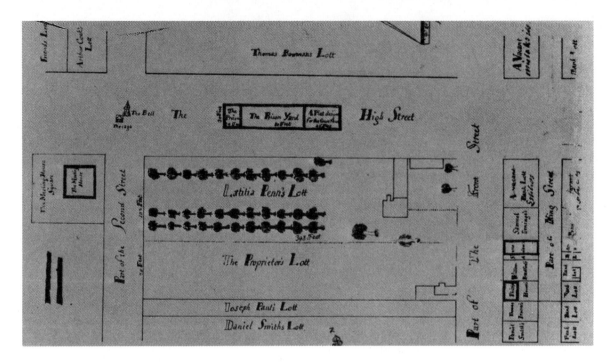

A map of lots in Philadelphia drawn for William Penn and his daughter, 1698 (Library of Congress, Map Division)

ment suited immigrants who needed work and proprietors who needed settlers. Some landowners provided initial provisions, farming equipment, and livestock as an enticement. A customary practice that involved livestock was to share the increase of stock. In addition to the rental payments, some tenant farmers had to make capital improvements on the property they farmed. That could include building a house, planting an orchard, raising a fence, or cultivating the soil. This was a particularly efficient way for landowners to improve their property. Men like Stepahnus Van Cortland and Robert Livingston developed massive tracts of land in New York this way. Another form of payment, common in New York, was the provision of services such as maintaining roads or hauling wood. Tenant farmers agreed to varying terms of time, knowing their rates could go up or they could face eviction at the whim of the owner. Because tenants were subsistence farmers, they had little cash to pay their annual rent. This cycle of poverty prevented tenant farmers from improving their economic status. Their lack of money also prevented tenant farmers from changing to nonagricultural occupations or to resettling on distant frontiers. By the end of the colonial period tenants in long-settled areas of Maryland and Pennsylvania equaled nearly half of the men who did not own land. They could not climb out or move away from their economically precarious situations.

Indian Occupation. Colonial expansion occurred because of the depopulation and dislocation of Indians who occupied the territory all along the Atlantic Coast. Initial encounters were friendly as the Indians sought to engage in trade and in some cases support the immigrants in their feeble attempts at settlement. As it became clear that the settlers were interested in claiming the Indian land and not in promoting a commercial relationship, violence erupted. Opechancanough led the Chesapeake Algonquians against Virginia settlers in 1622. Battles ensued for twenty-three years before the Algonquians signed treaties relinquishing their land to the English. While intermittent skirmishes between New England settlers and Indians obstructed western expansion, English officials compelled Indians to surrender land throughout New England. Tensions increased to the point that war exploded in 1675 between the English colonists and the Wampanoags and Narragansetts. One year later, four thousand Algonquians and two thousand settlers lay dead. In 1711 Tuscaroras attacked a Swiss frontier village in North Carolina because of land encroachment. More than one thousand Tuscaroras died or were enslaved before they surrendered their land in 1713. Two years later the Yamasees attacked South Carolina settlers out of frustration over trade violations. In all of these cases settlement and expansion to the frontier were temporarily halted. Pennsylvania was the only colony to maintain peaceful relations with Indians, as a result of William Penn's attempts to negotiate for inhabited lands in 1682–1683. Coercion and deceit altered that relationship between 1729 and 1735 when colonists made false claims to land they later sold to speculators. Eventually many tribes migrated further west to avoid the spreading settlement. Those Indians who remained behind became economically dependent on the settlers.

Sources:
Peter A. Coclanis, *The Shadow of a Dream: Economic Life and Death in the South Carolina Low Country, 1670–1920* (New York: Oxford University Press, 1989);

Wayland F. Dunaway, *A History of Pennsylvania,* second edition (Englewood Cliffs, N.J.: Prentice-Hall, 1964);

Jack P. Greene and J. R. Pole, eds., *Colonial British America: Essays in the New History of the Early Modern Era* (Baltimore: Johns Hopkins University Press, 1984);

Sung Bok Kim, *Landlord and Tenant in Colonial New York: Manorial Society, 1664–1775* (Chapel Hill: University of North Carolina Press, 1978);

James T. Lemon, *The Best Poor Man's Country: A Geographical Study of Early Southeastern Pennsylvania* (Baltimore: Johns Hopkins University Press, 1972).

MERCANTILISM

Economic Practice. Nations established colonies as outposts to promote their interests in their expanding empires. Rather than actual gold and silver, the British sought natural resources for their factories. They also wanted to develop markets to purchase their manufactured goods, goods they could tax to increase revenue. By controlling trade with colonies the parent nations wanted to establish a balance of trade that would bring national benefits to the government. Initially this economic strategy proved beneficial for both England and her colonies. The demand for labor to process the abundant natural resources of North America provided opportunities for English workers who could not find employment in England. The efficient efforts of immigrant labor provided the raw materials England needed to avoid reliance on other nations. The growing population in the British colonies increased the flow of consumer goods from England to the colonies, which in turn stimulated the English economy. Ultimately this expanded trade and its revenue produced the much sought after gold and silver.

Exchange of Goods. The British colonies provided a variety of foodstuffs, minerals, and forest products for English consumption and manufacture. Furs and raw tobacco were the first commodities in demand. Whether traded with Indians or harvested in colonial fields, the commodities were exported to England, where they were processed. The finished product, tobacco or fur hats, could then be reexported in the international free market. The ideal trading situation for a nation and its colony was the production of what a colony did not need to use and the consumption of what they could not produce. The southern colonies came closest to the ideal since they produced rice and tobacco for export and imported consumer goods from other colonies and England. Eventually the colonies exported fish, furs and pelts, grain, indigo (blue dye), livestock, lumber, naval stores (masts, pitch, tar, turpentine), rice, and rum. England's primary market lay in its colonies. Half of the copperware, ironware, glassware, earthenware, silk goods, printed cotton, and flannel that England exported went to British America. Between two-thirds and three-quarters of cordage, iron nails, beaver hats, and linen went there, too. Although these exchanges were privately fi-

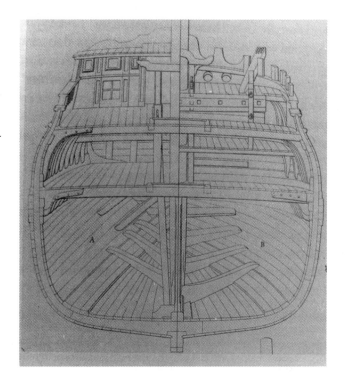

Cross section of an eighteenth-century British merchant vessel

nanced, the government needed to intercede to protect the British economic interests at home and abroad.

Government Regulation. In order to protect British trade and imperial gains, it was essential that the government impose regulations and restrictions on colonial trade. Between 1651 and 1733 the English Parliament directed those restrictions to both the domestic and overseas economy. With regard to colonial trade, Parliament enacted a series of navigation laws that controlled shipping and markets. In 1651 Parliament specified that colonial commodities be carried only in British-owned ships. This was an effort to prevent Dutch domination of the seas. In 1660 certain goods, such as furs, indigo, naval supplies, rice, sugar, and tobacco could be sold only to England or other English colonies. An act in 1663 stipulated that goods imported into the colonies must first pass through English ports. Finally, Parliament prohibited the colonies from manufacturing goods that would have directly competed with English exports. The Woolen Act of 1698, the Hat Act of 1731, and the Iron Act of 1750 limited the mass production of these specified goods for export. This intentional effort to control imperial trade prevented a competitive free market that would shape the American economy in the nineteenth century.

Sources:

Ralph Davies, *The Rise of the Atlantic Economies* (Ithaca, N.Y.: Cornell University Press, 1973);

John J. McCusker and Russell R. Menard, *The Economy of British America, 1607–1789* (Chapel Hill: University of North Carolina Press, 1985).

SLAVE TRADE

Early Efforts. The first slaves to be purchased in the British colonies in the seventeenth century were sold by Dutch slave traders. By the latter half of the seventeenth century England was able to prevail over Dutch control of the Atlantic Ocean. The English Crown sponsored a trading company in 1660 which they reorganized and rechartered in 1672 as the Royal African Company. For the next twenty-six years this group maintained a monopoly over the sale of African slaves. With the termination of the monopoly, New England merchants became active in the colonial slave trade. They sent goods to West Africa, where they traded for slaves whom they then sold in the West Indies or Carolina. Their slave trade was particularly active in Barbados. Puritan John Winthrop attributed the salvation of the New England economy to trade with the Caribbean. "It please the Lord to open to us a trade with Barbados and other Islands in the West Indies." Part of that success was based on the sale of African slaves. New England slavers sailed primarily from Massachusetts until 1750, when the center of American slave trade shifted to Rhode Island.

Statistics. Between the sixteenth and nineteenth centuries, ten million to eleven million African slaves crossed the Atlantic Ocean. Relatively few of those slaves arrived in the English continental colonies. Most of the slaves (85 percent) went to Brazil and the Caribbean colonies of the British, French, Spanish, Danish, or Dutch. Nine percent of the slaves went to the Spanish mainland. Six percent, or 600,000 to 650,000 Africans, went to the American colonies. Most of the slaves were from the coast of West Africa or from the Congo/Angola area further south. At best a trip between Senegambia and Barbados lasted three weeks. Storms or becalming waters could delay a ship so that the transatlantic voyage took three months and exhausted the food and water supplies. Between 5 and 20 percent of the slaves died in transit during the seventeenth century, but the mortality rate declined in the eighteenth century. Merchants made money only if the slaves arrived alive, so they sought captains who could deliver healthy slaves.

Middle Passage. Sailors referred to the shipboard experience of enslaved Africans across the Atlantic Ocean as "the middle passage." On board ships men were usually chained, while women and children were allowed some freedom of movement on deck. Captains chose one of two methods for transporting slaves: tight packing or loose packing. Tight packing squeezed as many slaves into a space as possible. Male slaves lay in spaces six feet long, sixteen inches wide, and two-and-one-half feet high. Female slaves lay in spaces five feet long, fourteen inches wide, and two-and-one-half feet high. Such tight spaces prevented the slaves from moving about or even sitting up. Captains who chose this style of storage did not want to waste space. They believed that their net receipts were higher from the larger cargo even if a higher ratio of slaves died. Part of the profit derived from less food and a smaller crew. The Reverend John Newton observed, "The poor creatures, thus cramped, are likewise in irons for the most part which makes it difficult for them to turn or move, or attempt to rise or to lie down without hurting themselves or each other. Every morning, perhaps, more instances than one are found of the living and dead fastened together." Other captains chose loose packing. They believed that more room, better food, and a degree of liberty reduced the mortality of slaves. Healthy slaves increased the profit. Some captains insured their stock of slaves against drowning. Because

European and African slavers bargaining in the Cape Verde Islands, circa 1700 (Victoria and Albert Museum)

insurance did not cover slaves who died aboard a ship, some captains dumped dying slaves overboard and claimed drowning to collect insurance benefits.

Auction Block. The goal of the slave merchants was to make a profit from the quick sale of the enslaved Africans. In some cases an entire cargo might be consigned to a planter or group of planters, which would close the sale to anyone else. A more common circumstance for the sale of slaves was an auction. Prior to bidding, slaves walked before prospective buyers for public inspection, to be poked and prodded. Upon completion of the examination an auctioneer would sell the slaves to the highest bidder. A second method was the scramble. Merchants would establish a fair market price before buyers rushed aboard ships to select slaves. Olaudah Equiano, an emancipated African, remembered, "On a signal given, the buyers rush at once into the yard where the slaves are confined, and make choice of that parcel they like best. The noise and clamor with which this is attended, and the eagerness visible in the countenances of the buyers, serve not a little to increase the apprehension of terrified Africans."

Sources:

Winthrop Jordan, *White Over Black: American Attitudes Toward the Negro, 1550–1812* (New York: Norton, 1977);

Peter Kolchin, *American Slavery, 1619–1877* (New York: Hill & Wang, 1995);

Allan Kulikoff, *Tobacco and Slaves: The Development of Southern Cultures in the Chesapeake, 1680–1800* (Chapel Hill: University of North Carolina Press, 1986);

Edmund Morgan, *American Slavery, American Freedom* (New York: Norton, 1975).

STAPLE ECONOMIES

Types. The term *staples* refers to resources or crops produced in mass quantities for sale or export. There are two types of staples: primary and secondary. Primary staples are goods produced predominantly for export, such as rice and tobacco. In the colonial period these crops grew in tropical and semitropical regions on plantations where indentured servants or slaves planted and harvested the crops. The Navigation Acts protected these crops that were essential to the trade between the colony and the homeland. Secondary staples were produced first for personal use and second for sale in both local and distant markets. Crops such as corn and oats grew in temperate zones where farm families with a few servants labored.

Regional Economies. Regardless of occupations in England and Europe, most settlers in the seventeenth century turned to farming for their livelihood. This condition would persist throughout the colonial era, with 90 percent of the economy being agricultural. But the crops they produced varied from one geographic region to another. The settlers found that it was weather and topography that determined the kinds of crops that they could grow and harvest. Fertile riverbanks, rocky terrain, verdant pastures, sandy hillocks, and fruitful forests determined what could be grown best in a specific area. The success or failure of experimentation led to an aggressive program of cultivating the profitable crops in those colonies whose goal it was to make a profit. Other colonists were satisfied with a subsistence culture that sustained families. The different economic goals and cultural values shaped the development of distinct labor forces. The colonial relationship

An advertisement for Virginia tobacco, circa 1750

African slaves processing indigo (from Pierre Pomet, *Compleat History of Druggs,* 1725)

with England and a growing international market secured the agricultural choices and reinforced regional economies.

New England. The New England Puritans wanted to create a new community far from the Anglican Church so that they could pray and practice their beliefs without interference. They envisioned family farms that supported their self-contained communities. They condemned excessive profits that promoted greed. In a cool climate that limited the growing season, Puritan farmers planted wheat, oats, and barley on just enough land to sustain their families. The town of Dedham allotted sixty-five acres outside of town to each family along with a one-acre house lot in town. Cattle, sheep, and hogs ranged freely in community fields and woodlands. After disease blighted the wheat in 1660, the New England farmers relied on maize (corn) to sustain their families. Relatively short growing seasons and rocky soil prevented the development of a staple crop for export. Farmers had not yet copied the Indian practice of rotating crops, so New Englanders found that their soil was depleted after five or six years. While some families moved, others turned to fishing, the first large-scale commodity New Englanders could export. Eventually many of the farmers would turn to dairy and meat production.

Mid Atlantic. With a combination of industrious families and deeply rich soil, Pennsylvania and New Jersey thrived after initial settlement in 1681. British, Dutch, and German farmers continued traditional agricultural practices on farms from one hundred to two hundred acres in size. It was not until the 1720s that Pennsylvania pursued an active export market. It was their wheat, flour, and bread that was in high demand in Ireland and southern Europe. Their balanced trade is evident in a description by a merchant in 1741:

> We make our Remittances a great many ways, sometimes to the West Indies in Bread, flour, Pork, Indian Corn, and hogshead Staves, sometimes to Carrolina and Newfoundland in Bread and Flour sometimes to Portugall in Wheat, Flour and Pipe Staves sometimes to Ireland in Flax seed Flour, Oak and Walnut Planks and Barrel Staves and to England in Skinns, Tobacco, Beeswax, staves of all Kinds, Oak and Walnut Planks, Boat Boards, Pigg Iron, Tarr, Pitch, Turpentine, Ships, and Bills of Exchange.

The Dutch and Swedes who first settled New Netherland and New Sweden developed a thriving fur trade with various Native American tribes. Wheat exports would supplant the fur trade in the early eighteenth century. One reason for that delay was the preference of Dutch patroons to hold on to their land rather than develop it for the commercial market. They were more inclined to lease the land to tenants who raised enough to feed their families and pay their rent.

Upper South. Investors in the stock company that financed the settlement of Virginia wanted to make money. Within twelve years of the first settlement in 1607, John Rolfe developed a marketable strain of tobacco. Virginia and Maryland were the first colonies to rely on a single crop that was dependent on an external market. Because tobacco fetched a high price at the beginning of the seventeenth century, Chesapeake growers planted primarily tobacco and imported everything they needed to live except food and timber. The tobacco boom ended a short ten years later, in 1629. During the 1630s the price of tobacco fell from sixteen to five pennies per pound. By 1670 the price of tobacco fell to one penny per pound. Tobacco remained profitable but would never again command the exorbitant prices of the first quarter-century. In 1619 planters exported 20,000 pounds of tobacco, and by 1700 they exported 38 million pounds. During the eighteenth century the exports of tobacco fluctuated between 25 million and 160 million pounds. To maintain a profitable venture planters needed to grow and export more tobacco. The reduction in profit was made even worse by soil depletion. Tobacco was even harder on the soil than the New England crops, so the Chesapeake planters found that their crop yield declined after only three or four years. That problem resulted in planters either moving further inland or switching to wheat.

Lower South. West Indian planters who needed land to produce foodstuffs to support their sugar economy migrated to Carolina. Cavaliers promised land by King Charles II joined the Barbadians. Before they established a staple crop, English settlers relied on the trade of deerskins with neighboring Indians. Between 1699 and 1715, two hundred traders sent an average of fifty-three thousand skins a year to England. In addition to the flourishing trade of skins, England also sought naval stores: bowsprits, masts, pitch, resin, tar, and turpentine. Although these commodities supported Carolina settlers, they did not bring the kind of profits the proprietors envisioned. A systematic search for a staple crop eliminated silk, sugarcane, ginger, tobacco, and grapes. Rice emerged in the 1720s as the crop that would thrive best in the Low Country. Planters exported twelve thousand pounds of rice in 1698, an amount dwarfed by the eighteen million pounds they sold in 1730. Caribbean planters supplied capital to develop the plantations and slaves to work the crop. The production of rice increased with the advanced knowledge of African slaves from Senegambia who were accustomed to harvesting rice in their home countries. Production of rice also increased with the development of irrigation, improved seed, and innovations in the cleaning process. Prudent experimentation by Eliza Lucas in the 1740s produced a quality crop of indigo (a blue dye) that could compete with French indigo grown in the West Indies. Indigo would become the fifth most valuable commodity exported from the mainland colonies, following grain, tobacco, rice, and fish.

Sources:

Peter A. Coclanis, *The Shadow of a Dream: Economic Life and Death in the South Carolina Low Country, 1670–1920* (New York: Oxford University Press, 1989);

Ralph Davies, *The Rise of the Atlantic Economies* (Ithaca, N.Y.: Cornell University Press, 1973);

Alice Hanson Jones, *Wealth of a Nation to Be: The American Colonies on the Eve of the Revolution* (New York: Columbia University Press, 1980);

Allan Kulikoff, *Tobacco and Slaves: The Development of Southern Cultures in the Chesapeake, 1680–1800* (Chapel Hill: University of North Carolina Press, 1986);

John J. McCusker and Russell R. Menard, *The Economy of British America, 1607–1789* (Chapel Hill: University of North Carolina Press, 1985).

TRANSPORTATION

Across the Atlantic. The manner in which colonial America's increasingly mobile population got from place to place depended on where the person was traveling; wherever possible, however, colonists preferred to travel by water. Watercraft could carry more people and goods than any form of land transport. Spain established regular trade routes with its American possessions during the sixteenth century. Travel between the home countries and their Dutch, English, and French possessions in America increased steadily during the seventeenth century as sugar plantations in the West Indies and tobacco plantations in the Chesapeake became well-established, producing lucrative yearly crops for export. As colonial commerce increased, shipwrights learned to make their vessels larger, faster, and more seaworthy. As transatlantic traffic increased, each European nation developed systems of regulations designed to keep the flow of goods and profits out of other nations' hands. England's piracy acts, along with those of other European nations, also helped make it safer to travel across the Atlantic in peacetime. The speed of transatlantic travel also increased during the seventeenth century thanks to improved ship designs and greater knowledge of Atlantic winds and currents. By 1740 a traveler embarking for London from Boston could expect to reach his destination within eight weeks, a good speed by the standards of the day. Travel conditions on shipboard were poor, however: except for the few who could afford private quarters, passengers had to stay with the crew. The area was unsanitary, poorly ventilated, hot in summer, cold in winter, and cramped. Food was often worm-eaten by the journey's end and usually consisted of hard biscuits, salt pork, and peas. Drinking water was often scarce and contaminated as well.

Coastal and River Navigation. Throughout the period 1600–1754 travel from colony to colony was likewise accomplished most quickly and easily by boat. In the early seventeenth century vast tracts of virgin forest separated the small centers of English settlement in New England, New York, and the Chesapeake. French and Spanish settlements were similarly separated. Only the most hardy souls could make a trip between them by land. Everywhere in colonial America settlements sprang up first near navigable rivers. As the population and commerce grew, a bustling coastal trade arose with it, usually carried on by small operators who plied the inlets and coastal waters in single-masted pinnaces or schooners. Travel up the rivers was more difficult. Colonists built a variety of canoes, barges, and rafts to manage river voyages. Two types of river vessel were common along rivers of southeastern English, Spanish, and French colonies: dugout canoes called pirogues carried small cargoes, while long (up to forty feet), flat-bottomed boats known as bateaux handled larger loads. Further north in New England and Canada the birch-bark canoe was preferred. French traders often traveled the Saint Lawrence

River and the Great Lakes in eight-man canoes up to thirty-five feet long. River travel everywhere in America was slow and fraught with danger. To travel inland a boat crew had to paddle or pole upstream. Floating debris could tip a boat; submerged rocks could sink it; and sandbars could catch and hold it fast. Ice floes in northern rivers made travel impossible during the winter. Nevertheless, rivers served colonists everywhere as routes for their goods, travel, and communication.

Travel by Land. On land travel between seventeenth-century colonies could be difficult as well. The number and condition of roads varied widely from colony to colony, depending heavily on the density of settlement and the support provided by the various colonial legislatures. In many places roadbeds were poor and bridges few. During the rainy seasons shallow fords became deep, treacherous torrents, and roads became impassable tracks of mud. Persons on horseback or on foot might make the journey at other times of the year, but the going was still tough and became tougher the further inland one traveled. In the winter of 1738–1739, for example, it took George Whitefield more than a month to journey 660 miles from Philadelphia, Pennsylvania, to Charleston, South Carolina, by horseback (an eleven-hour automobile trip today), and his route took him through almost trackless forests, treacherous swamps, and flooded rivers. Some of these roads could be traveled by sturdy ox- or horse-drawn wagons, especially those developed specifically for eighteenth-century hauling by German immigrants living in the Conestoga region near Lancaster, Pennsylvania. Conestoga wagons trekked further each year as roads stretched more into the backcountry. By the 1760s one of the longest roads, the Great Wagon Road, stretched nearly eight hundred miles along old Indian trails through western Pennsylvania and Virginia's Shenandoah Valley to Georgia. The longest road in North America was the Camino Real, which connected Mexico City to Santa Fe, an eighteen-hundred-mile trip which took wagon trains six months to complete. By 1700 a well-developed system of shorter roads was developing in the coastal Chesapeake, Middle Colonies, and New England. This system extended further inland every year as commerce and communication among new towns demanded it. Wealthy Americans traveled these roads in elegant carriages which they imported from Europe or purchased from colonial craftsmen. Travel by horseback could take a person where a carriage could not, but horses were not always cheap. Ordinary farming families often used oxen rather than horses to draw their plows and wagons. Poorer colonists who wanted to travel from place to place or colony to colony often had to walk.

Sources:

William L. Richter, *The ABC-CLIO Companion to Transportation in America* (Santa Barbara, Cal.: ABC-CLIO, 1995);

Ian K. Steele, *The English Atlantic, 1675–1740: An Exploration of Communication and Community* (New York: Oxford University Press, 1986).

HEADLINE MAKERS

THOMAS HANCOCK

1703-1764
MERCHANT

Lowly Beginnings. Thomas Hancock was born on 13 July 1703 to a poor parish minister, the Reverend John Hancock, and his wife, Elizabeth Clark. They lived in a settlement called Cambridge Farms, which would be known later as Lexington, Massachusetts. His education was limited to what his father was able to offer him. When Thomas was thirteen years old he accepted an apprenticeship with a Boston bookseller and bookbinder. In 1723 he established his own bookshop.

Diversification. Hancock's success led to other ventures. With various partners he engaged in paper manufacturing; he exported codfish, whale oil, logwood, and potash; he supplied rum, molasses, and other supplies to the Newfoundland fishing fleet; and he controlled a group of fishing vessels. His marriage in 1730 to Lydia Henchman, the daughter of a prominent Boston merchant, had a positive influence on his business dealings in Boston. The combination of that favorable marriage with his business skills increased his business transactions significantly. As a result he accumulated a considerable fortune. One activity that contributed to his ample wealth was his participation in smuggling. It was not uncommon for merchants who wanted to avoid the restrictions of the English navigation laws to turn to illegal smuggling. He transported tea and paper from Amsterdam to the West Indies and then concealed French molasses that traveled to the Boston ports.

Legacy. Thomas Hancock had no children to inherit his substantial wealth, so he named his nephew, John Hancock, the patriot leader, his equal partner in 1763. Only one year later Thomas Hancock died from a stroke at the Massachusetts State House, where he served as member of the Governor's Council. Thomas Hancock was a central figure of the wealthy merchant class of New England who dominated the seaborne trade.

Source:
William T. Baxter, *The House of Hancock: Business in Boston, 1724–1775* (New York: Russell & Russell, 1965).

ROBERT LIVINGSTON

1654-1728
FUR TRADER AND LANDHOLDER

A Foreign Shore. Robert Livingston was born on 13 December 1654 in Roxburghshire, Scotland, to John Livingston, a Presbyterian minister, and Janet Fleming, the daughter of an Edinburgh merchant. When Robert was nine years old, the Livingston family migrated to Rotterdam, Netherlands, where they could practice their faith. Robert lived with other Scottish refugees among the Dutch community. In 1673, one year after his father died, nineteen-year-old Robert sailed for New England. It was his intention to travel to the New York frontier, a region that Dutch settlers and fur traders controlled. By the time he arrived in the village of Albany in 1674, the Treaty of Westminster had awarded New Netherland to the British.

Marriage. Equally fluent in English and Dutch, Robert Livingston made a place for himself among the Dutch settlers. A shrewd fur trader and knowledgeable frontiersman, Livingston served as town clerk of Albany and secretary of the Board of Commissioners for Indian Affairs. In 1679 he purchased choice tracts of land along the Hudson River. He extended his holdings and secured his standing in the community by making a favorable marriage. Many ambitious men in the colonies improved their conditions by marrying the daughters and widows of other successful men. Alida van Rensselaer was the daughter of the prosperous Schuyler family and a widow of the wealthy van Rensselaer family. His marriage aligned him with two of the most prominent Dutch families in the region.

Investments. In 1686 he secured a patent to turn his 160,000 acres into a manor, which King George I officially recognized. Livingston purchased his land with money he had accumulated from two different sources: wages for his public offices and fur trade with the French and Indians. All of this money multiplied because of his astute investments.

New York Elite. Livingston continued to be involved in both appointed and elected government offices until his death on 1 October 1728. Livingston is a vivid example of an ambitious immigrant who joined the ranks of proprietors of extensive estates. These landholders held tightly the fertile land that they were not willing to sell. Instead they contracted with tenants to work their vast landholdings as a way of developing the colony of New York. In doing so Livingston established a large family fortune that enabled his heirs to influence economic development and political issues in New York.

Source:
Lawrence H. Leder, *Robert Livingston, 1654–1728, and the Politics of Colonial New York* (Chapel Hill: University of North Carolina Press, 1961).

ELIZA LUCAS PINCKNEY

1722-1793
INDIGO PLANTER

Responsibility. Eliza Lucas was the daughter of Lt. Col. and Mrs. George Lucas. She was born on 28 December 1722 on Antigua in the West Indies, but only part of her childhood was spent in that warm climate. Eliza traveled to England to pursue an education, an unusual activity for young women at that time. In 1738 Lieutenant Colonel Lucas settled his wife and two daughters in South Carolina because of his wife's poor health. He returned to Antigua after he left his two sons in England, where they attended school. A competent seventeen-year-old, Lucas assumed the management of her father's three Carolina plantations.

Dedication. A curious and industrious Lucas experimented with growing ginger, cotton, alfalfa, cassava, and indigo, a deep-blue dye product. Planters' frustration with indigo convinced them to invest time, money, and labor in rice cultivation. In 1740 she received West Indian seed from her father. It took Lucas four years to develop a promising grade of indigo seed. Frost ruined the first crop. Her second crop was very small. Her harvest in 1742 was barely enough to produce seed for the next planting. The 1743 crop was also unsatisfactory. It was not until 1744 that she harvested a successful crop that she could share with her neighboring planters. Her local supply of seed was critical because the French West Indians outlawed the export of indigo seed to competing English planters.

Success. In addition to developing good seed, Lucas worked closely with skilled laborers her father sent to process the dye. They were able to improve on the timely and delicate production of indigo. They needed to convert the plant to liquid dye and dry the liquid into dye-cakes that could be shipped to England. Eliza Lucas's painstaking experimentation and vigilant supervision produced a staple crop that was invaluable to South Carolina's export economy.

Renown. After she married widower Charles Pinckney in 1744, Eliza continued with her experimentation. She was more successful with the production of silk than with hemp and flax. Following her husband's death in 1758, Eliza resumed the management of family plantations that would belong to her three children. Eliza Lucas Pinckney died on 26 May 1793 in Philadelphia, where she had gone for medical care. Her funeral is noteworthy in that President George Washington was one of her pallbearers.

Source:
Frances Leigh Williams, *A Founding Family: The Pinckneys of South Carolina* (New York: Harcourt Brace Jovanovich, 1978).

JOHN ROLFE

1585-1622
TOBACCO PLANTER

Hard Life. Little is known about John Rolfe's life before he came to the British colonies. He was born in Norfolk, England, on 6 May 1585. In 1609 he and his wife left England aboard the *Sea Adventure*. They were stranded temporarily in Bermuda, where their daughter was born and died. Upon arriving in Virginia, John Rolfe's wife died, as did most new settlers in the colony.

Cash Crop. By 1612 Rolfe was sampling native tobacco for cultivation in Virginia. It was harsh when smoked, and many Englishmen said it was "unpalatable." Rolfe experimented with imported tobacco seeds from the West Indies and developed a tobacco leaf that was "as pleasant, sweet, and strong . . . as any under the sunne." Its success resulted in tobacco quickly becoming a staple crop for export to England. Tobacco became the first profitable crop on the mainland, laying a foundation for the mercantilist policies of the British Crown. Rolfe deserves credit for the early prosperity of Virginia.

Pocahontas. In 1613 John Rolfe met Pocahontas, the daughter of the powerful chief Powhatan. They received permission from her father to marry in 1614. This alliance resulted in peaceful coexistence with Powhatan's tribe for the next eight years. Pocahontas gave birth to a son before she died in 1616 during a trip to England. Rolfe returned to Virginia, where he remarried a third time, to Jane Pierce. In 1622 Native Americans attacked the English settlements in Virginia, and Rolfe was killed in the fighting.

Sources:
Frances Mossiker, *Pocahontas: The Life and the Legend* (New York: Knopf, 1976);

John Rolfe, *Virginia in 1616* (Richmond: Macfarlane & Fergusson, 1848).

PUBLICATIONS

Robert Briscoe, *The Merchant's Magazine; or, Factor's Guide, Containing, Great Variety of Plain and Easy Tables* (Williamsburgh, Va., 1743);

John Mair, *Book-keeping Methodiz'd; or, A Methodical Treatise of Merchant-Accompts, According to the Italian Form* (Edinburgh: Printed by T. & W. Ruddimans for the author, 1736);

John Oldmixon, *The British Empire in America, Containing the History of the Discovery, Settlement, Progress and Present State of all the British Colonies on the Continent and Islands of America* (London: Printed for J. Brotherton & J. Clarke, 1741);

Charles Snell, *A Guide to Book-keepers, According to the Italian Manner* (London, 1709);

William Weston, *The Complete Merchant's Clerk; or, British and American Compting House* (London, 1754).

COLONIAL AMERICANS

by JESSICA KROSS

CONTENTS

Sidebars and tables are listed in italics.

1602

- The Englishman Bartholomew Gosnold sails from England to New England with thirty-two men who intend to set up a colony; they return home when their food runs out.

1605

- Pierre du Guast, Comte de Monts, establishes a Huguenot colony at Port Royal (Annapolis), Nova Scotia; the settlement founders and is sacked by the English in 1614.

1606

- King James I of England is persuaded by wealthy investors to charter a joint-stock company with two branches, the Plymouth Company and the Virginia Company.

1607

- Over 140 men and boys form a settlement at Jamestown, Virginia; approximately one-half die before the end of the year. Jamestown will become the second oldest town in North America, after Saint Augustine, and the first permanent British settlement.

- Two ships of male settlers arrive at Sagadahoc River in Maine; the colony is abandoned within two years.

1608

- At least two women arrive with subsequent parties of settlers to Virginia.

- The comte de Monts and Samuel de Champlain establish a trading post at Stadacona on the Saint Lawrence River. It will become Quebec, the capital of New France.

1609

- Spaniards abandon San Gabriel and move the town to Santa Fe, the third oldest town in what will become the United States.

1610

- Henry Hudson sails his ship the *Half Moon* up the river that will bear his name, thereby laying Dutch claims to present-day New York.

1612

- Juan Rodrigues, a mulatto from the West Indies, sails with a Dutch trader to the Hudson River and stays behind with trade goods for a year, living among the Indians.

1619
- The first Africans arrive in Virginia.

1620
- Pilgrims and other colonists found Plymouth, Massachusetts.

1621
- The States General of the Netherlands charters the Dutch West India Company, which is to have a monopoly on trade and settlement in North and South America and West Africa.

1624
- The Dutch West India Company sends thirty families of Walloons, French-speaking Protestants from Belgium, to New Netherland; they construct Fort Orange at Albany, New York.

1626
- The Dutch West India Company builds a fort on Manhattan Island and calls the settlement New Amsterdam.
- The first slaves are brought to New Netherland.
- The village of Salem, Massachusetts, is settled.

1629
- The Massachusetts Bay Company forms in England with the idea of establishing a colony for religious dissenters called Puritans.
- Kiliaen Van Rensselaer, a wealthy Amsterdam merchant, receives a patroonship (land grant) and the right to settle families around Albany, New York.
- Samuel de Champlain surrenders Quebec to the Scotsmen Lewis and Thomas Kirke, but they are uninterested in colonization. At the treaty of Saint-Germain-en-Laye all French territory seized by the English is returned to France.

1630
- English Puritans, sponsored by the Massachusetts Bay Company, found Boston and ten other settlements in Massachusetts.

1632
- The French return to Quebec.
- King Charles I grants his friend George Calvert, first Baron Baltimore, lands in America upon which he can settle Roman Catholics.

1634

- Cecilius Calvert, second Lord Baltimore, establishes the colony of Maryland to be a haven for Roman Catholics who are mistrusted in England; the first settlers, however, are predominantly Protestant.

- Several families leave Massachusetts and create the towns of Hartford, Windsor, and Wethersfield in Connecticut.

1636

- Roger Williams is expelled from Massachusetts over matters of religious orthodoxy and founds Providence in Rhode Island.

- Swedish king Augustus Adolphus grants a charter for a trading company, the New Sweden Company, to open a post on the Delaware River.

1637

- Reverend John Davenport and his congregation establish New Haven, Connecticut.

1638

- The New Sweden Company founds its first settlement at Fort Christina, near Wilmington, Delaware.

1639

- Anne Hutchinson, banished from Massachusetts, and William Coddington, a friend of Roger Williams, found Portsmouth, Rhode Island.

1640

- The island of Montreal is given to the Société de Notre Dame de Montréal to establish a mission settlement with a church, school, and hospital; settlers including Jeanne Mance, a nurse, arrive the next year.

- The "Great Migration" to Massachusetts ends with the collapse of the reign of King Charles I and the beginning of the English Civil War; an estimated ten thousand Englishmen had come to New England by this time.

- Small settlements begin in Maine.

- Englishmen, dissatisfied with religious intolerance in Massachusetts, petition the Dutch for land on western Long Island.

1641

- William Coddington establishes the town of Newport, Rhode Island.

1643

- Samuel Gorton establishes the town of Warwick, Rhode Island.

- Johan Printz, governor of New Sweden, arrives with one hundred Swedish and Finnish settlers.

1653

- The Dutch town of New Amsterdam is officially created as a municipality.

1654

- Twenty-three Jews arrive in New Amsterdam from Brazil, joining two others who had arrived earlier in the year.

1655

- The Dutch under Peter Stuyvesant, director general of New Netherland, take control of New Sweden, ending Swedish control over any part of North America.

- The Spanish have nine missions in Apalachee, near modern Tallahassee, Florida.

1660

- The Stuart monarch Charles II is restored to the English throne.

1661

- The Dutch settlements at Bergen, New Jersey, and Kingston, New York, are granted town courts.

1663

- Charles II issues a grant to eight proprietors for the region known as the Carolinas.

1664

- The Dutch found Schenectady, New York.

- During the second Anglo-Dutch War the English take New Netherland and rename the colony New York.

1670

- The Carolina proprietors found a settlement called Charles Town on the Ashley River; some of the new settlers come from Barbados and bring African slaves with them.

- Some twenty-eight hundred Spaniards live in the upper valley of the Rio Grande, many of them in Santa Fe.

1673

- Spaniards at Saint Augustine start construction of the stone fort of San Marcos; they finish in 1687.

- Sieur Louis Jolliet and Father Jacques Marquette descend the Mississippi River and almost reach the Gulf of Mexico.

1676

- William Penn and others purchase West New Jersey, hoping to create a haven for Quakers.

1678

- Jews in Newport, Rhode Island, buy land for a cemetery. By 1685 many of these people, who had originally lived in Barbados, will leave Rhode Island.

1680

- Lowland Scots begin to arrive in New Jersey.
- The Charles Town settlement of Carolina is moved to the junction of the Ashley and Cooper Rivers.
- An Indian uprising, known as the Pueblo Revolt, forces the evacuation of Santa Fe, and many refugees flee to El Paso.

1681

- Charles II grants William Penn lands to pay off a debt owed to his father, Adm. Sir William Penn. Pennsylvania, or Penn's Woods, will be a refuge for Quakers and other religious minorities.

1682

- Robert Cavelier, Sieur de La Salle, and a large band of Frenchmen and Indians descend the Mississippi River to the Gulf of Mexico.

1683

- Francis Daniel Pastorius and a small contingent of Germans settle in Germantown, just north of Philadelphia, Pennsylvania.

1685

- King Louis XIV revokes the Edict of Nantes, which had protected French Protestants. They flee France, migrating to England, the Netherlands, Massachusetts, New York, and South Carolina.

- Robert Cavelier, Sieur de La Salle, with several hundred colonists, lands at Matagorda Bay in what is now Texas; the settlement ends in disaster.

1686

- German Pietists, such as Mennonites and Dunkers, arrive in Pennsylvania.
- Spaniards are beginning to abandon the missions along the Georgia coast.

1690

- Jews begin filtering back to Newport, Rhode Island.
- German Protestants flee the Palatinate after their prince converts to Roman Catholicism.

1693

- The Spanish repopulate Santa Fe.

1695

- Congregationalists from New England move to South Carolina.

1698

- The Spanish found the settlement of Santa Rosa Pensacola in Florida.

1699

- French priests from Quebec found the Mission de la Sainte Famille at Cahokia, Illinois.
- A French fleet under Pierre Le Moyne d'Iberville sails into Pensacola Bay, and a settlement begins at Biloxi, Mississippi.

1700

- Father Eusebio Francisco Kino founds the mission of San Xavier del Bac, near modern Tucson, Arizona. He introduces cattle and wheat culture to the Indians living around the mission.
- The French begin establishing more villages on the banks of the Mississippi between Cahokia and Kaskaskia. By 1735 there are six settlements and the area becomes the center of French life in the middle Mississippi valley until the founding of Saint Louis in 1764.

1701

- Delaware, which had been part of Pennsylvania, is granted a separate charter, although it will continue to share a governor with Pennsylvania.

1702

- East and West New Jersey become a single united royal province.

- The French establish the town of Saint Louis on Mobile Bay in the Gulf of Mexico.
- The French establish a mission at Kaskaskia.
- As part of the War of the Spanish Succession, known as Queen Anne's War in America, the English governor of South Carolina, James Moore, attacks Saint Augustine, burning outposts and missions in Apalachee, or northern Florida.

1707

- The Act of Union unites Scotland and England, allowing Scots to migrate more freely to America.

1708

- Blacks outnumber whites in South Carolina and will continue to do so through the American Revolution.

1709

- Swiss Mennonites first migrate to Pennsylvania.

1710

- Rhinelander Germans settle on the Schoharie River in New York, but most leave for Pennsylvania after a brief stay.

1711

- French colonists establish a permanent settlement at Mobile, Alabama.

1715

- The Jacobite uprising in Scotland causes many Scots to immigrate to America.

1716

- The Spanish set up four missions and a presidio, or fort, in East Texas.

1717

- Scotch-Irish settlers arrive in the Delaware River valley, Massachusetts, and New Hampshire.

1718

- The Spanish found the presidio of San Antonio de Béjar and the mission of San Antonio de Valero at San Antonio, Texas.

- France creates the province of Louisiana, which includes the Illinois country of the middle Mississippi; New Orleans becomes the capital.
- Pennsylvania grants land to Scotch-Irish settlers to found the town of Donegal.

1720

- German Lutheran, German Reformed, and Scotch-Irish immigrants begin arriving in Pennsylvania.

1729

- North and South Carolina become royal colonies.

1730

- Jews begin to settle in Philadelphia.
- Settlement of the Shenandoah Valley begins.

1731

- Sixteen families from the Canary Islands settle around the mission and presidio of San Antonio.

1732

- The English Crown approves a charter for the colony of Georgia.

1733

- James Oglethorpe arrives with the first English settlers in Georgia.
- Jews arrive in Georgia.

1734

- Germans from Salzburg settle in Georgia.

1735

- Moravians arrive in Pennsylvania and Georgia after their expulsion from Austria.

1736

- Highland Scots are recruited to settle at Darien on the Altamaha River in Georgia.

1738

- Former slaves who had escaped from South Carolina and converted to Catholicism are formed into a regiment by Spanish authorities and placed in a settlement called Gracia Real de Santa Teresa de Mose just north of Saint Augustine; they remain there until 1763.

1740

- Settlers, including the Scotch-Irish, move into the piedmont of North Carolina.
- The last of the Moravians leave Georgia for Pennsylvania over a misunderstanding about their pacifism.

1745

- A second Jacobite uprising in Scotland fails, and many Highland Scots leave for America.

1750

- Settlers, including the Scotch-Irish, move into the backcountry of South Carolina.

1752

- Congregationalists who had resettled in South Carolina from New England leave unfertile lands and begin moving to Georgia.
- The Crown takes over Georgia from the trustees, and it becomes a royal colony.
- Moravians settle in North Carolina.

1754

- Royal officials are appointed in Georgia, two years after the Crown takes over the colony.

OVERVIEW

Old Worlds and New. The settlement and peopling of what would become the United States cannot be understood without some knowledge of what was happening in the Old Worlds of Europe and Africa. The Crusades of the late Middle Ages introduced Europeans to the learning of the Moslems in the Middle East and the luxury goods such as silks and spices that came from the Far East. This knowledge enabled Europeans to use more-accurate maps of the known world, build more maneuverable ships, and find out where they were by observing the sun at noon. The availability of new goods offered those willing to take risks large profits. The emergence of the nation-states of Portugal and Spain ended civil wars and allowed the monarchies to concentrate energies and look for further revenues. Spain also took it upon itself to be Europe's great defender of and proselytizer for Roman Catholicism. France and England lagged behind but would in time also follow in the footsteps of the Iberian states. Portugal was the first to explore. Merchants, with the blessing of the Crown, inched their way down the African coast finding gold, ivory, and slaves. There was a small slave trade to Europe largely through Muslim traders even before Europeans encountered the Americas. Christopher Columbus's discovery of a continent previously unknown to Europeans opened the way for European expansion and exploitation, but both were continuously impacted by the ongoing affairs of the European states. Within Europe were large rivalries based on religion, economics, and emerging nationalism and ethnicity. The years 1600–1754 were marked by wars whose victories and defeats shaped New World boundaries. Domestic turmoil within European states also affected migration. European and African settlement of the New World was part of the restlessness ánd acquisitiveness of Old Worlds. Who settled where and what happened to them cannot be grasped by looking only at America.

Europe and Africa. The Spanish were the first to settle in the Americas, but most of Spain's energy went into her Latin American holdings. The riches extracted from Mexico and Peru were enormous. Spanish settlements to the north—what have been called borderlands—in Arizona, New Mexico, Texas, and Florida had two goals: Christianizing the Indians and protecting the wealth Spain had already found. Other Europeans' entry into the New World was a response to Spain's great discoveries. Unfortunately, by the time anybody else could get mobilized, Spain and later Portugal had secured South America. The first explorers of the North looked for gold and silver, but even more important, they searched for a way through the continent for a shorter route to the wealth of the East Indies and China. France found fish and furs, which brought some limited prosperity, and the great rivers—the Saint Lawrence and the Mississippi—were gateways to a continent, but the French lost both to the British in 1763. The Netherlanders set out to find the Northwest Passage through America and then settled in as a fur- and grain-producing outpost of the Dutch West India Company. In the process they created a multiethnic, multireligious, and multiracial society. Dutch political hopes ended in 1664 when the English took New Netherland without firing a shot. Many of those living there remained and prospered under the English. England—and after 1707, Great Britain—came to dominate North America. Divided into several different colonies and able to recruit from home, the English established viable settlements. They brought with them prejudices against Roman Catholics, Jews, Indians, and Africans but also a willingness to work and to take economic and political risks. They exploited the various environmental niches opened to them: fishing for cod in New England, growing wheat and cattle in the Middle Colonies, raising tobacco in the Chesapeake, and growing rice and indigo in South Carolina and Georgia. Throughout the period of colonization they thought of themselves as Englishmen, endowed with all the rights of the people back in the mother country. Among those rights was the sanctity of private property—a right that included the ownership of other people. Africa might well have sent more people to the New World than Europe did. These settlers were unwilling migrants, enslaved in Africa and sold to hard labor in America. They came from many different nations, spoke different languages, and worshiped different gods. They were settled by every European nation in almost every colony from the outset.

False Starts. The settlement and peopling of America is a story of trial and error, false starts, and early failures. Most of colonial settlement was left to private individuals, not the various European monarchs. Private money and initiative rather than the state underwrote colonization. Because the earliest venturers had little idea of what American conditions were actually like, they could imagine whatever they wanted. Since most of North America lay in moderate or semitropic latitudes, they speculated that New York would have a warm climate like southern Spain. They could visit Maine in the summer and decide that it must be more or less like that in winter. They could hope to find gold and precious stones just lying around or conclude that those landing in late summer or even autumn would have time to plant and harvest. They seemed to believe that they could mistreat the Native Americans without possibility of retaliation and even be aided by them when colonists' supplies ran out. Most important, and most consistently, they grossly underestimated how much it cost to set up a colony. Underfinanced, whether as "gentlemen adventurers" or joint-stock companies, colonizers could not raise enough money to keep a settlement going for the years it would take before it made a profit. Even the colonies that succeeded rarely made any money for their investors.

Economic Motives. People came to America for many reasons, and even single individuals might have had mixed motives. John Winthrop, whose Puritan principles in the end led him to America, also looked at his diminishing fortune when it came to thinking about what was best for his family. Most of those who financed colonies or settled in them came for economic reasons. They might have faced brutal conditions at home such as periodic famines, plagues, and wars. Crop failures created large migrations within Europe, and leaving for someplace overseas was just another step. Disease disrupted markets and trade as states quarantined areas and pestilence killed off populations that were both producers and consumers. Wars dislocated people: men left the labor force to fight and die in armies, and many never returned or were disabled when they came home. Civil strife also disrupted markets, closing off communication and trade. Moreover, wars changed the topography of an area, ruining fields and pastures, leveling forests, or destroying villages. Monarchs increased taxes to pay for their armies. Even if conditions were not as dire because of famine, plague, or war, economies moved in cycles with better times, when wages were high and rents and foodstuffs were low, alternating with hard times, when there were few jobs, low wages, high rents, and loaves of bread were costly. Many feared for their children's futures and felt that someplace new might hold out a brighter future. English men and women of the early seventeenth century and Germans, Scots, and Scotch-Irish in the eighteenth century thought so.

Religious Motives. The dictates of religion were also a powerful motive in bringing people to America. For Spanish friars, saving souls was the primary reason to settle in a lonely outpost far from home. French missionaries undoubtedly felt the same way. Dissidents came because they were persecuted in Europe, where nations usually supported only one religion and forced their citizens to belong or face dire consequences. Spain and Portugal permitted only Roman Catholics to settle in the New World as did France after the revocation of the Edict of Nantes in 1685. German principalities were often Protestant but could revert to Roman Catholicism if the ruler changed, as in the case of Salzburg. Since church and state often supported one another, a threat to the church was seen as a threat to the state. Catholics, Quakers, and Puritans in England were persecuted during the seventeenth century. In Germany exotic sects such as the Mennonites and the Moravians faced problems. America, with its seemingly empty land where religious communities could find a place away from the corrupting influences of others, beckoned.

Religious Pluralism. Those who came to America to establish their own version of the godly life did not necessarily want that freedom granted to others. Pilgrims in Plymouth and Puritans in Massachusetts felt that their way was the only way and that God would punish them if they allowed other religious ideas into the colony. While forced by the English government to be more open by the end of the seventeenth century, Massachusetts and Connecticut never attracted many with different religious views. But some colonies, especially those originally owned by private individuals (proprietors), became havens for many different religious beliefs. Maryland, New York, New Jersey, Pennsylvania, and the Carolinas all were open to settlers with different religious views. A major reason for this was that the proprietors needed settlers in order to make money, and restricting colonies to one religious denomination would have made profits less likely. Most of those who came to British North America were Protestants, with a sprinkling of Roman Catholics and Jews. The French and the Spanish settlements were Roman Catholic. Even from the beginning, then, colonial America was a jumble of religious beliefs. In most places Jews and Catholics were not given political rights, but the freedom to practice their religion at all was a major step forward. Later, when the Bill of Rights promised freedom of religion, it was building on a long tradition of religious toleration and the presence of many different religious groups.

Ethnic Pluralism. Colonial America was also a place with many different ethnic groups. The Illinois country and Louisiana were settled by the French. Various outposts in Arizona, New Mexico, Texas, and Florida were inhabited by Spaniards, and in the case of San Antonio, Texas, people from the Canary Islands. New Netherland was a colony of not only Dutch settlers but also Germans, Swedes, Finns, Norwegians, English, Scots, Jews, Walloons (French-speaking Protestants from Belgium), and even a Croatian; eighteen different languages were spoken in the province. Swedes and Finns settled on the Delaware. The English colonies attracted not only the English, Scots, Scotch-Irish, and Welsh but also Germans, Jews, French Huguenots, and the occasional Italian. In the Middle Colonies large numbers of Dutch colonists remained after the conquest of 1664. The larger migrations of European people tried to settle with others like themselves and thus created ethnic enclaves in the countryside that spoke the language, wore the clothing, built the homes, and cooked the food of the old country. Those who settled in cities such as New York and Philadelphia had to adapt more to the dominant culture. But from the outset, except in New England, the colonies were ethnically diverse and managed for the most part to live together peacefully and be outwardly tolerant of one another.

Racial Pluralism. Almost all of the colonies, regardless of nationality, used slave labor. Africans, like Europeans, came from many different nations. They had a variety of religious beliefs including Moslem, Roman Catholic, and animist (belief in the existence of spirits). Africans in America had the most difficult time of any of those who came over. Whether slavery caused racism or racism caused slavery might never be fully disentangled, but early in each colony's history Africans were considered unequal to white people. No attempt was made to keep family members, if there were any, together or to settle people in ethnic enclaves. Indeed, some effort was made to keep them apart since that way they were considered less dangerous. The number of slaves in any given colony depended upon economic factors. Where slavery was most profitable, there were more slaves. The North needed fewer slaves, the South more. South Carolina had a slave majority by 1708. In the North the slaves lived in the cellars and attics of their masters; in the South they had separate slave quarters. Indians also made up a small part of the slave force in the seventeenth century, but few Indians chose to live among the whites. By the eighteenth century many European colonists interacted with Africans on a daily basis.

Settlement Patterns. The North American colonies drew various ethnic and religious groups to settle in what seemed a place far away from home. Their reaction to this perception was to band together. Moving usually as groups of families, rarely as isolated individuals, the colonists looked for fertile lands, good water, meadows for cattle, and woods for lumber to build houses and fences. In New England and the Middle Colonies (New York, New Jersey, and Pennsylvania) they often established towns, elected local officials, and organized church congregations. In the Chesapeake (Virginia and Maryland) the first settlements were overwhelmingly male, as young men were sent over to serve as indentured (contract) laborers, especially after tobacco was found to be profitable after 1618. Still these work gangs were kept together on the plantations, partly because that was where their labor was needed and partly because the Native Americans quickly became hostile to Europeans. A few female indentured servants might serve as cooks, house cleaners, and laundresses. French settlements usually had more men than women and were situated near forts that colonists supplied with foodstuffs. Like many of the English, the French sought stability and tried to establish the trappings of civilization. In the Illinois country the villages established parish meetings of household heads to run internal affairs and chose a Jesuit priest to be their spiritual leader. The Spanish tried to settle families in El Paso and Santa Fe. The first colonists in present-day New York were thirty Walloon families sponsored by the Dutch government. Germans and Scotch-Irish moving into the piedmont regions of Pennsylvania, Maryland, Virginia, and the Carolinas came as families, often with other families whom they already knew.

A Moving Frontier. When John Smith of Virginia, William Bradford of Plymouth, and John Winthrop of Massachusetts Bay first stepped ashore in America, the lands before them were the frontier. As coastal areas filled up, settlers needed to look farther inland for farmlands. The easiest way to move was by water, so they looked to rivers—the Hudson, Connecticut, James, Ashley, Cooper, Savannah, and Mississippi, as well as the Rio Grande. During the eighteenth century English, German, Scots, and Scotch-Irish settlers began to look farther west, beyond the first rows of mountains. Again they tried to find the shortest and least difficult path. The great Shenandoah Valley, which stretched from Pennsylvania to the Carolinas, provided colonists with a broad, fertile, relatively flat landscape that lent itself to horse and wagon. By 1756 the Great Philadelphia Wagon Road, which began at the Schuylkill River Ferry opposite Philadelphia, reached Salisbury, North Carolina, opening up trade in cattle and goods and bearing settler families. French settlers from Canada looked south and found good lands in the middle Mississippi valley where they grew wheat. Spanish settlers moved north from Mexico into what is now New Mexico and Texas, where they found fertile soils and grazing lands for cattle and sheep. As lands filled and each new acre became more expensive, people looked farther away. This expansion brought them into conflict with Native Americans who never acknowledged that Europeans had rights to these lands which superseded Indian claims. By 1754 the colonials claimed vast acreage, much of it as yet undeveloped. One of the reasons they would fight a revolution against Great Britain was to preserve those claims.

TOPICS IN THE NEWS

AFRICANS

Slave Trade. Slavery had existed in Africa long before Europeans arrived on its West Coast. Individuals were captured in wars, sentenced to slavery as punishment for crimes, or chose slavery over starvation when famines and disease made it impossible to grow enough food or earn enough to buy it. Women were more desirable than men since most slaves were put to work raising crops, considered by many African nations as women's work. There were also enslaved craftsmen, warriors, and even a few individuals who acted as advisers to tribal chiefs and kings. In time Europeans would change the dynamics of the slave trade, but that would not be until the great exportations of people in the eighteenth century. Even at its height, however, the trade was not all that well organized; nor was it controlled by Europeans, who found that West Africa was too unhealthy for white settlement. The coast of Africa that provided slaves was more than three thousand miles long, stretching from the Senegambia River in the North to the Congo River in the South—a distance greater than that between New York and California. Mozambique Island off the coast of East Africa also supplied a few slaves. While a small slave trade existed between Africa and Europe prior to the discovery of the Americas, a significant trade began almost as soon as the Spaniards discovered that the West Indian Islands could grow desirable tropical products such as sugar. Disease quickly killed off the Native Americans, leaving the Europeans with land but no labor. As a result they turned to Africa.

Statistics. The exact number of Africans imported into the New World is uncertain, but estimates begin with the Spaniards who imported slaves into America as early as 1521. Between 1521 and 1550 some 500 Africans a year came to Spanish America. This number increased because the West Indies and Latin America, regardless of which European nation owned them, were unable to regenerate their slave populations through natural increase. More slaves died than were born; thus population was replenished and built through fresh importations of slaves from Africa. The North American mainland colonies, except for South Carolina, did better by the early eighteenth century, and Africans were able to replace themselves through their children. It is esti-

A female slave being weighed to determine her monetary value, circa 1750

mated that some 9.5 million slaves were imported into the New World by the nineteenth century—more people than came to the Americas from Europe. Of that figure some 5 million went to areas controlled by the Spanish and Portuguese—3.5 million to Brazil alone. What became the United States imported relatively few slaves—427,000, or 4.5 percent of total slave imports. Of these Africans roughly 399,000 arrived in the British colonies and 28,000 in the French possessions, mainly in Louisiana but also in the Illinois country. There were

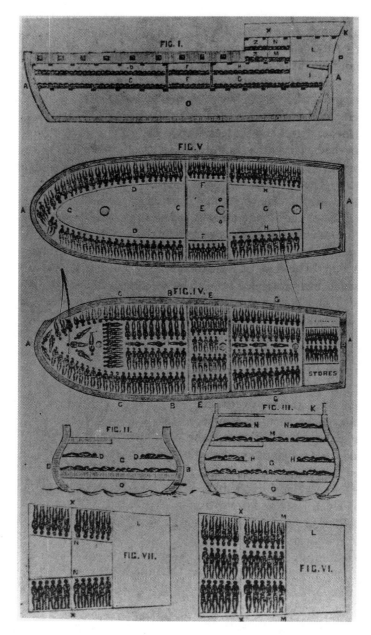

Diagram for stowing slaves aboard *The Brookes,* circa 1750

also a few slaves in the Spanish North American hold-ings, but these were negligible since the settlements were small and Native Americans provided the labor. Any-where from 8 to 23 percent of those captured in Africa died before they reached the Americas, so the number of Africans captured was larger than the 9.5 million who unwillingly settled in the New World.

Senegambia. The region between the Senegal and Gambia Rivers, south of the Sahara Desert, was known as Senegambia. This area was one of the first that Euro-peans found. On the coast they encountered two groups: the Mandingo, traders who establish themselves on the rivers that controlled West African trade, and the Jolof (also called Wolof). Farther up the Senegal River were the Fulbe and Bambara. The great African kingdoms of Ghana, Mali, and Songhai were also found in this re-

gion. At one time the Senegambia had been part of the Islamic Almoravides empire, and many of the people there, including some who found themselves slaves in America, were Moslem. For the eighteenth century, about 13 percent of all slaves imported into North America were from Senegambia. These peoples, espe-cially the tall Bambara, were the preferred slaves in South Carolina and Virginia. They also composed two-thirds of those brought to Louisiana.

Guinea Coast. The term *Guinea Coast* had no exact meaning in the colonial period and referred to the whole slave coast of West Africa as well as the area be-tween Senegambia and Angola. During the seventeenth and eighteenth centuries parts of this coast were known as Sierra Leone, the Malaguetta (pepper) Coast, Grain Coast, Ivory Coast, Gold Coast, Slave Coast, the Bight

William Snelgrave, the author of *A New Account of Some Parts of Guinea and the Slave-Trade* (1734), made several voyages to Africa as captain of a ship collecting slaves and bringing them to the West Indies. Snelgrave was an experienced slaver, having made the voyage many times. He considered himself a humane man—although he shared the racism and prejudices of his time—and also a savvy one. The excerpt that follows is part of a discussion of slave mutinies that he had either witnessed or heard about. He attributed such problems to harsh treatment and incompetence. What he describes is probably the best that slaves could hope for on the long Middle Passage from Africa to America.

Wherever therefore I have commanded, it has been my principal Care, to have the *Negroes* on board my Ship kindly used; and I have always strictly charged my white People to treat them with Humanity and Tenderness: In which I have usually found my Account [profit], both in keeping them from mutinying, and preserving them in health.

And whereas it may seem strange to those that are unacquainted with the method of managing them, how we can carry so many hundreds together in a small Ship, and keep them in order; I shall just mention what is generally practiced. When we purchase grown People, I acquaint them by the Interpreter, "That, now they are become my Property, I think fit to let them know what they are bought for, that they may be easy in their Minds: (For these poor People are generally under terrible Apprehensions upon their being bought by white Men, many being afraid that we design to eat them; which I have been told, is a story much credited by the inland *Negroes*;) So after informing them, That they are bought to till the Ground in our Country, with several other Matters; I then acquaint them, how they are to behave themselves on board, towards the white Men; that if any one abuses them, they are to complain to the Linguist, who is to inform me of it, and I will do them Justice: But if they make a Disturbance, or offer to strike a white Man, they must expect to be severely punished."

When we purchase the *Negroes*, we couple the sturdy Men together with Irons; but we suffer the Women and Children to go freely about: As soon after we have sail'd from the Coast, we undo all the Mens Irons.

They are fed twice a day, and are allowed in fair Weather to come on Deck at seven in the Morning, and to remain there, if they think proper, till Sun setting. Every *Monday* Morning they are served with Pipes and Tobacco, which they are very fond of. The men *Negroes* lodge separate from the Women and Children; and the places where they all lye are cleaned every day, some white Men being appointed to see them do it.

Source: William Snelgrave, *A New Account of Some Parts of Guinea and the Slave-Trade* (London: Frank Cass, 1971).

---

of Benin, and the Bight of Biafra. About 60 percent of those taken to North America in the eighteenth century came from these areas, with the Bight of Biafra supplying more than one-third. Trade along this coastline was hazardous because of contrary winds and sandbars. Since there were no anchorages for large ships, there were few places that slaves could be gathered for bulk sales to traders. Instead, the ships cruised offshore until hailed by small-scale African traders on land. Longboats were then rowed to the shore, and a few slaves were picked up and carried to the larger ship. When weeks or months later the ship had enough slaves to sail to America, it left the African coast with peoples from many different villages speaking different languages and worshiping different gods.

Congo and Angola. Congo and Angola furnished about a quarter of the slaves who came to North America. These two areas, while next to each other, had different histories from the rest of Africa. While Europeans were kept isolated on the coast in most of Africa, in Angola the Portuguese actually defeated and occupied the country in 1575. Once there they kept up a series of raids and wars with neighboring groups, always with large numbers of Angolan allies, seizing slaves in the process. The kingdom of Congo to the north was first reached by Portugal in 1483. In 1491 the king of Congo and some of his nobles converted to Roman Catholicism, and he took the Portuguese name João, after the king of Portugal. While many slaves exported through Congo were from more-inland territories, a series of civil wars meant that some slaves came from Congo and were Christians. Europeans, who claimed to have scruples against enslaving fellow Christians, did not seem to look too closely into the religion of those they bought and sold in Congo. These African Christians found their way to America as did those who practiced the animism prevalent throughout most of Africa.

Sources:

Philip D. Curtin, *The Atlantic Slave Trade* (Madison: University of Wisconsin Press, 1969);

Gwendolyn Midlo Hall, *Africans in Colonial Louisiana: The Development of Afro-Creole Culture in the Eighteenth Century* (Baton Rouge: Louisiana State University Press, 1992);

Anne Hilton, *The Kingdom of Kongo* (Oxford: Clarendon Press, 1985);

John Thornton, *Africa and Africans in the Making of the Atlantic World, 1400–1680* (New York: Cambridge University Press, 1992);

Thornton, *The Kingdom of Kongo: Civil War and Transition 1641–1718* (Madison: University of Wisconsin Press, 1983).

THE CAROLINAS

Earliest Attempts. The first interest in what would become the Carolinas came not from the English but from the Spanish and the French. While Spaniards had reached the coast of the Carolinas in 1520–1521, they did not actually establish a presence there, content instead to raid the local Indians, capturing seventy of them and bringing them back to Hispaniola (now Haiti and the Dominican Republic), where they were freed. In 1540 the explorer Hernando de Soto landed in Florida but proceeded on foot into the interior, reaching the Indian town of Cofitachequi (modern-day Camden, South Carolina), and then on into North Carolina. Spanish interest in a settlement on the Carolina coast sprang from the need to find an emergency haven for the treasure fleet bound from Mexico to Spain through the Bahama Channel—a narrow, fast-flowing passage east of Florida that was plagued by hurricanes and European marauders. Spanish efforts came to little, however, and it was actually the French who settled the area first, albeit temporarily. In 1562 the French commander Jean Ribault with a small contingent of male settlers arrived in Port Royal Sound and built Charlesfort, a small fort, on what is now the Parris Island Marine Station golf course. Ribault then left hoping to return shortly but found France engulfed in one of the religious wars between Protestants and Catholics that marked the last half of the sixteenth century. Those left behind deserted Charlesfort, and a few of them made their way back to France. Meanwhile, the Spanish, aware of French interest on the coast, decided to try again to establish their own presence on Port Royal Sound. In 1566 Pedro Menéndez de Avilés arrived and built a fort, San Felipe, on the ruins of Charlesfort. Supporting the fort was the town of Santa Elena, which included a mission, farming community, and such industries as a pottery kiln. But the Spanish hold on the whole coast was tenuous, and hostile Indians and English raiders, such as Sir Francis Drake, undermined Spanish efforts. They abandoned Santa Elena in 1587, retreating to Saint Augustine, the only surviving Spanish settlement on the East Coast.

New Efforts. English attempts at colonization in the Carolinas began with Sir Walter Raleigh during the years 1585–1587 and what has become known as the Lost Colony of Roanoke. The next colonizing venture to get settlers actually as far as the New World was not until 1632 when Sir Robert Heath, then proprietor of this large area, entered into negotiations with some French Protestant refugees. They were to build a saltworks, and some forty colonists actually arrived in America, but not in Carolina, disembarking instead in Virginia. It was not until after the restoration of the monarchy in 1660 that Charles II's grant to the Lords Proprietors would result in actual settlements. The first occurred in 1665 on the Cape Fear River in what is now North Carolina. Settled by Barbadians and a few New Englanders who quarreled among themselves, the settlement was abandoned when

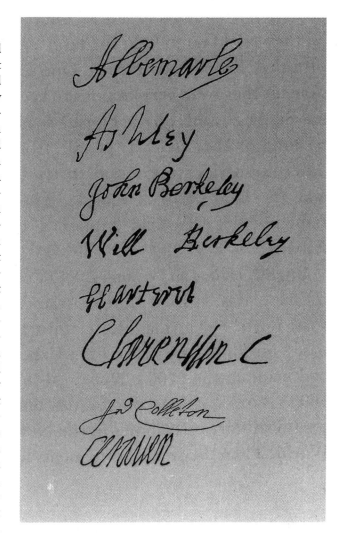

The signatures of the eight Lords Proprietors of the Carolinas, 1669

reports of better land and easier ocean access farther south in Port Royal Sound filtered back to the colonists.

Stuart Kings. The early part of the 1600s found various Englishmen interested in lands north of the Spanish ones. In 1629 King Charles I granted to Sir Robert a tract of land located between Virginia and Florida that extended west to the Pacific Ocean. He named the tract Carolana, but this early grant came to nothing since Sir Robert was unable to find either settlers or financial backing. A few years later he assigned his grant to Henry, Lord Maltravers, who ran into the same problems. In 1640 the English Civil War broke out and ended interest in the area. The Restoration of Charles II in 1660 brought to the throne a king indebted to those who had stood by him in his years of exile. One way to show his gratitude was to grant them lands in America that he owned only nominally and that he could offer at no cost to himself. Among the lands granted by the "Merry Monarch" were New York and New Jersey, given to his brother the duke of York, later James II; Pennsylvania to William Penn; and the Carolinas to a consortium of eight friends. All of these colonies would survive, al-

The earliest English efforts at settlement overlapped Santa Elena. In 1584 Queen Elizabeth gave Walter Raleigh the right to colonize in North America those lands not already claimed by Christians. Raleigh first sent out an exploratory expedition, which landed on Roanoke Island off the coast of North Carolina. It returned home with glowing reports of the "goodliest soile under the cope of heaven" and two Native Americans who then became walking advertisements for the new colonial venture. Queen Elizabeth, much impressed, knighted Walter Raleigh and named the whole area Virginia, in honor of herself, the Virgin Queen.

Second Attempt. Raleigh managed to put together a second expedition of 108 men in 1585 including the artist John White, whose watercolors excited the interest of those in Europe and provide us today with charming depictions of the plants, animals, and Native Americans of the late-sixteenth-century southern coast. This second expedition built housing and explored the surrounding area, but promised supplies were late in coming—an all-too-common problem for early settlements—and when Sir Francis Drake stopped off, many of those on the island chose to return with him to England.

A Third Effort. In 1587 Raleigh put together a consortium of investors to launch another colony of 17 women, 9 children and 94 men; White was appointed governor. Their destination was not supposed to be Roanoke Island, although they were to stop there, but farther north on Chesapeake Bay. As it turned out, their pilot refused to go farther than Roanoke, so the colonists, having little choice, disembarked there. In August the first English child was born in the Americas to Eleanor and Ananias Dare. Named Virginia, she was the grandchild of Governor White. But this auspicious omen of new beginnings was deceptive. The Roanoke colony arrived too late to plant crops, and it found that the surrounding Native Americans were also short of foodstuffs. White sailed back to England for supplies while those left behind sought a better site for the colony. White's swift return was prevented by the outbreak of war between England and Spain and the imminent threat of invasion from the Spanish Armada. He was able to smuggle out two small ships only to have their captains turn pirate and then be captured by the French. He returned to Roanoke in 1590 to find the place abandoned with the word *CROATOAN* carved on a tree—a prearranged signal to let him know where the colonists had moved.

Mystery. But White never did find Croatoan (now Hatteras Island) or any of the settlers. A storm forced his ships to leave. Years later the Indian sachem Powhatan told Capt. John Smith, founder of the first successful English settlement at Jamestown, Virginia, that the settlers had perished on their trek north, accidentally caught between two warring bands of Indians. Like so many of the earliest attempts at settlement, Roanoke was a victim of ignorance, poor planning, and bad luck. Its failure helped to bankrupt Sir Walter Raleigh, who met his own unlucky fate at the hands of the state executioner in 1618.

Source: Hugh Talmage Lefler and Albert Ray Newsome, *The History of a Southern State: North Carolina,* third edition (Chapel Hill: University of North Carolina Press, 1973).

though not necessarily in the form envisioned or under the control of the original proprietors.

Lords Proprietors. The eight proprietors granted Carolina in 1663 were politicians and men of state rather than colonial visionaries. Looking neither for religious freedom nor a way to help the downtrodden of England, they, like the investors of the Virginia Company or Thomas Weston and Associates, who financed the Plymouth settlement, hoped to make money from their new venture. The charter, granted in 1665, gave them extensive powers in America including the right to make war and deprive the inhabitants of life and limb. Their ability to make law was restricted by a clause that mandated the consent of the "freemen" of the province. They also had permission to grant religious toleration and to establish a hereditary nobility. Given the need for settlers in order to make the colony profitable, the Lords Proprietors promised many concessions—an elected assembly with the sole right to tax, freedom of conscience, and land grants—to those who came over and brought others with them. Yet they were unwilling to spend money to promote their colony, and England was suffering from plague and war, which made emigration more difficult.

Legal Experiment. In 1669 Anthony Ashley Cooper, soon to be Lord Shaftesbury, with the help of the great political theorist and his secretary, John Locke, proposed the "Fundamental Constitutions," a unique document meant to lure settlers by proposing a hereditary nobility, religious toleration, and the sanctity of private property, including slaves. Cooper also persuaded the other proprietors to contribute money, and in August of that year three ships with one hundred settlers, including some nineteen women, left England for Carolina. Accident and disaster scattered the ships, but by March 1670 all arrived, some via the Bahamas and Virginia. By the 1670s the colony was yet to make money, and the proprietors again had to invest rather than profit. Attempts by the proprietors to remain friendly with the local Indians and to monopolize the fur trade failed as the colonists provoked war and encouraged an Indian-slave trade. Proprietary interests clashed with those of the most aggressive colonists, making Carolina hard to govern. Moreover, the colonists were unwilling to pay even minimal rents. Wars in the early part of the eighteenth century created security problems and governmental debts that the proprietary government was unable to pay. In 1719 the Crown appointed a provisional governor, and in 1729 it bought out the remaining proprietors, although their effectiveness had been nullified ten years earlier.

Barbadians. While many of the earliest settlements drew their populations from England, Carolina also attracted colonists from England's West Indian islands, mainly from Barbados. Some of the proprietors, including Anthony Ashley Cooper and Sir John Colleton, also had Barbadian interests. The first unsuccessful settlement at Cape Fear in 1665 had included Barbadians, as did the first successful one on the Ashley River in 1670. Many congregated on Goose Creek, above Charleston, earning themselves the designation "Goose Creek men." Of some 680 settlers who came to the Carolinas between 1670 and 1680 and whose origins can be identified, over half came from the West Indies. These men had important resources at their command. By 1680 Barbados was a small but wealthy sugar island whose landed and merchant elite families had no way of giving younger sons land. Many turned to the Carolinas, whose semitropical climate promised, they erroneously thought, a healthier environment in which plantation agriculture and slavery would flourish. They brought both slaves and a slave code to control them—the only mainland colony formed in this way. The Barbadian elites did well: seven of the Carolinas' twenty-three governors between 1669 and 1737 had Barbadian backgrounds. Other less wealthy Barbadians also looked to the Carolinas for economic opportunity. Among the early settlers were small planters, artisans, and even indentured servants. The lure was land, and as it turned out, Barbados and other West Indian islands provided a market for the beef, corn, and lumber that the Carolinas produced.

Slaves. Whites chose to move to the Carolinas; blacks had no choice. Black slaves arrived in the region along with the first whites, although initially in few numbers. The first recorded slave, a "lusty negro man," arrived from Virginia within months of the first settlement on the Ashley River in 1670. The first slave family arrived from Bermuda a month later. Trade with the islands included slaves. In March 1671 Sir John Yeamans arrived from Barbados with eight blacks. These bound laborers

Anthony Ashley Cooper, first Earl of Shaftesbury, one of the Lords Proprietors of the Carolinas (portrait after J. Greenhill; National Portrait Gallery, London)

worked on his wooded lands, defending them against Indian and Spanish enemies when the whites were called back to defend Charles Town. When Yeamans died in 1674, he owned at least twenty-six slaves. By 1671 as much as 30 percent of the population was slave, mainly male; by 1708 more than half of the non-Indian population was slave, making the Carolinas the only colony with a black majority. In some low-country parishes the ratio of blacks to whites was as high as four to one—much like the West Indies. In 1769 Lt. Gov. William Bull estimated that South Carolina had some 45,000 whites and 80,000 blacks.

Charleston. In August 1669 three ships left England to sail via Barbados to the new colony of Carolina. Aboard were 93 passengers that included four gentlemen, servants, and artisans. Among the craftsmen represented were surveyors, carpenters, blacksmiths, masons, surgeons, and even "an ignorant preacher." The fleet first stopped in Ireland, vainly hoping to attract colonists, then sailed across the Atlantic to Barbados, where rough weather scattered the ships and destroyed one. Next stop was Bermuda, and finally Carolina, where friendly Indians enticed the colonists to consider a site up the river that the English renamed the Ashley. On a high defensible bluff with the river on one side and marshes on the other, the 130 settlers decided to settle and named the site Charles Town. This first settlement was crude and haphazard—the average house was fifteen by twenty feet, or the size of a modern American living room. Energy went into building a palisade, not growing crops, and early Charles Town, like so many first settlements, relied upon imported foodstuffs, in this case from Virginia, to survive. In 1670 and 1671 more settlers arrived, some from Barbados but others from New York. In 1672 the population amounted to 268 men, 69 women, and 59 children. Ethnic diversity was already a factor as this group included English, Barbadians, Irish, Dutch, and black slaves. In 1680 colonists moved the town to the peninsula formed by the junction of the Ashley and Cooper Rivers. This site became more defensible as the town expanded. In surveying the town, the settlers used a grid pattern following the "grand Model" sent from England and enacted various rules concerning house size and height. Thirty wooden houses and the guns from the old settlement made the new one habitable and seemingly safe. French Huguenots soon arrived, and three years later Scots settlers moved to Charles Town. Presbyterians and Baptists were also drawn by Carolina's promise of religious tolerance. While many left for the countryside, some stayed in the city, making eighteenth-century Charles Town culturally diverse and the largest urban settlement south of Philadelphia. By the mid eighteenth century highly skilled artisans and artists found patrons of taste and discernment. By the time of the American Revolution, Charleston was a city of elegance and culture with theater, music, libraries, and a social season that allowed the elite to view and be viewed by one another. It might well have been the wealthiest city in British North America.

North Carolina. Not until 1729 was Carolina divided into the two colonies of North Carolina and South Carolina. Geography inhibited North Carolina's growth since the colony had no large port and a long coastline marked by barrier islands, shifting sandbars, and treacherous currents. In an age in which any major travel and all commercial trade relied on ships, the lack of harbors was an almost insurmountable liability. The first settlers dribbled into northern Carolina from Virginia during the 1650s (boundaries were indistinct, and the Virginia-Carolina border would not be settled until 1728). When the Lords Proprietors acquired their tract, they found these people already in the Albemarle Sound area. Attempts to settle in the Cape Fear River area between 1662 and 1667 failed. The good harbors of the southern portion of the grant attracted most of the attention the Lords Proprietors gave to their property. They appointed governors to Albemarle County and then to what became known as North Carolina in 1689. The population grew slowly. A few French Huguenot families from Virginia moved near the Pamlico River in 1690–1691 and were followed in 1707 by a much larger group. In 1710 German Palatines settled New Bern but were attacked by Tuscarora Indians the next year, and the settlement was abandoned; it was rebuilt in 1723. In 1672 Quakers arrived and became a powerful political force. By the 1720s Indians and other problems were under control, and more immigrants found their way to North Carolina. The colony came under royal control in 1729. Initial settlements, mostly of Englishmen, stayed near the ocean until the 1740s, but after that the upper Cape Fear River and the backcountry opened and Scotch-Irish, Germans, Scottish Highlanders, and the Welsh moved in. The Great Wagon Road from Philadelphia opened up the Shenandoah Valley of Virginia as well as North and South Carolina in the 1750s. Slavery also flourished in North Carolina, although not in anywhere near the same numbers as the plantations of South Carolina. Estimates of the population of North Carolina in the 1760s suggest some eighty thousand whites and maybe twenty-six thousand blacks, but these figures may be even less reliable than other colonial-population statistics. North Carolina was of little interest to royal officials, so information on the colony remains elusive.

Sources:

Richard S. Dunn, "The English Sugar Islands and the Founding of South Carolina," *South Carolina Historical Magazine*, 72 (1971): 81–93;

Hugh Talmage Lefler and Albert Ray Newsome, *The History of a Southern State: North Carolina*, third edition (Chapel Hill: University of North Carolina Press, 1973);

Charles H. Lesser, *South Carolina Begins: The Records of a Proprietary Colony, 1663–1721* (Columbia: South Carolina Department of Archives and History, 1995);

William S. Powell, *North Carolina: A Bicentennial History* (New York: Norton, 1977);

Joseph I. Waring, *The First Voyage and Settlement at Charles Town 1670–1680* (Columbia: Tricentennial Commission by the University of South Carolina Press, 1970);

Richard Waterhouse, "England, the Caribbean, and the Settlement of Carolina," *Journal of American Studies*, 9 (1975): 259–281;

Robert M. Weir, *Colonial South Carolina: A History* (Millwood, N.Y.: KTO Press, 1983);

Peter Wood, *Black Majority: Negroes in Colonial South Carolina from 1670 through the Stono Rebellion* (New York: Norton, 1974).

LA FLORIDA

Unsuccessful Ventures. Spain's exploration of the region known as La Florida began in 1513 when Juan Ponce de León sailed to the area looking for riches and slaves. Within the next three years at least three other expeditions explored both the Atlantic and Gulf Coasts. In 1521 Spanish slavers made it as far north as the Santee River in South Carolina. Other explorers also made their way to and through these southeastern regions. In 1528 Pánfilo de Narváez set out with some four hundred black and white men to explore and perhaps settle the Florida Gulf Coast. Only four men survived and in one of the great heroic sagas of the century made their way back to Mexico City after wandering for eight years. Between 1539 and 1543 Hernando de Soto and five hundred followers covered an area from Tampa Bay to Tampico,

The Castillo de San Marcos in Saint Augustine, Florida, a castle begun by the Spanish in 1672

Mexico. Two unsuccessful colonizing ventures also preceded the Spanish settlement of Saint Augustine. In 1526 Lucas Vásquez de Allyón led five hundred European settlers with African slaves and some Dominican friars to a colony near what is now Sapelo, Georgia. They lasted only three months before disease, starvation, hostile Indian attacks, and the loss of Allyón forced them back. Fewer than two hundred made it back to their base in Santo Domingo; some of the Africans chose to remain with the Indians. In 1559 Tristán de Luna y Arellano tried again, this time on the Gulf Coast in Pensacola Bay. He sailed with thirteen ships carrying five hundred soldiers and one thousand settlers, but they found insufficient foodstuffs on the coast, and a hurricane destroyed their supply ships. Moving into the interior proved useless, and the group broke up; some returned to New Spain, and the others were killed in a storm while attempting to relocate on the Atlantic Coast. In 1561 Philip II of Spain, having recently made peace with France, called off these settlement attempts whose aims had been to keep the French from establishing a beachhead so close to Spanish territory.

Saint Augustine. Philip II had misjudged the French, who were occupied with a series of religious wars at home but nevertheless had covetous eyes on the wealth Spain was extracting from the Americas. In 1562 and 1564 French Huguenots had tried to establish settlements on the Atlantic Coast both at Charlesfort on what is now Parris Island, South Carolina, and Fort Caroline, near modern Jacksonville, Florida. In 1565, in response to these threats, Pedro Menéndez de Avilés sailed with a fleet intent not only on destroying the French, which he did, but also on establishing a permanent settlement protecting this whole area. On 8 September 1565 Menéndez and his officers, announced by trumpets and an artillery barrage, knelt to kiss the cross carried to them by their chaplain, who then celebrated a mass in honor of the Nativity of Our Lady. With due ceremony Menéndez then took possession of the territory for the king of Spain. Menéndez had planned carefully: he had supplies, and among those with him were farmers as well as carpenters. Still, the first winter brought disease and starvation to Saint Augustine. The fort was little more than a ditch. In 1566 the Spanish began building a town that they laid out in a grid with narrow streets and small blocks. The houses were correspondingly narrow. Thus was settled the oldest city in North America. Saint Augustine grew slowly. Always vulnerable to attack by the French and English—in 1669 the pirate John Davis killed sixty townsfolk—the Spanish constructed eight or nine wooden forts before beginning in 1672 work on the great Castillo de San Marcos, which still stands. Saint Augustine was a presidio—a garrison town—and its population reflected its purpose. Its three hundred inhabitants included soldiers, craftsmen, traders, Native Americans, black slaves, and an occasional Frenchman or Portuguese. Religious needs were met by the Franciscans. In 1605 Bishop Juan de las Cabezas Altamirano arrived.

Population. By 1700 Saint Augustine's population numbered around one thousand, and by 1763 some thirty-one hundred Europeans, Native Americans, Africans, and Canary Islanders lived there. Many had been born in America, especially the women since Spain continued to send over soldiers but had stopped sending women in the sixteenth century. Some three hundred black slaves lived in the city. The Indians lived outside the city in their own villages. In 1738 there were enough freed slaves, most of them escaped from South Carolina, to form a town of their own, Gracia Real de Santa Teresa de Mose. Saint Augustine was in many ways an anomaly born of the defensive needs of the Spanish Crown. Never self-sufficient in foodstuffs, goods, or population, it depended upon government subsidies to keep it going. This lifeline was cut off at various times during the many wars which plagued the sixteenth, seventeenth, and eighteenth centuries. Hostile Native Americans, sometimes allied with European enemies, also threatened the city. In 1702 South Carolina's governor, James Moore, attacked with a combined force of English, Creek, and Yamasee and destroyed everything outside the walls of the fort. What human enemies left standing was periodically leveled by the hurricanes that battered Florida from both the Atlantic Ocean and the Gulf of Mexico. Epidemics killed Europeans but were especially disastrous to native populations, including the Christianized Indians around the city. As part of the 1763 Treaty of Paris that ended the Seven Years' War, Florida was given to Britain, and all three thousand of Saint Augustine's residents chose to evacuate to Cuba or Campeche, Mexico, even though they could have stayed. Florida would return to Spain in 1783 and remain Spanish until sold to the United States as East Florida in 1821.

Catholic Church. La Florida exemplified two of Spain's colonial objectives: forts to protect the valuable exports of Mexico and Peru and missions to fulfill the Pope's charge to the Spanish Crown of converting the native peoples to Roman Catholicism. Early explorers had brought along priests, soon followed by missions and missionaries sent to America by the various religious orders. The 1521 expedition of Ponce de León marked the arrival of both secular (those not in one of the monastic orders) and regular priests to the shores of Florida as Ponce de León attempted to follow the instructions of his king "in every possible way to convert them [the Indians] to our Holy Catholic Faith." This expedition failed,

UNIQUE COMMUNITY

Gracia Real de Santa Teresa de Mose was a free black town in Spanish Florida just north of Saint Augustine. While freed and escaped blacks had settled themselves in other towns in the Caribbean and parts of Latin America, Mose, as it was called, was the only town of its kind in what would become the United States. In 1693 Charles II of Spain offered freedom to slaves who made their way to Spanish territory and converted to Roman Catholicism. This promise was known to at least some blacks living in South Carolina and later Georgia and was also known to white masters who feared its consequences. The earliest inhabitants of the town of Mose escaped from South Carolina in 1724 and included the man who would be the military and civilian leader of Mose, Francisco Menéndez. The actual town was established in 1738 by Gov. Manuel de Montiano two miles north of Saint Augustine. A military outpost, at its center was a fort. Settlers cultivated the lands nearby, hunted in the woods, and fished in Mose Creek. A Franciscan student priest, the only white person living there, attended to the community's spiritual needs. Escaped slaves from the English provinces were sent to Mose by the Spanish authorities so that at its height perhaps one hundred persons lived there. English predations forced the evacuation of Mose from 1740 to 1752, and the inhabitants moved to Saint Augustine. When the Spanish governor had the town rebuilt, the former inhabitants resisted his orders to return. After living in the capital city for twelve years, they viewed Mose as a mark of second-class citizenship. Forced back to the segregated settlement, the former slaves remained there until 1763 when the Treaty of Paris ending the French and Indian War gave Florida to the English. The residents of Mose, along with most others, were relocated to Cuba, still free people but soon to lose their identity as members of a cohesive settlement as they merged into the population of Havana.

Source: Jane Lander, "Gracia Real de Santa Teresa de Mose: A Free Black Town in Spanish Colonial Florida," *American Historical Review*, 95 (1990): 9–30.

as did the next venture in 1526 of Lucas Vásquez de Allyón, among whose members were two priests and a lay Dominican brother. Hernando de Soto had brought twelve priests with him, of whom five lived to return to Mexico. The first successful mission came with the founding of Saint Augustine, but Pedro Menéndez de Avilés also raised crosses at various points on the Florida and Southern Atlantic Coast and left Spaniards there as lay missionaries to instruct the Indians. Without a mutual language it is hard to see how this might have worked. Menéndez set up three settlements with diocesan priests, but only Saint Augustine survived, under the pastorate of Father Francisco López de Mendoza Grajales. He was joined in 1566 by five more priests. One of these, Father Sebastian Montero, would become the first missionary in the Southeast, living at the Indian town of Guatari in what is now South Carolina for six years and teaching the Indians to read, write, and speak Spanish. In 1566 the first attempt by the Jesuits to establish themselves in Florida met the problems that plagued so many early settlers. Missing the harbor at Saint Augustine, they encountered hostile Indians onshore, and the boat bringing them was forced back by storms. The first Jesuit in Florida was killed within two weeks of landing. Two more arrived the next year and began missionary work. In 1568 about a dozen more came, but their major mission near Fredericksburg, Virginia, was destroyed by the Indians, and in 1572 the Jesuits were recalled to Spain.

Franciscans. The next year Franciscans arrived, and in 1595 they began a large-scale missionizing effort. By 1655 they had created a chain of thirty-eight missions from south of Saint Augustine, northward to South Carolina, and westward to Alabama. The Franciscan missions reached their peak in 1675 and then began to decline, helped by the expansion of the English into South Carolina and then south into Georgia. English trade goods proved to be too enticing for some of the Indian villages that chose to cast their lots against the Spanish. Warfare with English allies either destroyed whole groups or forced them to abandon their homes and move farther into the interior. European diseases continued to decimate Indian populations. In 1703 former South Carolina governor James Moore destroyed the Apalachee missions. The English also engaged in an Indian slave trade capturing and removing native peoples. By 1708 there were no more Florida missions. The remaining three hundred Christian Indians moved to Saint Augustine. In Saint Augustine itself the church followed another path since the people there were already Roman Catholics. A church structure undoubtedly existed, probably made of wood, but there are no descriptions. Sir Francis Drake destroyed this church in 1586. Thirteen years later a Franciscan monastery burned, and by 1606 another building, including a small seminary, housed the monks. Moore's 1702 attack on Saint Augustine destroyed all the religious structures of the city, which included the church, a hermitage, convent, chapel, and library. The church was never rebuilt, and Mass was said in the chapel of the hospital until the Spanish left in 1763. Construction of a new monastery began in 1724 and was completed in 1737. With twenty-five cells it was too large for the number of friars in the city.

Rivalries. The fortunes of Roman Catholicism in La Florida were battered from within as well as from without. Franciscans and the secular clergy both wanted control over the church there. In 1746 the secular clergy finally won. By the 1720s the Franciscans were divided over the question of whether creoles (native-born friars), or peninsulares (Spanish-born friars) should control the order in Florida; the Crown sided with the latter. In 1738 twenty-five priests served all of the province; in 1759 ten remained. After the Spanish left in 1763 there were only eight Roman Catholics in all of La Florida.

Sources:

John Francis Bannon, *The Spanish Borderlands Frontier, 1513–1821* (New York: Holt, Rinehart & Winston, 1970);

Amy Bushnell, "The Noble and Loyal City, 1565–1668," in *The Oldest City: St. Augustine Saga of Survival*, edited by Jean Parker Waterbury (Saint Augustine, Fla.: Saint Augustine Historical Society, 1983), pp. 27–55;

Kathleen Deagan, *Spanish St. Augustine: The Archaeology of a Colonial Creole Community* (New York: Academic Press, 1983);

Michael V. Gannon, *The Cross in the Sand: The Early Catholic Church in Florida 1513–1870* (Gainesville: University of Florida Press, 1965);

John W. Griffin, "The Men Who Met Menéndez, 8000 B.C.–1565 A.D.," in *The Oldest City: St. Augustine Saga of Survival*, edited by Waterbury (Saint Augustine, Fla.: Saint Augustine Historical Society, 1983), pp. 1–26;

Jean Parker Waterbury, "The Castillo Years, 1668–1763," in *The Oldest City: St. Augustine Saga of Survival*, edited by Waterbury (Saint Augustine, Fla.: Saint Augustine Historical Society, 1983), pp. 56–89;

David J. Weber, *The Spanish Frontier in North America* (New Haven, Conn.: Yale University Press, 1992).

FRENCH ILLINOIS AND LOUISIANA

Exploration. The French presence in the American interior was initially launched from their settlements in Canada. In 1672 Louis de Buade, Comte de Frontenac et Palluau, governor of New France, wrote to his superiors in France that he was sending Louis Jolliet to discover the "South Sea" through Indian country "and the great river they call Mississippi, which is believed to discharge into the sea of California." The next year the expedition, joined by Father Jacques Marquette and various Indians who served as their guides, left Saint Ignace on the Straits of Mackinac (now in Michigan's upper peninsula) in birchbark canoes and paddled and portaged their way down various rivers and streams until they reached the upper Mississippi. They then made their way down the Mississippi, meeting with various Indians, some of whom had already had contact with Europeans. Marquette and Jolliet, fearing the Spanish, did not go all the way to the sea but, a few days shy of the river's mouth, turned around, ending their travels at Green Bay, now Wisconsin. Their voyage established French claims to the region and also made clear that the river did not empty into the sea of California but rather the Gulf of Mexico. The voyage of Robert Cavelier, Sieur de La Salle, in 1682 ended at the Gulf of Mexico. La Salle claimed all of the lands to the headwaters of the Mississippi and all of the river's drainage basin for France under the name Louisiana.

Le Pays des Illinois. The Illinois country, or le pays des Illinois, was a series of settlements on the Mississippi

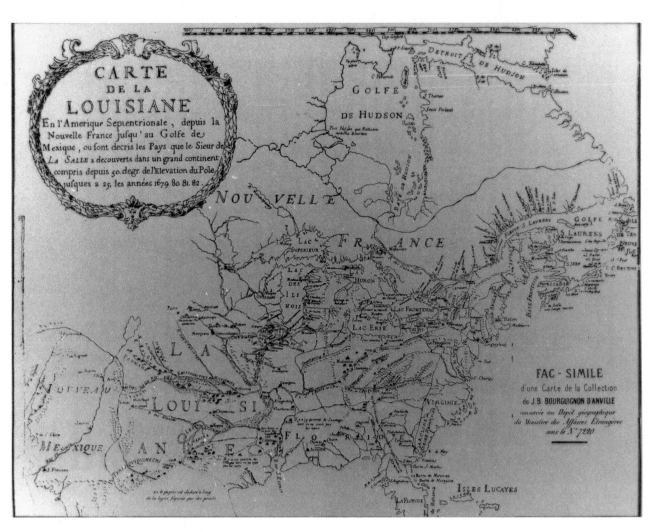

CARTE DE LA LOUISIANE
En l'Amerique Septentrionale, depuis la
Nouvelle France jusqu'au Golfe de
Mexique, ou sont decris les Pays que le Sieur de
LA SALLE a decouverts dans un grand continent
compris depuis 50. degr. de l'Elevation du Pole,
jusques a 25, les années 1679. 80. 81. 82.

FAC-SIMILE
d'une Carte de la Collection
de J.B. BOURGUIGNON D'ANVILLE
conservée au Dépot géographique
du Ministère des Affaires Etrangeres
sous le N° 7220.

Louisiana in 1679–1682, a 1720 map published in Pierre Margry, ed., *Découvertes et Etablissements des Français dans l'oest et dans le sud de L'Amerique Septentrionale* (1876)

River that stretched from Cahokia, across the river from what is now Saint Louis, to Kaskaskia, some fifty miles downriver. Cahokia was initially a mission founded in 1699 to convert the Indians; Kaskaskia was a fort established in 1703. Both settlements began to attract a few Frenchmen from Canada, the so-called coureurs de bois. These "woods runners" were trappers and traders who spent much of their time living among the Native Americans. At Cahokia they began to settle down, often with Indian wives, away from the government of New France in Canada and most other authority. In 1718 the region began to prosper as a result of the French Gulf Coast settlements that provided them with a market for wheat, beef, and pork. New interest and authority led to the founding of Fort de Chartres and the villages of Chartres, Saint Philippe, and Prairie du Rocher. In 1740 the last of the French towns, Sainte Geneviève, completed the six French settlements of the Illinois country. By 1752 some 58 percent of the white settlers came from Canada, 38 percent from France, and the small remainder from Switzerland, Italy, and Louisiana. There was also a considerable black slave population. By the mid

1760s there might have been some 1,100 whites, 500 black slaves, and also a few Indian slaves in the Illinois country.

Lower Louisiana. The settlement of Louisiana began slowly, as the French were in no position to put money or people into a new colony. The first census of Biloxi, Mississippi, in 1699 listed only 82 persons, all male, of whom 13 were Caribbean pirates and 40 were soldiers or sailors. By 1708 there were 278 persons in Louisiana, of whom 80 were Indian slaves and 28 were white women. In 1718, when Louisiana became a province, the colony had 400 Europeans. During the next few years Louisiana became a penal colony and also the temporary home to indentured servants, but high mortality rates kept the population low. While between October 1717 and May 1721 the Company of the Indies embarked 7,020 colonists, only 5,420 survived the crossing. By 1726 a census showed that only 1,952 French comprised the colony—the rest had died. The company lost control of the colony in 1731, and slave imports ceased. By 1763, when France surrendered Louisiana to the Spanish, the population stood at some 3,654 whites and 4,598 slaves. Some

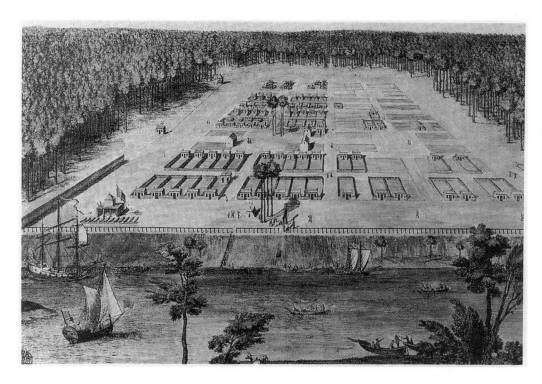

Savannah, Georgia, circa 1734

of these whites were West Indian pirates, Canadians who had traveled south, and recent European immigrants. Most of the slaves had come from the Senegambia region of Africa and included Bambara; others came from the Bight of Benin, with a few from the Congo and Angola.

Sources:

Susan C. Boyle, "Did She Generally Decide? Women in Ste. Genevieve, 1750–1805," *William and Mary Quarterly,* 54 (1987): 775–789.

Winstanley Briggs, "Le Pays des Illinois," *William and Mary Quarterly,* 47 (1990): 30–56;

W. J. Eccles, *France in America,* revised edition (Markham, Ontario: Fitzhenry & Whiteside, 1990);

Gwendolyn Midlo Hall, *Africans in Colonial Louisiana: The Development of Afro-Creole Culture in the Eighteenth Century* (Baton Rouge: Louisiana State University Press, 1992);

Carl O. Sauer, *Seventeenth Century North America* (Berkeley, Cal.: Turtle Island Foundation, 1980);

Daniel H. Usner, *Indians, Settlers, and Slaves in a Frontier Exchange Economy* (Chapel Hill: University of North Carolina Press, 1992).

GEORGIA

Trustees. Georgia was the last colony founded by the British in what would be the United States. By the 1730s authorities in England had a fairly good idea of what it meant to create settlements even though in many ways Georgia would be an experiment. Unlike the earliest colonies, which were either underwritten by joint stock companies (Virginia, Plymouth, Massachusetts Bay, New Netherland, and New Sweden) or were held as the semiprivate property of proprietors (Pennsylvania, Maryland, the Jerseys, New York, and the Carolinas), Georgia was entrusted to twenty-one trustees. Its 1733 charter, to run for twenty-one years, prohibited the trustees from making any profit or taking any salary. Money for the colony was raised in England, initially through the churches and schoolchildren since the idea being promoted was that Georgia would be a place where the deserving poor could find a second chance. (Most of these people were not the debtors jailed in England that popular myth has assigned to early Georgia.) Contributions fell off, however, and less than 10 percent of the £260,000 that the trustees ultimately spent came through donations. Other expectations by the trustees also failed to materialize, and Georgia proved hard to govern, especially through trustee meetings held three thousand miles away. In 1752, one year sooner than their charter called for, the trustees turned the colony over to the Crown, and royal officials arrived two years later.

Oglethorpe. The man most responsible for the creation and administration of Georgia was James Edward Oglethorpe. Born to a wealthy family in 1696, he began his career in the army of Prince Eugene of Savoy fighting against the Ottoman Turks. By 1719 he was back in England, and in 1722 he was elected to the House of Commons. A turning point for Oglethorpe came in 1728 when a close friend, Robert Castell, was committed to London's Fleet Street prison for debt, where he contracted smallpox and died. Oglethorpe had visited Castell in prison and was appalled by what he saw, so he began to agitate for prison reform. His efforts attracted the attention of Thomas Bray, the Anglican clergyman in charge of the church's missionary effort in America. Bray had conceived of a philanthropic colony for England's poor and released debtors. After his death his friends be-

The Trustees of Georgia (1734), by William Verelst (The Henry Francis du Pont Winterthur Museum, Winterthur, Delaware)

gan working with Oglethorpe and helped push the charter through. Oglethorpe was a man of action, and he accompanied the first boatload of 114 settlers to Georgia in 1732. While not officially governor, his leadership abilities in fact made him so. He would also be a military leader against the Spanish in Florida and take part in all the important events of the young colony. By 1738 Oglethorpe's authority was diminishing. Political dissent and economic problems in the colony led the trustees to look to others for guidance. Oglethorpe left the colony in 1743 to answer charges of military mismanagement against him. The ensuing court-martial cleared him, and Parliament granted the colonial leader the £66,109 that he had spent of his own funds for the public good of Georgia. He continued to attend meetings of the trustees in England until 1749, but he never returned to Georgia.

Buffer Zone. While Oglethorpe and many of the trustees hoped that Georgia would be a place for the poor to acquire a "necessary sufficiency," they and others also realized that the Spaniards and neighboring Indians were a threat to the increasingly prosperous colony of South Carolina. By the early 1700s Spaniards were concentrated south of the Saint Johns River (modern Jacksonville, Florida) and Frenchmen were settling the Gulf of Mexico. A series of European wars in the late seventeenth and early eighteenth centuries also contributed to English fears of enemies at their backs. Indian problems that culminated in the Yamasee War (1715–1716) convinced South Carolinians that they needed white frontier settlements that not only would prevent the French from

monopolizing the Mississippi but also would supply militias to forestall or repel Spanish or Indian forays into Carolina. Georgia was therefore settled on South Carolina's southern and southwestern flank abutting the Spanish in La Florida.

Failure of Idealism. While colonies such as Plymouth, Massachusetts Bay, Maryland, and Pennsylvania all were founded to some extent as idealistic ventures, their underpinnings were religious. Georgia's founders, while godly, were looking not to establish a protected religious enclave but a moral one. Chief among these moralists was Oglethorpe. He and the trustees envisioned a colony of sober, industrious, small landholders. To this end they prohibited strong liquors, large landholdings of more than five hundred acres, and slavery; the colonists disagreed. Not only did these constraints rankle many settlers, but also the restrictions on land acquisition and slave labor made Georgia unappealing to those with capital who wanted to take advantage of the area's potential for rice plantations. South Carolinians especially eyed the rivers and marshes, and a few even went so far as establishing illegal slave-based plantations. A colony without colonists was a colony that failed. In 1750 the trustees allowed slavery, and two years later the five-hundred-acre restriction on grants ended. The rum trade was never completely suppressed because Robert Musgrove and his wife Mary sold liquor less than a mile from Savannah. Georgia's trustees had learned what other utopians would learn throughout American history,

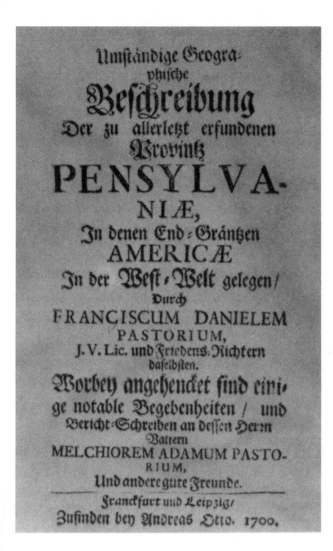

Title page for a description of Pennsylvania by Francis Daniel Pastorius, who founded the first German settlement there in 1700

which was that ideals in competition with economic realities rarely survived.

Savannah. By the time Oglethorpe and his settlers arrived in America they knew what locations would be good sites for towns. Probably aided by the South Carolinians he had met, Oglethorpe settled on Yamacraw Bluff, high above the Savannah River some seventeen miles from the ocean. As Oglethorpe told the trustees, "The Lannskip is very agreeable, the Stream being wide, and bordered with high Woods on both sides." The local Indians were few in number and peaceful. Oglethorpe then proceeded to lay out a town with public squares, blocks of ten lots each, and streets. Savannah also boasted an experimental garden where exotic crops such as olive trees, grape vines, coffee berries, tea, oranges, and Egyptian kale were planted. The planned city of Savannah was unlike almost any other town in British America and looked then, and still looks now, European. By 1754 it seemed to have some 150 houses and 600 inhabitants, black and white.

Sources:

Kenneth Coleman, *Colonial Georgia: A History* (Millwood, N.Y.: KTO Press, 1989);

Evarts B. Greene and Virginia D. Harrington, *American Population Before the Federal Census of 1790* (Gloucester, Mass.: Peter Smith, 1966).

GERMANS

Earliest Settlers. German-speaking people were among the first people to settle the eastern coast of North America. Even among the first colonists to Virginia in 1607 there were a few Germans. Others settled in New Netherland and were among those speaking the "eighteen different languages" heard in New Amsterdam by the French Jesuit priest Father Jogues. By 1673 New York had as many as 2,400 Germans. Most came because of economic hardship in their homeland made even worse by various European wars, but some came for religious freedom. This earliest trickle of peoples was largely disorganized as families or individuals found their way to America. These included men such as Johannes Kelpius, one of the religious hermits who lived in caves on the banks of the Wissahickon Creek in Pennsylvania and practiced fortune-telling. Later migrations were more organized. Between 1683, when Francis Daniel Pastorius established Germantown outside Philadelphia, and 1783, some 125,000 German speakers came to British North America. Especially important was the immigration of German pietists in congregations, such as the Lutherans and Moravians. Some were driven out of Europe by overpopulation and land scarcity; known as hard workers and good farmers, they were actively recruited to come to America. Other nations also tried to recruit Germans. Between 1717 and 1721 the French Company of the Indies would send some 1,300 German speakers to the Gulf Coast. Most of these immigrants would die shortly thereafter of disease, and those who were left would abandon the lower Mississippi.

Palatines. From 1709 to 1714 approximately 3,000 Germans from the Palatinate, pushed out of their Rhineland homes by the aftermath of war and lured by promotional literature and the promise of free passage, sailed to New York and North Carolina. The 2,300 or so Palatines sent to New York were settled on the Hudson River to engage in manufacturing lumber and naval stores. Unfortunately, promised economic support did not materialize because of political changes in England that called for an end to this kind of expenditure. The New York Germans saw themselves as oppressed, and their attempts to settle on what seemed to be unoccupied lands on the Schoharie River failed. Disgusted at what they considered to be breaches of contract and frightened by potential religious persecution, they moved to Pennsylvania. The 600 or so Palatines who left for North Carolina eventually joined with some German-speaking Swiss, and together they founded the town of New Bern. This settlement made an inauspicious beginning as illness, French privateers, mismanagement, and an Indian war in 1711 all wreaked havoc on those who survived. Nonetheless, New Bern was rebuilt and incorporated in 1723.

Salzburgers. In 1729 the archbishop of Salzburg decided to convert the Lutherans in Salzburg to Roman Catholicism. Over the next three years some 30,000 Protestants left, most of them fleeing to England. There they seemed like good prospects for the new colony of Georgia, and with a grant from Parliament, and two German ministers, the first group of 42 families sailed for America in 1734. They created Ebenezer and New Ebenezer on the Savannah River, and by 1742 both towns had 250 settlers.

Moravians. The people called Moravians were German Protestants who lived on the lands of Count Nikolaus Ludwig von Zinzendorf of Saxony. Religious persecution caused them to look elsewhere, and in 1735 and 1736 some 35 young men arrived in Savannah, Georgia. The outbreak of a war with Spain made these pacifists suspect, and between 1738 and 1740 they moved to Pennsylvania. Count Zinzendorf, one of the few European noblemen to come to America, traveled to Pennsylvania to set up a settlement even though he did not stay. In 1741 the Moravians bought land in Pennsylvania and founded the community of Bethlehem. In 1752 they also bought a tract of land in North Carolina that they called Wachovia, named for their lands in Europe. The first group of male brethren arrived in 1753 and celebrated their arrival by composing a song that began "We hold arrival lovefeast here / In Carolina land; / A company of Brethren true, / A little pilgrim band." Married couples first arrived in 1755. The settlements survived, and Moravian influence can still be seen today.

Sources:

Kenneth Coleman, *Colonial Georgia: A History* (Millwood, N.Y.: KTO Press, 1989);

Aaron Spencer Fogelman, *Hopeful Journeys: German Immigration, Settlement, and Political Culture in Colonial America, 1717–1775* (Philadelphia: University of Pennsylvania Press, 1996);

Adelaide L. Fries, *The Road to Salem* (Chapel Hill: University of North Carolina Press, 1972);

Gillian Lindt Gollin, *Moravians in Two Worlds: A Study of Changing Communities* (New York: Columbia University Press, 1967);

Hugh Talmage Lefler and Albert Ray Newsome, *The History of a Southern State: North Carolina,* third edition (Chapel Hill: University of North Carolina Press, 1973);

A. G. Roeber, " 'The Origin of Whatever Is Not English among Us': The Dutch-speaking and the German-speaking Peoples of Colonial British America," in *Strangers within the Realm: Cultural Margins of the First British Empire,* edited by Bernard Bailyn and Philip D. Morgan (Chapel Hill: University of North Carolina Press, 1991), pp. 220–283;

Daniel H. Usner, *Indians, Settlers, and Slaves in a Frontier Exchange Economy* (Chapel Hill: University of North Carolina Press, 1992).

HUGUENOTS

Early French Protestants. The migration of French Protestants to America was closely tied to the religious climate in France. The Edict of Nantes, promulgated in 1598 and revoked in 1685, guaranteed limited religious toleration for Protestants. Even before the Edict of Nantes, however, some individuals close to the government realized that Protestants might be in danger. As early as the 1560s French Huguenots looked to the New World as a potential area for settlement. Unfortunately, they chose places claimed by Spain and were thus seen as threats by the Spanish. In 1562 a small group built Charlesfort on what is now Parris Island, South Carolina, but abandoned the site shortly thereafter. In 1564–1565, 900 Huguenots tried to establish a colony near what is now Jacksonville, Florida. They were discovered and routed by a Spanish fleet, thus ending French Protestant attempts to set up their own separate colonies. Those who came to America in the seventeenth and eighteenth centuries, after toleration was abolished, would join already ongoing English colonies.

Revocation. In 1589 Henry of Navarre, a Protestant, became a Roman Catholic and was then crowned Henry IV of France. That same year he tried to protect his Protestant subjects by giving them some limited freedoms through the Edict of Nantes, but French Protestantism was not really safe, especially after Henry died. During the seventeenth century Protestants faced growing restrictions and by 1675 outright suppression. Many had already converted to Roman Catholicism. Louis XIV brought an official end to French Protestantism when in 1685 he revoked the Edict of Nantes and sent troops to Protestant villages. Ministers were forced either to convert or leave. By the time Louis XIV died in 1715 there were few Protestants in France. Most had become Catholics, at least outwardly, while maybe some 160,000 fled—no official figures were kept. Emigrés went first to Protestant countries in Europe: German principalities, the Netherlands, and England. In these places the exiles found life hard and sometimes, as in England, encountered prejudice. Perhaps because of these problems, most of those who would migrate to America came from the Huguenot communities in England.

Northern Colonies. The Huguenots were not the first French Protestants to settle in the northern colonies. In New Amsterdam the first settlers had been Walloons, French speakers from what is now Belgium. A small number of families from the Channel Islands, which lie between France and England, had also come to New England. But the real French migration began after 1680. New England had perhaps 200 Huguenot men, women, and children in 1700. New York had a larger population, one capable of creating a French church, the Eglise Française à la Nouvelle York, in 1688. By 1695 there were about 800 French Huguenots in New York, some 300 of which probably lived in New York City.

Southern Colonies. As in the northern colonies, there were some small clusters of French speakers such as those in Manakin, Virginia, but the majority stayed together in larger groups. South Carolina provided a home for French Protestants in the South, and by 1697 there were 450 in that colony. About 45 percent lived in Charleston, and the rest populated three settlements in the countryside. Immigration to South Carolina was not an accident. The Carolina proprietors advertised their colony in pamphlets, boasting that "for salubrity of Air, Fertility of Soyl, for the Luxuriant and Indulgent Blessings of Nature, [travelers' accounts] justly rendered Carolina Famous." Perhaps it was this kind of tract, translated into French, that lured Pierre Giton to leave Germany with his mother, brother, and sister, and after stops in Amsterdam and London, board a ship for Charleston. South Carolina proved to be not quite the paradise promised. His mother and brother died of disease within a year and a half. The sister recalled "sickness, pestilence, famine, poverty," and hard labor, yet in the end she survived and apparently prospered. The establishing of French churches in the colony must have helped to ease the transition from Europe to America.

Assimilation. The Huguenots were among the first ethnically discrete groups to migrate to the British colonies, but they did not keep their French identity for long. Those, such as Philip L'Anglois, who lived in Salem, Massachusetts, with few other Frenchmen around him, Anglicized their names: Philip L'Anglois became Philip English. In both New York and South Carolina, Huguenot cohesion had eroded by 1710. Both men and women married non-Huguenots and joined other churches, especially the Church of England. New Yorkers elected the wealthy Huguenot Stephen De Lancey assistant alderman as early as 1691. His family would become one of the most powerful in eighteenth-century New York, with James De Lancey serving as both a supreme court justice and lieutenant governor. In South Carolina some Huguenots such as Jean Boyd and Benjamin Godin sat in the Commons House of Assembly, South Carolina's house of representatives. In 1710 the merchant Isaac Masyck asked the colony's governor to be his daughter's godfather. By the time of the American Revolution, Huguenots were known by their French names, but in most other ways they were no different from English colonists.

Sources:

Jon Butler, *The Huguenots in America: A Refugee People in New World Society* (Cambridge, Mass.: Harvard University Press, 1983);

Joyce D. Goodfriend, *Before the Melting Pot: Society and Culture in Colonial New York City, 1664–1730* (Princeton, N.J.: Princeton University Press, 1992).

JEWS

New Netherland. The first recorded Jews in North America came to the Dutch West India Company's settlement of New Netherland in 1654. They did not all come together but instead represented the two major immigrant streams of Jews that came to early America—the Ashkenazim, or European Jews, and the Sephardim, or Spanish Jews. In the summer of 1654 Solomon Pietersen and Jacob Barsimson, both traders, arrived in New Amsterdam. Barsimson had sailed from Amsterdam. That same year twenty-three Sephardic Jews fled Brazil after the Portuguese defeated the Dutch there. While not exactly welcomed in New Amsterdam, they were not permitted as non-Catholics to remain in Brazil. The next year, 1655, Jewish merchants from Amsterdam arrived in New Amsterdam. In 1656 they petitioned local authorities for permission "to purchase a burying place," which was granted. By 1663 the Jewish community in New Amsterdam was unraveling, mainly because New Netherland was a backwater with decreasing appeal to Jewish merchants. All told, before the English conquest of 1664 there might have been as many as fifty Jews in New Netherland although not all at the same time.

New York. By the time the English took over New Netherland in 1664 there was no Jewish community left there, but Jews trickled into New York so that by 1682 there were enough to purchase land for a cemetery. Between 1690 and 1710 Jews of Anglo-German extraction migrated to New York so that by 1692 they worshiped as the congregation Shearith Israel at a house on Beaver Street. In 1730 they built the first synagogue in North America. At the time of the American Revolution some four hundred Jews lived in New York City. Single families also settled in various New York towns, but the city remained the heart of the Jewish community.

Rhode Island. The Jews in Newport, Rhode Island, began as an offshoot of the New York group. In the 1740s some of New York's Jewish merchants, such as the Harts, Isaackses, and Polocks, began paying Rhode Island taxes as transients. By 1743 Moses Lopez had moved there, and five years later he was joined by his brother-in-law, Jacob R. Rivera. By 1756 the Jews had organized a synagogue. They built a school in 1763, yet the community comprised only fifteen families. The synagogue provided seating for sixty adult men. By 1761 the town even boasted a Jewish social club, yet there were never many Jews in Newport. By 1774 the community had about two hundred people.

South Carolina. The first of the British colonies to openly provide for a religious toleration that included Jews was South Carolina. Anthony Ashley Cooper, one of the proprietors, and his secretary, the great philosopher John Locke, composed the Fundamental Constitutions of 1669 with an eye toward drawing people, including Jewish merchants, from Barbados. Four Jewish shopkeepers were naturalized in 1697–1698. Jews continued to trickle in during the early eighteenth century, but there were no organized schemes for a Jewish settlement until 1737. While this fell through, Sephardic Jews from London and the West Indies arrived in Charleston in the late 1730s. They were joined in 1740 by Jews fleeing Savannah, Georgia, and rumors of Spanish invasion. In 1749 the Jewish community organized a Sephardic-rite synagogue, Beth Elohim. (It would not have a building until 1794.) On the eve of the Revolution some two hundred Jews lived in Charleston.

A reconstructed seventeenth-century tobacco house, in Historic St. Mary's City, Maryland

Georgia. The first Jews in Georgia represented the only organized migration of their people to British North America, and they arrived as part of a settlement scheme organized by the Bevis Marks Sephardic congregation in London. On 11 July 1733, 41 Jews of Sephardic, Germanic, and Italian stock landed in the new colony, only the third or fourth boatload of people to do so. These individuals brought with them the ritual objects necessary to form a congregation and organized a synagogue, Mickva Israel, in a rented room. While neither James Oglethorpe nor the Georgia trustees wanted Jews, the charter did not actually exclude them, and they proved to have skills valuable to the new colony. Samuel Nunez was a doctor who helped the colony through an epidemic its first summer. Abraham De Lyon was a vintner. More Jews arrived later in the year, and the community grew until the War of Jenkins' Ear broke out in 1739, pitting England against Spain. Spaniards had been the chief cause of the Jewish New World diaspora, and Oglethorpe's unsuccessful assault on Saint Augustine raised the specter of a Spanish threat to Savannah. The Jews departed, leaving only the family of Benjamin Sheftall in Savannah in 1741. Jews began trickling back into Georgia in the 1760s, after the end of the French and Indian War and the resurrection of trade. On the eve of the Revolution the Jewish population lay somewhere between 27 and 240.

Sources:
Kenneth Coleman, *Colonial Georgia: A History* (Millwood, N.Y.: KTO Press, 1989);

Joyce D. Goodfriend, *Before the Melting Pot: Society and Culture in Colonial New York City, 1664–1730* (Princeton, N.J.: Princeton University Press, 1992);

James William Hagy, *This Happy Land: The Jews of Colonial and Antebellum Charleston* (Tuscaloosa: University of Alabama Press, 1993);

Jacob R. Marcus, *The Colonial American Jew: 1492–1776* (Detroit: Wayne State University Press, 1970);

David De Sola Pool, *Portraits Etched in Stone: Early Jewish Settlers 1682–1831* (New York: Columbia University Press, 1952).

MARYLAND

Proprietor. George Calvert was a favorite of King James I, who had knighted him and appointed him a secretary of state. Calvert's interest in America began long before he had a colony of his own. He bought stock in the Virginia Company in 1609 and in 1620 an interest in a group planning to settle Newfoundland. A trip to Newfoundland changed his mind about the merits of that island's climate, and he petitioned the king in 1629 for a grant of land in Virginia. By that time Calvert's life had changed: he had converted to Roman Catholicism in 1625, a move that had cost him his royal positions and precluded any other official duty. In friendship and as a mark of compensation, James I had granted him the Irish title of Lord Baltimore. James I also, against the protests of many in England and in Virginia, granted Calvert's petition for land in what was then thought of as northern Virginia. Calvert left it up to Charles I to name this new grant—Mary's Land, after Queen Henrietta Maria. Calvert did not live long enough to see his new project actually begin; Maryland's charter was signed on 20 June 1643, a month after he died. It awarded the proprietary to Calvert's son and heir, Cecilius, second Baron of Baltimore. The Lords Baltimore thus received the first proprietary grant issued by the English for lands in America. They undoubtedly hoped to make money from their new estate. They also hoped to provide a place in America where Roman Catholics could freely practice their religion and enjoy other political and legal freedoms.

Earliest Settlements. It is difficult to know who were among the 150 who sailed on the *Ark* and the *Dove*, the first ships to Maryland. A few women, "mades which wee brought along," were among them. Unlike any other colony, however, those first settlers included a few Roman Catholic laymen and two Jesuit priests. They arrived at Saint Clements Island on 25 March, Lady Day, the Feast of the Annunciation, and celebrated Mass. They then moved on to settle at Saint Mary's. Within the next few years large land grants called "hundreds" were worked by both tenants and paid laborers. The suitability of Maryland's land for tobacco set it on a course much like Virginia's economy. Those with some capital or connections amassed large landholdings, usually on one of the many rivers that eventually reached Chesapeake Bay. Those without came to work for them, often as indentured servants—laborers who had contracted to work for a set number of years. Most of these settlers were young men. By 1648 the civil war in England, which had reduced migration, and the disease environment, which killed off many of the settlers, had kept Maryland down to a mere 350 people. But immigration and natural reproduction helped the colony's population grow. Even so, life expectancies in Maryland were far lower than in New England. By 1660 the colony had an estimated 2,500 people; in 1675, 13,000; and in 1701, when an official census was undertaken, 32,000. By 1760 population estimates had reached 162,000. Most of these people lived in scattered settlements or villages with only one significant town, Annapolis.

Ethnicity and Race. Maryland's earliest settlers were English, but as in almost all of the proprietary colonies, the owners tried to recruit as many colonists as possible. By the 1730s Irish, German, and Welsh were granted lands along the northern border that the Lords Baltimore disputed with the Penn family. Scottish merchants came to live along the coast as they began to dominate the tobacco trade in the 1750s. On the eve of the American Revolution, Maryland attracted more immigrants, many of them artisans from various parts of England, than any other colony. The major change in Maryland's population patterns took place, however, around 1700 when slave labor began replacing white indentured labor, especially on the larger tobacco plantations. By 1760, 46 percent of planters owned slaves, with half of these whites holding five or fewer. Few planters owned large holdings of more than one hundred slaves, and these men, women, and children lived on smaller holdings called quarters. In the 1750s approximately forty-five thousand black slaves lived in Maryland.

Religious Pluralism. Just as the proprietors welcomed various nationalities in order to gain settlers, so they also allowed various religions. Maryland was founded as a haven for Roman Catholics, although Catholics were never a majority, even on the *Ark* and the *Dove*. Lord Baltimore tried

Interior of a reconstructed poor planter's house, circa 1700, with a dirt floor and unglazed windows, at Historic St. Mary's City, Maryland

to protect his coreligionists by asking that no Christian be "troubled [or] molested" and that such protection be made law. Jews and other non-Christians were excluded from these legal rights. Catholic immigration to Maryland was meager, but other religious groups took advantage of toleration. In the 1650s the Quakers found a welcome. Presbyterians, Independents, Baptists, and the Church of England all were represented by the 1670s. This early toleration did not last, and Catholics lost the right to hold political offiāe and to vote in the twenty or so years after 1692. Dissenting Protestants like the Quakers fared better.

Sources:

Bernard Bailyn, *Voyagers to the West: A Passage in the Peopling of America on the Eve of the Revolution* (New York: Vintage, 1986);

Patricia U. Bonomi, *Under the Cope of Heaven* (New York: Oxford University Press, 1986);

Aubrey C. Land, *Colonial Maryland: A History* (Millwood, N.Y.: KTO Press, 1981).

NEW ENGLAND

Financial Backing. The survival of the Plymouth Colony planted in 1620 spurred others to think about settlements in the same area. In 1622 Thomas Weston gave up on Plymouth and financed another group at Wessagusset in Boston harbor. The next year the Dorchester Adventurers, a group of investors who were interested in the codfish industry, attempted to set up a

Both men and women lived longer in New England than in the Chesapeake Bay area during the early colonial period. This table shows at what age a person on average would die if he or she reached various ages.

One can expect to live until age

Age	Middlesex Co., Va.		Maryland	Andover, Mass.		Plymouth	
	M	F	M	M	F	M	F
	N=259	N=258	N=153	N=192	N=108	N=645	
20	48.8	39.8	46.0	64.6	62.1	69.2	62.4
25	48.7	41.3	47.7	-	-	-	-
30	49.4	43.6	50.4	69.3	65.3	70.0	64.7
35	50.8	45.7	53.0	-	-	-	-
40	53.0	48.6	55.6	71.8	68.7	71.2	69.7
45	55.0	54.2	59.5	-	-	-	-
50	57.7	59.3	62.0	73.5	72.1	73.7	73.4
55	62.7	62.7	65.6	-	-	-	-
60	65.8	67.9	69.3	75.6	76.4	76.3	76.8
65	70.0	70.0	74.4	-	-	-	-
70	73.6	73.7	77.0	80.3	81.9	79.9	80.7
75	77.9	80.2	78.5	-	-	-	-
80	-	-	-	86.6	89.6	85.1	86.7
85	-	-	-	-	-	-	-
90	-	-	-	95.0	95.8	-	-
95	-	-	-	-	-	-	-
100	-	-	-	-	105.0	-	-

M = Males; F = Females; N = Number of Males or Females

Source: Darrett B. Rutman and Anita Rutman, "'Now-Wives and Sons-in-Law': Parental Death in a Seventeenth-Century Virginia County," in *The Chesapeake in the Seventeenth-Century: Essays on Anglo-American Society,* edited by Thad W. Tate and David L. Ammerman (Chapel Hill: University of North Carolina Press, 1979), p. 172.

permanent base on the mainland, but only a small settlement arose at Naumkeag. In 1628 the New England Company for a Plantation in Massachusetts-Bay received a grant that included some of the lands already given. John Endicott led fifty new colonists in June to the Naumkeag settlement, which would become Salem, Massachusetts. The most important group, The Governor and Company of the Massachusetts Bay in New England, received a royal charter in 1629. Many of its stockholders were Puritans, people who believed that the Church of England still had too much of Roman Catholicism in it and who wanted instead something simpler and purer like the earliest Christian congregations. Like the Pilgrims at Plymouth they were looking for a place to bring families and start life again without the laws which interfered with their form of worship. The company that financed them sympathized with their aims but also hoped to make a profit. While it might not have lost money, it did not make much either. The Massachusetts Bay Company charter omitted to specify where the company's meetings were to be held. Since one of the underlying ideas was to provide a place where settlers were free of English control, the company decided to take the charter to America and hold meetings there, three thousand miles from royal intervention. This shrewd move allowed the governor and General Court of the company to become the political leaders of the colony.

Reasons to Migrate. One of the early promoters of settlement was Robert Cushman, who had arrived in Plymouth aboard the Mayflower but then returned to England as the colony's business agent. There he published a pamphlet outlining why English people, "here born and bred, and hath lived some years, may remove [themselves] into another country." After assuring would-be settlers that God was not opposed to such a move he went on to say, "a man must not respect only to live and do good to himself, but he should see where he can live to do most good to others." Immigrating to America was not only best then for oneself but also for others as well. First, it would bring Christianity to the Indians. Second, the land was not well used by the Indians and was empty, a belief common among Europeans who did not acknowledge that Indian land-use patterns were legitimate or adequate. Third, England was overpopulated. The towns had too many young tradesmen, "and the hospitals are filled with old laborers"; everywhere there were beggars. Fourth, England had become a land of religious contention and strife that brought neighbor against neighbor and consumed energies better spent converting the heathen. Fifth, times were hard, and it became more difficult not only to live but to leave some legacy to one's children. In America things could be different:

> To conclude, without all partiality: the present consumption [deadly illness] which groweth upon us here, whilst the land groaneth under so many close-fisted [stingy] and unmerciful men, being compared with the easiness, plainness [honesty and simplicity], and plentifulness in living in those remote places, may quickly persuade any man to a liking of this course, and to practice a removal—which being done by honest, godly and industrious men, they shall there be right heartily welcome.

There were many reasons to come to America, and Cushman appealed to them all. They were not mutually exclusive. People could leave England for religious freedom—at least for themselves—and in the hopes that they and their children would have a better economic future. They could migrate overseas in the pious anticipation of converting the Indians to Christianity. The decision became easier for some as the religious climate in England deteriorated and many ministers intent upon purifying the English Church were relieved of their congregations or imprisoned. Congregations looked around for a place where they and their ministers would be left in peace.

Great Migration. Between the first settlers to Massachusetts Bay in 1630 and the outbreak of the English Civil War in 1640, some ten thousand English folk—men, women, and children—came to New England in what is known as the Great Migration. The leader of the Massachusetts migration was John Winthrop, a well-educated and wealthy country squire whose grandfather had purchased one of the abbeys confiscated by Henry VIII when he left the Roman Catholic Church. Winthrop sailed with the first fleet of seven hundred persons who arrived in Massachusetts in June—early enough to begin planting crops. These earliest arrivals spread out since they needed fresh water and realized that keeping that many people together led to poor sanitation and disease. Indeed, two hundred died the first

Seal of the governor and Company of Massachusetts Bay, 1629

year, and another hundred returned to England. But others continued to come even though some of these went back as well. The Puritan migrants, like the Plymouth settlers, intended to settle permanently in America. This meant that they often came as families or if single were placed in family groups. For example, in 1635 the Reverend Joseph Hull sailed from Weymouth, England, for New England with his wife Agnes and his two sons, five daughters, two male servants, and one female servant. Hull was forty years old. Most of those on the ship with the Hull family were younger; many were children under fourteen, but both Richard and Elizabeth Wade were in their sixties, the oldest people on board. New England's population as a whole was somewhat younger than old England's, but it still had the full range from newborn to those in their eighties. The Great Migration also brought over those of different social and economic status. While the wealthiest and poorest elements of society generally did not leave England, there were some exceptions. As a wealthy man Winthrop was one of these exceptions, and he and the rest of those early migrants agreed that God never intended for men to be equal. The towns that the first immigrants established filled quickly, and those who came on later ships spread out. Rather than individuals going alone into the wilderness, these New Englanders formed themselves into corporate bodies which bought land from the Indians, petitioned the legislature for the right to become a town, and then moved there as households. Husbands, wives, and their children set up housekeeping immediately, and those men and women who were as yet unmarried boarded in the houses of those who were.

Ethnic Homogeneity. Once the English Civil War, which pitted Parliament and the Puritans against the king and the Church of England, began, migration to New England nearly ended. Many, although not all, had come to America partially to escape religious persecution. Now that Puritans controlled England, those still there felt no need to leave. Indeed, some in Massachusetts felt that they should return and help in the fight against the Crown. Those in New England tried to preserve their religious base and even hanged four Quakers who would not leave the colony. Massachusetts's soil was relatively poor and its growing season short. Few newcomers arrived in New England, and most of its population growth would be due to high fertility and low mortality rates. Most of the eighteenth-century migrations did not occur in Massachusetts, and the colony boasted no sizable German or Scots populations. There were African slaves, however, although never in large numbers. In the cities they worked as laborers and as helpers in bakeries and storehouses. They also served aboard ships, and in the countryside they performed farm labor. African women worked as domestics. In 1776 Massachusetts, which then included Maine, had some 330,000 whites and maybe 5,200 blacks.

Connecticut. Not everybody who first came to Massachusetts stayed there. Some looked for fertile lands elsewhere, while others found Massachusetts's brand of Puritanism not strict enough. In 1634 and 1635 Massachusetts migrants settled the Connecticut River valley and founded the three towns of Wethersfield, Windsor, and Hartford. The well-known Puritan minister Thomas Hooker brought some of his English congregation to the area in 1636. Three years later the three towns joined together as Connecticut and adopted the Fundamental Orders "to maintain and preserve the liberty and purity of the gospel." Meanwhile in 1638 the minister John Davenport and the merchant Theophilus Eaton, with powerful friends in England, purchased land from the Indians along the coast and called their settlement New Haven. Finding the Puritans in Massachusetts somewhat lax, they adopted a government based on Mosaic Law. The two colonies coexisted, but in 1662 the Crown granted a charter that allowed Connecticut to incorporate New Haven against its will. Connecticut, without a major harbor, could not grow as did Massachusetts. Its population relied mainly on farming and raising livestock. Called "the land of steady habits," it had neither the wealth nor the poverty of its neighbor. Most of its population came from Massachusetts and so shared its English orientation. An exception were the few African slaves that helped work the farms of the wealthy. In 1774 the white population numbered 191,000; nonwhites (including Indians) totaled 6,450.

Rhode Island. Like Connecticut, Rhode Island began its existence as various smaller settlements. Unlike Connecticut, or any of the other New England colonies, it served as the refuge for those who were unwelcome in those places. The Dutch called it the "latrina [sewer] of New England," while Puritans labeled it "Rogues Island." The most famous of Rhode Island's founders were

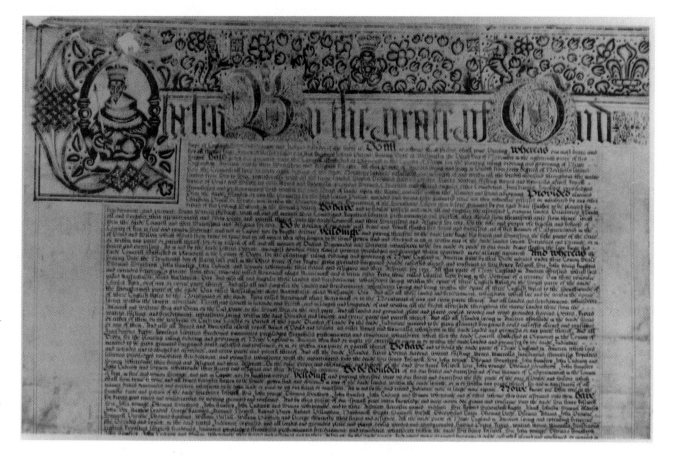

The first page of the royal charter for the Colony of Massachusetts Bay (1629). Charles I, the grantor, is depicted in the upper left corner (Massachusetts State Archives).

Roger Williams and Anne Hutchinson, but they were not the only ones to find that their religious beliefs resulted in their banishment. Williams was a young minister who arrived in Massachusetts in 1631. Everybody, including Winthrop, admired him, but Williams soon developed unacceptable ideas, including the unlawfulness of taking land from the Indians and the sinfulness of interaction with those whom God had not saved. He was a separatist—one who wished to break from the Church of England—whose views finally led him to believe that the church and state should be completely separate because the state would corrupt the church. He maintained that since it was unclear who the saved actually were—he believed that he could be sure only of himself and his wife—maybe the church should be open to everybody. Informed by Winthrop that he was about to be arrested in 1635, he fled Massachusetts and lived for a winter with the Narraganset Indians. He bought land from them and was joined by some of his followers in founding the town of Providence.

A Different Heresy. Hutchinson's beliefs were different from Williams's but just as dangerous to Massachusetts. She held that some of Massachusetts's ministers were preaching Arminianism, a gospel of works which said that people could influence God's will about their salvation through good behavior. She also felt that those who were saints should not obey the laws that were made by those who might not be saints. Her final heresy came out in a lengthy trial when she claimed to know through direct revelation from God who was saved. Puritans did not believe this, and of course it was dangerous to have people claiming that this minister or that magistrate was not among the chosen few. Hutchinson and her followers were banished on 7 November 1637 and founded the town of Portsmouth soon afterward. Hutchinson did not stay in Portsmouth long because religious squabbles plagued the community. Controversy centered around William Coddington, a political leader and former Hutchinson advocate, and Samuel Gorton, already persona non grata in Plymouth and Massachusetts. Gorton believed in the divinity of all human beings and rejected both a church restricted to saints and any form of social hierarchy. His contentiousness proved too much for Coddington, who left in 1639 to found Newport. Gorton finally left in 1641 and established the town of Warwick, the last of the original Rhode Island towns, in 1643.

Charter. Roger Williams meanwhile traveled to England to secure a charter for this menagerie of religious and political misfits. A skillful politician, he succeeded both with the Puritan Parliament in 1644 and the newly restored Charles II in 1663. The charter gave Rhode Island more autonomy than other colonies and was the most tolerant in New England. Quakers found acceptance there, and a small Jewish community emerged.

The seal of New Netherland, adopted by the Dutch West India Company on 28 December 1630. The beaver is surrounded by a belt of wampum.

Rhode Island never had a large ethnic population, but it was the most heterogeneous colony of the region. Newport was a cosmopolitan port town with Scots, French, Dutch, Germans, Portuguese, and Italians. Rhode Island also had the largest percentage of nonwhites in New England. Nevertheless, the numbers of people involved were small since Rhode Island contained only 1,214 square miles, about one-eighth the size of Massachusetts. In 1755 the colony had 36,000 whites and 4,700 blacks and Indians.

Sources:

Richard Archer, "New England Mosaic: A Demographic Analysis for the Seventeenth Century," *William and Mary Quarterly,* 47 (1990): 477–502;

Bruce C. Daniels, *Dissent and Conformity on Narragansett Bay* (Middletown, Conn.: Wesleyan University Press, 1984);

Benjamin W. Labaree, *Colonial Massachusetts: A History* (Millwood, N.Y.: KTO Press, 1979);

William D. Pierson, *Black Yankees: The Development of an Afro-American Subculture in Eighteenth-Century New England* (Amherst: University of Massachusetts Press, 1988);

Robert J. Taylor, *Colonial Connecticut: A History* (Millwood, N.Y.: KTO Press, 1979).

NEW NETHERLAND AND NEW YORK

Fur Trade. When in 1609 Henry Hudson sailed his eighty-ton, three-masted carrack, *The Half Moon,* into New York Bay and up the river that would bear his name, he and the other eighteen or twenty men with him were looking for the Northwest Passage, a mythical water route through North America to the East Indies. Instead he and his men found a navigable river on whose banks lived native peoples "who had an abundance of provi-

sions, skins, and furs, of martens and foxes." Thus the fur trade began early. Until 1621 when the Dutch West India Company was incorporated, the fur trade allowed individuals such as the West Indian mulatto Juan Rodrigues to come to the area and work for one firm, leave it and stay with the Indians, and sign on with another company that would pay him better once the winter ended and ships again sailed from the Netherlands. Early settlements both up the river at Fort Orange (Albany) and on "the Manhates," or Manhattan, were glorified trading posts with soldiers and farmers. Because beavers, the most important fur-bearing animals, were fewer around Manhattan, Albany became the center of the Dutch fur trade. Each year when the fur-trading season opened, merchants from New York awaited the coming of the Indians with their pelts. Albany boomed, and even ordinary people tried to buy and sell furs before the season ended and the town was again left to the few who lived there all year around. The fur trade would outlast the Dutch, who surrendered New Netherland in 1664, but in time the fur-bearing animals close by were killed off, and Indians either had to trap farther away or buy from more distant tribes whose lands still supplied plenty of beavers. Albany merchants engaged in an illegal fur trade with the French in Montreal by 1700. The Hudson River valley turned its attention to growing wheat, and the fur trade, so crucial in the earliest years, became increasingly less important to the economy of the colony.

Dutch West India Company. The States General of the Netherlands chartered the Dutch West India Company in 1621 as a private trading monopoly and as a countermeasure against the Spanish, with whom a treaty had just ended. Initially its mission was seen as harassing the Spanish and Portuguese, not overseeing New World settlement. It looked for wealth on the African coast and in the West Indies rather than areas north of Virginia. The company's operation in New Netherland, roughly between the Connecticut and Delaware Rivers, was incidental and received few resources since it could produce only furs. The director general and a few other officers were appointed by the company to oversee the fur trade and whatever else was necessary. They acted as the government, rented out company lands to farmers, chartered towns to those who wanted to settle, traded with the Indians, and tried to keep the peace among the Europeans. Their authority was somewhat compromised since settlers could appeal directly to the company. By 1629 it was clear that the company monopoly did not work in keeping the colony solvent, and private investors were allowed large landholdings called "patroonships." The fur trade was thrown open to other merchants in 1639, and by the 1660s the colony occupied little company time or interest.

Settlement Patterns. The first settlements, as opposed to seasonal trading posts, were undertaken by the Dutch West India Company, who paid thirty Walloon families to come to the New World in 1624. They were

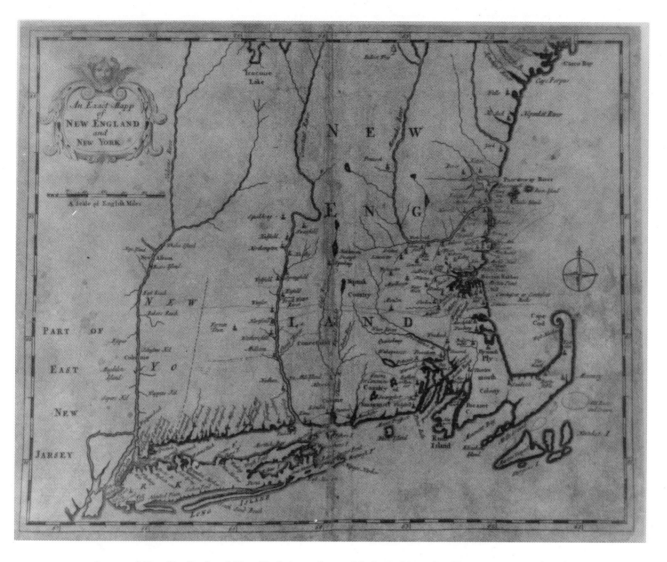

A map of New England and New York from Cotton Mather's *Magnalia Christi Americana* (1702)

scattered on farms among Manhattan Island, Fort Orange, and the Connecticut River valley, where the company also had a fort. Two years later, after the company purchased Manhattan Island, they were brought back to stay there. New Amsterdam, as the settlement was named, was the center of Dutch control of New Netherland; by 1664 nineteen hundred people lived there. Fort Orange was a struggling post manned by fewer than twenty men until the 1630s when the company granted to Kiliaen van Rensselaer, one of its directors, the right to bring over settlers. Rensselaerswyck, which surrounded Albany and included vast acres on both sides of the Hudson River, was the only patroonship to have any success. Rensselaer recruited some tenants, and one hundred persons lived on his property by 1646. Schenectady, located just west of Albany, was the last Dutch village founded in 1661. Down the Hudson stood the village of Esopus (Kingston). On Long Island both Dutch and some English settlers applied for and received town charters, thereby forming farming villages in the 1640s

and 1650s. Slightly to the south in what is now Jersey City, New Jersey, was the town of Pavonia. Finally, the Dutch nominally controlled the Swedish settlements on the Delaware River near what is now New Castle, Delaware.

Diversity. In 1646 the French Jesuit priest and missionary Father Isaac Jogues found himself temporarily in New Amsterdam. "On the island of Manhate, and in its environs, there may well be four or five hundred men of different sects and nations: the Director General told me that there were men of eighteen different languages. . . . No religion is publicly exercised but the Calvinist, and orders are to admit none but Calvinists, but this is not observed: for besides the Calvinists there are in the colony Catholics, English Puritans, Lutherans, Anabaptists, here called [Mennonites]." Part of what Father Jogues saw was the result of the difficulty that the Dutch West India Company and various patroons had in enticing Dutchmen to leave the Netherlands. Half of those in New Netherland later called Dutch were in fact German,

Swedish, Finnish, Norwegian, French, English, or even as exotic as Abraham Stevenson, alias Crabaat/Crowaet, the Croatian. During the 1640s and 1650s New England dissenters, sometimes expelled from more-orthodox towns, petitioned the Dutch authorities for town grants and settled as families on Long Island at Gravesend, Newtown, Jamaica, Oyster Bay, and Hempstead. Some of these were the Anabaptists, those who believed in adult rather than infant baptism, and English Puritans noted by Father Jogues. In 1654 Jews arrived, and even though Director General Peter Stuyvesant would have expelled them, they appealed to coreligionists who as major investors in the Dutch West India Company successfully pressured the company's directors to override Stuyvesant's prejudices and allow them to stay. The 1655 conquest of New Sweden on the Delaware brought in even more Swedes and Finns. Africans also entered New Netherland.

Enslaved. The Dutch West India Company imported Africans to work on their farms, storehouses, and ships. Women performed domestic duties as well as gardening and light farmwork. Almost all of the Dutch settlements had at least a few slaves taken from various parts of Africa. In 1664 some 300 slaves and 75 free blacks lived in New Amsterdam. A census of 1698 lists 2,170 blacks, mostly slaves, in the whole colony.

The English. The conquest of New Netherland in 1664 as part of the Second Anglo-Dutch War meant that the scattered settlements were now under English control. King Charles II gave the territory to his brother James, Duke of York, hence the name New York. James, like other proprietors, understood that his colony would succeed only if it had a population growing crops and buying goods. The surrender of New Netherland guaranteed that those living there, of whatever nationality or religion, were protected even if they did not all have equal rights. New York continued to attract different groups; Quakers found religious tolerance after some early persecution and Huguenots arrived before 1700. German Palatines were offered sanctuary, even if in the end they left for the greater security of Pennsylvania. On the eve of the Revolution, Scotsmen with their families poured into upper and western New York, lured by speculators who wanted to sell them farmland. African slaves continued to make up a substantial percentage of the population, being as much as one-fifth in the seventeenth century. They came from all regions of Africa including the island of Madagascar. Many had first lived in the West Indies, and some were born there. A census of 1771 lists 148,000 whites and almost 20,000 blacks, most of them slaves.

Sources:

Bernard Bailyn, *Voyagers to the West: A Passage in the Peopling of America on the Eve of the Revolution* (New York: Vintage, 1986);

Thomas E. Burke Jr., *Mohawk Frontier: The Dutch Community of Schenectady, New York, 1661–1710* (Ithaca, N.Y.: Cornell University Press, 1991);

Joyce D. Goodfriend, *Before the Melting Pot: Society and Culture in Colonial New York City, 1664–1730* (Princeton, N.J.: Princeton University Press, 1992);

David G. Hackett, *The Rude Hand of Innovation: Religion and Social Order in Albany, New York 1652–1836* (New York: Oxford University Press, 1991);

Michael Kammen, *Colonial New York: A History* (New York: Oxford University Press, 1975);

Thomas Elliot Norton, *The Fur Trade in Colonial New York 1686–1776* (Madison: University of Wisconsin Press, 1974).

PENNSYLVANIA

Proprietorship. Pennsylvania, like Maryland, New York, and the Carolinas, was a proprietary colony, the gift of the monarch to an individual or group of individuals. In the case of Pennsylvania the land north of Maryland and west of the Jerseys repaid a debt that the Crown owed to the Penn family. Adm. Sir William Penn aided the Stuart princes in exile during the English Civil War. The admiral's son, William, was a friend of both Charles, who would be restored to the throne in 1660 as Charles II, and his younger brother James, Duke of York, later James II. William Jr. had also become a Quaker, a religious sect feared and persecuted in England. With the grant of territory in 1681 Charles II had repaid a debt without it actually costing him anything

PROMOTIONAL LITERATURE

One of the ways that proprietors and land speculators lured settlers to America was through published descriptions of the richness of the lands. Some descriptions were clearly fantastic, promising health, wealth, and happiness with little work. Women usually made only half of what men made in wages, and the marrying age for women was in their early twenties. Notwithstanding the facts, Gabriel Thomas, hoping to lure both men and women to Pennsylvania, wrote in 1698:

They pay no Tithes [church taxes] and their Taxes are inconsiderable. . . . I shall add another reason why Womens Wages are so exorbitant: they are not yet very numerous, which makes them stand upon high Terms for their several Services in Sempstering [seamstress], Washing, Spinning, Knitting, Sewing, and in all the other parts of their Imployments . . . moreover they are usually Marry'd before they are Twenty Years of Age, and when once in that Noose, are for the most part a little uneasie, and make their Husbands so too, till they procure them a Maid Servant to bear the burden of the Work, as also some measure to wait on them too.

The Christian children born here are generally well-favoured, and Beautiful to behold; I never knew any come into the World with the least blemish on any part of its Body, being in the general, observ'd to be better Natur'd, Milder, and more tender Hearted than those born in England.

Source: "An Historical and Geographical Account of Pensilvania and of West-New-Jersey, by Gabriel Thomas, 1698," in *Narratives of Early Pennsylvania, West New Jersey and Delaware 1630–1707*, edited by Albert Cook Myers (New York: Barnes & Noble, 1967), pp. 329, 332.

Map of Philadelphia by William Penn, circa 1681

since he had never invested in American lands. He also provided a means of getting rid of Quakers because Admiral Penn gave the proprietorship to his son. Penn and his heirs were granted large powers over their new land, but they found, as did the Lords Baltimore and the Carolina proprietors, that having this authority on paper and being able to exercise it were different things. Politically, the proprietors and the settlers were often at odds. Penn, a genuine reformer and true believer in religious toleration for most groups, understood that his family's fortune depended upon his attracting settlers to his colony. Promotional literature extolled the richness of the land, healthiness of the air, and convenience of river transportation and ocean access for trade. But Penn also promised personal and religious freedoms, thereby attracting not only Quakers but also other persecuted minorities. Upon his death in 1718 the proprietorship descended to his son, Thomas.

Philadelphia. William Penn realized that his colony needed a port city that would attract merchants and artisans as well as provide a market where farmers could sell their goods. It helped that many of those who became Quakers in England had urban backgrounds and skills. The model he did not want to follow was overcrowded, dirty, disease-ridden, and dangerous London. To this end Philadelphia (the name means "brotherly love" in Greek), unlike Boston or New York, was a planned city, and Penn sent commissioners to find a good location and provide the knowledge necessary to lay out his "green country town." They chose a peninsula between the Delaware and Schuylkill Rivers, thus giving water access both to the Atlantic Ocean and to the hinterland. The peninsula lent itself to the grid plan that Penn and his surveyor, Thomas Holme, chose as the best way to order the city. A one-hundred-foot-wide street in the middle (Market) intersected another one-hundred-foot-wide street that ran lengthwise (Broad) with smaller streets at regular intervals. Rather than honor human beings, the

streets were either named after trees (Chestnut, Walnut) or given numbers (First, Second). The middle of town had a square. In 1683 the town had 600 people and 100 houses; two years later there were 357 houses, "divers of them large, well built, with good Cellars, three stories, and some with balconies." The town also had seven "ordinaries," inns which served food, rented rooms, and most important, gave men a place to drink. Philadelphia would become the major port and largest city in British America on the eve of the Revolution with some 31,500 people, of whom about 850 were blacks, slave and free.

Quakers. The people called the Society of Friends, or Quakers, began in England in the early 1650s, when George Fox, a cobbler and shepherd, received what he felt to be an immediate awakening to the Inner Light, Truth, and God. These were years of civil strife in England, and Fox's message was one of pacifism. The Friends were also evangelical, spreading the good news of their beliefs and calling on those around them to renounce the Church of England, or state church, and follow them. The Restoration of the monarchy in 1660 brought to power those who saw Quakers as a threat to the church and the state. Fox and many of those around him spent time in jail. Some of the wealthier and more well connected followers, such as William Penn, began to look for a place of refuge where Quakers could worship as they liked—without baptism, liturgy, and ministers—but also where they could make decent livings for their families. They first looked to West New Jersey, part of the holdings of James, Duke of York. James had given this land away already, but Quakers still settled there. The proprietorship of Penn held out more promise in the long run. He arrived at his colony in 1681 with other Friends, and his land policies encouraged wealthy Quaker merchants and farmers to come to America. English, Irish, and Welsh Quakers flocked to Pennsylvania. They quickly established meetings (congregations) along the lines that Fox had laid out in England. Tightly

Penn's Treaty with the Indians (1771), by Benjamin West (Pennsylvania Academy of the Fine Arts, Philadelphia)

organized, Quaker meetings did well in Pennsylvania. The Quaker elite also kept its power base in the legislature, the only colony where Quakers were politically important. They managed to keep Pennsylvania out of the colonial wars until they were forced to compromise in the 1750s. Their basic tolerance of other religious and ethnic groups made Pennsylvania attractive to Europeans. It was the fastest growing colony of the eighteenth century.

Diversity. The area of land that became Pennsylvania had hosted European settlement long before Penn was granted his charter. New Sweden, founded in 1638, was conquered by the Dutch in 1655. After the conquest Dutchmen, Germans, and Scandinavians settled in the region. In 1685, four years after Penn's grant, he wrote, "The People are a Collection of divers Nations in Europe: As, French, Dutch, Germans, Swedes, Danes, Finns, Scotch, Irish and English; and of the last equal to all the rest." These people were also of various religions that included Swedish Lutherans, Dutch Reformed, German Lutherans, Anglicans, Quakers, Anabaptists, and Presbyterians. In the eighteenth century German Mennonites and Moravians, Presbyterian Scots, and Welsh Baptists filed into Pennsylvania's backcountry. Indentured servants served as laborers in Philadelphia and on the farms in the counties that supplied the city. While there were no large settlements of Roman Catholics or Jews, there were enough individuals to hold small religious services in private homes. In 1744 the Maryland

physician and gentleman Alexander Hamilton, traveling north for his health, "dined att a tavern with a very mixed company of different nations and religions. There were Scots, English, Dutch, Germans, and Irish; there were Roman Catholicks, Church men [Church of England], Presbyterians, Quakers, Newlightmen [evangelicals], Methodists, Seventh day men, Moravians, Anabaptists, and one Jew. The whole company consisted of 25 planted round an oblong table in a great hall." Pennsylvania's ethnic diversity created the audience and the market for a German-language press. The large numbers of non-English speakers in Pennsylvania had some, such as Benjamin Franklin, worried. In the end he was unable to convince the legislature to take steps against immigrants. Most realized, as had Penn, that a province's prosperity lay in its people. An open and tolerant society brought in people to work the land and provide the grains and beef upon which Pennsylvania's economy was built. They in turn provided the markets for goods made by artisans in the colony and merchandise imported from Britain through the great and wealthy merchants of Philadelphia. Finally, Pennsylvania was also home to those who had never wanted to come at all—African slaves. While Quakers became increasingly uncomfortable with slavery from the 1750s onward, they were slave owners up until the eve of the Revolution. Non-Quakers had fewer doubts about the morality of owning other human beings. Pennsylvania did not take any censuses during the colonial period. Estimates from the 1770s and data from the first federal census of 1790 place the white population at about three hundred thousand and the black at about ten thousand.

Sources:

Hugh Barbour and J. William Frost, *The Quakers* (New York: Greenwood Press, 1988);

Joseph Illick, *Colonial Pennsylvania: A History* (New York: Scribners, 1976);

Sally Schwartz, *"A Mixed Multitude": The Struggle for Toleration in Colonial Pennsylvania* (New York: New York University Press, 1987);

Jean R. Soderlund, "Black Importation and Migration into Southeastern Pennsylvania, 1682–1810," *The Demographic History of the Philadelphia Region 1600–1860, Proceedings of the American Philosophical Society*, edited by Susan E. Klepp, 133 (1989): 144–153.

PLYMOUTH

Exploring. The area that would become New England was claimed by England on the basis of voyages of discovery by John Cabot in 1497. By 1502 fishermen exploiting the great cod banks off Labrador and New England had brought their catch to the port of Bristol, England. As early as 1508–1509 Sebastian Cabot had explored the coast, but England's attention was elsewhere, and aside from the fisheries nothing much happened until almost one hundred years later. In 1602 the English were again ready to look west. Bartholomew Gosnold left Falmouth with thirty-two men who intended to colonize in New England. They eventually settled on an island which separated Buzzards Bay from Vineyard Sound (Massachusetts), but like so many others who made early colonizing attempts, they were unprepared to live where they landed. As foodstuffs ran out they decided to return home, but the reports of the venture that were eventually published spoke of "the goodliest continent that ever we saw, promising more by farre than we any way did expect." The description of such bounty led to the formation of business ventures that hoped to exploit it. In 1606 James I chartered the Virginia Company, whose wealthy investors hoped to establish colonies along the coast north of the Spanish. The Virginia Company divided into a northern division, the Plymouth Company, and a southern, the London Company. In 1607 the Plymouth Company outfitted an expedition to Sagadahoc, Maine, which had been described in the most glowing terms by an earlier voyage whose men had seen the place only in summer. Most of this group managed to survive the Maine winter, but one of its leaders died, and when the other was called back to England the settlement broke up. It was not until 1620 that the English established a permanent foothold in New England.

Religious Origins. Protestantism began in England in 1531 when Henry VIII, heretofore a staunch supporter of Roman Catholicism, wished the Pope to annul his marriage to Catherine of Aragon so that he could marry again and father a son and heir. Catherine was a Spanish princess, and the Pope was dependent upon Spain for the monies he needed to fight Protestantism in Europe. He could not afford to alienate the Spanish so

Sketches of an early Plymouth, Massachusetts, meetinghouse, circa 1685 (The Pilgrim Society, Plymouth, Massachusetts)

did not grant an annulment to Henry. The English king broke with Rome, declared himself the head of the Church of England, closed the monasteries, and confiscated church lands. But Henry's quarrel with Roman Catholicism was political, not religious. He did not want to change the church all that much, and he kept some of the ceremony and especially the pomp and fancy vestments (clothing). His daughter Elizabeth I continued her father's lead. She loved the grand processions and ritual of the church. Her successor, James I, also proved unwilling to make major changes. Other English Protestants chafed under what they considered to be too much Catholicism. They wanted a simpler church with less wealth. Under James I some ministers and their congregations refused to organize their worship as the Church of England required. Most of these felt that what was needed was a purification of the national church, not a separation from it. They became known as Puritans. A

THE FIRST THANKSGIVING

One of England's celebratory traditions was for a village to come together in feasts of thanksgiving when it seemed that God had been especially merciful. Good harvests, a year without major epidemics, the end of a war, or the birth of an heir to the throne called for a day in which God could be thanked for care and kindness. The Plymouth thanksgiving in 1621 comes down to us through a letter that Edward Winslow, one of the colony's leaders, sent back to England:

Our harvest being gotten in, our Governor sent four men on fowling, that so we might after a more special manner rejoice together, after we had gathered the fruit of our labours. The four in one day killed as much fowl as, with a little help beside, served the Company [inhabitants] almost a week. At which time, amongst other recreations, we exercised our arms [weapons], many of the Indians coming amongst us, and amongst the rest their greatest king, Massasoit with some 90 men, whom for three days we entertained and feasted. And they went out and killed five deer which they brought to the plantation [Plymouth] and bestowed on our Governor and upon the Captain and others.

Given the sources, we cannot know when the Pilgrims actually celebrated this feast of plenty. It would not become a regular American fall harvest festival until the nineteenth century. What we can see from this letter is the richness of the environment, at least in the autumn months, since birds and deer were readily available. It also shows that Indian-European relations were friendly enough in 1621 that they could sit down one with the other, each side still keeping its weapons.

Source: William Bradford, *Of Plymouth Plantation 1620–1647*, edited by Samuel Eliot Morison (New York: New Modern Library, 1967), p. 90n.

---

few dissenters felt that the Church of England was too corrupt to be saved, and they wanted to get away from it entirely. Unfortunately, since the church and the state were linked and the king headed both, such an action was considered a crime against the state. In the small town of Scrooby in northern England, a congregation became separatist. In 1607 the persecutions against some of Scrooby's leaders began, and the congregation resolved to leave England and go to the Netherlands, the most tolerant of the European states.

Exiles. While life in Holland was pleasant and there was religious freedom, the Scrooby congregation became uneasy. The children were becoming Dutch rather than English; economic opportunities were limited; and the twelve-year truce between Spain and the Netherlands was ending, causing great concern that war might erupt. Many decided to move again, not to England and not to New Netherland where they were urged to go, but to a place in America where they might bring up their children in the English language with their own understanding of the kingdom of God.

Finances. The Leyden separatists were not wealthy, and they certainly had nowhere near the wherewithal to finance a migration from Holland to America, much less pay the costs of founding a colony once they arrived. There was already one English colony in America which, if not thriving, was at least surviving, and that was Virginia. They decided to settle at the northernmost end of the land granted to the Virginia Company. In 1619 they found financing through a consortium of investors, Thomas Weston and Associates. In 1620 a small group of the religious separatists left Holland to emigrate. Stopping in England first, they found that only one of their ships, the *Mayflower*, was seaworthy. One hundred and two men, women, and children boarded the ship for America, but not all of these were Pilgrims. Many represented Thomas Weston and Associates and did not share the Pilgrims' religious outlook. No minister sailed with them, nor did one come for some years after. The *Mayflower* took eleven weeks to cross the Atlantic, only to arrive north of the intended destination and beyond the jurisdiction of the Virginia Company. Technically, they had no right to be there and were outside any charter. Fearing that some among them might take advantage of the fact that they were beyond the law and under no civil authority, the free adult males drew up what has become known as the Mayflower Compact, in which they promised to create a new government and obey it. Plymouth, like Virginia, would disappoint its investors. Its first ship home with goods intended to provide its backers with some profit—clapboards and beaver and otter skins—was seized by the French. Thomas Weston pulled out of the company in 1622. In 1627 the colony reached an agreement with the remaining investors to buy out their interest. To pay for this some of the colony's leaders personally assumed the debt in return for a monopoly of the fur trade. This economic scheme would prove expensive, and it was not until 1642 that debts were liquidated, partly through the colony's wealthier men selling land they still owned in England. They did better than most since they had the satisfaction of seeing Plymouth, born out of religious necessity, survive.

First Settlement. Aside from landing too far north, the Mayflower settlers arrived in winter, and nearly half of them died—the fate also of the earliest settlers in Virginia. However, some things worked out right for them. Unlike many ships bringing settlers, the *Mayflower* remained with the Pilgrims, furnishing housing until they could create shelters on their own. The first houses were small one-room dwellings made of boards (not logs).

While the weather worked against them, the careful selection of a settlement site did not. Rather than facing a "howling wilderness" they settled on a hillside where the Indians had once lived. Good water was close by, and they would utilize the fields cleared by the Indians before epidemics killed most of them. They also ate the stored ears of corn—a new food to them—that the Indians had put away for winter. Those who survived were helped in the spring by the Patuxet Indian Squanto, who years earlier had been kidnapped and taken to England. He was returned to America only to find that his entire people had died of disease. Squanto taught the colonists how to grow corn. The next fall was a time of plenty, and the settlers and Indians joined together to help celebrate what we call the first Thanksgiving, although thanksgiving celebrations were common in England. After the initial problems of food and shelter had been solved, Plymouth turned out to be remarkably healthy but a backwater. There were few fur-bearing animals, and the soils were poor. The Pilgrims had come to America to practice religion the way they thought God wanted. They did not extend this right to others so Plymouth was not a haven for those who were persecuted for their religious beliefs. Few emigrants, almost all from England, settled there, but families were large and mortality rates low. The population grew slowly but steadily, reaching seven thousand persons when the colony was absorbed by Massachusetts in 1691.

Sources:

Benjamin W. Labaree, *Colonial Massachusetts: A History* (Millwood, N.Y.: KTO Press, 1979);

George D. Langdon Jr., *Pilgrim Colony: A History of New Plymouth 1620–1691* (New Haven, Conn.: Yale University Press, 1966).

SCOTS AND SCOTCH-IRISH

Scotland. The emigration of individuals from Scotland, regardless of their destination, was a product of conditions at home and the aftermath of various wars and rebellions against England. Scotland was roughly divided into the Lowlands, the flatter and rolling lands closest to northern England along the east coast, and the Highlands to the North and the West, which were mountainous. Lands were poor and growing seasons short. Almost any traveler visiting Scotland was struck by its poverty: "The ordinary country houses are pitiful cots built of stone and covered with turves [sod], having in them but one room, many of them no chimneys." In the Lowlands, which furnished the majority of the settlers to America, most of the land was owned by a small group of the wealthy who rented it out to farmers. These tenants raised oats and barley and kept a few animals. While some tenants could rent larger holdings many had barely enough to survive, especially during periodic years of famine such as the late 1690s, 1709, 1740, and 1760. Laborers fared even worse than tenants. Given the lack of economic opportunity, at many levels, Lowlanders were willing to move to northern Ireland (Ulster), the Netherlands, and other parts of Europe. Until the Resto-

ration of the Stuarts and the 1707 Act of Union, which united England and Scotland, Scots were not allowed to trade with the American colonies. Scottish Highlanders enjoyed even fewer opportunities since fertile lands were scarcer there and poverty even greater. Their political and social structure was based upon clans whose chiefs had great power over their members.

A New Life. The Act of Union in 1707 opened up the possibility of immigration to North America. Lowlanders took greater advantage of this opportunity. They could be found almost everywhere although they tended to cluster in the Middle Colonies and the Shenandoah Valley of Virginia. The Highlanders' fate was more problematic. Supporters of the Stuart king, James II, who lost his throne in England's Glorious Revolution of 1688 (called Jacobites since James's name in Latin is Jacobus), Highlanders fought against the Crown in 1715 and 1745. Both rebellions ended in disaster with some of those taken prisoner sent to the colonies as exiles. The 1745 uprising in particular had dire consequences for the Highlands. After the defeat of "Bonnie Prince Charlie" at the Battle of Culloden in 1746, the English took the opportunity to undermine the power of the clans by changing inheritance patterns that had given chiefs the land to reward their followers, forbidding weapons and outlawing the wearing of the tartans (the plaid clothing that identified each clan). With the end of the clan system a more profit-oriented relationship to the land and to the people on it emerged, which allowed more opportunity for some, less security for others, and greater ability to leave a hard and harsh environment. Those Highlanders who came to America in the eighteenth century tended to settle in the South, especially in North Carolina. They did not join the Lowlanders who had come earlier.

Scots in Ireland. The southwest coast of Lowland Scotland and the east coast of Ireland are culturally and linguistically related. (On a clear day the two coasts are in sight of one another.) The first major movement of Scots to Ireland took place about 1400 when some of the clan chiefs married into the Irish nobility and acquired land. Further large grants to Scotsmen were part of the English Crown's program of pacifying the native Irish who opposed both English and Scottish settlement. In 1609–1610 a large push for a non-Irish settlement resulted in planting Scots and English in Ulster. By the 1650s there might have been forty thousand or fifty thousand Scots in northern Ireland. Religious difficulties in Scotland also sent migrants to the Protestant parts of Ireland. By 1700 there were one hundred thousand Scots there. Ireland proved to be no safe haven for dissenters because Queen Anne authorized the Test Act in 1703 that required all officeholders to be members of the Church of England. The Irish, both Catholic and Protestant, also contended with various economic problems. England began undermining the Irish economy through trade barriers that prevented American or European goods from going directly to Ireland. Instead they had to go through England, thus raising the prices and keeping merchants in Ireland out of the wholesale trade. Protective policies restricted Irish trade in some goods, such as woolens, only to England. Rents also rose in the early eighteenth century as rent controls, passed in 1607 for the period of one hundred years, expired. Poor harvests occurred sporadically through the eighteenth century.

To America. The first major attempt at Scottish colonization took place in New Jersey when Lowland Scots Quakers and Scottish Episcopalians became the proprietors of East New Jersey in the 1680s. These men envisioned a settlement like those in northeast Scotland with large landholdings subdivided among tenants. They did not want a colony of independent small landholders. Of the seven hundred or so people who migrated in the 1680s, over half were indentured servants who came in family groups. While the large estates did not work out as the original proprietors had imagined, Scots were more likely than other groups to remain tenants after their labor contracts were over and less likely to buy their own farms. By the mid eighteenth century three thousand inhabitants of Scottish descent lived in New Jersey. Scots also dominated the politics of earlier eighteenth-century New Jersey through their connections with the proprietors and their friendship with the Scottish governors sent over by England. The proprietors of East Jersey did not keep control of their colony which merged with West Jersey in 1702. After initial efforts at colonization, they left it to others to settle their lands. Scots, and after 1725 Scotch-Irish, dribbled in, settling near other Scots rather than among the English or Dutch in New Jersey. In time they came to identify even more strongly as Scots, and as Presbyterians, than they had at home. In 1750 central New Jersey had forty-two hundred Scots and Scotch-Irish, more than 20 percent of the population. Lowland Scots also settled on Port Royal Sound in South Carolina in the early 1680s, but the Spanish forced them out in 1686. Eighteenth-century Lowland Scots settlements into the backcountry and the South are harder to trace since historians tend to speak about the Scotch-Irish rather than the Scots. Likewise it is difficult to know how many Scots there actually were since population has been estimated based on last names that might or might not actually be Scottish. The largest Scots migrations occurred from 1763 to 1775 and consisted of around twenty-five thousand people, excluding the Scotch-Irish.

Another Wave. Highland Scots furnished the fewest of the Scottish immigrants. Highland emigration indirectly resulted from the fight over the British Crown between the Protestant Hanovarian kings who succeeded Queen Anne, the last of James II's daughters from his Protestant first marriage, and the Jacobites who looked to the Roman Catholic heirs of James II from his second marriage to the Catholic Mary of Modina. This branch of the family had been excluded from succession to the throne by the Glorious Revolution of 1688, which had deposed James II and crowned his older daughter Mary and her husband, the Dutch Prince William, joint monarchs of England. While some of those on the losing side were forced into exile or years of indentured servitude, these political emigrants were relatively few. Economic motives drew most of the Highlanders to America beginning in 1732 with a settlement on the upper Cape Fear River in North Carolina. In 1739 another group settled nearby on Cross Creek. The great migration to North Carolina began in 1749 and ended only with the American Revolution. This exodus from the Highlands was led by those known as "tackmen" who had once served as middlemen between the clan chiefs and ordinary people. With the end of the clan system in 1746 they found themselves with no position in the new society, and many not only organized the emigration of others, for a fee, but also moved themselves. The Highlanders wanted to be with other Highlanders, and they tended to settle together, entering North Carolina through the Cape Fear River and not through the Valley of Virginia as the other Scots did.

Last Group. Scotch-Irish immigration began in 1717, and by the next year 5,000 Ulster Scotch-Irish left for America. In 1728 another 3,000 boarded ships. Undoubtedly, smaller groups had embarked for America in the intervening years. Their destinations were Delaware and Pennsylvania, places where they had heard there were ample farmland and religious toleration. Initial settlements centered in southeastern Pennsylvania, encouraged by an active recruitment campaign on behalf of the province. In time the colony's leaders came to see their effort to entice these folk as misguided since many of them were poor and unable to pay for the lands they squatted on. Moreover, they continued to follow the valleys west, putting pressure on the Indians, which made the frontiers more dangerous. The Valley of Virginia opened up to the Scotch-Irish in 1736, when Virginia's governor, William Gooch, gave huge land grants to proprietors who then began selling off smaller landholdings. Hard times in Ireland in 1739–1740 led to a large migration that made its way to the backcountry of Virginia. During the 1740s settlement reached the geographic limit of the Valley of Virginia, and settlers looked farther south to the Carolinas, which welcomed immigrants. The number of Scotch-Irish who came to America is problematic. They might well have been the largest number of migrants other than the English. An educated guess is that in 1783, at the conclusion of the American Revolution, there were 250,000 people of Scotch-Irish heritage in America.

Sources:

Ian Adams and Meredyth Somerville, *Cargoes of Despair and Hope: Scottish Emigration to North America 1603–1803* (Edinburgh, Scotland: John Donald, 1993);

Bernard Bailyn, *Voyagers to the West: A Passage in the Peopling of America on the Eve of the Revolution* (New York: Vintage, 1988);

Ian Charles Cargill Graham, *Colonists from Scotland: Emigration to North America, 1707–1783* (Ithaca, N.Y.: Cornell University Press for the American Historical Association, 1956);

Carlton Jackson, *A Social History of the Scotch-Irish* (Lanham: Madison Books, 1992);

Ned Landsman, *Scotland and Its First American Colony, 1683–1765* (Princeton, N.J.: Princeton University Press, 1985);

James G. Leyburn, *The Scotch-Irish: A Social History* (Chapel Hill: University of North Carolina Press, 1962);

Duane Meyer, *The Highland Scots of North Carolina 1732–1776* (Chapel Hill: University of North Carolina Press, 1957).

SPANISH IN THE SOUTHWEST

Explorations. When the Spanish found the great empire of the Aztec in Mexico in 1519 and understood both its immediate riches and its potential to generate wealth into the future, they naturally sought out other great empires. They found the Inca in Peru in 1529 but could not then know that the Aztec and the Inca were the only two such prizes. Exploration also turned north into what would become Texas, Arizona, and New Mexico. The first trek through the Southwest was accidental. In 1528 Alvar Núñez Cabeza de Vaca (literally "head of a cow") was part of a colonizing expedition to the Gulf Coast of Florida. The expedition foundered, and he and three of the others washed up on the Texas coast and lived with various Indian groups, all the while traveling west and south. In 1536, eight years later, they finally found other Spaniards and made their way to Mexico City. They told of large cities with great populations. The Spaniards hoped these would be Cíbola, the famed Seven Cities of Gold. The next major expedition, 1540–1542 under Francisco Vásquez de Coronado, attempted to find these cities. With three hundred soldiers, six Franciscan friars, hundreds of Indians, one thousand horses, and six hundred pack animals, Coronado marched to the Indian pueblos, first reaching the Zuni, who had already shown their hostility to the Spanish invasion by forcing back the missionary Fray Marcos de Niza the year before. Coronado was better prepared and was able to defeat various Zuni and Hopi villages. During the winter of 1540–1541 he got as far as Barnalillo, New Mexico, and had managed to antagonize most of the Native Americans in the area. In 1541 he returned to Mexico, leaving behind two friars who were soon killed by the Indians. In 1573 Philip II of Spain, distressed by the Indian deaths in the wake of Spanish colonization, promulgated a new ordinance that outlawed destructive military ventures such as Coronado's and required missionary efforts. Some historians consider this the third and final period of Spanish colonization: conversion and settlement.

New Mexico. The first major colonizing venture in what would become New Mexico was a private undertaking sanctioned by the Crown but under contract to the wealthy Juan de Oñate. He grew up in New Spain, and his father had invested in the great silver mines of Zacatecas. In 1598 he set out with 400 soldiers, colonists, missionaries, and Mexican Indians for the Rio Grande

The church (begun in 1744) at the Alamo, a Franciscan mission founded in 1724 in present-day San Antonio, Texas

valley. There he established a settlement but soon ran afoul of the Pueblo Indians from whom he demanded food and other goods. They revolted, and in time Oñate lost control of his colony. In 1610 he was replaced as governor by Pedro de Peralta, who moved the settlers to Santa Fe, the third oldest permanent European settlement in the United States after Saint Augustine and Jamestown. By the 1630s there were 250 Spaniards, 750 Indians, and about two dozen Franciscan friars who serviced twenty-five missions. Santa Fe, and indeed all of the Southwest, proved to be lands of few mineral resources, leaving the labor that could be forced from the Indians the only road to wealth. Forced labor included herding, farm labor, blacksmithing, silverworking, and domestic labor. Spanish-Indian relationships were thus built upon exploitation, which led to resentment. In 1680 the Pueblo Indians formed a confederation and drove out the Spanish in what is known as the Pueblo Revolt. They killed 21 of 33 Franciscans and 401 settlers. The remaining 1,946 whites fled to El Paso del Norte, now Ciudad Juarez across the Rio Grande from Laredo, Texas. The Spaniards gradually retook control of the pueblos and in 1693 set about resettling Santa Fe, making it a presidio (fort) with 100 soldiers. In 1695 families left to establish New Mexico's second town, Santa Cruz de la Cañada; eleven years later Albuquerque was founded. Twenty-one missions were also reestablished. By 1749 New

Mexico's Spanish population had risen to about 4,300 persons. Meanwhile, the Indian population declined drastically; estimates of 17,000 in 1679 gave way to about 9,000 in 1693. Pueblo populations declined slowly as late as 1860.

Texas. While Spain worried about Indian hostility in West Texas, it had to fear other Europeans along East Texas's Gulf Coast. In 1682 Robert Cavalier, Sieur de La Salle, had come down the Mississippi River claiming it for France. The Mississippi divided Spain's claims into La Florida in the East and New Mexico in the Southwest. The French in the Mississippi Valley also put pressure on the Native Americans to move farther west, where they trespassed into Apache and Navajo hunting grounds. The Spanish responded by strengthening their forts. Early settlements in East Texas included an outpost at San Francisco de los Neches. In 1691, 6 missionaries and 16 soldiers were posted there, but the settlement was abandoned by 1693. Missionary-presidio complexes marked the path the Spanish took in East Texas. In 1716, in response to the French in Louisiana, some 80 persons, including 11 Franciscans, 25 soldiers, and 40 men, women, and children, were sent to establish missions and the presidio of San Juan. The settlement itself was called Los Adaes. These areas were close to the French. In 1718 the presidio of San Antonio de Béjar and mission of San Antonio de Valera were established. A town was created near them in 1731 that would become San Antonio. Sixteen families of Canary Islanders, some 55 people, helped start this settlement. Finally, a third presidio-mission complex was begun in 1721 near Espíritu Santo Bay at La Bahí on the Guadalupe River. These were the only three settlements that survived. In 1760 there were 1,190 non-Indians living in Texas.

Arizona. The northern part of the large area known in Spanish as Pineria Alta is present-day Arizona. Like New Mexico, it was first explored by Alvar Núñez Cabeza de Vaca in 1530 and by Francisco Vásquez de Coronado. By the end of the sixteenth century Franciscans had established missions among the Indians. The Jesuits, however, had control over this part of the world, and in 1651 the Franciscans left. For twenty-four years Father Eusebio Francisco Kino worked among the Indians with mixed results. Those who depended upon the irrigation agriculture were easier to Christianize than the nomads and hunters. The Spanish push to establish Indian towns was counterproductive since these towns were easy targets for Apache raiders. The Sapnish finally settled in Arizona in 1752 when they built a presidio at Tubac. They built only one at Tucson in 1776 near what had been one of Father Kino's missions. California lagged even farther behind and had no European settlements in this era.

Sources:

John Francis Bannon, *The Spanish Borderlands Frontier, 1513-1821* (New York: Holt, Rinehart & Winston, 1970);

Carl O. Sauer, *Seventeenth Century North America* (Berkeley, Cal.: Turtle Island Foundation, 1980);

David Hurst Thomas, ed., *Columbian Consequences: Archaeological and Historical Perspectives on the Spanish Borderlands West*, volume 1 (Washington, D.C.: Smithsonian Institution Press, 1989):

David J. Weber, *The Spanish Frontier in North America* (New Haven, Conn.: Yale University Press, 1992).

VIRGINIA

The Virginia Company. Even before there was a Virginia Company there was Sir Walter Raleigh and his dream of a colony in America. The colony at Roanoke had been his venture, and even though it failed he still had hopes for an English settlement in the New World. But Raleigh was bankrupt, and in seeking support for a colony he turned to traders and businessmen such as Sir Thomas Smith, first president of the East India Company, which had just been chartered in 1600. It would be men like Smith, wealthy merchants, rather than men like Raleigh, gentlemen-adventurers, who bankrolled early colonies as business ventures. That they all lost money must be attributed not to their foolishness but to ignorance of what settlements in the New World truly cost. By 1605 England was poised for greater adventures overseas. That year it had signed a peace with Spain that meant energy and monies could go elsewhere. Several investors petitioned the Crown to incorporate two companies—the London Company and Plymouth Company.

Silver frontlet (for use on an armband or headband) presented to the queen of the Pamunkey Indians in 1677 (Association for the Preservation of Virginia Antiquities)

In 1606 the Virginia Company of London and of Plymouth was chartered, gfiving them rights to the land between the Cape Fear River of North Carolina and Bangor, Maine. The northern part of this huge grant fell to the Plymouth part of the company, the southern half to the London part. Government of each colony was administered by a thirteen-man council in America that took its orders from a joint royal council of thirteen in England. The charter further provided that the colonists and their descendants "shall have and enjoy all liberties, franchises and immunities" as if they had been living in England—in other words, the rights of Englishmen.

Valuable Lessons. Experience soon showed that the council in Virginia was unworkable, and in 1609 the company rewrote the charter, putting one man in charge. Gone too was the royal council, and instead the company in England took charge. It also reorganized its stockholders since it needed more money. Now called The Treasurer and Company of Adventurers and Planters of the City of London for the First Colony in Virginia, or the Virginia Company for short, it counted among its investors various corporations such as the Company of Ironmongers and the Company of Fishmongers (*mongers* means sellers) as well as 659 individuals. Yet problems in the colony undermined these efforts as well. Once tobacco was found to be a profitable crop, those hired to work the company lands chose to work their own instead, and laborers sent to work for the company found their way onto the personal farms of local officials. By 1616, the year that profits were to be divided among those who

invested in 1609, no profits existed. Since Virginia needed people the company promised free land. In 1618 the company reorganized again, this time promising a more liberal and less authoritarian government and division of Virginia into four large settlements. The next year the company sent over 1,216 people of whom about half were laborers for the company; it also permitted a general assembly. Called the House of Burgesses, it was the first representative elected body in America. But the days of the company were limited. Even though it continued to send over settlers, high mortality rates considerably reduced their numbers. In 1622 came the crowning blow when the local Indians rose up and murdered one-third of the settlers, 347 "men, women, and children, most by their owne weapons." On 24 May 1624 King James I dissolved the bankrupt Virginia Company, and Virginia became the first royal colony. Other companies in Plymouth, Massachusetts Bay, and New Netherland would try to underwrite colonies, but in the end the needs of such a complicated enterprise outstripped the available financial resources; none would succeed in North America.

Jamestown. The settlement of the new colony of Virginia began under an unlucky star. First, the three ships carrying the new settlers were kept by adverse winds for a full six weeks within sight of England. They finally arrived on the shore of Virginia almost five and one-half months later, in May 1607, only to place their settlement on a small peninsula on the James River surrounded by a marsh. This location proved to be especially unhealthy as

PARENTAL DEATH

Even in an age used to early death, the mortality rates in Virginia between 1655 and 1724 were considered disastrous. The following table shows what happened in Middlesex County. Along with parental death it shows child mortality (infants, who comprise the most deaths in any population, are not included here since the table picks up children already aged one year). Of the 239 children aged one who comprised the "population at risk," 164, or 69 percent, lived to reach the age of twenty-one or married, whichever came first. Of this 164, only 26.8 percent still had both parents living; 37.2 percent had only one parent still alive; and a full 36 percent had lost both parents.

Achieved age	Children known to survive to age	Children with both parents at age	Children with but one parent at age	Children orphaned at age
1	239 (100%)	222 (92.9%)	17 (7.1%)	0 (0.0%)
5	227 (100%)	174 (76.7%)	47 (20.7%)	6 (2.6%)
9	211 (100%)	124 (58.8%)	67 (31.8%)	20 (9.5%)
13	194 (100%)	90 (46.4%)	66 (34.0%)	38 (19.6%)
18	173 (100%)	57 (32.9%)	62 (35.8%)	54 (31.2%)
*	164 (100%)	44 (26.8%)	61 (37.2%)	59 (36.0%)

* indicates age 21 or age at marriage, whichever came first.

Source: Darrett B. Rutman and Anita H. Rutman, "'Now-Wives and Sons-in-Law': Parental Death in a Seventeenth-Century Virginia County," in *The Chesapeake in the Seventeenth-Century: Essays on Anglo-American Society*, edited by Thad W. Tate and David L. Ammerman (Chapel Hill: University of North Carolina Press, 1979), p. 161.

Portrait of Sir William Berkeley (painted 1677–1688), by Sir Peter Lely
(Berkeley Castle, Berkeley Springs, West Virginia)

during the late summer and early autumn the force of the water coming down the river from the mountains was not enough to get past the tide coming up from the Chesapeake Bay. Not only did the colonists suffer from salt poisoning by drinking brackish water, but also the river became an open sewer and a breeding ground for dysentery and typhoid. Disease was not the only problem facing this first English colony. The Virginia Company had organized a government by committee, but the names of those in charge were kept secret until the ships reached Virginia.

Smith. The seven-man council of state was composed of men who despised and feared one another. Capt. John Smith, the most able of the seven, was already under arrest when they landed. He eventually became the leader of the colony only because three of the seven had returned to England and the other three had died. It fell to Smith to organize his unruly and unsuitable settlers into some sort of workforce. The ships he arrived in had car-

ried 104 men, but 48 of these were gentlemen, defined as men who did not earn their living with their own hands. Only 24 were laborers. By September 46 settlers had died. Smith also had to contend with a well-organized and suspicious Indian population already living on the river. Relations were difficult from the beginning, with Smith eager to negotiate peaceful relations and wary of the excesses of his own men but also willing to force the Indians to provide grain for the settlers. Fall brought some relief as migrating wildfowl returned to the rivers and the Indians were willing to trade meat and corn. In January 1608 the town burned. Only the arrival of supply ships from England kept the colony afloat. In the fall of 1609 Smith was badly injured in a gunpowder accident and left for England, never to return. The colony quickly fell apart, and the winter of 1609–1610 became known as the "starving time," brought about by not only a shortage of foodstuffs but also the hoarding and selling of what there was so that some ate while others died. Of the 490 settlers in Virginia when Smith left, only 60 had survived the winter. In 1610 a new governor, Lord De La Warr, a seasoned soldier with experience in Ireland, arrived. Jamestown was now under a form of martial law, and the men there were forced to work. But Virginia's viability was not yet assured. In 1614 the settler John Rolfe was responsible for helping the colony find its moorings. First, his marriage to Pocahontas, daughter of Powhatan, head of a loose federation of neighboring Indians, brought about a truce. Second, Rolfe experimented with growing a West Indian species of tobacco and found that he could produce a crop of high enough quality to fetch good prices in England. Virginia's tobacco boom began, and Jamestown settlers started growing tobacco in the very streets of the town. With its economic destiny set, Jamestown and the Virginia colony began the path toward a plantation economy that it continued throughout the colonial period.

Tobacco. The emergence of tobacco as a cash crop changed the destiny of Virginia. Whereas in 1616 the colony exported 2,300 pounds of tobacco, by 1626 it sent to England 260,000 pounds of tobacco. What James I had called a "stinking weed" and threatened to outlaw now paid enough in taxes that he quickly came to rely upon it. The emergence of an export crop changed the labor situation in Virginia. Even before the tobacco boom the company had sent over indentured servants, who usually worked four to seven years in exchange for free passage to Virginia, room, board, and maybe a little land at the end of their service. With the discovery of tobacco the need for labor increased. Virginians also fanned out, occupying small settlements along the James River. Many of these were crude, and life was harsh and often short. Indentured male servants aged fourteen to forty worked on meager rations and less protection. As Richard Frethorne wrote to his parents in 1623, "And when we are sick there is nothing to comfort us; for since I came out of the ship I never ate anything but peas, and loblollie (that is water gruel). As for deer or venison I never saw any since I came into this land. There is indeed some fowl, but we are not allowed to go and get it, but must work hard both early and late for a mess of water gruel and a mouthful of bread and beef."

Field Hands. The labor needs of tobacco were met by Englishmen for the first fifty years or so of Virginia's history, but beginning in the 1660s black slaves began to replace white indentures even though there had been a few slaves in Virginia since 1619. Reasons for this shift in labor included Virginia's reputation as a death trap for whites, better job prospects in England, the opening of new colonies in America that needed labor, and the increasing availability and decreasing cost of slaves. Virginians also learned that tobacco impoverished soils, and in order to grow a high-quality plant they needed to put fresh lands into cultivation. Planters spread out along the various rivers since this was where the better soils lay and rivers provided the easiest way to transport the heavy casks of tobacco leaf. This settlement pattern assured a

more scattered population and an isolated one. Virginia did not attract many nationalities other than the English until after the 1740s when the Great Wagon Road from Pennsylvania brought in Scotch-Irish and Germans. For the tidewater region the chief diversity was racial. Close ties to England forged by tobacco also affected the religious diversity of the colony. Most were members of the Church of England, although Quakers were tolerated. In the eighteenth century Presbyterians and Baptists emerged, especially in the backcountry.

Mortality. The history of colonial Virginia (and Maryland as well) was in many ways shaped by the high mortality rates for those who lived there. The earliest years under company rule were a disaster as far more people died than came in and few children were born to offset the losses. More than half of those who stepped off the boat with Captain Smith died within a few months. Dysentery and typhoid did most of the damage, but poor nutrition, overwork, and occasional losses to Indians added to the chance of early death. Richard Frethorne listed 20 people who had died in his master's household in a four-month period. He estimated that of the 150 that come over with him, two-thirds had died before the first year. In the three years before the Indian massacre of 1622 some 3,470 people had been sent to Virginia to join the 700 already there, for a total of 4,170. But right after the massacre only 1,240 survived. The Indians had killed 347, but another 2,700 souls had also perished in three years. Virginia's climate, marshes, and seasonally slow rivers undermined the colony's health.

Malaria. Once malaria was introduced into America, first a less virulent strain from England and then a more deadly type from Africa that came with the slaves, rivers and swamps provided the breeding grounds for the mosquitoes that carried the disease. (South Carolina and Georgia, which both grew wetland rice in low-country marshes, fared even worse.) High mortality rates had an especially depressing effect upon family formation, already undermined by the high ratio of men to women sent to the colony. In late-seventeenth-and early-eighteenth-century Middlesex County, Virginia, of 239 children born between 1655 and 1724, only 44 reached either marriage or age twenty-one (whichever came first) with both parents alive. In some cases the parents had died; in some the children had died. Grandparents rarely survived long enough to know their grandchildren. Men and women married serially as spouses died, leaving them with young children. Children, in turn, lived in households with stepparents and stepsiblings. Many growing up had no adult relative to turn to for help and advice. Among the indentured servants, age at first marriage was high since servants were not allowed to marry. Late marriages for women also meant fewer births. For those not servants, men and women married younger than they did in Old England or New England where ages at death were much higher and more parents lived to see their children into adulthood. Virginia's population grew relatively slowly. In 1625 the total population was 1,300; in 1653, 14,300; and in 1699, 62,800. These figures include Africans, but their number is hard to determine; one estimate suggests that by 1699 there were between 6,000 and 10,000. The eighteenth century saw a large growth in the black population. In 1754 there were 168,000 whites and 116,000 blacks in Virginia.

Sources:
Philip L. Barbour, *The Three Worlds of Captain John Smith* (Boston: Houghton Mifflin, 1964);

Edmund S. Morgan, *American Slavery American Freedom: The Ordeal of Colonial Virginia* (New York: Norton, 1975);

Richard L. Morton, *Colonial Virginia*, volume 1 (Chapel Hill: University of North Carolina Press for the Virginia Historical Society, 1960);

Darrett B. Rutman and Anita H. Rutman, "'Now-Wives and Sons-in-Law': Parental Death in a Seventeenth-Century Virginia County," in *The Chesapeake in the Seventeenth-Century: Essays on Anglo-American Society*, edited by Thad W. Tate and David L. Ammerman (Chapel Hill: University of North Carolina Press, 1979), pp. 153–182.

HEADLINE MAKERS

ROBERT COLE

1628?-1662?

MARYLAND PLANTER

Early Life. Robert Cole, an early settler in Maryland, was not a man of special achievement or renown, but his life was more typical of colonists than some of those who are better known. Cole was born in Heston, Middlesex, England—his mother, Joan, lived there in the early 1660s. His father, William Cole, died in 1633 or 1634, when Robert was young. He was apparently the only surviving child in the family. Heston lay in a fertile agricultural region, and the Cole family, long resident there, had shared in the local prosperity. Robert Cole could read and write, and, unlike many immigrants, he arrived in the colonies with enough money to buy land and to bring servants. Between 1649 and 1652 Cole married Rebecca Knott, a widow with two children.

Family. While it is impossible to know why Cole immigrated, it is likely that his Catholicism played a role. The 1650s was the interregnum—the time between reigns—when Charles I had already been executed and Charles II was still in exile. A Puritan Parliament and the Protector, Oliver Cromwell, tried to instill a more Protestant vision of England. It was not a particularly good time to be a Roman Catholic there. Maryland, on the other hand, was the proprietorship of the Roman Catholic Lords Baltimore and a haven for the likes of Cole. Cole arrived in Maryland in 1652 with his wife, four children (two of whom were stepchildren), and two servants. A son, Robert Jr., was born in 1652. Four more children lived to survive their parents; all were raised Roman Catholic.

Planter. Cole was a tobacco planter and originally purchased 300 acres on Saint Clement Bay and surveyed 350 acres more that he sold without developing. His Saint Clement's land was within distance of a Jesuit mission and several neighboring families. Cole owned uncleared forest, and his first task was to carve a farm out of the woods. He needed a house where he and his wife, children, and servants could find shelter. He also built a tobacco-curing shed. This half-acre site provided some household vegetables and herbs. Here Cole's wife kept chickens and other fowl. The earliest Chesapeake settlers also cleared land for an orchard and planted apple trees since apple cider was their major beverage. Cattle and swine ran loose in the forest. For his own dependents Cole needed about six acres of corn. For a cash crop he and two or three servants would have been able to handle six or seven acres of tobacco. By his third year in Maryland, Cole had cleared enough land and done well enough to buy another servant, a twelve-year-old boy. In 1657 he also brought over a kinswoman to help his wife, who that year had her fourth child born in Maryland. The women also had a twelve-cow dairy herd that supplied milk, butter, and cheese. In 1661 the kinswoman-servant Mary Mills had served out her time and married. She was replaced with two female servants. At the height of his plantation in 1662 Cole had twenty-two acres under cultivation in corn and tobacco that he worked alongside three male servants and his stepson. He also acquired the rights to an additional eleven hundred acres. Cole's position in the top half of his society carried with it some forms of public service. He held the minor offices of provincial court juror and manor court juror. He was also an ensign in the militia.

Life and Death. In 1662 Cole's world changed. Sometime between March and April his wife, Rebecca, not yet forty years old, died. Cole himself was planning on leaving for England, taking care before he left to inventory his assets and make out a will, just in case. He died by September 1663, leaving behind seven children, five of his own and two by his wife's previous marriage. The oldest of his own children was only ten at the time Cole died in his mid thirties. He had accumulated an estate that would allow his children a start in life better than that of the indentured servants whom he had hired, but his eldest son died at the age of forty-one, worth less than half of what his father had left him. His second son was bound out an apprentice and died at the age of thirty-three, leaving behind no record of landholdings. His youngest son did the best of all. Edward Cole, planter and merchant, lived to be around sixty years old and was given the title of Mr., which denoted respect and status. At his death in 1717 he owned 575 acres and had personal property, including seven slaves, worth more than three times what his father had owned. He had changed with the times, diversifying his occupations to include both farming and wholesaling—he was the representative of a London firm at the time of his death. He also had made the leap from indentured white labor, which was cheaper but also only good for a contracted number of years, to slave labor, which lasted for not only the lives of the slaves but also of any children a slave woman might have. Francis Knott, the stepson, did not receive the same opportunities as Robert Cole's natural children. He inherited land rights but no land. He lived to be fifty-six, married, and had children. He died with a long-term lease for one hundred acres and a personal estate less than 30 percent that of his stepfather.

Source:

Lois Green Carr, Russell R. Menard, and Lorena S. Walsh, *Robert Cole's World: Agriculture and Society in Early Maryland* (Chapel Hill: University of North Carolina Press, 1991).

FATHER EUSEBIO KINO

1644-1711
SOUTHWEST MISSIONARY

Education. Father Eusebio Francisco Kino was born in the Valley of Nonsburg in the Austrian province of Tyrol, but he spent most of his adult life living in the borderlands claimed by a Spanish king. Kino was well educated. At a time when many could not read or write he studied at the universities of Ingolstadt and Freiburg, where he showed an aptitude for mathematics. Although offered a professorship in mathematics at the University of Ingolstadt, Kino had already made his decision about his life. In 1665 he joined the Jesuits in order to become a missionary, as did one of his relatives. He hoped to go to China but was sent to Mexico instead, although he stayed there only a short time.

California. Spain claimed present-day California but had been unable to do much in the way of securing this land. The conquest of the Philippines in the 1560s had paved the way for a Pacific Ocean trade between Mexico and Manila. The ocean route to the Philippines skirted the California coast because of the currents, and therefore Spain looked for a harbor there as a way of making the voyage shorter and thus healthier. Both English and Dutch pirates also sailed this coast, hoping to pick off heavily laden Spanish ships, so a safe harbor would be welcome. California itself offered a pearl fishery for the Crown to grant to private patentees to exploit. Unfortunately, the Spaniards had alienated the Indian tribes living there. By 1678 there were as yet no permanent Spanish settlements in California. That year the Crown was willing to grant the rights to try again. The spiritual responsibilities for the enterprise fell to the Jesuits, and Father Kino became one of two missionaries to California. His mathematical abilities also made him a royal astronomer, surveyor, and mapmaker. The expedition sailed in 1683 to what is now part of Baja California in Mexico. For the next two years Kino and various others explored the region, making frequent reports. In 1685 the whole enterprise was dropped. Father Kino was sent to the area known as Pimería Alta, now northern Sonoma, Mexico, and southern Arizona.

Pimería Alta. Father Kino's work in Pimería Alta began in March 1687 and was wholly concerned with living and traveling among the mainly Yuma and Pima Indians. There were no European settlers initially. He explored, built a mission, and attended to his religious duties. Moving beyond the last mission at the town of Cucurpe, he founded the mission of Nuestra Señora de los Dolores. Here he would stay for almost twenty-five years, and from this outpost he established new missions, pushing north to the Gila and Colorado Rivers. In April 1700 he founded the first mission within the present state of Arizona, San Xavier del Bac, now Tucson. Kino did more than just direct the establishing of missions. His explorations confirmed that California was a peninsula and not an island. It could therefore be reached and explored by land, and this is what Father Kino did. Kino traveled thousands of miles on horseback, sometimes with Europeans and other times with Native Americans. In 1695 he rode to Mexico City, taking fifty-three days to make the fifteen-hundred-mile journey.

Ranching. Father Kino was more than just a priest, an explorer, and a cartographer. He was also responsible for establishing ranching as a viable economic enterprise in Pimería Alta. The older missions had supplied him with a few animals, but Kino went on to establish cattle ranches in at least six river valleys in northern Mexico. The missions bred cattle, horses, mules, and sheep. Indeed, one historian credits him with establishing the cattle industry in at least twenty places where it still exists, including Tucson. These animals belonged to the church, not Father Kino, and not only fed Indians but also enabled the missions to be self-sufficient. This last factor was most important because it meant that they could survive regardless of what was happening politically and economically elsewhere in the Spanish domains. It also allowed Father Kino to develop new missions without relying on help from anybody else. For example, when creating San Xavier del Bac he was able to send along seven hundred animals—a large herd for the time.

Simplicity. Father Kino seems to have exemplified the simplicity and faith that marked the most devout of those in holy orders. He took his vows of poverty seriously and owned little. He ate and slept sparingly. He was unafraid to die, secure in his belief in the promise of salvation. His companion for the last eight years of his life, Father Luis Velarde, wrote of his death, which occurred on a visit to his mission at Santa Magdalena where he had gone to dedicate a chapel:

> He died as he had lived, with extreme humility and poverty. In token of this, during his last illness he did not undress. His deathbed, as his bed had always been, consisted of two calfskins for a mattress, two blankets such as the Indians use for covers, and a pack-saddle for a pillow.

He was sixty-seven years old.

Source:
Herbert Eugene Bolton, *Kino's Historical Memoir of Pimería Alta*, volume 1 (Cleveland, Ohio: Arthur H. Clark, 1919).

FRANCISCO MENÉNDEZ

DATES UNKNOWN
LEADER OF GRACIA REAL DE SANTA TERESA DE MOSE

Renegade. Francisco Menéndez is the Spanish name for the man who was the military and political head of the free black town of Gracia Real de Santa Teresa de Mose. Nothing is known of Menéndez's early life. He might have been born in Africa or as a slave in the Carolinas or the West Indies. As an adult he lived as a slave in South Carolina but at some point made his way to the Indians and fought against his former masters in the Yamasee Indian War of 1715. What became of Menéndez between 1715 and 1724 remains hidden, but in 1724, helped by the Yamasee, he and nine others arrived in Saint Augustine, Florida, then owned by Spain. They claimed to know of the Spanish king's promise of 1693 that if they converted to Catholicism they would be freed.

Saint Augustine. Menéndez's initial status in Saint Augustine must have been unclear, but in 1729 Gov. Antonio de Benavides sold him and the nine other escaped slaves at public auction. Some remained in Saint Augustine; others were taken to Havana. Slavery in the borderlands, like Florida, was not as harsh or as rigid as it was in the plantation colonies. Governor Benavides recognized Menéndez's abilities and appointed him commander of a slave militia in 1726. In 1728 these slaves helped defend Saint Augustine against the English. Appeals for freedom were finally granted in 1738 by the new governor, Manuel de Montiano.

Mose. Governor Montiano made other changes as well and in 1738 established a new town for the former English slaves known as Gracia Real de Santa Teresa de Mose, two miles north of Saint Augustine. Menéndez was the town's leader, a task he was well suited for since it was in reality a military outpost, poised to stall or repel an attack from the English. Officially designated captain, Menéndez exercised considerable authority and autonomy over Mose. He would be its militia captain for forty years.

War. The struggle with England touched off by the War of Jenkins' Ear (1739) found Captain Menéndez on the front lines. The governor even made a point of commending him to the king, perhaps as a means of paving the way for a petition Menéndez would send asking for rewards for services rendered. Menéndez apparently wrote this and a second petition, in Spanish, by himself. Unfortunately, the Spanish authorities ignored him.

Slavery Again. The evacuation of Mose brought Menéndez back to Saint Augustine where he became involved in privateering. This legalized piracy, practiced during wartime by all nations, brought rewards when things went well but disaster when they did not. In 1741 the ship Menéndez was aboard was captured by the English, who recognized him as the leader of a "Comp'y of Indians, Molattos, and Negroes" at Mose. He was given two hundred lashes and a dousing of salt water to make the wounds even more painful. He and several others were then taken to the Bahamas where the Admiralty Court declared them slaves and ordered them sold. For many people that would have been the end of the story, but Menéndez was more resourceful than most. What happened to free him is unknown, but by 1752 he was back in Mose.

Exile in Cuba. In 1763, when the Spanish evacuated Florida, Menéndez, along with the others from Mose, sailed to Cuba. He presumably died in Havana, certainly a man whose life had taken him from slavery to freedom more than once and whose abilities must indeed have been exceptional to propel him, against many odds, into positions of leadership and responsibility.

Source:
Jane Lander, "Gracia Real de Santa Teresa de Mose: A Free Black Town in Spanish Colonial Florida," *American Historical Review*, 95 (1990): 9–30.

WILLIAM PENN

1644–1718
FOUNDER OF PENNSYLVANIA

Background. William Penn was born to the ranks of privilege, connection, and wealth. His father, Sir William Penn, was a friend of the Stuart kings, an admiral in the Royal Navy, and a large landowner in Ireland. Penn's mother was Margaret Jasper Vanderschuren, daughter of a merchant living in Ireland and widow of a Dutch merchant. She and her family fled Ireland for London in 1641 when the Catholic Irish began war against immigrant Protestants. There in

1643 she met and married William Penn Sr. Their elder son and major heir, William, was born in 1644, a time of troubles. The English Civil War was raging, and the king was a prisoner in Scotland. There was religious turmoil as well, and some, such as George Fox, the founder of the Society of Friends, were preaching throughout England. The elder Penn himself was arrested on suspicion of treason but shortly thereafter released. In 1654 the admiral headed for the West Indies in what was to be a strike against Spanish Hispaniola. This grand expedition ended in failure, and on his return Penn Sr. was imprisoned again. Upon his release Penn Sr. decided that England was not safe, and in 1656 he moved the family to Ireland. The end of the civil war and the restoration of the Stuart kings in 1660 were good for the Penn family since the admiral was friends with both Charles II and his brother and heir, James. That same year William was sent to study at Christ Church, Oxford.

Religious Doubts. William Penn Jr. had his first religious experience at the age of ten or eleven. When he was thirteen Thomas Loe, an itinerant Quaker, visited Ireland and was invited to the Penn home. It was Penn's first brush with Quakerism, although it did not lead then to his conversion. At Oxford, Penn realized his need for a more personal faith than the Church of England provided him. In the spring of 1662 he was expelled for absenting himself from compulsory chapel. Meanwhile, laws were passed against the Quakers. Sir William's answer to the increasingly religious bent of his son was to steep him in worldly society, so young Penn was sent off to France, the center of polite culture. But William left Paris and the royal court at Fontainebleau and enrolled in the Protestant Academy of Saumur where he stayed for a year and a half.

The Quaker. In 1666 Penn Jr. sailed for Ireland to handle the family estates. The next year he again encountered the Quaker minister Loe and this time underwent an intense religious awakening. He began attending Quaker meetings and was briefly imprisoned in Cork because of them. He also wrote his first public statement against religious intolerance, protesting the injustice of such treatment for the sake of conscience. His father called him back to England where it was reported, "Mr. Will Pen, who is lately come over from Ireland, is a Quaker again, or some very melancholy thing; that he cares for no company, nor comes into any." But Penn did care for Quaker company and at age twenty-four became a minister. He preached, was arrested and jailed, and published various tracts about his beliefs, the most famous being *No Cross No Crown* (1669). In 1670 Adm. William Penn died, leaving young William not only a tidy fortune but also a considerable debt from the Crown. After yet another stint in jail he left to spread the word in Germany and Holland. He would later urge these people to settle in Pennsylvania.

The Proprietor. In 1680 Penn reminded Charles II of the account owed him, but rather than money Penn asked for a tract of land north of Maryland. Knowing persecution firsthand, he hoped to establish a refuge for Quakers where other religious and ethnic minorities would also be welcome. The next year Penn was named proprietor of Pennsylvania (literally Penn's Woods). In 1682 he arrived in America, stayed two years, but then returned to England to help fellow Quakers fight a renewed round of persecution and to settle the southern boundary of his colony, which was also claimed by Lord Baltimore. The overthrow of James II in 1688 and the installation of William and Mary meant trouble for Penn, who now no longer had a personal relationship with the Crown. His absence from Pennsylvania also fostered discontent, and his authority slipped there as well. In 1692 the Crown stripped Penn of his proprietorship, but it was restored two years later. Penn was back in Pennsylvania by 1697 and faced growing opposition from those who wanted the Crown to take over the colony. Again he stayed for two years, during which he presided over legal reforms that gave some power to an elected assembly, and signed one of the few treaties with the Native Americans that brought a prolonged peace. But affairs in England again called him home; Penn returned there in December 1701, never again to see his colony.

Last Years. Penn's last years were spent fighting those in America who wished to end the proprietary and dealing with debts at home that threatened to ruin him. The colony was a success, yet it had not made much money for Penn. Rents and land purchases went unpaid. In 1707 Penn chose debtor's prison rather than pay what were probably justifiable debts. Five years later he began negotiating with the Crown for the sale of Pennsylvania, but during these arrangements he suffered a series of strokes that disabled him. He lingered on until 1718, and his colony remained in family hands until the American Revolution.

Sources:

The Diary of Samuel Pepys, edited by Robert Latham and William Matthews, 11 volumes (Berkeley: University of California Press, 1970–1983).

Richard S. Dunn and Mary Maples Dunn, eds., *The World of William Penn* (Philadelphia: University of Pennsylvania Press, 1986);

Catherine Owens Peare, *William Penn: A Biography* (Philadelphia: Lippincott, 1957).

CAPT. JOHN SMITH

1580-1631

LEADER OF JAMESTOWN COLONY

Military Calling. John Smith was born in Lincolnshire, England, to George and Alice Rickards Smith. His father was a farmer who, while not wealthy, lived comfortably, owning one small farm and leasing another from Peregrine Bertie, Lord Willoughby. Smith, unlike a majority of English children, attended grammar school where he learned to read and write. He also attracted the attention of Lord Willoughby, whose patronage helped him leave the farms of Lincolnshire. At the age of fifteen he was apprenticed to a merchant in the seaport of King's Lynn where Smith learned what he did not want to do with his life. The death of his father and remarriage of his mother left him with a small inheritance. The first thing he did was end his apprenticeship, thus freeing him to follow a military career.

Service. In late 1596 or early 1597 John Smith left England for the Netherlands as a soldier in a company under the command of an in-law of the Willoughbys. This venture was short-lived as peace broke out, and by 1599 Smith was out of the army and back in England. There he began a program of self-education that included not only reading about the art of war from Niccolò Machiavelli and Marcus Aurelius but also training himself in hunting and horsemanship. In this latter he had the teaching of the Italian Theodore Paleologue, riding master to the earl of Lincoln and a descendant of Constantine XI, the last Greek emperor of the Eastern Roman Empire. From Paleologue he not only learned some Italian but also heard tales about the Ottoman Turks. None of these opportunities would have been possible for a man of Smith's station in life without the help of Lord Willoughby. They also prepared him in ways that few of his time were prepared for the unusual challenges of colonization.

Early Travels. Smith was not only educated but also well traveled. By 1699 he had been to the Netherlands, France, and Scotland. In 1600 Smith again left England looking for adventure and wealth. He turned toward Italy and then sailed throughout the Mediterranean to North Africa and the Near East. His real destination was the Holy Roman Empire, and his purpose was to fight the Ottoman Turks. Eventually he joined the count of Modrusch, then forming a regiment in Vienna.

Captaincy. Smith's first encounter with the Ottoman Turks occurred during a relief expedition to a fortified town on the border of western Hungary. Smith was pivotal in the Christian victory because he had remembered secret signals and diversionary tactics from his military reading. As a reward he received a captaincy and the command of 250 horsemen. While the Europeans were laying siege to one of the Turkish strongholds in Transylvania, one of the Turks challenged them to a duel to the death on horseback. The Europeans drew straws to select their champion and Smith won. He decapitated this Turk and two others. In time the siege was completed, and the Europeans were successful. Prince Zsigmond of Transylvania reviewed the victory and granted to Smith the right of a coat of arms with three Turk heads and named him "a gentleman." Smith's next adventure ended less happily for him. At the battle before the Red Tower Pass in Romania the Europeans were soundly defeated, and Smith, injured but alive, was captured and sold into slavery. He lived first in Istanbul, Turkey, and then Russia as both a galley and agricultural slave. In time he killed his master, escaped, and journeyed west until he eventually found Zsigmond. With a present of gold ducats from his Transylvanian pa-

tron, Smith toured Germany, France, and Spain. He reached Gibraltar, from which he sailed to Tangier and Morocco. After narrowly escaping from French pirates Smith returned home.

Virginia. Smith arrived back in England around 1605. His connections with the Willoughby clan brought him into contact with Bartholomew Gosnold, one of the visionaries who dreamed of a colony in the New World. Smith became part of this venture and was named one of seven members of its council in America. He was among those on the first voyage in 1607. The crossing was difficult, and he crossed swords with one of his social superiors who then had Smith arrested onboard and kept a prisoner for the majority of the trip. Once in Virginia, Smith was still under suspicion, but his military experiences made him too valuable not to use. During his stay in Virginia he explored the rivers and traded with the Indians, made maps, and kept detailed notes that he later published. Modern historians know much about early Jamestown because of his writings. He was also one of the first Englishmen to see Native Americans with some clarity as human beings trying to survive. His capture in 1607 and meeting with Powhatan, head of a confederacy of local Indians, must be read as part of a larger religious and communal ceremony, but Smith was in no position to know what was really going on. His death during this ritual appears to have been prevented by Powhatan's daughter, the eleven-year-old Pocahontas. He survived not only the Indians but also his fellow English settlers and the diseases that ravished the colony. By September 1608 he was the only councilor still in Virginia, so he became president by default. But while Smith was able to keep an underprovisioned colony together, he did so at the expense of his own popularity. He coerced, rather than persuaded, the other colonists, causing much resentment and bitterness. In 1609 new orders arrived from England along with several of his old enemies. Smith might have been able to weather these changes in Virginia, but he had been severely wounded when a stray spark from a fire lit his gunpowder bag as he lay napping. The explosion and fire burned him so badly there was a question of his survival. Just before October the little fleet that had brought news of a new government to Virginia sailed back to England with one gravely injured and dispirited Smith.

Worlds Lost. Smith survived and made his reports to the Virginia Company in London, but he would never see Virginia again. In 1614 he sailed to New England, named it that, and mapped part of the coastline. Two further excursions to America failed, although Smith acquired the title of admiral of New England. What Smith hoped to do was establish a colony in New England, and he wanted to go to Plymouth with the Mayflower settlers, but none of this worked out. Smith never went back to America. In 1624, just about the time that the Virginia Company went bankrupt and James I took over Virginia as a royal colony, Smith published his greatest, although not his first, work, *The Generall Historie*, an attempt to recount English colonization up to that point. Two years later he wrote a general handbook for sailors, followed a year later by a more comprehensive volume. A narrative of his life and travels appeared in 1630. In 1631 his last work appeared, discussing the problems of Virginia and New England and giving advice on how a colony should be run. That same year Smith, staying in the home of one of his wealthy patrons, died; he was fifty-one. The passion of his adult life was America. As he himself wrote of Virginia and New England:

> By that acquaintance I have with them, I may call them my children; for they have been my wife, my hawks, my hounds, my cards, my dice, and in total my best content, as indifferent to my heart as my left hand to my right: and notwithstanding all those miracles of disaster [which] have crossed both them and me, yet were there not one Englishman remaining (as God be thanked there is some thousands) I would yet begin again with as small means as I did at first.

Source:

Philip L. Barbour, *The Three Worlds of Captain John Smith* (Boston: Houghton Mifflin, 1964).

MARIA VAN CORTLANDT VAN RENSSELAER

1645-1689

OVERSEER OF RENSSELAERSWYCK

Dutch Expectations. Women of the Netherlands were considered the freest in Europe. In part, this freedom was the unintended consequence of their being educated and trained to manage the accounts of their households in good times, and the businesses of their husbands if they died. Dutch women in the New World were also expected to know how to keep a family's wealth together so that when the children were old enough to take over there would be something there for them. Maria van Cortlandt van Rensselaer lived her life in accordance with these expectations and was able to secure for her children one of the largest estates in colonial New York.

Rensselaerswyck. In 1629 the Dutch West India Company realized that in order to attract settlers it would need the private initiative of those wealthy enough to provide funding. Among those who came forward was one of the directors of the company, Kiliaen van Rensselaer. The large land grant the company awarded him formed the basis of Rensselaerswyck, located around what is now Albany, New York, up the Hudson River some 160 miles from New York City. Kiliaen never visited America, but the care of Rensselaerswyck was entrusted to various sons who made the long journey over to become resident managers and, most important, to guard title to the land from other speculators. They lived at the fur-trading outpost of Fort Orange. In 1654 Jeremias van Rensselaer, younger son of Kiliaen by a second marriage, settled in America, and in 1662 he married Maria

van Cortlandt. They remained at Rensselaerswyck the rest of their lives.

Marriage. Maria van Cortlandt was born in America in 1645, the daughter of the wealthy New Amsterdam (later New York City) merchant Oloff Stevensen van Cortlandt and Anna Loockermans. She was thought to be too young to marry. As her husband explained in a defensive letter to his mother, "You may think perhaps that she is still a little young and therefore not well able to take care of a household. She is only entering her eighteenth year, but nevertheless we get along together very well in the household." Jeremias had actually been patient: "I had been thinking of her already a year or two before, when now and then I did an errand at the Manhatans." The young couple then left for Albany where they lived in the patroon's house, the best dwelling in Rensselaerswyck, consisting of two cellars, two rooms, and an attic.

Family. The Dutch placed a high premium on family and looked forward to the birth of children. In May 1663 Jeremias wrote to his brother in Holland, "You may perhaps be longing to hear whether we have any baby yet. My answer is no, but that my wife is pregnant and that, please God, she will be in childbed in two or three months at the longest." Maria gave birth to Kiliaen, named for his grandfather, on 24 August; he was baptized two days later. Both godfathers and godmothers were close family, but none of the four lived in Albany so surrogates stood in for them. Life in America often meant separation from loved ones rather than easy access to them. The birth of her son also marked the beginning of illness, lameness, weakness, and pain that Maria van Rensselaer lived with for the rest of her life. For a time one leg was paralyzed, although by the spring she could walk with a crutch. This condition restricted her mobility and kept her from family and friends, as her father was informed in March 1664, "We would have gone to see you by this yacht, but owing to the little improvement in my wife's walking, this could not take place." It was not until April 1664, almost nine months after Kiliaen's birth, that she was "churched," the ceremony of the first going to church after a birth which symbolized a woman's return to the community. Maria's health did not keep the couple from having more children. When Jeremias died in 1674 he left behind five children, the eldest eleven years old, and a pregnant wife.

Businesswoman. The death of Jeremias van Rensselaer left his wife not only a large family but also significant business responsibilities. In 1664 the English had conquered the province from the Dutch, which meant learning a new language and new laws and political customs. The van Rensselaers were faced with the task of procuring a land grant that would guarantee the family possession of the almost twenty-four square miles that was Rensselaerswyck. Others, including heirs of old Kiliaen, the original patroon, also had their eye on this land. Claims were not settled until 1685. Unlike many widows with young children, Maria van Rensselaer did not remarry so did not have the help of a resident male. Instead she relied upon first her father and then her brother, Stephen van Cortlandt, when she could, but they lived in New York City, not Albany. It was up to her to negotiate the day-to-day concerns of the holding by leasing lands to tenants; buying and selling land, wheat, and cattle; and keeping up the houses, barns, mills, and fences. It was her responsibility to entertain distinguished visitors, such as the governor, "to keep up the dignity of the colony." She was also responsible for the future of her children. Kiliaen was apprenticed to a New York silversmith, and two other children were sent to New York City to live with her parents. Four of her children married well, two to cousins. Through marriages and the childlessness of other van Rensselaer heirs her son Kiliaen eventually became the sole owner of Rensselaerswyck. She lived to see this, dying in 1689 at the age of forty-three.

Sources:

The Correspondence of Jeremias Van Rensselaer, 1651–1674, edited by A. J. F. Van Laer (Albany: University of the State of New York, 1932);

The Correspondence of Maria Van Rensselaer, 1669–1689, edited by Van Laer (Albany: University of the State of New York, 1935);

Robert G. Wheeler, "The House of Jeremias Van Rensselaer, 1658–1666," New-York Historical Society, *Quarterly*, 45 (1961): 75–88.

JOHN WINTHROP

1588-1649
GOVERNOR OF MASSACHUSETTS BAY

Youth. John Winthrop was born to privilege as a member of the English gentry. His grandfather had benefited from Henry VIII's confiscation of Roman Catholic monasteries by buying Bury Saint Edmunds in Groton, Suffolk. John's father, Adam Winthrop, was also a shrewd businessman, and in addition to his Groton estate he rented and bought lands close by and grew cash crops that he sold to nearby London. He was trained in the law although he did not have a legal practice; presumably he dispensed justice on his estate. Adam's second wife, John's mother, was Anne Browne, the daughter of a wealthy merchant. John was Adam's only son, so he knew that the manor at Groton would one day be his. His education befitted his station. His first years were spent under the tutelage of a local minister, but he was being groomed for Cambridge University, where his father had gone and was auditor for Trinity and Saint John's Colleges. In 1603, at the age of fifteen, John entered college. He left within two years without a degree, but such was expected of a young gentleman such as himself. He also spent some time at Gray's Inn, one of the famed Inns of Court where the elite studied law. Again he left without a degree. College had apparently been an unpleasant experience, "For being there neglected, and despised, I went up and down mourning with myself."

Country Squire. Winthrop returned to Groton Manor at the age of seventeen and quickly made the arranged and advantageous marriage expected of a man of his estate. His wife was Mary Forth of Great Stambridge, Essex. He became a Puritan, and at the age of eighteen he was a father. Before his wife died in 1615 they had six children. He married Thomasine Clopton within six months of Mary's death, but she lived only another year. Winthrop married for a third time in 1618 when he was thirty years old. His new wife, with whom he lived for almost thirty years, was Margaret Tyndal, daughter of Sir John Tyndal of Much Malstead, Essex. Margaret shared his religious convictions. The couple lived first at Groton and then on the lands in Essex that she had brought him as a dowry. At both places Winthrop learned through hands-on practice how to manage large estates. By 1617 he was a justice of the peace and began a more serious study of the law since as lord of Groton Manor he would hold manorial court for his tenants. Winthrop was thus on his way to living his life as a pious but nonetheless provincial country squire when larger events brought Puritanism to the center of his life and took him far from Groton.

Difficult Times. Both religiously and economically the England of the 1620s was heading for trouble. Since Henry VIII's break with Rome, Protestants in England had wanted further reforms in the church. Queen Elizabeth had followed in her father's footsteps. James I, Elizabeth's successor, lacked her strength and political skills. He disliked Puritans, seeing them as a threat to the church and to the Crown. Puritans predicted the ruin of England. Economic problems seemed to bear out their dire warnings as textiles, England's major industry, suffered a depression that rippled through the entire economy. Suffolk, where Groton Manor lay, was hit especially hard, and Winthrop saw his own finances decline. To make matters worse his family was growing. Four of his six children from his first marriage had survived, and the oldest, John Jr., came of age in 1627. Winthrop already had three sons from his third marriage, and more children would come. In 1627 his connections rewarded him with an appointment as attorney in His Majesty's Court of Wards and Liveries—the board that controlled the estates of orphaned children until they came of legal age. This job took him away from his wife and family and also let him see governmental corruption firsthand. In 1625 Charles I replaced his father, James I. Charles was not only more rigid and less tolerant of both Puritans and Parliament but also married to a Roman Catholic. Charles accepted a new direction for the Church of England that promoted good works as a means of salvation. Puritans were horrified since they believed that human beings could not affect their future and God had predestined who was saved and who was damned. It seemed to them as though England were headed straight down the path to ruin. Puritans began to look for a place where a saving remnant might keep faith with both God and human beings. They looked toward America.

New England. Winthrop was not among the earliest promoters of the Massachusetts Bay Company, but once it was clear that the charter did not have to remain in England and that any colony the company founded would be self-governing, he joined and quickly became one of its leaders. In August 1629 Winthrop pledged to move his whole family to Massachusetts. In October he was chosen governor of the company and took charge of organizing the fleet that would sail. To help underwrite it he sold Groton Manor. Leaving most of his family behind to come in 1631, he sailed with the first settlers aboard the *Arbella* and while on ship delivered one of the most famous sermons in American history, "A Modell of Christian Charity," in which he likened their new enterprise to "a Citty upon a Hill," with the eyes of the world upon them. For Winthrop it was a holy errand, and this sense of providential responsibility would allow him to lead others through hard times. It would also make him a fanatic who lost sight of human needs and tolerated few other opinions.

Colonial Leadership. Winthrop arrived in America as governor of the new colony, and he remained so for four years. The first order of business was how to organize the colony religiously. The decision that each congregation establish itself and call its own minister (congregationalism) set the stage for what would become an unwanted religious diversity. Winthrop also established the colony's government, keeping power in his own hands with the aid of a few assistants. He gave little authority to those men called freemen who sat as a general assembly. In 1634 the freemen challenged Winthrop to show them the company's charter and saw that they had been granted more power than he had allowed them. They formed a representative assembly, elected men from each town, and voted Winthrop out of office. During the next three years Massachusetts was racked by religious controversy. In 1637 the colony turned to Winthrop and elected him governor again. Three years later he was replaced only to be elected again in 1642, demoted to deputy-governor in 1644–1645, and elected governor again from 1646 to his death at age sixtyone. His wife Margaret had died in 1647, and he quickly married a fourth time. Within a year Martha Coytmore Winthrop had borne him a son, his sixteenth child. John Winthrop died in 1649, the same year that Charles I was beheaded. His colony had survived, but he was a member of an older generation, schooled in the religious persecution of pre–Civil War England. Massachusetts would outgrow the narrow authoritarianism that Winthrop brought to America and that had been useful in the precarious first years of its founding.

Sources:

Richard S. Dunn, *Puritans and Yankees: The Winthrop Dynasty of New England 1630–1717* (Princeton, N.J.: Princeton University Press, 1962);

Edmund S. Morgan, *The Puritan Dilemma: The Story of John Winthrop* (Boston: Little, Brown, 1958).

PUBLICATIONS

A Brief account of the province of East New Jarsey in America (Edinburgh: Printed by J. Reid, 1683)—an early piece of promotional literature;

Daniel Coxe, *A description of the English province of Carolana* (London: Printed for Edward Symon, 1727)—a travel account of the Mississippi Valley;

Pierre Francois Xavier de Charlevoix, *Histoire et description generale de la Nouvelle France, avec le journal historique d'un voyage fait par ordre du roi dan l'Amerique septentrionnale* (Paris: Rolin, 1744)—a description of New France including discussions of Native Americans and a history of an unsuccessful Huguenot colony in Florida in the sixteenth century;

Louis Hennepin, *A new discovery of a vast country in America extending above four thousand miles, between New France and New Mexico. With a description of the Great Lakes, cataracts, rivers, plants, and animals, also, the manners,* *customs, and languages, of the several native Indians, and the advantage of commerce with those different nations* (London: Printed for M. Bentley, J. Tonson, H. Bonwick, T. Goodwin, and S. Manship, 1698)—translated work which describes the geography and native peoples of the Great Lakes and Mississippi River;

Benjamin Martyn, *Reasons for establishing the colony of Georgia, with regard to the trade of Great Britain, the increase of our people, and the employment and support it will afford to great numbers of our own poor, as well as foreign persecuted Protestants* (London: Printed for W. Meadows, at the Angel in Cornhill, 1733)—describes the area and enumerates several reasons for its settlement;

Nathaniel Morton, *New-Englands memoriall, or, A brief relation of the most memorable and remarkable passages of the providence of God manifested to the planters of New-England in America: with special reference to the first colony thereof, called New-Plimouth* (Cambridge, Mass.: Printed by S.G. and M.J. for John Vsher of Boston, 1669)—an early history of the Plymouth colony and biographies of some of its settlers;

William Penn, *Some account of the Province of Pennsilvania in America: lately granted under the great seal of England to William Penn &c. : together with priviledges and powers necessary to the well-governing thereof : made publick for the information of such as are, or may be disposed to transport themselves, or servants into those parts* (London: Printed and sold by Benjamin Clark, 1681)—a promotional account of Pennsylvania designed to lure settlers;

John Smith, *Advertisements for the unexperienced planters of New-England, or anywhere. Or, The path-way to experience to erect a plantation. With the yearely proceedings of this country in fishing and planting, since the yeare 1614. to the yeare 1630. and their present estate* (London: Printed by Iohn Havilland, 1631)—Smith's history of the colonies to the year 1630 with advice on how to start a successful settlement;

Smith, *The Generall Historie of Virginia, New-England, and the Summer Isles: with the names of the Adventurers, Planters, and Governours from their first beginning, in 1584, to this present 1624* (London: Michael Sparkes, 1624)—Smith's history of the Virginia Colony, Plymouth, and Bermuda;

Captain William Snelgrave, *A New Account of Some Parts of Guinea and the Slave-Trade* (London: Printed for James, John, and Paul Knapton, 1734);

Gabriel Thomas, *An historical and geographical account of the province and country of Pensilvania, and of the West-New-Jersey in America . . . with a map of both countries* (London Printed for and sold by A. Baldwin . . . , 1698)—promotional literature luring settlers to the Quaker colonies of Pennsylvania and what was then West New Jersey;

Andrew White, *A Relation of Maryland; together, with a map of the countrey, the conditions of plantation, His Majesties charter to the Lord Baltemore, translated into English.* (London, 1635)—an early description of Maryland and some of the Native American inhabitants;

Edward Winslow, *Good newes from New-England: or, A true relation of things very remarkable at the plantation of Plimouth in Nevv England. Shewing the wondrous providence and goodnes of God, in their preservation and continuance, being delivered from many apparant deaths and dangers. Together with a Relation of such religious, and civill Lawes and Customes, as are in practise amongst the Indians, adjoyning to them at this day. As also what commodities are there to be raysed for the maintenance of that and other Plantations in the said Country* (London: W. Bladen and J. Bellamie, 1624)—an early account of Plymouth along with a description of the Native Americans.

EDUCATION

by RONALD HOWARD

CONTENTS

Sidebars and tables are listed in italics.

1636

28 Oct.   Harvard College is founded in Boston by an act of the Massachusetts General Court. Officials allow £400 for the school's establishment and appoint the Reverend Henry Dunster as the first president.

1639

20 May   The town of Dorchester, Massachusetts, establishes the first school supported by community taxes.

1647

11 Nov.   The colony of Massachusetts Bay passes the first compulsory school law in America. The statute requires every community of at least fifty families to maintain free elementary schools; communities with more than one hundred households have to provide secondary education as well.

1655

- Illiteracy among women in Massachusetts Bay is about 50 percent; the rate in New Netherland is 60 percent and in Virginia is 75 percent.

1656

- Harvard College formally accepts the Copernican theory (the belief that the Sun and not the Earth is the center of the solar system).

1669

- The first Sunday school is opened in Plymouth, Massachusetts.

1674

- Increase Mather is appointed a fellow at Harvard College. During his distinguished career Mather promotes the study of science while maintaining the college's strong Congregationalist ties.

1675

- Cotton Mather, the twelve-year-old son of Increase Mather, becomes the youngest person ever admitted to Harvard College.

1680

- Thomas Brattle, a Boston mathematician, accomplishes a major scientific achievement by calculating the orbit of a comet.

1685

- Increase Mather becomes acting president of Harvard College. The next year he becomes rector, a position he will hold until 1701.

1689

- The William Penn Charter School is founded in Philadelphia. The first public school in America, it charges tuition, but only for those students who can afford it.

1692

- Increase Mather receives from Harvard College the first divinity degree conferred in the British North American colonies.

1693

8 Feb. A charter for the College of William and Mary in Williamsburg, Virginia, is signed. James Blair receives a grant to "furnish Virginia with a seminary of ministers, to educate the youth in piety, letters and good manners and to propagate Christianity among the Indians." The school opens the next year.

1701

16 Oct. Congregationalists dissatisfied with the growing liberalism of Harvard College establish the Collegiate School in Killingworth, Connecticut. The school awards its first degrees fifteen years later.

1710

- The Society for the Propagation of the Gospel opens Trinity School in New York City.

1721

- A Jesuit College is founded at Kaskaskia, in present-day Illinois; its library contains many volumes by leading French philosophers.

1723

- The first permanent Native American school is established at the College of William and Mary. The school, housed in Bafferton Hall, is maintained by funds from the famous English scientist Robert Boyle.

1727

- Harvard College endows the first chair in mathematics and natural philosophy, and the first incumbent, Isaac Greenwood, lectures on calculus.

1731

- Benjamin Franklin founds the first circulating library in the Western Hemisphere, the Library Company of Philadelphia.

1737

- John Winthrop IV replaces Isaac Greenwood as professor of mathematics and natural philosophy at Harvard College.

1743

- The American Philosophical Society is formed in Philadelphia "for the promotion of useful knowledge among the British planters in America." Thomas Hopkinson serves as president and Benjamin Franklin as secretary.

1745

- The Collegiate School of Killingworth, Connecticut, moves to New Haven and changes its name to Yale College.

1746

- John Winthrop IV gives the first laboratory demonstration of magnetism and electricity at Harvard College.

22 Oct.
- The College of New Jersey receives a charter, and the next year it opens in Elizabethtown. President Jonathan Dickinson teaches the first classes in his home. The school later moves to Princeton and changes its name to Princeton College.

1751

- Through the efforts of Benjamin Franklin, the Academy and Charitable School of Philadelphia is established; it later becomes the University of Pennsylvania.

1754

- King George II grants a charter for King's College in New York City; it later becomes Columbia University.

- Americans are the most literate people in the British Empire. Approximately 90 percent of adult white males and 40 percent of the females in New England can read and write. In the other British North American colonies the literacy rate among men varies from 35 percent to more than 50 percent.

OVERVIEW

Cultural Distinctions. Education was at the heart of European efforts to colonize America. Whether Spanish, Portuguese, French, Dutch, or English, colonists from the Old World found success only as they adapted familiar ways of life and their own expectations to the peoples, geography, and natural resources they found in this strange New World across the Atlantic Ocean. Driven by a mixture of motives, aptly captured in the phrase "God, Gold, and Glory," Europeans wanted to teach the Indians about Jesus, to exploit economically both the people and natural resources they discovered in America, and to advance the strategic interests of their respective nations. The later inclusion of large numbers of Africans, most of whom were imported as slaves, into this cultural cauldron significantly influenced the lives of Indians and Europeans as well as the Africans themselves. Despite their unequal status and their suspicion—if not outright hatred and fear of one another—Europeans, Indians, and Africans together forged an increasingly complex, many-layered civilization. The educational process—which included ideas, practices, and institutions—at once reflected and regulated the interaction of all three peoples and shaped in many ways the evolving societies in which they lived and labored.

Christian Perspective. Throughout the colonial American era Christian theism remained the dominant worldview of the European settlers. The fundamental purpose of education, both formal and informal, was to explain the ways of God to humankind and the duty of men and women to God; human salvation was the ultimate goal. Everything else, including scholarship and occupational training, was deemed secondary. "The end then of Learning," wrote John Milton in 1644, "is to repair the ruines of our first parents by regaining to know God aright, and out of that knowledge to love him, to imitate him, to be like him." In the fifteenth century elements of Renaissance humanism, especially as conveyed by Erasmus of Rotterdam and other Christian humanists who were inspired by the Greek and Roman classics, became incorporated into the mainstream of Western Christian thinking. In the early sixteenth century the Protestant Reformation broke the hegemony of the Catholic Church. Protestants rejected the conventional wisdom that the path of eternal salvation was only through the sacraments of the Holy Catholic Church. Instead reformers such as Martin Luther and John Calvin emphasized the priesthood of all believers, God's sovereignty, original sin and human depravity, and salvation through grace. Like Martin Luther himself, most Protestant reformers advocated literacy training so that the faithful might seek God's guidance for themselves from his Holy Word, in their own language. Competition between Protestants and Catholics over evangelizing the American Indians contributed considerably to the European colonization of the Americas.

The New Learning. During the Renaissance the humanistic revival of Greek and Roman knowledge laid the foundation for the emergence of modern science. Critical of the deductive method of reasoning, especially as advocated by Christian scholars of the Middle Ages such as Thomas Aquinas, European thinkers in the sixteenth and seventeenth centuries found they could improve upon the knowledge of the ancient world through inductive reasoning based upon empirical inquiry. Applying inductive methodology, scientists such as Copernicus, Johannes Kepler, and Galileo discredited the theory that the sun and stars revolved around the Earth (geocentric view) and advanced the proposition that the sun is the center of our solar system (heliocentric view). This scientific method, or "new learning," as the seventeenth-century English scientist Francis Bacon called it, prepared the way for Sir Isaac Newton's path-breaking *Philosophiae Naturalis Principia Mathematica* (1687), which identified and explained the law of gravity. "Man, as the minister and interpreter of nature," wrote Bacon in 1620, "does and understands as much as his observations on the order of nature . . . permit him, and neither knows nor is capable of more." The impact of the new learning on western thought proved nothing less than revolutionary.

The Enlightenment. Newton's discovery made scientific inquiry the catalyst for modifying the European worldview. If there were laws governing the physical universe, might not the principle of cause and effect also provide insight into human nature, human thought and behavior, and social interactions? Inspired by Newton, the great mathematician's good friend, John Locke, applied the scientific method to his own seminal work in human psychology, education, and politics. Locke's political thinking on natural law and natural rights put governmental authority squarely in the hands of the people. His ideas on human nature and psychology inspired fundamental change in child rearing and teaching generally. Along with Locke and Newton, other thinkers in various fields, such as René Descartes in philosophy and Adam Smith in economics, contributed to this Age of Enlightenment, whose consequences profoundly influenced educational thought in America as well as Europe.

Natural Religion. Native American religious beliefs, institutions, and practices were diverse and complex and defy easy characterization. Subsistence patterns, usually either hunting, agriculture, or a combination of the two, did much to shape religious expressions. So did the level of social and political integration of the particular nation or tribe. Despite its many and various manifestations the religious life of Indians did reflect certain common themes that make for interesting comparisons with European Christianity. Native Americans saw the material world of nature and the supernatural world of the spirit as constantly intersecting and interacting so that they became different expressions of the same reality. Some Indians possessed rather elaborate creation myths, even identifying a specific creator; others did not, or referred to the spiritual realm in vague and ambiguous terms. But mythologies connecting the natural world and the present with the spiritual world and the past abounded. Some tribes spoke of a pervasive spiritual presence, variously called *orenda* by the Iroquois, *manitou* by the Algonquians, and *wakan* by the Lakota. Virtually every plant, animal, rock, or object in the sky was thought to possess a spirit. Rituals were usually performed over animals slain in the hunt lest their spirits become angry and bring bad luck upon the hunters. Unlike Europeans, Indians saw themselves as a part of nature rather than having dominion over the natural world. Shamans, or priests, were called upon to perform various rituals to assure the harvest or the success of the hunt or to ward off evil spirits thought to bring disease and death. Many Indian tribes worried that the spirits of the dead would haunt the living, though a few, like the Pueblo tribes in the Southwest, saw the spirits of their departed friends and family as assisting the living. Religion in general upheld the communal standards and conformity among the various tribes and nations.

Catholicism. The Catholic Church played a major role in uniting the principalities that became Spain. King Ferdinand and Queen Isabella particularly looked to the church to supervise the removal or conversion of the Moors and Jews. In the Americas the Spanish Crown relied upon the Catholic Church to Christianize and civilize Native Americans. The clergy also tried with only limited success to protect the Indians from abusive treatment by the conquistadors, who used them as slaves and forced laborers. The church similarly intervened in later years on behalf of African slaves, whose status was also defined and protected by Spanish-Roman law. The church became the primary agency for propagating both Christianity and Spanish culture among the Indians and settlers alike. Its clergy ministered not only to the spiritual but also to the medical and educational needs of the people, whether Spanish, Indian, African, mestizo, or mulatto. Outside the family—and to a considerable degree within it as well—the church dominated formal education in Spanish America, including the Spanish borderlands in North America that were later incorporated into the United States.

Catholic Schooling. The Catholic Church founded and regulated not only primary and secondary schooling but also the ten major and fifteen minor institutions of higher learning in Spanish America. In Mexico City in 1536 the College of Santa Cruz, initially designed for Indian students, was the first institution of higher learning founded, followed by universities at Mexico City and Lima, which were chartered in 1551. Regular clergy such as the Jesuits and Franciscans led the missionary efforts among the Indians and settlers in the borderlands, but parish clergy who were not in the orders but answered directly to the local bishop also contributed considerably to the establishment of schools. In Brazil the Catholic Church was not nearly as well established as in Spanish America. However, it did organize primary and secondary schools there, though not a university during the colonial era. Much like Spanish America, in seventeenth-century New France the Catholic Church presided over an extensive system of schooling, including college and university training. In British America, Catholic priests, despite the threat to their lives should they be discovered, periodically ministered the sacraments and conducted schools among the settlers, particularly in Maryland and the larger British American port cities.

Spain's Rivals. North of Mexico, where the Spanish had explored and found little worth exploiting, the English, French, and Dutch began their colonies, thereby encouraging Spain to pay greater attention to its borderlands. Spain's rivals found no rich native civilizations to plunder, and the intermingling of male colonists and female Indians did not occur to the extent that a formidable mestizo population ever developed, as was the case throughout Spanish America and Brazil. As English, French, and Dutch colonists came to America, they adapted elements of their respective national cultures to the New World environment. Many factors shaped the societies that began to emerge after the English established Jamestown in 1607; the French founded Quebec in 1609; and the Dutch West India Company brought settlers to New Amsterdam on Manhattan Island and Fort Orange farther up the Hudson in 1624. Educational institutions were fundamental to the colonial civilizations that began to emerge.

The English Chesapeake. Throughout colonial America the family was generally the chief educational institution, where boys and girls usually began their instruction in both religion and literacy. However, in Virginia and Maryland family formation was inhibited throughout the seventeenth century because planters recruited primarily young white males as indentured servants to work their tobacco crops. Family stability was also weakened by the harsh disease environment of the Chesapeake, where one or the other parent was likely to succumb before their children were raised. Not until after 1700 did sex ratios among whites come into equilibrium enough so the population could increase naturally. Scattered farmsteads or plantations became the rule in the Chesapeake, where slave labor replaced white indentured servants in the eighteenth century. Aside from regularly legislating apprenticeship regulations that increasingly called for literacy as well as occupational training, the provincial government did little to advance education in the Chesapeake, a pattern that would become characteristic throughout Britain's southern colonies. Educational efforts depended upon individual families, or families cooperating, though Anglican vestrymen increasingly intervened in the care and education of poor and orphaned children. Among the emerging planter elite the consensus was that education should be restricted, with "every man according to his ability instructing his children," as Gov. William Berkeley of Virginia wrote in 1671. "But, I thank God," continued Berkeley, "that there are no free schools nor printing . . . for learning has brought disobedience, and heresy, and sects into the world, and printing has divulged them, and libels the best government. God keep us from both." Charity, or free, schools would come to the Chesapeake, and the wealthy employed some fine tutors, but as late as 1724 Virginia reportedly had only two grammar schools, and as late as 1763 the governor of Maryland lamented that there was "not even one good grammar school" in his province.

Puritan New England. The Separatist Puritans who settled Plymouth in 1620 prepared the way for the major migration of English Puritans to Massachusetts Bay beginning in 1629. Estimates vary, but perhaps as many as twenty thousand people migrated from England to New England between 1630 and 1640. Perhaps as many as 90 percent of them came in family groupings. Unlike the Chesapeake, New England colonists settled in townships, with families given a "townspot" for their home garden plot and outlying fields for farming. Village life was encouraged, as were cooperative efforts in working the land. If all New England immigrants were not Puritans, Puritan ideology nevertheless dominated much of the thinking about church and state, and both institutions worked in tandem to fulfill this "Errand into the Wilderness." Education was central to the Puritan plan of building a society based on biblical principles. John Winthrop's vision of a "City Upon a Hill" required that the rising generation be well prepared to continue what their fathers and mothers had begun. Through the cooperative endeavors of the family, the school, the congrega-

tion, and the community in general, Puritan youth were expected to learn proper behavior, acquire literacy skills, and receive occupational training. Of all the European settlers to America, the Puritans were the most explicit and deliberate in tying educational efforts to their larger goals.

New Netherland. According to the Dutch their province of New Netherland included all the lands from the Connecticut River in the Northeast to Delaware Bay in the Southeast. Beginning as hardly more than a series of trading posts in the Indian fur trade, the Dutch colony remained thinly populated because the general prosperity of the Netherlands discouraged people from immigrating to America. It numbered no more than ten thousand settlers when the English conquered it in 1664. Like the Dutch republic itself, New Netherland from the outset possessed a heterogeneous population composed of many nationalities and Christian confessions. Passing through the Dutch colony in 1644, Father Isaac Jogues reported, "there may be four or five hundred men of different sects and nations; the Director General told me that there were persons there of eighteen different languages." The company brought over Dutch Reformed clergymen, who were encouraged to minister to the Indians as well as the colonists. It was a frustrating assignment. Of the Indians, Domine Jonas Michaelius, the first Reformed minister in New Netherland, complained in 1628 that they were "entirely savage and wild, strangers to all decency, yea, uncivil and stupid as garden poles." The settlers, mostly made up of adventurous and rowdy young men, were not much better. As late as 1648 Domine Johannes Backerus characterized his congregation in New Amsterdam as "very ignorant of true religion, and very much given to drink." In the later 1640s, thanks to property and trading concessions made by the Dutch West India Company, increasing numbers of young married couples began arriving in New Netherland, often with children. This shift toward domesticity encouraged Domine Backerus, who thought the young could be taught "to resist a bad world." From 1647 to 1664 Director General Peter Stuyvesant struggled to reform New Netherland, urging parents, pedagogues, and preachers to cooperate in educating the young for successful living. Stuyvesant secured more preachers and teachers for the Dutch colony, but his efforts to impose Reformed orthodoxy upon the heterodox settlers failed as education remained primarily in the hands of the family.

New France. In Canada fur trading, fishing, and farming the Saint Lawrence Valley secured the survival of French settlers. As in Virginia and New Netherland, females were also scarce in Canada, where the prohibition against Protestant immigrants kept the colonial population sparse. After making Canada a royal colony in 1665, the French government recruited indentured male servants, who got their freedom and received modest grants of land after three years, and orphaned females, known as the "king's girls," who easily found husbands. The colonial population grew, but slowly. Around 1700 the sex ratio among French colonists reached equilibrium. Outside the home formal education in New France was in the hands of the Catholic Church and its clergy. Jesuit priests early on established an extensive ministry among the Huron Indians. The Jesuits, various other religious orders, and the parish clergy not only continued their ministry among the Indians but also established educational institutions among the settlers, including several reading and writing schools, several grammar schools, and a few colleges and seminaries. The fur traders, called coureurs de bois ("runners of the woods"), frequently intermarried with the Indians, further strengthening Franco-Indian relations, which gave force to the French claim of the Mississippi Valley (christened Louisiana by Sieur de La Salle in 1682). As French settlements were established down the Mississippi Valley and along the Gulf Coast, Catholic schools, though relatively few in number, accompanied them. In 1718 New Orleans became the capital of Louisiana, where plantation agriculture and African slavery were expanding after 1720. By 1732 Louisiana possessed somewhat less than one hundred Indian slaves, four thousand African slaves, and two thousand whites. But the total population of New France remained small, numbering only seventy thousand settlers in 1754, compared to 1.2 million in British North America.

Spanish Borderlands. The outlying Spanish province in North America, Florida, with its troops and civilian settlers concentrated at Saint Augustine, scarcely progressed beyond a strategic military outpost. However, English and French colonization efforts encouraged the Spanish to pay more attention to the borderlands, especially New Mexico and Texas. Spanish expansion into the Southwest progressed slowly but steadily. Priests, usually Franciscans though some Jesuits were also involved, would first establish a mission among or near Indian encampments; then a garrison or presidio would be established; and lastly Spanish colonizers would be given mining concessions or extensive lands for cattle and sheep ranching. The colonists, sometimes with ecclesiastical or governmental assistance, were expected to recruit settlers, usually from Mexico or Spain itself. Catholic missions generally served both Indians and colonists alike, playing a major role in the religious instruction and formal education of their youth. In New Mexico the non-Indian colonial population increased from 2,800 in 1680 to 5,200 in 1750, but the Pueblo population decreased to 13,500 due to their prolonged but ultimately unsuccessful revolt against the Spanish from 1680 to 1692 and continued attrition because of disease. Due to their preoccupation with Mexico, Spanish officials did not establish any permanent missions and garrisons in New Mexico until 1716. As late as 1742 there were only one thousand Spaniards and thirteen hundred Indian allies in the province. The older colony of Florida was increasingly threatened not only by the French in Louisi-

ana but also the English in Carolina after 1670 and Georgia in 1733. Its Spanish population remained sparse even as its Indian population declined, due in part to raiders from Carolina who captured and sold mission Indians into slavery.

Demographic and Economic Expansion. Unlike either the French or the Spanish, the British did not maintain a restrictive immigration policy toward their American colonies. Catholicism was illegal, but hardly rooted out, especially in Maryland. English officials also encouraged the immigration of Europeans to America, recognizing that colonial settlements meant commerce and protection against invaders, whether European or Indian. In New England the population burgeoned, due less to immigration after 1650 than to the natural increase from high birth rates and a much less malignant disease environment. Massachusetts Bay served as the cultural heart of the other New England colonies: Connecticut, New Hampshire, and Rhode Island. As in Massachusetts Bay, the Congregational Church was established in Connecticut and New Hampshire, as were Puritan educational practices and institutions. Rhode Island, castigated by the more-orthodox Puritans as the "latrina of New England," followed Roger Williams's views of separation of church and state, but its settlers nevertheless shared much in common with fellow New Englanders. An expanding economy stimulated by trade and commerce brought change to New England, including its educational ideas and institutions.

The Middle Colonies. Wedged between growing British populations in New England and on the Chesapeake, New Netherland fell to the British during the Second Anglo-Dutch War in 1664. However, the Dutch settlers were encouraged to remain in the lands the English christened New York and New Jersey. Their religious freedom, property rights, and customs of inheritance were all protected. Consequently, Dutch cultural influence remained pronounced in many communities along the Hudson Valley, on western Long Island, and in eastern New Jersey. Of course continued emigration from New England, the British Isles, and Europe further variegated the cultural landscape of New York and New Jersey. As for the lands west and south of New York and New Jersey that the Dutch had also once claimed for New Netherland, King Charles II granted those in 1681 to William Penn in payment of a debt owed the young Quaker's father. The English and Welsh Quakers who first settled in the Delaware Valley brought with them a distinctive religious culture. According to historian Barry Levy the Pennsylvania Quakers were primarily concerned with the proper raising and educating of their children in the faith. Quakers were followed by thousands of Germans and Scotch-Irish immigrants attracted by the liberal politics, religious toleration, and cheap land available in Pennsylvania and Delaware. The cultural mixture found in the Middle Colonies called forth an educational pattern that maintained ethnicity even as it made compromises with the dominant English culture.

The Carolinas and Georgia. The Carolinas, granted by Charles II in 1663 to eight friends in his Restoration government, developed differently in the northern and southern parts of the huge territory, dictated largely by geography. The first settlers in northern Carolina came from Virginia, which was shifting to slave labor and larger-scale tobacco plantations. They were small farmers, often growing some tobacco but also grains and raising hogs and cattle. The treacherous coastline and lack of a good harbor inhibited the growth and development of North Carolina, though it would become a major supplier of naval stores in the eighteenth century. By 1700 some ten thousand settlers (including one thousand slaves) lived in North Carolina, which was treated as a separate colony after 1712. South of Cape Fear the coastal plain widens considerably and is distinguished by an excellent harbor, around which the town of Charleston grew. Among the first settlers in this area were British immigrants from the West Indies (especially Barbados), whose slaves apparently introduced the cultivation of both rice and indigo, which produced the richest planter aristocracy on the British mainland. By 1700 there were six thousand settlers (including at least two thousand slaves) in South Carolina. Not founded until 1732 and initially intended as a military buffer against Spanish Florida and as a haven for Englishmen imprisoned for debt, Georgia would begin developing along the lines of South Carolina after 1750 when its population numbered five thousand (including two thousand slaves). By 1760, 60 percent of South Carolina's ninety-four thousand population were slaves. As in Virginia, the style of life, especially the economic pursuits of settlers in the Carolinas and Georgia, would influence their culture and the educational institutions that transmitted that culture across the generations.

New Trends. Although the American colonies were cultural provinces of Europe, they nevertheless were influenced by the cultural and intellectual movements that swept through England and the Continent. Enlightenment ideas, for example, made their way to the Spanish borderlands and the Illinois country of New France as well as the coastal cities of British North America. During the revivals of the Great Awakening, American evangelicals were plugged into a pietistic religious network that stretched across the Atlantic through England and into Germany. After 1700 American thinking, like that of Europe, began to change regarding child rearing and pedagogy. It became less authoritarian, more child-centered, and secular in orientation. The expansion of trade and the growing economic and social complexities of colonial societies increased the demands upon educational institutions throughout the Americas. The importance of a classical education was questioned by those who wanted a more utilitarian turn given to school and college curricula. This was especially so in British North America, where the humanistic and scientific dimensions of the European Enlightenment were being widely discussed by the general population. By 1754 more than 80 percent of adult males in British America were literate, whereas literacy rates were considerably lower in the Spanish borderlands and New France. Throughout the colonial era, cities were the hubs of intellectual activity. As the eighteenth century wore on, the cultural influences of the cities penetrated deeper and deeper into the hinterlands, thereby lessening the cultural gap that separated them.

TOPICS IN THE NEWS

AFRICAN AMERICANS

Black Population. The number of enslaved and free Africans in both New France and the Spanish borderlands was small compared to the slave population of British North America. African slaves accompanied the Spanish who explored and settled the borderlands. In 1763 the Spanish evacuated from Florida eighty-seven free blacks and over three hundred slaves. Black slavery in the Spanish borderlands of the Southwest has not yet been studied extensively. Some black servants and slaves accompanied Juan de Oñate and the colonists he brought into New Mexico in 1598. Their numbers there in the colonial era do not appear to have been great since most slaves were Indian captives, as was the case also in Texas and Arizona. According to a census in 1779 there were 20 slaves out of a population of almost 4,000. Similarly, African slaves trickled into New France, numbering about 1,000 in Canada and 450 in the Illinois Country by

1750. Louisiana had perhaps 4,000 slaves by 1732 and an even larger number by the time France ceded the territory to Spain in 1763. In contrast, of the 1.2 million colonists in British North America perhaps 250,000 were African slaves by 1750. They numbered almost 500,000 by 1776. Most were located in the colonial South, where South Carolina had a black majority by 1730, but slavery existed in the Middle Colonies and New England as well.

Catholic Colonies. The Catholic Church mightily influenced the nature of slavery and slave education in both the Spanish and French colonies. In the Spanish borderlands the church catechized and baptized black slaves as well as Indian slaves, thereby acknowledging that bondsmen possessed souls and were not mere chattel. Under church law slaves could marry, and their family life was to be respected. Masters were expected to provide minimum care for their slaves and not punish them unreasonably. In Spanish America slaves were often allowed to earn money to buy their freedom, and manumission was rather commonplace. Moreover, because of the lack of Spanish women, Spanish men married African women. These conditions are the reasons there were more free blacks than slaves in Spanish America by the end of the colonial era. Aside from some religious training, slaves were usually educated in a particular calling, whether household servant, cook, carpenter, or other artisan. Their training began in childhood and led naturally into its adult role. Literacy training for all but the elite was scarce in the Spanish borderlands, and one may assume that few blacks, slave or free, received much schooling. A similar situation prevailed in New France, where the Catholic Church was much concerned with both public and private behavior of the colonists. In 1685 Jean-Baptiste Colbert, Louis XIV's chief minister, issued a Code Noir (Black Code) for the French West Indies that also applied in Canada and Louisiana. Indians as well as blacks were enslaved in New France, but after 1700 black slaves became the norm. All slaves were to receive religious instruction and be converted to Catholicism. As in the Spanish borderlands, slave marriages were allowed and family life respected. However, frontier conditions, especially in Louisiana, kept the Code Noir from being rigorously enforced. Particularly in Louisiana, some black women who became concubines to white men won their freedom and that of their children born under the union. Such free black children might be schooled and otherwise well educated, but generally slave children seldom got any schooling and were much more apt to learn through formal or informal apprenticeship their life's work.

New Netherland. Under Roman-Dutch law slavery was a recognized status with certain basic protections for those enslaved. There were both slaves and free blacks in New Netherland, and slavery became quite common, but a slave code was never instituted. Consequently, the status of a slave was more flexible in New Netherland than in most places of colonial America. The Dutch West India Company, which made huge profits importing Africans slaves into Brazil and Spanish America, owned most of the slaves before 1650. The Dutch West India Company was known to manumit bondsmen who served it well. Other slaves were granted "half-freedom" by the company, thus allowing them to live in family groupings and to own property while still working for the company when called upon to do so. As the white population increased in the 1650s, so did the number of privately owned slaves. Whether slave or free, most black parents taught their children the trades they knew, including housekeeping, farming, and craft. Blacks joined the Dutch Reformed Church at New Amsterdam, some of whom may well have been slaves. Whether enslaved or free, Africans were given religious instruction by the domines, though the latter sometimes suspected that slaves wanted baptism for themselves and their children to mitigate the hardship of their bondage. One might assume that few blacks got any schooling in New Netherland, but Peter Stuyvesant hired a schoolmaster for the slave children on his farm, where free blacks' children probably also received instruction. Free black parents, on occasion, apprenticed their children to whites who promised to treat them well and bring them up in a trade. In 1664, when the English captured New Netherland, there were about five hundred slaves scattered about the colony, concentrated in and around New Amsterdam, where at least seventy-five free blacks lived and worked. Despite the hardships of slavery and racial prejudice, blacks in New Amsterdam shared a community of interest that ran from slavery to freedom in which families and neighbors assisted one another in educating the young as in so much else.

British Colonies. In the Chesapeake colonies slaves were early on taught the laborious tasks that attended growing tobacco, stripping it from the stalk, curing it, and preparing it for shipment to England. Young slaves were also introduced by their elders to household work in the master's home and to the many arts and crafts that became an integral part of life on the larger plantations. However, literacy training was generally deemed inappropriate for blacks, given racial prejudice and their servile status. Even the issue of religious instruction aroused controversy because of the popular notion that Christians could not enslave fellow Christians. Would not conversion, symbolized by baptism, transform the infidel or heathen slave into a free Christian man or woman? That question made the catechizing of slaves problematic, especially in the colonial South. However, between 1664 and 1706 all the southern colonies, plus New York, passed laws declaring that baptism did not "alter the condition of the person as to his bondage or freedom."

Reluctance. Despite such legislative assurance most colonial slave owners remained reluctant to give their slaves religious instruction. In 1724 the Anglican rector of Dorchester, Saint George's Parish, in South Carolina, reported, "I have hitherto indeavored in vain to prevail with their masters to convince them of the necessity of having their slaves made Christians." In 1740 South Carolina prohibited teaching slaves to read and write under penalty of £100. Slave and free blacks were less likely to be catechized, or even to attend white Anglican congregations, in South Carolina than elsewhere. Some blacks were also given literacy training, but that was certainly the exception. In Virginia a charity school for orphans, poor children, and Negroes opened in 1750 and operated for a few years in Saint Peter's Parish, and there is evidence that several schools, especially after 1750, admitted at least some blacks, slave and free. Despite the law prohibiting teaching literacy skills to slaves, blacks were taught at schools in Charleston. Due largely to the work of Commissary Alexander Garden, the most significant of these was founded by the Society for the Propagation of the Gospel in Foreign Parts (S.P.G.) in 1743 and functioned for the next twenty years, having as many as sixty students at one time. S.P.G. missionaries scattered throughout the Carolinas and Georgia also provided religious instruction and some literacy training to slaves and free blacks on occasion. Quakers in Virginia and the Carolinas preached the Christian message to blacks and sometimes taught them literacy skills, as did various Presbyterian divines. However, without denigrating the impact upon the individuals involved, both white and black, such religious and educational activities were intermittent and affected relatively few African Americans.

New England. By the time of the American Revolution, less than 3 percent of the population of New England were African Americans; most lived in and around Boston. In the seventeenth century John Eliot was an early advocate of catechizing blacks, though there is little indication that his voice was much heeded in that regard. In 1717 Cotton Mather, who advocated more religious instruction for blacks, was a leading spirit behind the founding of a short-lived charity school for Africans and Indians in Boston. There is also evidence that some children of free blacks attended schooling with white children at various times in New England. Again, though, literacy training for blacks was quite limited and took place largely in the household rather than the classroom. A remarkable prodigy by any standard, the young Phillis Wheatley, a slave girl brought from Africa in 1761, learned both English and Latin in her master's household and became the leading black poetess of her day.

Middle Colonies. Because of the work of the S.P.G. and the Quakers, there may have been more formal instructions of slaves and free blacks in the Middle Colonies than elsewhere in British America. In New York, Dutch Reformed domines continued their limited ministry to catechizing blacks, slave and free. Much more systematic after 1700 were Anglican efforts, especially in New York City. Under the auspices of the S.P.G., Elias Neau, a Huguenot refugee and merchant by trade,

opened a catechetical school in the evening for adult slaves in 1704. Neau was an extraordinary teacher whose success at catechizing was roundly praised and prevailed against strong opposition in the wake of the slave revolt in New York City in 1712. Upon Neau's death in 1722 William Huddleston, master of the S.P.G.-sponsored charity school, continued Neau's work. Huddleston was followed by a succession of young Anglican clerics—James Wetmore, James Colgan, Richard Charlton, and Samuel Auchmuty. Between 1728 and 1734 John Beasley conducted an S.P.G. school for whites in Albany, where he also taught blacks reading, writing, and Christianity. Outside New York City S.P.G. ministers reported little instruction among African Americans, whether slave or free. In Pennsylvania prominent Quakers opened a school for black children in 1700. Growing Quaker opposition to slavery produced more opportunities for blacks to obtain schooling in Pennsylvania, though the extent to which this occurred is difficult to determine. In 1738 the Moravian brethren began a short-lived mission to blacks at Bethlehem. In Philadelphia the Anglican Christ's Church began a school just for black children in 1758, as did another Anglican congregation, Saint Paul's. The antislavery leader Anthony Benezet prodded Quakers to found a school for both black and white children in 1770.

Sources:

John Calam, *Parsons and Pedagogues: The S.P.G. Adventure in American Education* (New York: Columbia University Press, 1971);

Lawrence A. Cremin, *American Education: The Colonial Experience, 1607–1783* (New York: Harper & Row, 1970);

Donald Everett, "Free Persons of Color in Colonial Louisiana," *Louisiana History*, 7 (1966): 221–250;

Philip S. Foner, *History of Black Americans from Africa to the Emergence of the Cotton Kingdom* (Westport, Conn.: Greenwood Press, 1975);

Joyce Goodfriend, "Burghers and Blacks: The Evolution of a Slave Society at New Amsterdam," *New York History*, 59 (1978): 125–144;

Lorenzo Greene, *The Negro in Colonial New England, 1620–1776* (Port Washington, N.Y.: Kennikat Press, 1942);

Gwendolyn Midlo Hall, *Africans in Colonial Louisiana: The Development of Afro-Creole Culture in the Eighteenth Century* (Baton Rouge: Louisiana State University Press, 1992);

Edgar J. McManus, *Black Bondage in the North* (Syracuse, N.Y.: Syracuse University Press, 1973);

McManus, *A History of Negro Slavery in New York* (Syracuse, N.Y.: Syracuse University Press, 1966);

Gary B. Nash, *Forging Freedom: The Formation of Philadelphia's Black Community, 1720–1840* (Cambridge, Mass.: Harvard University Press, 1988);

Jean R. Soderlund, *Quakers and Slavery: A Divided Spirit* (Princeton, N.J.: Princeton University Press, 1985);

Robin W. Winks, *The Blacks in Canada: A History* (New Haven, Conn.: Yale University Press, 1971);

Donald R. Wright, *African-Americans in the Colonial Era: From African Origins Through the American Revolution* (Arlington Heights, Ill.: Harlan Davidson, 1990).

APPRENTICESHIP AND OCCUPATIONAL TRAINING

European Background. Children, both girls and boys, generally began their occupational education within the

The printing press used by Benjamin Franklin in London in 1726 (Smithsonian Institution, Washington, D.C.)

household of their birth. Most would remain there, being taught farming or housewifery as they grew to adulthood. Others, however, lived with relatives or friends and essentially acquired much of the same occupational instruction. A legal and contractual arrangement for occupational training, apprenticeship emerged from the European craft and trade guilds of the Middle Ages. In the apprenticeship system boys, usually between ten and fourteen years old, were trained under the supervision of a master craftsman or merchant in a particular trade or profession for several years, most often until they were twenty-one. Many guilds required that the apprentice's parents pay the master a fee for his services. Through apprenticeship the guilds regulated entry into the trades, maintained skill levels, and secured cheap labor for the masters. Under the terms of the indenture (contract), the master acted in loco parentis, and the apprentice promised to serve his master well, living in his household while learning the craft. A young man who had completed his apprenticeship successfully would be admitted by a specific guild as a journeyman and allowed to work with a master craftsman for wages. After serving a fixed tenure as a journeyman and having proven his craftsmanship, the journeyman could apply to the guild for master craftsman status, which allowed him to establish his own shop and ply his particular craft. Outside the guild sys-

tem girls were sometimes apprenticed by their parents to become seamstresses or housemaids, serving until they turned eighteen or got married.

Variation. Aside from the voluntary apprenticeship system described above, there was also a compulsory type which was almost always concerned with poor or orphaned children indentured by church or civil officials whose primary concern was finding a decent home for the child. Occupational training was often implicit in such indentures but decidedly secondary to custodial concerns. The guild might be involved but quite often was not in compulsory apprenticeship, which was an effort to maintain social stability in the face of dramatic economic changes. Both types of apprenticeship were transferred to the American colonies, but not the guild system, which exerted little influence except in parts of Spanish America.

Latin America. Of all the European powers Spain was most successful in transplanting its guild system in America, or at least in Mexico, where the sixty guilds functioning in the mother country exercised similar authority over the crafts in Mexico City. Only those of Spanish background were supposed to practice the skilled crafts, such as blacksmithing or carpentry. However, even in Mexico City, mestizos and mulattoes could on occasion get apprenticeship training, and out in the countryside racial mixture was of less concern than skills. In New Mexico and Texas the Indian missions often trained young native men and women in Spanish arts and crafts because such skills were so much in demand on the frontier, where beautifully decorated churches bespoke the skill of Indian and colonial artisans. However, the priesthood and the professions—together with the apprenticeship training and study required for them—were closed to Indians and African slaves. In the borderlands as elsewhere in Spanish America, most boys acquired occupational skills from their fathers or brothers, just as girls learned housewifery from their mothers and sisters.

New France. As in the Spanish borderlands, apprenticeship provided training in the crafts for boys or young men in New France. However, the regulations came not from the guilds, which exercised little influence in New France, but from the Supreme Council of the province. There are also records of young women who served apprenticeships with seamstresses. Among the leading crafts were blacksmithing, shoemaking, cooperage, and joinery. Apprentices were usually between the ages of thirteen and nineteen, and they typically served three years. Some indentures specifically exempted the apprentice from performing menial tasks, but other contracts spelled out such mundane duties as running errands, carrying wood, or farmwork. The master usually provided food, clothing, shelter, and some spending money to the apprentice, who seldom had to pay the master an enrollment fee. Moreover, if the apprentice was less than sixteen years old, the master was obliged to release him for catechism classes until his first communion. Contractual apprenticeship training centered in the population centers, such as Louisbourg, Quebec, or Montreal, where 25 percent of the population resided. More often than not, a craftsman trained his sons to his own or related trades. Apprenticeships in the professions—law, medicine, or commerce—were difficult to acquire and usually limited to relatives. Rather than an apprenticeship in the crafts or a career as a farmer, large numbers of young men opted for the adventurous life in the fur trade as coureurs de bois, much to the disappointment of clerics and government officials alike. After 1700 officials in New France discouraged racial mixing even though Indian and French liaisons had been encouraged before 1689, but it is unclear the extent to which discrimination became institutionalized in terms of occupational training.

New Netherland. In the absence of the guilds, apprenticeship in the Dutch province was not well regulated, like virtually everything else there, until the advent of Peter Stuyvesant, who served as director general from 1647 until 1664. As was the case in the Dutch republic, apprenticeship indentures in New Netherland, especially in the 1650s, generally called for the youth to be taught reading, writing, and perhaps arithmetic as well as a specific trade. For example, Evert Duyckinck agreed in 1648 to take young Cornelis Jansen for eight consecutive years, provide him with adequate food, clothing, and shelter, and teach him "the trade of glazer or such [other] trade as Evert can and to have him taught reading and writing." The poor and orphaned children in New Amsterdam were the responsibility of the orphan masters, who arranged apprenticeship for the unfortunate youngsters. In Beverwyck the Dutch Reformed consistory usually assumed that chore as part of its service to the poor.

British Background. Apprenticeship regulations in England were regularized by two Elizabethan parliamentary enactments. The first was the Statute of Artificers of 1562, which turned conventional trade practices and local employment regulations into national economic policy. According to this law persons between the ages of twelve and sixty who were not otherwise employed were compelled to service in husbandry. Another major provision fixed apprenticeship service at seven years and standardized the rights and duties of both the master and apprentice. The second statute, the Poor Law of 1601, dealt more explicitly with the economic dislocation and problem of vagrancy as tenants lost their traditional homesteads because of the enclosure movement. While restricting itinerant begging, this legislation called upon every parish to elect overseers of the poor who were empowered to erect workhouses where children of the poor worked as apprentices and learned a trade in the budding textile industry. The Statute of Artificers of 1562 and the Poor Law of 1601 were models for England's North American provinces in regulating apprenticeship. As in England, the master possessed the rights of a parent over the apprentice, who might be rea-

A 1722 essay written by Benjamin Franklin while he served as an apprentice on his brother James's Boston newspaper, *The New-England Courant*

sonably punished for misdeeds. By the same token, the apprentice did have the right to complain against unfair treatment. However, the British guilds were not transplanted to colonial towns, and consequently trade apprenticeships, whether in terms of tenure or quality of workmanship taught, were never as standardized, or as important, in America as in the mother country.

Chesapeake Colonies. In 1643 Virginia passed its first apprenticeship law. It sought to protect orphans, of whom there were many because of the Chesapeake's devastating disease environment, from unscrupulous guardians who might otherwise neglect their wards' inheritance and education. Guardians and overseers were instructed to educate such orphans "in Christian religion and in rudiments of learning and to provide for them necessaries according to the competence of their estates." In 1646, drawing extensively on the Poor Law of 1601, the Virginia assembly called upon officials to choose two poor children from each county, either male or female, and send them to Jamestown, where they would work in the public flax house and be taught carding, knitting, and spinning. Virginia's legal code of 1661–1662 instructed the parish vestries to apprentice out orphaned, illegitimate, or poor children. In 1668 vestries and individual counties were further authorized to set up a workhouse school. Finally, an apprenticeship law passed in 1672 left the county justices in charge of caring for poor children. Virginia apprenticeship statutes passed in 1705, 1727, 1751, and 1768 instructed masters to teach reading and writing respectively to male orphans, poor boys apprenticed, orphaned females, and illegitimate children of white females. Such regulations were not always rigorously enforced, but they could hardly be ignored. In 1668 Maryland passed legislation requiring orphans with sufficient estate to be schooled; other orphans less well off were to be apprenticed. Another Maryland statute of 1715 ordered justices annually to examine the relationship between masters and apprentices to make sure the former were teaching the latter their respective trades.

Lower South. None of the other provinces in the South demonstrated as much concern over apprenticeship as Virginia. In 1715 North Carolina's only legislation on apprenticeship, like the Maryland law of 1688, called for orphans to be schooled if they could afford it, but if not, to be bound out "to some Handcraft Trade" until they came of age. A South Carolina statute of 1695 allowed for poor children to be bound out but said nothing specifically about learning the trade. Georgia passed no provincial regulations before the American Revolution. Despite the paucity of pertinent provincial legislation—and most of that related to paupers—apprenticeship indentures found in the Carolinas and Georgia in the eighteenth century ranged from agreements for poor children, male and female, to craft and trade indentures that emphasized that the master would provide not only training in a craft but also instruction in reading and writing.

New England. In 1642, because of "the great neglect of many parents and masters in training up their children in learning, and labor and other imployments that may be profitable to the common wealth," the Massachusetts Bay General Court instructed town selectmen to make sure that parents and masters were properly educating the young. The 1642 law dictated that children should not only be prepared for future employment but also taught "to read and understand the principles of religion and the capital laws of the land." Negligent parents and masters might be fined, and selectmen were empowered to take apprentices and poor children from families that were incapable of fulfilling their responsibilities to them. A 1648 revision of the law added the requirement that children be exercised weekly in some orthodox catechism. Other New England colonies followed Massachusetts Bay's example and passed similar legislation: Connecticut in 1650, New Haven in 1655, and Plymouth in 1671, the latter adding a reading requirement to legislation it had passed in 1641 regarding the apprenticing of poor children. In 1703 Massachusetts required that poor children apprenticed by town selectmen learn writing as well as reading. Subsequent amendments passed in 1710, 1720, and 1731 specifically mandated that poor male apprentices be taught reading, writing, and cyphering (arithmetic). Of the New England colonies only Rhode Island, whose government embraced separation of church and state, refused to copy Massachusetts Bay's legislation on apprenticeship. None of New England's provincial laws set the number of years for apprenticeship service, but Boston tried in 1670 to require at least a seven-year term, though it later apparently abandoned its enforcement.

Middle Colonies. Following the English conquest of New Netherland in 1664, the Duke's Laws of 1665 endorsed the continuation of customary labor practices as the former Dutch colony became New York. Serving an apprenticeship was one way one could become a freeman of New York City, with the privileges of practicing a trade and voting in elections. Not until 1766 did New York's provincial assembly address the status of apprenticeship, basically just affirming its legality and restating the reciprocal rights and obligations of masters and apprentices or servants. In New Jersey the Quaker Assembly of West Jersey regulated apprenticeship as early as 1683. However, local town and county regulations prevailed, and not until 1774 did New Jersey's assembly require that masters and mistresses teach their apprentices to read and write. In 1682 the Pennsylvania legislature passed a similar act requiring masters to teach their apprentices to read and write, though the law itself was not enforced, and subsequent provincial laws on apprenticeship dealt with the disposition of various groups of poor children. Many Quaker charity schools were founded with the stated purpose of educating children until they were "fit to be put out as apprentices." Delaware generally followed Pennsylvania customs and law regulating apprenticeship.

Slavery. Although the southern colonies had the most enslaved persons, slavery existed throughout the colonies. Slave artisans were found in the northern cities of Philadelphia, New York, and Boston as well as southern cities such as Annapolis and Charleston. They often possessed considerable freedom, living apart from their master but paying him or her a portion of their income and sometimes buying their freedom and that of their wives and children. Such slave artisans were known to teach their sons the family trade. Young black males might be apprenticed to white artisans, or Anglo-American craftsmen might teach their own slaves. Southern plantations early on organized procedures for teaching crafts to young slaves. A review of the *South Carolina Gazette* from 1732 to 1776 provides a catalogue of twenty-eight different trades in which slaves were trained. Throughout the South and much of the North, slaves were involved in the clothing and building trades.

Aristocratic Trades. In British North America voluntary, legal apprenticeship became increasingly less important because skilled labor was so much in demand that a lengthy apprenticeship was no longer necessary. However, throughout British America legal apprenticeship remained the primary way of entering the aristocratic trades of commerce, medicine, and law. As the eighteenth century progressed, more and more formal schooling, including a college education or study at the Inns of Court, became standard for those in the elite. However, serving an apprenticeship for several years was the way to learn the craft and make the contacts necessary to succeed as a merchant, doctor, or lawyer. Parents usually had to pay substantial fees to secure such apprenticeships for their sons. The initial fee for entering a mercantile apprenticeship ranged from £50 to £100. Some lawyers, especially the wealthier ones, charged £200, and doctors might require even more of an initial payment from aspiring young men. Nor was it unusual for the tenure of an apprenticeship in commerce, medicine, or law to last seven years. By the middle of the eighteenth century, established and usually well-trained lawyers and doctors, worried by the lack of training and competition from other practitioners, began urging a college requirement for lawyers and licensing examinations for doctors.

Sources:

Edward Gaylord Bourne, *Spain in America, 1450–1580* (New York: Barnes & Noble, 1962);

Lois Green Carr, "The Development of the Maryland Orphans' Court, 1654–1715," in *Law, Society, and Politics in Early Maryland*, edited by Aubrey C. Land, Lois Green Carr, and Edward C. Papenfuse (Baltimore & London: Johns Hopkins University Press, 1977), pp. 41–64;

Margaret Gay Davies, *The Enforcement of English Apprenticeship: A Study in Applied Mercantilism* (Cambridge, Mass.: Harvard University Press, 1956);

William J. Frost, *The Quaker Family in Colonial America* (New York: St. Martin's Press, 1973);

Marcus Wilson Jernegan, *Laboring and Dependent Classes in Colonial America, 1607–1783* (Chicago: University of Chicago Press, 1931);

Richard B. Morris, *Government and Labor in Early America*, revised edition (New York: Harper & Row, 1965);

Dorothy H. Smith, "Orphans in Anne Arundel County, Maryland, 1704–1709," *Maryland Magazine of Genealogy*, 3 (1980): 34–42;

Mechal Sobel, *The World They Made Together: Black and White Values in Eighteenth-Century Virginia* (Princeton, N.J.: Princeton University Press, 1987).

CHILD-REARING PATTERNS

Overview. Fundamental to educational thought and institutions in British America, New Netherland, New France, and the Spanish borderlands were the attitudes of parents toward child rearing. In general there was a trend through the colonial era from rather authoritarian and repressive styles of parenting toward more-indulgent and liberating methods. This shift from repressive to liberating child-rearing methods was most pronounced among the upper classes, though exceptions could be found even there as well.

Spanish Borderlands. Despite the frontier circumstance of many settlers on the borderlands, their attitude toward child rearing reflected the strongly class-conscious, patriarchical family of Spain itself. Honor was at the heart of family relations. Children owed their parents honor and respect, and for children to disobey their parents was to dishonor the patriarch in particular and the family in general. Women were responsible for the religious education of children, especially catechetical training before puberty. Mothers trained daughters for their future roles as wives and mothers, with particular emphasis on chastity, modesty, and submissiveness. Children of the elite were usually taught reading and writing in church schools, but the literacy rate among the general population of settlers was low. Craftsmen were in high demand in the borderlands, and boys were required to read and write before beginning an apprenticeship. More often fathers taught sons the family trade and initiated them into the code of honor that governed males in the upper classes. While sons were taught to protect their sisters and other women relatives from predatory males, the machismo culture of the borderlands encouraged men to express their sexual prowess through seductions, whether with Indian or European women.

New France. National culture and the Catholic Church both conveyed a strongly patriarchical view of the family among French settlers in Canada, the Illinois country, and the Mississippi River valley. However, the shortage of labor in New France gave both children and wives more leverage in dealing with husbands and fathers. The labor of children was valuable, and for that reason alone the child's wishes in his or her work had to be heeded, at least to a degree. Between puberty and first communion children were rigorously catechized by the priest. Young women of the middling to upper classes went to school, usually taught by a priest or nun; boys of similar status were much more likely to work with their fathers or perhaps be apprenticed. Craft apprenticeship was the dominant form of secular education in New France, and family vigilance made certain that the master treated the apprentice fairly and taught him well. Because of the labor shortage, fathers could ill afford to alienate their offspring by being too restrictive when it came to career choices or marriage. Many an aging couple deeded over the family farm to an offspring in return for their care in later years, but not before they spelled out all the terms carefully in the contract.

New Netherland. In the seventeenth century the Dutch in both the Netherlands and their North American colony demonstrated progressive attitudes toward child rearing. In the arts and literature the Dutch celebrated infants and children and were accused by foreign observers of indulging and spoiling their offspring. Even Jakob Cats, the most famous Dutch Reformed moralist, made it clear in both prose and poetry that parents owed their children affection as well as discipline. By the 1650s, as family life in New Netherland was burgeoning, so were Dutch child-rearing attitudes and practices. Arriving in 1647, Director General Peter Stuyvesant described the children of New Amsterdam as wild and undisciplined. The personal correspondence of Jeremias and Maria Van Rensselaer reveal parents and grandparents who simply doted on their children, and similar evidence of deep and abiding parental affection may be found in New Netherland prenuptial agreements and joint wills. As in the fatherland, young men and women mixed and mingled in the Dutch colony without much parental supervision, and despite the freedom given them in courting, they generally married within their class.

British North America. Unlike many of the parents in New Netherland, Puritan parents in New England were likely to follow more-authoritarian, restrictive views of child rearing. Puritan moralists warned that the infant, tainted by original sin, possessed an evil nature that had to be disciplined again and again lest the unruly child grow up into a dissolute young man or woman. Catechetical training and reading and quoting from the Bible were encouraged among the young. The fear that parents might spare the rod and spoil the child no doubt encouraged the Puritan practice of farming out sons and daughters to live with friends or relatives who presumably would have fewer qualms about disciplining them during their adolescent years. "Children should not know, if it can be kept from them," explained the Reverend John Robinson, "that they have a will of their own, but in their parents' keeping." According to historian Philip Greven this Puritan-evangelical style of child rearing was just one of the three Protestant temperaments that determined adult attitudes toward children. The second, which Greven called the moderate temperament, saw the child as an innocent with a tendency toward sin but whose will could be made good by the affection and moral instruction of dutiful parents. This moderate temperament was especially manifested by many Quakers and most Anglicans, Greven believed, and was becoming the majority Protestant temperament after 1700 among Anglo-Americans. It owed much to the popularity of John Locke's writings on education, which were didactic but in a decidedly secular way. Finally, Greven described the emergence of the genteel temperament, characteristic of the upper classes generally in the eighteenth century but especially southern planters on the Chesapeake and in South Carolina. Rationalistic and self-confident, parents of the genteel temperament were permissive and loving; they encouraged individualism and self-expression in their children and were loved and respected in return. Although all three temperaments can be found in both the seventeenth and eighteenth centuries, the tendency in Anglo-America was movement over time from the evangelical toward the genteel temperament.

Sources:

Karin Lee Calvert, "Children in American Family Portraiture, 1670–1810," *William and Mary Quarterly,* 39 (1982): 87–113;

John and Virginia Demos, "Adolescence in Historical Perspective," *Journal of Marriage and the Family,* 31 (1969): 632–638;

Philip Greven, *The Protestant Temperament: Patterns of Child-Rearing, Religious Experience, and the Self in Early America* (New York: Knopf, 1977);

David Freeman Hawke, *Everyday Life in Early America* (New York: Harper & Row, 1988);

N. Ray Hiner, "Adolescence in Eighteenth-Century America," *History of Childhood Quarterly,* 3 (1975): 253–280;

Hiner, "The Child in American Historiography: Accomplishments and Prospect," *Psychohistory Review,* 7 (1978–1979): 13–23;

Peter Laslett and Richard Wall, eds., *Household and Family in Past Time* (Cambridge: Cambridge University Press, 1972);

C. John Sommerville, *The Discovery of Childhood in Puritan England* (Athens & London: University of Georgia Press, 1992).

COLLEGES

Background. In colonial America as in Europe, colleges were the primary institutions of higher learning. Their establishment in America was yet another manifestation of the European commitment to preserve Western culture despite the challenges of the wilderness and its "savage" inhabitants. In Spanish America and New France the Catholic Church led the way in establishing colleges, whose first priority was propagating the faith among both Indians and colonists. The religious motive was also dominant in the founding of Protestant colleges in British North America. Throughout the colonial era Latin and Greek classics dominated the curricula of American colleges. However, under the impact of Enlightenment thought, advances in mathematics and the natural sciences began to make their way into the college curriculum in the later eighteenth century.

Spanish, Dutch, and French. Although learned laymen as well as clergy settled in the Spanish borderlands, no college was established there in the colonial era. From Florida, children of the elite attended college in Santo Domingo or Mexico City, and those from the provinces of New Mexico and Texas went to Mexico City. It should be emphasized that the universities at Mexico City and Lima, both established in 1551, were by 1700 thriving institutions that rivaled the leading Catholic

A 1740 engraving of the College of William and Mary, Williamsburg, Virginia

universities in Europe. Returning to Spain for their college education was another option that some chose. New Netherland did not have a college, but several young men from the Dutch colony attended Harvard, and others returned to the Netherlands for their education. In New France the Jesuits founded a college in Quebec in 1635, though a genuine college curriculum was not instituted there until the 1660s. By 1712 the college was judged as good and perhaps better than Jesuit colleges in France and possessed the same standardized curriculum. There were five Latin classes, one each of rhetoric and humanity and three in grammar. Some history and geography were included in the grammar and rhetoric classes; science was taught along with philosophy, and the theories of Galileo, René Descartes, Blaise Pascal, and Sir Isaac Newton were explored in mathematics and physics. The course of study in letters at the College of Quebec usually took five years or more, and the science curriculum took three years. Students also studied drama and presented plays, including *Le Cid* in 1652 and Jean Racine's *Mithridate* in 1694. The College of Quebec, like other Jesuit colleges, did not award degrees, but students completing their studies regularly engaged in public disputation. Among those educated at the College of Quebec was Louis Jolliet, later famous for his explorations of the Mississippi River, who in 1666 argued his thesis in Latin before the leading figures of the province.

Early British Efforts. As early as 1622, plans were afoot and money had been collected in England for the founding of Henrico College in Virginia. The Indian uprising of that year and the subsequent takeover of the colony by the Crown in 1625 put an end to the project. The Puritans in New England were more successful in establishing colleges. In 1633 Reverend John Eliot called for the founding of a college in Massachusetts Bay. Eliot warned that "if we norish not Larning both church & common wealth will sinke." In 1636 the provincial legislature agreed, allocating some £400, and college instruction began in Cambridge in 1638. That same year John Harvard, a preacher and recent immigrant, died and left £780 and his library of four hundred volumes to the college, which took his name. According to a promotional pamphlet published in 1642, the purpose of Harvard College was "to advance Learning and perpetuate it to Posterity; dreading to leave an illiterate Ministry to the Churches, when our present Ministers shall lie in the Dust." Its charter of 1650 added another objective: the education of Indian youth. Money was collected in England for John Eliot's missionary efforts among the Indians, and President Henry Dunster used some to pay for the building called the Indian College. However, few Indians ever attended Harvard, and only one, Caleb Cheeshahteaumuch, ever graduated. In fact, Harvard College, like the Puritan vision of a "City Upon a Hill," had little to do with the Indians.

Harvard College: Structure. The Massachusetts Bay legislature put Harvard under the supervision of a board of overseers made up of local civil and ecclesiastical leaders. In 1650 the legislature granted Harvard a charter creating a corporation made up of the president and fellows and empowering it to grant degrees, which it had been doing without any official sanction since 1642. Thereafter, the overseers and corporation jointly governed Harvard. Its structure and curriculum were modeled after Emmanuel College, a fairly young foundation which had become a stronghold of Puritan influence at Cambridge University. Emmanuel and the other colleges at Cambridge and Oxford were rather small, including from twenty to fifty students, a president, two or three tutors, and a few servants. In 1638 Nathaniel Eaton, who had studied under the famed Puritan theologian William Ames, was appointed professor and charged with leading Harvard, which began with nine or ten students. After many complaints Ames was removed in late 1639 for mistreating the students. His successor, Henry Dunster, who had studied at Magdalene College, Oxford, served Harvard until 1655 as professor and president.

Curriculum. The three-year curriculum that Henry Dunster instituted at Harvard reflected four influences that were shaping higher learning in Europe: the seven liberal arts (grammar, rhetoric, logic, arithmetic, geometry, astronomy, and music), taught from Latin texts; Aristotelian philosophy, rediscovered in the later Middle Ages and transmitted in classes on ethics, politics, physics, and metaphysics; humanistic learning from the Renaissance, emphasizing the Latin classics of Cicero and Virgil and knowledge of Greek and other eastern languages; and the Reformation ideal that liberal learning should be devoted to explaining the religious doctrines of the Puritan faith. Dunster initially conducted all the

	1642–1658	1659–1677	1678–1689	1642–1689
Clergymen	76	62	42	180
Physicians	12	11	4	27
Public Servants*	13	17	12	42
Teachers	1	8	4	13
Merchants	3	6	1	10
Planters	4	5	2	11
Soldiers, Mariners	0	1	4	5
Miscellaneous	2	3	0	5
Died Young**	11	5	11	27
Unknown***	27	35	6	68
Total	149	153	86	388

*Governors, councilors, judges, deputies, and permanent officials.

**Died in college or within five years of graduating.

***Most of these individuals are nongraduates before 1663.

Source: Lawrence A. Cremin, *American Education: The Colonial Experience 1607–1783* (New York: Harper & Row, 1970), p. 221.

classes six days a week. In later years a tutor would be assigned an entering class and teach all the courses for that class as it moved through one sequence after another toward graduation. Dunster's successor, Charles Chauncy, who served from 1654 to 1672, added another year of study at the freshman level, which dropped the median age at entry to between fifteen or sixteen, the basic requirement for admission being a solid background in the Latin language.

William and Mary. The prime mover behind the establishment of the second college in British North America was the Reverend James Blair, commissary of the Church of England in Virginia. Appointed by the bishop of London to supervise ecclesiastical affairs in the tobacco colony, Blair had powerful friends in England who helped him secure a royal charter in 1693 and raise funds for the proposed college. According to its charter William and Mary was founded for three reasons: to train ministerial candidates for the Anglican ministry, to educate Virginia youth, and to convert the Indians. The latter objective may well have been disingenuous, calculated to capture a share of the scientist Robert Boyle's estate dedicated to Christianizing the Indians. Some Indians did attend the college, now and again, but the Boyle legacy was used primarily for the Brafferton Building and library books. Under the 1693 charter William and Mary was governed by a self-perpetuating board of eighteen members; its president until 1743 was James Blair. The charter also called for the creation of four schools (sacred theology, philosophy, Greek and Latin, and Indian instruction) with six professors. After some fits and starts, William and Mary became fully functional in the 1720s and followed the design of the charter until after the American Revolution.

Yale. In 1701 Harvard alumni became concerned that their alma mater had strayed from Puritan orthodoxy and wanted to found another college in southern New England. Fewer Harvard graduates were going into the ministry, and the proposed Connecticut college was expected to revive both piety and orthodoxy among New England youth. The new college was a modest affair at first, meeting in the home of its president, Abraham Pierson, for five years and moving among several towns for the next thirteen. By 1720 the college had built a permanent building at New Haven, taken the name of its most generous benefactor, Elihu Yale, a director of the East India Company, and had received the eight hundred volumes purchased by Connecticut's English agent, Jeremiah Dummer. The Dummer collection included books by John Locke, Sir Isaac Newton, René Descartes, Robert Boyle, John Milton, and more-recent writers, both clerical and lay. Despite its devotion to Puritan orthodoxy, Yale had a library that included the chief works of the European Enlightenment, and that library, especially the works of Locke and Newton, encouraged two young tutors, Samuel Johnson and Daniel Browne, to reject Congregational orthodoxy and turn to the Church of England in 1722. The apostasy scandal grew worse when

William Burgis's 1725–1726 engraving of Harvard College, Cambridge, Massachusetts

Yale's rector, Timothy Cutler, like Browne and Johnson, was found guilty of "Arminianism and prelatical corruptions." They were all summarily dismissed. However, the books remained, and others detailing rationalism and the scientific method would be added to the collection. Others, including conservative clerics such as Jonathan Edwards, read and had to come to terms with them.

Later Schools. After the establishment of Yale in 1701 demographic and economic expansion and shifting religious and intellectual currents brought forth the founding of six additional colleges in British North America. During the late 1730s and early 1740s the leadership of both Harvard and Yale opposed the revivalism of the Great Awakening. In response evangelical Presbyterians, breaking with the more conservative Synod of Pennsylvania and organizing the Synod of New York, founded the College of New Jersey (later Princeton University) in 1745. Its first president was the Reverend Jonathan Dickinson, followed by the Reverend Aaron Burr, a Yale graduate, during whose ten-year tenure the college became housed in the Nassau Building at Princeton. In Pennsylvania and New York civic pride and the mercantile spirit led to the founding of colleges. In

Philadelphia Benjamin Franklin organized the movement that led to the Philadelphia Academy in 1753 and which became the College of Philadelphia two years later. After a decade of discussion and two years of intense controversy, King's College (later Columbia University) was chartered in New York City in 1756. Under the presidency of the Reverend William Smith, the College of Philadelphia became identified with the Church of England. From the beginning, Anglican influence was dominant at King's College, where Samuel Johnson, one of the 1722 Yale apostates, became the first president. Evangelicals were also behind three more colleges: in 1765 the Baptists founded the College of Rhode Island (later Brown University); the Dutch Reformed Church obtained a charter in 1766 from New Jersey for Queen's College (later Rutgers University); and the Reverend Eleazar Wheelock, a Congregational minister, founded Dartmouth College in Hanover, New Hampshire, in 1770.

Curriculum. Although Latin and Greek classics remained at its heart, the eighteenth century brought changes to the traditional college curriculum. Among the thousands of Scotch-Irish immigrants to America were graduates of Scottish universities, which were among the leading centers of Enlightenment learning. They also led in pedagogical reforms such as offering instruction in English instead of Latin, having professors specialize in just one discipline instead of teaching all subjects, and utilizing demonstration and modern methods in teaching the sciences. Some of these innovations were applied in British North America, first in the academies run by Presbyterian preachers and later in the evangelical colleges. Locke's writing on education and psychology, no less than Newton's insights into mathematics and physics, were influencing the curricula of colleges both old and new. Americans such as Benjamin Franklin campaigned aggressively for a more practical education in both academy and college. Franklin's College of Philadelphia had perhaps the most "modern" curriculum of any American college, rivaled closely by King's College in New York, where William Livingston and other opponents of an Anglican establishment argued for a nonsectarian institution of higher learning. Despite their Anglican leanings, neither the College of Philadelphia nor King's College advertised itself as a divinity school. Instead each touted its broad plan of instruction, including the classical languages, grammar, rhetoric, logic, and mathematics as well as surveying, navigation, geography, history, husbandry, commerce, and government. King's College claimed its curriculum offered "everything useful for the comfort, the convenience and elegance of life, in the chief manufacturers relating to any of these things." Such extravagant claims aside, the college curriculum was becoming more secular, scientific, and concerned with nurturing leaders in the professions.

Sources:

James Axtell, *The School upon a Hill: Education and Society in Colonial New England* (New Haven, Conn.: Yale University Press, 1974);

Lawrence A. Cremin, *American Education: The Colonial Experience, 1607–1783* (New York: Harper & Row, 1970);

Mario Gongora, *Studies in the Colonial History of Spanish America,* translated by Richard Southern (Cambridge: Cambridge University Press, 1975);

Jurgen Herbst, "The First Three American Colleges: Schools of the Reformation," *Perspectives in American History,* 8 (1974): 7–52;

David C. Humphrey, *From King's College to Columbia, 1746–1800* (New York: Columbia University Press, 1976);

Howard Miller, *The Revolutionary College: American Presbyterian Higher Education: 1707–1837* (New York: New York University Press, 1976);

Samuel E. Morison, *The Founding of Harvard College* (Cambridge, Mass.: Harvard University Press, 1935);

David W. Robson, *Educating Republicans: The College in the Era of the American Revolution, 1750–1800* (Westport, Conn.: Greenwood Press, 1985);

Douglas Sloan, *The Scottish Enlightenment and the American College Ideal* (New York: Teachers College Press of Columbia University, 1971);

Thomas J. Wertenbaker, *Princeton, 1746–1896* (Princeton, N.J.: Princeton University Press, 1946).

LIBRARIES AND LEARNED SOCIETIES

Books. The cultural baggage of European immigrants to America included books reflecting the dominant literary trends of the age. Even the earliest settlers brought significant numbers of books with them, determined as they were to carry the best of their Old World culture into their New World homes. For some of them, books on law, history, and religion were deemed especially essential as they struggled to reconstitute society in the American wilderness. Books that instructed and uplifted, especially religious books, were most numerous. But learned political and theological works and belletristic literature could also be found in personal and college collections of the seventeenth century. As the eighteenth century progressed, institutional libraries grew in numbers and size, as did personal and family collections of books. In the English colonies the expansion of literacy gave rise to the phenomenon known as subscription libraries, whereby the general public had even greater access to a wider variety of books. The European Enlightenment contributed significantly to rising rates of literacy everywhere and brought forth increased intellectual activity, including the organization of learned societies such as the American Philosophical Society (1743) in British North America.

Spaniards. Among the first settlers into the Spanish borderlands were well-educated priests, military officers, and landowners. They saw themselves as promoters of Spanish culture and Christianity; books were crucial to their mission of transmitting European civilization to the American Southwest, Texas, and Florida. Juan de Oñate, who led the first European and Mexican settlers into New Mexico in 1598, carried books with him, as did several of his fellow officers, including Capt. Alonso de Quesada, who reported that he brought with him "seven books, religious and non religious." Another Spanish captain accompanying Oñate was Gaspar Perez de Villagra, who later wrote the epic poem *Historia de la Nueva Mexico* (1610) in blank verse. Villagra's work made its way into the private and mission collections of books in the province. Throughout the Spanish borderlands mission libraries contained at least some books, mostly liturgical works but also writings on philosophy, canon law, and ecclesiastical history as well as biblical commentaries and Latin classics. The library at Our Father Santo Domingo mission just southwest of Sante Fe included Diego de Baeza's *Commentaria moralia in Evangelicam Historiarum* (1624), Antonio de Solis y Rivadeneyra's *Historia de la conquista de Mexico* (1684), Fray Domingo de Soto's *In dialecticam Aristolelis commetarii* (1554), and Philipp Cluver's *Introductio in universam geographiam* (1624), as well as an assortment of Roman writers. Two governors of provincial New Mexico, Bernardo Lopez de Mendizabal (1659–1691) and Diego de Penalosa (1661–1664) both had impressive libraries and both were arrested and tried by the Inquisition. Having studied at the University of Mexico, Lopez was a learned man; he

A lecture in experimental philosophy, as illustrated in a 1748 issue of the *Universal Magazine*

and his wife, Doña Teresa, were accused of being Jews, and their reading habits came under scrutiny. Lopez's library also included poems by the Italian Ludovico Aristo which were widely read by Spanish intellectuals though they were claimed by New Mexican clerics to contain "English heresies." Governor Penalosa had an even more extensive library than Lopez. Besides devotional works and volumes on political philosophy, history, theology, and law, Penalosa possessed several novels, plays, and a volume on horsemanship. He too was accused of reading books listed on the Church's *Index of Prohibited Books*, though it must be said that the Holy Office of the Inquisition found little heretical reading materials in New Mexico. Devotional materials and almanacs came from the printing presses in Mexico City; most books were imported from Spain. The evidence is not conclusive, but the literacy rate was apparently higher in New Mexico than in Spain itself. Nevertheless, by the end of the eighteenth century no more than one-third of the men could sign their names. Of course, the literacy rate among women was considerably lower.

Frenchmen. Among the first settlers in Canada, Marc Lescarbot shared his extensive library with fellow colonists during the short life of their settlement at Port Royal in Acadia between 1606 and 1607. Lescarbot's library was destroyed, but later colonists were known to have books particularly related to their profession: lawyers and judges had collections of books usually including legal commentaries; merchants usually owned well-known accounting books such as *Le parfait negociant* (1675) or *Dictionnnaire universel de commerce* (1723). Attorney-general Louis-Guillaume Verrier shared his extensive collection of legal volumes with the students he taught law, and François-Joseph Cugnet, secretary to the governor and council of Quebec, probably had the finest library assembled in New France. Especially popular were works by Michel Eyquem de Montaigne, François de Salignac de La Mothe-Fénelon, Pierre Corneille, Molière, and Jean Racine. Voltaire and Jean-Jacques Rousseau were also widely read. In 1778 the estate of Pierre de Laclede Liguestor, Saint Louis's leading citizen, included a library of two hundred volumes. It contained titles by René Descartes, Fénelon, Charles Rollin and French translations of works by Francis Bacon, John Locke, and Benjamin Franklin on electricity. Educational institutions developed the largest libraries in New France. By 1750 the Jesuit College at Quebec had a library of over five thousand volumes on theology, ecclesiastical and classical history, the lives of the saints and devotional practices, and medicine. The Quebec Ursulines and Sulpicians' Seminary also had impressive libraries. New France did not have any learned societies, but Michel Sarrazin, a surgeon general in the army, regularly contributed observations on the flora and fauna of North America to L'Académie Royale des Sciences de Paris. In terms of literacy, travelers often observed that the daughters of landowners in New France were better schooled than the boys, the latter being drawn into farm labor or the fur trade while their sisters were attending church schools. Statistics on literacy in New France, however, are inconclusive and scarce.

Dutchmen. The Dutch colony between New England and Chesapeake Bay may well have possessed the most literate colonists in seventeenth-century America. Both their commercial economy and Reformed faith demanded schooling, where not only reading and writing but also arithmetic were regularly taught. Even among women in New Netherland, the literacy rate was much higher than in New England and elsewhere in colonial America, no doubt because of the emphasis upon schooling in the Dutch republic. As in the Spanish borderlands and in New France, New Netherland possessed more than a few learned men who brought books with them and sent for more. Primers, Bibles, and devotional works as well as scholarly and literary volumes regularly made their way to New Netherland. The Dutch Reformed domines, especially the Reverend Henricus Selyns, possessed respectable home libraries, as did Latin schoolmasters Carolus Curtius and Aegidius Lucyck; Dr. Johannes de la Montagne and his son Jan; and Jacques Cortelyou, a student of Cartesian philosophy and known as a freethinker. Among those who published were Adrian Van der Donck, a young lawyer and leader of New Netherland's political dissenters in 1650. In 1656 Van der Donck published *Description of the New Netherland,* a promotional pamphlet praising the potential of the colony. Another was merchant Jacob Steendam, already a poet of some note before moving to America. Steendam published *The Complaint of New Amsterdam* (1659), lamenting in verse the neglect of the Dutch colony by the West India Company. Domine Selyn was another New Netherland poet. Upon the marriage of his friend, merchant and former teacher Aegidius Luyck, Selyn wrote a long poem titled "Bridal Torch." However, not the poem or the promotional tract but rather the lampoon, usually laced with sexual innuendo or political satire, was the most popular writing done in New Netherland.

Van Imborck. The reading habits of New Netherlanders may perhaps be seen in the inventory of the estate of Dr. Gysbert Van Imborck, a physician and bookseller. Upon his death in 1665 Imborck had over 500 books, including 102 primers, 100 catechisms, and 154 other religious works. In 1643 the Widow Bronck's estate included books by John Calvin, Heinrich Bullinger, and Martin Luther, a book on medicine, a child's book, several moral and practical discourses, and a German Bible. For the use of the preacher at his patroonship, Kiliaen Van Rensselaer sent various books on theology and biblical interpretation, three on mathematics, one on philosophy, one on geography, one on history, another on economics, and two Bibles. More typical New Netherlanders possessed just a few books, like those in the inventory of the estate of Jan Jansen Damen, a well-off farmer who died in 1651: one folio Bible, one chronicle (probably on the Dutch wars for independence), and a quarto Bible.

Britons. By the middle of the eighteenth century British North America was one of the most literate societies on earth, well ahead of both New France and the Spanish Borderlands. Estimates vary, but literacy rates among the British settlers—not including Indians or slaves—was as high as 90 percent in some regions. Literacy was definitely encouraged by the Protestantism and commercialism of colonial culture, with religious controversy and economic expansion contributing significantly to the availability of schooling. Just as Protestantism placed a premium on reading the Bible, trade and commerce were facilitated not only by reading but also writing and arithmetic. The proliferation of newspapers, book and pamphlet printing, bookselling, and the development of libraries testify to the growth and importance of literacy in the English colonies. Even in the seventeenth century British Americans were a bookish people, especially the Puritans of New England. But whether in New England or on the Chesapeake, reading materials ran to the practical, the devotional or theological, and the Latin classic. Especially popular throughout English America was Lewis Bayly's *The Practice of Piety* (1611). In the seventeenth century the English poets most read in the British colonies were John Milton and George Herbert. All students studying Latin grammar read Greek and Roman histories, tragedies, comedies, and poems because they were part of the traditional Latin curriculum, even in a Puritan New England, which might otherwise have resisted such worldly writers. In the eighteenth century contemporary belletristic literature from England became common even among New Englanders. Indeed, anything of note published in Britain would shortly make its way to the colonies, including the works of Alexander Pope, Jonathan Swift, Joseph Addison, and Richard Steele. Most popular of all were almanacs filled with practical advice; practical guides to business, navigation, and surveying; and devotional pamphlets.

Collections. Among early New Englanders who owned personal libraries were William Bradford, William Brewster, and John Harvard. Among the fifty volumes Miles Standish owned were Sir Walter Raleigh's

History of the World (1614) as well as John Calvin's *Institutes of the Christian Religion* (1536). Harvard left his substantial library to the college that bears his name; at his death in 1644, Brewster owned over four hundred volumes. Both Harvard and Brewster owned Capt. John Smith's *Description of New England* (1616) and Francis Bacon's *Advancement of Learning* (1605). When he died in 1676, John Winthrop II, the first governor of Connecticut, possessed the largest and most variegated library in New England. Along with the classics and contemporary works on divinity, Winthrop's library was filled with works on alchemy, mathematics, and astronomy. In Virginia, Ralph Wormeley II also had an extensive library. Among his books were Ben Jonson's *Every Man in His Humor* (1618), Francis Beaumont and John Fletcher's *Fifty Comedies and Tragedies* (1647), and Michael Dalton's widely read *Country Justice* (1618). Among the great individual libraries of early-eighteenth-century America were those of William Byrd II of Virginia, James Logan of Pennsylvania, and Cotton Mather of Massachusetts. They were followed by those two great bibliophiles, Benjamin Franklin and Thomas Jefferson, whose libraries were extraordinary for both their size and range. By 1750 college libraries such as those of Harvard, Yale, and William and Mary were rich depositories of books and documents. The resourceful Anglican priest Thomas Bray led an effort by the Church of England to establish parochial libraries in Annapolis, New York, Boston, Philadelphia, and Charleston for the use of the clergy. In the late 1720s Benjamin Franklin and others of his junto in Philadelphia began a subscription library, and that effort prepared the way for Franklin's Library of Philadelphia in 1731, which had two thousand volumes by 1770. Similarly, the New York Society Library was chartered in 1754, and its members paid a subscription fee which allowed them access to hundred of books. However, public subscription libraries, even the one in Philadelphia, were perhaps less effective in making books available than the booksellers themselves, especially in the major colonial towns. Many of them loaned books for free or set up their own subscription library at a minimum fee to interested readers. Moreover, these entrepreneurs bought books in large numbers and often sold them at bargain prices. A casual glance at a colonial newspaper after 1750 makes clear the rising importance of the ubiquitous bookseller and the variety of titles available to the general public.

Meetings of the Minds. Interestingly enough, several early Americans with the most impressive libraries were invited to join the prestigious Royal Society of London, founded by Charles II in 1660 and devoted to the advancement of "physico-mathematical experimental learning." Among the American members of the Royal Society were Winthrop II, Cotton Mather, Byrd, and Franklin. Franklin's junto, in which young mechanics and apprentices began a program of self-improvement, was hardly a learned society, but it pointed toward the quest for useful knowledge that would distinguish American intellectual life. Of course, the colleges had their debating societies, and during the eighteenth century various professional organizations began to emerge in the port towns, including legal societies, where lawyers regularly debated issues. As early as 1739 Cadwallader Colden, New York official, doctor, mathematician, and botanist, suggested to Franklin and others that American scientists organize a learned society. In 1743 Franklin formally proposed the American Philosophical Society, which faced competition from another Philadelphia scientific society in the early 1750s. The two organizations combined as the American Philosophical Society in 1768. Meanwhile, New Yorkers established in 1748 the Society for the Promotion of Useful Knowledge, which was essentially a literary society. The American Philosophical Society corresponded regularly with the Royal Society, but not until 1771 did it produce its own *Transactions*, which Benjamin Franklin promptly sent to all European learned societies. In 1764 New Yorkers organized the Society for the Promotion of Arts, Agriculture and Oeconomy, which offered bounties for manufactured products normally imported from Britain. This society was primarily an economic measure provoked by the Stamp Act rather than a true learned society.

Sources:

Stephen Botein, "The Legal Profession in Colonial North America," in *Lawyers in Early Modern Europe and America*, edited by Wilfrid Prest (New York: Holmes & Meier, 1981);

Richard D. Brown, *Knowledge Is Power: The Diffusion of Information in Early America, 1700–1865* (New York: Oxford University Press, 1989);

Lawrence A. Cremin, *American Education: The Colonial Experience, 1607–1683* (New York: Harper & Row, 1970);

Bruce Curtis, "Some Recent Work on the History of Literacy in Canada," *History of Education Quarterly*, 30 (1990): 613–624;

Richard Beale Davis, *A Colonial Southern Bookshelf: Reading in the Eighteenth Century* (Athens: University of Georgia Press, 1979);

Kenneth Lockridge, *Literacy in Colonial New England* (New York: Norton, 1974);

Perry Miller, *Errand Into the Wilderness* (Cambridge, Mass.: Harvard University Press, 1956);

Joel Perlmann and Dennis Shirley, "Where Did New England Women Acquire Literacy?," *William and Mary Quarterly*, 48 (1991): 50–67;

Ellis Raesly, *Portrait of New Netherland* (New York: Columbia University Press, 1945);

Marc Simmons, "Authors and Books in Colonial New Mexico," in *Voices from the Southwest: A Gathering in Honor of Lawrence Clark Powell*, edited by Donald C. Dickinson, and others (Flagstaff, Ariz.: Northland Press, 1976), pp. 13–32.

NATIVE AMERICANS

Uneducated Pagans. The Spanish, English, Dutch, and French all professed their desire to teach Native Americans the gospel of Jesus Christ. Indeed, spreading Christianity to the benighted peoples of the New World was a prime rationale for European colonization. However, propagating the faith always took place within a broader cultural context peculiar to the nationality of the colonists involved. Both the Spanish and the English thought in terms of transforming the Indians' way of life, but only the Spanish pursued that goal rigorously and made it the foundation upon which much of Spanish American culture was based. Of course it was arguably much more the result of European and Indian sexual intermingling than the monumental educational efforts jointly undertaken by the Catholic Church and the Spanish Crown. Moreover, in the borderlands of Florida, Texas, and New Mexico, Spanish success at acculturating the Indians was limited at best. The British too aimed at civilizing as well as Christianizing the Indians, but compared to the Spanish, whose mighty missionary efforts were driven by the powerful Catholic Church, the British commitment to propagating their faith and culture among Native Americans was desultory. Also bringing together the resources of their Catholic Church and Crown, the French missionary adventure in North America was extensively pursued through the Saint Lawrence River valley, the Illinois country, and down the Mississippi River valley to Louisiana and the Gulf of Mexico. Less intrusive and generally more accommodating than Spanish clerics, French priests nevertheless garnered thousands of converts and played a crucial role in forging a Franco-Indian alliance that dominated much of North America. The European missions to the Indians aside, the most fascinating educational story regarding the Indians concerned their adjustments to the European invasion of America that began with Columbus's arrival in 1492.

Florida. During their war against the Aztec empire in the 1520s, Spaniards developed attitudes toward the Indians that would shape their policy in the borderlands. Before the Aztecs could be taught the gospel, the Spanish conquerors believed, their old religion, which sanctioned human sacrifice and idolatry, had to be crushed. The Franciscan priests carried this conquest mentality into the borderlands, bound and determined not just to convert the natives but to civilize them. Because of its location near the Bahamas channel used by Spanish treasure ships, Florida was of strategic importance. After the French established a Huguenot settlement there in 1564, Spain struck back. The French fort was destroyed; Saint Augustine was established in 1565; and presidios and missions gradually multiplied through central and northern Florida. Numbering perhaps as many as five hundred thousand in 1500, the Indians in Florida—the Calusa, Tequesta, Tocobaga, Timuca, and Apalachee—declined rapidly in response to disease, warfare, and enslavement. By 1650 Franciscan friars had disrupted traditional tribal life and established thirty-eight missions, to which were attached twenty-six thousand Indian converts. Intent upon advancing both Christianity and Spanish culture, the Franciscans tightly regulated mission life, teaching not only religious doctrine but handicrafts and farming skills. Several tribes such as the Guales and Westos never accepted Spanish domination and resisted fiercely the expansion of Franciscan missions. The Creek Indians and English settlers from the Carolinas raided the Flor-

ida missions, seizing the Indian converts and selling them into slavery in the Caribbean.

Eighteenth Century. By 1750 Florida was garrisoned by four hundred soldiers, but the Indian population may well have declined to no more than a few thousand, and the civilian population remained slight. Deerskins were the chief export, and Saint Augustine had to be continuously supplied from Cuba. Threatened by growing English populations in South Carolina and Georgia, Spanish officials in Florida granted freedom to runaway slaves from Carolina and Georgia, who joined with friendly Indians and Spanish troops in defending the province. In 1763, when Florida was surrendered to the English at the end of the French and Indian War, the Spanish government evacuated some thirty-one hundred settlers and Indians to Cuba and New Spain.

New Mexico. As in Florida, demographic catastrophe reduced the Pueblo Indians in New Mexico from eighty thousand in 1598 to seventeen thousand in 1679. Some twenty-four Pueblo towns survived the conquest, and they were divided into seven districts by the Franciscans, who were determined to root out the idolatrous religion they believed the Indians practiced. Everything about Pueblo life had religious significance, from irrigating the fields and working the corn crops to annual hunting trips. The gods were collectively known as the kachinas, and many voluntary associations, dedicated to one of the kachinas, were formed to pass along crucial knowledge about daily life and work which this or that particular god had supposedly passed along to the people once upon a time. Just as parents taught their young basic skills and kinship traditions, so did the associations initiate the young into the myriad of rules and regulations that governed the village. Taught to obey and conform, Pueblo Indians appeared to take the teaching of the Franciscans to heart, increasing numbers accepting Christianity and working at the missions, where they practiced their traditional arts and also those Spanish handicrafts introduced by the friars. Although the Franciscans confiscated ceremonial masks, prohibited the traditional rituals which took place in the kiva (underground religious chambers), and punished native religious leaders who dared to defy them openly, the Pueblo accepted Christian baptism but continued to keep their customs.

Revolt and Aftermath. The uncompromising stand of the Franciscans, coupled with several years of drought and rising persecution of native religious leaders, led to the Pueblo Revolt in 1680, during which the Spanish colonists were driven from the northern Rio Grande, including Sante Fe, and the old religious ways were fully revived. A dozen years later the Spanish began to reconquer the Pueblo, taking a frightful vengeance upon the Indians. However, the Franciscans who returned with the soldiers did not try to dominate the Pueblo as before the 1680 revolt. The Pueblo continued to become more Hispanized, incorporating more and more Catholic doc-

The Brafferton, a dormitory for Native American students, built at the College of William and Mary in 1723

trine into their lives, but it was increasingly upon their own terms. As for the friars, they concentrated increasingly upon the general population, catechizing and nurturing the faith among the settlers and their children as well as the Indians. By 1750 the settlers numbered about four thousand and the Indians about ten thousand. As Pueblos and settlers alike banded together to resist marauding Apache and Comanche, cultural and religious compromise became more acceptable for the Pueblo and their Hispanic neighbors alike.

Arizona and Texas. The work of Father Eusebio Francisco Kino and two other Jesuit priests among the Indians of northern Mexico and southern Arizona proved a salutary contrast to the Franciscan missionaries in New Mexico. Unlike the Franciscans, who generally thought that Indian culture was incorrigible and must be totally transformed, the Jesuits believed that they could engraft Christianity upon the religious views of the Indians. Ministering among the Pimas and their northern neighbors, the Papagos, the Jesuits were much more gentle and positive in their missionary approach than the Franciscans. Father Kino established some twenty enclaves of Christian Indians, introduced wheat and other European cereals, and brought cattle and other livestock into the region. Carefully catechizing and preparing the Indians for baptism, Father Kino also utilized other Christian Indians to spread the gospel. Altogether, despite their cautious approach to proselyting, Kino and his Jesuit cohorts baptized more than thirty thousand Indians between 1687 and 1711. However, following his death his missions among the peoples of the Pimeria Alta were neglected and failed. Fear of French expansion into Texas in 1714 shifted Spanish attention, both civil and ecclesiastical, toward the region northeast of Mexico which had been declared a frontier province in 1691. Between 1717 and 1724 the Franciscans established ten missions and the Viceroyalty of New Spain established four presidios in Texas, with San Antonio de Bejar as its capital. In the mission communities converts were not only instructed in Catholicism but also taught various trades that would enhance the self-sufficiency of the mission itself. Mission work among the nomadic and warlike Apache, Comanche, and various Indian bands known collectively as Norteños was challenging and dangerous. The Spanish settlements were vulnerable to marauding Indians and the French, both of whom came well armed. As late as 1742 there were only eighteen hundred Spaniards and thirteen hundred Native Americans in Texas.

Early French Missions. As Samuel de Champlain, the entrepreneur who founded Quebec in 1609, made trade agreements with the Indians of Canada, he obtained their approval to send missionaries among them. The Recollects and the Capuchins, both reform branches of the Franciscans, were the first French missionaries in Canada. However, the Franciscans thought in terms of root-and-branch reformation of the Indians, that is, transforming them into good Christian Frenchmen, something that was quite impossible to do as long as French colonists remained few in number in the province. In short, the Indians had to be civilized before they would become good candidates for Christianity. So the Recollect and Capuchins encouraged the Huron and Montagnais to give up nomadic habits and settle near European villages, become farmers, and send their children to Catholic schools. They educated some Indian boys themselves in Canada and sent others to France for schooling. However, they had little success. Between 1615 and 1627 the Recollects reportedly baptized only fifty-four Indians, forty-one of whom had stopped coming to church services.

French Jesuits. Clerics of the Society of Jesus were better equipped to preach and teach among the Indians of New France. In 1625 the Jesuit mission to the Huron began in earnest with the arrival of Fathers Charles Lalemand, Jean de Brebeuf, and Ennemond Masse. In 1639, thanks largely to the encouragement of the Jesuits, the Ursulines and the Soeurs Hospitalières of Dieppes founded a school for girls and a hospital in Quebec. The school was initially intended for Indian girls, but their parents were resistant. Rather than simply dismissing Indian culture as worthless paganism, the Jesuits learned to build upon certain traditional elements in Indian religion to bring them around to Christianity. So the Jesuits traveled and lived with the Indians and accepted much of Native American culture as legitimate. They generally found it did little good to complain about the lack of sexual inhibitions of young girls, easy divorce practices of adults, or ritualistic torture and cannibalism. Unlike the Franciscans, who were usually rotated around every five years, the French Jesuits would spend many years—often the remainder of their lives—ministering to the same Indians. Such methods won not only converts but respect for the "blackrobes," whose gentle ways and strange dress had initially led the Indians to ridicule them. Altogether, 115 Jesuit fathers came to New France during the seventeenth century.

Later Mission Efforts. The Jesuits early on concentrated their efforts among the Hurons, who dominated the fur trade in Canada and who lived in a vast area bounded by Georgian Bay and lakes Huron, Erie, Ontario, and Simcoe. They learned their language, nursed them through illnesses, assisted them with farming, and began to gain a following among the thirty thousand Hurons by discrediting native religious leaders. However, between 1648 and 1650 the Iroquois from the Finger Lakes region of western New York invaded Huronia and either killed or dispersed all its people, including some Jesuit priests, who claimed twelve thousand Huron converts before the Iroquois massacres. After gathering together the remnants of the Huron people, the Jesuits continued their ministry among the Indians in the east and the west, often traveling with explorers and fur-traders to tribes who had not heard the gospel. As with the Huron, the Jesuits learned the languages of other tribes; translated the Catholic catechism, creeds, and set prayers into the local Indian dialect; and exercised native catechumens orally in the doctrines of the faith. Indian languages, though wonderfully suited to the style of life of their speakers, were ill equipped to convey the often abstract meaning of European Christianity. Sin, for example, as an offense before God, was simply not in their vocabulary. Jesuits overcame this linguistic obstacle by living with the Indians, by learning many of the nuances of their oral cultures, by the use of ritual and singing, and by using familiar occurrences to convey Christian principles. Images, especially ornamental crucifixes, vessels, vestments, pictures in Bibles, and token figures of Mary and the baby Jesus given to the Indians, were important instruments of propagating the faith.

Mississippi Valley Missions. As the Jesuits moved west into the Illinois country and down the Mississippi River, they taught not only Catholic doctrine but also French and on occasion would send a bright Indian boy

Eleazar Wheelock, founder of Moor's Charity School for Indians in Lebanon, Connecticut
(Dartmouth College Library)

back to Quebec or Montreal for study. A few of these young men continued to be transported to France to attend a grammar school or college. However, the results of such a French education were not encouraging, for when the educated young Indians returned, they found themselves creatures torn between two worlds, neither of which fully accepted them. Those who learned French and remained with their respective tribes, however, often became important cultural mediators. Jesuit missions were established among the Ojibwes at Keweenaw Bay on Lake Superior in 1660 and on the western shore of Lake Superior at La Pointe du Saint Esprit in 1665. Opposition of the warlike Lakota forced Father Jacques Marquette to abandon La Pointe and establish another mission on Michilimackinac Island in the straits between Lakes Michigan and Huron in 1671. Having explored the Mississippi River with Louis Jolliet in 1673, Father Marquette established a mission he called Immaculate Conception among the Illinois Indians at Kaskaskia in 1674, the year before his death. Other Catholic missions were established at Detroit, Vincennes, and Saint Louis, with Christian Indians always congregating nearby. However, despite the French colonization along the Gulf Coast in the eighteenth century, French missions among the Muskogean Indians of the area never flourished, in part because ecclesiastical jurisdiction over the region was disputed for decades by the bishop of Quebec, the Congregation de Propaganda Fide in Rome, and the Society for Foreign Missions.

New Netherland. Dutch traders and Iroquois chiefs early on formed a military and economic alliance that proved mutually beneficial. The Iroquois served as the middlemen in the fur trade between the Dutch and the western Indians, performing much the same role as their traditional enemies, the Huron, did for the French. The Provisional Articles for New Netherland, promulgated by the Dutch West India Company in 1624, expected the colonists to lead the Indians to Christ. "By the example of godliness and outward discipline on the part of the Christians," wrote the commissioners of the company, "the heathen may sooner be brought to a knowledge of the same." The first Dutch Reformed preacher in the colony, Jonas Michaelius, who arrived in New Amsterdam in 1628, found ministering to the Indians especially frustrating. Domine Michelius stated that they were "entirely savage and wild, strangers to all decency, yea, uncivil and stupid as garden poles, proficient in all wickedness and godlessness; devilish men, who served the Devil." The only way to Christianize the Indians, Michelius believed, was to separate the young from their parents and teach them both the Dutch language and Christian principles before they learned "the heathenish tricks and deviltries" of their elders. But the domine doubted that such a plan could ever be implemented, given the reluctance of Indian parents to be separated from their offspring. In 1642 Domine Johannes Megapolensis became the minister for Rensselaerswyck, the patroonship located up the Hudson surrounding Fort Orange. Megapolensis learned the Mohawk tongue and wrote a small book about them, but he apparently had little success converting them to the Christian faith. In 1649 Megapolensis was called to New Amsterdam, where he was joined shortly by another preacher, Domine Samuel Drisius. In 1657, having worked for two years instructing their single Indian convert in the Christian doctrine, the two domines sadly reported that their once prized neophyte had become a drunk, sold his Bible, and "turned into a regular beast, doing more harm than good among the Indians." Domine Gideon Schaets, who had replaced Megalpolensis at Rensselaerswyck in 1652, was asked to "use all Christian zeal there to bring up both the Heathen and their children in the Christian religion," but his success was negligible.

Virginia. The English mission to the Indians in Virginia began promisingly enough as the Reverend Alexander Whitaker converted the Indian princess Pocahontas to Christianity. The latter's visit to England, which ended tragically with her death, built public support for the establishment of an Indian college at Henrico, a project that collapsed with the massacre of settlers around Jamestown in 1622. "The way of conquering them is much more easy than of civilizing them by fair means," reported officials of the Virginia Company after suppressing the Indian uprising, "for they are a rude, barbarious, and naked people, scattered in small companies, which are helps to victory, but hindrance to civility: Besides that, a conquest may be of many and at once; but civility is in particular, and, slow, the effect of long time, and great industry." Despite such sentiments, the charter granted the College of William and Mary in 1693 called for the establishment of a school with one professor to teach Indian boys reading, writing, arithmetic, and religion. The latter provision qualified the college for funds from the legacy of Robert Boyle, and an Indian school was established.

Mayhew and Eliot. In New England, given their rigorous theology with its emphasis upon the conversion experience, biblical knowledge, and disciplined living, the Puritans found proselytizing the Indians especially challenging. Few were converted before the 1640s when Thomas Mayhew Jr. of Martha's Vineyard and John Eliot of Roxbury began their respective ministries to the local Indians in Massachusetts. By 1652 Mayhew had 283 Indian converts. Convinced that it was "absolutely necessary to carry on civility with religion," John Eliot established the first town for his "praying Indians" in 1651. Over the next fourteen years thirteen towns of praying Indians were established, but only two of them had churches with covenants that fully met the approval of neighboring Puritan congregations. Eliot also established English schools in the towns of the praying Indians. Both Mayhew and Eliot were assisted by the Society for the Propagation of the Gospel in New England, chartered by Parliament in 1649 and having collected almost £16,000 by 1660. Rechartered after the restoration of the Stuart monarchy as the "Company for Propagation of the Gospell in New England and the Parts Adjacent in America," under the leadership of the scientist Robert Boyle, this organization underwrote the publication of several books in the Algonquian language, including Eliot's Algonquian edition of the Bible. By the early 1670s approximately twenty-five hundred Christian Indians lived in New England, roughly 20 percent of the remaining Indians in the region. During King Philip's War perhaps a third of the praying Indians joined in and attacked New Englanders. Although the assistance of the other two-thirds of the praying Indians was crucial in the death of King Philip and the defeat of his forces, wartime hostilities destroyed most of their towns and brought the praying Indians under considerable suspicion. Even before King Philip's War, Eliot and other New England mission leaders had come to doubt the wisdom of relying upon native teachers and made plans for establishing English schools. Given what they perceived as the "idle ways" of the Indians, New Englanders generally had decided that Indians would have to be Anglicized before there was hope for them to be truly civilized and Christianized.

Missions in the South. In 1714, to curry favor with the Siouan-speaking tribes along Virginia's vulnerable southwestern frontier, Gov. Alexander Spotswood of Virginia established Fort Christina, where reportedly as many as seventy-seven Indian children were also taught English and exercised in the Anglican catechism. After political feuding in 1717 led the Virginia Burgesses to refuse further funding of the frontier outpost, the teacher at Fort Christina, Charles Griffin, became master of the Indian school at the College of William and Mary. Over the years Indian attendance varied, from a reported high of twenty-four in one year to one in another. In fact, well into the 1730s William and Mary itself was not much of a college, hardly more than a grammar school for planters' sons. In 1721 there were no Indian students, but money allotted by the Boyle fund for Indian education in Virginia kept accumulating, so President Blair took £500 from the Boyle fund in 1723 to build Brafferton Hall, the fine two-story structure designated to house the Indians. In 1732 Blair tapped the Boyle account again, this time for the purchase of books to upgrade William and Mary's small library, where Indians as well as white students would presumably use them. However, relatively few Indians were housed in Brafferton until intercolonial warfare in the 1740s and 1750s brought young Cherokee and Shawnee hostages there to be taught reading, writing, and religion. Many of them died there, victims of the unfamiliar and deadly disease environment despite considerable effort to give them the best medical care. Others simply ran away. As Gov. Robert Dinwiddie wrote in 1756 of some Cherokee boys, they had "no Inclination to Learning" and "could not be reconciled to their books." William Byrd II complained of the Indian schoolboys that once back with their people they "immediately Relapt into Infidelity and Barbarism themselves." Indeed, Byrd believed, "since they unhappily forget all the good they learn, and remember the Ill, they are apt to be more vicious and disorderly than the rest of their Countrymen." In the rest of the colonial South, the Society for the Propagation of the Gospel in Foreign Parts (S.P.G.) encouraged its missionaries to teach God's Word to the Indians, and some surely did, though most stayed along the coastal settlements where relatively few Indians lived. In the late colonial period the Presbyterians in Virginia especially and the Moravians in North Carolina and Georgia also engaged in missions to the Indians, though their impact was probably even slighter than that of the S.P.G. in the South.

New England Missions. Few of Eliot's Indian-language translations were published after 1700. There was little enthusiasm even for reprinting Eliot's Indian Bible. "It is a very sure, the best thing we can do for our Indians is to Anglicize them in all agreeable Instances," wrote Cotton Mather, "and in that of Language, as well as others." The Indians could not retain their language, Mather insisted, "without a Tincture of other Salvage Inclinations, which do but ill suit, either with the Honor, or with the design of Christianity." Although much diminished, the work that Eliot had begun continued

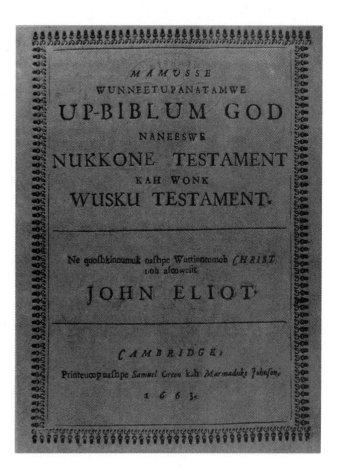

Title page for John Eliot's first complete Indian Bible

among the declining praying Indians as English-language instruction became the order of the day. During the seventeenth century, while Indian missions were flourishing in Massachusetts, they were largely nonexistent in Connecticut. At the behest of Cotton Mather, whose influence with the Company for the Propagation of the Gospel in New England was significant, the Connecticut General Assembly founded a school on the Mohegan reserve in 1726. Shortly thereafter another English school for Indians was funded by the Company at New London.

The Godly. However, Mather and Connecticut governor Joseph Talcott believed the best method of "civilizing and Christianizing" the Indians would be putting native children as apprentices in "English and Godly Families." Their respective masters would be required to educate them. When the reluctance of the Indians to part with their children killed the apprenticeship scheme, those pushing the Connecticut missions next advocated boarding schools that separated Indian youth from their primitive, heathen habits. Not only Indian boys but Indian girls too were to be educated at boarding schools because male graduates needed civilized mates or else they would likely leave the faith and return to their native ways. Not only John Mason's school at New London but also the Reverend Samuel Whitman's school at Farmington took Indian boarders. A few of their Indian students, like John Mettawan of Whitman's school, became teachers themselves. The Stockbridge mission in Massachusetts's Housatonic River valley, under the leadership of the Reverend John Sergeant and Timothy Woodbridge, the Indian schoolmasters, made plans for an Indian boarding school which opened in 1749, shortly after Sergeant's death. Jonathan Edwards, who succeeded Sergeant as missionary, had to do battle with relatives of Sergeant's widow to take control of the boarding school, which in 1752 was directed by Gideon Hawley, whose students included several Mohawk children from New York. The school was burned under mysterious circumstances in early 1753, ending its educational mission to the Mohawk. That same year the Reverend Eleazar Wheelock, a New Light Congregationalist, opened his Indian free school in Lebanon, Connecticut. Among his early students was Samson Occom, easily the most famous Indian preacher in colonial America, who established Presbyterian congregations among the Montauk Indians on Long Island. Wheelock's school was later endowed by Col. Joshua More and became known as "Moor's Charity School," where ten Indian students were studying in 1761. After the French and Indian War, Wheelright convinced Sir William Johnson, the British superintendent of Indian affairs, to send him several Mohawk boys, including Joseph Brant, later famed as an Indian leader during the American Revolution. With the money that Occom and others collected for him during a successful fund-raising trip to England, Wheelock, who was growing weary with his Indian school, turned his efforts toward the founding of Dartmouth College in New Hampshire.

Middle Colonies. Following the conquest of New Netherland in 1664, the British governors of New York encouraged the Dutch Reformed clergy of Albany and its environs to cultivate the faith among the nearby Mohawk and other Iroquois nations, for diplomatic as well as religious reasons. The Iroquois had been crucial political and commercial allies of the Dutch against the French. In the 1680s Gov. Thomas Dogan, himself a Catholic, considered introducing English Jesuits among the Iroquois to counter the influence of French priests. However, the overthrow of James II in 1688 in the Glorious Revolution ended any thought about English Jesuits, though King William's War made it all the more important to the English to cultivate the Iroquois. In the 1690s Gov. Benjamin Fletcher encouraged Domine Godfriedus Dellius, the Dutch Reformed minister at Albany, to preach to the Mohawk. Dellius baptized more than a hundred; admitted sixteen to communion; and translated the Ten Commandments, creeds, and psalms into the Mohawk language. After 1700 Domine Bernardus Freeman of Schenectady and Domine Johannes Lydius of Albany were likewise encouraged by New York governors to minister to the Indians. The Anglican Society for the Propagation of the Gospel in Foreign Parts (S.P.G.), founded in 1701, sent Thoroughgood Moore

as its first missionary to the Iroquois in 1705. Moore left his post after one frustrating year. "Tis from the behavior of the Christians here that they [the Indians] have had and still have their notions of Christianity, which God knows has been and generally is such that I can't but think has made the Indian hate Christianity." After Peter Schuyler brought four Mohawk chiefs to London in 1710, the S.P.G. responded to popular enthusiasm for the Indians and in 1712 sent missionary William Andrews to Fort Hunter, in the Mohawk Valley, where a handsomely outfitted chapel had been built for the Indians, thanks to Queen Anne. Andrews established a school for Indian youth, shortly reporting more than forty students, and made good progress for a couple of years in preaching and teaching to the Mohawk. But the school began to fail, and as the gifts Andrews brought began to run out, so did attendance at his church services. The failure of the Christian Indians to give up such heathen ways as torturing captives and getting drunk angered the young cleric. "Heathen they are," wrote the exasperated Andrews as he left in 1718, "and Heathen they shall be." In the other Middle Colonies there was little organized effort to Christianize the Indians before 1740, though the Quakers, who preferred to influence by example, did establish good relations early on with Indians in both Pennsylvania and New Jersey, and there is evidence that a few Indians, mostly orphans or indentured servants, received some schooling in the other Middle Colonies as well as New York.

Later Efforts. The religious revivalism known as the Great Awakening reinvigorated Indian missions and the educational efforts directed toward Indian youth which usually accompanied them. In the 1740s the Moravians, whose missionary work among the Indians in many ways resembled that of the French Jesuits, taught both the young and the old. Moravian missionaries were active in New York and Pennsylvania. Accused of being Catholics in disguise, the Moravians aroused quite a stir in New York, especially because of their work among the dispirited Shakomeko Indians in Dutchess County between 1740 and 1744. In Pennsylvania the Moravians established several Christian Indian towns along the western frontier and beyond into the Ohio Territory, several of which survived until the American Revolution. In 1741 the Presbytery of New York, acting on behalf of the Society in Scotland for Propagating Christian Knowledge (S.S.P.C.K.), appointed Azariah Horton, a recent Yale graduate, as minister to the four hundred or so remaining Indians on the southern shore of Long Island. The next year David Brainerd, another Yale alumnus, gained the sponsorship of the S.S.P.C.K. and began his ministry in New Jersey and eastern Pennsylvania, working primarily among the Delaware Indians. Upon his death in 1747 his younger brother, John, became pastor to the Christian Delaware, whose primary reservation was named Brothertown in Burlington, New Jersey. The Anglican mission to the Indians in New York was picking up even before the Great Awakening. At Fort Hunter, after William Andrews left in 1718, various Anglican clerics from Albany had preached and exercised Indians young and old in the catechism. However, in 1735 another Yale graduate, Henry Barclay, whose father had earlier been Anglican minister to Albany, was named catechist to Fort Hunter. After eighteen months on the job he reported that he taught more than forty students to read and write their own language. Barclay continued to visit Fort Hunter after he became the Anglican missionary to Albany, where served from 1738 to 1746. Between 1736 and 1777 John Jacob Oel, a German minister with Anglican ordination, assisted significantly in the Mohawk mission. Taking charge of Indian affairs in New York in 1746, William Johnson worked hard to get both missionaries and schoolmasters for the Iroquois. Johnson and Henry Barclay secured the publication of a Mohawk Prayer Book in 1769, and despite his suspicions of New England Congregationalists, Johnson initially encouraged the work of Eleazar Wheelock among the Iroquois, including that of his protégé, Samuel Kirkland. The Reverend Kirkland began his ministry among the Oneidas near Brothertown, New York, in 1766, and due in no small measure to his missionary labors, the Oneidas generally sided with the Americans during the Revolution. Similarly, John Stuart, an Anglican priest, began his labors among the Mohawk Indians in 1770, and his ministry played a major role in keeping the other nations of the Iroquois Confederations generally loyal to Great Britain after the Americans declared their independence.

Sources:

James Axtell, *The Invasion Within: The Contest of Cultures in Colonial North America* (New York & Oxford: Oxford University Press, 1985);

Henry Warner Bowden, *American Indians and Christian Missions: Studies in Cultural Conflict* (Chicago: University of Chicago Press, 1981);

John Calam, *Parsons and Pedagogues: The S.P.G. Adventure in American Education* (New York: Columbia University Press, 1971);

Henry F. Dobyns, "Indians in the Colonial Spanish Borderlands," in *Indian American History: An Introduction,* edited by Frederick E. Hoxie (Arlington Heights, Ill.: Harlan Davidson, 1988), pp. 67–93;

W. J. Eccles, *The Canadian Frontier, 1534–1760,* revised edition (Albuquerque: University of New Mexico Press, 1983);

Cornelius J. Jaenen, *Friend and Foe: Aspects of French-Amerindian Cultural Contact in the Sixteenth and Seventeenth Centuries* (New York: Columbia University Press, 1976);

James McCallum, *Eleazar Wheelock: Founder of Dartmouth College* (New York: Arno, 1969);

Edgar McInnis, *Canada: A Political and Social History* (New York: Rinehart, 1947);

Edward H. Spicer, *Cycles of Conquest: The Impact of Spain, Mexico, and the United States on the Indians of the Southwest, 1533–1960* (Tucson: University of Arizona Press, 1962);

Margaret C. Szasz, *Indian Education in the American Colonies, 1607–1763* (Albuquerque: University of New Mexico Press, 1988).

SCHOOLING: AN EVOLVING VARIETY

Characteristics. From the seventeenth to the eighteenth centuries, schooling played an increasingly important part in the education of young Americans. More colleges were founded, of course, but the greatest proliferation of schooling came below the college level. In both New France and the Spanish borderlands the Catholic Church continued to control formal schooling, generally making sure that academic standards and religious orthodoxy were maintained. In New Netherland as well as the British colonies schooling was closely allied with the various Protestant denominations throughout the seventeenth century. During the eighteenth century schooling proliferated and became more accessible and diverse in subject offerings than in either New France or the Spanish borderlands. Throughout the Americas, though, education reflected the class system, and except in Canada, boys were much more likely than girls to have schooling. Young men from the lower classes might attend some elementary school and go into apprenticeship training. On the other hand, sons of the gentry were expected to study Latin grammar and the Greek and Roman classics. Latin grammar schools were scarce in the Spanish borderlands, where sons of wealthy families had private tutors or attended school in the more settled provinces of New Spain. Most of the schoolmasters in New France and the Spanish borderlands were priests, but in New Netherland and British North America teachers were usually laymen, though preachers sometimes instructed a few boys in Latin grammar. Teachers were valued, and Latin masters often made a better than middling living. However, masters of primary schools teaching reading, writing, and arithmetic were usually poorly paid. Indeed, most schoolmasters plied several vocations to make ends meet or until they could establish themselves in another more lucrative vocation.

New Netherland. In 1638, at the behest of Domine Everardus Bogardus, the Dutch Reformed pastor at New Amsterdam, the West India Company employed a schoolmaster, Adam Roelantsen, whose credentials were certified by the Classis of Amsterdam, the ecclesiastical body having jurisdiction over New Netherland. Roelantsen's school was for young children, both girls and boys, and emphasized the Heidelberg Catechism and reading and writing. Roelantsen turned out to be a disappointing teacher. However, from 1638 on the company and the Reformed clergy generally cooperated in securing qualified teachers as immigration brought more families to the Dutch colony. "In order to best help the church of God here, and to resist a bad world," wrote Domine Johannes Backerus in 1648, "I think we must begin with the children, for many of the older people are so far depraved they are now ashamed to learn anything good." Bogardus found a ready ally in Director General Peter Stuyvesant, who arrived in 1647 and immediately began recruiting both clergymen and schoolmasters for the colony. More often than not the village schoolmaster was associated with the local Reformed congregation as sexton and clerk, much as was the case in the Dutch republic. By 1664, when the English conquered New Nether-

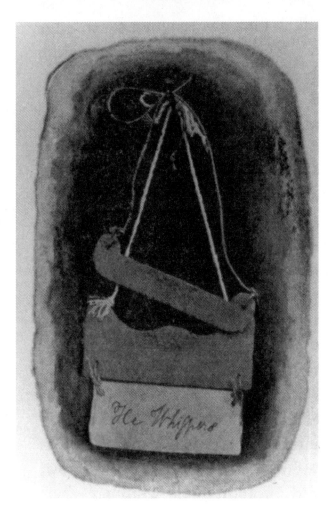

Whispering sticks, circa 1700, used to quiet noisy school-children. The wooden gags fit in the mouth somewhat like a horse's bit (from Alice Morse Earle, *Child Life in Colonial Days*, 1949)

land, of the eleven Dutch chartered towns (including New Amsterdam), all but two are known to have had schoolmasters usually associated with the Dutch reformed congregations. There was also a schoolmaster at New Amstel on the Delaware River, where the city of New Amsterdam maintained a settlement that was under Stuyvesant's jurisdiction as well. In addition Stuyvesant licensed several individuals who conducted private schools unattached to the local congregations. In 1659 the directors of the West India Company sent Alexander Carolus Curtius, a professor from Lithuania, to open a Latin school in New Amsterdam. After a dispute over his salary, Curtius was replaced by Aegidius Lucyck, formerly pastor at New Amstel and tutor to Stuyvesant's children, whose school attracted students from Virginia and continued until 1664.

New France. Most children in New France got little formal education beyond the year of catechetical instruction that most children received as preparation for their first communion, which usually occurred at age ten. Some of the priests also conducted primary schools for both girls and boys in which they taught reading, writing, and arithmetic as well as the catechism. Among the ordinary farmers and fur traders, known as the *habitants*, young women were more apt to get additional schooling than young men, whose labors were much in demand for farmwork, apprenticeships in the trades, or the fur trade. Especially active in establishing schools for girls were the Sisters of the Congregation of Notre Dame, which founded ten such schools by 1707, especially in the rural parishes. More than half the parishes had at least one girls' schools by 1763. Some apprenticeship agreements required masters to teach their charges to read and write. Boys of the upper classes might attend the Jesuits' college at Quebec, founded in 1635, or the Sulpicians' Latin school at Montreal, where they were grounded in the Roman and Greek classics. Bishop François Laval de Montigny began a seminar in 1659 mainly for the education of priests, but young men not especially interested in the priesthood were allowed to attend. Laval's seminary, however, was rigorous, and of 843 who entered only 188 stayed and went into the priesthood. The Jesuits at Quebec also established a school of hydrography for preparing young men as pilots, navigators, and cartographers. Young ladies from the upper classes were likely to attend the various schools founded by the Ursuline sisterhood in Quebec, Trois-Rivières, and Montreal. There they were taught reading, writing, mathematics, chemistry, biology, and botany and rigorously instructed in Latin before being taught French grammar and literature. Some of them would later teach their own children and those of their neighbors, though never establishing schools as such. Besides the priests and nuns, educated young men from France were sometimes allowed to teach, but only under the supervision of the Catholic clergy. The only permanent school at Louisbourg was for girls, founded by the Sisters of the Congregation of Notre Dame in 1727. Schooling was generally neglected in Louisiana, which did not even have a Catholic seminary. However, a Capuchin monk, Father Cecil, did operate a school in the territory from 1725 to 1731. Young men from wealthy families generally went to France for their classical education. In 1727 the Ursuline sisters established a hospital and boarding school for girls in New Orleans. It relocated in 1734 to a building on Chartres Street that still stands.

Spanish Borderlands. The Catholic clergy supervised schooling in present-day New Mexico, Texas, Arizona and Florida among both the settlers and the Indians. Schools were scarce outside the Indian missions until near the end of the eighteenth century. Parents were required by law to provide religious training to their children and servants, and it was common among the upper classes to have live-in tutors for their children. During the conquest of New Spain, children of the Indian elite were educated in the missions and served as a bridge between the Spanish rulers and other Indians. This system, known as the Calmecac, was also followed in the borderlands. The young Indians so educated were called *doctrineros,* and they were utilized in the missions as teachers. Around 1700 Fray Alvarez established a school for reading and writing in Santa Fe. In New Mexico private teachers were often contracted by the mission communities to conduct primary schooling for not only the Indians but also mestizos, mulattoes, Africans, and Spaniards living outside the pueblos. Private tutoring aside, education above the primary level did not exist in the borderlands. However, Durango, in northern Mexico, was one of the places where children of the borderland elite might go for Latin schooling and seminar training.

British North America. The rich variety of schooling that emerged in English America reflected not only its large and growing population but also the economic diversity of the region and the growing importance of literacy in the lives of its people. From the seventeenth to the eighteenth centuries the nature of schooling, and education generally, changed as Anglo-American colonial society expanded and matured. Regional differences in the way schools were founded and maintained remained pronounced, but the trend was everywhere the same: schooling generally became much more accessible. While Latin schools remained the primary institution of secondary education, the "English school" emerged with a curriculum designed to serve the economic ambitions of the growing British American middle classes. While elementary schooling in reading, writing, arithmetic, and the catechism continued to be sponsored in large part by the various religious denominations, the English schools were usually run by private entrepreneurs who offered not only English grammar but also mathematics, modern languages, and practical subjects related to commerce, navigation, and surveying. Especially located in the larger colonial cities and towns, the English schools manifested larger educational trends away from both the classical and the religious and toward the practical and the secular.

Puritan Beginnings. In Britain schooling was the responsibility of the Church of England. Rejecting episcopacy and embracing congregationalism, the Puritans did not have a central ecclesiastical organization that could take the leadership in schooling. Given the communal ethos that dominated Puritan culture in New England, it is not surprising that government, both local and provincial, would exercise authority over education in New England that the Anglican Church did in old England. Eager to secure regular Latin instruction for prospective ministers and other young gentlemen, several Massachusetts towns, led by Boston, began in 1635 establishing schools to teach Latin grammar. However, the General Court, as the Massachusetts provincial government was called, felt that Latin schooling was hardly enough to bring forth the reformation of society the Puritans hoped to achieve. So the General Court passed the famous law of 1642 requiring parents and masters to teach their children, apprentices, and servants to read and understand the Bible and capital laws of the land. This was followed by the famous "Old Deluder Satan" law of 1647 calling upon towns of fifty or more families to establish a school to teach reading and writing. Towns of a hundred or more families were also required to provide a Latin grammar school. Over the next decade all eight of the large towns complied with the grammar-school requirement, but perhaps less than one-third of the towns with fifty families set up petty schools. As the population grew and became geographically extended, magistrates hired teachers and required them to hold classes in different sections of the towns over the space of a year. This "moving school" method made the teacher less accountable to the people of any given district and limited the time their children were likely to have access to schooling. The next stage, which clearly became the rule as the eighteenth century progressed, was the development of the district system, whereby the legislature delegated authority over schooling not to the town but to the various districts of the township. In terms of schooling, Connecticut, Plymouth, and New Hampshire followed the lead of Massachusetts. But in Rhode Island, where religious diversity was celebrated and protected even before 1650, the government did not mandate schooling for fear that one religious sect might be favored above another.

The South. In the Chesapeake, where the Anglican Church was established, the civil government dealt with education only when it came to poor children and orphans. As early as 1642 Virginia began legislating apprenticeship of poor children, much of which called upon masters to teach their apprentices to read and write. However, schools were not mandated. Few parishes built schools or paid a teacher to instruct the poor. As part of their catechetical efforts, some preachers felt compelled to teach reading and writing, but they were the exceptions rather than the rule. During the colonial era nine schools were established by endowments left by generous Virginians specifically for the education of poor children. The other southern colonies followed Virginia's apprenticeship legislation for poor and orphaned youth. In 1696 Maryland set up a government-sponsored corporation to raise funds and implement policy for establishing a Latin school in every county. The trustees of the corporation founded King William's School (later called St. John's) in Annapolis but was able to do little else. Another Maryland law in 1723 encouraged the establishment of schools in several counties, but the religious differences of the settlers worked against the success of this legislation. Similarly, South Carolina tried several times to establish free Latin schools, but class differences and growing religious heterogeneity undermined public support for such measures not only in the Carolinas but throughout the South until after the American Revolution.

The Middle Colonies. Religious and ethnic diversity limited the involvement of the provincial governments in education in the Middle Colonies. In New York, created

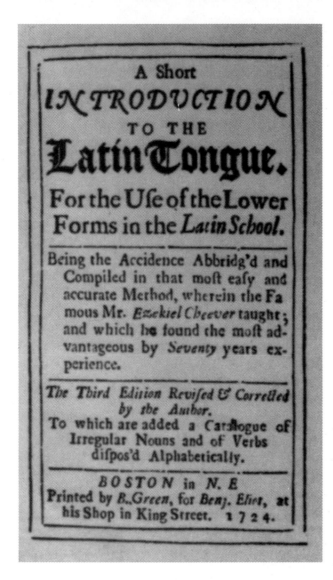

Title page for the third edition of Ezekiel Cheever's influential Latin textbook, first published in 1709

by the conquest of New Netherland in 1664, schooling became the special preserve of the various religious groups; such was also the case in Pennsylvania, where English and Welsh Quakers lost their majority with the immigration of German and Scotch-Irish settlers. Towns and counties did exercise authority over orphans and poor children and apprenticeship generally, but school legislation ran into fears that public funds might help one sect over another. A Latin school was legislated for New York City in 1702 and again in 1732, but neither lasted because of the lack of consensus over religious disposition. In both New York and Pennsylvania non-English settlers were concerned with perpetuating elements of their culture, particularly their respective religious confessions and languages, through schooling. Indeed, the educational dimensions of denominationalism, particularly as it was manifested in schooling, emerged first in the Middle Colonies.

Religious Sponsorship. The proliferation of petty, or elementary, schooling on reading, writing, and arith-

metic after 1700 was largely due to the efforts of various religious groups. Schooling was increasingly seen as essential to keeping children in the faith. It was also useful in terms of proselytizing. In Congregational New England, Baptists and other dissenters claimed the right to maintain their own schools, as did Baptists, Presbyterians, and Lutherans in the Anglican South. The Society for the Propagation of the Gospel in Foreign Parts (the S.P.G.) was a major propagator of the Anglican faith in the Middle Colonies and did more than any provincial government to encourage schooling throughout the southern colonies. The S.P.G. generally subsidized established schoolmasters, requiring them to teach the Anglican catechism along with reading, writing, and arithmetic. Educational rivalry between the Anglicans and Presbyterians became quite intense in the Middle Colonies.

Financing. In New York Anglican influence kept Presbyterian congregations from gaining corporate charters, which made it more difficult for them to raise money and undertake such activities as schooling. But in Pennsylvania the law encouraged religious groups to undertake educational efforts. The Moravians established several foreign-language schools in the Quaker colony, including Nazareth Hall and Christopher Dock's famous school. The German Reformed Church, led by Michael Schlatter, and the Lutherans, led by Henry Muhlenberg, established schools conducted in German that also taught the catechisms of their respective faiths. In Virginia endowed schools like those established by Benjamin Symnes in 1634 and Thomas Eaton in 1659 were given corporate charters in 1753 and 1759, respectively. In the eighteenth century girls as well as boys sometimes attended these schools. In South Carolina a free school was established by the planter organization known as Winyaw Indigo Society. In Georgia the evangelist George Whitefield endowed the Bethesda Orphan House, which served as a free school. Endowed schools were less common in New England, but Edward Hopkins, former governor of Connecticut, provided funds for grammar schools at New Haven, Hartford, and Hadley. The Dummer Academy in Massachusetts, incorporated in 1782, began with an endowment from Lt. Gov. William Dummer in 1761. In Connecticut Joshua Moor endowed the Indian Charity School at Lebanon, taught by the Reverend Eleazar Wheelock. Endowed schools, bolstered by corporate charters, became rather commonplace by 1750 in British America.

Petty Schooling. Most colonial parents, if they were literate themselves, began literacy training of their young in the home, often in conjunction with teaching the catechism. Apprentices sometimes received additional literacy training from their masters, or sometimes the latter sent the former to two or three months of evening school in the winter. Poor children might attend a church school for free, whereas children of the faithful would pay a small fee. Wealthy parents hired tutors or perhaps

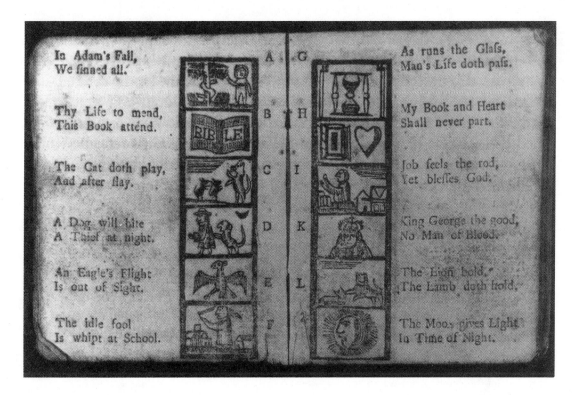

	A	G	
In Adam's Fall, We finned all.			As runs the Glafs, Man's Life doth pafs.
Thy Life to mend, This Book attend.	B	H	My Book and Heart Shall never part.
The Cat doth play, And after flay.	C	I	Job feels the rod, Yet blefses God.
A Dog will bite A Thief at night.	D	K	King George the good, No Man of Blood.
An Eagle's Flight Is out of Sight.	E	L	The Lion bold, The Lamb doth hold.
The idle fool Is whipt at School.	F		The Moon gives Light In Time of Night.

Pages from an early edition of the *New England Primer*, a widely used spelling book first published in the late 1680s

prevailed upon a Latin master to teach English as preparation for the classical languages.

Reading. Elementary education in early New England was sometimes separated into reading and writing schools. Reading was the first to be taught, usually through recitation of the alphabet as the catechism was being learned. This was the method followed in New England and also in Pennsylvania in the German-language school run by the pious Christopher Dock, one of the most remarkable teachers in colonial America. The hornbook, so called because it was a single parchment page covered by transparent horn, usually contained the alphabet, simple syllables, and the Lord's Prayer. Parents used hornbooks, as did female teachers who ran so-called dame schools. Usually the dame schools were more custodial than educational, though there were exceptions. In the dame schools the girls were often given lessons in cooking and sewing as well as reading.

Writing. When students were learning how to write, the primer replaced the hornbook. Its content was decidedly religious, building upon the rudimentary doctrine conveyed through the hornbook and oral recitation of the catechism. *The New England Primer* (1690), the most famous of such texts, combined in a single volume the alphabet and an approved catechism. The most popular catechism, repeatedly printed in *The New England Primer,* was John Cotton's famed *Spiritual Milk for Boston Babes in Either England* (1656). A typical primer began with the alphabet followed by lists of syllables. Woodcuts adorned *The New England Primer,* many of them illustrating the alphabet and accompanied by sim-

ple rhymed verse. For example, a woodcut of a figure picking an apple from a tree is followed by "In Adam's Fall, We sinned all." Next came moral lessons for children, the Lord's Prayer, the Apostles' creed, the Ten Commandments, the names of the Books of the Bible, and finally the Westminster Catechism and Cotton's famed catechism. Children were expected to read, re-read, and recite from the primer. Much of the recitation was done in unison so that the more-advanced students could encourage those less skilled. In virtually all petty schools prayer and Bible readings marked both the beginning and end of the day. The towns' schools and schools sponsored by the various religious groups required that the masters bring their children to church Sunday for catechizing by the pastor.

Attendance. Few children went more than three years to such petty schools, and then seldom more than a couple of months each year. Children from wealthy families were placed in grammar school at age seven. Poor rural parents had little money to spend on education and usually needed their children to assist on the family farms. Nevertheless, the fact remains that petty, or elementary, schooling was becoming increasingly available in British North America by 1750. Indeed, its ubiquitousness surely contributed substantially to the burgeoning literacy rates that the British colonies enjoyed after that date.

Grammar Schooling. As in England, boys destined for college or leadership in the professions had to study Latin and some Greek, the languages of scholarship and learning. In the seventeenth century New England, of all the regions of British North America, was most conscientious in establishing grammar schools. The 1647 Massachusetts law calling for the establishment of grammar as well as petty schools reflected not only the Puritan desire for an educated ministry but the presence in the community of many college graduates. In the Middle Colonies and the South knowing Latin and at least some Greek was a mark of upper-class status, one that gentleman planters no less than clergymen cultivated. The wealthy and urbane Virginia planter William Byrd II seldom began the day without reading or rereading something in Latin, Greek, or Hebrew. The upper-class association with Latin schooling remained paramount throughout the colonial era, and the curriculum of the grammar school changed little, though private tutors who lived with wealthy families and town masters varied their approach somewhat. Reading, memorization, oral recitation, and writing were the techniques most heavily relied upon, with an emphasis on rote memory. Girls in the upper classes occasionally learned some Latin by studying along with their brothers under the guidance of a tutor, but females were generally not taught the language.

Years of Study. Typically, young boys began grammar school at age seven or eight, and the course of study lasted seven years, usually six days a week, throughout the year. For the first three years boys memorized a Latin primer called an "accidence." In their fourth year boys studied Latin grammar, often using William Lily's classic text from the sixteenth century or the more recent one done by Ezekiel Cheever, the legendary master of the Boston Latin School; students also began to read more-advanced works by Erasmus, Aesop, and Ovid. The fifth year emphasized writing Latin prose and verse as well as continued reading in Erasmus and Ovid as well as Cicero's letters. The sixth year was usually devoted to classics such as Cicero's *De Officiis*, Virgil's *Aeneid* (30–19 B.C.), and Ovid's *Metamorphoses* (A.D. 1–8), and both Greek and rhetoric were also introduced. In the final year students added other Greek authors to their reading list, including Horace, Juvenal, Homer, Isocra-

tes, and Hesiod and also the New Testament in Greek. Considerable care was also given to translating Latin into Greek and to writing Latin dialogues, verses, and essays. Hebrew was also often introduced in the seventh year. While studying Latin grammar, most students continued learning English grammar as well. They might spend part of the early morning or late evening attending an English reading-and-writing school, or else the Latin master might teach English grammar along with the classical languages. At the end of seven years a young man was expected to be ready to pass the language requirement for college admission.

Private English School. The Latin grammar school remained the paramount form of secondary schooling throughout the colonial era. However, the expansion of trade and commerce and the Enlightenment emphasis upon science, modern history, languages, and contemporary literature gave rise to an increasing demand for more practical subjects taught in the vernacular. The middling classes, which clearly predominated in the British North American colonies, were especially attracted to education that tied the classroom to the demands of trade and commerce. As the eighteenth century progressed, the seaport towns in particular reflected the increasing variety of school available in English America. Some of these schools emphasized English grammar, often using Thomas Dilworth's *A New Guide to the English Tongue* (1740), but they typically offered other subjects as well. Schoolmasters increasingly advertised instruction in surveying, accounting, navigation and mathematical training necessary for road and bridge building. Instruction in the "practical arts and sciences" was always in English, so the entrepreneurial schools became known as "English schools." However, the masters of such establishments often advertised the teaching of many different subjects, including college-preparatory courses in Latin, Greek, Hebrew, and rhetoric. These schools were especially intended for young men, but girls were frequently invited to attend. Women were more likely to attend schools where sewing as well as reading and writing were taught or where young gentlemen and ladies were taught music and dancing.

Academies. Many of these English schools, with their emphasis upon English, modern languages, and technical subjects, paved the way for the academies that began to emerge by the 1750s which tried to combine both the Latin school and English school curricula. In such combinations the Latin curriculum usually won out. However, as historian Robert Seybolt noted many years ago, the English schools became the forerunners of the high schools that would rise to dominance in nineteenth-century America. Another scholar, Lawrence Cremin, argued persuasively that the proliferation of English schooling after 1750 played a major role in the liberating literacy that has remained a vital force in shaping American culture ever since. The English school influenced what was being taught in town schools, by private tutors, and ultimately in college. It played a major role in making the English language a paramount nationalizing force in the American colonies, and its involvement with both young men and women made it a remarkably democratic force in the distribution of knowledge through society.

Teachers. A varied lot, teachers usually came from the middling or lower classes but had the intelligence and good fortune to acquire some formal education. They were always in demand, and during the early days of settlement some of the leading figures of the community taught school lest the young be deprived of the wisdom of the ages in the American wilderness. Later on, teaching frequently became a stop on the way to another occupation or profession. In the seventeenth century provincial governments generally tried to license teachers, largely in an effort to protect established pedagogues from unqualified competition and to preserve religious orthodoxy. However, after 1700 provincial licensing requirements for teachers tended to go unenforced. Although there were women throughout the colonies who kept petty schools, most teachers were men. They had generally gone to school themselves, though their preparation and qualifications for teaching were uneven.

Salaries. Their pay likewise varied, though it was seldom enough to sustain a growing family, even for the more-skilled Latin instructors. Schoolmasters in the cities were generally paid better. Throughout British North America petty or elementary schoolmasters were almost always bivocational, often serving as town clerks, farmers, or shopkeepers as well as teachers. Even the famed Ezekiel Cheever, who presided over the Boston Latin School for more than seventy years, had difficulty making ends meet. In eighteenth-century New England, grammar schoolmasters were usually young college graduates awaiting a call to pastor a congregation or else older preachers looking to supplement their pastor's salary. They typically made about forty pounds annually in addition to board, which gave them middle-class status. Elementary-school teachers made much less, seldom more than twenty pounds annually. Philip Fithian, the young College of New Jersey graduate who tutored the children of Col. Robert Carter in 1773–1774, was paid about forty pounds a year, about what a Latin schoolmaster in New England would make. Most tutors on Southern plantations made about thirty pounds annually. In New York City, Garrat Noel, Robert Leeth, and James Nathan Hutchins kept school while selling books, surveying, and writing almanacs, respectively. Although later becoming a wealthy attorney, the young Luther Martin was paid only twenty pounds colonial currency (often a third less than the English pound) for teaching a year in Maryland. However modest the pay, schoolmasters at least found their services even more in demand as the eighteenth century progressed. However poor their qualifications, the schoolmasters of British America contributed in manifold ways to the rich literary culture that characterized British North America.

Sources:

James Axtell, *The School upon a Hill: Education and Society in Colonial New England* (New Haven, Conn.: Yale University Press, 1974);

John Calam, *Parsons and Pedagogues: The S.P.G. Adventure in American Education* (New York: Columbia University Press, 1971);

Sheldon Cohen, *A History of Colonial Education, 1607–1776* (New York: Wiley, 1974);

Lawrence Cremin, *American Education: The Colonial Experience, 1607–1783* (New York: Harper & Row, 1970);

Bernardo P. Gallegos, *Literacy, Education, and Society in New Mexico: 1692–1821* (Albuquerque: University of New Mexico Press, 1992);

William H. Kilpatrick, *The Dutch Schools of New Netherland and Colonial New York* (Washington, D.C.: U.S. Government Printing Office, 1912);

Robert Middlekauff, *Ancients and Axioms: Secondary Education in Eighteenth-Century New England* (New Haven, Conn.: Yale University Press, 1963);

Stuart G. Noble and Arthur G. Nuhrah, "Education in Colonial Louisiana," *Louisiana Quarterly*, 32 (1949): 759–776;

Robert F. Seybolt, *The Evening Schools of Colonial New York City* (Albany: University of the State of New York, 1921);

Seybolt, *The Public Schools of Colonial Boston* (Cambridge, Mass.: Harvard University Press, 1935).

SAMSON OCCOM

1723-1792

NATIVE AMERICAN SCHOOLMASTER AND PREACHER

Two Worlds. Samson Occom, a Mohegan Indian born and raised near New London, Connecticut, was something of a novelty. A Native American who could write and speak English with grace and style, Occom has been called the father of Native American literature. He was also a preacher and schoolteacher who devoted his life to serving God and helping his people. Occom also knew the liabilities of being an Indian. His mentor, Eleazar Wheelock, abused his trust, and his own denomination lessened its support as he pushed harder to protect Indian lands, thus making clear the liabilities of being an Indian in a white man's world.

Early Life. Occom was the grandson of Tomockham and the son of Joshua Ockham. His mother, "Widow Sarah" Occom, was one of the first Mohegan converts of the Great Awakening. Samson, at sixteen years old, became a second-generation Christian. He converted to Christianity under the preaching of James Davenport, a friend and colleague of another evangelist, Eleazar Wheelock, who was beginning his school for young white and Indian males. Thanks to his mother and Davenport, Occom got enrolled in Wheelock's school at Lebanon, Connecticut. He had already begun to teach himself English and soon excelled at the difficult tasks of learning Greek, Hebrew, and Latin. Occom was a gifted student whose facility with languages allowed him to learn the Oneida tongue and later teach it among that Iroquois nation. Occom's progress as a student was said to have inspired Wheelock to found his famous Indian Charity School for educating Native American missionaries. Occom spent four years studying at Wheelock's school. Failing health and poor eyesight conspired to prevent him from going to college.

The Lord's Work. Occom began his teaching career near his home of New London and then transferred to Long Island, where he taught school and ministered to the Montauk Indians for eleven years. Supported by the Boston Board of Correspondents for Propagating Christian Knowledge, Occom was a popular and well-received teacher. Indicative of his creative pedagogy, he used singing and constructed card games as teaching devices for his students. Following the retirement of Azariah Horton, the white Presbyterian minister to the Montauk, Occom assumed his pastoral duties without any additional pay. While teaching at Long Island Occom met and married Mary Fowler in 1751; together they had ten children. To supplement his meager teacher's salary he bound books and carved spoons, pails, and gunstocks for his white neighbors.

Overseas. An eloquent preacher, Occom, despite some opposition because of his race, was ordained by the Long Island Presbytery in 1759. Under the auspices of the Scotch Society of Missions, arrangements were made for him to preach among the Cherokee in Georgia and Tennessee. However, fighting between the Cherokee and white settlers ended those plans. Instead Occom was sent to preach among the Oneida in New York, where he recruited young men to Wheelock's school. In 1765 Occom traveled with George Whitefield, regarded as the greatest preacher and missionary of the age, on his sixth preaching tour of the colonies. In late 1765 Occom sailed for England with the Reverend Nathaniel Whitaker to raise money for Wheelock's Indian Charity School. By all accounts British officials were taken by Occom's charismatic preaching. Over the next two years he delivered more than three hundred sermons through the British Isles. His preaching was the major reason he and Whitaker were able to raise more than £11,000, the most ever raised for an institution in British America. Truly ecumenical in his Christianity, Occom made friends with Andrew Gifford, London's leading Baptist; he also charmed the bishop of Gloucester, William Warburton, who approached him about Anglican ordination. Occom also spent several days visiting with John Newton, the composer of "Amazing Grace" and other hymns. The University of Edinburgh offered him an honorary degree, but the modest Occom gracefully declined.

Turmoil. Returning to America in the fall of 1768, Occom discovered that Wheelock had failed to live up to his promise of caring for Occom's wife and seven children; they were living in abject poverty. The relationship between Occom and his old mentor began to deteriorate. The breach was widened when Wheelock, using the money Occom had been so instrumental in raising, moved his Indian school to New Hampshire, began to exclude Indians, and renamed it Dartmouth. "I am very jealous," Occom told Wheelock, "that instead of your Semenary Becoming alma Mater, she will be too alba mater [white mother] to Suckle the Twanee, for She is already adorned up too much like the Popish Virgin Mary." With regard to Dartmouth, Occom bluntly told Wheelock "your present Plan is not calculated to benefit the poor Indians."

Writings. Throughout his career Occom was a writer, and his skills improved with time and experience. From 6 December 1743 to 6 March 1790 he kept a diary recording his work and activities, and it remains a remarkable historical document. On 2 September 1772 a Christian Indian was hanged for committing a murder while intoxicated. Occom preached a temperance sermon at the execution. It was subsequently published and became a best-selling book. He also published a collection of hymns, including some he wrote. Occom is generally recognized as the first Native American whose writings were published and widely known.

Decline. Ironically, Occom himself had been victimized by rumors that he was a heavy drinker, and some even claimed he was not a Mohegan. His biographer, Harold Blodgett, makes clear that both charges were patently false. They were started apparently by those who resented Occom for defending the land claims of the Montauk and Oneida against speculators. But he lost the support of his denomination and the several missionary societies who had underwritten his work. He wrote a short biography of his life defending himself against those baneful charges. Throughout the 1770s and into the 1780s Occom preached among the Mohegan and other remnant tribes of New England. His life during this period was hard and impoverished. After the American Revolution he began making plans for the settlement of Brothertown, New York, on lands deeded him and others by the Oneida as a reserve for New England Indians. The move to New York was made in 1791. The next year he established the first Indian Presbyterian church in Brothertown. Occom died soon afterward as he gathered cedar wood with which to finish the church building.

Impact. Occom's influence lived on through his children, converts, and students. Two of the latter became writers themselves, both of them Mahican Indians. Hendrick Aupaumut wrote a travelogue and a description of Mahican life. The other student, Joseph Johnson, wrote several letters that were published in New England newspapers.

Sources:

Harold Blodgett, *Samson Occom* (Hanover, N.H.: Dartmouth College Publications, 1935);

Michael Elliott, "'This Indian Bait': Samson Occom and the Voice of Liminality," *Early American Literature*, 29 (1994): 233–253;

Samson Occom, *A Sermon Preached at the Execution of Moses Paul, an Indian; Who Was Executed at New-Haven, on the Second of September, 1722; for the murder of Mr. Moses Cook, Later of Waterbury, on the 7th of December, 1771. Preached at the Desire of Said Paul* (New Haven, Conn.: Printed & sold by Thomas & Samuel Green, 1772);

Bernd Peyer, "Samson Occom: Mohegan Missionary and Writer of the Eighteenth Century," *American Indian Quarterly*, 6 (Fall/Winter 1982): 208–217.

PUBLICATIONS

Thomas Budd, *Good Order Established in Pennsilvania and New Jersey in America* (Philadelphia: Printed by William Bradford, 1685)—recommendations for a comprehensive plan of public education which were largely adopted;

Ezekiel Cheever, *A Short Introduction to the Latin Tongue* (Boston: Printed by B. Green for Benj. Eliot, 1709);

John Cotton, *Spiritual Milk for Boston Babes in Either England* (Cambridge, Mass.: Printed by Samuel Green for Hezekiah Usher, 1656)—a popular catechism written by a leading Boston minister and Puritan theologian;

Benjamin Franklin, *Proposals Relating to the Education of Youth in Pensilvania* (Philadelphia, 1749)—a discussion of subjects to be taught in an ideal secondary school. Franklin had a utilitarian view on the matter and recommended that students "learn those Things that are likely to be *most useful* and *most ornamental*";

Cotton Mather, *The Christian Philosopher* (London: Printed for Eman. Matthews, 1720)—a famous scientific treatise dealing with astronomy, physics, meteorology, geography, geology, and mineralogy;

Mather, *India Christiana* (Boston: Printed by B. Green, 1721)—an argument supporting the education of Native Americans;

Mather, *Magnalia Christi Americana* (London: Printed for Thomas Parkhurst, 1702)—one of the most significant books published in the entire colonial era. Mather glorifies the founders of New England, a group chosen for a special "errand in the wilderness";

Isaac Watts, *The Improvement of the Mind* (London: Printed for J. Brackstone, 1741)—the author's theory is based on John Locke's premise that sensation and reflection are the basic experiences that furnish knowledge. Maintaining that "all persons are under some obligation to improve their understanding," Watts developed five "eminent means" of improving knowledge: observing, reading, attending lectures, engaging in conversation, and studying.

Map from John Seller's *Atlas Minuiimus; or, A Book of Geography* (1679)

CHAPTER SIX
GOVERNMENT AND POLITICS

by SAMUEL SMITH

CONTENTS

Sidebars and tables are listed in italics.

1607

- Three vessels carrying 105 London Company passengers arrive in Virginia.

1608

- Capt. John Smith is elected president of the Jamestown Council.

1609

- Capt. John Smith reluctantly relinquishes authority with the anticipated arrival of Gov. Thomas Lord De La Warr.
- The Starving Time, a one-year period of severe malnutrition, disease, and disorder begins in the Jamestown settlement.

1611

- Virginia governor Thomas Gates implements a series of laws called Dale's Code to maintain order in Jamestown.

1614

- The first tobacco shipment is sent to England.

1619

- Martial law in Virginia is replaced by a general assembly of twenty-two burgesses, the first representative assembly in America.

1620

- Off of present-day Cape Cod, Massachusetts, forty-one male passengers on the *Mayflower* sign the Mayflower Compact, establishing a preliminary "civil body politic" and the authority to legislate laws as necessary.

1621

- William Bradford becomes governor of Plymouth and serves at that post for thirty years.

1624

- After the revocation of the London Company charter in May, Virginia becomes a royal colony.
- The first permanent settlers to come through the Dutch West India Company (approximately thirty families) arrive in the present-day New York Bay area.

1625

- Peter Minuit purchases land from Indians (Manhattan Island) and names it New Amsterdam.

1629

- The Massachusetts Bay Company is formed by English Puritans allowing the Company to have governmental autonomy once on the American mainland.

1630

- John Winthrop is elected first governor of Massachusetts Bay Colony.

1631

- One hundred and thirty male church members combine to make up the freemanship of Massachusetts Bay Colony.

1632

- Maryland is established as the first proprietary colony. George Calvert, first Lord Baltimore, sought the initial charter from Charles I, and upon his death, his son Cecilius Calvert, second Lord Baltimore, became the first proprietor of the colony.

1635

- The General Court of Massachusetts Bay banishes Roger Williams after he questions the government's authority in matters of religious conscience.

1636

- Plymouth colony inhabitants adopt the Great Fundamentals allowing for the establishment of a general court made up of the governor and two representatives from each town.
- Roger Williams founds Providence, Rhode Island, on Narragansett Bay.

1637

- In retaliation for the killing of the trader John Oldham the previous year, militiamen under Capt. John Mason destroy a large portion of the Pequot Indians in the New Haven area.

1638

- Anne Hutchinson is tried and banished from Massachusetts Bay for the promulgation of Antinomianism, which is seen by authorities as a threat to church dominance both politically and religiously.
- Backed by Dutch and Swedish investors, settlers from Sweden and the Netherlands disembark at present-day Wilmington, Delaware.

1639

- The Fundamental Orders are adopted by settlers of New Haven, Connecticut.

1641

- The Massachusetts Bay General Court adopts the Body of Liberties, a penal code closely aligned with Old Testament Law.

1642

- Sir William Berkeley begins his first term as Virginia's royal governor.

1643

- Massachusetts, Connecticut, New Haven, and Plymouth form a confederation called the United Colonies of New England.
- The colony of New Haven formally bases its government structure on the Mosaic Decalogue (Ten Commandments).

1644

- Massachusetts Bay adopts a bicameral legislature.
- Roger Williams receives an official charter granting inhabitants of the four primary towns of Rhode Island (Providence, Portsmouth, Newport, and Warwick) the right to establish a constitution through a general assembly.

1647

- Rhode Island adopts its first constitution which declares separation of church and state and freedom of religious expression.
- Peter Stuyvesant becomes director general of New Netherland.

1649

- After Charles I is beheaded, Virginia proclaims its loyalty to the Stuarts and becomes a safe haven for royal supporters.
- The Act of Toleration passed in Maryland affirms freedom of religion for all Christians in that colony.

1652

- Dutch official Peter Stuyvesant authorizes an independent government for the growing municipality of New Amsterdam.
- The General Court of Massachusetts Bay officially pronounces the territory of Maine as within the boundaries of the Bay colony.
- After authorizing a blockade on Virginia shipping, the English Commonwealth Parliament forces a new election for governorship, replacing Sir William Berkeley with a parliamentary appointee.

1653
- The earliest English settlers in the Carolinas come by way of Virginia. The settlement of Albemarle is established just north of Albemarle Sound; the colony is called North Carolina after 1691.

1655
- Peter Stuyvesant brings an end to Swedish rule in America by defeating Johan Classon Rising, New Sweden's governor, at Fort Casimir.

1659
- With the fall of Oliver Cromwell's Protectorate, the Virginia burgesses assume full control of the colony.

1660
- After the Restoration of the Stuarts, Charles II re-commissions Sir William Berkeley as Virginia's royal governor.
- Parliament passes the first of the Navigation Acts.
- The Lords of Trade (or Committee for Trade and Plantations) is commissioned to oversee commerce in the American colonies; it operates under the authority of the Privy Council.

1662
- Connecticut obtains a royal charter.

1663
- Charles II grants the lands consisting of South and North Carolina to eight proprietors.

1664
- Rhode Island receives a royal charter which honors the colony's preexistent declaration of religious liberty.
- English forces take New Netherland and rename it New York.
- John Lord Berkeley and Sir George Carteret receive a grant from the duke of York for land within present-day New Jersey.

1665
- New Haven becomes part of the royal colony of Connecticut.
- Philip Carteret, a relative of Sir George Carteret, is appointed the first governor of New Jersey.
- New York adopts the Duke's Laws which mark the transition from a Dutch to an English civil and legal code.

- Charles II sends four commissioners to New England to ensure that each of the regional colonies (Plymouth, Rhode Island, Connecticut, and Massachusetts) comply with royal prerogatives, one of which demands greater latitude for church membership. The royal commissioners also institute a separate government in Maine.

- Carolina proprietors adopt the Concessions and Agreements which allow for the formation of a representative assembly of freeholders, a system of land ownership, and freedom of conscience.

1668

- New Jersey convenes its first General Assembly.

1669

- Maine becomes part of Massachusetts.

- As a supplement to the Concessions and Agreements, Carolina proprietors adopt John Locke's Fundamental Constitutions.

1670

- An English settlement is established on the Ashley River at Albemarle Point called Charles Town. The settlement later relocates to the fork of the Ashley and Cooper Rivers, site of present-day Charleston, South Carolina.

1671

- The first assembly for the new settlement at Charles Town is established.

1674

- The Treaty of Westminster provides for the official surrender of Dutch forces which had retaken control of New York earlier in the year.

1675

- King Philip's War begins and pits the New England Confederation against Indian tribes led by Chief Philip of the Wampanoags. The two-year conflict results in great loss and destruction for both sides. Twelve New England towns are leveled, and for every sixteen white men of fighting age, one loses his life.

1676

- Bacon's Rebellion occurs in Virginia.

- As a result of proprietary transitions first initiated by Lord Berkeley's sale of his interests, New Jersey divides into two colonies, East and West Jersey.

1677

- Since the Lords of Trade do not recognize Massachusetts' claim on the territory of Maine, Massachusetts Bay authorities buy out the heirs of Sir Ferdinando Gorges who hold the land title. From this point until 1820 Maine remains part of Massachusetts.

- The proprietors of West Jersey institute the Laws, Concessions, and Agreements which stress the rights of religious liberty, trial by jury, and the requirement of public consent prior to taxation.

- In Charles Town an antiproprietary government, with John Culpeper as a principal leader, is formed to counter the perceived misappropriation of authority by the proprietary government.

1680

- The colony of New Hampshire is separated, by royal commission, from Massachusetts.

1681

- William Penn receives proprietary rights from Charles II for the land now known as Pennsylvania. The formation of this colony is what Penn calls a "holy experiment" due to the emphasis placed on the rights of Christian dissent.

1682

- William Penn establishes his Frame of Government which allows for the creation of an assembly, council, and governor's office in Pennsylvania.

1683

- Under the direction of the duke of York, the Charter of Liberties (drawn up by Mathias Nichols) provides for the establishment of a general assembly with the powers of taxation and independent legislation.

1684

- The Royal Court of Chancery decrees the Massachusetts Bay charter null and void.

1685

- Due to Charles Town's rejection of the Fundamental Constitutions, the Carolina proprietors disallow the settlement's local assembly.

- The Dominion of New England is formed, and the next year Sir Edmund Andros is appointed governor.

1689

- With the absence of Gov. Sir Edmund Andros and Lt. Gov. Francis Nicholson, Jacob Leisler, German trader and fervent Calvinist, assumes political and military control of New York.

1691

- Newly arrived Gov. Henry Sloughter defeats Jacob Leisler's forces in New York.

1696

- William III commissions the Board of Trade to oversee commercial (trade and fishing) and political (power of appointments and legislative review) concerns in the American colonies.

1697

- The Board of Trade establishes vice admiralty courts which have jurisdiction over colonial maritime cases.

1701

- Delaware becomes a separate government from Pennsylvania and convenes its first autonomous assembly three years later. Even so, a single governor administers both provinces until the American Revolution.
- The Charter of Liberties, the constitution of Pennsylvania until the American Revolution, establishes the only sustained unicameral (one-house) legislature in the colonies.

1702

- Both East and West Jersey become royal colonies.

1704

- The secretary of state for the Southern Department gains the prerogative to appoint royal governors in the colonies; this power had been previously held by the Board of Trade.

1712

- North Carolina appoints its first separate governor, Edward Hyde.

1721

- South Carolina becomes a royal colony with the appointment of Francis Nicholson as governor.

1729

- North Carolina becomes a royal colony.

1732

- Twenty trustees receive a royal charter for land south of the Savannah River, previously part of South Carolina; the new colony becomes known as Georgia.

1752

- The original charter granted to the Georgia trustees expires, whereupon Georgia becomes a royal colony.

James Lyne's map of New York City, published by William Bradford, 1731

OVERVIEW

English Precedents. It is vital when studying colonial history to recognize that the American provinces descended from and were still part of a rich Old World past. It is a mistake to automatically place the colonies into a single English context. Colonies such as New York and Florida had their beginnings with the Dutch and Spanish respectively. Many non-English settlers—German, French, Swiss, etc., populated much of the American landscape. Of course, the thousands of slaves living throughout the colonies did not have an English past. Yet, notwithstanding the rich ethnicity, one finds when examining the government and politics of the overall scene that by the mid to late seventeenth century a predominant English presence existed. Subjects pertinent to provincial and local government such as legal administrative structures (courts, judges, juries), law enforcement offices (sheriffs, constables, watches), legislative bodies (councils and assemblies), executives (governors), town, borough, and county offices simply cannot be understood apart from their English origins. The American colonists were and saw themselves as decidedly English.

Increased Anglicization. The often-asserted idea that colonists over time saw themselves less as English and more as autonomous Americans is questionable. The very fact that they did develop independent attitudes can arguably be attributed to an increased perception of their role in the world as Englishmen. This mentality became especially recognizable after the Glorious Revolution in 1688. From this momentous event, when Parliament asserted a more authoritative role, a two-edged sword hung over the British Empire. One edge slowly drew offense in the minds of provincial leaders. Nonrepresentative parliamentary jurisdiction in the colonies did not sit well with those prone to assert their rights as Englishmen. On the other hand, the renewed power of Parliament encouraged those same leaders to imitate that authority in their provincial assemblies. Thus, for example, the rise of the assembly in provincial America was not so much an assertion of Americanization as it was of Anglicization.

Diversity and Transition. Even with the strong English presence it is important to remember that colonial government and political structures were not static. That is, from province to province they were different, and through time each one experienced relatively significant transitions throughout the period. There were basically three types of English settlements: company-chartered, privately chartered (covenant or proprietary), and royal. Some of the earlier settlements (Jamestown, Plymouth, Massachusetts Bay, Rhode Island, and Connecticut) were company or privately chartered. Connecticut and Rhode Island, for example, were settled based on private, covenant-oriented charters with no direct royal sanction. In 1632, starting with Maryland, a different type of privately chartered colony emerged—the proprietary. Proprietary colonies, such as Pennsylvania, South Carolina, and Maryland, had royal charters, but they were charters that gave almost complete sovereignty (Pennsylvania excepted) to the individual proprietors. Each colony proprietary or privately chartered (company and covenant) reflected individual government structures unique to its own goals of settlement.

Royal Control. By the mid eighteenth century most colonies had made the transition to direct royal control. Even with this trend, differences in emphasis remained. This was particularly true of local government structures. New England colonies, for instance, which were the most resistant to royal control, conducted their civil business primarily through the town meeting. The Middle Colonies, possibly reflective of greater ethnic and religious heterogeneity, were more diverse in local government functions. No one system (town, borough, city, or county) seemed to dominate as in New England. The Chesapeake was more county-oriented, whereas the lower southern region, especially South Carolina, placed a greater emphasis on the parish vestry. Law-enforcement procedures also reflect the differences in the American colonies. Those regions with more proactive Christian enforcement (Puritan New England) tended to equate sin with crime. Elsewhere a greater differentiation between the two existed. The difference had a very noticeable impact on the crime rate, or at least the conviction rate, between New England and other regions (except possibly Virginia, which by the eighteenth century had developed an effective law-enforcement system through elite social control). The strongly Puritan New Haven colony, for example, from 1638 to 1658 had a 93 percent conviction rate, whereas North Carolina never went above a 25 percent conviction rate.

Similarities. Even with the significant differences on both the provincial and local levels, and particularly in law enforcement, there were certain common governmental characteristics throughout the colonies worth noting. The basic overall provincial structure included a governor, council, and assembly. Granted, the roles of these government entities may have differed from colony to colony, but essentially the functions of each, especially when most colonies became royal (a demonstrable commonality in itself), were, if not exactly the same, very similar. The governor was the chief representative of either the proprietor or the Crown. He often held executive, legislative, and judicial powers. The council, almost always appointed, served as the primary advisory board to the governor and, especially early on, as a prominent legislative and judicial body, often as a check on the assembly. The elected assemblies, modeled on the House of Commons, the lower house of Britain's Parliament, initiated all money and most other bills. The overriding similarity of the assembly throughout the colonies was its representative role for the common freeholder (or landowner). The assembly became the essential link for the common insistence of English rights, especially as those rights related to the private ownership of property. The increased call for greater representative government, especially after the Glorious Revolution, was parallel with a growing insistence to be treated as respectable Englishmen.

Attempt at Centralization. In 1685, an attempt from the Crown to centralize the colonies materialized in what was called the Dominion of New England. The Duke of York, who became King James II in 1685, sought to unite the Northern colonies in order to gain control of their governmental structures. The immediate objective was to bring the New England colonies into compliance with the Navigation Acts and to obtain a more unified front against the French. Once Edmund Andros took over as governor of the Dominion in 1686 (with headquarters in Boston), he nominally extended its authority as far south as New Jersey. The successful replacement of James II with William III and Mary in 1688 resulted in the collapse of the Dominion of New England. England never successfully reinstituted another centralization of colonial governments after that time.

Rebellions. The period of our study was checkered with rebellions. Some of the more significant ones were direct attempts to overthrow existing governments. Aside from the general similarity of wresting power, the motives were often different. In 1676 Bacon's Rebellion in Virginia was an attempt by Nathaniel Bacon and his followers to change Governor Sir William Berkeley's favored land policies both toward the Indians and the governor's inner circle elite. Leisler's Rebellion in New York, which came on the heels of the Glorious Revolution, was a reaction born of religious fervor and fear. Almost simultaneous to Leisler's Rebellion, the Protestant Association in Maryland managed to gain control over that colony's government and subsequently called upon the Crown to take it over. Thus, until 1715 Maryland was a royal colony until it reverted to the Calvert family's (who had by now turned Protestant) proprietary control. Not born of religious motives but with the same outcome as in Maryland was the 1719 revolt against the proprietary government in South Carolina. The rebellion ended with South Carolina becoming a royal colony in 1721. This was not the first rebellion in the Carolinas against the proprietors. In 1677 John Culpeper led farmers on the northern coast in protest of unfair customs duties. Possibly the most significant similarity among these rebellions is what was not present—anti-Crown sentiment. In fact, the very opposite was true. Granted, Leisler's Rebellion in New York and the Protestant Association's rebellion in Maryland were initially against James II because of his outspoken Catholicism. These rebellions did not get under way until their leaders perceived themselves in concert with parliamentary actions in England. Nathaniel Bacon did direct his actions against the existing royal government in Virginia, but his was a local dispute, not one with the Crown. It is significant, therefore, that royal governments, though at the provincial level, were the objects of attack, in no case were those attacks leveled at the concept of English rule, but rather at English rule that in their minds had gone awry. Moreover, the antiproprietary rebellions were in themselves appeals for royal intervention.

Political Stability. The growth of political stability is a most important factor in the study of colonial America. With Maryland and North Carolina as arguable exceptions, the mainland English colonies experienced increased political stability from early in the seventeenth century to around 1750. That stability did not wane significantly until the Seven Years' War (1756–1763). Most of the colonies, with the exception of Massachusetts, exemplified considerable instability early on. Contributors to this early political flux included a less viable economy and a sparse and gender-imbalanced population resulting in both a small pool from which to choose qualified leaders and a lack of community cohesion. From around 1710 through the 1750s, an increase in population and a decrease in direct Crown control, among other important factors, led to a considerable increase in political stability. Of course, it is always a mistake to treat this phenomenon as a blanket event. That is, its levels of actuality differed from colony to colony and period to period. But it is true that on balance, the American colonies, starting in the early 1700s, experienced several decades of growing political stability.

TOPICS IN THE NEWS

ENGLISH IMPERIAL SYSTEM

Roots. Before any in-depth study of the British American colonies can be done, it is necessary to first examine them in their English imperial context. In many ways the colonial governments that evolved over time reflected more and more their English roots. It is clear that the engine of time did not alter the average colonist's self perception that he was English. If anything, that perception increased with time. For that reason, a look at the British imperial system, especially as it related to colonial politics and government, is in order.

Direct Crown Control. Colonial governments were not uniform; that is, they varied substantially in settlement organization and in political maturity. Different circumstances dictated each colony's origin and function. Vital to understanding this fluctuation is to understand also the simultaneous fluctuations that transpired in England throughout the American colonial era. Yet, even with the changing royal scene through time, one motivation remained relatively constant: the English monarchs intended to have direct control of the American colonies.

Divine Right. The first permanent English settlements began during the reign of James I, who with his emphasis on the divine right of kings, held direct control over early colonial policy. James I's court administration of Jamestown was called "Our Council of Virginia." This royal council established in 1606 was the first of its kind for the exclusive purpose of administering the American settlements. Even though at this stage the English monarchy did not see the vital importance of the American colonies as much as it would later, the early Stuart doctrine of divine right at least partially explains the English notion of direct control over its new provinces. This does not suggest that the Jamestown (1607) and Plymouth (1620) settlements did not view their own existence, especially after their charter companies failed and lost jurisdiction, as strongly autonomous. Yet, from the early Stuart perspective the colonies answered ultimately to the Crown. It is important to note that such a strong royal prerogative early on left neither side believing that the provinces were "sister communities of England" but rather were "dependent local jurisdictions."

Privy Council. Under Charles I the administration of colonial policy initially came under the jurisdiction of the Privy Council, sometimes called the King in Council. The Privy Council had long served previous monarchs in advisory, judicial, and executive capacities. After 1634, due to the growing Puritan migrations to the Massachusetts Bay Colony, Charles I extended the Privy Council's operations by creating a separate standing committee under William Laud, Archbishop of Canterbury and out-

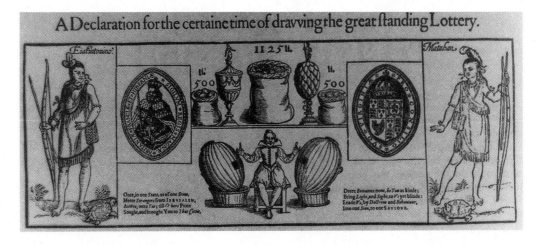

A London lottery ticket sold to raise money for the Virginia Company, 1607 (Society of Antiquaries, London)

Sir Edmund Andros, governor of the Dominion of New England (portrait by F. S. Batcheler; Rhode Island State Archives)

spoken critic of the Puritans, to deal more directly with colonial policies. This new committee of the Privy Council, called the Commission of Plantations, represented a degree of royal involvement that the colonies had not yet seen. Charles I, like his father James I, believed in the divine right doctrine. The Privy Council, with this newly created Commission of Plantations, served as a direct arm of the king's practice of this doctrine since it required his approval for any action. Although in reality Charles accomplished little with this committee, it nevertheless reflected the royal attitudes of dominion toward the American colonies.

Parliament. Charles, with his dire need for money to finance his policies, recalled Parliament in 1640 (it had been dissolved since 1629). Parliament then made its own attempts to govern the distant American settlements. It appointed the Committee of Plantations to operate under the direction of the earl of Warwick. This committee's effectiveness, however, was hampered by the ensuing Civil War (1642–1649), a war that would depose the monarchy for eleven years.

Committee for Trade and Plantations. In 1650 the Council of State, which directed governmental affairs in the three years prior to Oliver Cromwell's ascension as head of state, created the Committee for Trade and Plantations to oversee colonial affairs. This committee started out with considerable activity by sending com-

missioners into the Chesapeake region to gain greater administrative control. It also passed the first Navigation Act (1651) which stipulated that only English vessels could transport certain colonial cargo. Cromwell, who became the executive head of the Commonwealth in 1653, had high hopes that due to his sympathies with the Puritans he would be able to implement necessary levels of control. He replaced the Council of State, which was over the Committee for Trade and Plantations, with the Council of the Protector, and it became the primary administrative body over the American provinces. Yet, whether from the Crown, Commonwealth, or Lord Protectorate, early colonists consistently resisted complete subjugation by aligning with the Confederation of New England, which had been formed in 1643. In truth, during both the Interregnum and the Lord Protectorate there was little need for overt resistance on the colonists' part due to the attention England necessarily gave to internal as well as satellite colonial affairs (revolts in Scotland and Ireland).

Council of Plantations. In 1660 Charles II, who had been in exile for eleven years, ascended to the throne. In the first year of this Restoration era Charles created yet another bureaucratic body for colonial administration, the Council for Foreign Plantations. This committee was later (1670) renamed simply the Council of Plantations. This body proved ineffective. In 1672 the Committee of Plantations and the recently formed Council of Trade combined as one committee with commercial and governmental oversight duties. Finally in 1675, due to this body's budgeting problems, the renewed Privy Council once again assumed responsibility for the colonies and appointed a committee called the Lords of Trade.

Lords of Trade. Lasting for twenty-one years (1675–1696), the Lords of Trade proved to be the most effective colonial oversight board since the beginning of American settlement. One reason for this effectiveness was that the American colonies began to matter more to Britain. England came to see the colonies, due to their rapid growth in population, as much more vital to English military and economic interests. But the immediate success of the Lords of Trade was due to its specific objectives.

Goals. The Lords of Trade had three overall goals. One was to create greater Crown control of the then four royal colonies (Virginia, Jamaica, Barbados, and the Leeward Islands). This was done by careful oversight of gubernatorial appointments and by the subsequent issuance of instructions—specifically outlined orders that the governor was to follow strictly. Along with these controls, the Lords of Trade also sought to limit provincial assemblies, which had, in England's view, gained too much autonomy by assuming sovereignty over financial matters in the respective colonies. A second goal was to hamper further efforts for the creation of private colonies and to eventually transfer the existing ones under direct royal control. Massachusetts Bay lost New Hampshire, which became a royal colony under this policy. The policy was not always successful, as in the case of William Penn's charter in 1681, but Penn did have greater than normal limitations on his proprietorship. The most noted attempt in the implementation of this goal was the successful reversal in 1684 of the Massachusetts Bay charter due to that colony's failure to abide by the Navigation Acts. Two years later this reversal led to the third overall goal of the Lords of Trade: centralization of colonial control through the Dominion of New England. The Dominion of New England included all the colonies northeast of the Delaware River. Even with the advances made toward greater consolidation, however, the mistrust that plagued the relationship between Parliament and Charles II insured that the Lords of Trade could not satisfactorily consolidate colonial policy. With the ascension of James II, that mistrust intensified until his removal in 1688, which also led to the downfall of the Dominion of New England. Even with the unity that emerged between Parliament and William III after the Glorious Revolution, the Lords of Trade were given fewer and fewer responsibilities in colonial oversight until it was replaced in 1696 by the Board of Trade.

Board of Trade. William III commissioned the Board of Trade in 1696. The Board's longevity (until 1782) attests to its effectiveness in administering colonial affairs. The Board of Trade was of design made up of sixteen landed gentrymen, as opposed to the merchant class, to avoid possible conflicts of interest relating to colonial trade. Although the Board was not officially under the Privy Council, it issued reports both to it and to the Crown's assigned minister of colonial affairs, the secretary of state for the Southern Department. The Board of Trade was responsible for gubernatorial instructions, insuring that colonial legislation did not conflict with assigning members to colonial councils. The Board's effectiveness did wane from time to time, especially due to countermeasures employed by powerful ministers. Sir Robert Walpole, for example, whose ministry lasted from 1721 to 1742, stressed a relaxation of governmental intervention in colonial affairs except in extreme cases when major economic or political issues were at stake. This tendency gave the colonies room to expand while at the same time benefiting the mother country. The royal governors especially were able to operate in the best interest "of the parent state without having to be constantly on guard against reprimands from home for failing to enforce the 'long established Maxims' of the Board of Trade." In retrospect, therefore, the waning of the Board of Trade's power through a policy of less intervention, as in Walpole's ministry, at least gave the appearance that it was functioning effectively for both colonies and empire.

Admiralty and Vice Admiralty. Another English department important in the colonial governmental structure was the High Court of Admiralty. The Admiralty originated in the fourteenth century and was given the power in maritime affairs that the common-law courts had in land cases. As maritime issues and cases increased in the colonies over time, the need for a recognized Admiralty Court jurisdiction in the provinces became evident. In 1697 Vice-Admiralty courts were assigned to operate within the American colonies with considerable judicial powers relating to the high seas. Vice-Admiralty courts were placed in the colonies by the Board of Trade primarily to enforce the Acts of Trade and Navigation. Of particular offense to many colonists was the absence of trial by jury within this court. The Vice-Admiralty judge of a given region had sole authority in deciding cases that came to him. Over time the court's jurisdiction included matters only indirectly related to its original sphere of maritime authority. For example, under a 1722 act of Parliament the Vice-Admiralty courts gained authorization in New England to enforce the king's "broad arrow policy," which forbade the cutting of any white pines that had a diameter of at least twenty-four inches. Such trees were needed for the manufacturing of masts on English merchant ships. The surveyor general was to mark these trees with the king's "broad arrow." But even if he found such a tree felled without the marking, the perpetrators would face prosecution. Cases such as these as well as other overzealous seizures of ships and cargo by the Vice Admiralty have often clouded the positive role it played in the colonies. The judges had the responsibility to defend the human and economic rights of sailors during a time when such rights were often violated by ship captains. They also aided crews, foreign or otherwise, who were in distress from lack of food or an unseaworthy vessel. Though often justly ridiculed for improper actions, the Vice-Admiralty courts on the whole did serve a useful function in British colonial affairs.

Southern Department. Beginning in the early eighteenth century the one official most immediately concerned with colonial oversight was the secretary of state for the Southern Department. The secretary of state had long been a powerful intermediary agent for the king, particularly in foreign affairs. Eventually the office was divided between northern and southern European interests. Included in the southern geographic region were the American colonies. The secretary of state for the Southern Department had authority to personally go before the monarch to report on or petition for political, military, and economic concerns related to the colonies. He also communicated with the Board of Trade on a whole range of economic issues.

Governors. Of the powers held by the secretary, one of the most important was the appointment of royal governors. Although the Board of Trade issued the governor's instructions, a duty that opened the door to many patronage (to appoint for other than meritorious reasons) possibilities, the secretary's power of appointment left many would-be and incumbent governors beholden to him. He was also the channel through which the royal governors communicated to the king. All types of motives, often financial, drove aspirants to seek gubernatorial appointments from the secretary of state of the Southern Department. For example, in 1732 the duke of Kent wrote on behalf of Christian Cole for the governorship of North Carolina stating that Cole was "a very honest intelligent and knowing person in all business," but, the duke continued, "his misfortune has been to have lost in the South Seas . . ., which makes him desirous to leave his own country and to go abroad and would be very happy to have your Grace's favor and protection for his employment." One of the more unusual reasons to seek a governorship was that of the earl of Kinnoul. The earl had been stationed as a British representative in Turkey until his alleged bad reputation cost him the position. In 1738 he requested to become governor of Barbados to prove to others that his reputation remained intact. To the secretary he wrote, "My lord, if the king is so good as to give me the government of Barbados at this time, it will justify me in the eyes of all the world; whereas, if I do not soon receive some such public mark of his Majesty's favor, the greater part of mankind will have reason to think that my accusers were in the right and that I did not discharge my duty in Turkey as I ought to have done. . . . Therefore, as my reputation is concerned at this time as well as my support in the world, I must beg your Grace seriously to consider my case." In neither of the above cases did the applicants win the offices. These examples illustrate nonetheless the potential power of patronage the secretary of state for the Southern Department had.

Treasury. One of the least emphasized but important English governmental departments related to the colonies was the Treasury. The Treasury held the responsibility of collecting tariff duties. It also functioned as an auditing agency on accounts in the colonies. A constant dilemma in the royal colonies was that the governors, on the one hand, depended heavily on local assemblies to finance their administrations, and on the other hand faced the ever-present threat of giving too much power to that representative body. After 1680 the Board of Trade regularly included in the governor's instructions the requirement that twice a year he send to the Treasury certified "fair books of accounts" reflecting a complete showing of a given colony's financial records. With this ex post facto regulation was the requirement of the royal governor to receive preapproval from England for all appropriations originating in the assemblies. These regulations were primarily given as a check on the local assemblies and as a means to insure that the raising of revenue had the mother country's interest at heart. Other duties of the Treasury included expenditure authorization and the regulation of customs. Interestingly, the Treasury possessed more potential power in the proprietary and private-charter colonies since fewer royal officials existed in these provinces. Due to the local assemblies' ever-increasing assertion, especially after the Glorious Revolution in 1688, that they possessed the localized power of a House of Commons, royal attempts at fiscal control through the Board of Trade and the Treasury never reached their intended goals.

Sources:

Charles M. Andrews, *The Colonial Period of American History*, volume 4, *England's Commercial and Colonial Policy* (New Haven, Conn.: Yale University Press, 1938);

George Louis Beer, *The Origins of the British Colonial System, 1578–1660* (New York: Peter Smith, 1933);

Ralph Paul Bieber, *The Lords of Trade and Plantations, 1675–1696* (Allentown, Pa.: H. Ray Hass & Company, 1919);

George Dargo, *Roots of the Republic: A New Perspective on Early American Constitutionalism* (New York: Praeger, 1974);

Jack P. Greene, *Peripheries and Center: Constitutional Development in the Extended Policies of the British Empire and the United States, 1607–1788* (New York: Norton, 1986);

Leonard Woods Labaree, *Royal Government in America: A Study of the British Colonial System before 1783* (New York: Ungar, 1958).

THE FRANCHISE

Origins. In general, American colonial franchise structures were patterned after English precedents. The requirement of landholding, for example, known as the "forty-shilling freehold," was of English origin. The reasoning behind landholding requirements was connected to the complementary British precedents of individual interest and state benefit. That is, the person voting had to have stake in the outcome of the election and had to be one whose personal stake would be dependent on the overall political health of the colony. The 1716 South Carolina voting regulation stated that "It is necessary and reasonable, that none but such persons who have an interest in this Province should be capable to elect . . . members of the commons House of Assembly."

Residency. Although as cities grew and as time passed landholding requirements lessened, it was generally assumed that apart from landownership one did not have an interest in provincial elections. It should be added that not all provincial franchise structures were English. Residence requirement is a case in point. The strict residence requirements that eventually developed in most colonies did not derive from English origin. In fact, when colonies first began to make stricter residence rules, litigation and protests were forthcoming that stressed the practice as non-British. In New York and Virginia, if someone owned property in a county, regardless of his residence, he could vote in that county. Actually, he could vote in any number of counties in which he owned property. In 1737 a major dispute arose in New York City over an assembly race there. Adolph Philipse, a candidate for an assembly seat, funneled in outsiders to vote for him against his challenger, Cornelius Van Horne. Van Horne protested, but the assembly allowed the votes to remain, citing English precedent. In time, residence did become a requirement in several colonies, but the change was of local rather than British origin.

The Disenfranchised. Each colony had a different voting structure, but there are generalities that can be made. Voting was limited by citizenship, residence, and

EARLY PENNSYLVANIA GOVERNMENT APPOINTMENTS

The following table shows the relationship between large landholdings and government appointments in early Pennsylvania. It demonstrates the accommodation William Penn necessarily made from his original ideal to political reality.

Office	Name	Land Purchased (Acres)	Religion
Deputy Governor	William Markham	5,000	Anglican
Assistant	Silas Crispin	5,000	Quaker
Deputy Governor	Thomas Holme	5,000	Quaker
Commissioners for Settling the Colony	Silas Crispin	5,000	Quaker
	William Haige	500	Quaker
	Nathaniel Allen	2,000	Quaker
	John Bezar	1,000	Quaker
Keeper of the Seal	Thomas Rudyard	5,000	Quaker
	Thomas Lloyd	5,000	Quaker
Master of the Rolls	Thomas Rudyard	5,000	Quaker
	Thomas Lloyd	5,000	Quaker
Receiver-General	Christopher Taylor	5,000	Quaker
Receiver-General for the Lower Counties	Thomas Holme	5,000	Quaker
Register-General	Christopher Taylor	5,000	Quaker
Secretary and Clerk of the Council	Richard Ingelo	500	Quaker
	Nicholas More	10,000	Anglican
Treasurer	Robert Turner	6,000	Quaker
Chief Justice of the Court	Silas Crispin	5,000	Quaker
	Nicholas More	10,000	Anglican
Judges	William Welch		Quaker
	William Wood	2,500	Quaker
	Robert Turner	6,000	Quaker
	John Eckley	1,250	Quaker
Attorney General	John White	?	Quaker
Commissioners of Property	James Claypoole	10,000	Quaker
	Robert Turner	6,000	Quaker
	Thomas Lloyd	5,000	Quaker
	Samuel Carpenter	5,000	Quaker
Proprietary Secretary	Philip Lehnman	1,000	Quaker
Proprietary Steward	James Harrison	5,000	Quaker

Source: Gary B. Nash, "The Framing of Government in Pennsylvania: Ideas in Contact with Reality," *William and Mary Quarterly*, 23 (1966): 183–209.

age. In the British American colonies there were several additional limitations that considerably lessened the number who could vote. The most common limitation, and the one that excluded the most people, was gender. Regardless of a woman's status or landholdings, she could not vote. John Adams well represents the thinking of the time. "Their delicacy," Adams stated, "renders them unfit for practice and experience in the great businesses of life, and . . . the arduous cares of state. Besides, . . . nature has made them fittest for domestic cares."

Dissenters. One's religious affiliations also played a significant role in voting eligibility. Prior to 1689 one generally (there were exceptions such as in Rhode Island) had to belong to a respective colony's established church in order to vote. During this time Protestant dissenters such as Quakers, Presbyterians, and Baptists were usually barred from casting their ballots. With the Glorious Revolution many of the limitations on Protestant dissenter sects were dropped. But as restrictions eased on these, they intensified on Roman Catholics and Jews. As to Catholics, this is not surprising since the Glorious Revolution involved the defrocking of a Catholic king, James II. In every colony where a collective Catholic vote posed a possible influence on a political outcome, Catholics lost the right to vote. In 1718 Maryland, with the largest contingency of Catholics, disenfranchised them, fearing their vote "would tend to the Discouragement and Disturbance of his Lordship's Protestant government." Other colonies that disenfranchised Catholics were Virginia (1699), New York (1701), Rhode Island (1719), and South Carolina (1759). Many Jews also lost suffrage rights during this time. At least seven colonies excluded the Jewish franchise. Enforcement of the exclusion was often lax, especially in New York City after the mid eighteenth century. The colony most lauded as being based on religious freedom, Rhode Island, had and enforced the strictest disenfranchisement of Jews.

Blacks. Race was another determinant of suffrage rights in colonial America. Black slaves were not allowed to vote. The same, however, is not true for free blacks. Although there is no record of free blacks voting in Northern colonies, there were no official statutes prohibiting them. Evidently the cultural reality made prohibitive statutes unnecessary. In the Southern colonies, however, free blacks did vote. In early-eighteenth-century South Carolina (1703–1704), for instance, Berkeley County petitions stated that "free Negroes were received and taken as good Electors as the best Freeholders in the Province." Similar participation was recorded in Virginia and North Carolina. South Carolina disenfranchised free blacks in 1716 and Virginia in 1723; North Carolina did for a period between 1715 and 1734, after which free black suffrage remained until the Revolution. In Georgia free blacks could vote prior to 1761.

Source:
Robert J. Dinkin, *Voting in Provincial America: A Study of Elections in the Thirteen Colonies, 1689–1776* (Westport, Conn.: Greenwood Press, 1977).

LOCAL GOVERNMENT

England. In order to better understand local government in the British American colonies, it is instructive to consider first the English precedents that informed them. Before the Norman Conquest (1066), English local government was under a manorial system. Lords, under the authority of the king, ruled over their respective manors. Also in existence prior to 1066 were townships within the manors. The word *township* derived form the word *tunscipe,* which referred to a section of community marked off by a hedge. In theory, every parcel of land, hedged or not, was considered part of a township or *vill* (village). Whenever an Englishman laid claim to a piece of property he was required to name the town it was in. The borough derived from the Anglo-Saxon word *burh,* which referred to an enclosure designed for the protection of a house. A borough came to mean a protected or fortified town. Eventually, by the time of the Norman Conquest, a borough was the name given more particularly to the large marketplace within a township that had its own judicial courts for maintaining peace and safety.

Cornelis Steenwyck, who held several civic positions in New Amsterdam. After the English takeover he served two terms as mayor of New York City (New-York Historical Society).

Having realized that they were outside the jurisdiction of governmental authority as defined in their Virginia Company charter and fearing that some on board might use their freedom from governmental restraint as a license for unruly behavior, Separatist leaders decided to draw up a Compact (based on their familiar church covenants) allowing them to later establish a government with binding laws. On 11 November 1620, before ever disembarking their vessel, forty-one adult male passengers signed the Mayflower Compact. The following is the Compact in its entirety.

In the Name of God, Amen. We, whose names are underwritten, the loyal subjects of our dread Sovereign Lord King James, by the Grace of God of Great Britain, France, and Ireland King, Defender of the Faith, etc.

Having undertaken, for the Glory of God and Advancement of the Christian Faith and Honour of our King and Country, a Voyage to plant the First Colony in the Northern Parts of Virginia, do by these presents solemnly and mutually in the presence of God and one of another, Covenant and Combine ourselves together into a Civil Body Politic, for our better ordering and preservation and furtherance of the ends aforesaid; and by virtue hereof to enact, constitute and frame such just and equal Laws, Ordinances, Acts, Constitutions and Offices, from time to time, as shall be thought most meet and convenient for the general good of the Colony, unto which we promise all due submission and obedience. In witness whereof we have hereunder subscribed our names at Cape Cod, the 11th of November, in the year of the reign of our Sovereign Lord King James, of England, France and Ireland the eighteenth, and of Scotland the fifty-fourth. Anno Domini 1620.

Source: William Bradford, *Of Plymouth Plantation, 1620–1647*, ed. Samuel Eliot Morison (New York: Knopf, 1966), pp. 75–76.

It could also refer to any large portion of land, even land outside an enclosed area. Some towns were completely within a borough. Thus, that which had been a part of the township could eventually encompass it.

Characteristics. A key distinguishing point between a township and a borough was that the latter became corporate and the former did not. The borough, therefore, developed a more urban setting and was the forerunner of a city. The county also had English origins. After 1066 the old Anglo-Saxon *shire* (literally a division or share), over which a *shire-reeve* (shire headman), or sheriff, presided, became more commonly known as a county (or domain of a count). The county was a type of tribal division of land and might encompass several townships or boroughs. It became the largest local government division in Britain.

The Church. Another important precedent was the English parish. By the fourteenth century the manorial system as a local government structure began to give way to private property ownership. Even so, the manorial courts sought to maintain authority over inhabitants' affairs. The intervention of churches and their priests slowly evolved into an alternative structure for local authority. The parish priest, due to his social and academic position, often took it upon himself to protect the people's rights. Over time "the custom of meeting in the vestry led to the assembly becoming known as the 'vestry meeting,' or simply the 'vestry.'" By the eighteenth century, with the leadership of the parish priest in local secular affairs, the parish vestry had become integral within the local government structure. It, with all of the above structures, evolved in one form or other into the British colonial framework of local government.

New England Town. The New England town, though in many respects different from its English counterpart, did draw significant functional elements from English roots. The New England town served much the same function as the English manor and parish where jurisdiction extended to the surrounding countryside, not just to the local municipality. A typical size for a New England town was fifty square miles. One of the unique elements of the New England town was its function as an arm of Puritan interest. That is, the town institutionalized the Puritan ideal, and it was, for all practical purposes, a secular replica of a congregational church meeting.

The Town Meeting. All New England towns regularly (at least once a year) held town meetings. All white adult male property owners (in time the property stipulation lessened) of good character were eligible to vote in the town meeting. The meeting place was usually in a church or tavern. Majority rule was not the ideal for town business. The primary goal of a town meeting was to find consensus on as wide a scale as possible. The town meeting was not, therefore, as it is often described, a condensed form of democracy per se. Each year new town officials were elected. Offices included selectmen (chief executives), constables (similar to policemen), a clerk (town record keeper), tax officers, highway surveymen, fence viewers (assured fences were properly placed), tithingmen (monitored sabbath and other moral infractions), and cattle catchers.

The Chesapeake. Local government in the Chesapeake operated primarily under a county system. The governor appointed six to eight magistrates for each county. These justices of the peace had singular duties in their respective neighborhoods (where they often held hearings in their homes), and together they made up a county court. In this capacity the court could appeal decisions made by individual magistrates. This collective status also gave the county court a legislative and executive role whereby local regulations were created and carried out. The primary executor of local law was the sher-

A Song made upon the Election of new Magiftrates for this City.

To the tune of, To you fair Ladies now
on land

To you good lads that dare oppofe
all lawlefs power and might,
You are the theme that we have chofe,
and to your praife we write:
You dar'd to fhew your faces brave
In fpight of every abject flave
                with a fa la la.

Your votes you gave for thofe brave men
who feafting did defpife;
And never proftituted pen
to certify the lies
That were drawn up to put in chains,
As well our nymphs as happy fwains;
                with a fa la la.

And tho the great ones frown at this,
what need have you to care?
Still let them fret and talk amifs,
you'll fhew you boldly dare
Stand up to fave your Country dear,
In fpight of ufquebaugh and beer;
                with a fa la la.

They beg'd and pray'd for one year more,
but it was all in vain:
No malcontents you'd have, you fwore;
By jove you made it plain:
So fent them home to take their reft.
And here's a health unto the beft,
                with a fa la la.

A Song made upon the foregoing
Occafion.

To the Tune of, Now, now, you Tories
all fhall ftoop.

Come on brave boys, let us be brave
for liberty and law,

Boldly defpife the haughty Knave,
that would keep us in aw,
Let's fcorn the tools bought by a fop,
and every cringing fool.
The man who bafely bend's a fop,
a vile infipid tool.

Our Country's Rights we will defend;
like brave and honeft men;
We voted right and there's an end,
and fo we'll do again.
We vote all fignеrs out of place,
as men who did fatisfy
Who fold us by a falfe ...,
I'm fure we're right ...

Exchequer courts, as void by law,
great grievances we call;
Tho' great men do affert no flaw
is in them; they fhall fall,
And be contemn'd by every man
that's fond of liberty.
Let them withftand it all they can,
our Laws we will ftand by.

Tho' pettyfogging knaves deny
us Rights of Englifhmen;
We'll make the fcoundrel rafcals fly,
and ne'er return again.
Our Judges they would chop and change
for thofe that ferve their turn,
And will not furely think it ftrange
if they for this fhould mourn.

Come fill a bumper, fill it up,
unto our Aldermen;
For common-council fill the cup,
and take it o'er again.
While they with us refolve to ftand
for liberty and law,
We'll drink their healths with hat in hand,
whoraa! whoraa! whoraa!

Broadside, anonymously printed by John Peter Zenger, of two ballads celebrating the popular-party victory in the Saint Michael's Day election of 1734 in New York City. Since neither the author nor the printer could be identified, the government ordered all copies of this broadside to be burned in front of City Hall.

iff (one per county), who served under the magistrates. Court appointed constables also served with the sheriff. Other officers appointed by the governor were the coroner, clerk, and road supervisors.

Lower South. A dominant form of local government in the Lower South was the parish vestry. In South Carolina, where the parish system was most pronounced, magistrates appointed by the governor did serve, but the more powerful officers were parish vestrymen. In 1706 South Carolina was divided into ten parishes within the existent counties of Berkeley, Colleton, and Craven. Between 1706 and 1770 twenty-three were established. Each parish in the colony appointed seven men for the annual position whose social functions extended to education (oversight of parish schools), benevolence (care for the poor), and ethics (morality enforcement). Vestrymen also acted as parish law enforcement, both executive (police-type work) and judicial (as judges), and as tax collectors. The parish in South Carolina was in some ways like the New England town insofar as it too served as a secular arm of the established church. Unlike the Puritan counterpart, however, the Anglican Church in South Carolina and dissenters (non-Anglican Christians) often worked together in a considerably harmoni-

The lock and key for the powder magazine at Fort Orange, New Netherland, circa 1650 (Albany Institute of History & Art)

ous manner. This spirit of cooperation insured mutual support in the secular realm. Dissenters supported the secular functions of the church and received the benefit of public services in return. The parish vestry, even with county structures developing around it, remained the most powerful arm of local government in South Carolina from the early eighteenth century until the Revolution.

Pennsylvania. The Middle Colonies had a much more diverse system of local government than the other regions. This is not to suggest that the above mentioned regions did not also have diverse systems. Yet, in comparison the Middle Colonies had a greater mixture of systems, making any given one less dominant than in other colonies. In Pennsylvania there were four distinct local entities: township, city, county, and borough. The city, though a separate entity, was nevertheless under county authority (Philadelphia was the only exception to this rule throughout the colonial period). Each county was sectioned off into townships. The township's highest officer was the constable, and the county's was the sheriff. Pennsylvania townships, unlike New England towns, did not hold town meetings. The constable was appointed by the Court of Quarter Sessions while other officers were elected at the polls. The borough, on the other hand, did hold meetings similar to the New England town system. The borough officers (burgesses and councilors) conducted the meetings. In practical terms a borough was more like a village. On a smaller scale it functioned much like a city. It was also less beholden to county authority than was a township. A marked uniqueness about early colonial Pennsylvania's local government was the subordinate character of its judiciary.

Penn. William Penn, whose double exposure as an English court defendant and as a Quaker (who as a group had experienced much opposition within English courts), stressed a less technical, user-friendly court system. The influences of this attitude are reflected in the "Laws Agreed upon in England," which the colony adopted. In one section it is asserted "That in all courts all persons of all persuasions may freely appear in their own way, and according to their own manner, and there personally plead their own cause themselves, or if unable, by their friends. . . . That all pleadings, processed, and records in courts, shall be short, and in English, and in an ordinary and plain character, that they may be understood, and justice speedily administered."

New York. Somewhat different from Pennsylvania, New York demonstrated further local government diversity in the Middle Colonies. After Dutch rule ended in 1664, local government structure in New York tended to become less simplified. As New York's local government structures began to anglicize they also grew in complexity. After the period of the Duke's Laws, which served as a transition in the immediate post-Dutch years, and after the volatile years under the Dominion of New England (1685–1688) and then Leisler's Rebellion (1688–1691), New York's most enduring local government structures were established.

Authority. The county emerged as the highest entity of local authority, but within the county structure was a subdivision of authorities consisting of municipalities, manors, and towns. The sheriff was the most powerful official in a New York county. He was to execute court decisions, oversee elections, perform police duties, and collect taxes. Also important were the county Boards of Supervisors, who served an administrative role. County judges had little or no administrative or executive functions. Their duties were generally limited to trial court cases. The sheriff and judges (judges were usually members of the assembly) were appointed by the governor, whereas the Boards of Supervisors were elected yearly by freemen. Town government administration proved remarkably stable during New York's larger transitional periods (Dutch to English rule, the Glorious Revolution, and Leisler's Rebellion). During the change from Dutch to English rule "daily life continued unchanged," and some towns, "recognizing that not much was new, neglected to even note the conquest in the town minutes." Whereas smaller towns such as Newtown, Long Island, anglicized more slowly, the larger municipalities experienced swifter and more pronounced change as they developed strictly along English metropolitan lines (wards, aldermen, freemen status, etc.). What is true about all levels of local government (in every region) was that whether suddenly or gradually, they overall became more, not less, English over time.

Sources:

John J. Clarke, *A History of Local Government of the United Kingdom* (London: Herbert Jenkins, 1955);

Joseph E. Illick, *Colonial Pennsylvania: A History* (New York: Scribners, 1976);

Jessica Kross, *The Evolution of an American Town: Newtown, New York, 1642–1775* (Philadelphia: Temple University Press, 1983);

Frederic William Maitland, *Township and Borough* (Cambridge: Cambridge University Press, 1898);

M. Eugene Sirmans, *Colonial South Carolina: A Political History, 1663–1763* (Chapel Hill: University of North Carolina Press, 1966);

Robert M. Weir, *Colonial South Carolina: A History* (Millwood, N.Y.: KTO Press, 1983).

THE MILITIA

An Armed Citizenry. In 1622 the Virginia House of Burgesses legislated that all men "go under Arms." Likewise in 1628 the Massachusetts Bay charter allowed for the formation of a colonial militia: it would exist "to incounter, expulse, repell and resist by force of arms, as well by sea as by lands." Like the earlier settlements at Jamestown, Plymouth, Massachusetts Bay, and elsewhere (except Pennsylvania due to Quaker pacifism), the other provinces acted upon English precedent in establishing militias. Men sent over to give military protection such as John Smith in Jamestown and Miles Standish in Plymouth were often veterans of English warfare. They were familiar with the English system of militia readiness and of necessity employed that system in the provinces. The ancient Anglo-Saxon tradition emphasized that every able-bodied adult male was obligated to render service if called upon. Though possibly an exaggerated account of militia readiness during the attack of the Spanish Armada (1588), the following nevertheless at least illustrates the English ideal if not altogether the fact: "the rugged miners poured to war from Mendip's sunless caves . . . and the broad streams of pikes and flags rushed down each roaring [London] street."

Transition. An important English precedent that transferred into the colonies was the short-term utilization of the militia. English law forbade the king to possess a professional standing army lest he use it as a tool of subjugation. Although on the eve of the American Revolutionary era the colonial militias were in transition to that status, prior to 1754 they were very much like their English predecessors. That transition was "evolutionary and subtle in nature, involving as it did the gradual appearance and development of semiprofessional military forces, which provided a transitional link between the seventeenth-century militia and the Revolutionary Continental Army."

Differences. As there were similarities among the colonial militias themselves and with their English predecessors, there were also important differences. A key difference between the English and American militia was that the former was unified whereas the latter was diverse from colony to colony. "Let the New Yorkers defend themselves," said a North Carolinian, "Why should I fight the Indians for them?" The differences were not so much in militia makeup as in the different demographic realities in which the militias existed. For example, in seventeenth-century Massachusetts dense manpower

A French soldier of the early colonial period (from Jaques de Gheyn, *Maniement d'armes,* 1608)

and the cohesive nature of town communities provided a strong military defense for New England, whereas in Virginia the individual plantations and farms were much more susceptible to destruction. After English dominance in 1664, New York's needs were vastly different from those in New England and Virginia. Its heterogeneous settlements and its relative lack of community cohesion made New York more dependent on its allied relationship with the Iroquois confederation than on a strong militia.

Protection. South Carolina, even as late as the 1730s, had such a scattered populace that the strongest possible militia could not possibly provide adequate protection. As that colony's governor, William Bull, stated in 1738, an adequate militia defense was "Inconsistent with domestick or Country Life." The presence of many slaves (more than any other mainland colony) also played a significant role in South Carolina's militia duties. Slaves fought in the South Carolina militia during the Yamasee War. After the Stono Rebellion of 1739, however, with an ever-increasing ratio of blacks to whites, not only were slaves not allowed to fight, they became a major ob-

A cannon cast in 1630 by an Amsterdam gun-and-bell founder. The van Rensselaer family owned it until 1939 (New York State Museum).

ject of the militia's concern. Thus, the militia's role in each of these colonies was different. Not only did spatial and demographic differences cause variation among militias, time did as well. As time progressed, militia needs changed. By early eighteenth century, even with the Indian concerns in South Carolina, the overall threat to most colonies came principally from the French and Spanish. Virginia, on the other hand, faced very little danger from any enemies, rendering a strong and active militia virtually unnecessary for almost fifty years. Time also effected change in the overall type of recruits that occupied the militias by the 1750s. The makeup of a seventeenth-century militia consisted mainly of men whose vested interests (usually land) depended on local protection. By mid eighteenth century that was much less the case.

Strollers. Colonial militias tended to attract the less geographically and socially established. The Virginia and Massachusetts lawmakers called them "strollers." In 1755, when Virginia needed a stronger militia once again, it called for "such able bodied men, as do not follow or exercise any lawful calling or employment, or have not some other lawful and sufficient maintenance. . . ." At the same time, anyone "who hath any vote in the election of a Burgess or Burgesses" was excused from service. During the Seven Years' War (1756–1763) British officers disdained these stroller-type allies who made up this now semiprofessional American army. Their attitude would later come back to haunt them.

Sources:

Don Higginbotham, "The Military Institutions of Colonial America: The Rhetoric and the Reality," in his *War and Society in Revolutionary America: The Wider Dimensions of Conflict* (Columbia: University of South Carolina Press, 1988), pp. 19–41;

Louis Morton, "The Origins of American Military Policy," *Military Affairs*, 22 (1958): 75–82;

John Shy, *A People Numerous and Armed: Reflections on the Military Struggle for American Independence* (London: Oxford University Press, 1976).

THE NON-ENGLISH

Dutch. The Dutch in New Netherland came under the auspices of a private corporation, the Dutch West India Company, not the Estates General of the Netherlands. Political organization reflected these corporate origins. What the company needed was an inexpensive way to maintain order and insure the fur trade. It had no intention of replicating the kind of government enjoyed by the Netherlands. The first director of New Netherland was Cornelis Jacobsen May, who commanded the ship which brought the first thirty families to the company's New World holdings in 1624 and whose job was to coordinate trade. He was replaced in 1626 by Willem Verhulst. This director was supposed to be aided by an advisory council of company officials, but in fact he was the government. In 1629 the company decided to open up their colony to private investors, known as patroons, who were granted lands and allowed to bring in tenants and enter the fur trade. The only successful patroonship, Rensselaerswyck, near Albany, had its own government in the form of an appointed commissioner or commissioners, and in 1648, control by a director. In 1634 it established its own manorial court which functioned as a judiciary. In 1640, under pressure from the States General of the Netherlands, the company promised local autonomy to villages in New Netherland, allowing them to nominate magistrates from whom the director would choose. English settlers from New England petitioned the Dutch for town sites and took advantage of these freedoms. The Dutch were more reluctant and had to be encouraged to come together as villages. They were then able to nominate two kinds of town officers, the *schouts*, or magistrates, and a *schepen*, or sheriff.

Lack of Leadership. Meanwhile, central government languished since the company had difficulty finding able directors. Turnover was high and competence low as needy relatives of powerful company investors were given the position. In 1645 the company found its first, and as it turned out, its last, able governor in Peter Stuyvesant, a former military leader who arrived in the colony in 1647. His was a troubled tenure as he tried to keep control over a mixed lot of colonists, fought pressures from the English colonists for more self-government, dealt with Indian problems, tried to turn a profit for the company, and became the point man for all of the various discontents that an economically marginal colony created. He and a small council tried to rule autocratically, with mixed results since they had few ways to enforce their will. Stuyvesant's tenure closed when the English conquered New Netherland in 1664, thus ending Dutch rule.

French. The French presence in what would become the United States was mainly confined to the villages along the Mississippi River in what became known as the *Pays des Illinois* and Louisiana. The villages of Kaskaskia, Cahokia, Fort de Chartres, Saint Philippe, Prairie de Rocher, and Sainte Genevieve along the Mississippi

The city gates of colonial Saint Augustine, Florida

never had a large population and until 1718 were under the government in Canada. After that they were nominally under Louisiana, but in reality they were too far away from either for control to be exercised. Initially, what administration there was came from the Jesuit missionaries. In 1718, on orders from Paris, the government of the province of Illinois was to consist of a council made up of the commandant of the new fort being built, military officers, and various officials of the joint-stock company, first called the Company of the West and then the Company of the Indies, which was given a monopoly over Illinois and Louisiana that year. In 1721 it became a military district. Local concerns were in the hands of the villagers. They elected a syndic who represented the village in all lawsuits and took on other local responsibilities such as fencing the commons. Local decisions were discussed in a public open-air meeting of all males over the age of fourteen, and maybe widows. They decided when to plant and harvest, build and mark roads, keep up fences, and build and maintain religious structures.

Cadillac. Louisiana had a rockier start, perhaps because it did not grow organically the way the Illinois country did. First settlements under Pierre Le Moyne, Sieur d'Iberville, almost perished. What government there was lay in the hands of a commandant appointed by Iberville in 1699. In 1710 the king appointed a governor, Antoine Laument Cadillac. The new colonial administrator persuaded the entrepreneur Antoine Crozat to take over Louisiana as a proprietary colony so that like the earliest English and Dutch colonies this one had private capitalism trying to create and profit from overseas

settlements. Governor Cadillac was in charge of civil government and the military. A second official, a *commissaire ordonnateur*, was in charge of financial and commercial affairs and the administration of justice. Underneath these two positions was a judicial council called the Superior Council, whose members were appointed by the king. This arrangement of divided responsibility was unstable as the governor and commissaire were often jealous of each other, and both sometimes conflicted with the council. With the death of Louis XIV in 1715, both of the top officers were replaced. Antoine Crozat soon resigned his rights in America, but the idea of a company remained, and by 1719 the Company of the Indies was ready to put resources into Louisiana in yet another failed attempt to make a colony profitable for investors. It kept the system of dual administrators and a council, and these remained the system of government for Louisiana after the company turned the colony back to the Crown in 1731. There were no representative institutions of government at the provincial level.

Spanish. Like the French, the Spanish had only marginal settlements in what would become the United States. The real action for them in the New World lay elsewhere. Spain's governmental structures were centralized. Her northern holdings—the borderlands in the Southwest and Saint Augustine—were under the Viceroyalty of New Spain, whose headquarters was in Mexico City, too far away to act quickly and too busy to bother with such unproductive areas. New Mexico was under the more direct oversight of a military governor based in Santa Fe. He appointed alcal-

Depiction of Samuel de Champlain and Native American allies battling the Iroquois (from *Les Voyages du sieur de Champlain*, 1613)

des, or administrators, to the larger towns. Roman Catholic friars also supervised some of those who lived at or around the missions. Texas was also an internal province with a governor and administrators in the very few towns there were.

Florida. Saint Augustine was organized along more traditional Spanish lines. Admiral Pedro Menéndez de Avilés set up his city in the 1560s with a *cabildo*, or council, which could collect taxes and distribute house lots. He was the first of Saint Augustine's governors, a post that would be filled continuously under the Spanish. Saint Augustine would also be a fort with resident soldiers as well as a mission with friars. As in other Spanish holdings the church and the state clashed. Other officers included treasury officials, an accountant, and those who helped keep the garrisons organized. In some ways Saint Augustine was subsidiary to Cuba, where the governor had easier communication with Spain and the church enjoyed a resident bishop. Saint Augustine, like all the other Spanish outposts so far north, was a backwater, unimportant in the larger Spanish scheme of things. It was also, like many of the others, in constant difficulty through its exposure to hostile Indians and other Europeans, and its unsettled climate. To make matters worse, its lack of sufficient foodstuffs throughout its history made governing the settlement hard and thankless.

Sources:

Mathé Allain, *Not Worth a Straw: French Colonial Policy and the Early Years of Louisiana* (Lafayette: Center for Louisiana Studies, University of Southwestern Louisiana, 1988);

Natalia Maree Belting, *Kaskaskia under the French Regime, Illinois Studies in the Social Sciences,* 39 (Urbana: University of Illinois Press, 1948);

Amy Bushnell, "The Noble and Loyal City 1565–1668," in *The Oldest City: St. Augustine Saga of Survival,* edited by Jean Parker Waterbury (Saint Augustine, Fla.: Saint Augustine Historical Society, 1983), pp. 27–55;

Luis Navarro García, "The North of New Spain as a Political Problem in the Eighteenth Century," in *New Spain's Far Northern Frontier: Essays on Spain in the American West, 1540–1821,* edited by David J. Weber (Albuquerque: University of New Mexico Press, 1979), pp. 201–215;

Michael Kammen, *Colonial New York: A History* (New York: Oxford University Press, 1975).

New Netherland governor Peter Stuyvesant (portrait attributed to Henri Couturier, circa 1663; New-York Historical Society)

POLITICAL STABILITY

Virginia. Debate among colonial historians has often centered around the question of political stability in the British American colonies. This question has been especially pertinent to Virginia's history. Historians disagree, for instance, over the period from settlement to the 1730s whether the Chesapeake region was socially and politically unstable or relatively well established. Historian John Kukla has argued that early-seventeenth-century Virginia had a stable political structure exemplified by a fully established civil government by 1646. After this time, Kukla asserted, political stability continued to progress. Taking an opposite view, historian Timothy Breen has argued that early Virginia was characterized by the inherently unstable mentality of "looking out for number one." Due to the early tobacco boom in the colony the strong lure of wealth attracted the rogue type, who Breen called "an unusual group of Jacobeans." Largely because of these inhabitants, early Virginia was unable to develop into a stable society.

Sound Structure. Whatever the differences and merits of these positions concerning early Virginia, evidence is strong that by mid eighteenth century that colony had developed into a coherent social and political structure. Especially between the 1730s and 1750s strong standards of virtue and duty, a well-adjusted religious tolerance, and a strong economy all led to an unparalleled political stability in Virginia. Part of this later stability, it has been argued, can be attributed to slavery and so emerged not so much due to a rise in virtue as to "more effective forms of human exploitation." Once slaves replaced the rogue Jacobeans as the dominant labor force, Virginia transformed into a province of "personal liberty, a cult of manhood, and an uncompromising loyalty to family." It should be added that the stability began to decline after 1760. Economic debt due to falling tobacco prices and soil exhaustion, problems associated with slavery, the Seven Years' War, and the overt attention to gaining wealth all led to this pre-Revolutionary social and political decline.

New York. Between the years 1665 (just after the English takeover) and 1688 New York experienced a series of politically unsettling events. For most of this period there was no provincial assembly in New York. Not until 1683 did the instructions for the new royal governor, Thomas Dongan, make provision for an elected assembly. The first assembly convened in October of that year. An early accomplishment was the drafting of the Charter of Libertyes and Priviledges, which outlined a new government structure with a strong emphasis on individual liberties. This document drew from two early English documents, the Magna Carta and the Petition of

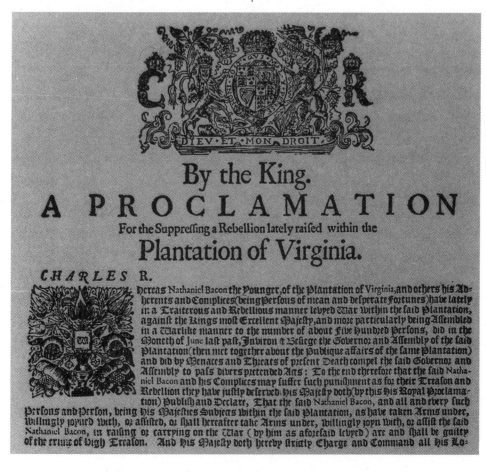

Charles II's October 1676 pardon for those involved in Bacon's Rebellion

The following was taken from a 1725 North Carolina court deposition. The plaintiff in the trial was the colony's governor, Richard Everard, and the defendant, James Burrington, had been the previous governor. The brash exchange revealed in this document may not be representative of the normal relationship between a former and sitting governor. Yet the depositions do show the earthy and often one-on-one personal encounter that typified many political disputes of that day. The following are depositions taken from the governor, his son (also named Richard Everard), and a resident named Susanna Parris.

The information of the Honorable Sir Richard Everard, Baronet, Governor, and Commander in Chief, etc., taken upon oath before us, Christopher Gale, Esq., Chief Justice, and John Lovick and Henry Clayton, Esqrs., Justices of the Peace, this third day of December, Anno Domini 1725. [He] sayeth that on the second of this instant December, about three or four of the clock in the morning, Mr. Burrington, the late Governor, with several ruffians in company, came to the back door of his house; and having made a violent knocking for some time, he called out, 'open the door'—which he repeated several times. But Sir Richard, knowing his voice, as did his servant who told him it was Mr. Burrington, Sir Richard advised him to go about his business or it would be worse for him; upon which Mr. Burrington replied after a rude and threatening manner, 'come out; I want satisfaction of you for saying you would send me to England in irons. Therefore come out and give it [to] me, you Everard, you a Knight, you a Baronet, you a Governor. You are a Sancho Panza, and I'll take care of you, numbskull head.' And upon Sir Richard's threatening him that if he offered to break into the house he would shoot him, or that if he did not go away quietly he would have him punished, he replied, 'you have not an officer [who

would] dare speak to me or look me in the face.' And so, defying Sir Richard and his authority, he went away, calling Sir Richard 'scoundrel' and several other abusive names.

The son's deposition reads as follows:

The examination of Richard Everard, Esq., aged about sixteen years, taken upon oath this third day of December, 1725.

The examinant sayeth that on the second of this instant December about three or four of the clock in the morning, [he] being in bed was wakened by his father's servant. And as he came downstairs he heard Mr. Burrington scurrilously abusing the Governor, Sir Richard Everard, saying, 'you send me to England in irons, you be damned. I will make your heart ache before I have done with you.' And then Mr. Burrington demanded whether the Governor would send him home to England or no; upon which the Governor desired him to go home, adding that he should see all things done in time, at which Mr. Burrington made a jest crying, 'ah! ah! ah! I am come to turn up my Cape Fair—to you, before it goes to take its leave of you, Dick D—, you, you a sorry fellow. I'll scalp your damned thick skull.' Whereupon the Governor again bid him depart, and soon after he went away, drumming against the window-shutters and weatherboards of the house.

Susanna Parris stated that former Governor Burrington on one occasion said, "are all you country men such fools as Sir Richard Everard? He is a noodle, an ape. . . ." Parris also reported that "further [he] said that he . . . was not more fit to be a governor than a hog in the woods."

Source: John Demos, ed., *Remarkable Providences: Readings on Early American History,* revised edition (Boston: Northeastern University Press, 1991).

Right. The lengthiest segment of the charter insured freedom of Christian conscience. It also gave the assembly a strong enough hand in the governing process that that body assumed the right of appropriations (originator of money bills). The governor, council, and Duke of York (later James II) approved the Charter of Libertyes and Priviledges and sent it on for Crown approval; due to Charles II's desire for closer scrutiny of his holdings, however, approval never came. New York was back to square one. Even when the duke himself became king of England (1685) he did not reinstate the charter but rather forced New York to go under the Dominion of New England. With this change the governor and council assumed the right to initiate taxation. Many inhabitants feared the prospect of being taxed by a nonrepresentative body.

Unrest. Two short-lived protests at Staten Island and

Jamaica demonstrated the growing unrest. Other factors, such as a slow-growth economy, land disputes, and safety concerns (close proximity to French rivals), led to considerable political instability in New York. As much or more than any of these, however, was the undercurrent of religious unrest. Since the duke of York was Roman Catholic, it is not surprising that during the 1680s New York received a considerable number of Catholic inhabitants. Their establishment in the colony's trade particularly alarmed the long-entrenched Dutch Calvinist merchants. By the time New York's government transferred to Boston in 1688, rumors of a Catholic conspiracy were swirling. One particular German merchant and ardent Calvinist, Jacob Leisler, determined to bring the perceived papal conspiracy to a halt. Once he learned that William and Mary had dethroned James II and that Bostonians had risen up against Gov. Edmund Andros and the Dominion of New England (April 1689), Leisler, in

A political cartoon drawn by Benjamin Franklin for the 9 May 1754 issue of the
Pennsylvania Gazette urging the colonies to unite in a federation

the absence of Lt. Gov. Francis Nicholson (who Leisler believed was in on the Catholic conspiracy), took control of the government through his position in the New York militia, which had seized New York City's Fort James. Leisler's regime ended in March 1691 when the newly arrived governor (appointed by William III), Henry Sloughter, demanded surrender of the fort. Leisler finally did surrender (after three refusals) and was summarily arrested, tried, and hanged.

Factions. New York's politics quickly factionalized into Leislerians and anti-Leislerians even though with time the original event and its causes became less and less relevant. Although there were times when stability seemed to be on the rise (such as 1709–1710 when the assembly held dominant control), problems of ethnic and religious factionalism remained a considerable source of political flux. Even with substantial economic growth (especially between 1713 and 1728), it was not until the 1740s that signs of sustainable political stability became evident. Key to the eventual rise in New York's political viability were the constitutional clarifications that were forthcoming by 1740. In 1735 the English Crown lessened the New York governor's role in legislative deliberations. Consequently, in 1736 the assembly began to reassert its authority of "power of the purse." Gov. George Clinton's repeated attempts to gain control over the assembly in the 1740s and early 1750s were not successful.

Rival. James De Lancey, possibly the most powerful New York politician from the 1730s through the 1750s, became Clinton's principal opposition as council mem-ber and chief justice. Even if for less than ideological reasons (De Lancey was an opportunist who delivered favors to assemblymen with landed interests), once he became lieutenant governor after Clinton's departure in 1753, he successfully wrested the royal prerogatives from the governor and council to the assembly, resulting in a more provincially focused agenda. If one judges political stability by the lack of conflict between the executive and legislative bodies, then New York had little. Yet the very fact that by the mid eighteenth century elected representatives, even if for their own benefits more than their constituent base, had effectively taken the royal prerogative into their own sphere was a large leap toward a more unified and stable government in New York. At least New York freemen perceived that their interests, more than the Crown's, were being served.

South Carolina. A most interesting case study of political stability is South Carolina. As noted earlier in this chapter, by the 1720s South Carolina had experienced considerable instability under its proprietary government. That dominant political factions demanded and received a royal government is evidence of South Carolina's prior lack of an efficient political structure. By the 1730s signs of political maturity and harmony were evident. A major contributor to this more civil state was the growing prominence of "country ideology." Country ideology was a body of seventeenth- and eighteenth-century English political and social thought that emphasized among other things a mutually limiting role for both the populace and the government. A primary function of government was to restrain human passion (or nonrational action), and a primary function of the populace was to limit governmental power. The practical result that emanated from country ideology was a strong inclination to work for the commonweal rather than individual self-interest.

Harmony. In South Carolina a unique working out of country ideology's balancing influence led to a stability through unprecedented harmony. Within the context of this ideal several factors played key roles in the evolution of political stability. The wide distribution of wealth by the 1730s led to a less divisive and competitive elite class. A pronounced toleration of religious differences helped to lessen political and social tensions and led to a "growing sense of community." The reality of shared internal and external threats also forced cooperation. South Carolina experienced within a five-year period (1738–1742) a series of potentially devastating emergencies, including a major slave revolt in 1739 and the immediate threat of Spanish and Indian attack. These realities led to "an unprecedented willingness by local leaders to compromise and cooperate with each other." Two other factors emerged that contributed to continued stability. The significant growth in literary influences, particularly from works such as *Cato's Letters* and *The Independent Whig,* buttressed the already-growing allegiance to country ideology. Finally, albeit closer to the Revolution, the growth of the local assembly's power with the decline of the royal council led to an increased attention to the wishes of the populace. "The more irresponsible the Council seemed to become, the more members of the Commons [assembly] felt their responsibility for the public welfare, because they alone appeared to have it at heart."

Pennsylvania. The Middle Colonies are often portrayed as being politically and socially disjointed due to the diversity in ethnic makeup and, in Pennsylvania's case, the late arrival of English dominance. This position has not gone unchallenged. Recent studies have shown that Pennsylvania, at least by the early eighteenth century, does not so easily fit into a political declension model. It is true that the early Holy Experiment (William Penn's name for his religious-political ideal) did not produce the desired stability, partly due to Penn's absence. It was not until 1701 that Pennsylvania's assembly achieved dominant control over local affairs. Also around this same time the increase in English control over proprietary concerns helped to bring relative stability to what had been a troublesome experience for Penn, who struggled to run the colony from afar. The role of the Quakers in Pennsylvania's political structure by the 1720s, rather than disjointed and ineffective, as some have maintained, was neither, but was substantial and stabilizing. Between 1726 and 1755 there were only three short-lived periods of substantial political conflict. Thus, as with the rest of colonial America, Pennsylvania, even with its diverse populace, was experiencing, if more subtly than most, anglicization, and with it, stabilization.

Assessment. From the early decades of the eighteenth century to around 1750 a considerable increase in political stability occurred. There are various general factors that help us to understand this trend. First, from around 1650 to 1710 British officials sought relatively stringent control. After that period Britain demonstrated a "casual posture toward the colonies." Second, after 1710 there was a marked growth in population and with it an overall increase in economic viability and therefore a more stable economy. Third, an increase in population, which on the surface might seem to have the opposite effect, was actually an asset to political stability by providing a greater number of quality leaders. Population growth also resulted in a greater "strength of community" overall. And fourth, of the reflectors of increased political stability, possibly none are clearer than that of a decrease in political elections. From the beginning of the eighteenth century to around 1750 there was a consistent trend of less and less electorate involvement. Such may seem unusual in light of the fact that parallel with this trend was an increase in the assembly's representative role in directing colonial policy. Paradoxically, this reflects freeholders' increased confidence and contentment with their political leaders. And with this level of trust freeholders naturally approved even greater degrees of representative authority.

Sources:

Timothy Breen, "Looking Out for Number One: Conflicting Cultural Values in Early Seventeenth-Century Virginia," *South Atlantic Quarterly,* 78 (1979): 342–360;

Douglas Greenberg, "Middle Colonies in Recent American Historiography," *William and Mary Quarterly,* 36 (1979): 396–427;

Jack P. Greene, "The Growth of Political Stability: An Interpretation of Political Development in the Anglo-American Colonies, 1660–1760," and "Society, Ideology, and Politics: An Analysis of the Political Culture of Mid-Eighteenth-Century Virginia," in his *Negotiated Authorities: Essays in Colonial Political and Constitutional History* (Charlottesville: University Press of Virginia, 1994): 131–162, 259–318;

Joseph E. Illick, *Colonial Pennsylvania: A History* (New York: Scribners, 1976);

Michael Kammen, *Colonial New York: A History* (New York: Scribners, 1975);

John Kukla, "Order and Chaos in Early America: Politics and Social Stability in Pre-Restoration Virginia," *American Historical Review,* 90 (April 1985): 275–298;

John Murrin, "Political Development," in *Colonial British America: Essays in the New History of the Early Modern Era,* edited by Jack P. Greene and J. R. Pole (Baltimore: Johns Hopkins University Press, 1984);

Alan Tully, *William Penn's Legacy: Politics and Social Structure in Provincial Pennsylvania, 1726–1755* (Baltimore: Johns Hopkins University Press, 1977);

Robert M. Weir, *Colonial South Carolina: A History* (Millwood, N.Y.: KTO Press, 1983);

Weir, "'The Harmony We Were Famous For': An Interpretation of Pre-Revolutionary South Carolina Politics," *William and Mary Quarterly,* 26 (1969): 473–501.

PROPRIETARY COLONIES

Revival. It has been said that around the mid seventeenth century England rediscovered the colonies that

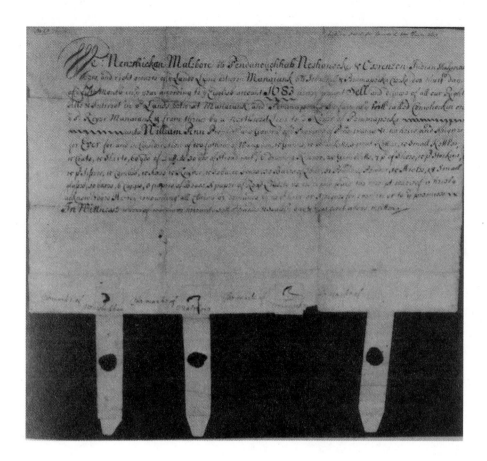

A 1683 deed in which William Penn received land from three Delaware chiefs in exchange for an assortment of goods, including beads, wampum, muskets, shoes, and pots and pans (Pennsylvania Historical and Museum Commission)

her people had previously settled. The early colonies were founded by the Virginia, London, and Massachusetts Bay Companies. It was not until the period of Stuart Restoration in the 1660s that England really began to take careful notice of the potential benefits these provinces could bring. The most common method by which the British colonial empire began to take shape at this point was through the royal issuance of proprietorships, either for provinces where the company charters had expired or failed, or as in the case of Maryland and Pennsylvania, where no previous claims were in force.

The Chosen. In 1632 the second Lord Baltimore's acceptance of Maryland made him the first American proprietor. In 1639 Sir Ferdinando Gorges received Maine, and in 1664 Charles II granted New Netherland (which included New York, New Jersey, and Delaware) to his brother James, Duke of York. That same year James granted New Jersey to John, Lord Berkeley, and Sir George Carteret. William Penn received the proprietorship for Delaware from the Duke of York in 1682. The previous year he became the proprietor of the colony that would bear his name—Pennsylvania. In 1663 and 1665 eight proprietors received a grant from Charles II for Carolina (land which included North and South Carolina and Georgia).

Holdouts. Pennsylvania is generally considered the last proprietary colony since it was the last directly granted by a sitting monarch. Georgia's trustees held in 1732 a limited (twenty-one-year) charter after the Carolina proprietors sold out their interests in 1729. Technically, therefore, Georgia was never a proprietary colony. In actuality, however, the trustees' function was similar to that of proprietors. Most proprietary colonies had come under direct royal dominion by the mid eighteenth century. Only two colonies remained under their proprietorship up to the Revolution: Pennsylvania and Maryland. Pennsylvania experienced a two-year period of royal rule (1692–1694) under King William III. This short period of direct Crown control came because Penn had developed a friendship with deposed Roman Catholic King James II and because of the pacifistic position Pennsylvania Quakers had taken in the recent war with France. In 1701 Pennsylvania adopted its Charter of Liberties, which established the only unicameral (one-house) legislature in the colonies. In that same year Penn returned to England and in 1708 tried to sell his proprietorship (although he retained a considerable amount of property in Pennsylvania) to trustees because of personal debt. In 1691, due to the petition of anti-Catholic leaders (the Protestant Association) in Maryland, the Lords of Trade revoked the proprietary rule of Charles Calvert, third Lord Baltimore, and Maryland became a royal col-

Cecilius Calvert, second Baron Baltimore, first proprietor of Maryland (portrait by Gerard Soest, Enoch Pratt Free Library)

ony. Upon Charles Calvert's death in 1715, the proprietorship was restored to his son Benedict Leonard, fourth Lord Baltimore, due to Benedict's appeal that he had renounced the Catholic faith for Anglicanism. His proprietary rule was short-lived, however. He died eight weeks later at age thirty-five. Rule then passed to his minor son Charles, fifth Lord Baltimore. Although Maryland remained a proprietary colony in name, the twenty-five-year royal rule had firmly entrenched a strong anglicization in the governmental structure. Maryland's assembly had gained significant power during royal rule and would not readily relinquish it. A strong antiproprietary movement held sway in Maryland throughout most of the remaining colonial years.

Power. A proprietary colony was one in which the English monarch granted to one or more persons (proprietors) a province over which they held feudal sovereignty. This privilege resulted from an official Crown bestowal of the ancient powers of the bishop of Durham. Since the Norman Conquest (1066) the bishop of Durham had held, by the king's authority, feudal lordship over a northern English county as a buffer against Scotland. Except for Pennsylvania, all of the proprietary charters in America contained a "Bishop of Durham" clause giving similar feudal rights to proprietors. In certain charters there were important limitations attached

to this clause. For example, in Maryland, whose original proprietors were Roman Catholic, the charter, with the words "to cause them [any churches] to be dedicated and consecrated according to the ecclesiastical [church] laws of our kingdom of England," prevented Catholicism from attaining established-church status. In Carolina the proprietary charter allowed for a certain degree of freedom in worship. In 1670 the Church of England became the established church of Carolina even though that province did not come under royal dominion until 1729.

Elite. Charters, again with the exception of Pennsylvania, allowed proprietors to grant titles of nobility. In Carolina, for instance, proprietors established an elaborate land-division scheme that was strictly based on hierarchical status, with them, of course, at the pinnacle. Also, the eight Carolina proprietors, who never actually came to the province, made up the Palatine Court, which, with its appellate judicial powers, also had the power to appoint governors and to rescind undesirable legislation. As for Pennsylvania, the king of England rather than William Penn had the power to disallow legislation. Also, unlike in Maryland, Pennsylvania could be directly taxed by royal prerogative. Overall, even with the greater limits placed on William Penn, proprietors held similar powers. They could appoint governors and depose them at will. Generally the governor of a proprietary province was there primarily as a political protector of the proprietor's landed interests. Each proprietor held certain executive, judicial, and ecclesiastical powers as mentioned above. Of the similarities they did possess, the most important was a limitation that all proprietary charters stipulated: in each colony all legislation required the assent of freemen. In a broad sense this common element of representation would be the ultimate undoing of proprietary and later royal rule.

Sources:

Aubrey C. Land, *Colonial Maryland: A History* (Millwood, N.Y.: KTO Press, 1981);

Samuel Lucas, ed., *Charters of the Old English Colonies in America* (London: John W. Parker, 1850);

Curtis P. Nettels, *Roots of American Civilization: A History of American Colonial Life* (New York: F. S. Crofts, 1945);

Carl Ubbelohde, *The American Colonies and the British Empire, 1607–1763* (New York: Crowell, 1968).

THE RISE OF THE ASSEMBLY

Representation. The imperial system was not designed for provincial assemblies to become the central governing force, but in all provinces (most had become royal by the mid eighteenth century) this is precisely what happened. In 1619 the first local representative body in British America assembled in Virginia. It was called the House of Burgesses (a burgess was an English representative from a local borough or corporate town). The words of Virginia governor Sir George Yeardley in 1618 concerning the formation of this new representative government could just as well have been said of the other colonial governments that would follow: they were,

The reconstructed Capitol at Williamsburg, Virginia, built 1701–1705

he said, "to imitate and follow the laws and administration of justice used in the realm of England as near as may be." The members of local assemblies, from the first in Virginia to the last in Georgia, saw their representative duties, even as they often conflicted with the governor and his council, as well within an English construct. Local assemblies assumed their powers from the body of English common law. This reliance on English precedent was intensified after the Glorious Revolution in 1688 when provincial assemblies slowly began to see themselves as reflections of Parliament. It was at this juncture that the various colonial representative bodies began to raise their own self-perception whereby they obtained what has been called "negotiated authorities." Such authorities would later strengthen their resolve to bypass Parliament and appeal directly to the king. They began, in other words, to see themselves as little Parliaments.

Power of the Purse. Of the powers the local assemblies had, none were more relevant to eventual royal decline than the power of the purse. In this vein historians have at times emphasized that the most important object of financial control was the governor's salary. As long as his income was at their disposal they could maintain the upper hand. This has been shown to be an oversimplification. Governors' salaries were often from sources other than local appropriations. Evidence has shown that even when pay was dependant on local legislation, rarely (although there were exceptions) was it withheld. The real power of the purse lay in the ability on a wider scale to control public finance through taxation. Assemblies gained "primary position in colonial money matters," which translated into control over public services as well as military, ecclesiastical, and judicial concerns. Again, this was not a break with English precedent. Ever since the Virginia House of Burgesses in 1624 had assumed the right to tax, the Crown proceeded to authorize the practice in all future royal colonies. Tensions arose between the Crown and the assemblies when the latter began to replicate the House of Commons's efforts to gain sole authority (as opposed to the governor or council) over appropriation initiatives. By the time of the Glorious Revolution the English House of Commons had won this right. In time the provincial assemblies would do the same.

Sources:

Jack P. Greene, *Negotiated Authorities: Essays in Colonial Political and Constitutional History* (Charlottesville: University Press of Virginia, 1994);

Greene, *The Quest for Power: The Lower Houses of Assembly in the Southern Royal Colonies, 1689–1776* (Chapel Hill: University of North Carolina Press, 1963);

Leonard Woods Labaree, *Royal Government in America: A Study of the British Colonial System before 1783* (New York: Frederick Ungar, 1958);

Carl Ubbelohde, *The American Colonies and the British Empire, 1607–1763* (New York: Thomas Y. Crowell, 1968).

ROYAL COLONIES

Crown Law. Royal colonies were those that in the absence or revocation of a private or proprietary charter came under the direct, everyday governmental control of the English monarchy. It is important to emphasize that the Crown and not Parliament held sovereignty over royal colonies. In theory their purpose, from the royal perspective, was in some ways similar to that of a medieval fiefdom. That is, the foremost function of a royal colony was to benefit the English Crown. Although most colonies started out as private or proprietary ventures, the majority became royal usually through revoked or time-limited charters well before the Revolutionary era. By the mid eighteenth century eight of the thirteen mainland colonies were royal: Massachusetts, New Hampshire, New York, New Jersey, Virginia, North Carolina, South Carolina, and Georgia. Of these, only New Hampshire actually started out as a royal province and then only after Charles II annexed it from the then-privately chartered Massachusetts Bay Colony. New

A nineteenth-century engraving of James Oglethorpe, the founder of Georgia

Dominion of New England. James II forced royal rule over Massachusetts in 1685. Boston became the headquarters for the centralizing efforts of this Dominion of New England under appointed Gov. Sir Edmund Andros. All the New England colonies, along with New York and New Jersey, were under Andros's royal regime for a time. With the fall of James II in 1688 and the ensuing Glorious Revolution in 1688, the Dominion of New England ended.

Commission and Instructions. The royal governor's role was in many ways precarious. First and foremost he was officially the king's representative in the colony. Although he bore the title His Excellency, he did not have the free will of a king. The governor's actions were not to originate with him but with the Crown, whose wishes were issued through a general commission (varying little from governor to governor) and subsequent instructions, which were outlined periodically in accordance to circumstances unique to a given colony. Unlike the commission, which was often read at the governor's induction ceremony, the instructions were not for public consumption. On occasion the council members had limited access, but generally the detailed contents of administrative policy and procedure contained therein were completely secret to all but the governor. The governor's instructions gave him and his council control of appropriations. Yet the general assemblies usually were successful hindrances to the effective execution of this power.

Judiciary. The governor had significant judicial powers as well. He, along with the council, had oversight of lower courts. Most important, the governor-in-council was the highest colonial court. Any appeals to this body's decisions were referred to the Privy Council in England. As legislative head of the council and assembly the governor had sovereign veto power, a power the Crown expected him to use with vigor for the advancement of British interests. But the governor who ignored provincial concerns, especially those expressed through the assembly, did so at his own political peril. A compromise between carrying out royal instructions and serving local interests was often an extremely difficult but necessary medium to attain. Sir Thomas Robinson's words, written in 1747 upon his recall as governor of Barbados, clearly express a royal governor's typical dilemma: "If a governor lies under the fatal necessity of disobliging a majority of representatives by doing his duty on one hand, or on the other of gaining their favor by a breach of duty, his doom is fixed, since he must either fall a victim to the unjust rage of those men for what is right or to his Majesty's just displeasure for doing what is wrong." In 1701 Gov. Christopher Codrington Jr. of the Leeward Islands summed it up well. It was as if, he said, he "were walking between red hot irons."

York, after its English takeover from the Dutch in 1664, if not technically then in practical function, started out as a royal colony since Charles II granted it to his brother, James, the duke of York, who would succeed Charles to the throne in 1685.

Instability. Some colonies became royal by the lack of proprietary governments' ability to provide stability. North and South Carolina, for instance, started out as one colony under eight proprietors. During the first two decades of the eighteenth century proprietary control steadily waned due to French, Spanish, and Indian threats. In 1719 South Carolina (regional distinction in the Carolinas had evolved by the eighteenth century) colonists deposed the proprietary governor Robert Johnson and appointed an interim. In 1721 South Carolina became a royal colony with the king's appointment of Francis Nicholson as governor. Once the proprietors sold their interests in 1729 North Carolina became a royal colony as well. In 1732 trustees received a twenty-one year royal charter for Georgia, which had belonged to the Carolina proprietors until 1729. With the expiration of this charter in 1752 Georgia became a royal colony (last of the thirteen colonies formed). Virginia, originally chartered under the Virginia Company, became a royal colony in 1624 upon that charter's revocation. Upon the Board of Trade's recommendation New Jersey, a proprietary colony since 1664, came under the Crown in 1702.

Decline. Given the delicate diplomacy required to successfully govern a royal colony, it is not so surprising that the governors began to decline in effective rule, as it is remarkable that they succeeded at all. The fact that governors were usually chosen for who they knew rather than for what they could do makes their relative longevity even more impressive. It should not be forgotten that colonists in such provinces as South Carolina and Maryland saw proprietary governorship as insufficient for stability and consequently discarded it for royal rule. Excluding, of course, the often-cited exceptions, it is to the royal governors' credit in finding a flexible medium that prior to 1763 Americans rarely expressed the notion to break away from the empire of Great Britain. But decline in royal governorship did eventually come, especially after the mid–eighteenth century mark. That decline did not come about, however, so much from personal inabilities as it did from underlying forces beyond immediate control, forces that were moving long before the governors' decline, was a discernable reality. None of the forces were more significant than the ever-increasing power of local colonial assemblies.

Royal Council. The men who made up the royal councils were usually provincials recommended by the governor, chosen by the Board of Trade, and appointed by the king. They ideally served for life, and the average number per council was twelve. Councilors received no pay for their services, but their position of power often secured them other paying positions within the government. Most councilmen were already men from families of considerable wealth. It was not uncommon for several relatives to serve on one council.

Problem of a Quorum. Five made up a quorum on island colonies and three on the continent in emergencies. One of the most acute problems for a governor was keeping a quorum. Absentee councilors became such a problem that after 1720 all governors were authorized to suspend a councilor if he was absent from the colony for twelve months without permission. Few governors acted on the instruction, however, even as problems of prolonged absenteeism were rampant by the mid eighteenth century. One thing that caused much consternation within the colonies was the immense power the council had in relation to its meager quorum requirement. Outside the governor, three men could determine the fate of legislation passed by an entire assembly. This, along with problems of absenteeism, caused voters to trust and support the elected assembly over the aristocratic governor and council.

Responsibilities. From the British perspective the most important governmental entity, apart from the royal governor, was the royal provincial council. It served both as a check and theoretically as an allied partner to the governor in practically every aspect of his duties. The council held judicial, legislative, and executive powers. It was the highest appeals court—the upper legislative house—as well as the governor's chief advisory board. With the council's advisory role it also held considerable power in certain areas where the governor could not execute his will apart from its consent. Legislatively and judicially the council was somewhat a replica of the House of Lords (the nonrepresentative upper house in England's Parliament), and in its executive role it had similar powers to the Privy Council in England. When the council served in its executive and judicial capacity, the governor was the presiding officer. But in its legislative role the council and governor were initially to be separate, especially since the governor held absolute veto power.

Intrusion. Even so, by the eighteenth century governors began to preside over the council's legislative functions, sometimes to that body's chagrin. In 1703 the Virginia Council complained about Gov. Francis Nicholson's undue control: "He is not only constantly present, but takes upon him to preside and debate, and state the question, and overrule as if he were still in council, which the said house takes to be a great encroachment on their liberties and privileges." Early on, virtually all royal governors' commissions gave the power, provided there was "good and sufficient cause," to remove councilors from active service. Due to the unusual control this gave to governors, the Board of Trade began to curb this power, as in 1698 when Nicholson's instructions set limitations to prevent "arbitrary and illgrounded recalls" from the council. After 1715 governors generally could not remove members of the council apart from a majority vote within that body. It should be added, however, that overall the governor and council worked in considerable harmony toward their shared ideals of royal and personal interests. The real effectiveness of the council, however, is debatable. Even with its varied legislative, judicial, and executive functions it was relatively powerless apart from a consenting governor. And as time progressed the governor's position of power increased while the council's power decreased. Nevertheless, over time both became victims of the elected assembly.

Sources:

Leonard Woods Labaree, *Royal Government in America: A Study of the British Colonial System before 1783* (New York: Frederick Ungar, 1958);

Carl Ubbelohde, *The American Colonies and the British Empire, 1607–1763* (New York: Thomas Y. Crowell, 1968).

RULING FAMILIES

Social Status. The role of social status must be considered in the development of the colonial political structure. It is important to remember that the earlier English and other European settlers did not conceive of government apart from a hierarchical social construct. Any semblance of egalitarianism was virtually foreign to most early provincials. "Social leadership and political leadership" were, in the minds of Englishmen, "so closely related" to the degree that "experience if not theory justified an identification between state and society." To most they were indistinguishable. This hierarchical relationship did not die easily in the American provinces.

Virginia as a Model. The settlers into Jamestown demonstrated this relationship of social status and political authority. The earliest leaders were of high social, economic, and educational standing. Within a generation, however, these leaders either departed or died not having left descendants to take their place. By the 1630s more rugged and self-made elite families arose who took the reins of governmental authority. But as with their more genteel predecessors they too failed to pass on their created hierarchy to descendants. In the latter half of the seventeenth century a third aristocracy began to arise in Virginia. Around 1650 sons of influential merchants and government officials (especially those connected in some way with Virginia) began to settle in the colony. Usually they came because their families had long held property or company stock interests within the colony. These sons bore well-known Virginia names such as Burwell, Byrd, Digges, Fitzhugh, Mason, Carter, Culpeper, and Berkeley. Within ten years of their relocation these sons generally dominated Virginia's county-level politics.

1660s. The Restoration in England had major ramifications in the way Virginia's political framework would develop. The Restoration government, desiring greater oversight of Virginia's economic and political life, began, through the governor, an elaborate system of patronage for positions on the council. Select members of this new elite were chosen for service. William Berkeley, the governor during this time, called his group the Green Spring faction, named after his plantation. Prior to this time the Virginia assembly had been aligned with the council to the degree that the two were, for all practical purposes, a unified house. With part of the ruling families within the governor's circle of central authority and the other part remaining at the local county level, a division between the assembly and council emerged. County leaders began to take seats in the House of Burgesses in order to share a degree of the central authority through local representation. This new hierarchical control of the council and the House of Burgesses caused significant problems. The main concern was not that those inhabiting the two houses were too elite but that they were not elite enough. "This social and political structure was too new, too lacking in the sanctions of time and custom, its leaders too close to humbler origins and as yet too undistinguished in style of life, to be accepted without a struggle." Within this whole system were several levels of discontent. The most famous, Bacon's Rebellion (1676), intensified the degree to which all segments involved themselves in government protest.

Bacon's Rebellion. Nathaniel Bacon, though a latecomer as opposed to the earlier "elite sons" who had taken their place among Berkeley's Green Spring circle, became a member of Berkeley's select council shortly after his arrival in Virginia. Bacon, well-educated and having strong kinship connections (cousin to Lady Berkeley and council member Nathaniel Bacon Sr.) within the colony, distanced himself from his colleagues on the council for their entrenched but, in his view, undeserved status which had been rewarded with prime landholdings.

Causes. The rebellion has most commonly been seen as starting from Bacon's dislike for Berkeley's protection of Indian land rights. Although this was a key to the first stages of the conflict, it was not the whole story. Bacon, along with other latecomers, took great offense to Berkeley's land policy because it favored the earlier members of the inner circle. Bacon wrote, "Let us trace these men in Authority and Favour to whose hands the dispensation of the Countries [sic] wealth has been commited [sic]. . . . let us observe the sudden Rise of their Estates [compared] with the Quality in which they first entered the Country." They were lacking in the proper education, Bacon continued, especially in light of their positions of authority. They were "unworthy Favourites and juggling Parasites whose tottering Fortunes have bin repaired and supported at the Publique chardg." The lack of contentment expressed by Bacon and others was duplicated by common settlers who perceived county-level elites as also possessing privileges that exceeded their actual social status. Thus, from this level of discontent came much of Bacon's following which empowered the eventual upheaval and destruction that transpired.

Impact. The end result of the rebellion, however, rather than culminating in a popular, more democratic structure, had the opposite effect. Since the disputes had largely been over who were the "real elites" deserving of authority, that same mentality of social status continued to inform future political selections for both the council and the assembly. This is evidenced by the entrenchment of an eighteenth-century Virginia aristocracy that existed in both houses up to the Revolution. The fact that the Virginia aristocracy did not practice primogeniture (estates passed to the oldest son) or entail made the potential for broad authority within few elite families greater. With any number of a family's sons inheritors of great wealth, that family's social and political status could strengthen significantly. The 1750s, for example, saw seven same-generation members of the Lee family in Virginia's assembly. Social status, therefore, controlled political authority not in spite of popular consent but because of it.

Source:
Bernard Bailyn, "Politics and Social Structure in Virginia," in Stanley N. Katz, ed., *Colonial America: Essays in Politics and Social Development,* second edition (Boston: Little, Brown, 1976), pp. 119–143.

TAXATION

Costs. As today, there were various costs that prompted colonial authorities to levy taxes on inhabitants. Local and provincial costs such as officials' salaries, schools (especially in New England), church expenses (New England and New York town taxes), benevolence efforts, road construction and maintenance, and the militia were paid through taxes. Unlike today, there were no income or sales taxes. In addition to trade duties indirect revenue was acquired largely through internal excise taxes. These allowed for lower individual taxation. The principle of individual (direct) taxation, in whatever form, was generally based on the concept of production. Both direct and indirect taxes were levied on the local and provincial levels. It should be remembered that taxation varied from region to region. The following, therefore, is an overall generalization.

Land Taxes. Both on the local and provincial level a primary measurement of taxation was land. Since land was most colonist's chief form of production, its value was taxed. The only way to avoid such a tax was to demonstrate that the property was at the time dormant. But for most a considerable amount of their property did produce income and was therefore taxable. On the provincial level a similar system was used with an additional system called quitrents. Quitrents were employed as a means of land taxation. The quitrent had its origin in feudal England. The prefix *quit* referred to one's payment obligation to the manor lord as quit or free once the annual rent was met. Royal and proprietary colonies often charged quitrents, which "emphasized the feudal dependence of the American colonies, and was the visible token of such a relation." Quitrents served as a necessary fixed rate of taxation (as opposed to labor rates which were variable and hard to enforce) for the transition of feudal England's inhabitants from tenancy to freeholdership. This system found its way first into Virginia and the Carolinas and later Pennsylvania. Some northern colonies adopted it, but it never reached widespread use as in the southern provinces. Quitrents are considered here as a form of taxation since colonial authorities looked to them as a primary means of income for governmental operations (and hopefully personal profit).

Poll Tax. The poll tax was an across-the-board flat labor tax imposed primarily on white adult males. This tax centered around the concept of income-earning labor. Anyone, most commonly white males, who earned an income was subject to this tax. For fathers who put their sons to work on the farm, their labor was also taxed; it was paid by the father as long as he drew the profit of their labor. Fourteenth-century England saw the earliest poll tax. Laborers above the age of fourteen were subject to the tax. Near the end of the seventeenth century the poll tax was abolished in England due to its perceived unfairness. Pennsylvania enacted its first poll tax in 1693 around the same time of its demise in the mother country. The Pennsylvania tax required sixteen-year-old white males who had been free from indentured servitude for at least six months and whose net worth did not exceed a certain amount to pay the tax. For many of the colonies the poll tax covered at least half of the government expenditures on the provincial (as opposed to local) level.

Excise Taxes. Another form of taxation that produced considerable income on the provincial level was the excise (internal) tax, especially on liquor and slaves. Since slaves existed for the owners' profit, they were a form of production subject to taxation. The most common excise tax in all the colonies was that paid by tavern owners on liquor, a cost passed on to the consumer. Provincial leaders eventually imitated the English Parliament, which established an excise tax on intoxicating drinks in 1643. This, of course, was the period of growing Puritan influence in Parliament, and the tax bore certain social implications. The records show Parliament increasing the excise of liquor in reaction to calls to limit excesses in alcoholic consumption. Although it cannot be shown that such, in England or the colonies, was the only or even the primary reason for the excise tax, the desire for moderation certainly was a motivating factor. One may be surprised to learn that the average alcohol consumption per person was much higher in the American colonial period than today. In 1733 Pennsylvania's lieutenant governor Patrick Gordon argued for an increase in the excise tax stating that the "debauchery introduced by the vast Consumption of it (liquor) is the crying Sin and disease of the Country; not only Numbers of Single Persons but Families are ruined by it." Gordon also asserted that the tax was "of much greater importance to the welfare of the Country, than the raising of Money from It."

Burden. Some assume that the burden of taxation in the colonial era was great due to the more stringent measures (Sugar Act, Stamp Act, Tea Act, and so forth) enacted in the Revolutionary period. The fact is, however, the average colonist's tax burden was moderate at best. After all, government operations were, compared to today's standards, low-budget affairs. There were very few full-time officeholders. During this period Massachusetts, for instance, employed around six full-time government officials. The highest salary in the colonies usually went to the governor, whose income might exceed, again by today's standards, $100,000. The absence of a standing army also meant minimal defense costs, costs that of course went up in time of war. On balance, military costs did not become a large concern until the Seven Years War. In short, taxation, though a sporadic concern in the early and middle colonial eras, never became a colonywide source of discontentment.

Sources:

Beverley W. Bond, *The Quit-Rent System in the American Colonies* (New Haven, Conn.: Yale University Press, 1919);

Patricia U. Bonomi, *A Factious People: Politics and Society in Colonial New York* (New York: Columbia University Press, 1971);

Jack P. Greene, "The Growth of Political Stability: An Interpretation of Political Development in the Anglo-American Colonies, 1660–1760," in Greene, *Negotiated Authorities: Essays in Colonial Political and Constitutional History* (Charlottesville: University Press of Virginia, 1994), pp. 131–162;

Lemuel Molovinsky, "Continuity of the English Tax Experience in Early Pennsylvania History," *Pennsylvania History*, 46 (July 1979): 233–244.

WILLIAM DAWSON

1704?-1752
ANGLICAN MINISTER

The Office of Commissary. The key role of established church officials in colonial governmental affairs should not be underestimated. This is especially true for the Reverend William Dawson. Between the years 1743 and 1752 Dawson served as commissary of the Church of England in Virginia. Commissaries were essentially extensions of the bishop of London's authority throughout the English empire. The bishop of London held considerable authority, especially in post-Restoration England. In 1689 the Anglican church in America came under the auspices of his office. In that same year commissaries were positioned throughout the American colonies to carry out the bishop's business. In 1728 by royal decree the bishop's customary jurisdictions were narrowed. With this limitation the American commissaries' duties were also confined. Prior to the royal commission a commissary, by virtue of his position under the bishop of London, held both ecclesiastical and civil authority. His ecclesiastical jurisdiction, like the Bishop's, included church appointments as well as church discipline, discipline that extended to the clergy as well as the laity. Also, a commissary's temporal or secular duties included jurisdiction over marriage licenses and probate. These duties generally fell to the royal governor after 1728. Although after that year the commissary's duties were limited, in one sense the powers he did possess held more authority than before since they were backed directly by royal decree.

Instructions. Bishop Edmund Gibson sent to each commissary detailed instructions for the implementation of their duties as well as a copy of his own royal commission from King George II. Included in these instructions was a stipulation requiring each commissary to keep the bishop abreast of all legislative activity related to the suppression of crime and vice. Since the bishop and commissaries no longer possessed direct lay control, at least they could stay informed on how well the colonial civil governments held wrong in check. Presumably the commissaries and the bishop of London could use their positions to influence legislation related to lay parishioners. Added to this function there existed in Virginia a unique custom of even greater civil authority for the commissary: in addition to customarily becoming president of the College of William and Mary, a position of considerable dignity, Virginia commissaries were appointed to the royal council. As a councilor, therefore, Virginia's commissary sat as a legislator, judge, and gubernatorial advisor. In this capacity he held considerable power not only in ecclesiastical matters but also in civil matters.

Early Success. Virginia's royal governor William Gooch heavily petitioned the bishop of London to approve the appointment of William Dawson, an English-born Oxford graduate (A.B. degree, 1725; A.M. degree, 1728), ordained Anglican minister, and professor of moral philosophy at the College of William and Mary. On 18 July 1743, three months after the death of Commissary James Blair, the bishop issued the commissary commission to Dawson. Once in office Dawson soon received an appointment to the twelve-member Virginia Royal Council. Commissary Dawson was able to demonstrate early his potential influence in civil matters by taking the lead in calling for loyalty to the Hanoverian Dynasty which was under threat by Charles Edward Stuart. In 1745 the Young Pretender, using Scotland as a base of operations, launched an attack into northern England in hopes of reaching London and claiming the throne for the Stuarts. The prospect of a Catholic monarchy caused considerable fear in the colonies, no less so in Virginia. Commissary Dawson sent out a letter to all Virginia Anglican clergy admonishing them to preach pro-Hanoverian sermons to their parishioners. He also called a special meeting (6 March 1746) in Williamsburg of the same clergymen. There he preached a moving sermon emphasizing again loyalty to the Crown. He also took the opportunity to speak to the Royal Council and House of Burgesses, an address received favorably by both bodies, thereby affirming his right to speak out and influence public affairs.

The Clergy Act. A study of William Dawson's actions surrounding the Clergy Act of 1749 provides an excellent window through which to examine the rising mid–eighteenth-century tensions between English control and provincial resistance. In 1749 the House of Burgesses debated a bill designed "For the better Support of the Clergy; and for the regular collecting and paying of the Parish Levies." The fundamental elements of the bill, which were largely designed to improve the financial status of clergy, had been written by Dawson. Once the bill passed the Burgesses, however, several amendments had been attached to it, including a provision that gave vestries a year as opposed to six months to hire a minister in the event of a vacancy. Dawson's larger concern was the vestry's sovereign prerogative granted in the amendment to choose or dismiss local priests apart from the governor's or the commissary's consent. Dawson was accurate in insisting that the act, because of this amendment, went against English custom and precedent. The royal authority vested in the governor and commissary would normally have secured their lead role in parish appointments and dismissals.

Gooch and Dinwiddie. Interestingly, Dawson, normally an ally with Gov. William Gooch, was not willing to sacrifice the entire bill for this one amendment. Soon after Gooch's successor, Robert Dinwiddie, arrived in the province (November 1752) Dawson successfully persuaded him that the Clergy Act was detrimental. Governor Dinwiddie wrote in complaint of the bill to the Board of Trade, the secretary of state, and the bishop of London. The Clergy Act, he argued, forced him to disobey his instructions, an action he was not willing to commit. The most damaging outcome of the Clergy Act to Dawson and Dinwiddie, however, concerned the loss of patronage power. In 1752 Governor Dinwiddie wrote that "the patronage, presentation [concerning ministerial appointments], and prerogative of the Crown and the ecclesiastical jurisdiction of the Bishop of London are quite destroyed." In the end Dawson and Dinwiddie were not successful in obstructing the Clergy Act of 1749. In retrospect, however, the act strengthened the Anglican Church's role in the colony by means of improving the clergy's financial lot. Even though Dawson opposed the act, he is credited for the improvements to the clergy that came as a result of it since he, after all, did write it. The larger significance from a civil-government perspective is that Commissary Dawson, as a councilor and advisor to the governor, strongly swayed Dinwiddie to such a firm stand on an issue in which he had previously not held a decided view.

The Kay Affair. On the surface it seems unusual that Commissary Dawson would oppose a bill he had written based solely on his fear of greater vestry control. After all, parishes across Virginia had long practiced a considerable amount of autonomy. An episode that began in 1745 no doubt influenced Dawson to take such a decided stand. A newly appointed priest in the Lunenberg parish, William Kay, preached a sermon on the sinfulness of pride. One of his more elite parishioners, a vestryman, Col. Landon Carter, took offense, believing the sermon was intentionally directed toward him. Carter became so

incensed that he eventually used his influence in the vestry to have Kay removed from the church. The affair turned ugly when Kay's opponents attacked his property and undermined his marriage. Commissary Dawson, who already believed that laymen in the vestry had far too much power over the clergy, convinced Kay to file suit against the vestry. As a councilor he used his civil authority within the court to help Kay win on 21 April 1749. Carter appealed the decision. A victory for Carter would mean another step away from the desired Anglican control that Dawson believed vital to the life of the church and colony. A minister aligned with Dawson, John Camm, expressed the high stakes involved. If Carter's appeal was successful, Camm wrote to the bishop of London, "it will be of very ill consequences to the clergy in general. Since there will remain very few in this colony who may not be driven out of their parishes upon the least disgust conceived against them, by the same method." To Camm the Kay affair was "a struggle to increase the power of the vestries, which almost universally exercise their power with too high an hand already." Commissary Dawson died before the failure of Carter's appeal. Largely due to Dawson's previous support, however, Kay not only defeated the appeal but also won a second suit a year later awarding him even more. What Dawson could not do legislatively, he did judicially.

Dual Role. The Young Pretender uprising, the Kay affair, and the Clergy Act show the extent to which an established church leader and government official such as Dawson could play a dual role. Once the bishop failed to renew Dawson's official commission in 1748, the commissary began to play an even more defined civil role in the colony's governmental structure. Dawson greatly enhanced the church's place in Virginia by "wielding the combined power of his ecclesiastical office as Commissary and his civil office as a member of the council." Overall, this dual role made him an exceptionally influential figure in eighteenth-century Virginia.

Sources:

Dan M. Hockman, "Commissary William Dawson and the Anglican Church in Virginia, 1743–1752," *Historical Magazine of the Protestant Episcopal Church*, 54 (June 1985): 125–149;

Hockman, "William Dawson: Master and Second President of the College of William and Mary," *Historical Magazine of the Protestant Episcopal Church*, 52 (September 1983): 199–214.

JAMES DE LANCEY

1703-1760

COUNCILOR, CHIEF JUSTICE, AND LIEUTENANT GOVERNOR

Royalist. James De Lancey was one of many Huguenot descendants whose families fled to New York after Louis XIV's revocation of the Edict of Nantes. Many Huguenots settled in New York and South Carolina and had a considerable influence on the direction of the

American colonies. James De Lancey was no exception. Born in America, De Lancey studied law in England and returned to New York in 1725. In 1729 he became a member of the royal council. In 1731 he took the position of associate judge on the colony's supreme court, and in 1733 he became the chief justice of the colony. Through the administrations of royal governors William Cosby (1732–1736) and George Clarke (1736–1743) De Lancey actively supported imperial prerogatives. His progression to justice and chief justice, all the while remaining on the council, spoke to his dedication to Crown objectives.

Zenger. His participation in the John Peter Zenger trial attests to his royal allegiance. In 1733 Zenger, the young printer of an opposition paper, the *New York Weekly Journal,* went on trial for libel due to his constant barrage against Governor Cosby. De Lancey, chief justice at the time, proceeded to disbar any lawyers he believed might represent Zenger's defense. Anti-Cosby leaders outmaneuvered De Lancey and bypassed his decision to a jury which decided that the chief justice did not have the authority to determine Zenger's fate. Zenger was acquitted and released. The Zenger case became a powerful precedent for later free-press issues. In 1736 Zenger published a work by his supporter Andrew Hamilton (who was most responsible for Zenger's acquittal) titled *Brief Narrative of the Case and Tryal of John Peter Zenger.* This work, excepting *Cato's Letters,* had the most far-reaching effect on royal-opposition thought in eighteenth-century America. Given De Lancey's role in this episode, one would not imagine that he too would become an instrument for royal opposition.

Political Transition. De Lancey's imperial loyalties did not change until well into Gov. George Clinton's ten-year administration (1743–1753). He began his opposition to Clinton primarily over their differing views of New York's role in King George's War. De Lancey strongly opposed Clinton's policy of heavy involvement in the war. This difference mushroomed into consistent opposition to most of Clinton's other policies. De Lancey's larger importance in American colonial history emerges at this point because he represents a transitional element common to many colonial leaders at this time. This particular time was crucial in the political life of New York. Governor Clinton sought throughout his tenure to gain control of the assembly. De Lancey was one of the reasons he did not succeed in this effort. In 1753 Clinton left his position as New York's royal governor. He delivered a commission that he had kept secret for six years that De Lancey was to be the lieutenant governor. Not long hence, Clinton's replacement, Sir Danvers Osborne, committed suicide (he hanged himself in despair over his wife's recent death), and the job fell to De Lancey to carry out Osborne's instructions.

Acting Governor. The instructions left for De Lancey to carry out were detrimental to large landholders, many of whom were in the assembly and council. More impor-

tant, the instructions directed the acting governor to seize appropriations control away from the assembly. De Lancey was to reinstate the "royal Prerogative and Authority," which the assembly had "trampled upon, and invaded in a most unwarrantable and illegal Manner." This was a particularly delicate position for De Lancey since he, during Clinton's tenure, had been a key proponent of the assembly's power of the purse. De Lancey was able to keep the authority of appropriations in the hands of the representative body. He always informed the assembly of imperial demands, but he never attempted to force their hand, walking a fine line between his duty as royal representative and that of provincial politician. In his periodic communications with the Board of Trade he would "always put the best possible face on the Assembly's actions, stressing its fundamental loyalty to the Crown. . . ." It is important to remember that neither De Lancey nor the assembly acted on purely representative or opposition ideals. This was never the case in any colony. In the early–eighteenth century New York Assembly, "Assemblymen sought to improve the position of the legislature for its own sake and for their own advantage, rather than in purposeful opposition to competitors within the colonial constitution."

Significance. Whatever the motive, De Lancey stands as an important transitional figure in New York politics. Through his efforts as lieutenant governor (he remained at that post until his death in 1760) he acted as a royal representative but one with keen provincial, if personal, interests, interests that would nevertheless operate toward political stability in the face of ever-weakening royal control. Much to De Lancey's credit the New York Assembly never lost its dominant role throughout the rest of the colonial era.

Sources:

Patricia U. Bonomi, *A Factious People: Politics and Society in Colonial New York* (New York: Columbia University Press, 1971);

Michael Kammen, *Colonial New York: A History* (New York: Scribners, 1975);

Stanley N. Katz, "New York Government and Anglo-American Politics," in Katz, ed., *Colonial America: Essays in Politics and Social Development,* second edition (Boston: Little, Brown, 1976): pp. 290–305.

ROBERT JOHNSON

1676-1735
SOUTH CAROLINA GOVERNOR

Early Life. Among his several marks of distinction Robert Johnson served both as a proprietary (1717–1719) and royal (1731–1735) governor in South Carolina. His father, Nathaniel Johnson, had served as South Carolina's proprietary governor from 1702 to 1708. Robert was born in England in 1676. As a young child he and his parents went to the Leeward Islands where his father served as governor. After his term Nathaniel moved to South Carolina to develop property he held there. He sent his family back to England expecting to meet them shortly in South Carolina once he had made the necessary preparations. On the family's voyage to England the French intercepted their vessel and held them as prisoners for a year. The children's mother died while in captivity. Eventually the children were reunited with their father, who, apart from his original intentions to be a private planter in the colony, agreed to serve as governor. Pleased with Nathaniel Johnson's service, the proprietors later (1717) selected his son to take the chief executive position.

Proprietary Governor. Robert Johnson had been characterized as "a person of Integrity and Capacity well affected to her Majestys Government and every way qualified for that Trust." Upon this recommendation the Board of Trade agreed to his becoming governor provided he would swear an oath and provide a bond to ensure that he would uphold the Navigation Acts earlier imposed on the colonies. With Johnson's oath and bond supplied, he was appointed. As capable a man as Johnson was, his first year in office reflected his inexperience. The proprietors had offered assemblymen a deal that if they would approve a new quitrent law (proprietors were losing money due to the ineffective implementation of the existing law) they would personally receive a two-year remission in past quitrent debts. The proprietors also directed Johnson to present before the assembly a plan to raise the price of land in South Carolina. The assembly completely rejected it. The young governor was furious and determined to retaliate by blocking their appointment for powder receiver. Johnson argued that as chief commander of the militia, he had the sole right for such an appointment. He eventually withdrew his demand but did scold the assembly by insisting that they should recognize the proprietors as their "masters." The assemblymen responded that they did not recognize the proprietors as such. This small episode illustrates the growing frustration already existent between colonial leaders and proprietors. Although Johnson was able to eventually work harmoniously with the assembly on subsequent financial matters, the assembly's determination to reject proprietary attempts at undue dominance remained a constant.

Road to Royal Rule. Provincial discontent intensified in the summer of 1718 when the proprietors began an assault on the assembly by disallowing many of its laws and by ordering Johnson to dissolve the assembly and make arrangements for new elections. Johnson recognized that the proprietors were out of hand, and he began to work with the assembly (which he did not dissolve) against proprietary prerogatives. Added to this was the refusal of the proprietors to help defend the colony against piracy. In that same summer pirate Edward Teach (Blackbeard) practically held Charleston captive for a week. When word spread that South Carolina's shores were vulnerable, other pirates made similar attempts. For a period of five months the colony was periodically terrorized by various sea bandits, with no help from the proprietors. Eventually the piracy all but ceased on the Carolina coast when Governor Johnson himself led an expedition that captured pirate Stede Bonnet along with forty-eight others. The pirates were convicted and hanged in Charleston.

Resentments. The proprietors' refusal to send aid during this crisis hardened the colonists' attitude toward them even further. And if that was not enough to cause an antiproprietary revolt, the subsequent actions taken by the proprietors did. In 1719 the proprietors attempted to completely reorganize the council by replacing antiproprietors with men more apt to comply with their wishes. Also in that year they reintroduced the earlier efforts of land reform and assembly reelections. This time Governor Johnson, albeit reluctantly, complied with their wishes, dissolved the assembly, and called for new elections. But the new assembly, which had convened on 10 December 1719, refused to recognize the reorganized council. They requested that Governor Johnson rather than the proprietors assume governorship under the Crown. He refused and gave the reason of "my honor as being Intrusted by their Lordships." On 21 December, the day of the militia muster in Charleston, Governor Johnson ordered the soldiers to go home; they refused. On that day the rebel factions were successful in dismissing Johnson from the governorship, replacing him with James Moore Jr. A revolution had occurred. Johnson made several efforts to regain control of the government. He had hoped to be named the first royal governor. Yet in 1721 the Board of Trade appointed sixty-six-year-old Francis Nicholson, the most tried and proven royal administrator available, as the first royal governor of South Carolina. But Johnson's career was not over.

Royal Governor. From 1724 Johnson had been in London seeking a royal governorship. In 1729 his connections and past experience gave him the opportunity to mediate the negotiations between the proprietors (who wanted to sell the Carolinas) and the Crown. Johnson helped to successfully negotiate the deal, which also helped him to win his second appointment as governor of South Carolina. There were two major plans for South Carolina that Johnson presented to the Board of Trade. He and his friend Samuel Wragg, the South Carolina Assembly agent to London, convinced the Crown authorities, because of hard-money policy failures, to allow for a more flexible currency system in the colony. This would ease many of the cash-flow problems that had almost shut down any semblance of effective government. One of the most important elements in Johnson's instructions from the Board of Trade was the authority to implement a new township system, a plan he had earlier introduced to the board. The system allowed for the formation of ten townships in the Carolina backcountry to be settled by exiled Protestants from Europe. As an inducement for settlement South Carolina would provide free land to the refugees. This would serve the colony in at least two important ways, Johnson argued.

It would mean a greater balance between whites and blacks in the colony. Also, the presence of new settlements on the frontier would enhance the colony's military defense. It is one thing to present new policy; it is another to successfully implement it.

Reasonable Harmony. Upon Johnson's arrival in 1730 he found a much more conciliatory attitude among the colonists. As one Anglican missionary stated, "I think the People have done with their former animosities, and have been in an indifferent easy quiet condition." South Carolina colonists had come to recognize the "futility of extremism." This attitude also existed with Johnson. Although the province faced much graver financial problems than previously known, Johnson's flexible interpretation of his instructions helped funnel necessary funds to pay off debts earlier than would have otherwise been possible.

Middle Ground. On other key issues Johnson compromised enough to bring most factions into a conciliatory position. For example, in accordance with his instructions he somehow convinced the assembly to allow the council to initiate and amend money bills. Albeit reluctantly, the assembly assented to the instruction; only once in Johnson's administration did it challenge the council's authority in this matter. The harmony that Johnson helped to bring about led to a more prosperous economy. Johnson and Wragg successfully gained concessions from Parliament for direct rice shipments to Europe, thus opening up a vast market for South Carolina planters. From 1732 to 1739 the rice economy in the province boomed. Also beginning in 1732 Johnson's township plan began to pay off. By the year of Johnson's death (1735) six of nine townships were populated with hundreds of productive Protestant immigrants from Europe. This was the beginning of a very large influx of Swiss, German, Welsh, Irish, and Scottish immigrants into the colony. Serving as buffers from Indians, the townships added to the already-growing harmony. The largest buffer against the Spanish in Florida, the new colony of Georgia, also materialized under Johnson's leadership. Had it not been for South Carolina's enthusiastic aid to James Oglethorpe, founder of Georgia, the new colony would not have succeeded. In addition to funds and supplies Johnson sent a very able councilor, William Bull, to assist Oglethorpe with Indian negotiations, militia establishment, surveying, and construction.

Land. Of course Robert Johnson's royal governorship was not without its problems. He spent much of his time trying to work out land disputes that the transition from a proprietary to royal government created. Critics accused Johnson of showing favoritism to the wealthy landed elite by giving them more land than was allowed and by not charging quitrents to some. Others blamed Johnson's instructions which outlined an incomplete quitrent law (1731). The new law left Johnson with a system of collection so incomplete that he had to improvise its execution. It is reasonable to lay the blame on both Johnson and the 1731 law. Wherever it should be laid, this failure in the land system was a blight in an otherwise successful administration.

The Good Governor. Johnson's service ended with his death on 3 May 1735. He had been the governor both under proprietors and under the Crown. He had taken his political knocks, especially in his first term. His is a story of reasonable compromise, a quality necessary for any colonial governor's success. He learned his lessons early, lessons that would win him another chance at leadership. The lessons learned helped him in no small way to lead the colony in transition from considerable tumult to reasonable harmony. For this he has long been known in South Carolina history as "the good Governor Johnson."

Sources:

Helen Kohn Hennig, *Great South Carolinians from Colonial Days to the Confederate War* (Chapel Hill: University of North Carolina Press, 1940);

Richard P. Sherman, *Robert Johnson: Proprietary & Royal Governor of South Carolina* (Columbia: University of South Carolina Press, 1966);

M. Eugene Sirmans, *Colonial South Carolina: A Political History, 1663–1763* (Chapel Hill: University of North Carolina Press, 1966).

JACOB LEISLER

1640-1691

MERCHANT AND MILITIA OFFICER

Conventional Explanations. Jacob Leisler was a German merchant and militia soldier employed by the Dutch West India Company when he came to New York (then New Amsterdam) in 1660. His rebellion and subsequent seizure of New York's government (1689–1691) is well known; what is less well known is why he did what he did. The standard explanations have focused on his inability to break into the higher echelons of New York's political world. Some have also focused on his supposed bitter disposition toward the Dutch merchants who were becoming anglicized. Each of these points has validity, but none adequately explores a central motivating factor behind Leisler's actions: religion.

Background. Jacob Leisler's family, on both his mother's and father's side, was from a long line of *magistri* (magistrate or lawyer class). Because of the close dependance John Calvin (French Protestant reformer) had on the magistri to maintain civil order, especially to limit secular rulers who would counter Protestant initiatives, many from that class became strong Calvinist Christians. Calvinism stresses the absolute sovereignty of God and absolute sinfulness of man. Because of this infinite separation between the two, the unmerited grace of God is required for reconciliation. As a branch of Protestantism, Calvinism was naturally in conflict with Roman Catholicism, which focused on the necessity of good works as a means of salvation. Many magistri closely associated with the Reformation in Germany and France began to see their legal function in an energetic religious context. Leisler's grandfather, Dr. Jacob Leisler, employed his Calvinistic zealotry as legal council to Prince Christian of Anhalt. Dr. Leisler sent his son Jacob Victorian Leisler to the University of Altdorf and later to Geneva University where he came under the powerful influence of Calvinist reformer Theodore Beza, author of the *Right of Magistrates* (1574). The younger Leisler became a reformed Calvinist pastor to many Huguenot exiles, a ministry that gained him considerable note. Since the 1560s the Huguenot role in French society had been in a constant state of flux, gaining and losing political, civil, and religious rights. The most recent event had taken place in 1629 when French Cardinal Richelieu rescinded the Huguenot's political and military rights in the Peace of Alias (1629).

Promising Youth. In 1640 his son Jacob Leisler was born. One can imagine the zeal for a Calvinistic world-view this young man would be prone to adopt. With this view came a fear of Roman Catholicism's potential secular dominance. Part of this fear resulted from the Catholic-Protestant conflicts associated with the Thirty Years War, a conflict that was in its most destructive stage in Germany at Jacob's birth. Just three years before he was born his parents fled the Roman Catholic Inquisition. By the retelling of this difficult time Jacob's parents instilled in him, as historian David Voorhees has described, "a lasting fear of Roman Catholics." While in New York, Leisler often spoke of the "Implacable malice & Violence" he associated with Roman Catholicism. Eventually, Leisler's father received a rather lucrative pastorate to a French congregation in Frankfurt. It was there that his father developed a wide reputation for strict Calvinistic orthodoxy. Jacob Leisler's "growth . . . was shaped by his family's social position, their Huguenot connections, his father's rigid orthodoxy, and the religious fanaticism rife in the war-torn German states." All this he brought to the colony of New York.

Radicalization. In 1683 New York's Catholic governor Thomas Dongan believed that by appointing the now-successful merchant and militia leader Jacob Leisler as a Court of Admiralty commissioner that he could help to ease tensions between the very diverse Protestant groups in the colony. Leisler reluctantly served in this capacity. He did not like serving under "a profest Papist," he later stated. His greater concern over Roman Catholic dominance intensified in 1685 when Louis XIV revoked the Edict of Nantes, a decision that caused almost two hundred thousand Huguenots to flee France. Also in this year a Catholic king ascended the throne of England, James II, formerly the duke of York. From this time forward Jacob Leisler radicalized his position and began to act within his ancestral tradition as a magistrate for the glory of God. Leisler viewed political action as spiritual warfare. He saw the apathy of Anglicanism as willful submission to Catholic sentiments, especially after New York came under the Dominion of New England during the reign of James II. Government was under obligation, Leisler stated, "to enforce the true faith of the Scriptures." The true faith to Leisler was Protestant Christianity. Many other Protestant groups, mostly German Pietists who would normally not have been in a close alliance with Leisler's Calvinism, began to see him as their spokesman. A strong coalition of anti-Catholicism was developing in New York, with Leisler at the head.

Road to Rebellion. In 1688 New York Protestants were dismayed when news came that James II had had a son. Now the prospects of a long Catholic rule in England were a reality. But the Glorious Revolution changed all that. With the invasion of William III, Protestant husband to James II's daughter Mary, the Protestant hopes in England and America revived. Dominion of New England lieutenant governor Francis Nicholson suppressed the news of William and Mary's invasion. Eventually the word came to Leisler through his own European connections, and he publicized the news. When word reached Boston of the Revolution, the Dominion of New England's governor Andros was overthrown and jailed. Once the rebellion had spread to New York, Nicholson appointed Leisler, because of his leadership position in the militia, to put a stop to the uprising. He accepted this position, because as a magisterial Calvinist he was committed to "legal structures." Soon after this appointment Leisler reversed his support for Nicholson upon learning of the lieutenant governor's support of James II and of a possible anti-Protestant plot between fallen Massachusetts governor Edmund Andros and Nicholson. At first reluctant to actively engage in confronting Nicholson's "violent caridge" and "malicious designe," Leisler eventually acted upon Calvin's famous counsel that the magistri exist "to withstand the fierce licentiousness of kings in accordance with their duty." It was in this context that Jacob Leisler took over New York City's Fort James in the absence of Nicholson. Many hailed him as a defender of the Protestant faith. He soon received the lieutenant governorship of the colony. Leisler had successfully taken control of New York's royal government in the name of God and the Protestant king, William III. His victory was short lived. The tables eventually turned when certain merchants harmed by Leisler's economic policies convinced King William III that Jacob Leisler was a traitor to England. Leisler further distanced himself from the monarchy when in 1691 he refused to transfer the command of the fort into the hands of a newly arrived royal commander. Leisler, with no other recourse, surrendered the fort to the newly arrived royal governor Henry Sloughter. On 31 March 1691 he was found guilty of "traitorously levying war against our Sovereign Lord and Lady the King and Queen" and was summarily hanged (16 May) until "halfe dead," then beheaded. Whatever else the rise and fall of Jacob Leisler may mean, especially its role in the subsequent emergence of a representative assembly in the colony, the religious context of his actions shows the extent to which Calvinists were willing to go "to obstruct what they saw as a threat by James II and Louis XIV to romanize the Atlantic world."

Source:
David Voorhees, "The 'fervent Zeal' of Jacob Leisler," *William and Mary Quarterly,* 51 (1994): 447–472.

PUBLICATIONS

Robert Beverley, *The History and Present State of Virginia* (London: Printed for R. Parker, 1705)—this is a readable, opinionated (in favor of Virginia), and at times humorous account from one who served as justice of the peace, clerk of the House of Burgesses, and member of the royal council. Section 4, titled "Of Civil Polity and Government of Virginia," is of special interest;

Cadwallader Colden, *The History of the Five Indian Nations of Canada, which are Dependent on the Province of New-York in America, and are a Barrier between the English and French in that Part of the World* (London: Printed for L. Davis, 1755)—this work includes information on government structures within the various Indian tribes, colonial legislation for the encouraging of British trade with the tribes, and Indian treaties in Pennsylvania, Maryland, and Virginia. Written partly to encourage a British/Indian alliance against the French;

The Lawes of Virginia Now in Force (London: Printed by E. Cotes, for A. Seile, 1662)—by order of the general assembly this volume was prepared by Virginia's governor Francis Maryson and the clerk of the House of Burgesses, Henry Randolph;

Daniel Neal, *The History of New England, Containing an Impartial Account of the Civil and Ecclesiastical Affairs of the Country, to the Year of Our Lord 1700*, 2 volumes, second edition (London: Printed for A. Ward, 1747)—includes information on municipal laws, issues of ecclesiastical discipline, a map, and an appendix with the then-present charter.

The New York City shipyards, circa 1717 (engraving by William Burgis, 1746)

LAW AND JUSTICE

by THOMAS T. TAYLOR

CONTENTS

Sidebars and tables are listed in italics.

1606

10 Apr.   James I issues charters to the Virginia Company of London and the Virginia Company of Plymouth to establish colonies in North America.

1607

Dec.   A conspiracy against the council in Jamestown, Virginia, is discovered; the leader of the rebellion, George Kendall, is executed for mutiny.

1611

•   "Dale's Code" is implemented in Jamestown, mixing military law with religious precepts to bring order to the poorly run colony.

1616

•   Edward Coke, one of the greatest commentators on English law, is forced to resign as chief justice of the King's Bench after contesting the authority of James I. Coke's *Reports* (1600–1615) and *Institutes on the Laws of England* (1628–1644) become the chief sources for Americans studying English legal principles.

1619

30 July   The House of Burgesses meets at Old Church, Jamestown, Virginia, becoming the first representative assembly in the American colonies.

1620

21 Nov.   Forty-one male passengers of the ship *Mayflower* sign a compact before establishing the colony of Plymouth. In the Mayflower Compact the settlers agree to frame "such just and equal laws . . . as shall be thought most meet and convenient for the general good of the colony."

1624

•   James I revokes Virginia's charter and makes it a royal colony with an appointed governor.

1630

30 Sept.   John Billington, a member of the original Pilgrim band, is hanged for murder.

1634

•   Cecilius Calvert, second Lord Baltimore, founds Maryland, the first permanent proprietary English colony.

1636 • The Reverend John Cotton proposes *Moses, His Judicials*, based largely on the Old Testament and English common law, as a legal code for Massachusetts; it is rejected.

1637 • Anne Hutchinson and several followers are tried by the Massachusetts General Court for sedition; they are convicted and banished from the colony.

1638 • Virginia enacts the first American statute regulating and licensing taverns.

1639 14 Jan. The first written constitution in the colonies, Roger Ludlow's Fundamental Orders, is adopted by representatives from Hartford, Windsor, and Wethersfield, Connecticut; it remains in effect until 1818.

1641 • The Reverend Nathaniel Ward proposes his *Body of Libertyes* as a legal code for Massachusetts. Like Rev. John Cotton's plan, it combines Old Testament laws with English common statutes; it is also rejected.

1642 • Margaret Brent is the first woman barrister in America.

1643 • The people of Rhode Island receive the Rhode Island Patent from Parliament, a document similar to a royal charter but without the requirement that the governor be appointed by the English government.

1647 • Massachusetts makes it legal to pass a debt from one person to another, in essence allowing the transfer of wealth by paper transactions.

1648 • Massachusetts adopts the *Book of the General Lawes and Libertyes*, its first complete legal code and a mixture of English common law and biblical rules. Based on the Reverend Nathaniel Ward's 1641 *Body of Libertyes*, it influences legal codes in Connecticut, New York, New Jersey, Pennsylvania, and Virginia.

1649

- The Act of Religious Toleration in Maryland recognizes the rights of both Catholics and Protestants to worship.

1651

- Parliament passes the first of many Navigation Acts, which regulate trade between the American colonies, England, and other parts of the world.

1656

22 Sept. The General Provincial Court in Patuxent, Maryland, impanels the first all-woman jury in the colonies. The defendant, Judith Catchpole, is accused of murdering her child, although she claims that she had never been pregnant; the jury acquits her.

1661

- The government of Barbados creates the first comprehensive slave code in the English colonies.

1662

- Virginia's House of Burgesses diverges from English law by making the children of enslaved women slaves, even if the father is free.
- New France becomes a royal colony.

1664

- A Maryland slavery law prevents slaves who had converted to Christianity from claiming their freedom on the basis of previous English court decisions; similar laws providing for the lifelong servitude of blacks are passed in Virginia, the Carolinas, New York, and New Jersey.

1665

28 Feb. Six months after England conquers New Netherland (and renames it New York), the Duke's Laws are implemented. Dutch mayoral, or burgomaster, courts combine with English manorial and county courts.

1669

- The Fundamental Constitutions of Carolina attempt to establish Carolina as a feudal colony with a representative assembly.

1682

5 May William Penn's Frame of Government goes into effect in Pennsylvania, providing for a governor, council, and assembly to be elected by freeholders. In addition a new legal code forbids capital punishment and imposes sentences and fines instead of bodily punishments, all designed to reform offenders instead of merely punishing them.

1686
- The New England colonies are combined into the Dominion of New England, and Sir Edmund Andros is appointed governor-general. All representative assemblies are replaced by a nonelective council nominated by the royal governor.

1688
- New York is included in the Dominion of New England.
- William and Mary initiate the Glorious Revolution and replace James II the following year.

1689
- The English Parliament adopts the Bill of Rights, which becomes the basis for the American Bill of Rights in 1791.

Apr. The Dominion of New England is dissolved.

June Jacob Leisler seizes control of New York.

1691
- Jacob Leisler is executed for treason.

1693
- The Salem witchcraft trials end in 342 convictions and 19 executions.

1696
- The authority of English vice-admiralty courts, which hear cases pertaining to maritime trade but without juries, is extended to America.

1735
- John Peter Zenger is found not guilty of seditious libel by a New York jury.

1740
- South Carolina residents, frightened by the Stono Rebellion of the previous year, enact the most complete slave code of the colonial era; it influences Southern slave laws until the Civil War.

1741
- Prompted by fears of the Negro Plot, colonial authorities in New York burn thirteen African Americans, hang eighteen others (plus four whites), and deport seventy more.

1750
- Georgia legalizes slavery.

OVERVIEW

Transplantation. The European settlement of the New World, with its subjugation of the native peoples between 1492 and 1900, constitutes one of the largest migrations of peoples in human history. Europeans who transplanted to the New World brought with them their native cultures, and in North and South America they attempted to transplant as much of the old culture as suited their purposes, which were many and varied. They brought with them Old World ideas about family, labor, religion, government, and gender as well as notions about right and wrong.

New Societies. At every step of the way the colonists utilized European ideas about law to justify their actions and to regulate the new societies they created. They did not simply transpose English, French, Dutch, or Spanish laws to America; the situation in America was too different, too rough and new, for that to work. Instead they borrowed heavily when European ways supported what they wanted and improvised when they did not. Where there was much internal variety among colonies, such as in the English colonies, departures from European laws were common. In colonies more closely aligned to the mother country, like New Netherland, New France, and New Spain, there were fewer differences.

Conquest. All the European powers justified their claims to new territories and their rights of conquest over the native peoples they called Indians by appeals to the laws of conquest. French and Spanish law, drawing on ancient Roman law, justified the conquest of foreign peoples and lands. They had a harder time justifying the enslavement of Indians, and many in Spain concluded that it was illegal even though it continued in the New World. But conquer they did—the Spanish, French, Dutch, and English—and they extended their legal systems to the New World, always relying on them for justification. There was no international law in the colonial era, only the law of power. Disputes by different peoples were settled either through negotiation or through war. Sometimes different legal cultures would be blended, as in New York in the late 1600s when the English took the colony from the Dutch. Most of the time the law reflected who was in control.

Native Americans. The original inhabitants of North and South America had their own systems for regulating behavior and punishing wrongdoers, but these were not consistently respected by Europeans. The practice in New England was common. There the colonial government treated Indians as though they were under the same laws as the English and subject to the same penalties. This application of the laws of conquest had especially unfortunate consequences. What to English settlers might seem as an exercise of the principle of law and order could seem to nearby Indians as high-handed and dictatorial. Indian customs emphasized concepts such as honor and retribution, and the taking of captives in warfare was a common way of replacing relatives lost in battle. The English, however, did not recognize such principles as legally relevant, and the settlers saw the adoption of captives simply as kidnapping.

Adaptation. Once colonies were established, basic governmental and legal systems were instituted. These tended to be simple, and they varied not only according to country but also among the colonies founded by the same country. The English colonies along the Atlantic seaboard shared some tendencies. Most utilized the English common law only sparingly at first, finding the English system of courts too complex for their simpler needs. Most gradually developed slave codes, which had no corollary in English law. As they became more economically sophisticated and their legal needs changed, they made greater use of English law, especially in the 1700s.

Variations. Nevertheless, there were differences among the colonies. Most of New England was dominated by the Puritans, and the laws reflected their religious convictions. For example, they made blasphemy a crime punishable by death, though in actual practice they did not execute blasphemers. And it was in the Southern colonies that the most extensive slave codes developed because of their greater concentration of blacks.

Profession. Law was dominated by part-time or amateur lawyers and judges in the 1600s, but by the late 1700s there were many well-trained lawyers in the English colonies, especially in and around the major port cities and towns. They constituted a valuable resource.

As early as 1700 the legal profession became noticeably more professional in the city of New York, and most of the colonies experienced the Anglicization of their legal systems. Despite misgivings in many colonies about lawyers, the increasing complexity of commerce and daily life made their presence ever more necessary. Americans found themselves explaining and defining their relationship to the mother country from the early 1600s onward. In times of political or imperial crisis, such as in the 1680s or the 1760s, legal knowledge could be invaluable. The debates in the 1760s and 1770s about rights, government, and authority, arguments that led to the American Revolution, occurred because by that time both lawyers and legal language were very much a part of the common culture.

Order and Abuse. Law served purposes other than maintaining order. As an expression of the values of a community it was used to maintain social arrangements thought by those in power to be appropriate. By the 1700s the institution of slavery was well grounded in, and well protected by, the legal system in all the English colonies. The Spanish used the law to sustain the enslavement of Indians and Africans. Although women often were better served by the legal system in America than they would have been in England, the law nonetheless expressed the dominant societal value that women should not enjoy rights equal to those of men. Children enjoyed even less protection. Some colonies used law to suppress the sentiments of those who dissented from prevailing religious beliefs: Puritans in Massachusetts persecuted Quakers in the 1650s, and Anglicans perse-cuted Baptists in Virginia in the 1750s. Most colonies attempted to regulate private morality through legislation and judicial enforcement.

Imperial Law. If law was an instrument of social control at the local level, it was an instrument of empire at a higher level. The Spanish, Dutch, French, and English possessions in America varied considerably, but their home countries each expected the colonies to serve them. England's Parliament began enacting colonial trade regulations in the 1650s and continued to pass such laws throughout the colonial period. Such regulations bound Americans, especially those in port cities, more closely to the economic destiny of England. But when such regulations exceeded what Americans would tolerate, they could just as easily divide the two peoples. By the 1700s royal officials were common sights in port towns, agents of an imperial bureaucracy that imperfectly expressed the will of the king and Parliament for the colonies' economic growth. Most Americans encountered imperial law infrequently, if ever. But those who did found it both a blessing and a curse, for while it benefited some economic enterprises, it could hurt others.

Local Restraints. Economic regulation was a fact of life locally, too. Craftsmen were not free to charge whatever they liked; disgruntled buyers could sue over high prices; and access to certain trades was legally restricted. Americans might have believed in liberty, but they also believed strongly in order, and one way of staving off economic changes was through legislation. This rarely worked in the long run but often succeeded in the short run.

TOPICS IN THE NEWS

THE ANTINOMIAN TRIALS

Puritan Mission. In a colony like Massachusetts Bay, religious disputes could become legal problems. Although the church and the state were formally distinct from one another, only members of the church could vote or hold office, and the colony had been founded to promote a Puritan vision of the ideal community as a model for religious reforms back in England. The Puritans expected some debates in their community, but when disagreements went so far as to threaten the religious harmony of the colony, the dissenters could be seen not merely as folks with different points of view but as threats to the social and political order.

Covenant. A few years after the colony's initial settlement a group of residents, whose leader was Anne Hutchinson, was tried for sedition. Hutchinson and her associates were accused of having criticized the colony's ministers for teaching a covenant of works, the doctrine that men and women achieve salvation not by the grace of God but through their own good works. This was a serious accusation because Puritans generally taught a covenant of grace, that individuals are saved by grace alone. But there were different ways of teaching this doctrine. Some Puritans emphasized the possibility of preparing for salvation even while admitting that only God's gift could actually save them. To Puritans like Hutchinson, this resembled a covenant of works. In turn Hutchinson and her friends sounded like Antinomians, those who believed that individuals have no obligations to follow the laws of the Bible because law has nothing to do with salvation.

Gender. Hutchinson offended people as well by the fact that she was a woman. Like most Christian groups of the time, Puritans did not allow women to instruct men in matters of theology, though women were expected to instruct younger women in matters of faith, with appropriate deference to the minsters. But Hutchinson had a sharp mind and a talent for theology. Discussions in her home about recent sermons quickly gathered an audience, and these audiences included men.

Politics. The timing of Hutchinson's meetings was bad. During the mid 1630s Massachusetts was at war with the nearby Pequot Indians. For a time the Antinomians seemed to have the upper hand, and in league with merchants who disliked the government's trade restrictions, they gained control of the council in the election of 1636. But they lost control the next year, and the new council moved against them. Convening as a general court, it accused them of various crimes, including sedition and aiding and abetting those who broke the laws of the colony.

Trial. Hutchinson herself, however, had avoided the political protests, and thus Puritan leaders had an awkward time bringing charges against her. The court eventually charged her with heresy, but this was hard to prove, in part because of her skill in handling the Scriptures. She was several months pregnant at the time, and as was the custom she stood through much of the trial.

Late in the proceedings Hutchinson condemned herself by stating that she had received revelations from God that she should be persecuted. Puritans did not believe in such revelations because they could undermine the authority of Scripture and the ministry, and this sealed her fate. Hutchinson was found guilty and, like most of the Antinomian leaders, was banished from the colony. The largest group, including the Hutchinson family, moved to Rhode Island. Anne and most of her children died in an Indian attack in New Netherland in 1643.

Source:

David D. Hall, *The Antinomian Controversy, 1636–1638: A Documentary History* (Middletown, Conn.: Wesleyan University Press, 1968).

CHURCH AND STATE

Established Churches. For hundreds of years the official church of western and central Europe was the Roman Catholic Church. After the Protestant Reformation of the 1500s divided Christians into different churches, the nations of Europe had to choose. Countries like France and Spain kept the Roman Catholic Church as the official, or "established," church of the nation. Other nations became officially Protestant: Scandinavian countries became Lutheran; the Netherlands became Reformed; and England created the Anglican Church, which combined elements of both Catholicism and Protestantism.

Non-English Colonies. The church therefore was actively involved in European expansion in North America. French and Spanish settlements included Catholic churches and various religious orders, and the Reformed Church enjoyed state sanction in Dutch New Netherland. The later American idea of separation of church and state was nowhere to be seen in any of these European colonies. Instead, the church actively participated in governmental affairs.

Confusing Example. But maintaining one official church became difficult. England itself had different established churches at different times. In the 1500s England went back and forth between Catholic and Anglican before becoming permanently Anglican in 1660. This vacillation helps explain why some English colonies became Anglican while others became Congregationalist.

English Colonies. The English settlers also expected to create an established church, and nearly all of the early colonies set up an official church, but it was not always the Church of England. The Anglicans constituted the official church in all the royal colonies, which by the end of the colonial period included all the colonies south of Maryland. The New England colonies, heavily influenced by the zealous Protestants called Puritans, usually made the Congregational Church the official one, as happened in Massachusetts, Connecticut, and New Hampshire.

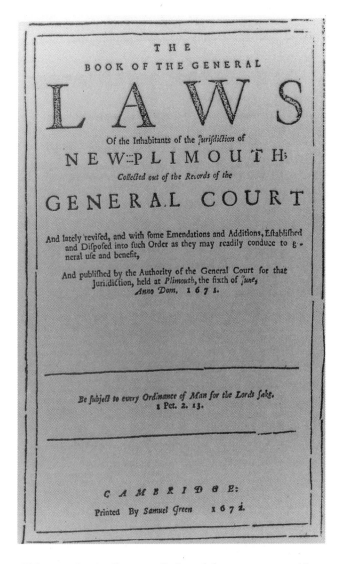

Title page for the first compilation of the statutes passed by the General Court in Plymouth Colony

Pluralism. But the mixture of peoples and ethnic groups in America made established churches even more difficult to keep. New York had two established churches after the English conquest in 1664, the Dutch Reformed Church (left over from the days of New Netherland) and the Anglican Church. And other colonies had different ideas about official churches. Many of Rhode Island's settlers disliked Massachusetts and its tough attitude toward religious dissenters, so Rhode Island had no official church. Pennsylvania was created in part as a refuge for Quakers, who had been persecuted by both Anglicans and Puritans back in England, so Pennsylvania did not establish an official church either. The American traditions of the separation of church and state and the respect for a mixture of religious sentiments was pioneered in colonies such as Rhode Island and Pennsylvania. Some officially Anglican colonies such as Georgia and North Carolina had few enough Anglicans that religious pluralism and toleration became the dominant practice, whatever the law might say.

Virginia. Even in colonies where there was little initial opposition to the official church, problems could arise in time. Virginia's established church faced little opposition until the mid 1700s. But beginning in the 1750s, after the revivals of the Great Awakening, other religious groups grew rapidly, especially the Baptists, even though the ministers of these other groups were not officially recognized by the colony, could not perform marriages, and could be jailed for preaching without a license. After the American Revolution, Virginia became one of the first states to disestablish its church. Massachusetts did not disestablish its church until 1833, making it one of the last of the original thirteen colonies to do so.

Sources:

Thomas Buckley, *Church and State in Revolutionary Virginia, 1776–1787* (Charlottesville: University Press of Virginia, 1977);

Thomas Curry, *The First Freedoms: Church and State in America to the Passage of the First Amendment* (New York: Oxford University Press, 1986).

CONFLICT RESOLUTION IN EARLY NEW ENGLAND

Methods. Legal systems serve as formal ways to resolve conflicts in communities. But going to court is not the only way to resolve a conflict. Indeed, one reason that the colonial legal systems remained fairly simple in the 1600s was that they did not grow until the society was large enough and faced conflicts that required formal processes. Most disagreements between human beings are settled directly, but some conflicts prove harder to resolve, so all communities develop mechanisms of conflict resolution that extend beyond the individual. Colonial New England had three such venues: the town, the church, and the courts.

Well-Ordered Communities. Many of the early New England settlements were dominated by Puritans, who showed much concern for well-ordered communities. They often viewed their churches as bound by covenants with God, and they saw their communities this way as well. The maintenance of order was very important to them, not only to promote security but also because they believed it to be their religious duty. Yet they knew from experience that the good intentions of people do not necessarily promote order, and so they accepted governmental and legal systems as necessary for the survival of the community.

Towns. When colonists were given permission by the colony's government to settle a new area, it was to create a town with farms around it. The town then became the focal point of local government, and through the local government and the annual town meetings that developed, the community could establish standards of behavior, control land development in the area, and resolve disputes that divided settlers.

Church. Townspeople often were church members, and the church actively addressed disputes among its

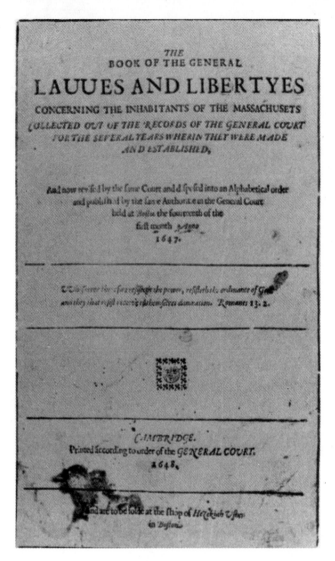

Title page for the book that became the basis of the legal codes in British North America

members and not infrequently took disciplinary action against members whose behavior was found unacceptable. The Bible, in which they passionately believed, taught them to resolve their differences with one another individually, and if that did not work, to take two or three other people along to assist. If that still did not produce satisfaction, the offended party was admonished to take the issue to the church.

Limits. But while the town and the church served as principal ways of regulating the community, by themselves they were not adequate. Town meetings might pass regulations to define the limits of acceptable behavior, but they did not meet frequently enough to enforce their decisions. The church could regulate disputes among its willing members, but its power was limited to those who would cooperate. As much as these people believed in their government and their churches, it took courts to fill the gap in conflict resolution.

Courts. The Puritans understood the need for a court system to settle disputes that could not be resolved through informal mechanisms. The complexity of land ownership and owners' rights made the courts indispensable to maintaining order within a few years of settlement. There was too much room for misunderstanding, and the stakes were too high to rely on oral agreements in these matters.

Gradual Independence. Early on, the courts reflected the values of the church to a strong degree. But by the 1660s the courts began to diverge a bit. The church's influence on the community was not as strong as it had been around the time of the founding of the early New England colonies in the 1630s. As a result the courts sometimes acted not in the interests of the church but instead to protect individuals from the church.

Source:

David Thomas Konig, *Law and Society in Puritan Massachusetts: Essex County, 1629–1692* (Chapel Hill: University of North Carolina Press, 1979).

CONQUEST BY THE RULES

Origins. The European societies who conquered the Americas had centuries of experience in conquering and subjugating other peoples, and with this experience came legal support for both conquest and governance of the newly acquired territories. In the Crusades of 1096–1291 Europeans attempted to "free" the Holy Lands from the control of Islamic peoples. Pope Innocent IV argued that he was given authority by Jesus himself over all peoples for the good of their souls, an authority first given to Peter and handed down from pope to pope. Obviously, not all peoples respected this authority, and the pope was to use it only to the degree necessary to protect the well-being of souls. A pagan people who disallowed the preaching of the Gospel, Innocent claimed, were subject to coercion for their own good. The Pope could, if necessary, even declare war on such a people.

Justification. This argument provided a theoretical legitimacy for the Crusades themselves, and in the centuries to follow it would be cited as justifying European conquests of other peoples as well. This meant that by the 1500s and 1600s a close connection existed between exposing other peoples to Christianity and the justification for conquest. In Innocent's eyes pagan peoples had rights, including the right to rule themselves. But they also had obligations, violations of which negated the right to self-rule. This amounted to saying that if alien peoples conformed to European notions of right and wrong they were not subject to conquest. Many Europeans sincerely believed that this was in the best spiritual interests of the conquered peoples; others merely manipulated the situation for their selfish ends. But however their motives might have differed, the result was the same: Europeans used religion to justify conquering other peoples.

Spain and Portugal. The Spanish and Portuguese were the first to adapt this philosophy to conquering the New World. Both nations' governments were intertwined with the Catholic Church and remained so after the Protestant Reformation of the 1500s. In the 1450s Pope Nicholas V affirmed the power of Portugal over the Canary Islands and empowered the Portuguese king to extend his power to the African mainland as well. The rationale used was the same as that of Innocent in the 1200s. The Pope assumed that Portugal would conquer Africa "more for the salvation of the souls of the pagans" than for personal gain. But once such a process was underway it could not be stopped. Spain's King Ferdinand II ordered that Indians be baptized in Spanish-controlled territories of the New World, "for this is the principal foundation upon which we base our conquest of these regions."

The *Requerimiento*. The Pope's authority also could serve as a check on abuse of New World Indians, and it sometimes did so. The explorer Christopher Columbus recognized that the Pope's support of conquest was not intended to justify harsh treatment of natives. Indeed, in the 1500s a fierce debate raged among churchmen in Spain over conquest, colonization, and the treatment of the Indians. If the church became a justification for conquest, it also could serve as a fierce critic. Ferdinand himself requested legal advice on his titles to New World lands from two noted legal scholars, Matias de Paz and Juan Lopez de Palacios Rubios. Both argued for legitimacy, and Lopez was instrumental in writing the Spanish document of conquest, the *requerimiento*. This document required the Indians of the Americas to accept the rule of the church and warned that they were subject to war if they refused to accept missionaries. The terms of the *requerimiento* were to be read to Indian peoples for their consideration before any conquest might occur. However reasonable this may have seemed in Madrid, in actual practice this requirement was either ignored or executed in a meaningless way. In the 1550s Spain stopped the practice and simply declared their entire colonizing effort to be a "missionary enterprise."

Vittoria. Nevertheless, some Spaniards objected. Led by Friar Antonio de Montesinos, Dominicans had objected to Spanish treatment of the Indians on Hispaniola in the 1510s. In the 1550s Franciscus de Vittoria argued in "On the Indians Lately Discovered" that all peoples, including those in America, enjoyed natural legal rights to freedom and that the Pope had no authority to grant the Americas to Spain. But even he held, in the tradition of Innocent IV, that a pagan people's violation of the laws of nature served as justification for the Christian conquest of those peoples. Vittoria, however, deemphasized the authority of the church, thus broadening the theoretical bases for conquest.

England. The English could hardly base their conquests on the same papal grounds as did the Spanish. They had no papal bull (an order from the pope) to support their claims to North America, and they eventually joined other nations in breaking ties with the Roman Catholic Church. By the time the English settled their first American colonies, England had become a Protestant nation, one at odds and often at war with Catholic Spain. The religious disputes between Catholics and Protestants served to spur the nations to compete even more heatedly for New World dominance. Protestantism may also have helped to advance capitalism, which in turn fueled the economic forces that drove expansion.

Black Legend. If Protestantism gave some Europeans added reasons to expand their national powers and to compete with other nations, it also influenced the legal language used to justify expansion. In the 1480s, under Henry VII, England used language similar to that used by Spain and Portugal, respectful of both papal and Iberian authority. But by the 1570s, when serious attention was given to settling the New World, England's monarch was the Protestant Queen Elizabeth. English justifications for conquest centered on their right to conquer peoples who violated the laws of nations, on the right to challenge Catholic and Spanish rule in the Americas, as well as on the desire for economic gain. The English felt particularly justified in opposing Spain after the 1583 publication of Bartolomeo de Las Casas's *Brief Narration of the Destruction of the Indies by the Spaniards*. Las Casas, a member of the Dominican order, excoriated his fellow Spaniards for their inhumane and un-Christian treatment of the Indians. One edition of the book contained a record of Las Casas's debate with Juan Gines de Sepulveda over the treatment of the Indians, with Sepulveda defending Spanish practices. Las Casas claimed Indian deaths to have been fifteen or twenty million at the hands of the Spanish. Las Casas thereby provided the English both a stinging indictment of Spanish colonization and a rationale for their own. The English did not blame the influence of religion in justifying conquest but blamed instead the evils of Roman Catholicism and of Spain. The "Black Legend," as it is called, was used by the English to justify their own efforts in the New World. Ironically, and tragically, their own record of the treatment of Indians was no better.

Perpetual Enemies. In its charter of 1606 the Virginia Company specifically empowered the company to settle "Virginia," a land "not now actually possessed by any Christian Prince or People." One of its authors, the famous jurist Edward Coke, had argued earlier that the king was entitled to ignore legal claims made by "perpetual enemies." The early English colonies in the Chesapeake Bay area and in New England generally took the same stand: they were entitled to occupy land because it was not owned by Christians. Some colonies, notably Rhode Island and Pennsylvania, attempted to deal with the Indians on a more equal footing, negotiating and abiding by treaties. But the general English pattern resembled the Spanish one: conquest justified in the name of religion.

Source:
Robert A. Williams Jr., *The American Indian in Western Legal Thought: The Discourses of Conquest* (New York: Oxford University Press, 1990).

CRIMES AND PUNISHMENT

The Condemned. The surviving court records from the New England area offer a glimpse of what crimes were being committed and punished during the colonial period. From 1630 to 1644 ninety-nine people were charged with drunkenness in Massachusetts, seventy-three of whom received a fine. For the fifty charged with theft, the most common punishment was whipping. About half of the twenty-two charged with fornication were whipped, while nineteen of the twenty-two servants charged with running away were whipped. The twenty-four accused of cursing or swearing received a fine or whipping. There were only nine assaults, three attempted rapes, one rape, and one murder. Of the four people executed, one cause was unspecified, two were for adultery, and one was for murder.

Fines and Humiliation. Crimes like drunkenness, fornication, and theft dominated most New England courts throughout the 1600s. Fines were common, but for more serious or repeated offenses bodily punishment like whipping was inflicted. It was also common to humiliate the offender. Such was the purpose of the bilboes, a bar and shackles used to raise an offender's legs off the ground in a position both uncomfortable and embarrassing. Over time these were replaced by the less expensive wooden stocks which did physical harm to the offender only if left on for too long. Colonies limited the number of hours in the stock, usually no more than three or four, though Rhode Island allowed six. The first man placed in the stocks in Boston was the carpenter Edward Palmer—for overcharging the town after building the stocks.

Public Spectacles. Punishment most often was a public affair because it also served, in theory at least, to deter others from committing the same crimes. In England this did not work well. Pickpockets, for example, were known to ply their trade aggressively during public hangings. In New England sermons often were preached before executions, and prisoners were known to offer moral advice to the crowd before meeting their deaths.

Capital Offenses. Colonial laws often appeared harsher on paper than in life. Adultery could be punished by death, but it seldom was so. Plymouth's laws of 1671 created twenty-one capital offenses, including cursing one's natural parent and "profaning the Sabbath provocatively." Massachusetts's list of 1686 was longer, including the return of a Jesuit or a Quaker after banishment and heresy. From 1641 on, Massachusetts allowed the death penalty not only for crimes such as murder and manslaughter but also for idolatry, blasphemy, and witchcraft.

Quakers. Exceptions to the violence of colonial punishments were found in Pennsylvania and East and West Jersey, all due to varying degrees of Quaker influence. William Penn and the Quakers who settled Pennsylvania had experienced much persecution in England. Quakers had their ears cropped or were executed in Massachusetts in the 1650s (usually for returning repeatedly after being banished), and thousands of Quakers languished in English jails in the 1670s. Seen as dangerous radicals at the time, they believed passionately that each human, though sinful, nonetheless possesses a spiritual inner light that must be nurtured. Just as this affected their child-rearing, making them more concerned about nurturing the child than rooting out his or her sinfulness, so too it committed them to emphasize reform more than punishment in criminal law. Pennsylvania criminalized social deviancy as did the other colonies, but in doing so its punishments were much less severe than those in any other area of the empire.

New Netherland. In the Dutch colony of New Netherland little violent crime occurred in the 1600s; death sentences were rarely pronounced and carried out. Often a pardon or order of banishment was announced just before the execution was to occur, in order to create a maximum effect upon the populace without actually killing the offender.

A scold's bridle used by the Puritans in Massachusetts to punish gossips, circa 1690. The headpiece originally had a tongue depressor that extended into the woman's mouth (New Haven Colony Historical Society).

Sources:

"Crime and Law Enforcement," in *Encyclopedia of the North American Colonies*, edited by Jacob E. Cooke (New York: Scribners, 1993);

Peter Charles Hoffer, *Law and People in Colonial America*, volume 1 (Baltimore: Johns Hopkins University Press, 1992);

Edgar J. McManus, *Law and Liberty in Early New England: Criminal Justice and Due Process, 1620–1692* (Amherst: University of Massachusetts Press, 1993).

THE DUKE'S LAWS

Conquered Territory. New Netherland became New York when England defeated the Netherlands in the Second Anglo-Dutch War of 1664. But English authorities confronted a delicate situation with the Dutch culture that had grown there since the colony's founding four decades earlier. They had to accommodate their new subjects and at the same time not alienate them.

Accommodation. The Dutch courts that had developed before 1664 were called burgomaster (mayoral) courts. They used a legal system derived from Roman law, unlike English courts, which used English common law. The burgomaster courts were awkward for the English, but the new governor, Francis Nichols, recognized that some accommodation would have to be worked out if he was to rule the colony. The agreements that resulted were known as the Duke's Laws because they operated under the authority of the proprietor, the king's brother, James, the Duke of York. Nichols agreed to preserve the authority of the Dutch courts if the Dutch citizens would swear allegiance to the English Crown; they agreed. Where English Puritans settled, Nichols created courts like the county courts of Massachusetts. And the prominent Dutch and English politicians who received enormous land grants on both sides of the Hudson River were allowed to administer their own manorial courts, just as the landed gentry had done in England since feudal times, although few in fact did.

Cultural Tensions. For several decades two different kinds of legal systems existed within New York simultaneously, but tensions between the Dutch and English settlers still did not disappear. The Dutch who gained economically from English rule formed an alliance with the English, but other Dutch residents felt alienated. An attempt in 1673 to restore Dutch rule failed. Members of the older Dutch community were particularly upset by the creation of the Dominion of New England in 1686, and after ousting the royal government some of them briefly ran the colony, in what became known as Leisler's Rebellion.

Sources:

Peter Charles Hoffer, *Law and People in Colonial America* (Baltimore: Johns Hopkins University Press, 1992);

Michael Kammen, *Colonial New York: A History* (New York: Oxford University Press, 1971).

THE ENGLISH BILL OF RIGHTS

Stuarts and Parliament. In the 1640s and 1680s members of Parliament struggled with the ruling monarchs, the Stuarts, over the relative powers of Parliament and monarch and the king's subjection to the laws of the land. The first struggle ended with the English Civil War, won by a Puritan-dominated Parliament which executed Charles I for treason in 1649. But rule without a monarch proved awkward, and the Stuarts were restored to the throne in 1660. The Restoration left many issues unresolved, as became all too clear when in 1685

Charles II died and was succeeded by his Roman Catholic brother James II. In 1688 Parliament forced James to abandon the throne, and they installed Prince William of Orange (the Netherlands) and his wife, Mary (James's daughter), as monarchs, an action afterward known as the Glorious Revolution.

Statement of Principles. Parliament enacted in 1689 a statement of principles addressing the issues that it believed lay at the root of the struggle with the Stuarts and their pretensions to extensive royal powers. The provisions of the English Bill of Rights were aimed in the first place at reducing the monarch's ability to interfere with or control Parliament. Laws or their execution could not be suspended or dispensed by the Crown; taxes could be levied and armies raised only with Parliament's consent; elections ought to be free; and parliamentary debates could not be challenged in court. Such principles eventually made their way into the United States Constitution of 1787 and became known as the doctrines of separation of powers and checks and balances. Other provisions affected all citizens. The Bill of Rights championed freedom of speech and the right to petition the king, and it prohibited excessive bail or fines as well as cruel and unusual punishments.

Rights of Englishmen. The idea that Englishmen had rights was hardly new. The early colonial charters required that the rights and privileges of Englishmen be protected, and several colonial legal codes of the 1600s described rights and liberties. Many, therefore, saw the English Bill of Rights as simply a statement of long-standing rights, not a declaration of new ones. Indeed, the rights of Englishmen were thought to be too many to be listed. Nonetheless, the English Bill of Rights of 1689 did influence the American states in the late 1700s to write specific lists of rights distinct from their legal codes or governing constitutions. This expectation became so strong that when the new U.S. Constitution was proposed in 1787, a Bill of Rights had to be added.

Source:

Kermit Hall, William Wiecek, and Paul Finkelman, *American Legal History* (New York: Oxford University Press, 1991).

ENGLISH CHARTERS, COMPACTS, AND GRANTS

Joint-Stock Companies. The authority of most of the early English colonies derived from legal devices that gave the colony standing in English law. Early colonies such as Virginia and Massachusetts Bay were issued charters by the king of England. These charters were initially given to a group of investors, usually no more than twenty in number, to form a joint-stock company, which enabled them to pool their money. In addition, a charter typically named the new corporation, specified its organization, granted specific economic advantages, and granted land and governing powers if the company was to run a colony.

The charter of Plymouth Colony, issued to John Pierce in 1621 (Pilgrim Hall, Plymouth, Massachusetts)

Virginia and Massachusetts. Under such a charter, the Virginia Company of London owned and administered the colony at Jamestown for seventeen years. The charter was revoked in 1624, and Virginia became a royal colony, allowing the monarchy greater control over the province. The charter of the Massachusetts Bay Company (1629) was unusual in that it failed to specify where the company would hold its annual meetings. The early stockholders used the loophole to hold the meetings not in England but in Boston, thus distancing themselves from supervision by the English government. The officers of the company who actually moved to Massachusetts decided in 1631 to expand the membership of the company by 116; later expansions had the effect of turning the company charter into a constitution. Massachusetts existed under this charter until 1683. In 1691 it was replaced with a royal one.

Unclear Legality. Other early colonies had no charters at all. Their settlers had no clear legal authority from the king, so they bound themselves to one another through compacts. The Mayflower Compact governed Plymouth from 1620 until 1691, when the colony was merged with Massachusetts Bay. The colonies of Rhode Island, New Haven, and Connecticut followed with their own compacts in the 1630s. These compacts had their drawbacks, because the inhabitants could not count on the English government recognizing them as binding.

Proprietary Colonies. The proprietary grant was also used as a means to initiate colonization of North America. Such a grant was issued by the monarch to one or more individuals, conveying to the recipient(s) large tracts of land and the power to rule that land as if the individual(s) were its monarch. This practice dated back to the Middle Ages, and hence these were known as feudal proprietary grants. Maryland was founded upon such a grant in 1632, issued to Cecilius Calvert and conferring upon him and his heirs extensive powers. In the second wave of colonization between 1660 and 1685 such grants were the chief means by which the Carolinas, the Jerseys, New York, and Pennsylvania were founded. By this time the earlier colonies all had some form of representative assembly in place, and the newer colonies followed suit. On paper a proprietary colony looked like a throwback to the Middle Ages. In actual practice these colonies all were practicing a limited form of representative government by 1700.

Source:
Alfred Hinsey Kelly, *The American Constitution: Its Origins and Development,* seventh edition (New York: Norton, 1991).

ENGLISH COMMON LAW

Origins. The English common law, from which Americans borrowed heavily in the colonial period, had evolved for centuries in England. Its principles and rules were extensive and complex, and they varied by region and locality. Common law developed through practical experience over time and thus became distinguished from a legal code in which the law was summarized all at once. The royal courts established by the Normans slowly harmonized the divergent laws and practices that had characterized the Anglo-Saxon courts before the conquest of England in 1066. Because the royal courts were in greater contact with one another than the older regional courts had been, there developed similarities in interpreting the law. This situation did not create one law for all of England, as regional and local variations continue even today, but it did overlay local variations with principles of interpretation that were common (hence the term *common law*) to the nation at large.

Coke. This kind of law was not legislated by assemblies but instead evolved through the decisions of judges as they confronted new situations requiring the applications of established principles. Perhaps the greatest of these interpreters was Sir Edward Coke, chief justice of Common Pleas and King's Bench from 1606 to 1616. He lost his position after arguing that the king, James I, was bound by the law like any other man. But his collection of common-law rulings, called *Reports* (1600–1615), and his later books, the four-volume series *Institutes* (1628–1644), became the definitive works on English law for succeeding generations.

Colonies. Bringing the common law to America was not easy. For one thing, a complex legal system did not easily meet the needs of the simple communities that were founded on the eastern shore of North America in the 1600s. Colonial lawyers and judges had little interest in the esoteric knowledge of those trained in common law, the principles of which seemed at times foreign and strange compared to local expectations. Wealthier colo-

Title page for Sir Edward Coke's influential treatise on common law

nial elites tended to control court appointments, and a looser, more open attitude toward legal interpretation often suited their economic interests better than the common law. In the early years the pattern was to borrow as much as seemed necessary and no more. Lawyers often were frowned upon as unnecessary at best, and at worst as nuisances who confused other people with silly legal intricacies.

Eighteenth Century. Not until the colonies were established and growing in social and economic complexity did interest mount in borrowing extensively from English law. As the colonial legal systems became Anglicized after 1700, the common law was used more widely. Unfortunately most colonial judges did not understand common law, and relatively few American lawyers studied in England. Not until Sir William Blackstone produced his *Commentaries on the Laws of England* (1765–1769) did there appear a reliable and thorough guide to the subject. Formal legal training did not improve appreciably until the late colonial and Revolutionary eras. By the 1800s English common law was accepted

by many as a part of the national legal heritage, especially in states like New York. But even then Thomas Jefferson argued that Americans had never adopted common law. Well into the nineteenth century leading politicians argued that the common law was undemocratic and that only experts with years of training could master it. Many maintained that it was better to be governed by legal codes adopted by the legislature than by an abstruse set of judicial rules.

Sources:

Daniel J. Boorstin, *The Mysterious Science of the Law* (Boston: Beacon, 1958);

Bernard Schwartz, *The Law in America* (New York: McGraw-Hill, 1974).

JOHN PETER ZENGER CASE

Seditious Libel. Freedom of the press as a legal protection did not exist in the colonial period. Under English and colonial law, to criticize the government in a way that lessened the public's esteem of it was to commit the crime of seditious libel. Under this practice the truth of the criticisms was unimportant; all that mattered was that they undermined public confidence in the government. Judges generally made the decision whether or not printed material was seditious.

Critics. In the 1600s several noted figures argued for greater freedom in printing, among them the poet John Milton and the philosopher John Locke. The most significant criticisms of the doctrine of seditious libel for colonial America were found in *Cato's Letters* (1733), written by the Englishmen John Trenchard and Thomas Gordon. These letters included defenses of the freedom of speech and criticisms of existing libel laws.

Alexander. An avid reader of *Cato's Letters* was James Alexander, a New York lawyer who wrote articles on free speech for John Peter Zenger's *New-York Weekly Journal*. Alexander also was a political foe of New York's royal governor, William Cosby. When Zenger ran articles criticizing Cosby's government, the governor had Zen-

---

WHAT IS LIBEL?

The following is part of defense lawyer Andrew Hamilton's comments to the jury in the John Peter Zenger trial in 1735:

And may I not be allowed, after all this, to say, That by a little Countenance, almost any Thing which a Man writes, may, with the Help of that useful Term of Art, called an Innuendo, be construed to be a Libel according to Mr. Attorney's Definition of it. . . . If a Libel is to be understood in the large and unlimited Sense urged by Mr. Attorney, there is scarce a Writing I know that may not be called a Libel, or scarce any Person safe from being called to an Account as a Libeller.

Source: Leonard W. Levy, ed., *Freedom of the Press from Zenger to Jefferson* (Indianapolis: Bobbs-Merrill, 1966).

Document signed by Zenger giving power of attorney to James Alexander and William Smith (from Livingston Rutherford, *John Peter Zenger, His Press, His Trial and a Bibliography of Zenger Imprints*, 1963)

ger jailed for seditious libel and ordered copies of the newspaper burned.

Defense. James Alexander and a colleague planned to defend Zenger, but when the attorney general managed to get them disbarred, they turned to Andrew Hamilton, a noted Philadelphia attorney and then speaker of the house of Pennsylvania. In the trial Hamilton admitted that Zenger had written the pieces in question but argued that their truthfulness should excuse the violation. The chief justice ruled that Hamilton could not attempt to prove their truthfulness since that was not in question. Hamilton then appealed to the jury, noting that "the facts which were offered to prove were not committed in a corner; they are notoriously known to be true: and therefore in your justices lie our safety." The jurors did not like Governor Cosby any more than did Alexander and Zenger, and they were only too happy to find in Zenger's favor.

Consequences. The verdict in the Zenger case did not change the law but rather was an exception to the law that prevailed throughout much of the eighteenth century. Alexander wrote and published a narrative account of the case, and thus the story was handed down to later generations who wrote freedom of the press into the Constitution of the United States itself. The significance of the Zenger case lies not in its immediate impact, which was small, but rather as an early example of a principle that would become law only much later.

Source:
Leonard W. Levy, ed., *Freedom of the Press from Zenger to Jefferson* (Indianapolis: Bobbs-Merrill, 1966).

LABOR

Economic Regulation. English society was heavily regulated by law. While the colonies created much simpler legal systems than had existed in the mother country, they brought with them expansive English notions about what could and should be regulated by law, such as prices and labor. In early America price-gouging was punishable by the courts; if a jury decided that an artisan's prices or workmanship had violated local community standards, fines or punishment could follow.

Guild System. In similar fashion laborers found themselves regulated by social expectations. Skilled laborers in Europe had long maintained monopolistic control over admittance to their trades through a system of guilds. This system came under legal fire by the early 1700s from people advocating freer trade. English law generally frowned upon efforts of either workers or masters to combine to artificially raise or lower prices, and this was true in the colonies as well. Craft guilds developed in places like Massachusetts, Philadelphia, and New York. Carpenters' guilds in Philadelphia published price scales. The Moravian communities in Georgia, Pennsylvania, and North Carolina combined craftsmen into what amounted to a general guild, though in the "Brotherly Agreement" of 1754 they stated that they joined not for wage gain but for spiritual reasons. Craft

A SELECTIVE LISTING OF AMERICAN COLONIAL RIOTS, 1654-1757

Year(s)	Colony	Cause
1654–1655	R.I.	Political factionalism
1663–1750	R.I.	Boundary dispute
1663–1750	Conn.	Boundary dispute
1663–1750	Mass.	Boundary dispute
1682	Va.	Tobacco cutters
1690	N.C.	Election
1699	N.H.	Sailors
1699–1700	N.J.	Land claims
1703	S.C.	Political factionalism
1703–1710	N.Y.	Religious differences
1704	Pa.	Young gentry
1705	N.Y.	Privateersmen
1710	Mass.	Food prices
1711	N.Y.	Religious differences
1711	N.Y.	Naval press gangs
1713	Mass.	Food prices
1718	N.Y.-Conn.	Boundary dispute
1718	N.C.	Seizure of official records
1719–1764	N.Y.-N.J.	Boundary dispute
1719	R.I.	Customs duties
1721–1737	Pa.-Md.	Boundary dispute
1722	Conn.	Jailbreak
1724	Conn.	Court seizure of a ship
1734	N.H.	Production of ship masts
1737	Mass.	Prostitution
1737	Mass.	Market prices
1737	N.C.	Quitrents
1738	Pa.	Construction of fish dams
1742	Pa.	Election
1745–1754	N.J.	Land claims
1747	Mass.	Naval press gangs
1750	Pa.	Election
1751–1757	N.Y.	Rent prices
1751–1757	N.Y.-Mass.	Boundary dispute
1754	N.H.	Surveyors of woods

Source: Richard Maxwell Brown, *Strain of Violence: Historical Studies of American Violence and Vigilantism* (Oxford & New York: Oxford University Press, 1975), pp. 301–302.

guilds attempted to maintain the exclusive right to practice their trades by defining precisely the individual trades and prohibiting working in more than one area. Such efforts, however, met with only limited success.

Licensed Workers. Some trades were licensed and regulated by local authorities in the public interest. Dutch and then English New York limited the numbers of porters working in weigh houses and beer houses. Coopers (barrel makers), butchers, and bakers likewise had to be licensed by the colonial government. New York bakers went on strike in the 1600s and also in 1741 over high wheat prices; the latter strike resulted in indictments but no convictions.

Bound Servants. If skilled workers in Northern colonies were successful for a time in combining with one another, bound servants were not. The most common form of servitude initially was indentured servitude, by which one person contracted to serve another for a specified period of years. The indenture was usually made in return for food, shelter, and transportation to America. Most laborers in the Chesapeake area in the 1600s were white indentured servants. In 1670, 43 percent of Virginia's House of Burgesses were former indentured servants. Masters began preferring slaves to indentured servants in the late 1600s, by which time slaves were seen as a better investment and easier to control. Yet indentured servitude lasted throughout the colonial era. Insurrections of indentured servants in Maryland and Virginia in the 1650s and 1670s resulted in statutes restricting their movements as well as their ability to meet in groups. Although legally and socially of a higher level than slaves, indentured servants nonetheless were seen as potentially dangerous should they band together. This attitude reflected English and American prejudices against poor, unskilled workers.

Source:
Richard B. Morris, *Government and Labor in Early America* (New York: Harper & Row, 1946).

LAWYERS

The Profession. Lawyers were few in the early English colonies because their skills were rarely required. In colonies like Massachusetts Bay the generally high level of education of the early inhabitants meant that some had experience in law. Gov. John Winthrop and the Reverend Nathaniel Ward were two such men. But there were no professional, full-time lawyers, and in colonies like early Virginia practically no one had any familiarity with English law. The demand for legal counsel came late in the 1600s and then only in the cities, usually fueled by merchants whose business interests were large enough and complicated enough to warrant seeking such help.

Attitudes. For most people in the 1600s, going to court meant representing oneself. Lawyers were suspect, seen as individuals who profited off other people's misfortunes and tried to confuse honest folk with legal intricacies. From a modern point of view this meant that legal affairs were terribly amateurish in the seventeenth century. But at the time the prevailing social attitude kept the law from getting too complicated and expensive. A few colonies even attempted to prohibit the use of lawyers or at least to outlaw lawyers' fees. All this allowed considerable room for experimentation, sometimes at the expense of innocent people, and it permitted lay people—both men and women—to handle their own legal affairs.

Brent. One of the most important lawyers of seventeenth-century Maryland was a woman, Margaret Brent, who as attorney for her brother's economic interests and as consultant to Gov. Cecilius Calvert handled more cases than any other lawyer in her lifetime. Brent's example reminds us that lawyers were needed, especially by the government and by those with sufficient wealth. New Netherland contained no practicing attorneys, despite much litigation, before English conquest made it New York in 1664. The Duke's Laws promulgated by Gov. Francis Nichols were actually written by a lawyer, Mathias Nichols (no relation), who had studied law in London. The result was that the Duke's Laws exhibited a superior understanding of the common law, which influenced New York's legal history more than any other colony.

The Few. By 1700 the major towns like New York, Philadelphia, Boston, and Charleston boasted several successful lawyers, but most of these had other business interests to explain their wealth. The small numbers meant that one wealthy client could retain all the local lawyers. In 1695, for example, New York had to impose restrictions on the number of lawyers available to any one litigant. Although New York's ranks of lawyers did grow, the colony licensed only around 170 lawyers between 1709 and 1776. Between 1695 and 1769 only 49 lawyers practiced in New York City. Virginia was slower in developing a qualified corps of legal professionals. A major reason was that the large landowners who dominated the colony's politics in the late 1600s did not want lawyers in their way. But after Virginia regularized its system of courts in 1705, the need for trained lawyers became more apparent. By the end of the colonial period Virginia was home to many distinguished legal minds, including Thomas Jefferson, John Marshall, and George Wythe.

Incomes. Most colonial lawyers did not get wealthy. The better lawyers in New York might earn around £700 per year in the mid 1700s. John Rutledge, lawyer to merchants in Charleston, South Carolina, made several thousand pounds per year, but that was unusual. Lawyers' wages were kept low in Virginia by legislation. In the 1760s men like Patrick Henry and Jefferson earned in their peak years less than £600 each and collected only little more than half. Lawyers did make more than doctors, though, and their social and political prominence had risen greatly by the end of the colonial period, as had the professional standards which they attained.

Sources:

Anton-Hermann Chroust, *The Rise of the Legal Profession in America: The Colonial Experience* (Norman: University of Oklahoma Press, 1965);

"The Legal Profession," in *Encyclopedia of the North American Colonies*, edited by Jacob Cooke (New York: Scribners, 1993).

LEGAL PRINCIPLES IN FRENCH AMERICA

New France. In the early 1600s the North American interests of France lay chiefly in the hands of explorers like Samuel de Champlain and the Company of New France, which possessed a royal monopoly on the French North American (Canadian) fur trade. But New France was reorganized in the 1660s, an effort led by Louis XIV's chief minister, Jean-Baptiste Colbert. It became a royal colony, with an appointed governor, an army, and a mandate to increase France's economic profit from the fur trade. The principle at work was the same as in the English empire—the colonies existed to further the interests of the mother country.

Government. As in the Spanish colonies, power in New France was shared among a governor responsible for military and Indian matters, an intendant responsible for civil and local government, and a bishop who headed the Catholic Church. Unfortunately the arrangement caused problems and struggles within the government, especially between the church and the secular authorities. Compared to the organization of the English colonies, it was a model bureaucracy, and it was undemocratic—not a single French official was elected by the people.

Judicial System. The governor, intendant, bishop, and several others formed the Sovereign Council, seated at Quebec, which served as the highest court in New France. The judicial system was the responsibility of the intendant, who could handle many cases on his own. Most matters were handled by the local, seigneurial courts, while appeals were heard by royal courts at Montreal, Quebec, and Trois Rivières. Royal court decisions could be appealed to the Sovereign Council, and some wealthy individuals appealed these decisions all the way to the Conseil de Parties in Paris, thus giving the wealthy a significant advantage over less-prosperous litigants.

Practices. Lawyers were even less well-liked in France than in England, and New France outlawed lawyers altogether. The intendant was trained in law, but notaries handled most routine legal matters at the local level. In court people represented themselves, as typically occurred in the English colonies. Witnesses were paid for their appearances, the fee varying according to social rank. Though their testimony could be challenged, they could not be cross-examined.

The Accused. French law allowed the accused to be interrogated and under some circumstances even tortured, neither of which was allowed under English law.

Torture in France usually entailed pouring water into the mouth of the accused, but French Canadians were more likely to use "torture boots"—wooden slats tied to the legs with wedges driven between the wood and the flesh. Three physicians were required to be in attendance, but this rule was not rigorously obeyed. Any confession obtained became invalid if not confirmed by the prisoner after he or she had recovered. The practice could be used only under strict circumstances, and only eight men are known to have been tortured.

Punishments. Executions were rare but could be inflicted through hanging, beheading (for nobles), or being broken on the rack. From 1665 until 1763 only eighty-five persons were executed. Hangings were not popular among the populace, and they were not nearly the public events they were in England and its colonies. Indeed, workers tried to avoid constructing the gallows or removing the corpse afterward. The stocks and lashing were infrequently used. Theft or breaking and entering might bring the punishment of banishment, branding, or service on a king's galley. Branding with a fleur-de-lis was not only painful but also served to permanently identify a convicted criminal.

Sources:

W. J. Eccles, *The Canadian Frontier, 1534–1760*, revised edition (Albuquerque: University of New Mexico Press, 1983);

Eccles, *France in America* (New York: Harper & Row, 1972).

LEGAL PRINCIPLES IN SPANISH AMERICA

Overlapping Authority. More so than the early English colonies, Spanish colonies were tied closely to the military, an imperial bureaucracy, and the church. The imperial bureaucracy had three components: the office of the viceroy, responsible for civil and military matters and the local governors; the *audiencias*, or appeals courts; and the episcopate, or church. Their powers overlapped, and in theory they worked to complement one another. In practice, however, disputes arose frequently over authority.

Underlying Theory. In part the jurisdictional confusion was intentional. The Spanish government knew that if the authority of these groups overlapped they would check each other and none would get too powerful. But another reason was that the agencies reflected the Spanish monarchy itself. The monarch was seen as both king and vicar of Christ, with secular and spiritual authority. In that sense both the church and the secular authorities could claim to be the emissaries of the king. The Spanish possession of New Mexico (present-day southwestern United States) exemplified this pattern. Franciscan friars first moved into New Mexico in 1581. Their positive reports prompted the king to award a *capitulacion* (charter) to Don Juan de Oñate in 1595 to conquer the region for Spanish settlement, which he did in 1598. In the years that followed, the Franciscans had the upper hand, but they admittedly relied on military power as a backup to their spiritual influence with the people. The result was

nearly a theocratic state until the Pueblo Revolt of 1680 temporarily ended both Spanish civil and religious authority in the region. Even after Spanish rule was reasserted in the 1690s, the lines of authority frequently were crossed.

Encomiendas. Another distinctive feature of Spanish colonization was the *encomienda*. An encomienda entitled its recipient not only to the use of the land but also to tribute (payments) from the inhabitants, much as might be received on a feudal estate in medieval Europe. The first encomiendas had been unregulated, but the Laws of Burgos (1504) had placed restrictions, including a prohibition against enslaving the Indians. In the 1540s, under the influence of Bartolomeo de las Casas, King Charles V attempted to sharply curtail and even to end encomiendas through the New Laws. These were repealed only a few years later, but many restrictions survived. Don Juan de Oñate's 1595 charter entitled him to award encomiendas to those who conquered New Mexico. Encomiendas could be inherited for up to two generations, but the ranches that their *encomenderos* (owners) created could be inherited indefinitely and became the basis of many large estates in the American Southwest. Governors and their regional subordinates, the *alcaldes*, often had little incentive to enforce Spanish law. As a result it was not uncommon for encomenderos to force the Indians, such as the Pueblos, into labor as well.

Roman Law. A third distinctive aspect of Spanish colonization was the influence of Roman law. Like other Continental nations, Spain had incorporated many Roman statutes during the sixteenth and seventeenth centuries, which in turn influenced Spanish colonial law. Some scholars believe the influence of Roman laws made slavery less harsh in Spanish America than in English America. Likewise, others note that Spanish women in the colonies enjoyed greater legal autonomy.

Sources:

Charles Gibson, *Spain in America* (New York: Harper & Row, 1966);

Ramón Gutiérrez, *When Jesus Came, the Corn Mothers Went Away* (Stanford, Cal.: Stanford University Press, 1991);

David J. Weber, *The Spanish Frontier in North America* (New Haven: Yale University Press, 1992).

LEISLER'S REBELLION

Insurrection. After James II was forced to leave the throne in the Glorious Revolution of 1688, Massachusetts overthrew the royal governor in charge of the Dominion of New England, and Dutch New Yorkers soon followed suit. The rebellious New Yorkers named a Dutch merchant, Jacob Leisler, to take charge of the province. He established control but in the process alienated the powerful English merchant families of the colony. Though Leisler's supporters were overwhelmingly Dutch, they had no desire to reinstate Dutch rule, only to alter the government under the recently created Dominion of New England. When the newly appointed governor arrived one evening in March 1691, Leisler refused to surrender the fort at New York City to him because it was after dark. His delay made him more vulnerable to the charge of treason, and a brief skirmish ensued. The next morning he turned the fort over to Gov. Henry Sloughter, who in turn had Leisler and nine others arrested for treason.

Trials. The Dutch leaders in the colony had miscalculated badly, and their trials demonstrated the difficulty of facing English criminal proceedings. The accused did not fully understand the intricacies of English legal procedure, and their opponents were after revenge. Two men were acquitted; six more were convicted, but later they were reprieved and pardoned. Leisler and his son-in-law, Englishman Jacob Milborne, were not so lucky. They refused to answer the charges, considering them without legal foundation. Leisler's domineering ways had weakened his support in preceding months, and those whom he had arrested while in command desired that he be punished. The jury was packed with men opposed to the Leisler faction, and Leisler and Milborne were convicted and, despite popular protest, executed.

Results. The executions did not end the matter. The anti-Leisler faction proceeded to seize the land of many Leisler supporters, a practice halted in 1695 by Parliament, which also reversed the convictions. But the passionate hatred among the surviving leaders of the two factions lingered, influencing New York politics for another twenty-five years.

Sources:
Peter Charles Hoffer, *Law and People in Colonial America* (Baltimore: Johns Hopkins University Press, 1992);

Michael Kammen, *Colonial New York: A History* (New York: Oxford University Press, 1971).

NEW YORK'S "NEGRO PLOT" OF 1741

Fear. In 1730 false rumors of an impending slave uprising swept through the colony of New York. That colony contained the largest number of slaves north of the Chesapeake colonies; one-sixth of New York City's residents were slaves. A strict slave code was adopted in the 1730s, but it was only partially successful in controlling the behavior of slaves in the city. Rumors circulated in 1740 of plans to poison the city's water supply, and the harsh winter of 1740–1741 further heightened anxieties.

Burton. In early 1741 a rash of arsons and thefts resulted in the posting of a reward of £100 for information leading to the arrest of the criminals. Mary Burton, a teenage indentured servant, claimed the reward with information about a theft ring that included her master. Subsequent evidence pointed to the existence of the ring, but Mary's claims went further: she reported a plot to burn the city, kill the white males, and place her owner in charge as mayor.

Trials and Torture. Many New Yorkers believed Burton, despite inconsistencies in her story. The trials that followed during the next year fully displayed the city's fear of a general slave uprising, as well as class and religious resentments. One hundred and fifty blacks and twenty-five whites were jailed. Eighteen slaves and four whites were hanged, and thirteen slaves were burned to death. Another seventy slaves were deported to non-English colonies after confessing. The confessions were extracted under threats—at least two while the fire was being lit beneath them—so the best way to save oneself from death was to "confess" and to implicate others. Truth mattered little, and pleas of innocence were ignored, as the law became an instrument of fear rather than of justice.

Aftermath. The trials came to an end when Burton's accusations became even wilder and were extended to include prominent citizens. She left New York soon afterward. In the years that followed, rumors periodically surfaced of other plots, and New Yorkers increasingly preferred free laborers over slaves, more out of fear than of sympathy for unfree laborers.

Sources:
Daniel Horsmanden, *The New York Conspiracy* (Boston: Beacon, 1971);

Michael Kammen, *Colonial New York: A History* (New York: Oxford University Press, 1971).

REGULATING TRADE WITHIN THE EMPIRE

Navigation Acts. From 1651 onward Parliament passed a series of laws called the Acts of Trade, or Navigation Acts, that attempted to regulate trade with the empire. The theory that underlay these acts was called mercantilism. The idea was that the colonies existed for the benefit of England and that their economic development should coincide with the interests of the mother country. Starting in 1651, the Navigation Acts established a system of regulations that worked both for and against colonial economic interests. Under these laws commodities transported to and from the colonies had to be carried on British ships commanded by British masters; three-quarters of a ship's crew had to be Britons. (In

SLAVE DISTURBANCES IN COLONIAL AMERICA, 1663-1741

Year(s)	Type	Colony	Place or Description
1663	SC	Va.	Gloucester County
1687	SC	Va.	Westmoreland County
1691	SR	Va.	Rappahannock County
1708	SR	N.Y.	Newtown, Long Island
1709–1710	SC	Va.	Surry, James City, and Isle of Wight Counties
1711	SR	S.C.	Band of rebels
1712	SR	N.Y.	New York City
1713	SC	S.C.	Goose Creek
1720	SC	S.C.	Charleston
1722	SC	Va.	Rappahannock River
1723	SC	Va.	Middlesex and Gloucester counties
1727	M	La.	Maroons of des Natanspallé
1729	M	Va.	Blue Ridge Mountains
1730	SC	Va.	Princess Anne County and Norfolk
1730	SC	S.C.	Charleston
1730	SC	La.	New Orleans
1738	M	Md.	Prince Georges County
1739	SC	Md.	Annapolis
1739	SR	S.C.	Stono River
1741	SC	N.Y.	New York City

Key for Types of Activity: SR = Slave Revolt / SC = Slave Conspiracy (without revolt) / M = Maroons or escaped slaves

Source: Richard Maxwell Brown, *Strain of Violence: Historical Studies of American Violence and Vigilantism* (Oxford & New York: Oxford University Press, 1975), pp. 320–326.

this case "British" meant anyone from the British Isles and American colonies.) This provision greatly aided American sailors and shipbuilders. Other provisions required that certain items called enumerated articles must be taken to England before they could be transported to European ports, while other goods could not be sold anywhere but in England. The latter included tobacco, rice, furs, indigo (a blue dye), and naval stores (masts, hemp, pitch, tar, and turpentine). The acts also included bounties to be paid to Americans for producing things that England needed, such as hemp for rope, iron, dyes, silk, and lumber, while imposing protective tariffs on the importation of the same commodities from other countries. Better enforcement of the Navigation Acts was one motive behind the creation of the Dominion of New England in the 1680s, just as avoiding their enforcement was one motive behind the colonial rebellions that followed the Glorious Revolution of 1688.

Enforcement. In order to enforce these laws Parliament created vice-admiralty courts in the colonies. Such courts handled maritime matters and were controversial in America because they did not include jury trials and took matters out of the hands of local courts. But the mildness of much of the legislation combined with lax enforcement meant that such regulations were rarely the object of protest after 1700, at least until the American Revolution. Parliament claimed first pick on the New England trees suitable for ships' masts in the White Pine Acts of the 1720s, restricted the American manufacturing of beaver hats in the Hat Act of 1731, and taxed the importation of French Caribbean molasses in 1733. Each of these prompted complaints, but none resulted in wide-scale rebellion.

Reassertion of Control. As the British began to reorganize their control over the colonies in the late 1740s, they created still more regulations. The Iron Act of 1750 outlawed the building of colonial forges for turning pig iron into steel. This law also dropped duties that had previously been laid on pig iron, so in theory the statute both helped and hindered the colonies. In truth it was not enforced anyway, so it had little effect. The Currency Act of 1751 seriously restricted the use of paper money, but it only applied to New England and for various reasons was not immediately perceived as a threat there. Eventually many Americans would come to see such measures as unnecessary and even unlawful interferences with their freedom. Not until the famous Sugar and Stamp Acts of the 1760s did united resistance to such legislation occur.

Source:

Edwin J. Perkins, *The Economy of Colonial America* (New York: Columbia University Press, 1980).

THE SALEM WITCH TRIALS

Charges. In 1692 some teenage girls in Salem, Massachusetts, accused a West Indian slave named Tituba and two white women of practicing witchcraft. The girls behaved strangely and were subject to bodily fits. Most Puritans believed in witchcraft, and witches had been prosecuted in Massachusetts several times in the preceding decades. By April the girls began to denounce others as witches, including a former minister.

Hysteria. The events that followed are notorious in American history. A special court was convened in which the judges were not trained in the law and in which the accused had no attorneys. The court violated precedent by agreeing to consider "spectral evidence"—testimony by an accuser that claimed that a specter (spirit) resembling the accused person was the source of the accuser's misery. Such a specter could only be seen, it was believed, by the victim, so the evidence could neither be refuted nor corroborated and for that reason had not been admitted in the past. The trials that followed resulted in hundreds of accusations, over one hundred guilty verdicts, and the executions of twenty persons, mostly women. Nineteen who refused to confess were hanged, and one man was pressed to death with stones for refusing to answer the charge, thereby saving his family's fortune. By early 1693 several ministers had expressed grave doubts about spectral evidence, and the governor pardoned those condemned and eventually suspended all the trials.

Causes. Even though the hysteria was not limited to Salem, a close analysis of the community reveals some patterns concerning witchcraft accusations throughout New England. Most of the accusers came from the more rural Salem Village, with a third of the accusations originating with members of the Putnam family. The accused generally were prosperous and from the commercially oriented Salem Town. Most of the young girls who made the accusations had lost a parent in Indian raids and now worked around Salem as servants, while most of the accused were prosperous, older women without husbands or sons.

Puritan Mission. More broadly, the witchcraft hysteria of 1692 reflected deep anxieties among Puritans that the idealized, pious way of life they had created was ending. They had lost their charter in the 1680s, and under the new charter of 1691 the male members of the Puritan (Congregationalist) churches had to share the vote and office-holding with Anglicans. The tight-knit religious communities of their founders

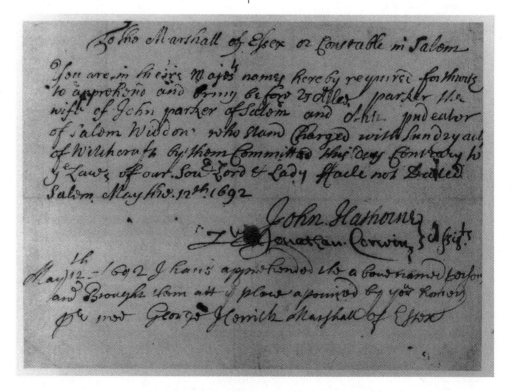

Warrant for the arrest of Ann Pudeator on charges of witchcraft, 1692 (Essex Institute, Salem, Massachusetts)

were giving way to more business-oriented and competitive towns. These changes, coupled with their sincere belief in a spiritual world in which good and evil fought for the souls of humans, made it easy to believe that there were witches among them causing all sorts of problems. Even so, the simple legal error of admitting spectral evidence turned what would have been isolated, ugly episodes into a yearlong horror for Massachusetts.

Sources:

Paul Boyer and Stephen Nissenbaum, *Salem Possessed: The Social Origins of Witchcraft* (Cambridge, Mass.: Harvard University Press, 1974);

Carol F. Karlsen, *The Devil in the Shape of a Woman: Witchcraft in Colonial New England* (New York: Random House, 1987).

SLAVERY AND SLAVE CODES

European Law. English common law did not describe slavery, though it did describe varieties of relations between superiors and inferiors, for example, masters and servants and parents and children. There were, therefore, no specific English legal precedents for slavery in the colonies. Yet slavery did develop in the 1600s, spreading to all the English colonies. The number of slaves grew rapidly in colonies such as Virginia, Maryland, and South Carolina. But a social system like slavery needed legal support in order to survive. Because Spain and Portugal had incorporated Roman law into their legal systems, those countries and their colonies could easily borrow from the ancient statutes to govern the Latin American slavery of the 1600s.

Development. Britain did not use Roman jurisprudence, and the common law's silence on the subject meant that the English colonies would develop their own law of slavery. Slavery developed in the Chesapeake colonies of Virginia and Maryland first as a socioeconomic practice and only afterward as a legal institution. The earliest Africans in Virginia were probably indentured servants—workers who labored for a set number of years. Gradually during the 1600s it became accepted that whites could be indentured servants but that blacks could be slaves or permanent servants, a status that would pass on to their children.

Virginia. After the mid 1600s slavery came to be sanctioned by statutes passed by the various legislatures. The first of these slave codes was enacted in Barbados in 1661; the most complete was adopted in South Carolina in 1740. Virginia's assembly passed several such laws. A 1662 statute made the child of a slave woman a slave, even if the father were free. A 1669 law declared that if a slave died while resisting his master, the master could not be charged with a felony; this was based on the assumption that no master would deliberately choose to kill his own slave, and therefore that the death must be presumed to have been unintended. And a 1680 law inflicted twenty lashes on any "negro or other slave" who chose to carry a weapon or to "depart from his master's ground without a certificate from his master, mistress or overseer."

South Carolina. The slave code of 1740 in South Carolina was passed after the infamous Stono Rebellion, an uprising that resulted in far more black deaths than white ones. The most comprehensive of the colonial codes, it greatly influenced the slave codes in the South from 1776 to 1861. It stipulated that negroes, mulattos (mixed white and black background), Indians, and mestizos (mixed Indian and white parentage) were to be assumed to be slaves "unless the contrary can be made to appear." Slaves could travel only with written permission of their masters and were subject to the death penalty for homicide or for attempting "to raise an insurrection." They could suffer death for lesser crimes as well, such as maliciously destroying "any stack of rice, corn or other grain" or setting fire to "any tar kiln, barrels of pitch, tar, turpentine or rosin." If accused of such a crime, the slave was entitled to a trial before two justices, but they benefited from fewer legal protections than did whites.

The Spanish. Spain transplanted its laws of slavery to its American provinces. The Spanish codes, since they grew out of Roman precedents, were not based on race, while English colonial statutes were decidedly racist. While slavery throughout the Americas was racist for its enslavement of non-Caucasians, English slave owners wrote this racism into the law itself.

Sources:

Kermit Hall, William Wiecek, and Paul Finkelman, *American Legal History: Cases and Materials* (New York: Oxford University Press, 1991);

Alan Watson, *Slave Law in the Americas* (Athens: University of Georgia Press, 1989).

WOMEN

Law of Coverture. Colonial women who married ceased to exist, legally speaking, as separate persons. Single women maintained much greater control over their own property than did married women. Under the English common law doctrine of coverture, upon marriage the wife became covered by the husband; that is, she could not act in legal matters except in concert with her husband. While the law allowed them to act together, the husband controlled all legal affairs and was under no legal compulsion to consult his wife. A husband could even be found liable for the wrongdoing of his wife on the assumption that it occurred at his behest. In some instances husbands could be whipped for the wife's crime, including adultery.

Colonial Departures. In the American colonies coverture was followed but with modifications, as in the case of dower rights. Under English law one-third of a deceased husband's estate, called a dower, had to be preserved for the support of his surviving wife. In Britain this law frequently was circumvented, but in America it was protected and strengthened. Often, es-

Elizabeth Eggington, a Puritan woman of Massachusetts, 1664
(portrait by an unknown artist; Wadsworth Atheneum,
Hartford, Connecticut)

pecially in New England, the court would enlarge the dower to more than one-third of the estate, so great was the concern for the protection of widows. In some courts women were allowed to sue in their own names.

Dutch Influence. The jurisprudence of the Netherlands was heavily influenced by Roman law and afforded women more protection. For example, Dutch women could sign joint wills with their husbands, something not allowed under English law. The joint will option meant that, until 1695, Dutch women in New York often had greater say in matters of inheritance than did English women.

Anglicization. During the 1600s it was not uncommon for women to appear in English colonial courts in their husband's stead, even as their attorneys. After 1700 the economic life of the colonies became more complex, and knowledge of English common law proved useful. With greater Anglicization came even greater sexism in the courts, and the acceptance of women in the courtroom lessened. On the other hand, divorce, though rare and difficult, was easier to obtain in America than it was in England.

Crime. It is possible that crimes committed by women were underreported, but from available data it appears that women were less likely to commit crimes of any category except witchcraft. In New England the only women accused of murder before 1660 had killed children. And women were particularly susceptible to be victims of crime. Female servants were susceptible to sexual harassment even though the law could and would strictly punish men who exploited such women.

Gender Differences. Women were commonly treated differently than men. Connecticut and Massachusetts laws against sodomy, perjury, and idolatry applied only to men on the theory that women could not commit them. Since fornication was most likely to be discovered by the pregnancy of the woman, women were at much greater risk of being charged with that crime. Unless she reported the name of the father, he would probably remain undetected and not receive punishment. It became common to question mothers during childbirth to ascertain the father's name, both to ensure his punishment and to guarantee his support of the child.

Sources:

Edgar J. McManus, *Law and Liberty in Early New England* (Amherst: University of Massachusetts Press, 1993);

David E. Narrett, *Inheritance and Family Life in Colonial New York City* (Ithaca, N.Y.: Cornell University Press, 1992);

Marylynn Salmon, *Women and the Law of Property in Early America* (Chapel Hill: University of North Carolina Press, 1986).

HEADLINE MAKERS

JAMES ALEXANDER

1691-1756
NEW YORK LAWYER

Arrival in America. James Alexander was born in the village of Muthill in Pertshire, Scotland, the son of David Alexander, sixth Earl of Stirling. (After his father's death he never claimed the title of seventh earl.) He studied science and mathematics at Edinburgh. Alexander's family was politically active and sided with the Jacobites in the rebellion against the British Crown in 1715. Alexander served as an engineering officer with the Scottish forces, and following their defeat he fled to America.

Government Positions. Alexander's connections and talents landed him an appointment as surveyor-general of New Jersey. He began studying law in 1718 and the next year surveyed the boundary between New Jersey and New York. During the 1720s he served on the governor's council and as the attorney general for both colonies. (Until 1738 New Jersey and New York shared the same governor and administrative offices.)

Political Opposition. Alexander's dislike for and opposition to Gov. William Cosby of New York helps explain his support of John Peter Zenger. In 1733 Alexander launched the *New-York Weekly Journal,* a newspaper printed by Zenger. Alexander wrote editorials on freedom of the press as well as pieces criticizing Cosby's administration. When Zenger was arrested for seditious libel in 1734, Alexander and William Smith volunteered to represent the printer in trial. But Alexander was to be denied his chance to appear in court. The government clearly was against Zenger, and his bail was set at £800, at least ten times his personal assets. When Alexander and Smith challenged the commissions of the judges hearing the case, the court responded by disbarring both men. Cosby also removed Alexander from his position on the governor's council. Andrew Hamilton of Philadelphia had to be called to represent Zenger in what became one of the most famous American trials of the century.

Political Rehabilitation. The death of Governor Cosby in March 1736 reversed New York's political climate, and Alexander was readmitted to the bar. He also returned to his position on the governor's council, although he still met with opposition from royal authorities. In 1744 he helped found the American Philosophical Society, and in 1751 he raised funds to establish King's College (now Columbia University). Alexander also sponsored several unsuccessful efforts to secure religious freedom for disfranchised Catholics, Jews, and Quakers. As one of the best-known lawyers of his day he had a large and lucrative practice, and his various appointed positions also brought him wealth. His obituary in 1756 called him "eminent in his profession of the law; and equally distinguished in public affairs."

Sources:

James Alexander, *A Brief Narrative of the Trial of John Peter Zenger*, edited by Stanley Nider Katz (Cambridge: Belknap Press of Harvard University Press, 1972);

Leonard W. Levy, ed., *Freedom of the Press from Zenger to Jefferson* (Indianapolis: Bobbs-Merrill, 1966).

MARGARET BRENT

1601-1671?
ATTORNEY AND LANDOWNER

Early Settler. Margaret Brent was born in Gloucester, England, the daughter of Lord Admington and Lark Stoke. Little is known of her mother. Brent was reared a Roman Catholic and given an education. She arrived in Maryland in 1638 with a sister, two brothers, and several servants. The Brents were well connected and had a letter from Cecilius Calvert, the proprietor of Maryland, which recommended they be given land.

Land Grant. Men usually received land grants, but Margaret and Mary Brent were also accorded land independently, a 70.5-acre property called the "Sisters Freehold" in St. Mary's City. In 1642 Margaret acquired one thousand acres, including a house, mill, and livestock, from her brother Giles in payment of a debt. Her brother Fulke returned to England and bestowed upon her full power of attorney, making her able to represent him in all legal and economic matters concerning his Maryland property. Few professional lawyers were to be found in Maryland in the 1640s, and individuals represented their own interests before the courts. Of these amateur lawyers Margaret Brent was perhaps the most successful of her day, and she often appeared in court representing her brother's or her own interests. Brent had connections in the elite circles of Lord Baltimore, and she came to advise the governor on all sorts of political and legal matters.

"Important Task." When Gov. Leonard Calvert died unexpectedly in 1647, Margaret Brent became the executrix of his will, making her responsible for seeing that his estate's financial affairs were settled and his final wishes were fulfilled. The court declared her to be "his Lordship's attorney," and as such she handled all the claims made against his estate as well as all the debts owed to the deceased governor. More important, in her capacity as attorney she had a responsibility not only to Leonard Calvert but also to his brother, the lord proprietor. These duties included maintaining order after a rebellion had been put down by troops imported from Virginia. Her shrewd handling of the situation gave the new governor the necessary time to get things in order. And while Cecilius Calvert later criticized her conduct—she had sold much of his cattle to pay the soldiers' salaries—the Maryland assembly defended her, saying that "the Colony was safer in her hands than any man's in the Province."

Limits of Gender. While Margaret Brent was a major landowner and in some ways acting governor, she was still discriminated against because of her gender. In 1647 she demanded two votes in the assembly, but the request was denied. Brent's influence became limited because, following the English Civil War in 1648, Puritans started discriminating against Roman Catholics. Moreover, her brother Giles was an outspoken Jesuit. As a result Brent and her family moved to Virginia; there she died around 1671, an unmarried, independent woman.

Sources:

Rosalyn Baxandall, Linda Gordon, and Susan Reverby, eds., *America's Working Women: A Documentary History, 1600–Present* (New York: Vintage, 1976);

Elisabeth W. Dexter, *Colonial Women of Affairs: Women in Business and the Professions in America Before 1776* (Boston: Houghton Mifflin, 1931).

DANIEL DULANEY

1685-1753
MARYLAND ATTORNEY

Career. Daniel Dulaney was born in Queens County, Ireland, and immigrated to Maryland around 1703 with his brothers. He arrived well educated but impoverished. A former attorney general of the province became Dulaney's mentor and trained him in the law. He soon was admitted to the Maryland bar, and for a time he studied law at Gray's Inn in London. He spent twenty years in the Maryland Assembly and several years on the Governor's Council before his death.

Rights of Englishmen. Dulaney was a leading figure in Maryland during a time when royal authorities debated to what extent English law should be operative in the colony. As an assemblyman Dulaney served on the important committee on laws and also as attorney general. In 1722 the proprietor refused to accept a new Maryland law that seemed to make all English laws applicable in the province, maintaining that he should approve any and all statutes first. But Dulaney and those he represented believed that the Maryland charter entitled them to certain privileges that could not be enjoyed without the protection of English laws. This dispute continued for several years, with Dulaney explaining his position in a pamphlet called *The Rights of the Inhabitants of Maryland to the Benefit of the English Laws* (1728). In 1732 Dulaney devised a compromise that satisfied most people.

Governor's Appointee. Before his death in 1753 Daniel Dulaney had become one of the wealthiest and most influential men in Maryland. His political skills earned other appointments, which included agent for the colony, receiver general, and commissary general. He was also appointed an admiralty judge and heard cases pertaining to smuggling and other maritime matters.

Sources:

Aubrey C. Land, *Colonial Maryland: A History* (Millwood, N.Y.: KTO Press, 1981);

Land, *Law, Society and Politics in Early Maryland* (Baltimore: Johns Hopkins University Press, 1977).

WILLIAM FITZHUGH

1651?-1701
VIRGINIA ENTREPRENEUR

Merchant and Planter. William Fitzhugh was born in Bedford, England, the son of a wealthy woolen draper. Little is known of his early life. Already a lawyer when he immigrated to Virginia in 1670, he acquired a large estate and proved successful as a tobacco grower and exporter. By 1672 he became the Stafford County representative to the House of Burgesses and gained a reputation as an expert on the colony's laws.

Beverley. In 1682 Fitzhugh served as defense attorney for Maj. Robert Beverley, the clerk of the House of Burgesses. The governor and the council (the upper house in Virginia) asked the major for copies of the Burgesses' journals. But Beverley, determined to protect the independence and authority of the Burgesses for whom he worked, refused to turn the journals over until that body had met and expressly authorized such an action. The governor became infuriated and had Beverley arrested. Fitzhugh defended Beverley to the best of his ability, but he was convicted in 1685.

Other Activities. Fitzhugh also served as a lieutenant colonel in the militia and a justice of the peace. As a supporter of the Stuarts and an accused Roman Catholic, he was forced to take the Oath of Allegiance in 1693. That same year he completed a brief history of Virginia, but it was never published and is no longer extant. In the late 1690s he attempted to recruit French Huguenot refugees to settle on his lands. Fitzhugh died on 21 October 1701 of dysentery after returning from a trip to England. In his lifetime he acquired 54,054 acres of land.

Source:
Richard Beale Davis, *William Fitzhugh and His Chesapeake World, 1676–1701* (Chapel Hill: Published for the Virginia Historical Society by the University of North Carolina Press, 1963).

ANDREW HAMILTON

1676?-1741
PHILADELPHIA LAWYER

Early Career. Andrew Hamilton, although well known in his own day, left little information about his early life. He was born in Scotland around 1676 and for some reason changed his last name from Trent to Hamilton. He came to America in 1697, opening a classical school in Accomac County, Virginia, and acting as a plantation steward. In 1706 he married the estate owner's widow, and two years later he bought six thousand acres in Maryland. He opened a law practice in Chestertown and was elected a member of the colonial assembly.

Philadelphia. In 1715 Hamilton arrived in Philadelphia after having spent some time in England, where he was admitted to Gray's Inn, one of the Inns of Court. In 1717 he was appointed attorney general of Pennsylvania. A close friend of the Penn family, the proprietors of the colony, he acted as their agent from 1724 to 1726. His reward, among other things, was 153 acres in the heart of Philadelphia, from which he created his well-known estate, Bush Hill. His associate James Logan described him as "a very able lawyer, very faithful to his client," who "generally refused to be concerned for any plaintiff who appeared not to have justice on his side." In 1727 Hamilton became chief clerk of the Court of Common Pleas and recorder of the city. The same year he won election to the Pennsylvania Assembly, serving there as speaker for close to ten years.

Zenger Trial. Hamilton is best known today for his successful defense of John Peter Zenger against the charge of seditious libel in 1735. When Zenger's lawyers, James Alexander and William Smith, were disbarred, they called upon Hamilton to act in their stead. The eloquent lawyer was able to convince the jury to take into account not only whether Zenger had printed material critical of Gov. William Cosby of New York (he had), but whether or not it was true. For his efforts Hamilton not only received his fees but also a naval salute, the freedom of the city, and a gold box. In 1737 he became a judge of the vice admiralty court, a position he held until his death on 4 August 1741.

Source:
Burton Alva Konkle, *The Life of Andrew Hamilton, 1676–1741: "The Day-Star of the American Revolution"* (Philadelphia: National Publishing Company, 1941).

PUBLICATIONS

James Alexander, *A Brief Narrative of the Case and Tryal of John Peter Zenger, Printer of the New-York Weekly Journal* . . . (New York: Printed by John Peter Zenger, 1736)—Alexander's account went through fifteen editions in both New York and London by 1800 and has been described as one of the most influential books in American history;

Robert Beverley, *An Abridgement of the Public Laws of Virginia* . . . (London: Printed for F. Fayram & J. Clarke & T. Bickerton, 1722);

Sir William Blackstone, *Commentaries on the Laws of England* (Oxford: Printed at the Clarendon Press, 1765–1769);

Michael Dalton, *The Countrey Justice* (London: Printed for the Societie of Stationers, 1618)—a manual commonly used by colonial justices of the peace;

Matthew Hale, *Pleas of the Crown. Or A Brief, but Full Account of Whatsoever can be Found Relating to That Subject* (London: Printed for Richard Tonson, 1678);

William Hawkins, *A Treatise of the Pleas of the Crown* (London: Printed by His Majesty's Law-Printers, 1716);

Henry Home, *Essays upon Several Subjects in Law . . .* (Edinburgh: Printed by R. Fleming & sold by James M'Euen, 1732);

Daniel Horsmanden, *The New-York Conspiracy: or, A History of the Negro Plot* (New York: James Parker, 1744);

John Mercer, *An Exact Abridgment of The Public Acts of the Assembly, of Virginia, in Force and Use . . .* (Williamsburg, Va.: Printed by William Parks, 1737);

George Webb, *The Office and Authority of a Justice of the Peace* (Williamsburg, Va.: Printed by William Parks, 1736)—also has descriptions of the duties of sheriffs, coroners, surveyors of highways, and militia officers and various legal procedures in Virginia.

Colonial engraving of a woman being punished by dunking

LIFESTYLES, SOCIAL TRENDS, AND FASHION

by TIMOTHY D. HALL

CONTENTS

Sidebars and tables are listed in italics.

1609

- In what is probably the first marriage in mainland British North America, Anne Burrows and John Laydon are wed in Virginia.

1618

- Women begin to arrive in Virginia.
- Deputy Gov. Sir Samuel Argall of Virginia forbids Sunday dancing, fiddling, card playing, hunting, and fishing.

1619

- The first Africans arrive in Virginia.

1623

- The main source of nutrition for the Plymouth colony is seafood. The colonists feast on "lobster or a piece of fish without bread or anything else but a cup of spring water." The lobsters weigh an average of twenty-five pounds and are so abundant that children can catch them.

1624

- The first Walloon families settle in New Netherland.

1628

1 May   A May Day celebration at Mare Mount (present-day Quincy, Massachusetts) is described by Gov. William Bradford as follows:

> They . . . set up a May-Pole, drinking and dancing aboute it many days together, inviting the Indean women, for their consorts, dancing and frisking together, (like so many faries or furies rather) and worse practices. As they had anew revived and celebrated the feasts of the Roman Goddes Flora, or the beastly practieses of the Madd Bacchinalians.

1631

22 Feb.   The first public thanksgiving, a fast day, is celebrated in Massachusetts Bay.

1634

- The Massachusetts General Court passes a sumptuary law prohibiting the purchase of woolen, linen, or silk clothes with silver or gold thread lace on them.

4 Mar.   Samuel Cole opens the first tavern in Boston.

1637

- Gov. Willem Kieft of New Amsterdam laments that one-quarter of all the buildings in town are "grog-shops or houses where nothing is to be got but tobacco and beer."

1638

- A Massachusetts law forbids smoking "out of dores" in towns and villages because "fires have beene often occasioned by taking tobacco."

1639

- Church elders in New England censure men for wearing "immoderate great breeches," broad shoulder bands, capes, double ruffles, and silk roses on their shoes.

- In Plymouth a woman convicted of adultery is sentenced to "be whipt at a cart tayle" and to "weare a badge upon her left sleeue during her aboad" in the community. (The badge consists of the letters AD.) If found in public without the badge the woman would be "burned in the face with a hott iron."

4 Sept. The General Court of Massachusetts passes a law against drinking toasts, maintaining that "The common custom of drinking to one another is a mere useless ceremony, and draweth on the abominable practice of drinking healths." Nevertheless, authorities find it impossible to suppress the time-honored custom, and they repeal the law six years later.

1644

- A public thanksgiving is celebrated in New Amsterdam to commemorate the safe return of Dutch soldiers from a battle with Native Americans in Connecticut.

1647

- Connecticut authorities limit individual tobacco use to once a day, after a meal or another time, "and then not in company with any other." Furthermore, it could only be used in one's own house.

- Rhode Island declares common-law marriages illegal.

1648

- After a rash of fires Gov. Peter Stuyvesant of New Amsterdam forbids the construction of chimneys made from "wood or plaister in any house." He appoints four firemasters to inspect chimneys and collect a three-guilder fine for each one found "neglected and foul." The fines are used to purchase hooks, ladders, and leather buckets for the Prowlers, a firefighting organization of eight men who patrol the streets at night.

1649

- A Boston statute requires that all fires be covered or extinguished between the hours of 9:00 P.M. and 4:30 A.M.

1653

- Two women in Newbury, Massachusetts, are arrested for wearing silk hoods and scarves but are released after presenting proof that their husbands each had net worths of £200.

1654

- Twenty-four Jewish immigrants arrive in New Amsterdam.

1656

- After returning from a three-year sea voyage a Boston ship captain kisses his wife in public on Sunday; he is made to sit for two hours in the stocks for his "lewd and unseemly behavior."

- Burgomasters in New Netherland pass a law forbidding the following activities on Sunday: drinking, sowing, mowing, building, sawing, smithing, bleaching, hunting, fishing, dancing, card playing, bowling, and jaunting in a boat or carriage.

1657

- The burgomaster of New Amsterdam outlaws the throwing of "any rubbish, filth, oyster shells, dead animal or anything like it" into the streets.

1660

- The estimated population of mainland British North America is sixty-four thousand, of which two thousand are of African descent.

- The first divorce occurs in Delaware and involves a Finnish couple. It is found that the husband is an adulterer and the "wife receives daily a severe drubbing and is expelled from the house like a dog."

- In order to ensure more stable marriages Connecticut courts decree that all married men must reside with their wives. Any man found to be separated from his wife for three or more years is expelled from the colony.

- A Virginia sumptuary law prohibits colonists from importing "silke stuffe in garments or in peeces except for whoods and scarfs, nor silver or gold lace, nor bone lace of silk or threads, nor ribbands wrought with gold or silver in them."

May   Massachusetts leaders forbid the celebration of Christmas and place a fine of five shillings on violators.

1662

- Town administrators hire Thomas Willsheer to keep the streets of Boston free of "all Carrion & matters of Offenciue natuer."

1664

- After taking control of New Netherland, English authorities continue the Dutch law of 1590 permitting marriages by justices of the peace.

1670

- The first coffeehouse in America is established when Boston authorities grant a license to a female proprietor to sell coffee and chocolate.

1675

- In Massachusetts, Indian attacks are blamed for the sins of the people, including "the manifest pride" of wearing periwigs.

- Thirty-eight women in Connecticut are brought to trial for wearing clothes not befitting their social stations. The magistrate accuses one young girl of "wearing silk in a flaunting manner, in an offensive way and garb not only before but when she stood presented."

1678

- An English clergyman notes the heavy use of tobacco on the part of Dutch colonists. They "are obstinate and incessant smokers, whose diet . . . being sallets and brawn and very often picked buttermilk, require the use of that herb to keep their phlegm from coagulating and curdling."

1681

- A dancing master arrives in Boston but is expelled by church elders who describe him as "a person of very insolent & ill fame that Raues & scoffes at Religion."

1682

- John Skene of Aberdeen, Scotland, settles in Burlington, New Jersey, and becomes the first Freemason to reside in North America.

1685

- A Huguenot minister is arrested for performing marriages in Boston.

1687

28 June — King James II knights William Phips in ceremonies at Windsor Castle. Phips, the first American colonial to be knighted, is so honored for his recovery of a treasure ship off the coast of Hispaniola.

1695

- A street cleaner is hired by the town of New York for thirty pounds sterling a year.

1699

June — Gambling is rampant in all the colonies despite the various laws against it. A few days after Judge Samuel Sewall of Boston breaks up a card game he finds a pack of cards strewn over his lawn.

1700

- The population of mainland British North America reaches 260,000, of which 21,000 are of African descent.

1704

- Women's fashion in New York is described by one contemporary as follows:

  The English go very fasheonable in their dress. The Dutch, especially the middling sort, . . . in their habitt go loose . . . leaving their ears bare, which are sett out with Jewells of a large size and many in number. And their fingers hoop't with Rings, some with large stones in them of many Coullers as were their pendants in their ears, which You should see very old women wear as well as Young.

28 Sept. A statute in Maryland legalizes the separation of a couple by a clergyman.

1705

- Intermarriage between white and black people is outlawed in Massachusetts Bay. A fine of fifty pounds sterling is assessed on any minister performing such a marriage. This statute remains in effect until 1843 when it is repealed.

1706

- Continual hunting almost eliminates the deer population on Long Island, New York, and results in a limited hunting season on that popular game. Two years later a similar restriction is placed on turkey, heath hen, partridge, and quail hunting.

1709

- An armed watch of ten men patrols the streets of Charleston, South Carolina, nightly.

1710

- One of the favorite nonalcoholic beverages in the colonies is chocolate.

- The fashion of colonial elites is extravagant, with both sexes wearing high heels, stiff stays, and large curled wigs. Men's coat skirts are stiffened with buckram (heavy cotton or linen fabric). Hoops are used by women to support layers of skirts. Hairstyles among women are characterized by the "tower," from the top of which hangs lappets, or lace pendants.

- Slave codes go into effect in Virginia.

- Waves of German immigrants begin to arrive in the colonies.

- New York City employs public cartmen to remove trash placed before houses.

1712

- Officials in Philadelphia levy against reckless coachmen the first fines for speeding.

1717

- A wave of Scots-Irish immigration begins.

1719

- The selectmen of Boston order that the town be "well fixed with Lights on all or Stormy Nights."

- All lotteries are banned in New England.

Mar. A law in New Jersey declares it illegal for persons under the age of twenty-one to marry without parental consent.

1721

May Connecticut passes a law prohibiting people from leaving their homes on Sundays unless to attend church or perform some indispensable community service.

1723

- In Boston the police force consists of twelve men who are instructed "to walke Silently and Slowly, now and then to Stand Still and Listen in order to make discovery. And no smoaking to be on their walking rounds."

1727

- Benjamin Franklin founds the Leather Apron Club, later called the Junto, in Philadelphia. This group of artisans and merchants holds meetings in taverns to exchange books and discuss morals, politics, literature, and science.

1728

- In order to preserve its grass from carts and horses, Boston Common is enclosed. Soon it becomes the custom of men and women to stroll the Common after having their midday tea.

- Drinking is extremely heavy in the colonies. In this year alone rum imports amount to 2,124,500 gallons, worth £25,000.

1730

- Summer resorts become popular among wealthy colonials, where they engage in horse races and have dances, tea parties, and lavish dinners. Some of the more well known resorts are Spring Garden, on the outskirts of Philadelphia; the Bath Spring, outside of Bristol, Pennsylvania; and New Shoreham and Prudence Island, near Newport, Rhode Island.

1735

- A Dutch burgher in New York, John van Zandt, horsewhips his slave to death for having been arrested by the night watch. The coroner's jury concludes the "Correction given by the Master was not the Cause of his Death, but it was by the Visitation of God."

1738

- Abraham Savage founds the first Masonic lodge in the colonies.

1741

- Funerals become more elaborate and expensive, and it is customary to give mourning rings or gloves at such events. At the funeral of Gov. Jonathan Belcher of Massachusetts his widow gives away one thousand pairs of gloves although the General Court had outlawed such "extraordinary expenditures."

- In an effort to suppress excessive drinking, town officials in Boston publish the names of those charged with drunkenness.

1743

- William Monat opens a coffeehouse in Charleston, South Carolina, where businessmen meet and notices of ship departures, sales, and other matters are posted. By this time all the major towns in the British colonies have coffeehouses.

1749

- The consumption of cider rivals that of beer in New York. A Swedish visitor notes the abundance of apple orchards and cider presses in the colony. In the winter hot cider is used, while in the summer it is mixed with water, sugar, and nutmeg.

- A foreign traveler observes that Dutch settlers in New York have tea, bread, butter, and beef for breakfast; porridge and salad with vinegar but no oil for lunch; and a supper of bread, butter, and milk.

1750

- African Americans represent 40 percent of the total population in Virginia and 60 percent in South Carolina.

1754

- The population of mainland British North America nears 1.5 million, of which nearly 300,000 are of African descent.

- Saint Valentine Day's custom entails a young girl pinning five bay leaves to her pillow; if she dreams of her sweetheart, then she will marry him within the next year.

OVERVIEW

Old World Customs. European colonists came to America with assumptions about what constituted a good house, family, farm, community, food, and entertainment. They drew these ideas from what they had known in the Old World, and they poured all of their energy into re-creating that manner of living in their new surroundings. Colonists exchanged exotic Algonquian names of rivers, hills, and places for familiar English, German, Dutch, or Spanish ones. They clustered traditional houses in the village patterns they had known in Europe, giving them familiar names such as Plymouth, Boston, and Ipswich. European settlers displayed loyalty to their monarchs by giving important towns names such as Jamestown, Charlestown, and Williamsburg. They sought to establish traditional European families and to eat, drink, dress, live, and be buried at death in European ways.

Adaptation. Yet for all their efforts to re-create Old World patterns in the New World, those who came to North America found it necessary to adapt to the different environment. The New World had climates they had not known, introduced them to unfamiliar but attractive new crops, and everywhere seemed to provide them an unlimited abundance of land. Interaction with Native Americans also demanded a variety of adaptations by incorporating native practices and products. The varying purposes and ways of living in different colonies resulted in a wide range of adaptations. Community-minded farmers in Massachusetts organized networks of remarkably orderly, stable towns and villages, while ambitious planters in Virginia scattered their settlements across the countryside in search of ever-larger landholdings. Settlers on the haciendas of the Spanish borderlands found themselves separated both from each other and from the Indian population. French settlers along the Mississippi and Saint Lawrence River valleys created entirely new cultures adapted to suit their environments, small numbers, and the proximity of large Native American populations. Great changes in European commerce, philosophical and scientific inquiry, technology, and warfare also reached across the Atlantic to shape the colonies.

Regional Societies. As successive waves of European settlers arrived in each region, the various patterns of adaptation produced strikingly different regional societies. The Spanish borderlands of the American Southwest and Florida were organized more or less systematically to advance Spain's control over that region of North America. The *encomienda* system created a society of Spanish soldier-settlers whose conquest of Native American populations gained them vast land grants from the Crown along with rights to extract tribute in foodstuffs, clothing, and labor from Native Americans of the region.

New France and the Chesapeake. As a result Spanish colonial society came to be organized as a racial hierarchy determined by biological intermixing of Europeans, Indians, and Africans. New France emerged as a trading society along the Saint Lawrence and Mississippi River valleys, loosely organized at first but reproducing the social hierarchy of France as towns such as Quebec, Montreal, and New Orleans emerged. Chesapeake society was profoundly shaped by the cultivation of tobacco, the main export crop of Virginia and Maryland. Those who wanted to grow wealthy through tobacco cultivation needed large tracts of land and a substantial labor force. A comparatively small group of great planting families came to occupy the peak positions in society and to control the bulk of Chesapeake wealth and property. The bottom rungs of the social ladder came to be occupied by unfree laborers: English indentured servants for much of the seventeenth century and African slaves after the 1680s.

New England and the Middle Colonies. New England, by contrast, became a remarkably stable society of small family farms and villages distributed among the colonies that eventually became Massachusetts, Connecticut, New Hampshire, and Rhode Island. The Middle Colonies of New York, New Jersey, Pennsylvania, and Delaware reflected great diversity in their origins and population. England captured New Amsterdam from Holland in 1664 and renamed it New York, but the Dutch population continued to shape the colony. The Swedes were the first Europeans to settle along the mouth of the Delaware River between what is now Pennsylvania and New Jersey. Later settlers from Scotland, Northern Ireland, England, and the Netherlands created ethnic and religious diversity among the settlements that became New Jersey. When William Penn established

Pennsylvania in 1681, he welcomed settlers from all over the European continent as well as Quakers from England, and the colony became quite diverse.

The Carolinas. North Carolina remained largely undeveloped until late in the colonial period, but South Carolina emerged as a second plantation society specializing in the cultivation of rice and indigo, which produced a deep blue dye. By 1760 slaves of African descent comprised 60 percent of South Carolina's total population.

Social Ranks. The process of colonization was enormously disruptive to Old World ways of life, especially the manner in which Europeans sorted themselves into social ranks and roles. The first generations of Englishmen to settle in America tried to preserve a traditional belief that only a few persons inherited the capacity to rule. Persons born below the lofty station of "gentlemen" sorted themselves into lesser ranks according to their landholding and occupation, designating their relative importance with titles such as Mr., Mrs., goodman, and goodwife. Persons in higher social ranks termed themselves the "better sort" or the "gentry." They expected deference from "the middling sort" and "lower orders," and ordinary people usually gave their "betters" their due. Farmers, artisans, and laborers took off their hats and bowed or curtsied to important people when meeting them in the street. They yielded the best seats in churches and public meetings to their betters, consistently elected gentlemen to the higher public offices, and dutifully accepted the elite's judgment in matters both public and private. Yet these traditional ranks were unstable in America. For one thing neither the highest orders of English society nor the lowest came to America in great numbers. Many immigrants, including most indentured servants, came from the ranks of urban artisans and shopkeepers along with a smaller number of farmers.

Upward Mobility. All were anxious to preserve or improve their lot in life, and widespread availability of land made it possible for a great majority to do so by becoming freeholders, designating them as outright property owners which was far less common as an achievement in England. While new opportunities in America made it possible for enterprising colonists to amass greater landholdings, wealth, and status than would have been possible in England, the perils of New World settlement also exposed some people from established families to financial ruin. Many new family names appeared in the ranks of the colonial elite. In Virginia families such as the Byrds, Madisons, Randolphs, Washingtons, Lees, and Carters rose from seventeenth-century obscurity to leadership of their eighteenth-century province. In Philadelphia a poor Boston chandler's son by the name of Benjamin Franklin amassed a fortune in publishing and assumed the place of a gentleman who could pursue philanthropy, governmental service, and scientific investigation. Ambitious young men were not content, as their fathers had been, to remain in the station to which they were born. They insisted on their right to make their own place in the world according to their character and abilities. The Spanish borderlands and New France likewise experienced some shifting of social ranks. The encomienda system in Spanish North America rewarded enterprising soldiers with land grants and rights to collect tribute from conquered peoples. This made it possible for some men to rise to the status in many ways comparable to a feudal lord. Similarly in New France the rank of seigneur was granted to many colonial families that had achieved wealth through trading or other colonial enterprises. Few European colonists anywhere in North America openly challenged the social structure of the homelands. Most instead regarded it as a mark of civilization and stability and sought to preserve it even while moving up within it.

Labor. Throughout the colonial period a scarcity of laborers profoundly shaped early American societies. Settlers turned to various options to fill their labor needs. In New England, the Middle Colonies, and the backcountry large families commonly consisting of six or more members provided most of the labor on the farms. This in turn produced a steady increase in the population, a growing density of settlement in coastal New England as farmers divided their lands among their male heirs, and a steady expansion of settlement throughout these regions. By contrast early Chesapeake planters relied on the unfree labor of single young men driven by hard economic times in England to sign indentures committing them to several years of servitude. Far more men than women came to cultivate Chesapeake tobacco. The population languished, and Virginia freedmen who had served out their terms eventually formed a large, volatile class of landless poor with insufficient resources to establish their own plantations.

Slaves. In the later seventeenth century a dwindling supply of English indentured servants prompted planters to meet their needs for labor by purchasing large numbers of African slaves. South Carolinians likewise relied on slave labor from the 1670s as many planters from Barbados brought their African slaves with them to carve out new settlements. By 1700 the Chesapeake and South Carolina had become slave societies, ones in which the economy depended almost exclusively on forced labor, and the great numbers of slaves shaped the entire social system. Northern colonists continued to rely on indentured servitude to meet the demand for skilled labor in the growing cities, domestic labor in wealthy households, field hands on farms, and manual labor in such enterprises as iron foundries. Some northern colonists also met this need with African American slaves, which was legal everywhere in colonial America. Yet the slave population in the Middle Colonies and New England remained relatively small, and the northern economy and society never came to depend on slavery as did the Chesapeake and Lower South. The French initially imported contract laborers similar to English indentured servants who worked for a stated number of years and then returned home. The Spanish generally harnessed the labor of Native Americans through a variety of devices. Slavery was technically illegal, but many Spanish settlers found ways around the law by using the encomienda to exploit the labor of Indian farmers and cattle herders.

African Americans. The variety of societies and conditions that existed in colonial America resulted in diverse experiences for people of African descent. African captives brought with them a range of languages, beliefs, and practices that they had to adapt both to their new environment and to each other, combining them with selected European elements to produce true African American cultures. In the South Carolina and Georgia rice country slaves worked on a "task system" that permitted them to devote time to other pursuits after daily completion of an assigned task. Slaves outnumbered Europeans in the Lower South, and plantation owners spent the hot summers on the seacoast away from their plantations. In this environment the slaves were able to form communities and shape a culture with a rich mixture of African customs. The lives and work of slaves in the Chesapeake were much more regulated in a "gang system" of labor that kept them in tobacco fields all day. Planter families outnumbered slaves in the Chesapeake and remained on the plantations year-round, bringing Africans into constant contact with their English masters. Nevertheless, Chesapeake slaves were able to form nurturing communities bound by a distinctive African American culture that they passed down to later generations. Further north the conditions of slavery were often milder, but the much smaller slave population made it difficult to create the kind of communities that could sustain the survival of African traditions. In the eighteenth century free African American communities began to emerge in parts of New England, in the Middle Colonies, and in Charleston, South Carolina. People living in these communities often faced discrimination from their white neighbors, finding themselves shunted into separate neighborhoods and onto poorer lands. In addition they were often denied rights enjoyed by the English inhabitants of their colonies. Nevertheless, they developed tightly knit communities held by bonds of culture, kinship, and faith.

Commerce, Culture, and Communication. The great European powers that settled North America did so for other reasons besides commerce, but trade became the engine that fueled settlement, population growth, communications, and cultural ties with Europe. French settlements along the Saint Lawrence River began to draw colonists and establish strong cultural links with France only after the fur trade became firmly established. New Orleans, however, was settled initially to secure French military and political control of territory. French inhabitants there and in sparse settlements along the Mississippi and Ohio Rivers struggled throughout the colonial period to establish viable commerce. Spain likewise settled the borderlands of North America for geopolitical reasons. Trade and communications networks followed far-flung military and mission supply lines, serving a small, scattered population. These networks remained inefficient for most of the colonial period. English and Dutch colonization, by contrast, served commercial purposes from the beginning. Commerce in both strengthened the ties the colonies had with the mother countries. Even the Plymouth settlers, religiously motivated as they were, traded avidly with Native Americans for furs during the colony's first years. Early Massachusetts Bay colonists made money selling lumber and agricultural goods to those who settled later, and their governor, John Winthrop, established an important export market for Massachusetts grain and meat in the British West Indies. The fur trade fueled New Netherland's early growth, and the colony formed a crucial link in a larger Dutch Atlantic trading network. As a result the colony became a valuable commercial prize for the English in 1664. Virginia planters prospered with tobacco, and the sugar trade made many West Indian planters fabulously wealthy. Nevertheless, England's colonial trade policy was haphazard, and until the 1660s Dutch shippers and merchants profited most from the plantation goods grown in English colonies. The British Navigation Acts, passed in part to wrest control of the colonial trade from the Dutch, laid the foundations for a more coherent commercial policy. By 1700 a system of colonial administration was in place to enforce British colonial trade policies, and it did so quite effectively. Trade flourished throughout the British North Atlantic, providing the colonists as well as England with a host of benefits. Travel became quicker and more reliable as English ship makers improved sailing technology and the number of ships sailing the Atlantic increased. Because American-built ships, captains, and crews were protected under the Navigation Acts, colonial shipping flourished, and transatlantic communication improved dramatically. Colonial exports also increased steadily year by year. Most significantly the burgeoning colonial population provided a ready market for English manufactured goods. Over time all these developments exerted a powerful impact on colonial society and culture.

Expanding Awareness. As the colonies grew from isolated seventeenth-century outposts to prosperous eighteenth-century provinces, travel, communication, and trade enabled colonists to learn more about each other as well as keep abreast of dramatic developments that were transforming life throughout the Atlantic world. Ships sailed along the coast and across the ocean with increasing frequency, distributing news from Europe and other colonies throughout colonial ports where it could make its way inland. Educated colonists purchased European books and journals to keep up with the latest advances in scientific knowledge, theology, law, and politics. Colonial newspapers began appearing to keep readers informed of the latest developments in European affairs as well as selected matters of interest from other colonies. Wealthy gentry families cultivated transatlantic friendships with persons of influence in European society, and the richest sent their sons to Europe for genteel educations in the liberal arts and law. As 1750 approached, colonists exhibited an increasing awareness of their place in a vast Atlantic world of exciting possibilities and daunting challenges.

TOPICS IN THE NEWS

BRITISH AMERICAN CONSUMERS

Seventeenth Century. Few settlers lived completely independent of imported goods at any time in the colonial period. Indeed, English settlement followed paths blazed by traders who acquired furs from Native Americans in exchange for European manufactured goods. Early colonists in New England and the Chesapeake tried to sustain this trade by introducing items such as new metal goods, woolen fabrics, and firearms. The new European trade goods rapidly transformed Native American ways of life. Settlers who arrived earlier also relied on a constant influx of later colonists who brought such goods as nails, gunpowder, lead shot, glass, cooking utensils, books, and cloth to trade for food and lumber. Seventeenth-century tobacco planters traded their crops with Dutch and English merchants for various European products while their contemporaries in Massachusetts traded grain and salt pork for West Indian sugar, molasses, and rum. A modest flow of English products arrived in colonial ports throughout the seventeenth century, much of it purchased by wealthier colonists for their own use and some for resale to their neighbors.

Eighteenth Century. In the early eighteenth century the flow of consumer goods began a slow rise, exploding to a full-blown consumer revolution during the 1740s. The rise in colonial consumption came not because of the English industrial revolution, for that remained some distance in the future; instead early-eighteenth-century British artisans learned how to increase production using traditional methods. The increased production lowered the prices of goods, so more buyers could afford them. Even more important, producers learned how to create a demand for those goods with appealing newspaper advertisements, innovative product exhibits, and attractive shop-window displays. By 1740 ever-increasing amounts

A silver sugar box, made by Edward Winslow of Boston in 1702, and a pewter quart tankard, crafted by Simon Edgell of Philadelphia, 1713–1742 (The Henry Francis du Pont Winterthur Museum, Winterthur, Delaware)

Many colonial families adorned their homes with imported goods although the elite often found such practices among the poorer classes to be pretentious. The Scottish physician and traveler Alexander Hamilton exemplifies this view in the following account of his visit to the household of a New Yorker, with a companion, "Mr. M——s":

This cottage was very clean and neat, but poorly furnished, yet Mr. M——s observed several superfluous things which showed an inclination to finery in these poor people; such as a looking-glass with a painted frame, half a dozen pewter spoons, and as many plates, old and wore out, but bright and clean, a set of stone tea dishes and a teapot. These Mr. M——ls said were superfluous, and too splendid for such a cottage, and therefore they ought to be sold to buy wool to make yarn; that a little water in a wooden pail might serve for a looking-glass, and wooden plates and spoons would be as good for use, and when clean would be almost as ornamental. As for the tea equippage it was quite unnecessary.

Source: Alexander Hamilton, *Itinerarium*, edited by Robert M. Goldwyn (New York: Arno, 1971).

of textiles, ceramics, glass products, paper, finished metal goods, and teas were becoming available at prices lower, and of a higher quality, than most American producers could match.

Shopping. English goods made their way into colonial households in a variety of ways. Throughout the era merchants such as the Long Island whale-oil exporter Samuel Mumford kept small stores of English imported goods that they could sell for cash or barter for country produce such as grain or tobacco, which they in turn sold on the international market. Many southern planters kept stores of imported goods for sale to their neighbors. The Virginian Ralph Wormeley, for example, kept a trunkful of goods under his bed. Northern port cities such as Boston and New York also boasted specialty shops where persons could purchase items such as fabric, pins, tools, and building supplies, but elsewhere people sold consumer goods mainly to supplement their primary livelihoods as farmers or artisans. As the volume of exports rose in the eighteenth century, specialized retail shops began springing up throughout America. Many were locally owned, but in the South many were virtual chain stores run by factors and owned by merchants based in Glasgow, Scotland. Owners learned to arrange their wares in attractive shop-window and indoor displays where prospective buyers could browse and compare. Itinerant peddlers also wended their way through the countryside, carrying wares to smaller communities and country farmhouses where imported items were harder to come by.

Customs and Decor. The consumer revolution exerted a powerful impact on the habits, tastes, and self-perceptions of British Americans. By midcentury many items once enjoyed as luxuries by colonial elites became an expected part of everyday life. In 1700, for example, tea rarely appeared outside the homes of colonial elites, whose servants poured it from expensive, specially made serving pots into special cups as refreshment for honored guests. By 1750 many ordinary farmers and artisans habitually enjoyed daily tea served from inexpensive ceramic such as delftware, sweetened with a lump or two of sugar (which fifty years before had likewise been a luxury). Imports began changing table manners as well. Family members who might once have shared meals from a single wooden trencher began eating from their own individual ceramic plates or bowls, lifting food to their lips with spoons or sometimes forks instead of fingers. Women and men began adorning their clothes with English lace and buttons, accenting their parlors with brassware, and covering their beds with linen. Wealthy householders covered their floors with fine rugs imported from Turkey by English merchants, adorned their walls with rich Oriental tapestries, and draped their windows with elegant Dutch fabrics.

Colonial Identity. As colonists dressed, ate, drank, and decorated more like their cousins on the other side of the Atlantic, they came to think of themselves as inhabitants of civilized provinces rather than rustic colonies. As British Americans they shared with their cousins in En-

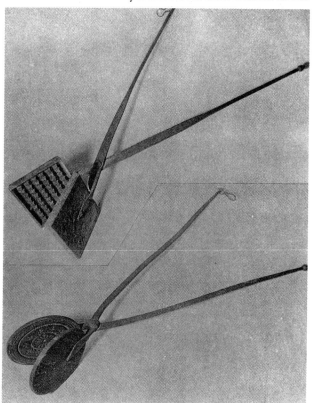

Waffle irons made in New Jersey in the late seventeenth century (Private Collection)

gland a common identity, an enjoyment of finery, and loyalties to king and Commonwealth. This effort to imitate things English resulted in a growing similarity among colonial cultures that had been strikingly diverse in 1700. At that time no colonist living in 1750 could have imagined his own province uniting with other American colonies to form a nation independent of the British Crown. Americans celebrated their place in what they regarded as the greatest, freest, most enlightened empire the world had ever known, and they increasingly looked to the British Isles as the source of the goods that they believed could make their lives decent, respectable, and civilized.

Sources:

John Brewer and Roy Porter, eds., *Consumption and the World of Goods* (London: Routledge, 1993);

Carole Shammas, *The Pre-Industrial Consumer in England and America* (Oxford, U.K.: Oxford University Press, 1990).

FASHION

Early Styles. The first generation of European settlers brought with them the fashions of their day, which functioned to place them within specific social ranks as well as to adorn them. Dutch settlers of all ranks wore clothing of similar style, but their social rank was distinguished by the relative coarseness or fineness of the fabric. French settlers distinguished their rank both by the type of cloth used and by the style. The early soldier-settlers of the Spanish borderlands clad themselves in

Dress gloves worn by Gov. John Leverett of Massachusetts circa 1645. Gold and silver threads are woven through the cuffs (Peabody Essex Museum, Salem, Massachusetts).

military attire but always kept an eye trained on the finery of the wealthy at home, whom they intended to emulate once they achieved New World wealth and position. Portraits of English settlers of this period depict gentlemen and ladies in dashing Elizabethan garments adorned with showy lace collars and cuffs and reveal that colonists of Massachusetts Bay shared Virginia adventurers' taste for fashionable clothes. Puritan ministers urged people to renounce the outer vanity of ostentatious dress for the inward adornment of a pious life. New England magistrates tried to enforce their ministers' teaching through laws regulating dress. Nevertheless, Puritans were not limited to somber clothing of black and gray. The laws aimed mainly at preventing ordinary farmers or craftsmen from dressing ostentatiously or "above their station" in clothing regarded as appropriate only for wealthy and important families. Puritans were generally free to clothe themselves in the range of colors and styles appropriate to their rank or position in society. The persistent anxiety of ministers and magistrates over clothing suggests that Puritan men and women never lost their eye for fashion and constantly pushed the limits of the law with fancy clothes and accessories.

American Influence. Fashions in the middle and later seventeenth century were dictated by the materials available to most settlers as well as by adaptations to their new environment. Settlers of the Spanish borderlands and New France sometimes adapted elements of Native American dress and adapted their apparel to the climate. French settlers often dressed in buckskin, and the hooded wool coat known as a capote characteristically shielded men from the icy Canadian winds. To enforce the racial caste system of New Spain, a law of 1582 prohibited mestizo women (those of mixed Spanish and In-

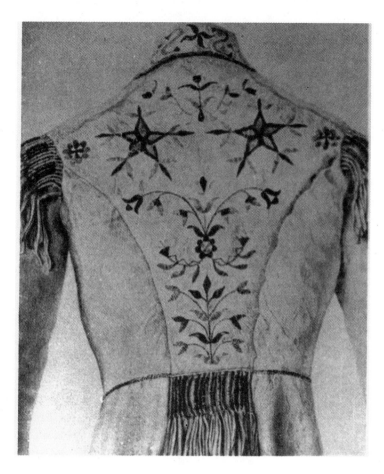

A buckskin coat made by the Cree Indians of Canada, circa 1750. While the design is European, the decorations are made from porcupine quills (Denver Art Museum).

dian blood) from wearing Native American dresses. These women adopted a shawl known as the rebozo, which over time came to be finely crafted and decorated. English colonists brought with them a knowledge of spinning and weaving. They never developed a large textile industry, however, and imported cloth was relatively scarce and expensive. Homespun woolens and linens became the common apparel of ordinary seventeenth-century Americans. Yet the bewigged figures of portraits reveal that prominent colonists—even Puritan ministers such as Cotton Mather—continued to imitate the styles of their English contemporaries.

London. After 1700 a growing range of English textiles began flowing into colonial ports; prices dropped so low that colonial producers could not compete; and some households no longer found it worthwhile to invest time and labor in producing inferior homespun cloth. Newspapers advertised the varieties of English and Dutch chintzes, silks, linens, damasks, woolens, velvets, and laces. They also included other items of apparel and accessories such as stockings, gloves, and buttons. Tailors placed their own advertisements nearby, enticing customers with their ability to cut and sew in the "latest London fashions." Diarists traveling the countryside often recorded remarks on the widespread imitation of

European fashion in America. In 1740 the Anglican preacher George Whitefield remarked on the fashionable dress of audiences from Massachusetts to Georgia, going so far as to declare that his followers in Charleston, South Carolina, dressed more extravagantly than gentry from the "court-end of London!" Portraiture of eighteenth-century gentry bears out the observations of diarists such as Whitefield, and historians studying wills and probate records have discovered that ordinary colonists imitated the fashions of their betters by buying and wearing an increasing range of cheap imported items. Many colonial leaders worried that the widespread wearing of fashionable wigs, fancy dresses, handsome waistcoats, silk stockings, and silver buckles was making it increasingly difficult to distinguish the gentry from their inferiors. Advertisements for runaways reveal that indentured servants and slaves were dressing in the cast-off fashions of the period.

The Frontier. Eighteenth-century backcountry apparel often contrasted sharply with that worn on the coast. Traders and settlers adopted certain articles of Native American clothing such as buckskin or woolen leggings both to establish cultural ties with them and because the clothing was better adapted to the environment. The Indian commissioner Sir William Johnson

A heavy oxhide coat made in the 1640s and once owned by Gov. John Leverett (Massachusetts Historical Society, Boston)

adopted Iroquois dress to help him gain trust and understanding as he pursued diplomacy among the Six Nations of upstate New York. Further south in the Carolina backcountry the Anglican missionary Charles Woodmason expressed shock at women who went about barefoot and immodestly dressed for that time in thin, tight-fitting garments that exposed their lower legs. Such women's apparel was partly the result of poverty and partly an adaptation to the hot southern climate. The adaptations were usually temporary as well: frontier settlers could seldom resist fancy eastern fashions when they became available at affordable prices.

Sources:

Cary Carson, Ronald Hoffman, and Peter J. Albert, eds., *Of Consuming Interests: The Style of Life in the Eighteenth Century* (Charlottesville: University Press of Virginia, 1994);

Jack Cassin-Scott, *Costume and Fashion in Colour, 1550–1760* (Poole, U.K.: Blandford Press, 1975);

Alice Morse Earle, *Costume of Colonial Times* (Detroit: Gale, 1974).

GENDER

Two Worlds. The historian Laurel Thatcher Ulrich has compared women's and men's roles in early British American society to a checked fabric of contrasting threads that could make a whole cloth—or a whole society—only when woven together. Men and women lived portions of their lives in separate, complementary spheres, but their daily experiences overlapped at many significant points. Within the colonial household women were expected to occupy a position of subordination to the authority of their husbands, who were conceived to be the heads of house and family in a system known as patriarchy. The realities of day-to-day living may have resulted in more-mutual cooperation than the ideal suggests. While men dominated the political and legal life of the world outside the household, women

were not excluded from larger social life. Only men could vote and hold office, while women were seen as perpetual dependents and therefore excluded from the political life of the community. Distinctive patterns of gender relations emerged in different areas, however, according to the ethnic background of the colonists and the circumstances of colonization. In New England, which was settled by family units, a rough imbalance in the numbers of women and men permitted many European patterns of gender relations to be imported with minor adaptations. New Netherland and the Chesapeake area, by contrast, were settled initially by single males. The imbalance between men and women resulted in much more adaptation. In New France a similar situation coupled with the trading nature of the colony resulted in significant intermarriage with the Native American population. Gender relations in the Spanish borderlands were marked by the presence of mixed-race marriages within a rigid social hierarchy.

Sexual Hierarchy. Throughout the European colonies of North America women occupied a subordinate place both legally and culturally. A woman in English colonial society operated as a *feme covert:* she could act as her child's guardian or as manager of the family's property, but she could receive pay for her labor only in the name of her husband. Single women might own property by inheritance or purchase, but marriage laws usually required them to transfer their property to their husband as the head of the household formed by their marriage. Dutch and French colonial law and custom likewise rele-

Albany patroon Abraham Wendell, circa 1737, portrait by an unknown artist (Albany Institute of History and Art, Albany, New York)

A sampler made by Mary Hollingsworth, Salem, Massachusetts, circa 1670 (Peabody Essex Museum, Salem, Massachusetts)

men the responsibility of managing the household and making a livelihood. Both might participate in the plowing and planting of a field, the harvesting and processing of the crops, or the care of livestock and poultry. Pioneer couples in New France shared tasks of clearing land and establishing a household. English men, however, tended to avoid domestic tasks such as food preparation and the tending of young children, sticking instead to the tasks of tilling land, mending fences, and maintaining buildings. As the farm became established, Anglo-American husbands and wives tended to divide other tasks more clearly. Men might herd and shear sheep, for example, while the women carded, spun, and wove or knitted the wool into fabric. Life in Franco-American households, by contrast, never became so sharply separated. Farming and the production of goods were tasks shared by the entire household.

Opportunities. In British colonial towns and cities trade and commerce were dominated by men as well, but women carried on significant commercial activities. Sometimes a woman ran a family shop during her husband's absence or owned outright a tavern or retail shop. A Dutch colonial woman likewise assumed the management of a husband's business during his absence and often operated it successfully upon his death. In New France a man's career in the military or government might provide his wife or daughter an opportunity to begin a lucrative business of her own. New France boasted women among the leading ranks of entrepreneurs: Agathe de Saint Père established Montreal's textile industry; Mesdames de la Tour and Joybert shipped furs from Acadia; and Louise de Ramezay ran a large Montreal lumber operation. A wife on a Spanish American hacienda often served as her husband's accountant, ran the estate in his absence, and frequently assumed the entire operation at her husband's death. Anglo-American midwives—women who assisted mothers in childbirth—provided a more humble but indispensable paid service in colonial health care. Their duties regularly carried them outside their own homes and families to tend to the needs of others, and their knowledge of health matters often extended beyond their skills in midwifery to treatments and herbal remedies for many ills. African women who were brought to the colonies as slaves were often put to work in tobacco or rice fields alongside men and expected to accomplish nearly as much daily work. In domestic work and trades, however, African men's and women's tasks were distinguished. Only men could become artisans, while women were put to domestic tasks such as cooking, nursing, and spinning.

Community of Women. In British American society females formed nurturing communities among themselves apart from the community of males. Older women in New England watched over the behavior and well-being of younger women, giving them advice, counsel, and protection in their dealings with husbands, children, and other members of the community. Religious groups

gated women to a subordinate social position, though in practice this hierarchy often broke down. In the Spanish borderlands the sexual hierarchy was both strongly asserted by men and resisted by women. The Virgin of Guadalupe came to symbolize for Spanish American women the ideals of charity, good mothering, and devoted wifeliness. La Malinche, a Native American woman who had been Hernán Cortés's translator and mistress, came to symbolize the betrayal of these ideals in Spanish borderland tradition.

Work. The patterns of work for women and men changed over time throughout the European colonies in America. Most free women in the English colonies lived and worked on farms, where they usually divided with such as Quakers and Baptists gave women formal authority over the conduct and welfare of young girls. Quaker women even held special meetings to deal with offenses such as unsupervised weddings, marriages to non-Quakers, and sexual relations before marriage. Offenders who refused to repent in these meetings could be cast out: forbidden to attend any further meetings or to associate with other Quakers. Women often came together at the birth of a child as well. While midwives took charge of delivering the baby, female neighbors and relatives would gather to assist, offer support, socialize, and celebrate or commiserate together as circumstances required. Less is currently known about the kinds of communities formed by women in non-English colonies, but the Roman Catholic Church did provide for two types of female community not found in Protestant colonies: convents and hospitals. Women could enter convents and devote their lives to serving the church. Daughters of rich colonists often brought with them their dowries—the portion of family wealth set aside to support them in their marriages. With this money they often established comfortable lives for themselves as nuns. They also provided important services in social welfare through hospitals that cared for the sick and indigent. French nuns ran such hospitals at Louisbourg, Quebec, Trois-Rivières, Montreal, and New Orleans. Spanish colonial laywomen as well as nuns centered much of their lives around the church or mission, participating together not only in religious processions or celebrations but also in mundane tasks such as cleaning sanctuaries and priests' robes and maintaining buildings.

Sources:

Carol Berkin, *First Generations: Women in Colonial America* (New York: Hill & Wang, 1996);

Clio Collective, *Quebec Women: A History* (Toronto, Canada: Women's Press, 1987);

Ramón A. Gutiérrez, *When Jesus Came, the Corn Mothers Went Away: Marriage, Sexuality, and Power in New Mexico, 1500–1846* (Stanford, Cal.: Stanford University Press, 1991).

HOUSING

European Designs. The structure and size of European houses varied widely throughout North America and changed dramatically as the period wore on. The first settlers brought the construction methods they had known in the Old World and adapted them to the materials and requirements of their New World environment. English builders of the first generations patterned dwellings on the English "hall and parlor" plan, in which each house had two equal-sized main rooms separated by a single fireplace. Dutch and French farmhouses shared this same basic floor plan, though their external appearance differed according to styles preferred by their countrymen. Both rooms had multiple uses. The parlor usually served as a bedroom as well as for various work and family functions. The other room in Dutch dwellings was called a *groot kamer,* or "best room," and served for social occasions as well as

SHARING ROOMS AND BEDS

People staying overnight in colonial inns or private houses often found themselves sharing their rooms and even their beds with total strangers. The traveling doctor Alexander Hamilton woke up one morning in a New York country inn to find

"two beds in the room, besides that in which I lay, in one of which lay two great hulking fellows, with long black beards, having their own hair, and not so much as half a nightcap betwixt both of them. I took them for weavers, not only from their greasy appearance, but because I observed a weaver's loom at each side of the room. In the other bed was a raw-boned boy, who, with the two lubbers, huddled on his clothes, and went reeling downstairs, making as much noise as three horses."

Source: Alexander Hamilton, *Itinerarium,* edited by Robert M. Goldwyn (New York: Arno, 1971).

sleeping. In the hall general-purpose activities occurred such as cooking, eating, and work. For English and French settlers it was often the core room of the house and was used for entertaining as well as work and eating. Many residents built lofts for additional sleeping or storage, and as a family grew, it might add rooms to house a separate kitchen, bedchamber, or storeroom. These floor plans encouraged communal living. Whole families commonly slept in the same room, the parents in a large bed and the children in a smaller one or on pallets by the hearth. Overnight guests often shared the family bed with their hosts. Even when family members slept in separate rooms they had to pass through one to reach another, and they carried out most of their daily activities in close proximity to each other. Dwellings in the Spanish borderlands varied considerably from region to region according to the climate and building materials available. In Saint Augustine a distinctive long, rectangular house emerged; inhabitants of New Mexico constructed long adobe houses only a single room deep.

Adaptations. As the seventeenth century wore on, house structures changed somewhat. New England builders came to locate the fireplace consistently at the center of the house, where the warmth of the chimney would heat the interior more efficiently, a practice also common in New France. Builders further south tended to place fireplaces at the ends, where the heat would be carried away during the hot summers, or even to build separate "summer kitchens" so that daily cooking would not make the main house intolerably warm. Timber, which had been scarce in England, was plentiful in America. Builders took advantage of this abundance by siding homes entirely in wood and roofing the houses with wooden shingles instead of thatch or slate. Almost no first-generation English settler had ever seen a log cabin, but by 1700 settlers in frontier

Westover Plantation, Virginia, built by William Byrd II around 1730–1735

New Hampshire were building log houses sided with clapboards, and settlers in the Middle Colonies were imitating the log-cabin design introduced to America by Swedish settlers. Dwellings in the Spanish borderlands of the Southwest were built of adobe or stone where available and were commonly adapted for purposes of defense in this thinly populated region. Inhabitants of towns commonly built their houses close together around a central plaza so that their outer walls could double as a fort. Haciendas were structured the same way for similar reasons, with dwellings and outbuildings arranged in squares around central patios.

Genteel Architecture. By 1700 wealthier English colonists were importing new European fashions in house design as they built larger, more formal structures planned by professional architects. The gentry wanted to display their wealth, importance, and civilized tastes in large structures graced with elegant, symmetrical lines and brick construction. They desired ornamental exterior woodwork and beautifully finished interiors. They forsook the simple hall and parlor floor plan for multiple rooms with specialized uses, separated by corridors to allow for greater privacy. Children and parents began to sleep in different rooms, and bedchambers were often located on the second floor, away from the parlors and halls where guests were entertained. Ordinary colonists gradually began imitating the symmetrical Georgian exteriors of gentry homes and began fulfilling a newfound desire for privacy with specialized rooms separated by corridors and partitions. Some mid-eighteenth-century

gentry also built great houses that incorporated various features of the Palladian style, with large porticos and modular, symmetrical plans.

African Americans. The dwellings of a growing population of Africans, the great majority of whom were slaves, contrasted sharply with the houses of great planters, though less so with those of many free white family farmers. In the eighteenth century many slaves built their own dwellings from materials provided by their masters. Whether they used English or African construction methods, slaves often organized their dwellings in patterns that supported communal ways of life they had known in Africa. Single-room structures were often built around a common central area where slaves could interact, share household work, and play together when time permitted. Free African Americans tended to adopt European designs in their housing.

Sources:

James Deetz, *In Small Things Forgotten: The Archeology of Early American Life* (Garden City, N.Y.: Anchor Press, 1977);

James Early, *The Colonial Architecture of Mexico* (Albuquerque: University of New Mexico Press, 1994);

Robert Lionel Séguin, *La Maison en Nouvelle-France* (Ottawa: National Museum of Canada, 1968);

Mechal Sobel, *The World They Made Together: Black and White Values in Eighteenth-Century Virginia* (Princeton, N.J.: Princeton University Press, 1987);

Dell Upton, *Common Places: Readings in American Vernacular Architecture* (Athens: University of Georgia Press, 1986).

Slave quarters at Mulberry Plantation, built in the eighteenth century near Charleston, South Carolina (Gibbes Museum of Art / CAA Collection, Charleston, South Carolina)

IMMIGRANTS ON THE MOVE

Mobility. No matter where a visitor to colonial America looked, he or she could find people on the move. For many individuals and families, in fact, the long move that brought them across the Atlantic to America was only the longest in a series of moves that began in the British Isles or on the European continent. The Pilgrims who settled Plymouth colony had first left England to seek refuge from religious persecution in Holland before embarking for the New World. Families who sailed from England to Massachusetts Bay could often remember when they, their parents, or their grandparents had first moved from country villages to larger English towns such as Ipswich and Great Yarmouth in search of jobs in manufacturing. Thousands of single young people traveled from the seventeenth-century English countryside to London in search of opportunity. Many of them took passage to Virginia and Maryland as indentured servants, hoping to learn tobacco planting and establish their own plantations after completing their terms of service. The mobility that brought settlers to America was not confined to England. In the 1680s German Anabaptists took advantage of William Penn's offer of cheap farmland in his newly founded colony of Pennsylvania, settling around Germantown. Waves of Mennonite and Amish immigrants soon followed. Around 1710 German refugees from the regions near the Rhine River arrived in London, and English officials relocated hundreds of them to settlements of the upper Hudson and Mohawk Rivers in New York to make pine tar for the Royal Navy. A steady flow of German Palatines poured into Pennsylvania in the following decades to compose more than a third of the colony's population by 1766. Scotch-Irish tenant farmers, whose parents or grandparents had left Scotland to settle in northern Ireland, also began a new migration to America as Ulster rents increased and Anglican officials persecuted them for their Presbyterian beliefs. Throughout the eighteenth century these Scotch-Irish settlers streamed onto cheap western lands in Pennsylvania, Virginia, and the Carolinas at a rate of four thousand per year.

Regional Differences. Once people arrived in British America their movements varied from region to region. New England settlers moved slowly and methodically across the countryside, establishing stable towns in which families remained for several generations. Chesapeake planters established their plantations along navigable rivers where ships could easily dock to take on each year's tobacco crop. Poor men who had worked off their indentures often pressed further west to set up hardscrabble farms. In New York, New Jersey, and Pennsylvania patterns were even more mixed. Earlier groups of settlers tended to establish stable communities, but as the eighteenth century wore on, the population became increasingly mobile, each year pressing further west toward the backcountry

---

AVERAGE TRAVEL TIMES BY SAIL IN 1730

Boston to London: 7.5 weeks

New York to London: 9.2 weeks

Philadelphia to London: 9.8 weeks

Source: Ian K. Steele, *The English Atlantic, 1675–1740: An Exploration of Communication and Community* (New York: Oxford University Press, 1986).

Copy of a colonial indenture binding Mary Elizabeth Bauer to five years of labor for Samuel Pleasants
(Historical Society of Pennsylvania, Philadelphia)

and further south along the Appalachian Mountain range. By the 1760s it was not uncommon for backcountry settlements to spring up rapidly, flourish for a few years, and then dwindle as their inhabitants moved on. Eastern leaders in Pennsylvania, Maryland, Virginia, and the Carolinas worried about how such a shiftless population could be governed or kept loyal to the colonies and the Crown. An increasing incidence of backcountry rebellion in the last decade before the Revolution seemed to confirm their fears. Colonial officials never satisfactorily resolved the problem.

Sources:

Bernard Bailyn and Philip D. Morgan, eds., *Strangers within the Realm: The Cultural Margins of the First British Empire* (Chapel Hill: University of North Carolina Press, 1991);

Edward Countryman, *Americans: A Collision of Histories* (New York: Hill & Wang, 1996);

A. G. Roeber, *Palatines, Liberty, and Property: German Lutherans in Colonial British America* (Baltimore, Md.: Johns Hopkins University Press, 1993).

MARRIAGE AND THE FAMILY

Variety of Experiences. Several important variables produced significant differences in family life from col-ony to colony. The health of the climate and the ratio of men to women were important environmental and circumstantial factors. The social and legal definition of family produced important differences as well. English colonists generally organized the household in nuclear families composed of mother, father, and their offspring. The Puritan colonists of New England were able to preserve this ideal in practice. Early settlers immigrated in whole family units, so they began with a relatively favorable balance in the numbers of men to women. This balance remained throughout the colonial period. In addition the climate of New England proved remarkably healthy, and the land supported a variety of crops that helped the people maintain excellent nutrition. All family members were consequently healthier than their counterparts in either England or other early colonies, so infant mortality was low, and people lived longer.

The South. In early Virginia and Maryland, by contrast, deadly diseases and an unbalanced sex ratio produced much different family patterns. In the early seventeenth century many more men than women came to the Chesapeake, most of them single indentured servants who worked in tobacco fields. The smaller number of

FORDING A FLOODED RIVER

Traveling could be hazardous in the sparsely settled backcountry. People usually moved by trails rather than roads. They crossed rivers and streams either by wading across at shallow fords or by ferry boat. The experience of Charles Woodmason, an Anglican minister in the backcountry of South Carolina, illustrates the hazards of crossing during spring floods. Woodmason arrived at Thompson's Creek in mid February 1767. He and his horse had already swum several creeks, but this one was too deep and rapid. His first hope of being ferried across failed when the rapids sank the ferry raft before he could get on board. A resident then found a "very large strong and High Horse" that could swim a spot where the waters were less rapid. Woodmason and his escort undressed, tied their clothes in a bundle over their heads, clambered on the horse, and entered the water. People lined both banks to fetch them out if they slipped off. They arrived safely on the opposite bank, but Woodmason "was almost stiff and torpid with the Cold, and being in the Cold Water—the Wind blowing very sharp at N.E. and Ground cover'd with Ice."

Source: Charles Woodmason, *The Carolina Backcountry on the Eve of the Revolution: The Journal and Other Writings of Charles Woodmason, Anglican Itinerant* (Chapel Hill: University of North Carolina Press, 1953).

young indentured women who came often found prospective husbands who paid off their terms of service early so they could marry. Plantation owners sometimes brought wives with them as well, but the overall ratio of women to men remained imbalanced, and there were not enough families to sustain the population until the 1680s. The unhealthy climate also took a heavy toll as many succumbed to diseases such as malaria, typhus, and dysentery. Few seventeenth-century Chesapeake families survived intact until the children reached adulthood. Families therefore came to extend beyond the nuclear unit to include step-siblings and cousins.

French and Spanish Colonies. In New Netherland, New France, and the Spanish borderlands family life was also shaped in important ways by the small number of women in proportion to men. Family life in New Netherland was unstable until Peter Stuyvesant became director general of the colony in 1647 and began working for policies that would encourage the formation of nuclear family units. New regulations encouraged more families to immigrate during Stuyvesant's term, bringing more stability to the colony as a result. New France achieved a relative balance in the sex ratio only after 1710, but the healthy climate contributed to stable nuclear family households. The small number of Spanish women in the

borderlands prompted the first soldier-settlers to take Native American women as wives. Yet the Spanish government worked hard to promote the immigration of Iberian women to marry and create an upper class of largely Spanish descent. This situation resulted in substantial diversity in family life and customs according to racial class, though extended families became quite common in the Spanish borderlands.

Matrimony. Like other social patterns in colonial North America, marriage habits and customs varied by colony, ethnic background, and social rank. Love was only one reason for colonists to wed and often not the most important. New England Puritans thought a happy marriage depended on love between prospective partners. Meanwhile other colonists did not think love a nec-

DAILY DIET

Well-to-do travelers' accounts of diet in America report what sounds deceptively like a delectable variety of poultry, pork, venison, fish, oysters, vegetables, and fruits among the dishes served by their hosts, often leaving unsaid that their hosts took special pains to feed them unusually well. Undoubtedly colonial gentry often enjoyed substantial variety in a cuisine that might include a number of separate dishes per meal. Most colonists, however, did not have the time, the available labor, or the inclination to lay out such fancy meals. Nearly every day they took their main meals from an iron pot that hung over the fire constantly and required little tending. Whatever food was in season went into the pot: beans, turnips, parsnips, carrots, onions, pumpkins, corn, and meat (when available) were all cooked together into a pulp. Seasoning—if it was done at all—consisted of parsley, hyssop, thyme, marjoram, salt, and sometimes pepper. Few English colonists developed a taste for the wide variety of vegetables enjoyed today, but maize, or corn, adopted from Native Americans, became a staple of colonial diet everywhere. In the summertime it was commonly eaten on the cob. Northerners pounded it into samp and made porridge out of it. In Southern households it was processed into hominy, which might be eaten whole kernel. It was also commonly ground into grits, which was then made into porridge. Beans were also adopted from Native Americans, who taught Massachusetts settlers how to cook them in clay pots. Pigs were brought from England and permitted to roam free in American woods, where they multiplied quickly. They provided inland settlers with the most common source of protein.

Source: David Freeman Hawke, *Everyday Life in Early America* (New York: Harper & Row, 1988).

A seventeeth-century marriage medal set in the lid of a tankard. The Dutch inscription reads: "See here, Lady, whom I love, here is my faith, my heart and my desire next to God alone" (Brooklyn Museum).

essary prerequisite to marriage, though they did expect it to follow the taking of vows. Throughout all European colonies marriage could serve to create alliances between important families. Indeed, Spanish American aristocrats labored hard to limit their children's marriages to persons of their own rank. In the English colonies marriage could sometimes provide a way for young men or women to climb the social ladder into the ranks of the gentry. It might also strengthen the position of young gentlemen, as in the case of George Washington, whose marriage to the widow Martha Dandridge Custis brought him the additional lands and wealth needed to establish his place as one of the leading figures in Virginia.

Households. For most English colonists marriage also meant establishing a separate household and bringing new children into the world to insure that the family name would carry on, the church and community would have a strong future, and the household would have plenty of workers to make it prosper. Young Anglo-Americans who wanted to marry usually could choose their partners, though the parents watched closely to make sure that they made a suitable match. People's age at marriage varied by colony. In New England teen marriages were rare because fathers controlled the distribution of land to their sons and used that power to keep them at home until their early to mid twenties. Daughters generally waited until their twenties to marry as well. New England marriages were usually stable and long-lasting, with couples generally establishing households in separate dwellings and beginning to bear children within the first nine to fifteen months. In the Chesapeake, by contrast, a striking number of young women entered their first marriage before their sixteenth birthday, seven to ten years sooner than their counterparts in

English Puritans and Quakers held simple weddings in brides' homes where local justices of the peace officiated, with no religious ceremony or exchange of rings. Spanish American brides and grooms, by contrast, got married in churches with great ceremony and festivity. The celebration opened with a great procession in which the veiled bride, her father at her side, made her way from her home to the church and up the aisle to the altar, preceded by her bridesmaids, family, and friends. At the altar the father physically gave his daughter's hand to the groom. The priest, after reading an appropriate passage from one of the biblical accounts of Jesus' life, would step down to the couple and explain the meaning of marriage to the couple and the gathered community. He would conclude these remarks with the Latin statement *ego vos in matrimonium conjugo* (I unite you in marriage). The groom then gave a ring to his bride, slipping it on her left thumb first with the words "In the name of the Father," then on the index finger saying "and of the Son," next on the middle finger with "and of the Holy Spirit," and finally on the fourth finger with "Amen." Wealthy grooms gave bands of gold to their brides, while commoners gave bands of wood or leather. After the ring was given the couple was often wound with a large rosary or rope to symbolize their union. If he had not already done so a groom then gave the bride an *arras*, a symbolic endowment of a pouch containing thirteen coins. The priest often rented this item to a wedding party who might not otherwise be able to afford the custom. The wedding was solemnized with a mass and concluded with the priest giving the kiss of peace to the groom, which the groom then gave to the bride. Afterward the couple left the church amid music, gun salutes, and loud celebration, which served both to congratulate the couple and to ward off evil spirits.

Source: Ramon A. Gutierrez, *When Jesus Came, the Corn Mothers Went Away: Marriage, Sexuality, and Power in New Mexico, 1500–1846* (Stanford, Cal.: Stanford University Press, 1991).

either New or Old England. Death frequently separated fathers, mothers, and children: only one in three early Chesapeake marriages lasted as long as a decade. Because of the sex ratio imbalance a widow whose husband died usually remarried fairly soon, bringing any children of her first marriage with her and blending the families if her new husband also happened to be a widower with children. A woman might lose two or three husbands to death, bringing additional children into a subsequent marriage and producing complex patterns of extended family relations. This situation often gave Chesapeake women unprecedented power over their families and property since their husbands often willed them control of their estates at death, and they often enjoyed a favorable range of choice in potential mates. Yet the circumstances under which many women first arrived in the Chesapeake and the fragility of life there also must have made many of them feel extremely insecure.

Growing up in America. The way children grew up in colonial America depended in part on where they lived, what the family occupation was, and the child-rearing practices of their parents. Children in the Chesapeake grew up in insecure circumstances: so many were left without parents that officials in Maryland and Virginia had to set up special orphans' courts to see to their upbringing and to administrate inheritances. Elsewhere life was more stable, with children commonly growing up in nuclear families of seven or more siblings, though family size declined in eighteenth-century coastal settlements. A child's most carefree, playful years were generally short, confined to the first few years of life. Boys six and older who grew up on family farms, as over 90 percent of colonial Americans did, were needed as field hands and were trained to perform various tasks as soon as they could manage them. Girls were likewise needed to help with domestic tasks. In many regions boys and girls were also taught to read and write during these years, though boys commonly received more schooling than girls. Most colonists also recognized the early teens as pivotal years. Male youths assumed more responsibility for labor on the farm, occasionally assisted neighbors, and were sometimes apprenticed to learn a trade. Female teenagers served their own sort of apprenticeships by being "put out" as domestic servants in separate households.

Preparation for Adulthood. Colonial parents believed it necessary to prepare their children for a hierarchical society by shaping their wills in various ways. Children growing up in New England farming and artisan families were seen as wayward subjects of their parents' love whose wills must be broken so that their souls could be prepared for salvation and they could learn obedience. Parents tried to use gentle measures to teach a child to obey, but if those did not work the child might be whipped or forced to wear a painful device in his mouth or on his nose accompanied with written signs that proclaimed his offense. Parents of similar "middling" families elsewhere may not have used the signs or devices the Puritans used, but they did use spankings, deprivation, and other means of punishment to break or conform their children's wills

A Dutch *kas* (wardrobe) made of oak and gumwood, circa 1720
(Metropolitan Museum of Art, New York)

in ways demanded by their communities. Children of Chesapeake or Carolina planters had their wills shaped to encourage competitive assertiveness but also to observe the elaborate social rules that governed planter society. They were taught to bow or curtsy and address their parents respectfully whenever they approached them, to submit to their social superiors, to show courtesy to their equals by strict observance of etiquette, and to display benevolence to their social inferiors.

Slave Practices. Meanwhile a significant slave population was also emerging in the Chesapeake and would soon emerge in South Carolina as well. Slaves adapted various traditional African family arrangements to the constraints of slavery, producing a distinctive African American family life. Masters tended to encourage monogamy among their slaves, though on many plantations the African practice of polygamy survived into the nineteenth century. Slave children were brought up by their parents in large families, and the traditional pattern of extended families provided a large network of nurturing and protection for young children. This extended family network was important even when families remained intact, for mothers were frequently put back to work soon after childbirth. It took on additional importance if families were sepa-

rated through death or through the sale of a parent or child, a frequent occurrence. Families provided slaves indispensable ways of surviving: companionship, love, sympathetic understanding, and lessons in how to avoid punishment, cooperate with other slaves, and maintain a sense of self-worth. In the North, where slaves tended not to live in quarters with other slaves but in the attics, cellars, and sheds of their owners, family life was more difficult. Husbands and wives tended not to live with one another, and children were often sold at a young age since they took time away from their working mothers.

Sources:

Ramón Gutiérrez, *When Jesus Came, the Corn Mothers Went Away: Marriage, Sexuality, and Power in New Mexico, 1500–1846* (Stanford, Cal.: Stanford University Press, 1991);

Barry Levy, *Quakers and the American Family: British Settlement in the Delaware Valley* (New York: Oxford University Press, 1988);

Gerald F. Moran, *Religion, Family, and the Life Course: Exploration in the Social History of Early America* (Ann Arbor: University of Michigan Press, 1992);

William D. Piersen, *Black Yankees: The Development of an Afro-American Subculture in Eighteenth-Century New England* (Amherst: University of Massachusetts Press, 1988);

Laurel Thatcher Ulrich, *Good Wives: Image and Reality in the Lives of Women in Northern New England 1650–1750* (New York: Oxford University Press, 1983).

PUBLIC CELEBRATIONS AND RITUALS

Life Cycles. Certain rituals in colonial America marked the stages of a person's life from birth to death. For the majority of colonists these included infant baptisms, weddings, and funerals. Other rituals, such as admission to full church membership for Puritans, communion for Anglicans or Presbyterians, or believer's baptism for Anabaptists, further served to mark important passages in life. Wherever infant baptism was practiced in colonial America it served both to confer certain religious benefits on the newborn and to initiate him or her into a particular position within the local community, a position sometimes signified by the person who stood as the baby's guardian or godparent. While baptisms were religious ceremonies with minimal celebration attached, weddings might or might not be considered religious affairs and were almost always occasions for large communal festivities. Anglicans in Virginia and elsewhere viewed weddings as sacred rites to be officiated by a minister either in a church or in the bride's home and sealed by an exchange of rings and elaborate vows. Virginians commonly celebrated a wedding with feasting, dancing, and gift-giving that involved the whole community and could last for days. Puritans, by contrast, considered weddings strictly civil in nature. They were usually conducted at home, officiated by the local justice of the peace, involved no exchange of rings (which Puritans regarded as a superstitious custom), and usually consisted of both partners answering a single question concerning mutual commitment and fidelity. Seventeenth-century New Englanders celebrated weddings with modest dinners (which some transformed into large feasts in the eighteenth century), and wedding guests often completed the festivities by conducting noisy charivari, banging pots, ringing bells, and cheering outside the couple's honeymoon chamber. Pennsylvania Quakers observed an elaborate, sixteen-stage process to complete a wedding, mingling celebration and ritual throughout. Quakers discouraged their members from marking the end of life with feasting and drinking at funerals.

Funerals. Puritans shared with Quakers a determination to avoid elaborate funeral ceremonies or extravagant coffins and tombs, but unlike Quakers they served large funeral dinners and so much alcoholic drink that on occasion entire communities, children included, became intoxicated. Over time New Englanders began wearing black memorial scarves, ribbons, cloaks, and gloves and making fine caskets and covering them with palls or shrouds, customs that could cost the mourners large sums. Virginians observed such customs throughout the colonial period, often going to great expense and trouble to honor the dead with funerals. The more important the person, the more elaborate was his funeral, sometimes accompanied by a great procession, usually punctuated with fusillades (the discharging of firearms), and nearly always concluded by consuming great quantities of food and drink.

WISHING FOR CHRISTMAS IN EARLY AMERICA

Outside of Puritan New England and the Quaker communities in Pennsylvania, inhabitants of British mainland America celebrated Christmas in a variety of ways. For many it was the greatest feast day of the year, with roast turkey or other fowl and plum pudding. Saint Nicholas rewarded good children among English colonists with small gifts for their year's behavior, while a separate devil figure called Old Nick punished bad children with gifts of switches or lumps of coal. The two figures were later merged into one. In Dutch households a somewhat unpredictable angel called the Christkind visited children with gifts on Christmas Eve. In Virginia, Christmas was a day for settling debts and for celebrating into the night with bonfires and the discharging of firearms. By the 1730s even some New Englanders were wishing they could join in the fun. Early in 1734 the Boston poet Joseph Green wrote a friend that people who could not be persuaded to embrace Christianity by argument "cannot withstand a Dish of Plum Porridge, and it is past all doubt with me, that a Christmas Sermon makes fewer Converts, than a Christmas Pye."

Sources: Hennig Cohen and Tristramm Potter Coffin, eds., *The Folklore of American Holidays* (Detroit: Gale, 1988);

Joseph Green to Captain Benjamin Pollard, 2 January 1734, Smith-Carter Papers, Massachusetts Historical Society.

Special Observances. Colonists readily interrupted their routine to celebrate important events in the life of their community or to beg God's mercy or give thanks when circumstances demanded, both informally and by official sanction. A new minister's ordination or installation was one such event that called for a special gathering to listen to sermons and then feast in the cleric's honor. Quaker and German farm families in Pennsylvania often gathered to build a new meetinghouse or to help a neighbor build a new barn at a raising, an event for women as well as men to socialize over food and drink while sharing their labor. Authorities in Connecticut and Massachusetts often responded to military defeats or natural disasters by proclaiming special fast days, and ministers were appointed to preach special sermons that reminded colonists of their duties to God while calling on them to abstain from food and to spend the day praying for divine forgiveness and help. Similarly they would commemorate relief from disasters, military victories, and favorable events with special thanksgiving days which were often accompanied by special sermons, feasting, and prayers of thanks. By the 1670s at least one such thanksgiving observance became a regular November custom among many New England families and was officially sanc-

The Old Plantation (circa 1744–1794)—African American slaves dancing and playing musical instruments (painting by an unknown artist; Abby Aldrich Rockefeller Folk Art Center, Williamsburg, Virginia)

tioned by the laws of many northern communities. Other colonial authorities made similar proclamations when circumstances demanded, though none outside New England came to celebrate a yearly thanksgiving.

Calendar Occasions. Since the Middle Ages, Europeans had depended on the church calendar to mark the weeks, months, and seasons of the year. In most New World colonies weekly cycles were officially punctuated with Sunday worship, which colonists were expected and often compelled by law to attend. Many did not attend, however, either through indifference or because a place of worship was too far away. Christmas, Lent, Easter, and Whitsuntide (the seventh Sunday after Easter, celebrating the Holy Spirit's coming) served as the most important markers. These holidays were supplemented in various ways by other religious, traditional, or national days of observance. Many European colonists continued to mark their yearly calendars by these days, fasting during Advent and Lent, feasting on fowl (often goose or turkey) and plum pudding at Christmas, and scheduling weddings, plantings, and harvests by saints' days and other holy days.

Lent. Shrove Tuesday, the day before Lent began on Ash Wednesday, was marked by feasting and celebration in the streets of many English Protestant colonial towns as well as French and Spanish Catholic ones. In French America this celebration was known as Mardi Gras and was accompanied by processions, great feasting, drinking, singing, and dancing. In the English colonies Shrove Tuesday became an opportunity for servants and artisans to fill the streets of port cities in noisy procession, sometimes throwing rocks at the windows of merchants, shop owners, and employers who they thought had wronged them.

Pinkster. Colonists in Albany, New York, celebrated Pinkster, the Dutch Whitsuntide, with rowdy slave-led processions through streets lined with the stalls of peddlers selling food, liquor, and trifles. The greatest celebration in Spanish America was reserved for the local patron saint on whatever day that happened to fall. The celebration usually occupied two days: the first involved religious services while bonfires were lit throughout the town; the second was marked by a great procession with a statue of the saint, celebration of a high mass in the church, feasting, music, dancing, and games. May Day was celebrated in many English colonies with feasting and dancing around a maypole, and April Fool's Day was commemorated with pranks. Some colonies were more austere, however. Settlers in frontier Virginia were reported to keep no holidays other than Christmas and Good Friday, not because they objected to the others but because conditions demanded that they work hard to survive. Puritans, on the other hand, repudiated observance of church holidays, May Day, and April Fool's Day as superstitious. Legislatures in Massachusetts and Connecticut passed laws that prohibited any special observance of Christmas, Easter, and other such holidays, and officials strictly enforced them by imposing stiff fines and other punishments on violators. In 1627 Plymouth governor William Bradford actually led a small invasion

A 1653 cartoon of Father Christmas being shunned by a Puritan while an
unidentified individual welcomes him

party into the neighboring colony of Merrymount to disrupt a May Day celebration by cutting down the maypole and seizing the settlement's leader, Thomas Morton. Puritans centered their religious calendar on weekly Sunday worship. Sunday was the Sabbath and any work or "frivolous activity" was prohibited. On all the traditional holy days, including Christmas and Good Friday, the Puritans worked hard; Quakers did likewise. New England's annual celebrations came instead to focus on various civic and governmental functions.

State Affairs. Colonists were inhabitants of great European empires as well as New World colonies, and they expressed their loyalty to both with enthusiastic participation in various governmental functions and celebrations. They mourned the passing of one monarch and the coronation of his or her successor with solemn processions accompanied by military guards, fusillades, and shouts of "God save the king." Colonists would carry these celebrations into the evening with elegant balls at the governors' mansions, where important people drank to the new monarch's health and danced the night away. Colonial governors were likewise celebrated. A new governor would arrive at the colonial capital amid great celebration, riding to his residence in great procession. Important local officials marched before and behind the governor's coach while throngs of cheering people lined the streets and tried to catch a glimpse of the monarch's representative in America.

Popish Plot. These opportunities to express loyalty to the sovereign were supplemented in many English colonies by the annual celebration of Guy Fawkes Day. The day commemorated the thwarting of the notorious Gunpowder Plot of 1605, in which English Catholics had attempted to assassinate King James I. Each 5 November brawling throngs gathered in the streets to celebrate the English Protestant monarchy with raucous processions featuring effigies of the Pope. Various other occasions punctuated the year as well. Settlers throughout British America met periodically to elect representatives to the colonial legislatures. Voters and their families took these opportunities to socialize over gingerbread and hard cider or rum punch. Massachusetts colonists also celebrated an annual Election Day in which the upper house of the legislature was elected by a special court. After the election the newly chosen "Assistants" went in solemn procession to the statehouse, where the whole assembly sat and listened to an election sermon delivered by a prominent minister who reminded them of their sacred duties as representatives of the people. Most colonies organized militias for local defense, and muster days also became social occasions. Men fit for military duty would convene, often on Sunday afternoons, for much socializing along with some practice in marching and firing weapons. New England militiamen elected their own officers. County court days provided people another opportunity to gather from miles around not only to present their cases before the county justices but also to meet their neighbors, compete in foot or horse races, watch or participate in fistfights, and socialize at the local taverns. When a trial at the courthouse resulted in a conviction for some capital offense, people would again gather on the day appointed for public execution. There they would visit with their neighbors, purchase goods and refreshments from peddlers, listen to a minister deliver a solemn execution sermon crafted to warn all against vice and crime, and finally, watch the condemned criminal swing by the neck from the gallows.

Sources:

Richard L. Bushman, *King and People in Provincial Massachusetts* (Chapel Hill: University of North Carolina Press, 1985);

Ramón Gutiérrez and Geneviève Fabre, *Feasts and Celebrations in North American Ethnic Communities* (Albuquerque: University of New Mexico Press, 1995);

David D. Hall, *Worlds of Wonder, Days of Judgment: Popular Religious Belief in Early New England* (New York: Knopf, 1989);

Rhys Isaac, *The Transformation of Virginia, 1740–1790* (Chapel Hill: University of North Carolina Press, 1982);

Myron Tassin and Gaspar Stahl, *Mardi Gras and Bacchus: Something Old, Something New* (Gretna, La.: Pelican, 1984).

HEADLINE MAKERS

WILLIAM BYRD II

1674-1744

PLANTER, ROYAL OFFICIAL, AND COLONIAL AGENT

Privileged Upbringing. William Byrd II was "born to one of the amplest fortunes" of late-seventeenth-century Virginia. His father, William Byrd I, inherited vast landholdings in America along with lucrative interests in the rum, slave, tobacco, and fur trades. The father's wealth and importance gained him a seat in the Virginia governor's council, a position of great influence that could be exploited to gain even more wealth. By the time of his death William Byrd I had amassed a huge estate of twenty-six thousand acres and had secured his family's place in the highest ranks of Virginia society. To prepare his heir for even greater achievements the elder William sent his son to London at the age of seven. There the younger William grew up receiving some of the best training England had to offer in commerce, letters, and law. He studied classics and modern languages with a leading schoolmaster in Essex, learned business in great merchant houses in Holland and England, and received his legal training in the renowned Middle Temple. He was admitted to the bar in 1695, a distinction few Englishmen of the time attained. Young William also toured the European continent, another essential element of a seventeenth-century English gentleman's education. He hobnobbed with important people in the drawing rooms, coffeehouses, and theaters of London, making friends and contacts that could help him make the Byrd name known and respected in England. Among his closest and most important friends were two men of science, Robert Boyle, Earl of Orrery, and Sir Robert Southwell. With their help William gained admission to the Royal Society at the age of twenty-two. His friendships, training, and honors all combined to make William Byrd II an influential man for his colony of Virginia.

Virginia Gentleman. In 1704 his father died, and William Byrd II returned to Virginia to inherit his fortune and place among the colony's leaders. He devoted the next eleven years to managing and enlarging his plantation, climbing the ladder of influence in public affairs, and establishing a family. He married Lucy Parke, daughter of another leading Virginian who soon became governor of the Leeward Islands. The marriage, though enduring, was not without difficulty. Two of their four children died in early childhood, and the couple frequently quarreled over Byrd's conduct with other women and his management of his slave workforce. His domestic misconduct was all too common among Virginia planters, with whom his political star continued to rise. By 1715 Byrd had so impressed his contemporaries that they appointed him the colony's agent in London.

London. Byrd remained in London to represent Virginia's economic and political interests before Parliament for more than a decade. His wife Lucy died of smallpox within a few months of his arrival, and he spent the next eight years as a widower. Byrd worked hard making business and political deals, lobbying on behalf of policies that could help Virginia and trying to prevent those that might harm the colony's interest, and renewing old friendships and cultivating new ones among men of influence in London. Byrd also enjoyed the many benefits of London's cultural and intellectual life while simultaneously falling in love with several wealthy women before winning the hand of Maria Taylor in 1724. He remained in London two more years after his marriage, returning to Virginia for good in 1726.

Patriarch. Byrd reaped the benefits of his hard work on his own and Virginia's behalf during the last eighteen years of his life. Like his father before him, Byrd served on the governor's council, of which he became president the year before he died. He also served as receiver-general of Crown revenues, a lucrative post overseeing the collection of customs that his father had likewise held. In 1728 he led a team of surveyors from Virginia and North Carolina to establish the boundary line between the two colonies, and he recorded this adventure in a pair of illuminating and entertaining diaries. This service on Virginia's behalf helped him gain a large grant of lands, which he added along with other land acquisitions to his already-huge estate. His landholdings totaled 180,000 acres by the time of his death. Shortly after his return to America, Byrd wrote to an English correspondent, "like one of the patriarchs, I have my flocks and my herds, my bond-men and bond-women, and every soart [*sic*] of trade amongst my own servants, so that I live in a kind of independence on every one, but Providence." His wealth in fact depended in great measure on his slave workforce, which in 1718 included well over two hundred men and women located on several plantations. The skilled "tradesmen" among them served Byrd in rebuilding Westover, the great family house on the James River, into a red brick Georgian mansion surrounded by beautiful English gardens. It remains to this day one of the most beautiful of the colonial-era plantation mansions. He and Maria raised four more children—three daughters and a son, William Byrd III, who inherited his father's wealth in 1744 only to gamble most of it away.

Sources:

William Byrd, *William Byrd's Histories of the Dividing Line Betwixt Virginia and North Carolina,* edited by Percy G. Adams (New York: Dover, 1967);

Kenneth Lockridge, *The Diary, and Life, of William Byrd II of Virginia, 1674–1744* (New York: Norton, 1987).

OLAUDAH EQUIANO

CIRCA 1745-1797
FREEDMAN, SAILOR, AUTHOR, AND ABOLITIONIST

Background. Olaudah Equiano (pronounced o-lah-oo-day ek-wee-ah-no), also known by his European name Gustavus Vassa, led a remarkable life as a slave in several English possessions, a veteran of the Seven Years' War, a widely traveled sailor, and an early abolitionist who worked to end the British slave trade. Equiano was born a member of the Ibo tribe in present-day Nigeria around 1745. At the age of eleven he was captured along with his sister by African slave traders. The two were soon separated as Equiano was traded from village to village, where he worked for a variety of masters. When he reached the coast of West Africa, Equiano was purchased by a European slaver and chained together with many other captives in the hot, stinking hold of a slave ship. He was then transported thousands of miles to the Caribbean island of Barbados, whose sugar plantations made it the richest British colony of the eighteenth century. When no Barbadian planter purchased Equiano he was taken to Virginia, where he worked briefly on a tobacco plantation.

Sailor and Veteran. Only a few weeks after his purchase in Virginia, Equiano was sold again to a British naval officer named Michael Henry Pascal. While sailing with Pascal to England in 1757 he met a Virginian named Richard Baker, who began teaching him to read and write. Equiano subsequently took every opportunity to improve his reading and writing skills and to add to his knowledge. The Seven Years' War had already begun, and his wartime years with Captain Pascal permitted Equiano to become a skillful sailor as he served on naval vessels in the Atlantic Ocean and Mediterranean Sea. At the close of the war in 1763 Equiano was again sold, this time to a Philadelphia Quaker merchant named Robert King. His skills as a sailor who could read, write, and calculate made him a valuable assistant in King's business: shipping sugar, slaves, and agricultural goods between the Caribbean, Georgia, and South Carolina. While sailing from port to port for King, Equiano was able to begin a small trading business of his own. He saved up the money he made, and by 1766 he had accumulated enough to purchase his freedom.

New Life. In the decade after his manumission Equiano continued to work as a sailor on merchant ships and visited various American ports. One time in Savannah, Georgia, he attended a service led by the great English evangelist George Whitefield. The clergyman's powerful sermon set Equiano to thinking about heaven, hell, and salvation, thoughts which troubled him for several years. Finally in 1774 he experienced a religious conversion while visiting Cadiz in Spain. This experience quieted his anxieties over his soul and instilled in him a desire for worship and Bible reading that brought him into contact with groups of people who shared similar experiences. The English and American Quakers, Anglicans, and Methodists whom he met also shared a determination to work against the slave trade in the hope of one day bringing it to an end. Equiano became an important contact person for these early abolitionists as he carried news between England and America of the horrors of slavery and of courageous antislavery activity. With the publication of *The Interesting Narrative of* the Life of Olaudah Equiano in 1789, Equiano himself became a powerful spokesman for the abolition of slavery. His autobiography catapulted him to international fame. In 1792 he married an Englishwoman, Susan Cullen, who bore him two daughters, Anna Maria and Johanna. Susan Cullen Vassa died only months after Johanna's birth, and Equiano died in 1797. Johanna died two months after her father, but Anna Maria survived him into adulthood.

Sources:

Ann Cameron, *The Kidnapped Prince: The Life of Olaudah Equiano,* introduction by Henry Louis Gates Jr. (New York: Knopf, 1995);

Olaudah Equiano, *The Interesting Narrative of the Life of Olaudah Equiano,* edited by Robert J. Allison (Boston: Bedford Books, 1995).

MARIE DE L'INCARNATION

1599-1672

BUSINESSWOMAN, MYSTIC, FOUNDER OF THE URSULINE CONVENT IN QUEBEC

Life in France. Marie de l'Incarnation exemplifies the mark an energetic woman could make as a missionary nun in New France. She was born Marie Guyart, daughter of a baker who sold his loaves in the French textile center of Tours. Marie enjoyed mystical experiences even in her youth and dreamed of entering a nunnery. Her father, however, disapproved and arranged a marriage for her to a silkmaker named Claude Martin when she was seventeen. She bore a son the next year, and before the child was a year old her husband died. Marie refused to marry again, devoting herself to religious exercises whenever she could free herself from other tasks in her sister's household, where she and her son Claude had taken up residence. She spent the next decade helping with her brother-in-law's carting business, grooming horses, keeping books, and writing correspondence. Sometimes during his absence Marie supervised all the work. All the while, however, she was seeking to dedicate her life to God's service as a nun, even though that would mean leaving her son Claude behind.

Sisterhood. Marie never gave up her longing to become a nun although family members worked diligently to dissuade her. Finally her brother-in-law agreed to act as legal guardian for her son, setting aside a fund for his upbringing in recognition that the family's recent prosperity owed much to Marie's "talent for business." In January 1631 she appeared at the door of a nearby convent kept by the Company of Saint Ursula, where she threw herself at the feet of the reverend mother. There she took the religious name Marie de l'Incarnation, and for the next few years she carried on a life of physical deprivation, constant devotion, and intensive spiritual training. She soon became an instructor of Christian doctrine in the convent, even writing explanations of the faith and a commentary on the Old Testament Song of Solomon. She also listened to the preaching of Jesuit fathers, some of whom had gone as missionaries to Canada and returned with stories of people who had no "knowledge of Jesus Christ." Eventually she had a vision in which God told her to go to Canada and "make a house for Jesus and Mary."

Missionary. On 4 May 1639 Marie de l'Incarnation embarked for Canada in partnership with the noble-born Madeline de La Peltrie, who had pledged to devote her wealth and life to missionary work "in the service of savage girls." When they arrived at Quebec in August, Marie kissed the soil on which she would spend the remainder of her life. She threw herself into the work of establishing a convent, painting altars, cooking, lugging logs for building, studying Native American languages, and teaching young Huron and Iroquois girls whenever possible. She served as the convent's superior for three six-year terms and held other offices. Marie also became a tireless promoter of the new convent through her writings. She carried on an extensive correspondence with her son, relatives, friends, religious officials, and potential donors in France. She composed accounts of her mission work for the *Jesuit Relations,* a popular collection of missionary narratives that were published annually in France to promote the Jesuits' work in Canada. In 1661 she began writing catechisms, prayers, and instructional materials in Algonquian and Iroquoian. The largest of these was a "big book of sacred history and holy things," written in Algonquian and titled *Sacred History.* Seven years earlier she had composed a spiritual autobiography at the request of her son, Claude Martin, charging him to keep it private. In 1677, five years after her death, he published it as *La Vie de la venerable Mere Marie de l'Incarnation.* The book's spiritual reflections and detailed accounts of mission life among the Canadian Indians made it a popular seller, spreading throughout France the fame of this enterprising woman. The autobiography remains an important source of information on how contact between two races changed the lives of Native American and European women in seventeenth-century Canada.

Source:

Natalie Zemon Davis, *Women on the Margins: Three Seventeenth-Century Lives* (Cambridge, Mass.: Harvard University Press, 1995).

PUBLICATIONS

Anonymous, *Directorium Cosmeticum, or, A Directory for the Female Sex: Being a Father's Advice to His Daughter* (London: George Larkin, 1684)—a good example of a late-seventeenth-century manual for young ladies. It promises to direct young women on "how they may obtain the greatest beauty and adorn themselves with holy conversation";

Samuel Clarke, *A True and Faithful Account of the Four Chiefest Plantations of the English in America: to wit, of Virginia, New-England, Bermudas, and Barbados* (London: Robert Clavel, 1670)—this travel account may not be as true and faithful as it claims, but it does provide a good example of an early visitor's observations of mid-seventeenth-century colonial life;

George Fisher, *The American Instructor, or Young Man's Best Companion* (Philadelphia: B. Franklin & D. Hall, 1748)—a handy guide on how to prosper in a variety of pursuits in colonial British America. It contains guides to spelling, reading, writing, arithmetic, bookkeeping, forms of indenture, letters, trades, descriptions of colonies, medicine recipes, and much more;

James Kirkwood, *The True Interest of Families, or, Directions How Parents May Be Happy in their Children, and Children in their Parents* (London: J. Taylor & J. Everingham, 1692)—throughout the seventeenth and eighteenth centuries ministers and gentlemen on both sides of the Atlantic wrote many advice books such as this one on methods of child-rearing;

Andrea Palladio, *The Four Books of Andrea Palladio's Architecture* (London: I. Ware, 1738)—this Italian architect lived in the sixteenth century but greatly influenced genteel architecture in eighteenth-century England and America. His influence can be seen in great American houses such as Thomas Jefferson's Monticello and James Madison's Montpelier;

Eliza Smith, *The Compleate Housewife: or, Accomplish'd Gentlewoman's Companion* (Williamsburg, Va.: William Parks, 1742)—a colonial cookbook; it includes recipes, instructions for preserving food, monthly menus, and over two hundred medicinal cures.

NATIVE AMERICANS

by   PATRICK RIORDAN

CONTENTS

Sidebars and tables are listed in italics.

1614
- The Dutch establish Fort Nassau near present-day Albany, New York, and begin a trading alliance known as the Covenant Chain with the League of the Iroquois, a confederacy of five tribes.

1622
- The Powhatan Confederacy attacks Jamestown, and the resulting war rages intermittently until a treaty is signed in 1646.

1624
- Over the next four years the League of the Iroquois pushes the Mahicans (or Mohicans) east of the Hudson River.

1637
- The Pequot War begins in New England, and the colonists nearly exterminate the tribe.

1648
- The Iroquois launch a massive attack on the Hurons of Lake Simcoe and Georgian Bay. Within a year dozens of Huron villages are destroyed and hundreds of their residents killed. The remaining Hurons flee west and gain sanctuary among the Ottawas.

1659
- According to a Spanish report approximately ten thousand Timucuans die of measles in Florida.

1660
- By the end of the Beaver Wars the Iroquois have destroyed the Hurons, Petuns, Neutrals, and Eries as political entities and adopted the captives and refugees from these tribes into their confederacy.

1663
- The Susquehannocks begin a series of raids into the heart of Iroquois country that lasts for the next thirteen years.

1675
- Metacom's War (also known as King Philip's War) begins in New England. When the war ends the next year, 10 percent of the adult male colonial population is dead.

1676

- Virginia colonists defeat the Susquehannocks, and the survivors seek refuge among the Iroquois and Delawares.

1677

- The League of the Iroquois and the colony of New York form a Covenant Chain.

1680

- The Pueblo Indians of present-day New Mexico revolt against the Spanish, driving them out for nine years.
- The western Iroquois attack the Illinois tribes.

1682

- René Cavelier de La Salle claims the Mississippi River valley for France and, three years later, stakes France's claim to land on the Gulf of Mexico.
- William Penn signs a treaty with the Delawares, opening a period of peace between Quakers and native peoples of the Middle Colonies.
- The governor of New France, Joseph-Antoine Le Febvre de La Barre, leads an army of eight hundred men to upstate New York in order to subdue the Iroquois; the campaign is a complete fiasco.

1683

- The estimated strength of the Five Nations of the Iroquois Confederacy is twenty-eight hundred warriors.

1687

- Two thousand troops led by Jacques-Réné de Brisay, Marquis de Denonville, the governor of New France, attack the Senecas in upstate New York, destroying villages and food supplies.

1689

- King William's War begins, the first in a series of conflicts among the French, Spanish, English, and their respective Native American allies; it ends in 1697.

1695

- The first Pima uprising against the Spanish in northern Mexico occurs.

1701

- The League of the Iroquois and New France sign a peace treaty.

1702
- Queen Anne's War begins; it ends eleven years later.

1711
- The Tuscarora War, a two-year conflict, breaks out in North Carolina.

1715
- The Yamasee attack white settlements but are eventually expelled from South Carolina.

1720
- Warfare erupts in the Mississippi River Delta region and goes on intermittently for the next thirty-two years, pitting Chickasaws against Choctaws and their French allies.

1722
- The Tuscaroras become the sixth nation of the Iroquois Confederacy. (They do not receive full membership until 1750.)

1729
- The French governor of Louisiana orders the Natchez to transform their principal town into a plantation for his use. The ensuing revolt leads to the virtual extinction of the Natchez people.

1734
- After three decades of sporadic fighting the French finally defeat the Fox tribe of Green Bay (on Lake Michigan).

1735
- Pennsylvania governor Thomas Penn produces a fraudulent document that states the Delaware tribe agreed in 1686 to sell their lands as far west as a man could walk in a day and a half. Penn organizes a relay of three men who run sixty miles in the prescribed time, and the Delawares are forced to cede twelve hundred square miles of land in what becomes known as the Walking Purchase.

1738
- A smallpox epidemic spreads among Native American villages from North Carolina to western Canada.

1739
- The War of Jenkins' Ear begins and lasts until 1742.

1740

- Gen. James E. Oglethorpe's raid on Spanish-controlled Saint Augustine results in the formation of a Creek settlement near present-day Gainesville, Florida, the nucleus of early Seminole towns.

1744

- King George's War begins; it ends four years later.

- In the Treaty of Lancaster the Six Nations of the Iroquois Confederacy claim suzerainty over the Delawares and sell their lands between the Susquehanna River and Allegheny Mountains to the colony of Pennsylvania.

1746

- A typhoid epidemic afflicts the Micmacs of Nova Scotia.

1749

- Pierre-Joseph de Céloron de Blainville leads an expedition down the Ohio River. Aside from claiming the area for France and expelling Anglo-American traders, he attempts to improve relations with the Native American tribes in the area.

1751

- A second Pima uprising occurs against the Spanish.

1752

- The French trader Charles Langlade and 250 Ottawas and Ojibwas from the Great Lakes raid the Miami village of Pickawillany (modern Piqua, Ohio) and destroy its British trading post.

1754

- Delegates from seven British colonies north of Virginia meet at Albany to discuss a proposal for colonial confederation. The Albany Congress also devises policies regarding military defense and relations with native peoples.

- The French and Indian War plunges the North American continent into a global conflict.

OVERVIEW

The People. In 1492 the native population of North America north of the Rio Grande was seven million to ten million. These people grouped themselves into approximately six hundred tribes and spoke diverse dialects. European colonists initially encountered Native Americans in three distinct regions. Eastern Woodland tribes included the Five Nations of the Iroquois Confederacy, Abenakis, Shawnees, Delawares, Micmacs, Mahicans, and Pequots. Some of these tribes were sedentary hunter-gathers while others grew maize (corn), beans, and squash. In the Southeast white settlers came into contact with Powhatans, Catawbas, Cherokees, Creeks, Natchez, Choctaws, and Chickasaws; these people were primarily agriculturalists. Pueblos, Zunis, Navajos, and Hopis represented some of the adobe-dwelling bands in the arid Southwest. Regardless of their differences, these groups shared some common characteristics. For Native Americans the family, clan, and village represented the most important social groups. In addition, religions revolved around the belief that all of nature was alive, pulsating with spiritual power.

Contact. When the various European nations reached the New World the encounters were predictably diverse. Culture, climate, and the location and timing of the contact all affected the nature of the experience. One common factor was disease, as large numbers of native peoples succumbed to the microbes that the Europeans unwittingly carried with them in virtually every encounter. Massive population declines undoubtedly placed great stress on economic, social, political, and religious systems of native peoples. From 1492 until the Revolutionary War, trade was a central theme of interaction between natives and Europeans. This relationship shifted over time, transforming native life by drawing North America into a web of global economic connections. The process began when the first traders offered textiles, glass, and metal products in exchange for beaver pelts and buffalo robes. The transactions did not end until Europeans had virtually dispossessed the native people of the land that produced the goods the foreigners desired. Relations between the different European nations and native peoples were often complex and contradictory. Spanish colonists developed a reputation for harsh treatment, but because the Spanish sent almost no women to the New World, Spanish men often intermarried with native women. The French have been portrayed as sensitive to the culture of native peoples, but under their influence, the Fox were all but destroyed.

Exchanges. In general, the interaction of native North Americans and Europeans began with a period of initial goodwill and trade, followed by armed conflicts in which native warriors demonstrated great courage, organization, and skill. Eventually, however, superior weaponry produced victory for the colonists. Throughout the period 1600 to 1754 the interaction was marked by biological, cultural, and material exchanges. Europeans were expected to bring "Indian presents" (glass beads, mirrors, hatchets, kettles, etc.) to any major negotiations, as a sign of their goodwill. These gifts were precursors to trade relationships that marked permanent change in native societies. By removing militant native leaders and replacing them with more-amenable rulers, the Spanish were able to take power and extract the gold and silver that made Central and South America attractive to Europeans. Spaniards sent priests to Christianize native peoples even as they stole their land and exploited their labor. Europeans initially mistook the natives of the Caribbean islands for inhabitants of Asia, the continent Columbus had expected to find, and called them Indians. Struck by the peoples' nudity and gentility, some Europeans considered them to be members of the lost tribes of Israel and the New World as the physical location of the Garden of Eden. As conflicts led to violence and colonization spread to the mainland, however, the view of Indians as naive innocents soon gave way to an image of native peoples as satanic fiends bent on the destruction of white colonists. Europeans engaged in formal academic debates on the nature of Native Americans and where they fit into the world.

Southwest. Spanish colonists pushed northward from their base in Mexico in search of precious metals and created the new colony of Nuevo México. In 1598 Juan de Oñate led a group of about four hundred colonists along the Rio Grande, where they settled among the residents of the pueblo of Yunque (to which they referred as San Juan Bautista). The Pueblo people accepted their presence without resistance, adopting some of their innovations in cooking, architecture, and town planning. These

Spaniards had profound effects on the local ecology. They brought cattle and sheep which grazed on the land. Their use of baking ovens greatly increased the need for firewood, depleting local supplies. And the Spanish organized Indian laborers to expand the existing network of irrigation canals. The Acoma Pueblo refused to submit to the interlopers, and hundreds of Indians were killed or enslaved. This policy of "blood and fire" produced a legacy of resentment. The Spanish never found gold or silver, struggled economically, and maintained an uneasy peace with their neighbors. But in 1680 Acoma warriors expelled the Spanish, driving them all the way back to Mexico and keeping them out for a decade. During the eighteenth century missionaries led by Friar Junipero Serra established twenty-one missions, a day's march apart, from San Diego to San Francisco, California. Military presidios, or forts, soon were added to each mission. Native religion was suppressed; Indians who resisted were physically abused; and traditional family relationships were discouraged. Native resistance took the form of poisonings, arson, and violent uprisings—with four thousand deaths recorded at Santa Barbara alone. The native population of coastal California, estimated at seventy thousand before the missions, declined to about fifteen thousand within three decades of their arrival.

Northeast. In the early 1600s Indians in the Saint Lawrence River valley established trading relationships with the French. The Montagnais and others obtained textiles and glass and metal goods in exchange for beaver skins. The French erected a fort at Quebec in 1608 to protect their trade from raids by the Mohawks. In the following years other nations entered into trade relations with the French, including the Hurons and the Algonquins. Against this alliance of French and natives were arrayed the Iroquois nations of Mohawks, Oneidas, Onondagas, Cayugas, and Senecas, which had united as the Five Nations under Hiawatha and Deganawidah in the previous century. The Iroquois gained an ally in 1609, when Dutch colonists led by Henry Hudson arrived in present-day New York, seeking to copy the economic success of the French. The Dutch supplied them with metal weaponry—hatchets, knives, and arrow points—needed to combat their native and French enemies. Dutch traders penetrated southern New England and the Delaware River valley in present-day Pennsylvania. Until 1620 the British were unsuccessful in their attempts to obtain a beachhead on the North Atlantic coast. After that date the Wampanoags accepted the colony of Plymouth, and British traders began to compete for native products. By the end of the second decade of the seventeenth century, the region bounded roughly by the Hudson River, the Saint Lawrence River, and the Atlantic Ocean was North America's most complex zone of interaction between natives and Europeans. The traders' influence grew considerably after the conversion of wampum, originally a sacred object used in religious rituals, into currency. The use of wampum accelerated the

pace of trade and heightened competition among native peoples, producing commercial rivalries that sometimes were settled through warfare. The Iroquois had overhunted their own territory in present-day upstate New York and needed skins to continue trading with the Dutch at Fort Orange. Further west, competition for hunting territory led to raids and counterraids. North of the Great Lakes, the Ottawas defeated the Winnebagos, forcing them to the western shore of Lake Michigan at Green Bay. Later a people known as the Neutrals drove out the Sauk, Fox, and Potawatomis, who also relocated to the Green Bay area, where the defeated Winnebagos—recovering from an epidemic—had little choice but to accept them. The native refugees at Green Bay grew into a strong anti-Iroquois, pro-French alliance. In the 1640s the Iroquois attacked the remaining Hurons, defeating them and driving the remnants of the nation and their allies toward Green Bay. Some of the Shawnee and Erie allies of the Hurons fled to the South, instead, where they would face still more conflicts with Europeans.

The Chesapeake. In Virginia early attempts to establish English colonies failed, but with the aid of the Powhatans the Jamestown colony survived. The Powhatan confederacy covered nearly all of eastern Virginia, and until 1609 relations with the English were peaceful. When white leaders attempted to dictate unfavorable terms of trade and colonization, the Powhatan chieftain retaliated by withholding corn, and war broke out. By 1611 the English had forced all native peoples out of their immediate area, and three years later a truce was implemented. Indian uprisings in 1622 and 1644 did not stop the tide of white settlers. By midcentury Virginia was experiencing a boom-and-bust economy as the price of tobacco rose and fell. Immigration remained high, however, and the area of settlements moved westward into Indian country. As the population grew, social divisions arose among the settlers. The colony's leaders tended to come from the men living near the coast and far from the Indians, representing established, relatively wealthy families. Those living farther inland tended to be more-recent arrivals, generally younger, and more hostile to their Indian neighbors.

Migrations. British trade goods were extremely attractive to the native peoples of the North. The French relied on military force to keep their native allies in line. In the first decade of the eighteenth century they built Fort Ponchartrain at Detroit in an attempt to enforce their monopoly of the fur trade in the northern Great Lakes region and keep the English at bay. But French attempts to block their partners from access to British trade made the Hurons and Petuns and other allies resentful and strengthened opposition to the French among the Iroquois. The Five Nations took part in two unsuccessful British attempts to invade Canada. In 1706 conflict pitted the Hurons, Petuns, and Miamis against the Ottawas, who relocated from upper Lake Superior to the Detroit River. The Miamis, meanwhile, returned to their former homes on the Maumee River in present-day Indiana. In 1712 the Fox people fled toward Detroit after being attacked by Ojibwas and Sioux. More than one thousand Fox arrived at Detroit to claim their traditional hunting grounds. Other Indians near Detroit resented the newcomers, and the Fox's historic links to the Iroquois fed French paranoia. The French supported their allies in a combined attack on the Fox in 1712, triggering a sequence of Fox wars that undercut French relations with native peoples during the balance of the century. In the second decade of the eighteenth century the Tuscaroras were driven from North Carolina after losing a war with the British. They journeyed to the territory of the Iroquois, who adopted the Tuscaroras and henceforth became known as the Six Nations. Two other groups—the Shawnees and Susquehannocks—also moved northward into Iroquois territory. Strengthened by the new arrivals, the Iroquois attempted to make peace with both the French and the British. This infusion of new people made the Iroquois a more formidable military power. Furthermore, the newcomers brought anticolonist sentiments that reinforced the views of those Iroquois who opposed cooperation with missionaries and Europeans generally. Finally, the influx coincided with a smallpox epidemic which the Iroquois leadership blamed on Europeans. Overall, Iroquois with "traditionalist" feelings, favoring isolation and withdrawal, became dominant over those who favored connections with traders and missionaries. For the next generation the Iroquois turned to the South, making war against the Cherokees (the Tuscaroras' old enemies), and lived in peace with the Hurons, Petuns, and other peoples of the Great Lakes.

Lower South. The colony of Carolina was founded in 1669 by investors seeking to prosper, in part, from the Indian trade. The proprietors assumed a monopoly on trade with the nearby Indians whom they called the Westos. (The Westos were, in fact, the surviving members of the Eries, driven from the Great Lakes region by the Huron-Iroquois conflicts.) Some colonists attempted to make slaves of the Westos, who retaliated with violent raids on white settlements. Colonists from the area known as Goose Creek, South Carolina, aided by the Shawnees, destroyed the Westos. The downfall of the Westos led to expanded trade between the English and the Creeks, who raided Spanish missions where Timucuans and Apalachees lived. In the 1680s Spanish raids against Coweta and Kasihta led those Creek towns to relocate into western Carolina. By the turn of the eighteenth century the Creeks were staunch military allies of the English. Led by the former Carolina governor, James Moore, English and Creek forces destroyed the Spanish mission villages in Florida. They took more than one thousand Apalachees and other Florida Indians to Charleston, where they sold them as slaves to Caribbean sugar planters. Afterward the Creeks achieved a balance of power in the region by playing European nations against each other and trading with the British, French, and Spanish alike. The British had the best trade goods at the lowest prices, however, and their economic strength and military advantages gave them the greatest staying power in North America. The Creeks' links to the British endured after their other alliances faded.

The Colonial Wars. From 1689 until 1754 a series of four colonial wars racked the North American continent and pitted the English against the French and sometimes the Spanish. Various tribes became embroiled in the conflict, fighting on behalf of one European power or another. In addition, old native enmities sometimes flared into open warfare, and new conflicts arose out of the indirect effects of colonization, such as trade and migration. By the early 1750s the native peoples of North America were squeezed between the French, who were gaining control of the Mississippi and Ohio River valleys and the British settlements along the Atlantic coast. In 1754, when the two powers went to war for the fifth and final time in North America, Indian country would be their battlefield.

TOPICS IN THE NEWS

EARLY VIRGINIA

Wahunsunacock. In 1607, after early attempts to establish English colonies in Virginia failed, the Powhatans and other native peoples of the Chesapeake region helped the settlement at Jamestown to survive, providing food and helping colonists find hunting and fishing spots. Even with their help the English suffered from high mortality and endured periods of starvation. When Capt. John Smith paid a visit to the Powhatan leader, or *werowance,* known as Wahunsunacock, the Indians engaged in a welcoming ritual in which the chief's daughter, Pocahontas, played a role. Smith interpreted this ceremony as an attempt to kill him, thwarted by Pocahontas's "rescue."

Powhatan Confederacy. Wahunsunacock used the British to enhance his position in native politics significantly. With British support he transformed what had been a loose confederacy of native peoples into a paramount chiefdom. The alliance was peaceful until 1609, when the English attempted to dictate unfavorable terms of trade and colonization. The Powhatans retaliated by withholding corn, and war broke out. By 1611 the English had forced all native peoples out of their immediate area, and in 1614 they captured Pocahontas and converted her to Christianity. Wahunsunacock reluctantly agreed to a truce, and Pocahontas married the planter John Rolfe and sailed to England, where she died of a respiratory illness in 1617. Her marriage probably helped to seal the uneasy peace. In the years following, however, the English started to grow tobacco, a field crop requiring huge tracts of land, and large-scale immigration put additional demographic pressure on the Powhatans.

Opechancanough. In 1622 the new werowance, Opechancanough, led a revenge raid against the English, killing more than three hundred colonists in retaliation for the execution of a Powhatan convicted of murdering a settler. In the ensuing conflict the colonists sought to exterminate the Powhatans or drive them as far inland as possible. The wars lasted until 1646, when the English finally captured the elderly Opechancanough and took him to Jamestown, where a guard shot him to death.

Sources:
Thomas Harriot, *A Briefe and True Report of the New Found Land of Virginia* (London: Robert Robinson, 1588);

Dutchman Wenceslaus Hollar's 1645 portrait engraving of a Virginia Indian later identified as a Munsee Delaware named Jacques, who was taken from New Amsterdam to Amsterdam in 1644

Helen C. Rountree, ed., *Powhatan Foreign Relations 1500–1722* (Charlottesville: University Press of Virginia, 1993).

FRENCH-ENGLISH RIVALRIES

Fur Trade. The trade in animal pelts between North America and Europe began in the late sixteenth century, after the French arrived on the Saint Lawrence River. The French supplied metal and glass goods, textiles, and firearms and ammunition while the Indians initially traded the beaver robes they used during the winters and annually discarded. After the arrival of the English in the

An early French engraving of Samuel de Champlain's 1615 attack on an Onondaga village in upstate New York

early seventeenth century native traders negotiated for the best deal, playing one European colony against another. Access to British firepower made the League of the Iroquois the most powerful native group in the Great Lakes region. In the mid 1600s they defeated the Hurons and Petuns, who were allied with the French, in a great war over furs. Following widespread custom, the Iroquois adopted members of the peoples they defeated. Expanded commerce placed pressure on wild-game populations. A pattern became established in which native traders journeyed farther and farther westward to find more fur-bearing animals. However, French traders seeking to cut out the middleman pressed westward to the source of the furs. By the mid eighteenth century Europeans had thoroughly penetrated the fur-producing regions. They stimulated rivalry among native peoples and brought guns and ammunition with which such conflicts could occur. At about the same time, the horse—a transportation innovation brought to Mexico by the Spanish—had reached the native peoples of the southern Great Plains.

Wars. Beginning in 1689, in the aftermath of England's Glorious Revolution, European conflicts repeatedly spilled over into North America. Spain was a nation in decline, but the continent's two major powers—France and England—were jousting for power, wealth, and empire. King William's War (1689–1697) turned partly on competition for the fur trade. Fearful of isolation, the French began to pressure the Iroquois to align with them or at least to observe neutrality. Conflict began as the result of England's provocations against the French and the Abenakis of northern New England, who responded by raiding British settlements. The war played out in a series of costly but inconclusive skirmishes. By 1700 each of the five nations of the Iroquois made peace separately with France. Queen Anne's War (1702–1713) was fought to determine who would be the Spanish monarch. Spain's alliance with France meant that native peoples in Spanish and French zones of North America would come into conflict with those living under British influence. Fierce fighting took place in New England, where

Contrary to popular belief, scalping was a Native American practice long before the arrival of Europeans in North America. (The only non-Indian people who are known to have scalped their foes were the Scythians, a nomadic Eurasian people of antiquity.) In recent years archaeologists have recovered human skulls from pre-1492 sites east and west of the Mississippi River that provide evidence of scalping. The skulls, some of which date from as early as 2500 B.C., exhibit circular cuts and scratches where scalps were traditionally lifted. Many of the first white explorers of the continent left written descriptions of this Native American custom. The Stadaconans along the Saint Lawrence River showed Jacques Cartier in 1535–1536 "the skins of five men's heads, stretched on hoops, like parchment." In 1540 a conquistador of Hernando de Soto's expedition to west Florida watched in horror as the Indians killed one of his comrades, then "removed his head, or rather all around his skull . . . and carried it off as evidence of their deed." Moreover, in the Algonquian, Iroquoian, and Muskogean languages, the ancient root word for "scalp" is cognate with the words for "head" and "hair."

Indian males considered scalps to be trophies. A scalplock symbolized the warrior's soul, and a young man earned honor and status by taking the scalp of an enemy. Although Europeans did not invent scalping they certainly promoted its spread and frequency by supplying Native American warriors with metal knives and offering bounties for not only Indian but European scalps as well.

Source: James Axtell and William C. Sturtevant, "The Unkindest Cut, or Who Invented Scalping? A Case Study," in Axtell, *The European and the Indian: Essays in the Ethnohistory of Colonial North America* (New York: Oxford University Press, 1981).

Abenaki warriors allied with France sacked Deerfield, the northernmost British settlement on the Connecticut River. In the South the French forged a durable alliance with the Choctaws and won over some of the many groups that made up the Creeks. In 1702 a British naval expedition sacked Spanish Saint Augustine, and two years later the British attacked a chain of Spanish missions in north Florida with more than one thousand Creek and Yamasee warriors. After capturing the missions they returned to Carolina with hundreds of native prisoners of war. The raid destroyed the Apalachee people of north Florida, who had survived as a chiefdom for hundreds of years. It also created lasting ill will among the surviving native peoples of the Southeast. The War of Jenkins's Ear (1739–1742) began when English captain Robert Jenkins claimed that a Spanish naval offi-

cer cut off his ear in an interrogation. The initial phase saw naval clashes between England and Spain in the Caribbean and soon led to all-out continental war in Europe. Meanwhile, the simmering trade rivalry in the Northeast had led the French and British to erect forts on their border, and a new conflict, King George's War, began in 1744. William Johnson, then a successful Indian trader and later the British Indian superintendent, persuaded the Mohawks to end their military neutrality and join him in raids against the French forts. In the South the Chickasaw resistance to the French and the Choctaws effectively disrupted trade routes, while the British-allied Cherokees battled the French-allied faction of the Creeks. A treaty ending the war was signed in 1748, but peace lasted less than ten years. In 1754 renewed hostilities led to the French and Indian War, the last great war between England and France for possession of the North American continent.

Sources:
Richard Middleton, *Colonial America: A History, 1585–1776*, second edition (Cambridge, Mass.: Blackwell, 1996);

Eric R. Wolf, *Europe and the People Without History* (Berkeley: University of California Press, 1982).

IROQUOIS

Early History. The League of the Iroquois was a confederacy of native peoples living in present-day western New York. Originally made up of five nations, the Senecas, Cayugas, Onandagas, Oneidas, and Mohawks, the Iroquois were united in the 1400s by Hiawatha. Along with his mentor, Deganawidah, Hiawatha helped the Iroquois to negotiate a peace that ended many generations of war among them. According to Iroquois tradition Hiawatha was deeply depressed and grief stricken by the deaths of all his daughters in quick succession. Wandering in the forest, eventually he met Deganawidah, the Peacemaker, who showed him new religious rituals that eased his mind and restored his sanity. Hiawatha believed that this new religion could unite the Iroquois and asked Deganawidah to share it. But Deganawidah was unable to speak in public, so the task of spreading the word fell to Hiawatha, who used Deganawidah's rituals to heal the old wounds among the Five Nations of the Iroquois and unite them in a Great League of Peace and Power. (They added a sixth nation in 1711, when the Tuscaroras of North Carolina migrated north and sought their protection.)

Covenant Chain. In the early years of the seventeenth century the French positioned themselves in Canada; the Dutch dropped anchor in New York harbor; and the British established settlements in New England. The Iroquois, therefore, held the strategically important central territory around which the European powers were arrayed. All sides needed them as trading partners and were willing to make concessions in exchange for their business. By maintaining unity and following a policy of playing one power off against the other two, the Iroquois

A ball-headed war club made by the Iroquois of New York or the Native Americans of southern New England, circa 1600

maximized their power and preserved their territorial integrity for many years, despite the inevitability of decline. In 1677 the Iroquois assumed a durable position of regional leadership with the establishment of a Covenant Chain with the British. (Earlier in the seventeenth century they had formed a Covenant Chain with the Dutch.) Through this series of treaties the British declared the Iroquois to be the leaders of all native peoples in most of present-day New York and Pennsylvania. This recognition empowered the Iroquois and made life simpler for Anglo-American colonists. While each tribe retained its own sovereignty for most purposes, they were willing to become clients of the Iroquois and Britain in order to obtain arms and trade goods at low prices. Further, by placing the Iroquois in the role of "first among equals," the Covenant Chain created a mechanism for resolving native differences peacefully. The Covenant Chain operated in practice through meetings between the colonial governor of New York and the Iroquois sachems, or leaders, who would often speak for other Indians in attendance. The Chain promoted the social and political authority of native peoples, but it also acknowledged the limits of native power in the context of superior European technology. In the eighteenth century the Chain empowered the Iroquois to avoid war by agreeing to give away the lands of the Delawares and Shawnees over the objections of those tribes. Despite the Chain, however, the Iroquois consistently tried to show the British that their loyalty could not be taken for granted. Although they sided with the British against the Dutch and later the French during wartime, the Iroquois always attempted to preserve at least a posture of independence during peacetime. In addition to commercial and military factors, the alliance was strong because of warm personal relationships. Sir William Johnson, the British Indian superintendent for the Northern District, lived in Iroquois territory, participated in ceremonial life, and had for a consort Molly Brant, sister of Joseph Brant.

Sources:

Daniel K. Richter, *The Ordeal of the Longhouse: The Peoples of the Iroquois League in the Era of European Colonization* (Chapel Hill: University of North Carolina Press, 1992);

Neal Salisbury, "Native People and European Settlers," in *The Cambridge History of the Native Peoples of the Americas*, volume 1, *North America*, edited by Bruce C. Trigger and Wilcomb E. Washburn (Cambridge: Cambridge University Press, 1996), pp. 440–453.

METACOM'S WAR

Origins. Also called King Philip's War (1675–1676), Metacom's War was a bitter and bloody conflict named for Metacom (or Metacomet), a chieftain of the Wampanoags. It arose out of cultural conflict and population pressure, as English settlers slowly surrounded the ancestral lands of the Wampanoags on Narragansett Bay. Concerned about encroachments and the divisions in native culture caused by missionaries, the Indians attacked nearby settlements. Metacom led a campaign that completely destroyed twelve of the ninety Puritan towns and attacked forty more.

Brass gorget (or pendant) presented by Massachusetts Bay to Native American allies during King Philip's War

Capt. John Underhill's diagram of his attack on a Pequot fort along the banks of the Mystic River in 1637

Significance. In the spring of 1676 Wampanoag forces evacuated to New York, but the Mohawks refused to help them, and the colonists gained the upper hand. Metacom was captured and killed, and his head was severed and kept on public display for twenty years. Many of the Wampanoags, including Metacom's wife and son, were sold into slavery in the Caribbean. The war not only broke the power of the coastal tribes in New England but also led to political changes in the colonies. Massachusetts's colonial charter was revoked. Also, before the conflict was over about 10 percent of the total adult male population of New England was killed—making it the most costly war in American history, measured by the proportion of casualties to total population.

Sources:

Alvin M. Josephy, "The Betrayal of King Philip," in *The Patriot Chiefs: A Chronicle of American Indian Resistance* (New York: Viking, 1969), pp. 31–62.

Richard Slotkin and James K. Folson, eds., *So Dreadfull a Judgment: Puritan Responses to King Philip's War, 1676–1677* (Middletown, Conn.: Wesleyan University Press, 1978).

THE PEQUOT WAR

Beginnings. Between 1634 and 1638 the population of the Massachusetts Bay Colony rose from about four thousand to more than eleven thousand all as a result of migration from England. As new arrivals began to crowd the coastal areas, Puritan colonists began to look to their west, into territory controlled by the Pequots and their allies, for additional lands. In 1635 colonists led by the former Baptist minister Thomas Hooker left present-day Cambridge, Massachusetts, and established the colony of Hartford. Simultaneously, a group of squatters—settlers with little or no legal claim to the land—from Watertown moved near the Pequot town of Pyquag and renamed it Wethersfield. At the same time, a group of English investors called the Saybrook Company built Fort Saybrook near the mouth of the Connecticut River, near the Pequot village of Mystic.

Native Allegiances. The Pequots were the dominant native people in the region, allied with the Niantics and others. They were frequently at war with the Narragansetts, who were friends with the English colonists. As

Puritan colonists began their westward expansion, tensions with the Pequots peaked. Despite an earlier treaty English authorities sought to humiliate and provoke the Pequots, seeking a pretext for a war that would sweep the Connecticut Valley of native peoples. The desired provocation came when some Indians, whose tribal identities are still uncertain, killed two English colonists, John Stone and John Oldham. English raiders attacked Pequots and their allies on Block Island, in Long Island Sound, in September 1636. The Pequots responded by laying siege to Fort Saybrook. The conflict remained low-key for some time, as the eastern colonists were caught up in a major religious dispute, with implications for gender roles and commerce, known as the Antinomian controversy. As a result the colonists temporarily ignored Indian affairs in Connecticut, as the breakaway settlements were becoming known. But impassioned pleas from the westerners claimed that the "roaring lions" would soon exterminate all English colonists if they were not stopped at Fort Saybrook, and reinforcements soon arrived.

Dawn Attack. The war ended at Mystic, where between three hundred and seven hundred women, children, and old men were left on their own. The English encircled the village at dawn to prevent escape and burned every structure. Only seven Pequots escaped the fire, which Puritan authors described as divine retribution. The remainder of the Pequots were hunted down and exterminated in the following months. In 1638 the Treaty of Hartford declared the Pequot nation to be dissolved.

Sources:

Alfred A. Cave, *The Pequot War* (Amherst: University of Massachusetts Press, 1996);

Francis Jennings, *The Invasion of America: Colonists, Culture, and the Cant of Conquest* (Chapel Hill: University of North Carolina Press, 1976).

PURITAN MASSACRE

On 26 May 1637 the Puritans and some Native American allies attacked a Pequot village at the mouth of the Mystic River in Connecticut. One of the leaders of the expedition, Capt. John Mason, believed that the Pequots, like the Philistines of the Old Testament, had been justly put to the sword:

Thus were they now at their wits end, who not many hours before exalted themselves in their great pride, threatening and resolving the utter ruin of all the English, exulting and rejoicing with songs and dances. But God was above them, who laughed his enemies and the enemies of his people to scorn, making them as a fiery oven. Thus were the stout-hearted spoiled, having slept their last sleep. . . . Thus did the Lord judge among the heathen, filling the place with dead bodies.

And here we may see the just judgment of God, in sending (even the very night before this assault) 150 men from their other fort, to join with them of that place; who were designed—as some of themselves reported—to go forth against the English at that very instant when this heavy stroke came upon them, where they perished with their fellows. So that the mischief they intended to us came upon their own pate. They were taken in their own snare, and we through mercy escaped. And thus in little more than one hour's space was their impregnable fort with themselves utterly destroyed, to the number of six or seven hundred, as some of themselves confessed. There were only seven taken captive and about seven escaped.

Thus the Lord was pleased to smite our enemies in the hinder parts and to give us their land for an inheritance; who remembered us in our low estate, and redeemed us out of our enemies' hands. Let us therefore praise the Lord for his goodness and his wonderful works to the Children of men!

Source: John Mason, *A Brief History of the Pequot War* (Boston: S. Kneeland & T. Green, 1736), pp. 9–10, 21.

RESERVATIONS

New Haven. Early in the colonial period Europeans conceived the idea of taking most of the land in a particular area for their own use and setting aside undesirable lands for use by native peoples. In New England a combination of military defeats and diseases weakened native peoples' will to resist. In November 1638 the Puritan leaders of the colony of New Haven forced the surviving members of the Quinnipiac tribe (who numbered fewer than sixty) to surrender land around the mouth of the Quinnipiac River and its harbor. The Indians were allowed to keep about twelve hundred acres east of the river's mouth. The Quinnipiacs agreed to have little or no contact with the English and were required to obtain the consent of the Puritan colonists before admitting any outside Indians to their reservation. The English had the right to appoint a superintendent to oversee the Quinnipiacs' affairs. While the Native Americans could hunt outside the reservation so long as they caused no inconvenience, the English retained the rights to the timber on their land. Quinnipiacs were responsible for any English livestock they killed, but they were not compensated for any damage that free-ranging cattle might do to native crops. In addition to a requirement that they accept Christianity and renounce their own religion, the Indians could not purchase alcohol or firearms.

Massachusetts Bay. Additional reservations were established in New England. After Metacom's War the surviving Wampanoags, Narragansetts, and Mohegans were reduced to about fifteen hundred people and confined to the reservation towns of Natick, Punkapoag, Hassamesitt, and Wamesit. Colonial officials expected native leaders to run these towns just as other New England settlements operated, with annual town meetings and elected officers, but the plan failed. Town living was

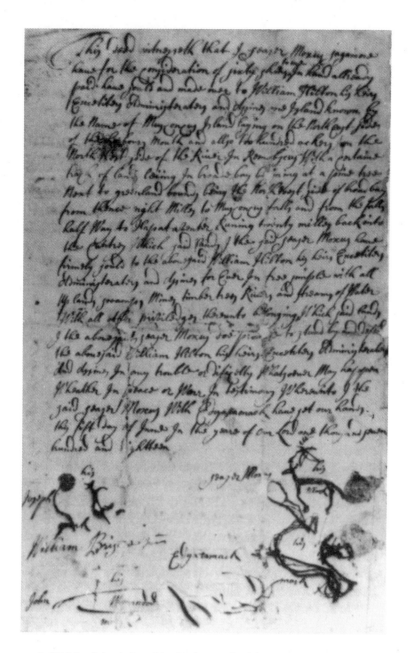

A 1718 land deed signed by Puritan authorities and Native American chieftains using pictographs (Henry E. Huntington Library and Art Gallery, San Marino, California)

incompatible with the native hunting economy, and living under European law was impractical. Native peoples used land and other property communally while Europeans strictly enforced laws protecting private property. Moreover, native practice allowed offenders to make retribution for their crimes by paying some form of mutually acceptable compensation to the victim or his family. European law was far more complicated and rigid. Also, Native Americans living on early reservations were often cheated out of their lands. Within a few generations the towns set aside for native peoples were under the control of Europeans and eventually lost their native character.

Other Groups. In Virginia the Powhatans and other groups also relocated to reservations after Bacon's Rebellion in 1676 and suffered a similar fate to that of the native peoples of New England. Elsewhere native peoples relocated westward to lands on the frontier rather than reservation islands surrounded by Europeans. In Maryland the Piscataway were forced to move to the Ohio Valley in the 1690s. The Tuscaroras left North Carolina to join the Iroquois after fighting against colonists in 1711–1713. And in Pennsylvania the Delawares moved westward in 1737 after they were defrauded in the Walking Purchase. As a model for relations between natives and whites, reservations failed miserably. It is not hard to understand why the idea of a colony of Christian Native Americans within a colony of Europeans was not a durable pattern. Native peoples numerous enough to resist would not agree, and the reservations of smaller groups were located on marginal land and inhabited by people afflicted with poverty, alcoholism, and oppression. The idea of reservations, however, became a key element of the Indian policy of the new United States after the American Revolution.

Sources:

Neal Salisbury, *Manitou and Providence: Indians, Europeans, and the Making of New England* (New York: Oxford University Press, 1982);

Salisbury, "Native People and European Settlers," in *The Cambridge History of the Native Peoples of the Americas,* volume 1, *North America,* edited by Bruce C. Trigger and Wilcomb E. Washburn (Cambridge: Cambridge University Press, 1996), pp. 420–424.

THE SOUTHEAST

Cherokees. Native Americans in the Southeast may have had contact with Europeans, or at least the microbes they brought to the New World, as early as 1526. In that year the Spanish conquistador Lucas Vásquez de Ayllón led a slave-raiding party from the Caribbean to the Carolina and Georgia coasts. In 1540 Hernando de Soto and his troops marched through Cherokee country, and in 1566–1567 Capt. Juan Pardo explored Cherokee territory. For nearly a century after that, the Cherokees were free of European interference. In 1654 Cherokees attacked the English colony of Virginia for reasons that are not clear, forcing the settlers to negotiate a peace treaty. Thereafter the Cherokees appeared frequently in the British and Spanish colonial records. Prior to European influences the Cherokees were surrounded by other powerful native groups and were often at war with them. The Cherokees spoke a language classified as part of the Iroquoian family. They developed three dialects, each associated with one of the three geographical regions into which they divided themselves. The Lower Towns were located in South Carolina and northeast Georgia. The Middle Towns and Valley Towns were clustered along the Tuckasegee River and the headwaters of the Little Tennessee River. The third group of settlements was known as the Western, Upper, or Overhill Towns, found in eastern Tennessee. The introduction of firearms made ancient enmities, which spawned the Tuscarora and Yamasee wars, more bloody. War with the Creeks, which arose out of the Yamasee conflict of 1715–1722, persisted for several generations. In 1749 the Upper Creeks and the Cherokees reached an accord, but the Lower Creeks pressed on, intent on acquiring new hunting lands. The Creeks attacked the Cherokees while their supplies were low and conquered several towns. In a treaty at Coweta in April 1754 the Cherokees acknowledged their weakened position by giving up lands between the Little River (in North Carolina) and Broad River (in Georgia).

Creeks. The Muskogee-speaking or Muscogulge peoples inhabited the interior Southeast. English settlers in Carolina called them Creeks because they lived on the tributaries of the Oconee and Ocmulgee Rivers in central

Portrait of the Creek chief Tomochichi and his nephew, 1734 (Smithsonian Institution, Washington, D.C.)

Georgia. The Creeks were highly diverse, encompassing many distinct peoples united loosely by language and broad cultural and political patterns. From the late seventeenth century through the early nineteenth century the Creeks adapted to the coming of Europeans, using their central geographical position to play European powers against each other. Initially they reacted to conflicts with the Spanish to the South by relocating and trading with the British in the Carolinas. After the Yamasee War that nearly destroyed the British, Creek leaders retreated westward to a zone equidistant from the French, the Spanish, and the British. From the 1720s until well after the Revolutionary War they struggled to protect their territory, adapting culturally to the presence of European neighbors and their trade goods.

Founding of Georgia. In 1732 a London-based society of Christian missionaries and philanthropists established the colony of Georgia. Intended in part as a second chance for debtors, Georgia's founding had three profound effects on native peoples of the Southeast. First, Georgia represented a new trading partner and additional access to superior British goods. Second, immigration to Georgia created population pressure on the Creeks, just at the same time when the Creeks began to fall into debt to the traders. The result was repeated cessions of land. Third, the colony was a pathway for escaping African American laborers to reach safety and freedom in Florida. The growing population of free people

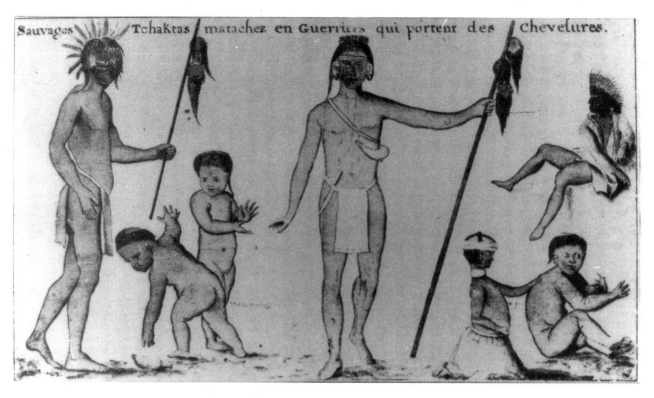

Choctaw children at play while warriors bear scalp trophies, circa 1730, drawing by A. de Batz (*Smithsonian Miscellaneous Collections*, 1927)

SEMINOLES

The Seminole people developed a separate identity in the eighteenth century, at a time when many other tribal bands withered away, either through loss of population or absorption into a larger group. The name Seminole is a variant of the Spanish *cimmaron*, meaning wanderer or runaway. It was applied to groups of Native Americans from the Oconee River area of Georgia who took up temporary residence in Florida, beginning perhaps as early as the 1500s. Permanent, continuous settlements were well established by the early to mid 1700s. The Seminoles of Florida, like many native groups in the conglomeration that the British considered to be Creeks, were friendly to newcomers.

In the aftermath of the Yamasee War of 1715–1722, a Creek leader named Brims relocated his Carolina towns to Georgia and developed a policy of neutrality with the French, Spanish, and English colonists. Another chief named Secoffee was friendly with the Spanish and began making regular visits into Florida. He was probably among the Creek delegations that visited Cuba and Mexico from time to time. His hunting camp, on the banks of Lake Miccosukee near present-day Tallahassee, began to coalesce into a permanent settlement over time, developing into one of two early Seminole locations; the second site was near present-day Gainesville. In the early 1740s a Creek named Ahaya (the Cowkeeper) founded a settlement known as Cuscowilla. Unlike the other settlements, Ahaya's village consisted of warriors opposed to the Spanish and friendly with the English. Their location, just inland from Saint Augustine, tended to hem the Spanish along the coast during much of the eighteenth century. Both Cuscowilla and the Lake Miccosukee towns were adjacent to wetlands where fish were plentiful and near woods where wild game abounded. In addition both were relatively remote from European settlements.

Throughout the eighteenth century escaping slaves from Carolina found their way into Indian country in Florida. After Georgia permitted slavery in 1755 slaves from this colony likewise slipped across the border into Spanish territory. The Seminoles treated African Americans neither as slaves nor exactly as equals. The refugee slaves lived in separate communities that raised their own crops, hunted with firearms, and apparently participated in the ceremonial life of Seminoles. The black Seminoles may have been required to pay an annual tribute in corn or other goods. But they clearly preferred such a second-class citizenship to no citizenship at all as slaves.

Source: James W. Covington, *The Seminoles of Florida* (Gainesville: University Press of Florida, 1993).

of color lived among the emerging Seminoles, who gradually developed a separate identity from their Creek relatives during the early eighteenth century.

Choctaws. The Choctaws were a large group who lived in present-day central and southern Mississippi, near the mouth of the Mississippi River and along the Gulf Coast. They were known for their prowess in agriculture. Raising more than enough maize to support both a large population and a sizable herd of cattle, they regularly had a surplus of corn to trade. They depended on hunting for only a small part of their diet and therefore were less mobile than hunter-gatherer societies. Their settlements were large and permanent, with residences made of logs and stucco. Choctaw territory was divided into southern, northwestern, and northeastern districts. They built towns on the boundaries of districts to repel intruders. Within the districts, settlements were sparse. The men of each district elected a *mingo* as the leader, based on military prowess, administrative skills, and ancestral connections. Large council meetings included all three mingos, the war chiefs, and the captains and subcaptains, who would assemble in the town square of the host mingo. After an initial wariness the Choctaws responded to French overtures of friendship. French settlers were more interested in the fur trade than in taking Choctaw lands and treated native peoples roughly as equals, sharing knowledge of hunting and farming and encouraging intermarriage. The alliance with the French generally benefited the Choctaws, despite involving them intermittently in war with the Chickasaws and the pro-British faction of the Creeks.

Chickasaws. The Chickasaws lived in present-day northwestern Mississippi, along the banks of the river. They spoke a language in the Muskogee group but distinct from that of the Creeks. Small in numbers compared to their neighbors, the Chickasaws maintained their culture partly by developing a reputation for ferocity. By the late 1600s the British had established their settlement in Carolina and traveled overland to Chickasaw territory, establishing an alliance that endured throughout the eighteenth century. A small group of Chickasaws, led by the Squirrel King, settled in South Carolina early in the 1700s to facilitate trade. From 1720 until the mid 1730s the Chickasaws were frequently at war with the French and their allies, the Choctaws. They defeated two French-Choctaw armies separately before they could link up. In the late 1730s a French army of three thousand was unable to attack because of poor weather. Finally, in the 1750s the Chickasaws defeated the French for the last time, and they remained undefeated until the American Revolution.

Sources:

Kathryn E. Holland Braund, *Deerskins and Duffels: The Creek Indian Trade with Anglo-America, 1685–1815* (Lincoln: University of Nebraska Press, 1993);

Verner W. Crane, *The Southern Frontier 1670–1732,* revised edition (New York: Norton, 1981);

Tom Hatley, *The Dividing Paths: Cherokees and South Carolinians through the Era of Revolution* (New York: Oxford University Press, 1993);

Richard White, *Roots of Dependency: Subsistence, Environment, and Social Change among the Choctaws, Pawnees, and Navajos* (Lincoln: University of Nebraska Press, 1983).

TRADE

Intra-Indian Activity. Archaeological evidence clearly establishes that by the time of the Hopewell people, about 200 B.C. to A.D. 500, Native Americans engaged in trade on a continentwide basis. Artists in the Ohio Valley used shells from the Gulf Coast, mica from the Pacific Northwest, and copper from the Great Lakes. Furthermore, art objects traveled thousands of miles through many hands to end up in the burials of native leaders of many cultures. Over the centuries small family-based groups came together to trade goods and find mates. Some particularly popular locations, such as The Dalles on the Columbia River, apparently attracted crowds numbering into the thousands. As Europeans entered North America, their metal, glass, and textile ob-

A Mohawk chief wearing a mixture of European and Native American garb. The wolf indicates that he belonged to the Wolf Clan.

A cloak of animal skin decorated with seashells. It is called "Powhatan's mantle," but its exact origin is unknown (Smithsonian Institution, Washington, D.C.).

jects all entered native commerce and were widely traded among the Indians.

Furs. The trade in the Great Lakes area was the initial entry of North American goods into the world economy. Great Lakes Indians swapped their beaver robes for technologically advanced goods ranging from guns and kettles to beads and cloth. The fur trade set the pattern for other trade relationships between natives and Europeans, as both sides maneuvered and negotiated for the best price. Typically, as the populations of fur-bearing animals died out, Europeans wanted to trade directly with the Indians whose furs were still plentiful. At the same time, native peoples whose own fur stocks were depleted positioned themselves as middlemen to broker deals and continue their involvement in the trade. In the Southeast the pattern was repeated, with deerskins replacing furs, in the first half of the eighteenth century.

Luxury and Necessity. In a relatively brief time what had been novelties became essential parts of native culture. Guns supplanted the bow and arrow; woolen cloth substituted for buckskin; and glass beads took the place of natural adornments. Durable cast-

iron pots soon replaced fragile pottery. When the pots reached the end of their lives, warriors flaked the metal to make knives, arrowheads, and other tools. By the early eighteenth century native groups from Maine to Louisiana were culturally dependent upon goods—everything from fishhooks to gunpowder—which they had no way to make for themselves. With no market for their products, many craftsmen died without passing on their skills, so that within a few generations many arts and crafts were all but lost in many native groups.

Alcohol. By far the most destructive aspect of the Indian trade was alcohol. Native Americans had virtually no exposure to beverage alcohol before 1500 and were as vulnerable to alcoholism as they were to smallpox, measles, and other diseases. Alcohol became an important medium of exchange by the late seventeenth century, and virtually every Indian trader sold it. Usually consumed in the form of rum or brandy, alcohol played a destructive role in native culture. Many Indians found alcohol highly addictive and were willing to do anything to get it. In 1774 William Bartram described a group of Creek warriors who were carrying twenty five-gallon kegs of liquor as trade goods. They kept it intact until reaching a trading post, where traders persuaded them to have drinks in celebration. They remained drunk for ten days. Bartram described the ensuing events: "White and red men and women without distinction, passed the day merrily with

CHEATING THE INDIANS

During the colonial period unscrupulous whites frequently robbed intoxicated Indians of trade goods and defrauded them of their lands. Such a case arose in New Jersey in 1716, and fortunately for the Native Americans involved, the governor restored their lands.

Myself [John Kay] with several others sent for John Weitherill and heard the Indian's complaint against him, which was that said John Weitherill had come to said Indian King and treated him with cyder and made him drunk, and that he came again to him the next morning and would have given him more cider and told him he sold him some land the night before, being land which said Indian King and other Indians lived on, and had set his hand to a deed or writing for the sale of said land. The said Indian King declared he remembered nothing of selling any land to said John Weitherill or setting his hand to any paper and further said he had always refused to sell that land and had reserved it for himself and the Indians to live upon and that the Indians had a right in it and would never suffer him to sell it. . . . If John Weitherill had got him to sign any paper it was by defraud and cheating him and that he could neither eat, drink, nor rest with quiet until that writing or paper was destroyed.

Source: W. Keith Kavenagh, ed., *Foundations of Colonial America: A Documentary History*, 3 volumes (New York: Chelsea House, 1973),

Seneca antler comb, circa 1650, decorated with the figure of a Dutchman (New York State Museum)

these jovial, amorous topers, and the nights in convivial songs, dances, and sacrifices to Venus, as long as they could stand or move; for in these frolicks both sexes take such liberties with each other, and act, without constraint or shame." When they ran low, women would sell recycled rum, which they had covertly spat out into a bottle after pretending to drink. The demand for alcohol caused distortions in the native economy, as hunters would trade skins for alcohol and go into debt for the trade goods that had become necessities. In the Southeast so much debt accumulated by the early 1770s that the London merchants withheld shipments of goods until receiving two million acres as payment.

Land. Trade provided a framework for negotiations between native peoples and Europeans in which land was a principal topic. Europeans and native peoples fundamentally misunderstood each other's ideas about land ownership. In general, native peoples did not consider land something that any could own, buy, or sell. In their view land was given to the people to live on and was often revered as sacred and inseparable from the people who lived on it. Initially, at least, Native Americans were usually willing to share their land with Europeans. But the colonists mistook native willingness to share as an agreement to sell. They would draw up legal sales agreements, which Indians thought were agreements to live in peace. Plying native leaders with alcohol, colonists used so-called whiskey treaties to assert a claim to native lands. As white settlers moved in, conflicts often erupted in which native warriors demonstrated great courage, organization, and skill. Eventually, however, the superior weaponry of the Europeans produced military victories and a steady westward movement of the line of white settlement.

Sources:

William Bartram, *Travels through North and South Carolina, Georgia, East and West Florida* . . . (Philadelphia: Printed by James & Johnson, 1791);

Christopher S. Peebles, "Moundville from 1000 to 1500 AD as Seen from 1840 to 1985 AD," in *Chiefdoms in the Americas*, edited by Robert D. Drennan and Carlos A. Uribe (Lanham, Md.: University Press of America, 1987), pp. 33–36;

Richard White, *The Middle Ground: Indians, Empires and Republics in the Great Lakes Region, 1650–1815* (Cambridge: Cambridge University Press, 1991).

HEADLINE MAKERS

JOSEPH BRANT (THAYENDANEGEA)

1743?-1807
MOHAWK TRIBAL LEADER

Family Connections. Named Thayendanegea ("He Places Together Two Bets") by his people, Joseph Brant was born into a prominent Mohawk family on the New York frontier. His father was Tehonwaghkwangeraghkwa, or Nickus Brant, while his grandfather was Sagayeeanquarashtow, one of the four native "kings" who visited London in the early eighteenth century. Molly, his older sister, was the influential consort of the wealthy landowner and merchant Sir William Johnson, superintendent of the Northern District for Indian Affairs. Brant married Margaret, the daughter of the Oneida leader Skenandon. When she died he wed her sister, Susana; when he was widowed a second time he married Catherine Croghan, the half-Mohawk daughter of Col. George Croghan, an interpreter in the Indian Department.

Accomplishments. Joseph Brant is remembered as a military leader, a diplomat, and a linguist. Missionaries taught him how to write Mohawk, and in 1761 he was recruited by the Mohegan teacher Samson Occom to attend Eleazar Wheelock's charity school in Lebanon, Connecticut. Brant attended the school for several terms and instructed white youths in the Mohawk language, emerging as a skilled interpreter. His formal education ended in 1763 when his sister Molly persuaded him to return home. Until 1775 he served Johnson as an aide and translator and informed him of American overtures for Iroquoian neutrality in the war between England and her colonies.

Ties with England. Brant visited London during the winter of 1775–1776. He apparently concluded from his visit that the British were the best protection for native peoples, who feared the rebellious Americans. During the Revolutionary War he helped keep the majority of Iroquois warriors in the royal camp, and he led several raids against the frontier settlements. Afterward Brant led some of the Mohawks into Canada along the Grand River, north of Lake Erie. While there he fused the roles of traditional Iroquois sachem and colonial lord of the manor. He and his family lived in a grand style, speaking English, wearing European clothes, and hosting elegant dinners served by well-dressed slaves. He encouraged missionary efforts and wrote Mohawk translations of the Anglican Book of Common Prayer and the Gospel of Mark. During conflicts with the new American government in the 1790s he lost his influence among the western tribes and died on 24 November 1807.

Sources:

Isabel Thompson Kelsay, *Joseph Brant, 1743–1807: Man of Two Worlds* (Syracuse, N.Y.: Syracuse University Press, 1984);

James O'Donnell, "Joseph Brant," in *American Indian Leaders: Studies in Diversity*, edited by R. David Edmunds (Lincoln: University of Nebraska Press, 1980), pp. 21–40.

MEMESKIA

?-1752
MIAMI TRIBAL LEADER

Old Briton. Memeskia was a leader of the Piankashaw band of the Miamis, a tribe living in present-day northern Indiana and Ohio. As a youth he traveled extensively on the Ohio River and lived on the lower Wabash River. Later he lived in a village in northeastern Indiana, near present-day Fort Wayne. Known as Old Briton because of his affinity for the British and their superior trade goods, Memeskia believed that his people would be better off severing ties with their former allies, the French. Both the French and British settlements were thinly spread over the Ohio territory, and the Miamis had a degree of independence regardless of their alliance. Memeskia may have been motivated by the hope of manipulating the two European powers to his advantage.

British Ally. In early 1747, when a British-sponsored uprising against the French failed, Memeskia led the Miamis to the new village of Pickawillany. Strategically located at the confluence of the Great Miami River and Loramie's Creek in western Ohio, it was far enough east that any French raiders would be detected before they got close. But it was near enough to the Potawatomi, Kickapoo, Illinois, and other tribes living in present-day Michigan, Indiana, and Illinois for trade and accessible to the British traders of Pennsylvania and Virginia.

Diplomacy. During the winter of 1749–1750 Pickawillany became a large center of the Indian trade, attracting new residents, including three hundred Weas and Piankashaws who arrived in the spring. During the summer Memeskia accepted gifts from the French but ignored their demands to relocate nearer to them; that November the British sent their own presents to assure his loyalty. By 1751 Memeskia declared war on the French and made plans to meet the British to formalize an alliance. But Memeskia feared to leave his village unguarded and could not attend the planned council. French raiders reached Pickawillany while Memeskia and his warriors were out on the fall hunt, but with too few troops to attack. Returning from the hunt, Memeskia executed three French prisoners and had the ears cut off a fourth; the ears were sent back as a warning.

War. In the spring of 1752 the French attacked Pickawillany in strength, capturing women in the cornfields, disarming men in the village, seizing property, and forcing Memeskia and twenty warriors into the stockade. Outnumbered ten to one, Memeskia reluctantly accepted the French leader's offer of a cease-fire and the return of his Miami prisoners in exchange for the surrender of the stockade and its British trading post. Once the prisoners were exchanged, however, the French and their Indian allies took bitter revenge. Ottawa and Ojibwa (or Chippewa) warriors killed Memeskia and mutilated his body. After cutting out his heart and eating it they boiled his body and consumed it in front of the villagers.

Sources:

R. David Edmunds, "Old Briton," in *American Indian Leaders: Studies in Diversity,* edited by Edmunds (Lincoln: University of Nebraska Press, 1980), pp. 1–20;

Neal Salisbury, "Native People and European Settlers in Eastern North America, 1600–1783," in *The Cambridge History of the Native Peoples of the Americas,* volume 1, *North America,* edited by Bruce G. Trigger and Wilcomb E. Washburn (Cambridge: Cambridge University Press, 1996), pp. 440–441.

METACOM

1640?-1676
WAMPANOAG SACHEM

Interlopers. Metacom (or Metacomet), whom white colonists knew as King Philip, was a war leader of the Wampanoags, an Algonquian-speaking people who lived in present-day Rhode Island and Massachusetts. Metacom was a member of the third generation of Native Americans since the arrival of English colonists. By the time he reached his teen years relations with the settlers had become dictated by land seizures, mistreatment, and the pressures of missionaries to subvert native customs and religion.

Tribal Leader. Metacom was one of five children of Massasoit, a Wampanoag chieftain who had cooperated with Pilgrim colonists in Plymouth. Massasoit died in 1661 and was succeeded by Metacom's older brother Wamsutta, who died a year later. Metacom assumed leadership in his mid twenties and for the next decade kept the English on edge. In 1671 Massachusetts Bay and Plymouth forced him to sign a treaty that bound him to their authority; he complied, hoping to buy time before the war that seemed inevitable started. When war did come in 1675, the Wampanoags had not completed their native alliance against the white settlers who virtually surrounded them.

King Philip's War. Hostilities were triggered by the murder of Metacom's assistant, a Christian Indian who had revealed the sachem's war preparations to the English. His death led to the trial and execution of three Wampanoags, which provoked further bloodshed. Facing a war of extermination, Metacom responded by attacking and burning nearby settlements. As native groups chose sides, some joined the colonists in hopes of economic betterment while others took up the Wampanoags' cause and destroyed white settlements from central Massachusetts to the Connecticut River valley. Terrified colonists revised their images of native peoples, with pictures of bloody tomahawks and severed scalps replacing scenes of cooperation and the first Thanksgiving. Colonists themselves took up scalping, offering bounties for the scalps or entire heads of their enemies.

Defeat and Death. The decisive battle was fought in a swamp near Narragansett Bay in December 1675, where the largest army the colonists had ever raised overran a Narragansett stockade, burning some six hundred native men, women, and children inside. When the survivors retreated toward present-day Albany, New York, Iroquois warriors forced them back into Massachusetts before they could recover from their losses. A series of smaller battles led to Metacom's ultimate defeat and death in August 1676. His killers dismembered his corpse and took pieces of it as trophies, publicly displaying his severed head for more than twenty years. His wife and son suffered the fate of hundreds of Wampanoags, Nipmucs, and Narragansetts: they were sold as slaves and transported to the sugar islands of the Caribbean, where they died. Metacom's forces had attacked more than half of New England's ninety settlements and destroyed twelve of them. His defeat marked the end of effective Native American resistance in southern New England.

Sources:

Russell Bourne, *The Red King's Rebellion: Racial Politics in New England, 1675–1678* (New York: Atheneum, 1990);

Alvin M. Josephy, "The Betrayal of King Philip," in *The Patriot Chiefs: A Chronicle of American Indian Resistance* (New York: Viking, 1969), pp. 31–62.

Grace Steele Woodward, *Pocahontas* (Norman: University of Oklahoma Press, 1969).

POCAHONTAS

1596?–1617
POWHATAN "PRINCESS"

European Connections. The daughter of Wahunsunacock, chief of the Powhatan people, Pocahontas ("the Playful One") is remembered as the first native woman to marry an Englishman in the North American colonies. Her connection to the Europeans arose in the context of Native American foreign relations. In the autumn of 1607, when the newly arrived colonists at Jamestown were starving, the Powhatan chief sent corn to help them. The Powhatans viewed the English as potentially powerful allies although Capt. John Smith and the other colonists felt so powerless that they considered all native peoples as threatening.

Smith. In December 1607 Smith was captured during an exploratory expedition. The Powhatans staged a mock execution ceremony (designed to dramatize native power and friendship) by pretending to cut off Smith's head. At the crucial moment, Pocahontas, then age twelve, intervened, throwing herself on Smith's body. Smith and the other Virginians interpreted this as a spontaneous demonstration of love (probably divinely inspired) while recent historians see it as part of a cultural drama of power and an offer of alliance.

Rolfe. In 1613 Capt. Samuel Argall, a member of the Virginia council, led a raid against the Powhatans and captured Pocahonatas. John Rolfe, a prosperous tobacco planter, fell in love with the young Indian woman and asked permission from Gov. Sir Thomas Dale to marry her. Their union occurred during a time of few white women in Virginia. It also served as an attempt to improve relations between the whites and native peoples.

England. In 1616 Rolfe and Pocahontas traveled to England on a voyage to encourage future colonization of Virginia. The following spring, as they were preparing to return to North America, Pocahontas became ill, probably from pneumonia, and died at the approximate age of twenty-two. A statue in the cemetery of Saint George's Church at Gravesend in Kent is believed to mark her grave. Her death, and that of her father, led to a deterioration of relations that resulted in war and the destruction of the Powhatan people.

Sources:
Frances Mossiker, *Pocahontas: The Life and the Legend* (New York: Knopf, 1976);

POPÉ

1630?–1690?
PUEBLO RELIGIOUS AND POLITICAL LEADER

Early Spanish Contact. Popé was a revolutionary leader of the Pueblo peoples of present-day southwestern United States. When conquistadores under Francisco Vásquez de Coronado passed through Pueblo territory in 1540–1542 the Pueblo peoples were forced out of their homes temporarily but returned to them for a full generation before the Spanish reappeared. Rumors of gold and the desire to avenge old wounds stimulated Spanish interest, and by 1590 a short-lived Spanish colony was established near the village the Europeans named Santo Domingo. Finally in 1591 the scion of a wealthy immigrant family, Don Juan de Oñate, moved to the Rio Grande and Chama River. He established his capital at the town he called San Juan and ordered the Indians to disperse to nearby villages. As friars delivered religious instruction, troops searched for plunder and provoked a rebellion at the Pueblo town of Acoma. The villagers reacted by throwing the Spaniards over the side of the cliffs of their mesa. More Spanish troops arrived, and in the subsequent fighting more than one thousand native warriors died. Others were tried, convicted, and had their hands and feet chopped off as punishment; Acoma women were enslaved.

Christianity. Spanish officials established the capital of Santa Fe a few miles northeast of Santo Domingo. They imposed an *encomienda* regime, treating Indians like European serfs and demanding annual payment of tribute in addition to forced labor. Some Pueblo people began to accept Christianity, although traditionalists continued to resist. Disputes among the colonists over the authority of the governor and the priests weakened the authority of both.

Resistance. By 1660 droughts began to reduce the food supply for a growing colonial population, causing some Indians to fear that their old gods were offended. Starving Apaches attacked Pueblo peoples for food. At this point an older Tewa religious leader named Popé emerged in San Juan. The Spanish had seized and enslaved his older brother as punishment for Popé's rejection of Christianity and his persistence in observing the old religion. Popé told the people that the drought was caused by the Spanish friars; only their departure would end the shortage of rainfall, he warned. As word spread of his preaching, his audience grew, and attempts to suppress him only fed the rising panic. When Popé and other priests were imprisoned in Santa Fe, a delegation obtained their release by threatening outright rebellion.

Popé urged the execution of all informers, even if they were members of his own family. He dramatized the anger of the gods by arranging for a symbolic costumed dance in a kiva (ceremonial pit). He sent cords with knots tied in them as a signal for the number of days remaining before a general revolt.

Attack on Santa Fe. Coordinated attacks began on 10 August 1680 and were highly successful. In a few days time, the entire Spanish community had retreated to Santa Fe. After several days of fierce fighting the Pueblo Indians burned Santa Fe to the ground and forced the white settlers to flee southward hundreds of miles to El Paso. In the Pueblo towns the Spanish language and the Christian religion were banned, and all converts were ritually cleansed of their sins. Eventually Popé lost the support of his followers, who had become accustomed to European trade goods. In addition they were vulnerable to attacks by Apaches who seized their horses and introduced them to other native cultures north of the Pueblo region. Popé died sometime around 1690, and Pueblo unity eroded. In 1691 the Spanish returned in force and reasserted their authority in the Southwest.

Sources:

Ramón Gutiérrez, *When Jesus Came the Corn Mothers Went Away: Marriage, Sexuality, and Power in New Mexico 1500–1846* (Stanford, Cal.: Stanford University Press, 1991);

Joe S. Sando, *Pueblo Profiles: Cultural Identity through Centuries of Change* (Sante Fe, N.M.: Clear Light, 1995).

PUBLICATIONS

Andrés González Barcía, *Ensayo Cronológico para la Historia General de la Florida, 1512–1722* (Madrid, 1723)—a Spanish study of interactions with Native Americans and European rivals in the 1500s and 1600s;

John Mason, *A Brief History of the Pequot War* (Boston: S. Kneeland & T. Green, 1736)—a firsthand account of the 1637 war on the Connecticut River, written by an English officer but not published until a century after the fighting;

Mary Rowlandson, *The Soveraignty & Goodness of God . . .* (Boston: Printed by Samuel Green, Jr., 1682)—a captivity narrative of a victim of Metacom's War in New England;

John Smith, *A True Relation of Such Occurences and Accidents of Noate as Hath Hapned in Virginia since the First Planting of That Collony . . .* (London: Printed for John Tappe, 1608)—contains descriptions of the Powhatan tribe;

John Underhill, *Nevves from America; or, A New and Experimentall Discoverie of New England* (London: Printed by J. D. for Peter Cole, 1638)—an account by a participant in the near extermination of the Pequots.

RELIGION

by ELIZABETH NYBAKKEN

CONTENTS

Sidebars and tables are listed in italics.

1620

- Plymouth colony is settled by separatist Pilgrims who had been living in Holland since 1608 when they fled persecution in England under Charles I.

1625

- The Jesuit order of Catholic priests comes to North America and attains success in converting the Indians because they do not demand that the Indians abandon many of their own religious beliefs and practices.

1630

- Massachusetts is founded by Puritans under Gov. John Winthrop to serve as a new world example for the Church of England.

- The Great Migration of Puritans to New England begins. They emigrate in order to escape persecution under Charles I, and over the next ten years they spread out and establish other colonies in the area.

1632

- Cecilius Calvert, Lord Baltimore, receives a charter for Maryland, which he intends to use as a haven for Catholics who are being persecuted in England.

1634

- The first Roman Catholic church in the English colonies is erected in Saint Mary's City, Maryland.

1636

- Roger Williams is banished from Massachusetts Bay colony and founds Rhode Island, which is based on freedom of religion and separation of church and state.

- Massachusetts establishes Harvard College to provide education for Puritan ministers.

- The Antinomian Crisis begins in Massachusetts Bay, resulting in the banishment of Anne Hutchinson and her followers, most of whom settle in Rhode Island the next year.

1639

- Roger Williams establishes the first Baptist church in America at Providence, Rhode Island.

1640

- The English Civil War starts as Puritans rise up against Charles I.

1643

- The Westminster Assembly meets and over the next five years formulates a "Confession of Faith," the "Directory of Public Worship," the "Form of Church Government," and the "Longer and Shorter Catechism," which are adopted by the Presbyterian and other colonial churches.

1647

- Massachusetts passes the "Old Deluder Satan" Act, which instructs each town to establish schools to enable all to read the Bible.

1649

- The Toleration Act institutes freedom of religion in Maryland so that the Protestant majority cannot discriminate against the Catholic settlers for whom the colony was founded.

1651

- John Eliot founds the first "praying village" for Indian converts in Massachusetts.

1653

- Oliver Cromwell becomes Lord Protector of the Commonwealth of England, Scotland, and Ireland.

1656

- The first Quakers arrive in Massachusetts from Rhode Island to proselytize but are arrested and condemned to death by the Puritan government.

1660

- The Restoration of Charles II to the English throne occurs. He reinstitutes the old Anglican Church and rewards his favorites with proprietary colonies in America.

1661

- Charles II begins to introduce the Clarendon Code into England and Ireland to force conformity to the Church of England.

1662

- The synod of Massachusetts recommends the Half-Way Covenant to New England churches whereby children of non–church members can be baptized and remain in ôhe churches as "half-way" members; not all congregations adopt it.

1680

- The Pueblos in the present-day southwestern United States rebel against Spanish attempts to suppress their religion. The Spanish abandon the area around Santa Fe but reconquer it ten years later.

1681

- William Penn receives a charter for Pennsylvania and establishes a government based on Quaker principles that guarantee freedom of conscience.

1685

- Louis XIV revokes the Edict of Nantes, which had protected French Protestants.
- James II forms the Dominion of New England.

1688

- The Glorious Revolution occurs in England, in which James II is replaced by the Protestant monarchs William and Mary. They recharter the New England colonies as royal colonies, which in turn marks the end of Puritan control of the area.

1689

- James Blair is appointed the personal representative of the bishop of London in Virginia and begins the reform of the Anglican Church in the colonies.

1691

- George Keith creates a schism among the Quakers, whom he accuses of being too lax. Quakers respond by tightening up their organization and becoming more formal. Keith becomes an Anglican missionary in the colonies.

1692

- The Salem witchcraft trials begin and result in mass hysteria of people who think that God is allowing Satan to hurt them.

1699

- The first Lutheran church in America is organized in Wilmington, Delaware. It was named Holy Trinity but is now called Old Swedes Church.

1701

- The Society for the Propagation of the Gospel in Foreign Parts (S.P.G.) is founded and pays for Anglican missionaries to come to the American colonies.

- Orthodox Connecticut clergy establish Yale College to guarantee more conservative ministerial education than liberal Harvard College is providing.

1706

- Francis Makemie forms the first American presbytery in Philadelphia and marks the beginning of the organized Presbyterian church in the colonies.

1708

- Connecticut adopts the Saybrook Platform, bringing Congregational churches together into an organization of consociations and limiting some of the autonomy of individual congregations.

1719

- The first German Reform church opens in Germantown, Pennsylvania, with services conducted by laypeople.

1722

- The Reverend Timothy Cutler, president of Yale College, announces his conversion to Anglicanism. He and his followers become the leading Anglicans in the northern colonies.

1729

- Presbyterian factions compromise over subscription to the Westminster Confession of Faith and set the first standards for the Presbyterian church in America.

1734

- Jonathan Edwards stimulates a series of revivals in the Connecticut River valley.

1739

- George Whitefield arrives in Pennsylvania and sparks the revivals that lead to the Great Awakening. It lasts until 1743 in the middle and northern colonies and divides many denominations into "Old" and "New" factions.

1740

- Gilbert Tennent preaches "The Danger of an Unconverted Ministry," which attacks learned clergymen, making an educated ministry the focus of the Great Awakening among the Presbyterians.

1741

- Jonathan Edwards delivers a sermon on "Sinners in the Hands of an Angry God," which portrays the terrors of hell. It becomes the most popular sermon of the period in New England.

- The Presbyterian synod splits; the Old Side remains in the Synod of Philadelphia, while the New Side forms the Synod of New York in 1746.

- Count Nikolaus Zinzendorf arrives in Pennsylvania to promote the Moravian unification of all denominations.

1742

- The first school for training slaves to be ministers opens in South Carolina under the sponsorship of the Reverend Alexander Garden, the Commissary of the S.P.G. It remains open until 1764.

- Connecticut passes anti-itinerant legislation to stop roving preachers of the Great Awakening.

- Henry Melchior Muhlenberg arrives to minister to the Lutherans in America.

1743

- Jonathan Edwards publishes "Some Thoughts Concerning the Recent Revival of Religion," which defends the emotionalism of the Great Awakening. Charles Chauncy responds in "Seasonable Thoughts on the State of Religion in New England," which sums up the Old Light objections to the revivals.

1744

- The New London Academy, conducted by Francis Alison, is adopted as the official seminary of the Old Side Synod of Philadelphia and offers free collegiate instruction to any Protestant.

1746

- Michael Schlatter arrives in Pennsylvania to unify the German Reform congregations. He convenes the first synod, or coetus, within a year.

1748

- The Pennsylvania Ministerium, the first synodical organization of Lutherans in America, is established under the leadership of the Reverend Henry Muhlenberg.

1750

- Jonathan Edwards is dismissed by the Northampton Congregationalist Church and moves to the frontier outpost at Stockbridge, Massachusetts, where he writes his treatises on "Original Sin" and "Freedom of the Will."

OVERVIEW

Native Peoples. When the Europeans began their colonization of the North American continent after 1500, one of their goals was to convert the native peoples to Christianity. The Spanish in the Southwest and the French in the North brought Catholic priests and friars with them, for Catholicism was their state religion. The English on the East Coast practiced several varieties of Protestantism and relied more on the settlers themselves to bring their interpretation of Christianity to the Native Americans. Although there was a wide variety of religious beliefs among the native peoples, all believed in a supreme creator who continued to maintain a presence in their world. The Europeans did not recognize the basic similarity of these religious beliefs to their own, and each nation attempted to convince the natives that its interpretation of God was correct and its religious practices were the most valid. The Spanish created missions in the Southwest, gathering the native peoples into communities where the friars could teach the European ways of living and thus make it easier to convert them to Catholicism and suppress their traditional religious practices. Those who did convert usually practiced their traditional religion as well. The French were more successful among the northeastern Woodland nations, particularly after the Jesuit order of priests arrived in 1625. They allowed the native converts to retain their traditional cultural practices and incorporate some Christian ideas into their own belief system.

Early Outposts. In the seventeenth century the eastern coastal colonies were little more than outposts of English immigrants. The settlers brought with them religious belief systems which had been formed in England and which reflected the variety of emphases spawned by the English Reformation. They lived in primarily two areas. To the north were the Pilgrims and Puritans in New England who translated Calvinist directives into a formula for creating religious communities independent of England. Their way of life was centered on the church, and their religious beliefs dictated the structure of families, society, economy, and government. These "Bible Commonwealths" spread throughout present-day Massachusetts, Connecticut, and New Hampshire and constituted a "New England Way." Rhode Island attracted people who disagreed with the prevailing view in these communities, primarily Baptists and Quakers. To the south, around the Chesapeake Bay, the Puritan emphases of the Anglican Church were present in Virginia, but the settlers practiced their religion privately because the dispersed settlements precluded the community organization found in New England. After Virginia became a royal colony in 1624, the Church of England was established as the official religion but did not affect the lives of the settlers much. The clergy who came were inferior, and the planters were more interested in making money than in practicing religion. In this area religion occupied a comfortable niche within a society orientated toward more secular concerns. Maryland developed in a different manner. This land was granted in 1632 to an individual, George Calvert, Baron of Baltimore, who intended it to be a haven for his fellow Catholics who were being persecuted in England. Yet non-Catholics always outnumbered Catholics in the colony, and to insure that Catholics would not suffer at the hands of the majority, the assembly passed a Toleration Act in 1649, which guaranteed the free exercise of religion. Yet Catholics continued to hold important offices and ran the colony in its early years.

English Developments. The shifts in the religious scene in England had a direct effect on American religious life, particularly in seventeenth-century New England. The move to purify the Anglican Church of England of its Catholic practices that had begun with the English Reformation gained momentum until it culminated in a Puritan victory against Charles I in the English Civil War and during the Puritan rule in the Interregnum (1640–1660). All of the varieties of puritanism that arose in this period appeared in New England to challenge the Puritan Orthodoxy there. The Stuart monarchs were restored to the throne in 1660, and their determination to reestablish a more Catholic Anglican Church threatened the very existence of the religious communities in New England. Although James II was deposed in the Glorious Revolution of 1688, the new Protestant monarchs, William and Mary, supported the unpurified Anglican Church and removed the New England colonies from Puritan control.

Continental Conflicts. American religion was also influenced by religious strife on the European continent that intensified during the seventeenth century. In an effort to unify their countries, rulers persecuted any who dissented from the state religion. German princes forced their pietistic sects to seek new homelands; in 1685 Louis XIV revoked the Edict of Nantes, under which Protestants had been tolerated, and drove the Huguenots from France; from 1661 to 1665 Charles II introduced the Clarendon Code into England and Ireland to force conformity to the Church of England. These efforts, coupled with the ensuing religious-political wars, drove many Protestants to the colonies, enhancing the religious pluralism that already was forming. During the Glorious Revolution the colonists did not know for several months whether the Catholic James II had prevailed over his Protestant challengers. Rumors that his royal governors were directed to deliver the colonies to the French papists fueled Leisler's Rebellion in New York and Puritan rebellions in New England in which the colonists imprisoned the royal officials and took over the governments. Fearful of a French-Indian invasion, the inhabitants of Maryland formed a Protestant Association, removed all Catholics from government offices, and even convinced the Crown to deprive Lord Baltimore of his proprietorship for twenty-six years. Once in control, however, the Protestants abided by the Toleration Act and did not persecute the resident Catholics. Wars between England and France became a contest for a religious empire, which extended to America. The colonists joined in the battles as much to protect their Protestant religion from the hated Catholicism as to attain political control of North America.

Pluralism. When Charles II was restored to the throne in 1660, he rewarded his loyal supporters by granting them land in America. New York, taken from the Dutch in 1664, already contained settlers with a variety of religious orientations, but New Jersey, Pennsylvania, and the Carolinas were relatively vacant. In order to attract the most settlers, all of these proprietary colonies guaranteed freedom of religion to those immigrants who were fleeing wars and religious persecution in their homelands. They came in droves, bringing their Old World religions with them and creating religious diversity in these newer colonies. Even a few Catholics and Jews came, although the latter were denied political rights. The appearance of larger farms or plantations which could no longer count on indentured European servants as a labor force also led to an increase in African slaves, which added African religion and Islam to the spiritual brew. Adherents of a variety of religious belief systems were forced to coexist, sharing ideas and empha-

ses and blending in the beliefs in magic and the power of the supernatural held by many of the common folk of all origins.

Colonial Problems. In the early part of the eighteenth century immigrants were mixed, scattered, and unable to support a settled minister of their traditional denomination, even if they could find one. There was a shortage of clergy, often caused by ministerial requirements set by Old World churches. Thus the religious scene was fluid, with settlers attending whatever Protestant church was within their reach. For instance, Presbyterians and Baptists in Philadelphia met together in a storehouse and listened to any Presbyterian or Baptist minister who happened to be in town. The most desirable clergy in the middle colonies were those who could preach in English, Dutch, and German. Most denominations directed their settled ministers to officiate in the smaller, outlying congregations and ádopted temporary measures to increase the number of qualified clergy. Anglican ministers could only be ordained by a bishop who resided in England, so the Church of England paid its ordained clergy to come as missionaries. The Dutch Reformed Church created a subsidiary body just to oversee the American ordination of ministers for both the Dutch and German Reformed Churches. Presbyterian clergy were required to have a university degree, which was difficult to obtain in the colonies, so the synod allowed ministerial candidates to take an examination instead.

American Denominations. The growing numbers of immigrants in the eighteenth century joined earlier settlers and slowly blended their divergent practices into the American denominations of Congregational, Presbyterian, Baptist, Quaker, Lutheran, Anglican, German Reform, and Dutch Reform. The Great Awakening of the late 1730s and early 1740s influenced and accelerated this development as traveling revivalistic preachers both challenged the nature of existing denominations and hastened their spread into new regions. The result by midcentury was a geographical diversity of denominations, each of which formed intercolonial ties. This development occurred in the same period in which the American provinces were being reintegrated into the transatlantic world in religious and Enlightenment thought, as well as in politics and economics. Americans were on the threshold of defining themselves as distinctively American in their unique blend of the secular new learning and old religious affiliations. Awareness of this distinctiveness became more conscious in the period after 1750.

TOPICS IN THE NEWS

AFRICAN RELIGIONS

Traditional Beliefs. Most Africans came to the American colonies as slaves from the western areas and held a variety of religious beliefs. There were some common patterns, however. Africans believed in one High God, who created the world. He was often associated with the sky and remained somewhat uninvolved in the lives of humans. Lesser gods and ancestral spirits, however, were actively involved with the daily lives of individuals and the society. Groups of gods were associated with natural phenomena, such as thunder, earth, and especially water. Gods of nature resided in trees, hills, and animals. They were as kind, cruel, arbitrary, or willful as humans and had individual personalities and preferences. Humans had to maintain proper relationships to them by establishing shrines, wearing certain colors, eating particular foods, and conducting religious ceremonies that pleased them. Ancestral spirits were more varied and personal. Whether they had lived long ago or recently, they were honored as the founders of villages and kinship groups and served as custodians of culture and laws and as mediators between humans and the gods. It was within their power to grant or deny fertility and health to their devotees. They were reincarnated in one of their descendants, but their souls returned to the High God after that human died. Elderly people were revered, in part because they preserved the memory of the dead and in part because they were chronologically closer to the ancestors. Burial rites ensured that the dead entered the spirit world and did not linger in the natural world as restless and malevolent ghosts. Funerals were long affairs. After death the ancestors demanded offerings of food and drink in ceremonies of varying degrees of complexity. Priests served as mediators, able to read the fates of individuals, to divine the wills of gods and ancestral spirits, and to identify all manner of witchcraft. They prescribed the charms and amulets which were charged with magical power to protect and help humans as well as those natural herbs and roots which promoted healing. Priests also conducted the religious ceremonies devoted to the individual gods and ancestral spirits. Interwoven with these rituals was a vibrant pattern of music—dancing, drumming, and singing.

Islam and Christianity. Some Africans were practicing Muslims and Catholics when they came to America. The trade networks of northwest Africa brought the Islam religion, which drew on Judeo-Christian roots but viewed Jesus as only a minor spiritual leader and Mohammed as its greatest prophet. Muslims followed the teachings of the Koran, observing dietary restrictions and praying in the direction of Mecca five times a day. The Portuguese explorers converted some to Catholicism. Many Africans blended these religions into their traditional belief systems. To them, God and Allah were just different names for the High God; Mohammed, Mary, and Jesus served the intermediary function of their lesser gods, and the Catholic saints were uncommonly similar to their ancestor spirits. The importance of water in their religious ceremonies prepared them for the sacrament of baptism. The magical power of charms was easily viewed in the donning of crosses or scraps of Koran parchment to protect oneself in battle.

Conversion. In the American colonies Africans were unevenly dispersed. The relatively small numbers in the northern colonies often blended into households and adopted the variety of Christianity practiced there. Puritans, as might be expected, were particularly anxious to convert their charges and enforce Christian mores, but this concern transcended denominations. The tobacco and rice colonies of the South had more Africans where concerted efforts at proselytizing occurred, particularly in the eighteenth century by the Anglican-supported Society for the Propagation of the Gospel (S.P.G.). It was created to bring salvation to those with the least prior access to the Scriptures. Some slaveholders were reluctant to expose their laborers to a religion that proclaimed the equality of all humans before God, in the fear that those who were baptized would claim that they were now free. One of the most effective missionaries in New York City lost his appointment when he was blamed for a 1712 slave uprising. The S.P.G. established schools to train blacks for the ministry so that they would proselytize among their own people. The most famous of these schools was in South Carolina and lasted over twenty years. Other denominations became more active during the Great Awakening, and Presbyterian, Baptist, and Methodist evangelicals sought to awaken blacks as well as whites and encourage all of them to found churches. The Presbyterian Samuel Davies was particularly assiduous and successful in Virginia in midcentury.

Blending of Tradition. Africans selectively adopted Christianity by modifying its theology and practices to include elements of their traditional regions. They sought conversion when the spirit of God entered their souls, much as it did during ancestral reincarnations. Satan was just a malevolent lesser god and needed to be held at a safe distance through the use of charms and the intercession of more friendly, ancestral spirits. Enslaved Africans related best to the Old Testament where God remained with his chosen people during their slavery in Egypt and delivered them to freedom. The image of water figured prominently and assumed the near-magical powers assigned to it in Africa. They created families of nonrelated kin to provide protective ancestral spirits and encouraged the fertility that would provide those spirits with human forms for reincarnation; they revered the elderly, and they followed the elaborate funeral rituals and grave offerings that marked religious practices in their homeland. They endured the stilted, silent, and formal services in European churches and then met in separate services at night which were much more participatory. Percussion and musical instruments provided the backdrop for their traditional singing, dancing, and shouting. Preachers from among their ranks performed all of the roles of priests, although some of their duties as "root doctors" and charm creators passed to others. Not surprisingly, Africans responded to the evangelicals of the Great Awakening, for their practice of extemporaneous praying and preaching, open-air meetings, and verbal participation were much more congenial to the African traditions.

Sources:

Albert J. Raboteau, *Slave Religion: The "Invisible Institution" in the Antebellum South* (New York: Oxford University Press, 1975);

Mechal Sobel, *The World They Made Together: Black and White Values in Eighteenth-Century Virginia* (Princeton: Princeton University Press, 1987);

Peter Wood, *Black Majority: Negroes in Colonial South Carolina from 1670 through the Stono Rebellion* (New York: Knopf, 1974).

ANGLICANS

Early Arrivals. Anglicans were first centered primarily in the Chesapeake colonies of Maryland and Virginia. They were included in the diocese of the bishop of London, who paid them little attention in the seventeenth century. Because their clergy had to be ordained by bishops, all of whom resided in England, the provincials depended on whatever ministers would come to the colonies. Few of them wanted to exchange their comfortable parishes at home for the ill-paid appointments, dependent status, and primitive conditions of the southern colonies. Here the laity controlled the church, elected their ministers, and refused to offer them a permanent appointment. Congregations employed the preachers year by year so that they could maintain control. Most of

Old North Church, or Christ Church, in Boston, built in 1723, with a spire added in 1741

the clergy who came were the dregs who were unable to find a parish in England. Few offered religious instruction, discipline, or even a moral example to their parishioners. If a minister struck a spiritual cord in individuals, they remained private in their piety and coexisted with their more apathetic neighbors within a formalistic church.

Church and Society. The Church of England was important in Chesapeake life but in a way different from that of the Puritan church in New England or the Quaker meetings in the middle colonies. In the South it served to reinforce the power of the gentry class, who served as the vestrymen of the parish. These men handled all church finances, determined who was to receive public assistance, investigated complaints against the minister, and generally conducted the day-to-day business of the parish. The vestry position was the first rung on the ladder of political power that individual members of the gentry climbed on their way to colonywide offices. Taxpayers were assessed a fixed rate to pay for the minister and the parish activities. Often the tax was figured in tobacco, which almost everyone grew and which the ministers could sell for their support.

Worship. Church services provided the communal rituals that bound these scattered peoples together. The services consisted of prayers from the Book of Common Prayer, reading of the Scriptures, and a sermon; communion was served four times a year. Anyone who had been confirmed as a church member and seemed to be of sound moral character could participate in the Lord's Supper. Sermons stressed the desirability of deference to social superiors and the moral order of the hierarchical society. Services provided an opportunity for all to gather to exchange news and conduct business before the service began. Once the lower classes had settled down for worship in the church, the gentry paraded in to take their choice pews; sometimes they did not enter at all.

Blair. The arrival of Reverend James Blair in 1689 marked the beginning of the sustained growth of the Anglican Church. He was the Commissary, or personal representative, of the bishop of London, who supervised the colonial church. This energetic and capable man was determined to centralize all church authority and administration into his hands and use it to promote religion and mold the clergy into true spiritual leaders. The gentry in the vestry resisted his centralization efforts, but he did improve the conduct of the existing clergy and attracted more educated ministers to the colonies. As a result of his efforts Maryland established Anglicanism in 1702, as did South Carolina in 1706, creating ten new parishes in the process and encouraging the Charleston elite to erect the elegant St. Philip's Church.

S.P.G. Blair's efforts received support in 1701 when Reverend Thomas Bray established the Society for the Propagation of the Gospel in Foreign Parts (S.P.G.) specifically to reverse the embarrassment that the colonial Anglican Church had become to the mother church. The Society provided partial support to ministers in existing parishes and fully funded itinerant missionaries whom it sent to organize congregations and evangelize among Native Americans and slaves. The quality of Anglican ministers improved markedly under this centralized direction, and they spread throughout the colonies, bringing Anglicanism into new areas and reinforcing congregations already in existence. Missionaries brought the message to the southern Yamasee and northern Iroquois with mixed success. However, they made steady progress in converting and baptizing slaves. In New England the S.P.G. expended much of its energy in trying to weaken the dominance of the Congregational Church. The middle colonies provided an exceptionally fertile ground with their large population of recent immigrants who were hungry for religious services conducted by any Protestant minister. When the former Quaker George Keith returned to the colonies as a missionary, many of his former supporters joined him in the Anglican Church. With the full power of the Church of England behind the S.P.G., the missionaries felt secure in emphasizing piety, disciplining immoral laymen, and reporting any ministerial laxity to their superiors in London. In short they began to reinstitute the organization and structure that they had known in England. They were most successful in the urban centers where the wealthy elite was attracted to the broad and liberal rationalism, the dignified worship, and the lenient church discipline that characterized Anglicanism.

Great Defection. At first the missionaries in New England were viewed as outsiders: Englishmen sent to foist the hated Church of England on unwary colonists. This view, however, changed after Timothy Cutler, rector of Yale College, concluded the commencement exercises of 1722 with an Anglican prayer and then led three of the most promising graduates into the Anglican fold. They sailed for England to be ordained and returned to lead churches in the cities. They suffered local harassment and did not enjoy the social status and governmental support of their Congregational colleagues, but their commitment was firm. They were overjoyed at the increase in membership that resulted from the Great Awakening, when those who were tired of emotional excesses sought refuge in the rational theology and orderly worship services of the Anglicans.

Sources:

Jon Butler, *Power, Authority, and the Origins of American Denominational Order: The English Churches in the Delaware Valley, 1680–1730* (Philadelphia: American Philosophical Society, 1978);

Dell Upton, *Things Holy and Profane: Anglican Parish Churches in Colonial Virginia* (Cambridge, Mass.: Harvard University Press, 1987);

John F. Woolverton, *Colonial Anglicanism in North America* (Detroit: Wayne State University Press, 1984).

BAPTISTS

Origins. Roger Williams and his fellow refugees from Puritan Massachusetts formed what is generally called the first Baptist church in America in 1639. They baptized each other by immersion after each had undergone a conversion experience. They came by their belief in adult baptism and separation of church and state on their own and were not influenced by the English and Welsh Baptists that had emerged from the English Reformation.

Variations. General Baptists, who believed in free will, emigrated from England, as did Particular Baptists from Wales, who believed in predestination. Some Puritan congregations came to believe in adult baptism and proclaimed themselves as Baptists. General (or Six Principles) Baptists were strongest in Rhode Island and formed a Rhode Island Yearly Meeting in early 1700 to serve as an advisory body to those churches. In 1701 the Particular Baptists formed the Philadelphia Baptist Association, which consisted primarily of Welsh Baptists in the area. They worked closely with the Presbyterians, whose beliefs on predestination and an educated clergy comported with their own. The Philadelphia Baptist Association soon attracted other newly organized churches in Virginia and North Carolina, many of which were composed of General Baptists from England, who modified their practices and beliefs to better conform to the Association. Later they changed their name to Regular

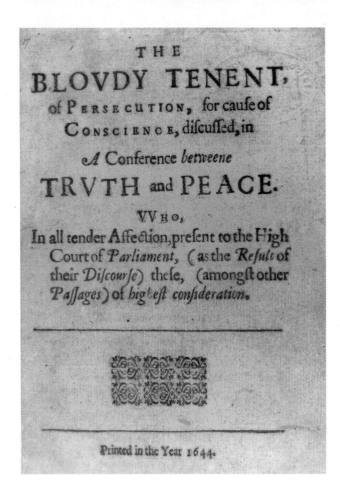

THE BLOVDY TENENT,

of PERSECUTION, for caufe of CONSCIENCE, difcuffed, in

_A_ Conference betweene TRVTH and PEACE.

VVHO,

In all tender Affection, prefent to the High Court of _Parliament_, (as the _Refult_ of their _Difcourfe_) thefe, (amongft other _Paffages_) of _higheft confideration_.

Printed in the Year 1644.

Title page for Roger Williams's treatise on religious liberty

Baptists to distinguish themselves from the evangelical Baptists spawned by the Great Awakening.

Great Awakening. Baptist congregations remained small and weak until the Great Awakening when conversion came to be viewed as the decisive Christian experience, leading many to reject the baptism of infants too young to have undergone conversion. The revivalists also protested against an educated ministry and a tax-supported clergy, which hit a responsive cord in New England, Virginia, and other areas with established churches. In New England, New Light members separated from their congregations and formed voluntary churches which entered into the Baptist fold, where they could continue their emphasis on revivalism. The most influential leader in this region was Isaac Backus, who was converted in 1741 and launched a half-century of service as a pastor, evangelist, and historian in the cause of Baptists and religious freedom. These efforts bore fruit throughout the eighteenth and nineteenth centuries as itinerant evangelicals spread their message southward.

Sources:

Jon Butler, _Power, Authority, and the Origins of American Denominational Order: The English Churches in the Delaware Valley, 1680–1730_ (Philadelphia: American Philosophical Society, 1978);

Robert G. Horbert, _A History of the Baptists_ (Philadelphia: Judson, 1950);

Norman H. Maring, _Baptists in New Jersey: A Study in Transition_ (Valley Forge, Pa.: Judson, 1964);

William McLoughlin, _New England Dissent, 1630–1833: The Baptists and Separation of Church and State_ (Cambridge, Mass.: Harvard University Press, 1991).

CONGREGATIONALISTS

Variety of Practices. With the disappearance of a Puritan orthodoxy at the beginning of the eighteenth century, the Congregational churches began to follow a variety of practices that church fathers tried to homogenize into some sort of uniformity. They had little success in Massachusetts, where coastal merchants gravitated toward churches which followed a "broad and catholic path," stressing a moral life over community piety and admitting to full church membership all who professed a Christian belief. Solomon Stoddard in western Massachusetts also abandoned church covenants, dispensed the Lord's Supper to all as a means of conversion, and advocated a presbyterial organization to prevent doctrinal errors in local congregations. His sermons were more emotional, however, and were designed to effect individual conversions rather than to create a community consensus. Other congregations continued to uphold the old traditions and would not even accept the Half-Way Covenant that middle-of-the-road churches adopted. The clerical party in Connecticut enjoyed the support of the governor and in 1708 was able to enact into law the Saybrook Platform. This plan provided for a presbyterian-type structure with county consociations to enforce discipline and doctrine in the local churches, ministerial associations to supervise them and their ordination of ministers, and a general association of ministers to set standards and procedures and generally oversee all church affairs. Yet the colony still had to abide by English law and tolerate other religions. It grudgingly passed a Toleration Act that few communities actually followed.

Churches. In the coastal cities throughout New England the physical appearance of churches changed, reflecting the growing wealth and sophistication of the members. Structures became larger and more luxurious and even sported steeples. Balconies accommodated more worshipers; tall windows flooded the interior with light. Altars appeared in the front of the church, with an elaborate, winding staircase leading to a pulpit which was placed high above the heads of the worshipers.

Revivals. In spite of the appearance of order, formalism, and rationalism that seemed to counter the old Puritan way, the earlier piety and longing for conversions continued. News of the powerful preaching of Solomon Stoddard and his revivals passed by word of mouth. The stirring increased under the pastorship of Jonathan Edwards and motivated other ministers to strive for awakenings in their congregations. By 1737, when Edwards published his _Faithful Narrative of the Surprising Work of God_ describing the 1735 revival in his parish, local awakenings were regular occurrences. However, it took the

Old South Meeting House, Boston, built in 1729–1730

appearance of George Whitefield in 1740 to fan these scattered fires into the general conflagration called the Great Awakening.

Sources:

Francis J. Bremer, *The Puritan Experiment: New England Society from Bradford to Edwards*, revised edition (Hanover, N.H.: University Press of New England, 1995);

James Jones, *The Shattered Synthesis: New England Puritanism Before the Great Awakening* (New Haven: Yale University Press, 1973);

J. William T. Youngs Jr., *God's Messengers: Religious Leadership in Colonial New England, 1700–1750* (Baltimore: Johns Hopkins University Press, 1976).

EASTERN WOODLAND NATIVE AMERICAN RELIGION

Great Spirit. Native American tribes of the eastern woodlands believed that a Great Spirit had created a harmonious world of plenty of which they were only one part. All of nature contained this divine spirit and was to be respected. Thus the native inhabitants managed the land so that it would be productive for all living creatures but changed it little, taking only want they needed. They thanked a tree for dying and providing them with wood for a fire and thanked an animal they had killed for giving up its flesh to feed them and its skin to clothe them. The Judeo-Christian view that humans dominated nature and could change it for their advantage made no sense to these people. Access to the spirit world came through dreams, which shamans would interpret for them. Often these shamans were women, who seemed to be more in contact with the spiritual world because of their role in the miracle of childbirth.

Efforts at Christianizing. To the Puritans, Native Americans were heathens and savages who, nonetheless, could be converted to the Christian faith and English civilization. To the natives, the Englishman's God was just another name for the Great Spirit, and they were quite happy with their own culture. However, the decimation that they suffered from smallpox and other diseases led them to view the English God with a healthy respect. Besides, the metal goods that the Europeans exchanged for Indian furs were useful and necessitated some interaction with the Puritans. Colonial officials supported the missionary activities of such clergymen as John Eliot and Thomas Mayhew, who established more than fourteen "praying villages" where Native Americans followed an English style of life and underwent religious instruction, often under the tutorship of a converted Indian. Eliot even provided an Algonquian translation of the Bible for those who could not read English.

King Philip's War. As the fur trade increased in New England, it demanded that Native Americans defy the Great Spirit by slaughtering many more animals than the tribes needed. Such a heavy emphasis on furs also disrupted their traditional culture and economy and fostered intertribal wars over trapping grounds. By 1675 tribal leaders were ready to push the Puritans out of their land and regain the integrity of their traditional religion and culture. In King Philip's, or Metacom's, War various tribes united in this mission. They destroyed outlying settlements, pushing the Puritans back to their coastal strongholds. At first the colonists attacked the praying villages, which they believed were dens of spies and sympathizers for Metacom. Yet gradually these "civilized" Indians were used successfully against their hostile countrymen. In fact, it was a Christian Indian who eventually killed Metacom in 1676, which ended the war.

Sources:

Francis Jennings, *The Invasion of America: Indians, Colonialism, and the Cant of Conquest* (Chapel Hill: Institute of Early American History and Culture, University of North Carolina Press, 1975);

Neil Salisbury, *Manitou and Providence: Indians, Europeans, and the Making of New England, 1500–1763* (New York: Oxford University Press, 1982);

Alden T. Vaughan, *New England Frontier: Puritans and Indians, 1620–1676*, second edition (New York: Norton, 1979).

Cross section of the *Mayflower,* showing the crowded conditions below deck (Plimoth Plantation, Plymouth, Massachusetts)

ENGLISH REFORMATION

Uneven Course. The Reformation came late to England and began only because the Pope refused to annul the marriage of Henry VIII so that he might marry again and have a male heir. Henry broke with the Pope in 1533 and 1534, pressuring Parliament to dissolve his marriage and proclaim him supreme head of the Church of England. He retained the theology, church organization, ecclesiastical courts, and religious practices of the Catholic Church. As the Reformation spread on the Continent, many Englishmen called for more-substantive changes that might purify their church of its Catholic aspects and return to the theology and religious practices that were sanctioned in the Scriptures. Under Edward VI these Puritans prevailed as the archbishop of Canterbury, Thomas Cranmer, established contacts with John Calvin and other continental leaders of the Protestant movements who aided him in introducing such Protestant reforms as sanctioning clerical marriages, adopting the Book of Common Prayer for use in worship services, and endorsing the Forty-two Articles, which codified church doctrine. The pendulum swung in the other direction under Queen Mary, a Catholic monarch who executed Protestants and forced others to flee to the Continent. Elizabeth I maintained a Protestant doctrine but retained much of the ceremony and structure of Catholicism. Under the "Elizabethan Settlement" puritan groups began to separate into particular groupings according to the manner and degree of reform they sought. This process continued during the reign of the Stuart monarchs. James I was unfavorable toward puritans, while Charles I was downright hostile. He instructed his archbishop of Canterbury, William Laud, to enforce a more high, or Catholic-oriented, Anglicanism. In response the puritans joined forces and rose up against him and won control of the country by 1648. Their leader, Oliver Cromwell, was a commoner who had no legitimate claim to the throne and so instituted a commonwealth which, by the time of his death in 1658, had degenerated into a military dictatorship under his son, Richard. Seeking some stability, the English Parliament restored the son of Charles I to the throne. The time between the accession of Elizabeth in 1558 and the Restoration of Charles II in 1660 has often been called the "Puritan Century" because of the growth, influence, and proliferation of many reforming groups who wished to purify the Church of England, albeit in a variety of ways and to different degrees. Some reformers gave up on the existing church and separated from it (separatists); others remained within the Church of England (nonseparatists). Some wanted each congregation to have complete autonomy (congregationalists), while others wanted a more national and centralized church (presbyterians).

Presbyterians. Presbyterianism was introduced into Scotland by John Knox in 1558 and into Ireland in 1606 when James I gave the lands of rebellious Irish Catholics to Scottish Presbyterian settlers. Presbyterians accepted the episcopalian notion of the Catholic and Anglican churches that the church should be centralized and nationally governed. They wanted to replace bishops and archbishops with representative assemblies in a similar hierarchical arrangement. In this plan congregations maintained a great deal of autonomy but operated within guidelines set by the higher councils, which also operated as courts of appeal from decisions made at the lower levels. The most important of these councils was the presbytery, which was composed of local ministers and their elders. Synods encompassed a wider area, and a General Assembly drew representatives from the nation. When the puritans controlled England, they called an assembly of divines to meet in Westminster and recommend a statement of beliefs and ecclesiastical structure for all churches in England, Scotland, and Ireland. The Westminster Assembly recommended a Confession of Faith with the basic and essential tenets of theology, the Directory of Public Worship for the order of services, the Form of Church Government, and the Longer and Shorter Catechism for religious instruction. In the end Parliament neither adopted these documents nor established Presbyterianism in England and Ireland, but the separate kingdom of Scotland did, implementing the rigid dogma and hierarchy of a state church. In Ireland, Presbyterianism remained as a voluntary church, and its adherents were persecuted as dissenters from the Anglican Church, which was reestablished under Charles II. They absorbed the sentiments of the variety of Protestants who fled to Ireland during this time of persecution, creating a more flexible ecclesiastical structure which emphasized congregational autonomy and allowed variations in nonessential theological doctrines.

Congregational Pilgrims. One separatist group went to Holland during the reign of Charles I to avoid persecution in England. When group members had trouble making decent livings and their children began to adopt Dutch ways, they boarded the *Mayflower* in 1620 and sailed to the New World to establish a settlement where they could practice their religion in isolation. No minister accompanied the settlers of Plymouth in the early years, but they gathered themselves into a church to pray, read the Scriptures, and listen to sermons even though they had no one to administer the sacraments. Another group settled in Salem. When the Puritans settled nearby, their larger colony overshadowed Plymouth and absorbed Salem. The distinction between the separatist Pilgrims and the nonseparatist Puritans soon faded, and they became indistinguishable from each other.

Congregational Puritans. Refusing to separate from the Church of England, puritans still hoped to reform the church from within and strove to lead moral and exemplary lives within an English society which they feared was becoming increasingly corrupt. These efforts became more difficult under Charles I, who forced everyone to conform to the Church of England, which was reinstating earlier Catholic practices. A group of puritans decided to move to America, practice their religion freely, and create a model society, a "citee upon a hill," which would be an example to England. In 1629 they sailed to Massachusetts Bay, led by John Winthrop, whom they chose as governor. They brought their charter with them so that they could govern their Bible Commonwealth with no outside interference. A great migration of puritans followed until 1640 when the English Civil War erupted and Puritans fought for control of England and her church. If the Puritans in New England had been serious about purifying the Anglican Church, they should have returned to England and done so; most did not. In reality they had become as separatist as the Pilgrims, and the two groups merged.

Congregational Baptists. Emerging from the puritan movement were the Baptists. They rejected infant baptism, believing that this sacrament should be the seal of conversion in adults. General Baptists were separatists, yet they continued the Anglican belief that everyone had the free will and ability to be saved. In spite of persecution they grew in numbers and spread throughout England and, eventually, to the colonies, settling mainly in Rhode Island. Particular Baptists retained the nonseparatist views of the Puritans, as well as the Calvinistic acceptance of predestination, and remained in fellowship with the Puritans. Their creed was patterned closely after the Westminster Confession. They mainly clustered in Wales and emigrated from there to many of the American colonies.

Sources:

Patrick Collinson, *The Birthpangs of Protestant England* (New York: Macmillan, 1988);

Christopher Hill, *Society and Puritanism in Pre-Revolutionary England* (New York: Schocken, 1964);

Diarmaid MacCulloch, *The Later Reformation in England, 1547–1603* (New York: St. Martin's Press, 1990).

EUROPEAN REFORMATION

Catholicism. There was only one church in western Europe from the death of Jesus until the Reformation; in fact, the term *catholic* means universal. After the fall of the Roman Empire the institution of the church was the one unifying force in a Europe fragmented into local fiefdoms. After the eastern branch separated in 1054, the western branch of the church became known as Roman Catholic because the bishop of Rome, or Pope, was considered to be Jesus' representative on earth and a successor to Peter, whom Jesus chose as the rock upon which the church was to be built. The Pope appointed bishops as the successors of the other apostles to oversee large dioceses, and they, in turn, appointed clergymen or priests to officiate in local parishes. Some clergymen were chosen by the Pope to serve as cardinals and advise him. Specialized orders arose to advance particular missions of the church, whether within the walls of monasteries and nunneries or in the outside world. All of these church officials were to remain celibate, dedicated to the life of the spirit rather than to the concerns of a secular world. The church, under divine inspiration, interpreted the will of God and explained to laymen what they could do to be saved and enter heaven. Any who questioned this interpretation of doctrine and practice were called heretics and were persecuted. The church was an integral

Lutherans from Salzburg before embarking for Georgia, 1732

part of the world, for secular and spiritual aspects of life were thoroughly meshed, and worldly practices crept in, sparking periodic reform movements. The Protestant Reformation of the early 1500s was, perhaps, the most important of these movements, for it ignited a Counter-Reformation among the Catholics that cleansed the church of many abuses, inspired the creation of many more orders devoted to Christian service, and led to a reformulation of doctrine and a reform of practices.

Lutheranism. Martin Luther sparked the Reformation by publicizing his objections to the practices of the Catholic Church in 1517 and defending them at the Imperial Diet held at Worms in 1521. In the process he set down many of the basic affirmations of the Reformed tradition in the Augsburg Confession of 1530. According to Luther salvation came only to those who had the faith, love, and hope in God's unbounded mercy that leads to a new birth in Christ. It could not come by one's own moral efforts and good works, church laws, or intercession by priests. The Bible was the only source for learning about God, so Christians had to be able to read and interpret the Holy Scriptures for themselves. The writings of Luther and news of his deeds spread throughout northern Europe and the Baltic states, opening the floodgates of reform and spawning evangelical movements which proliferated into sects that carried the movement far beyond what Luther had intended or desired. However, Lutheranism retained vestiges of Catholicism, such as the belief that all human institutions, including government, were divinely ordained and that during the sacrament of the Eucharist (communion), Christ was actually present in the bread and wine.

Calvinism. John Calvin erased much of Luther's conservative tone and exercised the main influence over the second generation of reformers in the 1530s. It was his interpretation of the Reformed tradition that formed the core of the major colonial Protestant denominations. The confessions, or statements of faith, that these denominations adopted shared similar themes. All emphasized the vast chasm that separated God from humans, who could enter heaven only by his grace. According to the Reformers, the trap that the Catholic Church fell into was the arrogant assumption that humans understood God and influenced him by their manmade rituals. According to Calvinism, God created Adam and Eve in his image so they might understand and follow his will, promising them an everlasting and joyful existence in return. When they disobeyed, God justly withdrew his spirit, leaving them and their descendants to sin, suffer, and die. The consequences of Original Sin could only be reversed by God, who did so by sending Jesus to take upon himself the guilt of the sin of humans so that they would escape punishment and attain that salvation promised to Adam and Eve. The Holy Spirit infused the souls of the "elected" with the saving grace that allowed them to regain some of their original faith in and obedience to God. One found his directives on how humans were to live by following Christ's example and teachings in the Bible. Thus each individual had to read the Scriptures constantly, for they progressively revealed more of God and how He operated in the world and their lives. There was no intermediary between an individual and God, as the Catholic Church had maintained.

Sources:

Sydney E. Ahlstrom, *A Religious History of the American People*, 2 volumes (Garden City, N.Y.: Doubleday, 1975);

Harold J. Grimm, *The Reformation Era, 1500–1650* (New York: Macmillan, 1965);

John T. McNeil, *The History and Character of Calvinism* (New York: Oxford University Press, 1954).

GREAT AWAKENING

A Key Event. The Great Awakening was the pivotal event in the eighteenth-century religious scene. It was an offshoot of a transatlantic revival of piety that arrived on American shores with George Whitefield, an evangelical itinerant preacher from England who sparked his own revivals, legitimized those of others, and publicized them all as one great awakening. It took on various emphases within the different denominations and regions, exposed existing fissures and caused others, precipitated realignments both within and among religious groups, and settled the religious landscape onto new ground. Although it affected all denominations, the Great Awakening had its greatest initial impact on the Presbyterians in the middle colonies and the Congregationalists in New England. In the northern colonies it only lasted for about three years, but its ripples continued to affect all regions throughout the century.

Middle Colonies. Revivalistic preachers in several denominations already were engaged in attempts to awaken religious fervor among their own flocks and the unchurched when Whitefield arrived in 1739 on a preaching tour to raise funds for his orphanage in Georgia. The Presbyterian revivalists in particular had already heard of him and rushed to enlist his support. Their leader, Gil-

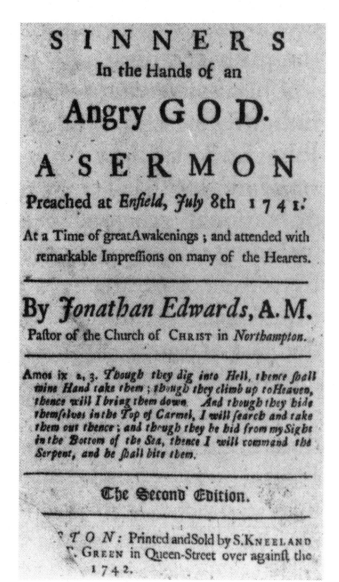

Title page for the best-known sermon of the
Great Awakening

SINNERS BEWARE!

The God that holds you over the Pit of Hell, much as one holds a Spider, or some loathsome Insect, over the Fire, abhors you, and is dreadfully provoked: his Wrath towards you burns like Fire; he looks upon you as worthy of nothing else, but to be cast into the Fire; he is of purer Eyes than to bear to have you in his Sight; you are ten Times so abominable in his Eyes, as the most hateful venomous Serpent is in ours. You have offended him infinitely more than ever a stubborn Rebel did his Prince; and yet 'tis nothing but His Hand that holds you from falling into the Fire every moment.

O Sinner! Consider the fearful Danger you are in: 'Tis a great Furnace of Wrath, a wide and bottomless Pit, full of the Fire of Wrath, that you are held over in the Hand of that God, whose Wrath is provoked and incensed as much against you as many of the Damned in Hell. You hang by a slender Thread, the Flames of divine Wrath flashing about it, and ready in a Moment to singe it, and burn it asunder.

Source: Jonathan Edwards, *Sinners in the Hands of an Angry God . . .* (Boston: Printed & sold by S. Kneeland & T. Green, 1741).

bert Tennent, led Whitefield in a tour of Pennsylvania, New York, and New Jersey, observing closely his rousing preaching style and simple message: repent, seek Christ, and be saved by the Holy Spirit in so sensible a manner that you will have immediate and definite assurance of your salvation and that of everyone else, including your minister. This ecumenical message, which dismissed theology, denominational distinctions, and the authority of the clergy, drew crowds. Tennent and his followers accompanied Whitefield to conduct revivals around the countryside and then to Philadelphia, where he filled Independence Square. His booming voice reached them all, even Benjamin Franklin, who had come as a spectator determined to give nothing to the collection for the orphanage and ended up emptying his pockets. This tour reenergized the revivalists, especially those among the Presbyterians, who became insistent on lowering the educational requirement for ministers so that more of their followers could be ordained, take over the synod,

George Whitefield preaching (portrait by John Wollaston, 1741; National Portrait Gallery, London)

and silence any opposition to them. Tennent sounded the call to battle in a 1740 sermon titled "The Danger of an Unconverted Ministry," in which he labeled all of his learned opponents as damned men who were leading their flocks to hell. Within a year the synod had split over this issue of the necessity of a highly educated clergy.

New England. From the middle colonies Whitefield set off for New England, making it a point to preach in the church of Jonathan Edwards, the intellectual cornerstone of the revivalists whose writings had received transatlantic acclaim. Local ministers at first welcomed the evangelist, applauding his ability to arouse the laity from their apathy and mimicking his style within their own flocks. Then he began to attack them as "dead men." Itinerant preachers such as Tennent and James Davenport who followed in his wake concentrated on this theme to the extent that the Great Awakening increasingly focused more on castigating settled clergy than on inciting conversion and personal piety. Such men raised the pitch of radicalism and encouraged laymen to take the stage and preach on the horrors of damnation on every available street corner. Davenport reached new heights when, after he had already been judged as "disturbed in the rational faculties of his mind" and expelled from Connecticut, he returned to New London and built bonfires which consumed classical works, sermons by Puritan divines, and even the clothes shed by his followers. The resultant animosities split churches so that most communities had a regular and a Separatist congregation

by 1743. Many of these Separatists later entered the Baptists' fold, while some of the more formalistic joined the Anglicans. Among mainstream Congregationalists there arose a deeper concern with the spiritual life and pious conduct that revitalized that large denomination.

Opposition Arises. As the Great Awakening became more extreme, moderates in all denominations publicly dissociated themselves from these New Light revivalists and fought back. Old Light Congregationalist Charles Chauncy and Anglican Timothy Cutler in New England were joined by two Old Side Presbyterians, Francis Alison and John Thompson, and an Old Light Baptist, Ebenezer Kinnersley in Pennsylvania, in denouncing the misguided theology and un-Christian behavior of the revivalists. Many of their arguments were based on those Calvinist foundations that Enlightenment thought reinforced: man can never have absolute knowledge of anything, much less the gracious states of others that are only known to God; God had revealed his will only through the Holy Scriptures and not through impromptu rantings by humans; and humans must glorify God by developing virtuous Christian habits that are best formed in the harmonious and settled environment similar to the one in the original creation. The governments of Massachusetts and Connecticut, where the Congregational Church was established, tried to force seceding congregations to continue to pay the legal tithes to their old churches. The Connecticut General Assembly even passed laws requiring ministers to have degrees from Yale or Harvard, prohibiting itinerancy and banning lay preachers from administering the sacraments.

Fading Movement. The emotionalism that underlay the spate of revivals had already begun to die by 1743 as people experienced the single emotional event defined as conversion, felt a release, and settled down to pious lives. In New England they continued their revivalistic emphasis within Baptist congregations. In the middle colonies some revivalistic leaders such as Tennent were shocked by the consequences of their actions and recanted, settling down to minister quietly to their own flocks. The people they had aroused often gravitated to the Moravians. Others, such as John Cross, were discredited, in his case for fathering an illegitimate child. Even Whitefield, in his subsequent tours, apologized and tried to heal the wounds caused by his zeal.

Legacy. The Great Awakening left different footprints on all of the colonial denominations and sects. Its general legacy was a renewed concern with individual salvation and piety, defining religious beliefs for oneself rather than accepting them from clerical authorities, selecting a minister for his charisma and preaching style rather than for his theology and counseling, and accepting those who shared a similar style and concerns no matter what the denomination. Women became more influential in many congregations which believed that, if females were converted, they would lead their children and menfolk to salvation. Itinerancy and clerical responsibility for multiple congregations became more common among the smaller congregations that resulted from the divisions in churches. Both the Old and New persuasions formed intercolonial and interdenominational networks that helped to break down provincialism and isolation and prepared Americans for accepting the denominational pluralism that was on the horizon. Baptists and Presbyterians spread into New England and the South, which had been strongholds of established churches. Evangelicals reached out to Native Americans and Africans and encouraged others to Christianize these peoples. Smarting from charges that they were ignorant and unlettered, revivalists founded colleges for their ministers, which coincided with the general movement for widespread education that the Enlightenment and increasing commercialization were effecting. Given the centrality of the Great Awakening to the development of an American culture, some historians have gone so far as to label the Great Awakening as the key to the society that later mounted the American Revolution.

Sources:

John B. Franz, "The Awakening of Religion Among German Settlers in the Middle Colonies," *William and Mary Quarterly*, 33 (1976): 266–288;

Edwin S. Gaustad, *The Great Awakening in New England* (New York: Harper, 1957);

C. C. Goen, *Revivalism and Separatism in New England, 1740–1800: Strict Congregationalists and Separate Baptists in the Great Awakening* (New Haven: Yale University Press, 1962);

Martin E. Lodge, "The Crisis of the Churches in the Middle Colonies," *Pennsylvania Magazine of History and Biography*, 95 (1971): 195–220;

Sally Schwartz, *"A Mixed Multitude": The Struggle for Toleration in Colonial Pennsylvania* (New York: New York University Press, 1987).

JEWS

Origin. The history of Judaism in America began with the arrival of Dutch Jews at New Amsterdam in 1654. They had been active in the Dutch West India Company settlement in Brazil and were expelled when the Portuguese retook the post. The Netherlands had provided a place of refuge for the Sephardic Jews (those of Iberian descent) after Spain had expelled them in 1492 and Portugal in 1496. In the Netherlands they flourished as merchants and tradesmen.

Early Clusters. There were no rabbis among these colonial Jews. This fact did not present much of an obstacle, however, because only ten adult males were needed to form a synagogue. As soon as they were granted the right to public worship in New York at the end of the seventeenth century, they established a congregation and by 1729 had built a house of worship. Others arrived in small groups, especially after 1740, when the British Parliament allowed them to be naturalized. In some colonies they were denied political rights because they were not Christians and could not take the required oaths on the Bible. They settled primarily in the coastal cities and practiced their faith unobtrusively. Cantors took on the

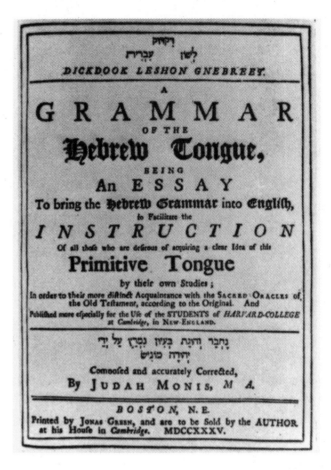

Title page for a Hebrew textbook for Harvard students

role of ministers, and the highly literate laity preserved their teachings and traditions.

Sources:

Ruth Gay, *Jews in America: A Short History* (New York: Basic Books, 1965);

Jacob R. Marcus, *The Colonial American Jews, 1492–1776*, 3 volumes (Detroit: Wayne State University Press, 1970).

LUTHERANS

New Sweden. The first Lutherans in America were Swedes who assembled on the banks of the Delaware River in 1638 in the settlement of Sweden's West India Company. New Sweden was served by a continuous line of ministers, the most famous of whom was John Campanius, a missionary to the Native Americans who translated Martin Luther's Catechism into the Delaware language. The church languished after the Dutch drove the Swedes out in 1655. When the king of Sweden realized that the church had no ministers, he sent a large supply of books and three ministers, who arrived in 1697 and established the Holy Trinity at Tranhook Church near Wilmington, Delaware, and Gloria Dei at Wicaco near Philadelphia. For seventy-five years all national branches of the Lutheran Church were supervised by a provost or personal deputy of the archbishop of Sweden, who was allowed to ordain ministers. Unfortunately none was appointed between 1730 and 1748, which left the Luther-

George II of England meeting with Count Nikolaus von Zinzendorf before his departure for America in 1741 (National Portrait Gallery, London)

ans with no government during the most crucial years of their growth. Dutch laymen organized churches in New York, but the rules of the Amsterdam Consistory did not allow the ordination of a minister for America until 1657, and that man was expelled at the behest of the established Dutch Reform Church. After the English took over New York in 1664, more churches sprang up (fourteen by 1719) but with only one minister. Deacons and overseers were running these congregations just as the great emigration of Germans began. These loosely organized congregations were the prime targets of the pietistic sects who appeared at the same time. The pleas of laymen to the University of Halle for ministers went unheeded until Count Nikolaus von Zinzendorf arrived in 1741. He was an ordained Lutheran minister but was more interested in promoting the ecumenicalism of the Moravians and directed them to fill the pulpits. When Henry Melchior Muhlenberg, an energetic missionary with impeccable credentials, was sent by Halle in 1742, he found the pulpits of his three congregations occupied by others, including Count von Zinzendorf himself. After a month's time he had reclaimed all three; within six years he joined Swedish and German pastors and lay delegates in the Pennsylvania Ministerium, which outlined a synodical organization, ordained ministers, consecrated churches, and prepared a book of common prayer. At the next meeting the delegates elected an overseer for all Swedish and German Lutheran churches.

Muhlenberg held this office for many years, thus ensuring the firm roots of Lutheranism in America. However, the shortage of ministers continued, encouraging lay participation in simple services held in homes and barns which consisted of a sermon, prayer, hymns, Scripture reading, and benediction.

Sources:

Fred W. Meuser, *The Formation of the American Lutheran Church* (Columbus, Ohio: Wartburg Press, 1958);

Sally Schwartz, *"A Mixed Multitude": The Struggle for Toleration in Colonial Pennsylvania* (New York: New York University Press, 1987);

Abdel R. Wentz, *A Basic History of Lutheranism in America* (Philadelphia: Muhlenberg Press, 1955).

MAGIC AND THE SUPERNATURAL

Folk Beliefs. Most colonists had little understanding or control over their natural environment and so looked for all of the supernatural help they could muster. Some employed magical techniques to solve particular problems that were too mundane for the notice of God. To Native Americans, Africans, and some Europeans, magic and religion were cut from the same cloth and often coexisted, shading into each other. Their religions included both benevolent and malevolent spirits, intermediaries between these spirits and humans, and manipulation of supernatural forces through prayer and ritual. What seemed to work for one belief system was often appropriated by another, so magical practices were quite similar.

The Man of Signs, from Benjamin Franklin's first almanac (1732).
The diagram illustrates how the stars affect human health.

Predicting the Future. Astrology was the most popular means of prediction among Europeans, and it was practiced widely. This entailed the belief that the Earth was a microcosm of the heavens, so that the motions of the stars affected all aspects of human life. Individual horoscopes were cast to reveal everything—when to plant, marry, sail, conceive, or bleed people as part of medical practice. Christian mystics, who believed that they were a part of all of the spiritual world, incorporated astrology into their mainstream belief systems. For instance, Johannes Kelpius and his hermit community of Rosicrucians, who migrated from Germany in 1694 and occupied caves along the Wissahickon Creek outside of Philadelphia, regularly used astrology to order their lives as they awaited the second coming of Christ. But there was also a wide variety of other fortune-telling devices such as "reading" the pattern of tea leaves, the shape of a raw egg white dropped into a bowl, the entrails of a fowl, or the arrangement of special pebbles cast on the ground. Almost everyone interpreted dreams as an entry into the spiritual world which encompassed the future. Among the Africans and Native Americans, priests or shamans were specialists in interpreting these dreams.

Charms. Particular objects used to ward off evil came

In a 1692 essay titled "A Brand Pluck'd out of the Burning," Cotton Mather described the possession of a young woman named Mercy Short. Mather had taken her into his home and observed one of her fits and conversations with evil spirits:

Reader, If thou hadst a Desire to have seen a Picture of Hell, it was visible in the doleful Circumstances of Mercy Short! Here was one lying in Outer Darkness, haunted with the Divel and his Angels, deprived of all common Comforts, tortured with most cruciating Fires, Wounded with a thousand Pains all over, and cured immediately, that the Pains of those Wounds might bee repeated.

Her Discourses to *Them* were some of the most Surprising Things imaginable, and incredibly beyond what might have been expected, from one of her small Education or Experience. In the Times of her Tortures, Little came from her, besides direful Shrieks, which were indeed so frightful, as to make many people Quitt the Room. Only now and then any Expression of marvellous Constancy would bee heard from her; *e.g.* "Tho' you kill mee, I'l never do what you would have mee.—Do what you will, yett with the Help of Christ, I'll never touch your Book.—Do, Burn mee then, if you will; Better Burn here, then [than] Burn in Hell." But when her Torturer went off, Then t'was that her senses being still detained in a Captivity to Spectres, as the only object of them, Wee were Ear-witnesses to Disputacions that amazed us. Indeed Wee could not hear what They said unto her; nor could shee herself hear them ordinarily without causing them to say over again: But Wee could Hear Her Answers, and from her Answers Wee could usually gather the Tenour of Their Assaults.

Source: George Lincoln Burr, ed., *Narratives of the Witchcraft Cases 1648–1706* (New York: Barnes & Noble, 1946).

in a bewildering array and occupied different levels of importance among the colonists. Talismans protected one in battle, be they verses from the Koran, a crucifix, bags of herbs, or magical stones. Horseshoes nailed over a threshold or stones hung over a stable rack protected both humans and livestock. Magic lines and circles kept evil from designated geographical areas. Divining rods found water, hidden treasures, or lost objects. One only had to hold the two ends of a freshly cut, forked branch, point the main branch away, and coax it with soothing requests. Bags of unidentified objects could unleash passion, promote fertility, or induce sickness.

Healing. Sickness or accidents, whether in humans or animals, were a horror to all before the days of modern medicine. The Africans were not alone in believing that illness and death came from spiritual as well as natural causes. Thus occult as well as natural remedies were seen as effective. Healers were often identified as "white," or good, witches who used their charms and knowledge of medicinal roots, barks, and herbs to aid the healing process. But there was a variety of other practices seen to be equally as effective. If a cow were going dry, a Christian might pour the milk over a red-hot iron poker while repeating the names of the Trinity. To employ the sympathy technique one simply took a hair from a sick or injured person or animal and used it in a ritual that promoted health and healing in its owner. Freckles might be removed by washing one's face with cobwebs.

Bewitchment. Spiritual possession of a person was viewed as either good or bad. Young Native American warriors welcomed the infusion of an animal spirit, which would serve as a protector. African religious ceremonies centered around evoking the possession of a worshiper by the spirit of a god who dictated the distinctive steps and voice of the human. Europeans believed that a "black," or evil, witch could control the thoughts and actions of others (even those whom she did not know) for her own malicious satisfaction.

Witchcraft. If no adjective was attached, the word *witch* usually meant an evil sorcerer or sorceress. Native Americans were more apt to blame evil spirits in general or an enemy in particular for their problems. Africans too were wary of evil witches whose spirits left them when they were asleep, entered the bodies of animals, and fled to a meeting of other witches where a human soul was consumed, thus killing that person. Europeans tended to single out a particular person, usually an old woman, who had made a covenant with the Devil, rather than with God, to cause all manner of trouble among good people. To them it seemed logical that if God were omnipresent in the world, then so was Satan. The American version of witchcraft was more staid than that of the Europeans, which involved witches flying through the air to engage in sexual orgies with the Devil and his minions. In the colonies it focused on a person who had signed a compact with the Devil just to get back at someone with whom there was an unresolved conflict. The witch was then empowered to cause the death of a child, crop failures, cream that could not be churned into butter, or the sterility of livestock. Witches could also bewitch others just for their malicious pleasure and enter the bodies of animals as "familiars" in order to prowl around undetected. Yet they could be discovered. A witch's cake of grain, mixed with a part of the afflicted body, such as urine, baked in ashes, and fed to a familiar would lead the animal to reveal the name of the witch. A rag puppet or clay model of the victim stuck with pins was a sure sign of guilt, as was a teat found in an unusual place on the woman's body with which she nursed her familiars. If such individuals confessed and repudiated their covenant with Satan, thus ceasing their harm and opening themselves to God, they were usually reaccepted into the community. The glaring exception was the witchcraft hysteria that erupted in Salem Village in Massachusetts.

ony. By the time it was over, 156 suspects had been imprisoned; 19 were hanged as witches; and 4 died in prison, one of whom was crushed to death during questioning. The clergy then reasserted its spiritual leadership, became more particular about evidence, and eventually ended the proceedings, which were roundly condemned. Some say that this ended the age of magic and superstition in the colonies and ushered in an enlightened age of more rational religion, although sporadic cases of witchcraft surfaced until well into the eighteenth century.

Sources:

Jon Butler, "Magic, Astrology, and the Early American Religious Heritage, 1600–1760," *American Historical Review,* 84 (April 1979): 317–346;

John P. Demos, *Entertaining Satan: Witchcraft and the Culture of Early New England* (New York: Oxford University Press, 1982);

Richard Godbeer, *Devil's Dominion: Magic and Religion in Early New England* (New York: Cambridge University Press, 1992);

Albert J. Raboteau, *Slave Religion: The "Invisible Institution" in the Antebellum South* (New York: Oxford University Press, 1978).

MINISTRY

Old World Connections. Almost all of the denominations in America looked to their Old World mother churches for ministers and models for ecclesiastical structure. Puritan Congregationalists were the exception because each congregation was autonomous and felt no obligation to imitate anyone's ecclesiastical practices. Colonial Anglicans were placed under the supervision of the bishop of London, who ignored them until the eighteenth century when he appointed a commissary to personally represent his authority, and the Society for the Propagation of the Gospel was founded and sent missionaries. The Lutheran and Reformed Churches, whose adherents flooded into the colonies in the eighteenth century, were governed by ecclesiastical bodies in their country of origin that retained the exclusive right to ordain clergy. Presbyterians were not formally tied to a European church, but they attempted to replicate the structure and practices they had experienced in their homelands. Their problem arose from the variations that existed in Scotland, Ireland, and England which had to be blended together. Even the Quakers looked to England for acceptable practices, which they tried to implement in the middle colonies. By the mid eighteenth century most denominations had developed some level of institutional and psychological autonomy from their mother churches, forming governing bodies to oversee the laity and clergy and developing practices that suited New World conditions.

Shortage of Clergy. The combination of control by Old World churches, small and scattered congregations, and primitive, frontier conditions all but insured that most religions that demanded an educated and ordained clergy would suffer from a chronic shortage of ministers. This problem reached crisis proportions in the eighteenth century among those denominations associated with the German and Irish immigrants who flooded into

The Flyer, a shaman or medicine man of an unknown North American Indian tribe, circa 1600 (American Museum of Natural History)

Salem. In the winter of 1691–1692 some young girls were trying to read their future in the shape of a raw egg white dropped into a bowl. They watched in horror as it assumed the shape of a coffin! Elizabeth Parris, the daughter of the local minister who was well aware of the Puritan condemnation of attempting to divine the will of God through magic, began to experience inexplicable sensations of pinching, suffocating, and hallucinations. The others soon followed suit. Physicians, finding nothing physically wrong with the girls, suggested that the maladies were caused by witchcraft. A concerned neighbor finally asked Tituba, the South American slave of the Reverend Parris, to bake a witch cake so that they might learn the identity of the witch and stop her; it did not work. When they first confessed to their actions, the girls pointed to Tituba and some old women as witches. They, in turn, implicated others, and the contagion of accusations spread to cover suspects throughout the col-

A depiction of a New England preacher on a gravestone, circa 1640

the backcountry of the middle and southern colonies. Congregationalists did not face this problem, for they could ordain their own ministers and founded colleges to educate their sons. Quakers, some Baptists, and the pietistic sects (Mennonites, Amish, Dunkers, and Moravians) also encountered no difficulty because they did not require a specially trained ministry and demanded no formal ordination. The Anglican Church required a university degree and ordination by an English bishop, and few of their clergy wished to travel to the colonial wilderness. The Society for the Propagation of the Gospel did offer some relief after 1702 by supplementing the salaries of settled ministers and fully funding itinerant missionaries who could officiate in several parishes on a regular basis. As the Anglican Church grew in prestige, it attracted educated ministers from other denominations. Anglicans supported the establishment of nondenominational colleges, which educated those native sons who were willing to accept the dangerous and expensive undertaking of traveling to England for ordination. In the more sparsely settled backcountry, however, most Anglicans remained unchurched and ignored. Presbyterians ordained any educated Calvinist and managed to keep their pulpits supplied until the 1730s when the scattered frontier congregations of Irish depleted the supply of qualified ministers. Settled clergymen organized small academies to educate potential ministers, while the synod allowed those candidates without a university degree to pass an examination on their learning. The synod

then adopted one academy as its official seminary and finally supported three nondenominational colleges with a curriculum that would meet its stringent requirements. Lutheran and German Reformed churches suffered the most, for they required both an educated ministry and one that had been ordained by the official bodies in Europe. This situation offered fertile ground for immoral, unqualified, and/or fraudulent men who foisted themselves upon congregations who were unwilling to dismiss them even if they were exposed. Most denominations responded to shortages by encouraging ministers to divide their time among several churches, designating settled ministers to officiate in vacant pulpits every few months, and calling some clergy to be itinerants who traveled from congregation to congregation and settled nowhere. Such sporadic attention, however, left believers open to the attraction of pietistic sects that emphasized an ecumenical spirituality that transcended denominational affiliation and the need for a specialized ministry.

Power of the Laity. The lack of clergy also reinforced the increased power of the laity, which distinguished American religions from their European counterparts. Most ministers depended on the voluntary support of their congregations, supplemented by a sideline occupation. Thus they followed the wishes of laymen, who could simply withhold their contribution or move to another church or sect if they became displeased. Even where churches were established in New England, the South, and parts of New York, the congregation exercised considerable control over its minister. In the middle colonies Pietists taunted congregations for their "hireling priests," engendering an anticlerical feeling that further undercut the authority of a clergy already denied the supportive mechanism of an ecclesiastical organization capable of enforcing deference. Congregations became accustomed to running their own affairs and even conducting services in the absence of ministers. They were reluctant to relinquish their power to a new minister or to an ecclesiastical body external to their community. Some historians have attributed the clergy's support of the Great Awakening to their desire to revitalize their authority by creating a personal allegiance among the laity for their charismatic preachers.

Sources:

Jon Butler, *Power, Authority, and the Origins of American Denominational Order: The English Churches in the Delaware Valley, 1680–1730* (Philadelphia: American Philosophical Society, 1978);

Elwyn Allen Smith, The *Presbyterian Ministry in American Culture: A Study in Changing Concepts, 1700–1900* (Philadelphia: Westminster Press, 1962);

Marilyn J. Westerkamp, *Triumph of the Laity: Scots-Irish Piety and the Great Awakening, 1625–1760* (New York: Oxford University Press, 1988);

J. William T. Youngs Jr., *God's Messengers: Religious Leadership in Colonial New England, 1700–1750* (Baltimore: Johns Hopkins University Press, 1970).

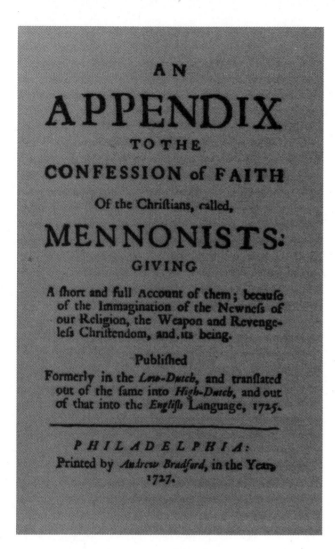

Title page for a tract on a pacifistic sect that settled in
Pennsylvania in 1683

PIETISTIC SECTS

Origin. A sect usually emphasizes some aspect of an orthodox faith that has been neglected in a denomination and depends on the perfection of its adherents, rather than church institutions, to effect salvation. Most of the pietistic sects that appeared in the colonies originated in central Europe in the latter part of the seventeenth century as an effort to revitalize and purify the growing intellectualism and formalism of the Protestant churches. Most of these groups settled in the tolerant climate of Pennsylvania and other proprietary colonies to the south.

Mennonites and Amish. The Mennonites arrived in Pennsylvania in 1683, settling in an area around Philadelphia which they named Germantown. They were joined by other pacifist sects who agreed with their goal of returning to the simple, primitive church of the early Christian communities. Such a life demanded discipline that could best be maintained when their adherents were separated from the rest of society and immune to its

changes. The Amish were even more socially conservative in their determination to retain simplicity in their separated agricultural communities and eschewed almost all contact with outsiders; the Mennonites tolerated some interaction as long as it did not dilute community cohesion.

Dunkers. The Church of the Brethren received the name "Dunkers" because they believed in complete immersion during baptism. Otherwise, they were quite similar to the Mennonites and worked closely with them when the Dunkers first arrived in 1719. Their intellectual leader, Christopher Sauer, established Sunday schools and a printing press which issued a German-language newspaper and an edition of Martin Luther's Bible, the first printed in America. Their most colorful leader was Johann Conrad Beissel, who left Germantown to establish the Ephrata Cloister, which practiced celibacy and a communal sharing of goods. In their belief Adam originally was androgynous, with the female wisdom coexisting with male divinity. Humans only exhibited carnal appetites after Adam was split into Adam and Eve. Only by transcending sexuality could humans return to a unity with God. Therefore, brothers and sisters lived separately, performing their separate but equal duties, which included printing, illuminating manuscripts, composing and performing musical pieces, and serving as a cultural center for all Germans in Pennsylvania.

Moravians. It is difficult to categorize Moravians or the Renewed Church of the United Brethren, but they operated much as a sect during this period, concentrating on awakening all to a spiritual pietism that transcended denominational boundaries. They preached that once people had the ecstatic experience of union with God, the converted could be assured of their inability to sin and their eventual salvation. The idea of a pan-Protestant union that would join all denominations probably originated with Count Nikolaus Zinzendorf, who opened his estate in Saxony to many pietistic and sectarian refugees. The first immigrants arrived in Georgia in 1735 to minister to Native Americans and slaves. Because they were pacifists, they were forced to leave and moved into Pennsylvania, where Zinzendorf joined them in 1741 and founded several missionary towns. In the course of the next decade some followed the backcountry route to North Carolina and founded villages there. In these settlements Moravians revived such early Christian practices as the love feast and foot washing. They held land and property in common and worked in cohorts organized by age and sex. Women exercised considerable power in their religious lives and secular pursuits. All surpluses went to support the extensive missionary networks, which particularly targeted Native Americans and enjoyed great success. Initially they also enjoyed good relations with the other pietistic sects and reformed denominations because they were willing to follow the particular customs in whatever congregation they were preaching. Later, however, they were suspected of trying to steal those members away and split existing congregations. They joined the early revivalists in the 1730s in riding the crest of the waves of the Great Awakening but then split with them over doctrinal issues. The United Brethren then turned their focus inward to their own settlements, which increasingly separated from neighboring communities.

Sources:

Gillian L. Gollin, *Moravians in Two Worlds: A Study in Changing Communities* (New York: Columbia University Press, 1967);

Walter C. Klein, *Johann Conrad Beissel: Mystic and Martinet, 1698–1768* (Philadelphia: University of Pennsylvania Press, 1942);

Ernest F. Stoeffler, ed., *Continental Pietism and Early American Christianity* (Grand Rapids, Mich.: Eerdmans, 1976).

PRESBYTERIANS

Beginnings. Among the earliest Puritan settlers in New England were many with a presbyterial orientation in which ministers and elders from congregations formed the governing body within a given district. When the Presbyterians gained ascendancy during the English Civil War, New England nearly adopted their view that church membership should be open to all who followed God's commandments and that congregations should relinquish some of their authority to higher councils of ministers and elders in order to maintain standards and prevent unscriptural practices and theological errors from creeping into the church. When this did not come to pass, individual congregations quietly followed presbyterian practices under either a Congregational or Presbyterian minister.

Makemie. The Irish Presbyterian minister Francis Makemie is credited with joining these scattered congregations into an organized denomination. An inveterate traveler, he first arrived in 1683 to journey throughout the mainland colonies and Barbados, preaching and organizing churches as he went. His appeals to his English, Scottish, and Irish brethren for clergy attracted much-needed ministers to these new churches. In 1706 he organized the first presbytery in Philadelphia, attended by seven local ministers and their elders. Within ten years there were four presbyteries and a synod operating. A few months after the first presbytery meeting, Makemie became the center of attention when Edward Hyde, Viscount Cornbury, governor of New York, had him arrested for preaching without a license. His defense was that he had been granted a license as a dissenting minister in Barbados, which was valid in all British domains. The court acquitted him, but a vengeful Cornbury charged him to pay the entire cost of the trial. New Yorkers were so incensed that the assembly passed a law prohibiting such assessments and got Cornbury recalled in disgrace. By this time Makemie had died, but the publicity brought the infant Presbyterian Church to the favorable attention of many dissenters who moved into the Presbyterian fold.

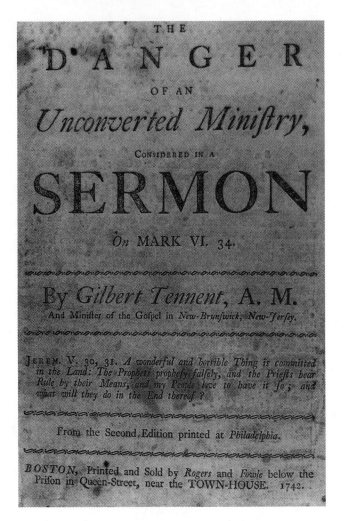

Title page for a treatise charging that many ministers were hypocritical agents of God

Adopting Act. From its inception the Calvinist theology and presbyterial organization of the Presbyterian Church attracted Protestants of many flavors, and the church worked closely with other denominations in worship, ministerial education, and mutual support. Within its fold were people from Scotland, Ireland, England, Wales, Sweden, Germany, and France. Bringing such diverse elements into a consensus on the essentials of an American denomination was a great challenge. The most divisive issues of congregational autonomy and subscription to the Westminster Confession of Faith found adherents settling into three identifiable positions. The Scots sat at one end of the spectrum, favoring a highly centralized government and strict adherence to the Westminster Confession; the New Englanders were poised at the opposite end, espousing more congregational autonomy and no subscription to any man-made creed; and the Irish occupied the middle ground. Debates raged from 1721 until 1729 when a compromise was reached in the Adopting Act. The synod adopted the Westminster Confession but required its members to subscribe only to the essential doctrines it contained and merely recommended the Westminster Directory as a guide to church government.

Growth. Presbyterians formed the fastest-growing religious group in the eighteenth century, primarily because of the large influx of Irish immigrants. As Dissenters these Presbyterians had endured religious persecution for decades in Ireland, but the eighteenth century also brought economic hardship. Waves of Irish Presbyterians flooded into the middle and southern colonies, which tolerated their religious beliefs, and flowed into the unoccupied western regions. Some were established congregations who brought their ministers with them; most immigrated as individuals or in small family groups and were followed by clergymen.

Congregations. Most of these immigrants dispersed into scattered farms and so had to travel some distance to attend services. They usually formed small congregations which had trouble supporting a minister. Before a congregation could call a minister, each family had to pledge what it could contribute to his salary in the form of money, firewood, food, or services. If this was not sufficient, two or three congregations shared a minister and conducted their own services when he was engaged at another church. Most clergymen had to find supplementary support and moonlighted as farmers, teachers, and physicians. The synod assigned settled ministers to hold services in the vacant congregations, but they often got lost trying to find them. Larger congregations relied on pew rents, with the more desirable pews going for a higher rent. Worship services were similar to those of the early Puritans and later Congregationalists in New England, except that several congregations might join in the sacrament of the Lord's Supper, which sometimes lasted for two days. One minister would preach a sermon of preparation, after which the local clergy dispensed communion tokens to worthy members. These were their ticket to sit at the rough tables which were roped off to keep out the undeserving.

Revivals. Within this porous, multinational, and loosely organized denomination the one common denominator was a desire for conversion. About 1726 a young minister in New Jersey, Gilbert Tennent, became acquainted with Theodorus Frelinghuysen, a neighboring Dutch Reform clergyman who was preaching emotional sermons urging personal conversion. Tennent wanted to spark his own revivals and was soon joined by his brothers and a few others who had been tutored by Gilbert's father in what later was known as the Log College. They began to intrude on other congregations and accuse the regular clergy of being unconverted and thus not able to lead others to regeneration. Several of Tennent's followers could not meet the stringent education standard required of ministers by the Westminster Directory and fought to rescind it. There was some sympathy for their position, for lowering these standards would make more ministers available for all those vacant con-

gregations. The synod compromised by passing an Examination Act in 1738, which served until it established an official seminary with the requisite course of study. Those ministerial candidates without a university degree were examined by a synod committee which could attest to their learning. When the supporters of revivals persisted and tried to repeal this act as well, the synod prepared to censor them.

Great Awakening. George Whitefield arrived in 1739, sparking his own revivals and lending legitimacy to the process. It grew and became more insistent on the irrelevancy of a settled and educated clergy. Eventually the synod split into the moderate Old Side Synod of Philadelphia and the revivalist New Side Synod of New York. After the emotions of the Great Awakening quieted, however, both of these synods maintained the standards and organization that had been set earlier: an educated ministry, adherence to the essential doctrines of the Westminster Confession of Faith, and a moderately centralized church government. They only remained separated until 1758 because of the hatreds engendered among local congregations who had split during the revivals.

Sources:

Jon Butler, *Power, Authority, and the Origins of American Denominational Order: The English Churches in the Delaware Valley, 1680–1730* (Philadelphia: American Philosophical Society, 1978);

Elizabeth Nybakken, "New Light on the Old Side: Irish Influences on Colonial Presbyterianism," *Journal of American History*, 68 (1982): 813–832;

Sally Schwartz, *"A Mixed Multitude": The Struggle for Toleration in Colonial Pennsylvania* (New York: New York University Press, 1987);

Leonard J. Trinterud, *The Forming of an American Tradition: A Reexamination of Colonial Presbyterianism* (Freeport, N.Y.: Books for Library Press, 1949).

PURITANS

Covenant Theology. Covenants were important in the religious communities of the Puritans in early New England. These were solemn and binding agreements which were patterned after the covenants they believed God had made with man. In the Covenant of Works, Adam and Eve agreed to obey God's will and obtain salvation by their own good works. They broke this covenant and lost God's favor. Through the Covenant of Redemption, Jesus agreed to take upon himself the guilt of the sins of men and save them from their fate. In the Covenant of Grace, God's spirit entered those predestined for salvation. God also made covenants with groups of people, such as Abraham and his descendants, to look on them with special favor if they strove to obey his will. The Puritans believed that they were one of these groups and employed covenants throughout their society in entering marriage, creating churches, forming towns, and establishing governments. All of these specific covenants added up to the society's covenant with God, who was quick to punish any infraction.

Congregational Organization. Churches were at the center of Puritan society. Believers settled close together in towns so that they could attend church at least twice a week and gather for prayers and theological discussions in private homes. Living in close proximity also allowed them to scrutinize each other's behavior and help everyone to lead the moral lives that would please God. Privacy was a luxury that striving Christians could ill afford. The first order of business in the town was to form a congregation. A few men were selected as pillars because of their probable conversion and virtuous conduct. They agreed to a church covenant and examined other applicants for membership in that covenant. Soon after they arrived the Puritans adopted the practice of admitting to church membership only those who could convince the pillars and the rest of the congregation that they had been saved. They followed a congregational form of government in which the congregation had absolute autonomy in admitting members, governing itself, selecting its leaders, and calling its minister, whose ordination was only valid in that congregation. The minister was the key in any church. He had to be a highly educated person so that he could provide the most accurate explanation of the Bible and how it related to all aspects of life. Humans could only be saved by hearing and understanding the word of God. But the minister also counseled his flock, leading them toward the saving faith that brought conversion and to the good works that characterized both a saved individual and a moral society. Because God spoke to humans only through the Bible, which the minister understood so well, people turned to him for advice on all sorts of matters, even economic and political. Faced with these awesome responsibilities, neighboring ministers met in informal support groups to discuss common problems of doctrine and governance. The decisions of these clerical consociations were not binding on individual congregation, but their suggestions usually were taken. In 1646 ministers and laymen from each church in Massachusetts met in a colonywide synod and issued the Cambridge Platform, which adopted the general tenets of the Westminster Confession of Faith and recommended that synods or consociations continue to meet and advise local churches. It was such a synod in 1662 that officially sanctioned a Half-Way Covenant whereby congregations could choose to baptize the children of non–church members and allow them to be "half-way" members of the church.

Worship. Puritan churches were simple, plain, square buildings. There were no steeples, stained-glass windows, or ornaments of any kind. Worshipers sat on hard, wooden benches facing the minister, who often stood on a raised platform. Later these benches were sectioned off into squares of family pews with partitions around them. This was designed to cut down on the cold drafts and retain the heat from warm bricks that the family wrapped in cloths and placed on the floor. Pews were assigned by the family's rank in society. Worship services went on all week, but the major services were on Sunday and were lengthy and formal affairs. In each the main feature was the sermon, which usually lasted about two hours and was bracketed by long prayers. The worshipers stood during the prayers and throughout much of the service. Sometimes the congregation would take a lunch break after the morning service and return for another in the afternoon. The singing or chanting of psalms was allowed but with no musical accompaniment. A "liner" would sing the line, and the congregation would repeat it in whatever tunes individuals chose to follow. Only those who had been saved and were members could take the sacrament of the Lord's Supper. There were no formal religious holidays, not even Christmas or Easter. The Bible provided no dates for the birth, death, or resurrection of Christ, and the Puritans believed that the Catholic Church had simply made them up to coincide with the celebrations of pagans whom the church was attempting to draw into the fold. To Puritans this was simply a whitewashing of heathen partying with a Christian hue. There were special days of Thanksgiving when things went well and fast days when they did not. These were called by a minister for local matters or by the ministerial meetings for colonywide concerns.

Family and Society. The family was the cornerstone of the society where the closest scrutiny and continuous religious instruction occurred. Thus people with no family were placed in one. The townsfolk carefully monitored activities within the households to insure that the family maintained the harmony that characterized God's original creation. If trouble arose, the church elders would intervene, removing children, apprentices, and servants. Government officials were empowered to grant a divorce so that a contentious husband and wife might enter more-pleasing matrimonial covenants, although it rarely happened. A hierarchy existed within a family so that all would know their places, thus avoiding competition and arguments. The husband was at the head and represented the family unit in all public and church affairs; the wife deferred to him and supervised the private household affairs. The husband also was responsible for raising the children in a strict fashion that would suppress their naturally sinful instincts. If any stepped out of their prescribed roles, it was believed that they would be vulnerable to the temptations of Satan. Similar hierarchies in the larger society were expected to promote the same harmony. The most important was the religious hierarchy, with the minister at the top and the church elders below him, followed by the church members; at the bottom were the non–church members. By law everyone had to pay taxes to support the minister, attend church regularly, and conform to Puritan practices and precepts.

Church and State. All government was in the hands of the saints because they alone could understand and follow God's will. Church membership was required of all adult men who wished to vote and hold political office. Female saints were excluded because they had men to represent their families. Local governance was most important in the lives of the townsfolk and was almost indistinguishable from the town church. Decisions were made in town meetings which adopted the consensus of the community, which they hoped was close to God's will. The state was formally separated from the church even though they shared the same mission. The colony government was to pass laws to insure that all would walk in the path of righteousness and to punish those who strayed. If the government failed to maintain proper standards, God would punish the whole society. For instance, wage and price controls were established so that one individual could not profit at the expense of others. All of these regulations were based on biblical directives. There was not even a written code of laws until 1641 because it was assumed that the Bible contained all the laws that were necessary. Government officials also directed the establishment of schools. Education was crucial for all Puritans because God revealed himself in the Scriptures, nature, and history, all of which they needed to learn. At the least everyone had to be able to read the Bible. In 1647 the colony government passed the "Old Deluder Satan" law, instructing towns to establish schools for this purpose. Harvard College was founded in 1636 to educate aspiring ministers.

Variations. Not everyone conformed to the New England orthodoxy. Some could not justify infant baptism, believing that this sacrament should be a seal of the conversion of adults. These Baptists, as they later came to be called, also demanded a complete separation of church and state, and some even suggested that humans had the freedom of will to choose whether or not they would sin. Others advocated the presbyterian position that church membership should be open to all who agreed to live according to God's commandments rather than only to those who were already saved and that congregations should relinquish some of their authority to higher councils of ministers and elders. In the interests of harmony, such deviants were counseled in love so that they might see the error of their disagreements, and if that failed they were banished from the colony. Roger Williams left Massachusetts Bay in 1636 and founded Rhode Island, where he established the first Baptist church. His colony welcomed people of all religious beliefs and allowed them to follow their consciences without fear of government interference. Such an environment attracted other exiles, such as Anne Hutchinson, who was banished from Massachusetts Bay in 1637 for adhering to a more mystical interpretation of Calvinism. The Society of Friends (Quakers), a more radical offshoot of puritanism, also settled on Rhode Island as a base from which they could fan out to proselytize through New England. The Puritan establishment considered the Friends to be the greatest threat, for they challenged not only its theology but also its society and government.

Decline. The challenges to Puritan control of New England increased after 1660 and exacerbated the internal threats to the cohesion of the society that accompanied a growth in population and economic prosperity. More people settled on isolated farms, away from churches and guardians of morality; merchants and wage workers put their individual needs above the community good; and non-Puritans arrived in greater force, seeking economic opportunity rather than religious cohesion. Fewer people believed they had been saved, and so smaller numbers were joining the church, thus denying their children the chance to be baptized. In desperation, some churches adopted the Half-Way Covenant, in which children of any baptized person could be baptized regardless of whether their parents were church members or not; others adopted the presbyterian position that anyone who led a moral life could become a church member and seek conversion within its fold. Meanwhile, Puritan officials were fighting to retain control of their colonies in the face of English threats to place them all under royal control. James II finally did so, revoking their charters and, in 1686, gathering Massachusetts Bay, Plymouth, Connecticut, Rhode Island, New Jersey, and New York into the Dominion of New England, ruled by a royal governor who was an Anglican. The Glorious Revolution ended this, but William and Mary did not restore their old charters. Instead Massachusetts Bay received a royal charter, which included Plymouth as well. Connecticut retained her self-government, but it too had to conform to the laws of England. The Puritans had become New Englanders, and their churches became known as Congregational.

Sources:

Francis J. Bremer, *The Puritan Experiment: New England Society from Bradford to Edwards,* revised edition (Hanover, N.H.: University Press of New England, 1995);

Stephen Foster, *Their Solitary Way: The Puritan Social Ethic in the First Century of Settlement in New England* (New Haven: Yale University Press, 1971);

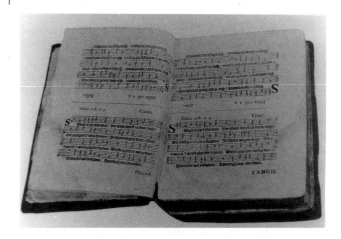

Psalm Book for Four Voices, printed in Holland, circa 1624, the ritual of the Protestant Reformed Dutch Church set to music

A *predickstoel* (pulpit) installed in the Blockhouse Church of Beverwyck and Fort Orange in 1657 (First Church of Albany, New York)

David D. Hall, *Worlds of Wonder, Days of Judgement: Popular Religious Beliefs in Early New England* (Cambridge, Mass.: Harvard University Press, 1990);

Carla Pestana, *Quakers and Baptists in Colonial Massachusetts* (New York: Cambridge University Press, 1991).

REFORM CHURCHES

Dutchmen. The Dutch Reform Church was Calvinistic and similar in theology and ecclesiastical structure to the Presbyterian Church. It was the established, or state, church of Holland, where its governing body, the Classis of Amsterdam, remained. This religion arrived in New York when the Dutch West India Company established it in its trading outposts in 1624. The first ordained minister, however, did not arrive until five years later. Followers were led by laymen appointed as *Krankenbesoeckers* (Comforters of the Sick). Although established, the church coexisted with denominations that were tolerated in the interest of attracting settlers. When the English took over the colony in 1664, there were only twelve struggling churches and six ministers, three of whom immediately left. Yet the church grew, spreading into New Jersey and later into Pennsylvania in spite of the lack of clergy, who could only be ordained by the Amsterdam Classis. They survived by welcoming any Reform or Presbyterian preacher and seriously considered joining with the Presbyterians in the early 1740s. The projected union failed because the church insisted that services be conducted in Dutch. Yet in New York several Dutch ministers did employ the English language and even adopted the more formalistic liturgy and practices of the Anglican Church. Churches in New Jersey went in the opposite direction after the arrival of Theodorus Jacobus Frelinghuysen in 1720. He and two other pietistic preachers spurred a series of Dutch revivals in 1735, marked by spontaneous prayers, evangelical preaching in Dutch, and a minimum of ritual. Frelinghuysen claimed to be able to recognize those who had not been saved and refused to allow them to take communion. He and his followers spread out, intruding on other congregations with their fervent preaching and lambasting their clergy as lifeless formalists. The New York ministers were their main targets. Congregations began to split into two warring factions as lay followers of Frelinghuysen preached and spread revivals throughout the area. This finally forced the Amsterdam Classis in 1748 to establish a subsidiary coetus, or synod, in America with the power to ordain ministers. Further autonomy was granted after 1750.

Germans. The German Reform Church was quite similar to that of the Dutch, and their histories are intertwined. It was established in the Palatinate and several Rhineland provinces and overseen by the Heidelberg Reform Group. Wars in the early eighteenth century drove many of them to the middle colonies, mainly Pennsylvania. Because few moved as organized religious groups, they lacked ministers and were ill-prepared to organize themselves; in the past, state authorities had directed ecclesiastical matters. Their earliest church, organized in 1719 in Germantown, operated without a minister, which was typical of later congregations. Nevertheless, churches were built and operated as community centers, with schoolmasters and pious laymen conducting services. John Philip Boehm, for instance, was a schoolmaster who rode a sixty-mile circuit to exercise pastoral duties in three churches. An ordained minister arrived in 1727 to found the Reformed Church of Philadelphia and convinced the Amsterdam Classis to accept responsibility for the Germans as well. It directed Dutch ministers in New York to ordain Boehm and in 1746 sent Michael Schlatter to establish a more comprehensive organization for the denomination. Within a year this energetic man brought together four ministers and twenty-seven elders representing twelve churches to form a coetus, which decided to meet annually for the general oversight of the church. Its actions could be vetoed by either of the two synods in Holland, and it could not ordain ministers, but it did put the church on a firmer foundation. Schlatter was untiring in his missionary efforts, organizing and overseeing congregations from northern New Jersey to the backwoods of Virginia and garnering financial and ministerial support from Holland.

Sources:

Randall H. Balmer, *A Perfect Babel of Confusion: Dutch Religion and English Culture in the Middle Colonies* (New York: Oxford University Press, 1989);

Dutch Calvinistic Pietism in the Middle Colonies: A Study in the Life and Theology of Theodorus Jacobus Frelinghuysen (The Hague: Nijhoff, 1967);

William J. Hinke, ed., *Life and Letters of Rev. John Philip Boehm, Founder of the Reformed Church in Pennsylvania, 1683–1749* (Philadelphia: Publication and Sunday School Board of the Reformed Church in the United States, 1916);

Sally Schwartz, *"A Mixed Multitude": The Struggle for Toleration in Colonial Pennsylvania* (New York: New York University Press, 1987).

ROMAN CATHOLICS

Spanish. The Catholic Church and the Spanish state were a team in the early exploration and settlement of America; conquest and conversion were assumed to go together. The Pope had granted such ecclesiastical power to the Spanish monarchs that they became virtually vice popes, and their religious fervor prompted them to evangelize and promote the church throughout their empire. The major Spanish settlements, however, were south of the present-day boundaries of the United States, although they did maintain footholds around Florida and in the Southwest. San Miguel in Virginia did not long survive its founding in 1526, but its chapel remained. Saint Augustine, Florida, prospered after its founding in 1565. Jesuits and Franciscans established missions, hospitals, and convents. By 1634 there were thirty-four Franciscan friars maintaining forty-four missions and ministering to over twenty-five thousand Native American converts within the present boundaries of the United States. In the Southwest the Spanish ventured into New Mexico, Arizona, and Texas after 1598 and slowly established missions whose existence was made precarious because of Indian hostility, jurisdictional conflicts within the church, and political intrigues in Spain which necessarily involved the church. Also, many missionaries refused to learn the language of the Indians and demanded that they abandon their traditional ways and adhere to the Spanish culture. They gathered their converts into missions, assigning their work and controlling their lives in a system that often approximated slavery. Especially in the borderlands, missions took on the militaristic characteristics of frontier forts. Because it embarked on an empire a full century before other countries, Spain transmitted a religion and culture that was more medieval in flavor, having been little affected by the Renaissance, Reformation, or commercial expansion.

French. The Protestant Reformation of the sixteenth century shattered the unity of Christendom and ushered in religious wars in France that impeded her efforts at colonization in the New World. When the dust settled in the early seventeenth century, French Catholicism underwent a resurgence of piety and the growth of old, and founding of new, orders dedicated to purifying the French church. In this new France the faith and institutions of the Roman church gained a centrality and importance that was equaled in no other country. This coincided with a renewed search for empire and the prominence of the Society of Jesus, or Jesuits, in making religion an integral part of this venture. The first Jesuit priests arrived in Canada in 1625 and, although most of their efforts were directed at settlers and Native Americans there, they spread out among the Iroquois and Hurons in the Great Lakes region. Some, such as Father Jacques Marquette, became explorers themselves. Unfortunately, when they ventured into the boundaries of the present-day United States and encountered the hostile English and Spanish, trade and military considerations often took precedence over religious objectives. This situation, plus the resistance of the Native Americans toward the adoption of European culture as a price for conversion, led the Jesuits in 1647 to relax their requirements for baptism, become more tolerant of traditional practices, and adopt stances admired in the native culture. Jesuits displayed oratorical skills, generosity with possessions, moral integrity, and patient suffering of adversity—all characteristics which the Indians admired. They also played on their ability to predict natural phenomena, such as eclipses, and on their ability to read and write, which seemed magical to members of an oral culture. They substituted religious icons for traditional charms, ascribing to a crucifix the power of healing simple diseases and flinging sulfur into campfires to illustrate their supernatural powers. Their effect on the religious beliefs of outlying tribes was questionable, but they left a legacy of piety and Christian commitment among French settlers in Canada and the northern boundaries of the United States.

English. Roman Catholics provided the foundation on which Maryland was founded and formed enclaves in New York, Pennsylvania, and other tolerant colonies, where they often were denied political rights. Charles I granted the Catholic Calvert family the proprietorship over Maryland in 1632 to settle debts, allow the persecuted Catholic population an outlet, and conciliate the European powers of the Counter-Reformation. Lord Baltimore instructed his governors to give Protestants no offense and advised Catholics to worship privately. Such toleration of other denominations was the only way that Catholics enjoyed any rights at all. A church building was immediately erected in Saint Mary's, the first settlement, in 1634, and within five years at least four other parishes had been erected. For the first decade the conduct of church affairs was in the hands of Jesuit priests, who converted both Protestants and Native Americans. However, their success antagonized the growing num-

Wampum belts presented by the Delawares to Quaker settlers in the 1680s (Museum of the American Indian and the Historical Society of Pennsylvania)

bers of Protestant setters, and the Calverts quietly began to limit their activities and invite the ministrations of other orders. The Catholic-dominated assembly passed an Act Concerning Religion in 1649 putting the long-practiced policy of toleration into precise and legal terms. Even though a Protestant Association arose during the Glorious Revolution and held power until 1691 when Maryland became a royal province, the colony reverted to the Calverts in 1715, by which time they had returned to the Anglican fold. Nevertheless, they maintained their earlier policy of toleration, and the small core of Catholics continued to attract priests and practice their faith in the face of Protestant threats. They were a landed and moderately wealthy group and enjoyed sufficient social prestige to sustain the work and worship of their church.

Sources:

W. J. Eccles, *France in America* (New York: Harper & Row, 1972);

John Tracy Ellis, *Catholics in Colonial America* (Baltimore: Helicon Press, 1965);

Colin M. MacLachlan, *Spain's Empire in the New World* (Berkeley: University of California Press, 1991).

SOCIETY OF FRIENDS

Radical Sect. The Society of Friends originated as a radical offshoot of puritanism that arose during the English Civil War of the seventeenth century. George Fox is usually credited as its founder and was ridiculed as a "quaker" when he told a judge to "tremble at the words of the Lord." Quakers first settled in tolerant Rhode Island, from which they sent missionaries to proselytize in Puritan New England. They preached extemporaneously, paraded in the streets, mocked the clergy, and generally challenged both the theology and society of New England. Quakers believed that all humans possessed the "Inner Light" of Christ, which was more important than the Scriptures in ruling one's life. They ordained no min-

isters, followed no formal liturgy in their worship, and recognized no sacraments. Instead they gathered and spoke at the prompting of their Inner Light, men and women alike. Believing in the equality of all people, Friends recognized no hierarchy and refused to engage in the customary rituals of deference, such as tipping their hats in the presence of their betters or referring to important people with the formal *you*. Instead they employed the more familiar *thee* and *thou* for everyone. They dressed plainly, eschewing any ornamentation, to signify that the material life was unimportant. As a matter of Christian principle they refused to bear arms or to take the oaths required in courts of law. The Puritans reserved the harshest penalty for these deviants and, for a time, hanged those who returned after having been banished from their colonies. In time Quakers moderated their attacks and settled down to a pious and sober Christian lifestyle that others admired.

William Penn. The man most responsible for creating a legitimate space for the Society of Friends and attracting them to the colonies was William Penn. He was one of the leading lights of the English Quakers and wanted to create a model colony based on their beliefs. He first joined other proprietors in founding West Jersey for Quakers and in 1681 was granted a charter for Pennsylvania (Penn's Forest). Penn immediately traveled through Europe, inviting all to come, offering generous grants of land and guaranteeing freedom of conscience by his Frame of Government and, later, Charter of Liberties. The right to vote and hold office in the assembly was open to almost every free man, and oaths were not required. Penn also set the tone that the colony would follow in dealing with the Native Americans. He considered Indians to be descendants of Old Testament Jews who practiced a primitive Christianity and treated them with the same respect that he accorded others. He purchased land from them at a fair price, prohibited the sale of alcohol to them, regulated the fur trade, and learned their language. The lavish wampum belt that the grateful Delawares gave him can still be seen at the Historical Society of Pennsylvania. Although open to all, Pennsylvania was dominated by the Quakers, both in population and control of political office. As other immigrants ar-

---

REJECTING LUST

Ye are called to peace, therefore follow it . . . seek the peace of all men, and no man's hurt . . . keep out of plots and bustling and the arm of the flesh, for all these are amongst Adam's sons in the Fall, where they are destroying men's lives like dogs and beasts and swine, goring, rending and biting one another and destroying one another, and wrestling with flesh and blood. From whence arise these wars and killing but from the lusts?

Source: George Fox, *Journal*, edited by John L. Nickalls (Cambridge: Cambridge University Press, 1952), p. 357.

rived, this dominance became increasingly difficult to maintain, and the Quakers withdrew into their subculture that separated themselves from these newcomers.

Meetings. Local Friends gathered at least once a week, usually in simple meetinghouses but also in private homes and barns. The meetinghouses were plain, rectangular buildings with windows high in the walls, which were often whitewashed to heighten spiritual intensity. They were also sparsely furnished, with no pulpits, altars, or ornaments of any kind. Members arrived quietly, with men and women entering by separate doors and sitting apart. Seating was by order of arrival, not rank, except for the elders. A time of silence allowed all to turn inward and tune into their Inner Light. As the spirit moved them, people rose and spoke spontaneously—men, women, and children alike. When there seemed to be no more messages, the elders rose, shook hands, and the meeting ended. Although all possessed the Inner Light, individuals were expected to employ their unique talents in following it. Those who had a gift for speaking of the spirit and leading others to contact it were called Public Friends (ministers). These men and women traveled around, ministering to Quakers and non-Quakers alike. Likewise, at monthly, quarterly, and yearly meetings men and women met separately and had different responsibilities. Men conducted the more-public business; women were responsible for charity, child rearing, marriage, and the moral conduct of the female sex.

Family and Community. Local meetings were almost synonymous with the community of extended families, for Quakers built their homes in clusters, or "loving neighborhoods," where they could monitor behavior. Those who did not behave as charitable Christians were required to stand before the meeting, shame themselves, and be forgiven in love. Individual families also relied on spiritual love rather than authoritarian hierarchy to maintain harmony. Families were openly affectionate and oriented to their children, regarding them as innocent and incapable of sin until at least eleven years of age. Then they used rewards and reason to encourage proper behavior. Adolescence was the most dangerous time, for Friends viewed lust as a sin and premarital sex as an abomination. Young people were watched closely by the elders, prohibited from physical contact, and married within the faith and only with the consent of their parents. Quakers spent little on formal education, other than learning to read and write and to perform in practical trades. They felt that too much book learning might obscure the Inner Light. Quaker homes were large by colonial standards, reflecting their family orientation, but were as plain as their dress. Because clothes were a badge of wealth and status in these times, rich and poor dressed in somber colors with no ornamentation—not even buttons.

Keithian Schism. George Keith arrived in Philadelphia in 1688 to head a Quaker Latin school and became active among the Society of Friends. By 1691 he was ac-

cusing ministers of downplaying the importance of a knowledge of the Scriptures and Christ, not inquiring into the spiritual state of members, and refusing to discipline their flocks. He demanded that the Quakers adopt a creed, require a relation of spiritual experience of all who attended meetings, and formalize the handling of discipline and finances in local meetings. He did all of this in a loud and censorious voice. His followers even organized separate local meetings, calling themselves Christian Quakers. Other Quakers called the Public Friends condemned them and fought to keep members from joining their schism. Eventually Keith returned to England, was forced out of the Society, and became an Anglican. He returned to Pennsylvania as a missionary with the Society for the Propagation of the Gospel and continued to plague the Quakers.

Formalization. Keith's charges struck a nerve among the Society of Friends, which responded by implementing much of what he advocated. Public Friends issued a statement of their beliefs which served as the orthodoxy, even though they did not force anyone to sign it. They became much more careful of whom they admitted to their meetings and more stringent in disciplining their own, especially the children. The Yearly Meeting began to circulate specific directives on what Quaker children could not do, such as wear "over long scarves" or their hair in bangs. Local meetings were directed to appoint Overseers to scrutinize behavior by asking standardized questions drawn up by the monthly meetings. Finally, the Philadelphia Yearly Meeting even prepared papers on discipline and practice which all of the lower meetings were directed to follow. Special quarterly meetings were instituted where the children were to be drilled in their duties. "Weighty Friends" (wealthy and respected elders) took a greater role in all of the meetings where the Public Friends had been dominant. The lines of authority were clarified: Overseers of local meetings, monthly meetings, quarterly meetings, and finally the Yearly Meeting. Decisions made at one level could be appealed at the next.

Decline. The Great Awakening of the 1740s had little impact on the Society of Friends. The theological emphasis on predestination and emotional preaching flew in the face of Quaker understanding of the Inner Light and practice of quiet contemplation. In addition Public Friends, or ministers, began sharing responsibilities with Weighty Friends and Overseers, so New Side and New Light attacks against ministers attracted little interest. Moreover, Quakers were less concerned with attracting converts, another goal of the various revivalists in the Awakening. Friends were more concerned about increased secularization. Prosperity was taking its toll on the Quaker lifestyle as wealthy merchants built bigger homes, purchased household items of exquisite craftsmanship, and acquired larger wardrobes of the finest and most expensive fabrics, even if they were still in dark colors and sported no ornamentation. It seemed as if the countinghouses of their businesses were attracting more of their attention than the meetinghouses of their faith. Young people followed suit, engaging in more games and social activities, often with non-Quakers. Some even married outside of the faith. Although they personally refused to bear arms, Friends in office were under increasing pressure to vote for military spending to defend the western frontier from Native American attacks. Some succumbed and voted for military stores; more defied the proprietor, which caused political conflict, or withdrew from office, leaving the governance of the colony to others.

Sources:

Hugh Barbour, *The Quakers in Puritan New England* (New Haven: Yale University Press, 1964);

Ewin B. Bronner, *William Penn's "Holy Experiment": The Founding of Pennsylvania, 1681–1701* (New York: Columbia University Press, 1962);

Barry Levy, *Quakers and the American Family: British Settlement in the Delaware Valley* (New York: Oxford University Press, 1988);

Frederick B. Tolles, *Meeting House and Counting House: The Quaker Merchants of Colonial Philadelphia, 1682–1763* (Chapel Hill: University of North Carolina Press, 1948).

SOUTHWEST NATIVE AMERICAN RELIGION

Pueblo. When the Spanish moved north from their Mexican strongholds into present-day New Mexico in the late seventeenth century, they encountered the many apartmentlike villages of the Pueblo. These farming people eagerly adopted the agricultural technology of the Spaniards and welcomed the Franciscan friars, according respect to these spiritual leaders as they did to their own. Religion was at the center of these people's lives as they irrigated the land, developed drought-resistant corn, and, in short, sought to control nature for their own purposes. They accomplished this through rituals led by their spiritual leaders, as the gods who brought them to the earth directed them to do before departing.

Creation Myth. The Pueblo believed that they had once lived in the center of the earth, which was the middle cosmos, with their mother and all living creatures. When it was time to leave, she gave them corn to take the place of her nourishment and appointed a priest to care for them. Helped by the birds, insects, and animals, they and their gods climbed up to the surface of the earth and entered the White House, from which they could view the sky, the third level of the cosmos. There two sisters contended to see who was the stronger. It was a draw, so one went to the east and became the mother of white people; the other became the mother of the Indians. The Pueblo remained at the White House with their gods who taught them how to farm and how to honor the gods by performing the sacred rituals and ceremonies that integrated humans into the forces of the cosmos. Then the people left the White House and established their villages.

Kiva. The kiva was the most sacred place in each of these villages, for it represented the hole in the earth through which they came, a hole which extended even to the underworld, the first level of the cosmos. It was through the kiva that they could communicate with their mother and the gods. The kiva was the center of each village from which all else was measured—the apartments, fields, and boundaries of the village. In this circular, semisubterranean room were held all of the ceremonies that marked the phases of the year when it was necessary to enlist the help of the gods and the cosmic forces. Next to it was a room where the sacred masks and other religious paraphernalia were stored. A chief priest cared for these and oversaw the rituals, aided by trained assistants.

Christianizing. Grafting Catholicism onto their religion was relatively easy, for the Pueblo considered the white friars to be the priests or assistants of the eastern sister. The Christian god took his place among their own gods; kneeling in prayer was added to the bodily movements; Catholic chants joined the other ritual sounds in their worship; and chalices were included among objects in the sacred warehouse. The Pueblo also saw similarities between crucifixes and their prayer sticks and between the use of incense and their smoking rituals. At first the friars were tolerant of this eclecticism, even creating boys' choirs to perfect their chanting. In periods of intense religious zeal, however, when the Spanish did battle with Satan by erasing any vestiges of pagan ritual, the Pueblos fought back and returned to their pure traditional religious practices.

Rebellion. In 1680 El Pope led the largest revolt against Spanish Catholicism. Five years earlier the Spanish began to raid the kivas, where no outsider was to venture, confiscate the sacred masks, burn prayer sticks, and execute the priests. This coincided with droughts and hostile attacks by other Native Americans. El Pope told the Pueblo that their god was stronger than the Spanish god and was punishing them for their inattention. He was able to unite most of the villages in burning churches, defacing statues of the Virgin Mary, destroying chalices, and driving the Spanish out. After more than fifteen years the Spanish returned, but the humbled Franciscans allowed the Pueblo to continue their traditional religious practices.

Sources:

Ramon A. Gutierrez, *When Jesus Came, the Corn Mothers Went Away* (Stanford, Cal.: Stanford University Press, 1991);

Andrew L. Knaut, *The Pueblo Revolt of 1680: Conquest and Resistance in Seventeenth-Century New Mexico* (Norman: University of Oklahoma Press, 1995);

David J. Weber, *The Spanish Frontier in North America* (New Haven: Yale University Press, 1992).

HEADLINE MAKERS

FRANCIS ALISON

1705-1779
ENLIGHTENED MINISTER

Irish Immigrant. The Reverend Dr. Francis Alison arrived in Pennsylvania in 1735 in the company of other oppressed Irish Presbyterians seeking religious and political freedom. He brought with him a deep commitment to the precepts and pedagogy of the Scots-Irish Enlightenment and to the desirability of religious diversity. Alison was born in Leck, in northern Ireland, in 1705, the son of a weaver. He was educated in a private academy, probably in Dublin under the Reverend Francis Hutcheson, the founder of the Scots-Irish Enlightenment. He earned his master of arts degree in Scotland at the University of Edinburgh in 1733 and started divinity studies under Hutcheson at the University of Glasgow. That institution later awarded Alison a doctor of divinity degree, an unprecedented honor for a colonist. He returned to Ireland, was licensed, and sailed for Pennsylvania. He settled in as minister to the New London Church in 1737 and opened an academy that introduced the progressive educational methods and curricula of the Scots-Irish Enlightenment to Americans.

Revivalists. An educated ministry was the main issue among Presbyterians in the Great Awakening, and Alison and his academy occupied center stage. The synod was planning to support a seminary that could prepare ministers to meet the standards required by the Directory. The revivalist faction knew that the New London Academy would be chosen, rather than the "Log College" of William Tennent, which most of them had attended. Alison, "the greatest classical scholar in America," was already teaching the higher branches of knowledge, which Tennent could not do. Tennent's son, Gilbert, the leader of the revivalist party, determined to destroy Alison's academy by convincing laymen to divert their financial support to his father. He opened his attack in 1740 by preaching one of the most in-

fluential and severely abusive sermons of the Awakening, "The Danger of an Unconverted Ministry." It targeted Alison but slapped a string of nasty labels on all educated ministers who dared to oppose the actions of the Log College faction. He announced that all learned clergymen were unconverted and would lead their flocks to damnation. True Christians, he proclaimed, must seek out pastors who had studied under an evangelical like the elder Tennent, channel financial support to the Log College, and choose only its alumni for their ministers. If deprived of support, the New London Academy would wither and nothing would be left for the synod to adopt. The Log College, in contrast, would grow and send out waves of revivalists to dominate the church.

Old Side Leader. When the Presbyterian Synod split in 1741 into the Old Side Synod of Philadelphia and the New Side Synod of New York, Alison assumed the leadership of the Old Side. In their effort to drive Alison from his pulpit, the revivalist faction broke synod rules and intruded on his congregation, hoping to draw away enough members so that the remainder would not be able to afford a minister and Alison would leave. The congregation was so incensed that it lodged a protest against the intruders in the synod of 1741. When the revivalists attempted to hinder consideration of the matter, the moderates issued a protest, which prompted the revivalists to march out of the synod. Alison tried for an immediate reconciliation and then worked for seventeen years to finally effect one in 1758. The Philadelphia Synod did designate the New London Academy as its official seminary in 1743 but opened it to students of all denominations. Alison left in 1752 to become the rector of the new Academy of Philadelphia and vice provost of the College when it was added. He boarded ministerial students at his home and continued the enlightened pedagogy and curricula in his instruction of a generation of moderate ministers. He preached a similar blend of Enlightenment ideas and Calvinism in the First Presbyterian Church of Philadelphia, where he served as a part-time minister until his death in 1779.

Enlightened Calvinist. Alison's opposition to the excesses of the Great Awakening stemmed from the combination of Calvinism and Enlightenment thought which he taught throughout his life from lectern and pulpit. He read the treatises of "the ingenious Mr. Edwards" and applauded them. However, he did not use the psychology of John Locke and the "new learning" to try to explain the process of conversion as Edwards did. Rather, he adhered to the Calvinist doctrine that humans could never know such divine matters and to Locke's contention that they could only have probable knowledge of the earthly world. Neither could humans have any control over whether or not they would be saved: that was all predestined. Yet Alison followed the Scots-Irish Enlightenment belief in the existence of a God-given sixth, or moral, sense that guided humans toward virtuous activity that brought pleasure. He also sought its goal of creating a society which would reward such Christian behavior. If humans developed their minds so that they could understand which acts were good and then do them, the conscience or moral sense would reward them with such pleasure that they would always want to follow God's commands. Soon, acting virtuously would become a habit for all of the society, which was what God had intended in the original creation. Alison's opposition to the Great Awakening was that its supporters opposed the liberal education that would develop this understanding and seemed to suggest that reading the Bible for God's directions was not necessary. Instead they encouraged their followers only to follow their emotions in making instantaneous judgments on the spiritual state of others and attack them with an un-Christian ferocity that bred chaos and conflict. This was the exact opposite of the harmonious world that God had intended and which Christians were obligated to re-create. To Edwards, who was concerned with the salvation of individuals, these emotional excesses and unwarranted attacks were simply a temporary and irrelevant spin-off from the revivals which could be ignored; to Alison, whose concern was the development of a Christian society, they were a major obstruction in its creation.

Sources:

Elizabeth Nybakken, "*The Centinel": Warnings of a Revolution* (Newark: University of Delaware Press, 1984);

Thomas C. Pears, "Francis Alison," *Journal of Presbyterian History,* 28 (1950): 213–225.

JONATHAN EDWARDS

1703-1758

THEOLOGIAN OF THE GREAT AWAKENING

Intellectual. Jonathan Edwards was born in 1703 in East Windsor, Connecticut, the only son of Timothy Edwards, a Congregational clergyman, and Ester Stoddard Edwards, the daughter of Solomon Stoddard, the famed evangelical preacher in Northampton. He illustrated incredible intellectual gifts at an early age. By the time he was twelve the precocious boy was reading Isaac Newton's mathematical works and gathering information on rainbows and spiders which he included in the short essays he wrote to prove the goodness and wisdom of the Creator. Less than a year later he began his collegiate studies under Timothy Cutler, president of Yale College. The scholarly and withdrawn lad did not join in the boisterous pranks of his classmates; instead he discovered the works of John Locke and deepened his knowledge of Newton. Not surprisingly, Edwards graduated at the top of his class in 1720, remained for three years of theological studies, and returned as a tutor for a year. He was astonished when Cutler and other ministers defected to Anglicanism and preached of free will. For him the rational inquiry of the Enlightenment only buttressed the Calvinist insistence that humans have no influence over the converting grace of God.

Pastor. In 1726 Edwards was called to Northampton to succeed his famous grandfather. At about the same time he married Sarah Pierrepont, daughter of one of the founders of Yale and granddaughter of Thomas Hooker, who had established Connecticut. Thus Edwards became as connected by marriage as he already was by birth to the most prestigious families of the Connecticut River valley. He had succeeded to the pastorate of one of the most desirable churches and seemed to be at the pinnacle of his social and religious world. Instead Edwards began to preach almost exclusively on the topic of Christian depravity and utter dependence on God's grace. In 1734–1735 he was rewarded by an amazing revival, which he described in *A Faithful Narrative of the Surprising Work of God* (1737). Revivals spread beyond Northampton and had engulfed the whole Connecticut River valley before they died. Energized by the apparent success of the Great Awakening, Edwards announced that he was reversing the policy started by his grandfather of admitting any moral person to membership in order to lead them to salvation within the church. Hereafter only those who could convince him of their conversion would be admitted and able to baptize their children. There would be no Half-Way Covenant in his church. Why Edwards took this action will remain a mystery until scholars can decipher the handwriting in his notebooks. If he was trying to spark conversions by creating parental fears for their children, the effort backfired. The congregation rose up in arms against him and appealed to an advisory council of ministers whose authority Edwards denied. The fight continued until 1750 when Edwards was fired and moved to the remote mission for Native Americans at Stockbridge.

An Angry God. Edwards was overjoyed at the apparent success of George Whitefield in awakening Christians from their lethargy and invited him to include Northampton on his 1740 tour. Unlike Whitefield, Edwards was no dramatic actor, but he began to dwell more and more on the punishment that they would suffer for rejecting God. This approach reached its zenith in 1741 with the sermon "Sinners in the hands of an Angry God." It was designed to give a vivid sense of the uncertainty of life and the certainty of eternal punishment for unrepentant sinners. This masterpiece of rhetoric bombarded the audience with vivid images of a hell filled with tormented souls who burned like livid coal forever. Sinners were likened to a spider dangling on one silken thread held fast only by God, who had every reason to let them drop. His hearers fell to such "great moaning and crying . . . What shall I do to be saved—oh I am going to Hell," that Edwards had to stop several times during each sermon. He repeated this sermon every time he was invited to preach in the aftermath of Whitefield's travels and published it to great acclaim. Edwards also wrote a series of pamphlets which defended the emotionalism of the Great Awakening as a natural result of God changing one's heart during conversion. The irresponsible judging of the spiritual state of others and attacks on the settled clergy Edwards dismissed as temporary spin-offs of no importance. To his mind the revivals were the genuine work of God and might well be the heralds of the millennium when all society would become holy in preparation for the second coming of Christ.

Reclusive Theologian. Exile in Stockbridge proved to be a blessing. Freed of his pastoral responsibilities, Edwards had the luxury of time to think, write, and resume his intellectual pursuits. In 1746 he had published *Treatise on Religious Affections*, which identified love of God as the fountain of all religious emotion. He also composed various tracts which drew on the psychology of John Locke and other Enlightenment thinkers. *A Careful and Strict Enquiry Into . . . Freedom of Will* (1754), *The Great Christian Doctrine of Original Sin Defended* (1758), *Two Dissertations, I. Concerning the End for which God Created the World. II. The Nature of True Virtue* (1765), and lesser treatises maintained that humans were not born with knowledge or ideas, contrary to the old view. Instead they were granted the faculties to form their own ideas from what their senses told them about the world around them and then to follow those ideas to do what brought them pleasure. Edwards used the concept of the faculties and the emotional pleasure that accompanied good actions to explain the Calvinist position on several ticklish issues: freedom of the will in the face of predestination and original sin, the nature of true or spiritual virtue, and the end for which God had created the earth. Philosophers and theologians have consulted, analyzed, and marveled at these treatises ever since. In 1757 the tracts catapulted him into the position of president of the College of New Jersey, founded by the New Side Presbyterians. He reluctantly accepted the honor but died in 1758 from a smallpox inoculation before he could assume his duties.

Sources:

Perry Miller, *Jonathan Edwards* (New York: Sloane, 1949);

Patricia J. Tracy, *Jonathan Edwards, Pastor: Religion and Society in Eighteenth-Century Northampton* (New York: Hill & Wang, 1979).

ANNE MARBURY HUTCHINSON

1591-1643
ANTINOMIAN LEADER

A Formidable Woman. Anne Marbury Hutchinson posed the greatest threat to the theology and society of Puritan New England. An astute, forceful, and committed Christian, she could explain Scriptures with such precision and follow theological principles to their logical conclusions with such clarity that she outshone all of the Puritan clergy who sought to squelch her voice. All we know of her was written by others, mainly those who wished to discredit her. Yet even John Winthrop, her most implacable enemy, complimented her as "a woman of ready wit and bold spirit." The Antinomian Crisis that she precipitated nearly destroyed his beloved colony.

Making of a Radical. Anne Marbury was born in 1591, the daughter of the Reverend Francis Marbury, an outspoken Anglican pastor in Lincolnshire, England. Although not officially a Puritan, he rejected most of the Anglican dogma and focused on the essential doctrines of the Scriptures. These he taught to his daughter, who received an education far superior to most girls of her time. She married William Hutchinson in 1612 but looked to the Reverend John Cotton and her brother-in-law, the Reverend John Wheelwright, for spiritual guidance after her father died. Both employed an evangelical style of preaching that focused on the mystical elements of conversion. Lincolnshire was a hotbed of puritans and other reforming Anglicans who could not be accommodated within the formal churches. Thus laymen who felt that they had received grace gathered together informally to discuss sermons, debate passages of the Scriptures, and pray without the presence of ordained ministers. Women played a particularly active role in these assemblies, and it was here that Hutchinson honed her natural intellect and leadership skills in the pursuit of religious truth. When Cotton was forced out of his ministry in 1633, he departed for New England and accepted a position with the Boston Church. Hutchinson packed up her family and followed in 1634, with Wheelwright close behind.

Crisis. Hutchinson quickly made her mark in the spiritual life of the colony, holding informal weekday meetings in her home to clarify and expand on Cotton's sermons to those who could not attend the services. Her audiences grew, and soon her followers comprised a majority in the Boston Church. She became increasingly bothered by the sermons of the copastor, John Wilson, who stressed moral activity as preparation for God's grace. To Hutchinson this smacked of the heresy of Arminianism, which claimed that good works earned salvation. Cotton's message deemphasized good works and stressed the incomprehensible grace of God in saving predestined individuals. Taken to its extremes, this bordered on the heresy of Antinomianism, which maintained that the mystical experience of grace bore no relationship to human conduct, either before or after salvation. Cotton and Wilson were both within the parameters of Puritan orthodoxy, which sought a balance: good works could not save, but the ability to perform them were the fruits of salvation, and all were obliged to lead the moral lives that glorified God's creation. Hutchinson, however, discerned important differences and exaggerated them. Her growing number of followers petitioned to appoint Wheelwright as a teacher and spokesman for their doctrines. When this failed, they openly shunned Wilson, walking out in the middle of his sermons and enlisting the support of those outside the congregation. Anne's skill as a midwife and healer endeared her to women who lined up behind her, joined by merchants who were undergoing criticism for their business practices and found solace in the view that their spiritual state was not dependent on their adherence to price and wage controls. Matters came to a head early in 1637 when Wheelwright urged the dissidents to separate from the Arminians. When summoned before the General Court, he refused to recant and was banished.

Trial. The General Court, however, knew that Wheelwright was not the main source of the conflict that was tearing their colony apart; they sent for his sister-in law. Hutchinson had played her cards so cleverly, however, that she could only be charged with the minor offense of having urged others to petition for the appointment of Wheelwright. The ensuing trial might have ignored the niceties of a proper judicial proceeding, but the court believed that it was fighting for the very existence of the colony. The written account of the proceedings records a defendant outshining her intellectually inferior accusers. Hutchinson deftly defended her actions on the basis of Scripture, contradicted her judges, poked holes in their reasoning, and generally displayed not a whit of the deference that she was supposed to pay to her superiors. In the final, stressful parry Anne blurted out that she had received a direct revelation from God for one of her statements. This was clearly a heretical claim for any Calvinist to make because it was believed that God spoke to humans only through the Bible. Even Cotton distanced himself from her extreme views and agreed to her banishment. Her husband and fifteen children plus over eighty families of supporters followed Hutchinson to Narragansett Bay in Rhode Island.

Lingering Threat. Hutchinson's beliefs, posture, and popularity threatened to unravel the entire fabric of this Puritan society and its covenant with God. If individuals could receive direct revelations from God, why bother with the Scriptures? If moral actions were totally unnecessary and no indication of salvation, then everyone was free to commit the most heinous crimes because, if they were predestined, they would be favored by God no matter what they did. What then would become of that moral society that collectively glorified God by its good works? By refusing to soften her extreme views which were causing untold conflict, Hutchinson was destroying the consensus that re-created the harmony of God's creation. When she continually defied the authorities, stepping out of her prescribed role as a woman, she endangered all of the hierarchical systems so necessary for order and harmony. This also left her vulnerable to the temptations of Satan, who was ever ready to pounce on a defenseless individual, as Cotton had insinuated. In fact some secretly considered her to be a witch. When Anne and most of her household were killed in an Indian raid after she left Rhode Island, John Winthrop smugly concluded that God had finally struck her down.

Sources:

Emery Battis, *Saints and Sectaries: Anne Hutchinson and the Antinomian Controversy in Massachusetts Bay Colony* (Chapel Hill: University of North Carolina Press, 1962);

William K. B. Stoever, *"A Faire and Easie Way to Heaven": Covenant Theology and Antinomianism in Early Massachusetts* (Middletown, Conn.: Wesleyan University Press, 1978);

Selma Williams, *Divine Rebel: The Life of Anne Marbury Hutchinson* (New York: Holt, Rinehart & Winston, 1981).

HENRY MELCHIOR MUHLENBERG

1711-1787
FATHER OF THE AMERICAN LUTHERAN CHURCH

Impact. The motto of Henry Melchior Muhlenberg, *"Ecclesia Plantanda"* ("Let the Church be Planted"), sums up the goal of the man and his achievements. Almost single-handedly he joined the scattered and directionless Lutheran churches and forged them into an American denomination that could effectively serve the flood of German immigrants in the latter part of the eighteenth century. Most agree that "the history of the Lutheran Church in America from his landing in 1742 to his death . . . is scarcely more than his biography."

Pietistic Beginnings. Muhlenberg was born on 6 September 1711 in Hanover into the pious family of a shoemaker who was active in the local Lutheran church. He attended a classical school and received a firm grounding in Latin. After his father died, a local minister taught him to play the organ, which began a lifelong love of music. Well-connected family friends, recognizing his talents, sent him to the University of Göttingen and then to Halle, the great citadel of German Pietism. At Halle he continued his studies in languages and music, helped found an orphanage, and taught. He was ordained in 1735 and settled into a church near the estate of Count Nikolaus von Zinzendorf. His former instructors at Halle convinced him that his calling lay in America.

Three forlorn Lutheran congregations in Pennsylvania, with neither church buildings nor pastors, had appealed to Halle for assistance; Muhlenberg was to be their answer.

A Stormy Arrival. The ocean voyage to Charleston in 1742, where Muhlenberg visited the Salsburger Lutherans and continued on to Philadelphia, took place amid one Atlantic storm after another. A different storm awaited him in Pennsylvania. His Philadelphia congregation had split, with some attaching themselves to the recent arrival, Count von Zinzendorf, who was a Lutheran but espoused beliefs that were also Moravian. Meanwhile some joined his other congregation at Providence, which was now led by the Reverend Valentine Kraft, who had been relieved of his church offices in Germany. The third congregation enjoyed the ministrations of an alcoholic charlatan known only as "Schmed." Rather than confront these usurpers directly, Muhlenberg relied on his superior authority, for he had been sent by the king of England (ruler of Hanover as well) and was the official missionary of Halle to fill a proper request. Muhlenberg presented his credentials to the followers of Kraft and Schmed and assumed authority over these congregations, after a series of wily maneuvers that displaced their former leaders. Zinzendorf was a more difficult adversary. He was a man of social and religious stature who led a blameless life of piety and self-sacrifice and was an ordained Lutheran minister. His goal of uniting Christians of all denominations under the ecumenical Moravian umbrella, however, was anathema to Muhlenberg, whose allegiance was to the traditional Lutheran Church. Yet even the mighty Zinzendorf had to back down in deference to Muhlenberg's credentials and his official licensure to the Philadelphia congregation.

Persistent Pastor. With incredible tact, patient firmness, spiritual power, and indefatigable traveling, Muhlenberg founded new churches and brought old congregations together. To rid the church of false and scandalous ministers, he kept up a steady correspondence with his patrons and the fathers at Halle, riveting their attention on the colonies. He attracted a stream of well-trained and devoted ministers to whom congregations naturally gravitated. He preached widely and constantly, in German, English, Dutch, and Latin as the occasion dictated, and quickly adapted the content and style of his preaching to the preferences of his audiences. He avoided all public controversies which might drive some away, instead focusing on the orthodoxy which was the common denominator of all factions. He catechized the unchurched, rallying congregations to erect or enlarge church buildings for regular worship. It did not hurt his standing that, in 1745, he married the pious daughter of Conrad Weiser, the commissioner of Indians affairs for Pennsylvania. They had eleven children, all of whom survived to occupy prominent positions.

Success. Muhlenberg's motto came to fruition in 1748 when six Swedish and German pastors and twenty-four lay delegates met in Philadelphia to form the Pennsylvania Ministerium. Guided by Muhlenberg, it outlined a synodical organization and prepared a book of common prayer that lasted into the nineteenth century. There were, of course, disputes which Muhlenberg, as "overseer" of the united congregations, mediated with surprising success. In 1760 he joined a close friend, the Swedish provost Karl Wrangel, in reorganizing the Ministerium, composing written constitutions for churches, and laying the basis for continuing cooperation between these two national churches.

Conclusion of Service. Muhlenberg remained a loyal Hanoverian subject of King George III until the Declaration of Independence and saw his sons do battle in the American cause. He died on 7 October 1787, the same year that the Lutheran and German Reformed Churches joined forces to found Franklin College in Pennsylvania with his son the Reverend Henry Ernest Muhlenberg as president.

Sources:

Henry E. Jacobs, *A History of the Evangelical Lutheran Church in the United States*, 4 volumes (New York, 1893);

Paul A. W. Wallace, *The Muhlenbergs of Pennsylvania* (Philadelphia: University of Pennsylvania Press, 1950).

GEORGE WHITEFIELD

1714-1770
REVIVALISTIC PREACHER

Transatlantic Revivalist. George Whitefield was an Anglican minister who scorned theology for whatever message would spark the conversion of people of all religious persuasions in England, Scotland, Ireland, and America. He used the increased ease of travel and the communications network of the eighteenth century to spread his message through a series of transatlantic revivals that became the Great Awakening in America. He preached the same sermons wherever he traveled, polishing them after each performance according to the reactions of his audiences. One of the first to capitalize on the emerging transatlantic press, he published his journals, sermons, and letters; directed his secretary to send press releases to newspapers, publicizing his tours and then giving his version of what had transpired on them; and inspired evangelical magazines that sprang up to extol his amazing successes. In public he subsumed his privately sweet and gentle personality beneath such dramatic preaching that it engendered an unearthly egoism in a man who was committed to bring salvation to all. He left a scorched earth in his wake, created by the fires of revivalism and the hot anger of those who saw only the excesses. The Great Awakening in America can ultimately be traced to this one man.

A Natural Preacher. Whitefield was born in 1714 in Gloucester, England, the son of innkeepers. He was a mediocre student but excelled in drama. At Oxford he met John and Charles Wesley (who founded Methodism), experienced conversion, and joined their pious circle. Following his ordination in 1736, he preached his first sermon and was amazed at the result, reporting that "I drove 15 mad." He had found his calling, and news of Whitefield's ability spread by word of mouth. Wherever he preached, crowds materialized out of nowhere. He began to preach in the fields, an innovation that delighted his listeners and forced him to employ a more powerful voice and style than even he thought possible. He also learned that by attacking the clergy, who had closed their pulpits to him, he could draw even larger crowds. A marvelous performer, he acted out his parts, used thunderstorms to punctuate his sentences, and created imaginary dialogues with biblical characters in sonorous tones that carried to the farthest edges of the crowd. He shouted, stomped, sang, and always wept. His cross-eyed stare (the result of a childhood case of measles) was viewed as a sign of supernatural presence which allowed him to keep one eye on heaven and the other on hell. His message was simple: "Repent and you will be saved." He neither understood theology nor considered it to be important in his mission of driving people to seek salvation. In the words of a young Maryland man, "he has the best delivery with the worst divinity that I ever mett with."

The Grand Itinerant. Whitefield began his traveling preaching career in America in order to raise money for an orphanage which he and the Wesley brothers had established in Georgia. When he arrived in Philadelphia in 1739, his reputation had preceded him, and the inhabitants rushed to meet this "boy preacher" who had attained such fame before he was twenty-five years old. Through Pennsylvania, New York, New Jersey, and New England he went, attracting large crowds and attacking clergy. Whitefield moved across the colonial landscape in a brilliant flash that lasted one month. He wintered in Georgia, but composed press releases to insure that he was not forgotten. In April 1740 he returned to Philadelphia and even captured the wily Benjamin Franklin with his oratory. Then he returned to Georgia for a well-publicized confrontation with Anglicans there, which kept his name in the news. In September he embarked on another tour of New England and then was off to Scotland, sparking revivals there.

Extremist Imitators. By 1744 Whitefield's meteoric rise to fame was ending. Many other preachers now gave sermons out of doors, mobs materialized and drowned out even his powerful voice, and former supporters either condemned his extremism or took it further. Gilbert Tennent adopted his attacks against ministers and brought them to new heights; James Davenport turned his dramatic techniques into a parody; lay preachers pro-

liferated, mouthing whatever their audiences wished to hear; and churches splintered into vitriolic factions. Even the newspapers turned against him, matching his press releases with unfavorable comments by his opponents. Many blamed Whitefield for causing all of this disorder.

Apologies. It was an older, wiser, and more sober Whitefield who returned to America in 1745. He apologized to everyone for his youthful egotism that had inadvertently unleashed all of this disorder and abuse of godly ministers. His heart had been in the right place, he maintained; it was just that his dramatic flair had gotten out of hand. He continued his evangelical tours, but in a less confrontational manner. His revivals became routine and even acceptable to society; more time was spent in quiet and pious conversations with individuals; and slaves became an object of his attention. He preached his last sermon in Boston on 29 September 1770, died at its conclusion, and was buried there.

Sources:

Frank Lambert, *"Pedlar in Divinity": George Whitefield and the Transatlantic Revivals, 1737–1770* (Princeton: Princeton University Press, 1994);

Harry S. Stout, *The Divine Dramatist: George Whitefield and the Rise of Modern Evangelicalism* (Grand Rapids, Mich.: Eerdmans, 1991).

ROGER WILLIAMS

1603-1683
CONSCIENTIOUS SEPARATIST

A Man of Vision. A warm, sweet-tempered, and rigid man, Roger Williams followed a spiritual journey that forced him to separate from first one group and then another. In the process he founded and governed the influential colony of Rhode Island, which was the first in America to advocate religious freedom and complete separation of church and state as matters of principle. He is also credited with starting the first Baptist church in America.

Puritans. Within five years of his arrival in Massachusetts in 1631, Williams had become an enemy to the Puritans. He was the son of a poor shopkeeper, but his intelligence so impressed some influential men that they sent him to Cambridge University, where he excelled in his studies, met John Winthrop, and followed him to the colonies. Several churches were interested in calling this brilliant and highly educated man to lead them. He refused a position in the Boston Church because the congregation would not sever all ties with the Church of England and settled in Salem. There he demanded that the church eschew the informal meetings that the clergy had been holding lest they compromise the congregational autonomy that the Scriptures described. He forbade members to worship or pray with any unregenerate persons, even family members. At the colony level he called for complete separation of church and state, arguing that any interference by the state in spiritual affairs only corrupted religion. In his view magistrates should have no power to maintain orthodoxy by enforcing laws, even the Ten Commandments. He threatened the physical existence of the colony as well by claiming that the king had no right to grant Massachusetts to the Puritans because the land belonged to the Indians.

Rhode Island. For five years Gov. John Winthrop and the magistrates argued with Williams, unsuccessfully, and finally banished him in late 1635. They had intended to ship him back to England, but, forewarned by Winthrop, he fled to the South. There he purchased land from the Narragansetts out of his own pocket and founded a colony based on his principles. He evenly distributed land to insure economic equality and instituted a government that was "democratical" under which "all men may walk as their consciences persuade them." In 1644 he made a trip to England and secured a charter for a self-governing colony, governing it from 1654 to 1657 just to guarantee that political and religious freedoms would continue. Many sought refuge there. Some were seeking complete purity in communal churches, in the tradition of Williams and typified by the Baptists; others were drawn to a more mystical strain which began with Anne Hutchinson and included Quakers.

Baptists and Beyond. In the first church that they organized, Williams and his friends baptized each other, probably by immersion, contending that the Scriptures spoke only of saints as church members and total immersion as the seal of membership. This is generally considered to be the first Baptist church in America. Later Williams condemned adult baptism but only because it was not administered by an apostle as the Scriptures described. Then he began to have doubts about the gracious states of others, finally reaching the position that he could only take communion with his wife. These same doubts drove him to the opposite extreme, and he administered the sacraments to anyone since no human can be certain who is saved. Finally he left the ministry entirely, noting that there was no official scriptural sanction for an organized church or official clergy.

Confrontation. Williams's tolerance was sorely tested by the Quakers because they seemed to ignore the Bible and the historical Jesus Christ in favor of a mysticism that relied totally on human divinity. When George Fox, the founding father of the Society of Friends, visited Newport in 1672, Williams was determined to confront him in a debate. Although over seventy years old, he dragged his fragile body into a boat and rowed alone the thirty miles to meet him. Fox had already departed, so Williams engaged his associates in a battle of published words. It seems fitting that Williams spent his last years in the midst of this pamphlet war over Christian principles.

Sources:

Edwin S. Gaustad, *Liberty of Conscience: Roger Williams in America* (Grand Rapids, Mich.: Eerdmans, 1991);

Edmund S. Morgan, *Roger Williams: The Church and State* (New York: Harcourt, Brace & World, 1967);

Ola Winslow, *Master Roger Williams* (New York: Macmillan, 1957).

PUBLICATIONS

William Bradford, *Of Plymouth Plantation, 1620–1647*, edited by Samuel Eliot Morison (New York: Knopf, 1952)—first published from Bradford's manuscript as *History of Plymouth Plantation* in 1856; the complete and detailed account of the founding and early years of Plymouth, including letters of the time, as written by its first governor;

Charles Chauncy, *Enthusiasm described and caution'd against. A Sermon Preach'd . . . after Commencement . . .* (Boston: J. Draper, 1742)—the most sustained condemnation of the revivals in the Great Awakening that expressed the universal sentiments of its opponents throughout the colonies;

Jonathan Edwards, *A Careful and Strict Enquiry into . . . Freedom of the Will* (Boston: Printed & sold by S. Kneeland, 1754)—a literary sensation when published and the most seriously analyzed of his works, for it employed the enlightened psychology of John Locke to defend the existence of free will within the bounds of predestination;

Edwards, *A Faithful Narrative of the Surprising Work of God . . .* (Boston: Printed by S. Kneeland & T. Green for D. Henchman, 1737)—the first detailed and widely read description of a revival he led in 1734–1735 which became the model for other revivals;

Edwards, *A Treatise Concerning the Religious Affections...* (Boston: Printed for S. Kneeland & T. Green, 1746)—an explanation of the conversion process and the role that emotions played in it which became a virtual textbook for revivalists in the Great Awakening;

Cotton Mather, *Magnalia Christi Americana* (London: Printed for Thomas Parkhurst, 1702)—a history of God's providences toward New England written by one of its foremost intellectuals who gathered documents, letters, biographies, and even myths into this magisterial work;

Henry Melchior Muhlenberg, *The Journals of Henry Melchior Muhlenberg,* translated by Theodore G. Tappert and John W. Doberstein, 3 volumes (Philadelphia: Muhlenberg Press, 1942–1958)—one of the most complete and informative records of a frontier missionary and church organizer by an acute commentator on the religious pluralism in the middle colonies;

William Penn, *No Cross, No Crown* (London: Printed & sold by B. Clark, 1682)—sets forth the very essence of the Quaker faith and was faithfully consulted by Friends throughout the colonial period;

Thomas Prince, *The Christian History* (Boston: Skneeland, 1743)—the most influential evangelical magazine of the Great Awakening, which published ministerial reports of revivals as they occurred throughout the British Empire;

Gilbert Tennent, *The Danger of an Unconverted Ministry, Considered in a Sermon on Mark VI. 34* (Philadelphia: Printed by Benjamin Franklin, 1740)—one of the "most abusive and scurrilous sermons ever penned," this attack on an educated clergy precipitated a division in the Presbyterian Church during the Great Awakening that lasted for seventeen years;

John Tillotson, *Sermons,* 14 volumes (London: R. Chiswell, 1695–1704)—these sermons by an Anglican archbishop during the Restoration were widely read in the colonies because they celebrated the use of reason to enrich Christianity and advocated a tolerance that downplayed minor differences between denominations;

George Whitefield, *The Christian's Companion: or, Sermons on Several Subjects . . .* (London: Printed & sold by the booksellers in town & country, 1739);

Whitefield, *A Continuation of the Reverend Mr. Whitefield's Journal, from His Arrival at Savannah, May 7 . . .* (Boston: Printed by G. Rogers & D. Fowle, 1741)—the second in a series of three accounts of Whitefield's awakenings and successes from 1737 to 1741; it spread his fame and elicited angry rebuttals from his opponents.

CHAPTER ELEVEN

SCIENCE AND MEDICINE

by RUSSELL LAWSON

CONTENTS

Sidebars and tables are listed in italics.

1602

- Sebastian Vizcaino sails from New Spain and explores the California coast as far north as Cape Mendocino.

- Englishman Bartholomew Gosnold explores the coast of New England from Maine to southern Massachusetts.

1603

- Samuel de Champlain arrives in New France (Canada) and explores the Saint Lawrence River valley.

- Englishman Martin Pring explores Cape Cod.

1604

- Edward Grimston's translation of José de Acosta's *The Naturall and Morall Historie of the East and West Indies,* a description of Central and South America, is published in England.

- Juan de Oñate leads a military expedition from New Spain and explores the Colorado River.

- Samuel de Champlain explores the northeast coast from Nova Scotia to Cape Cod.

1605

- George Weymouth of England explores the coast of Maine and Saint Georges Bay, Newfoundland.

1608

- John Smith explores the Chesapeake Bay.

1609

- Henry Hudson explores the Hudson River.
- Samuel de Champlain discovers Lake Champlain.

1610

- Dr. Lawrence Bohun of Virginia sets up the first botanical garden in the British colonies.

- Henry Hudson sails into Hudson Bay.

- The viceroy of Mexico, Luis de Velasco, Marqués de Salinas, draws a map of the North American Atlantic coast.

1612

- The first hospital in the British colonies is established at the James River.

- John Smith's *A Map of Virginia* is published in England.

- William Strachey pens *The Historie of Travaile into Virginia Britannia*, an account of the natural history of Virginia.

- Marc Lescarbot's *History of New France*, a description of the Saint Lawrence River Valley, is published in Paris.

1614

Apr.–July   John Smith explores the coast, observes the natural features, and studies the Algonquin tribes of New England.

1615

- Samuel de Champlain explores the region of Lake Huron and Lake Ontario.

1616

- English explorer William Baffin explores Baffin Bay in search of the Northwest Passage.

1619

- Ironworks are built at Falling Creek, Virginia.

1621

- The first gristmill is built at Jamestown, Virginia.

1622

- The population of Virginia is fifteen hundred.

1624

- John Smith's *The Generall Historie of Virginia, New England, and the Summer Isles* is published in England.

1625

- The Brigg's Map shows California as an island detached from the continent.

- Of the six thousand immigrants who have arrived in Virginia since 1607, only twelve hundred are still living.

1628

- The first gristmill is built in Massachusetts.

1634

- William Wood's *New England's Prospect,* an account of the topography and natural history of the region, is published in England.
- Frenchman Jean Nicolet explores Lake Michigan.
- Dutch explorer Harmen Van den Bogaert explores the Oneida country of up-state New York.

1636

- Harvard College opens.

1638

- The first American printing press begins operations in Boston, Massachusetts.

June The first recorded earthquake occurs in New England.

1642

- Darby Field and two Native American companions make the first ascent of Mount Washington, New Hampshire, the tallest peak in New England (6,288 feet).

1648

- Ironworks are built at Saugus, Massachusetts.

1651

- John Farrer publishes his *Mapp of Virginia,* which erroneously shows the Pacific Ocean just west of the Appalachian Mountains.

1652

- John Sherman and Jonathan Ince explore the Merrimack River and discover Lake Winnipesaukee in New Hampshire.

1658

- A hospital for Dutch soldiers is established at New Amsterdam.

1659

- The first argument in the British colonies for Nicolaus Copernicus's heliocentric theory is published by Zechariah Brigden in his almanac.

1660

- Frenchmen Pierre Radisson and Chouart des Groseilliers explore Lake Superior.

1662

- The Royal Society of London for the Promotion of Natural Knowledge is founded.

1663

- John Winthrop Jr. becomes the first American elected a fellow of the Royal Society of London.
- Naturalist John Josselyn climbs Mount Washington, New Hampshire.

1669

- Joseph West establishes an experimental garden in South Carolina on the Ashley River.

1670

- John Lederer reaches the foothills of the Appalachian Mountains in Virginia.

1671

- Thomas Batts and Robert Fallam are the first British colonists to explore the Appalachian Mountains.

1672

- John Winthrop Jr. presents Harvard College with a three-and-one-half-foot telescope.
- French Jesuits Claude Dablon and Claude-Jean Allouez map the Lake Superior region.
- John Josselyn publishes *New Englands Rarities Discovered.*

1673

- The French trader Louis Jolliet and the Jesuit priest Jacques Marquette explore the Mississippi River.

1674

- John Josselyn publishes *An Account of Two Voyages to New-England.*

1680

- Thomas Brattle uses the Harvard College telescope to study Newton's Comet.

1682

9 Apr.   After voyaging down the Mississippi River, French explorer René-Robert Cavelier de La Salle reaches the Gulf of Mexico.

Sept. Increase Mather and his sons Cotton and Nathaniel use a telescope to analyze Halley's Comet.

1683

- The Boston Philosophical Society is founded.

1685

- James Roseboom explores the region of Lake Erie and Lake Michigan.

1687

- Charles Morton publishes *Compendium of Physics*, the standard natural history text used at Harvard College.

18 Jan. The aurora borealis is seen in New England.

1693

- Dutch explorer Arnout Viele explores the Ohio River valley.

1697

- Louis Hennepin publishes the first engraving of Niagara Falls in his *New Discovery of a Very Great Country*.

1700

- John Lawson explores upper North and South Carolina.
- Spanish priest Eusebio Francisco Kino explores the region of the Gila and Colorado Rivers.

1708

- The first known copy of Sir Isaac Newton's *Philosophiae Naturalis Principia Mathematica* (1687) arrives in America.

1710

- The Pennsylvania rifle is invented by German gunsmiths residing in Pennsylvania.
- A packet boat establishes regular communications between England and New York.

1714

- French explorer Etienne Veniard de Bourgmont ascends the Missouri River.
- English explorer John Lawson publishes *A History of Carolina*.

1716

- Virginia governor Alexander Spotswood journeys up the James River through the Blue Ridge Mountains.

1718

- Guillaume Delisle prints a map of the territory of Louisiana.

1719

- Frenchman Bénard de La Harpe explores as far westward as Oklahoma.

1720

- Cotton Mather publishes *The Christian Philosopher.*

1721

- The first successful smallpox inoculation occurs in Boston.

1727

- New Englander Isaac Greenwood gives a series of sixteen public lectures on science.
- Earthquakes rattle New England.
- Benjamin Franklin's junto, the forerunner of the American Philosophical Society, is established in Philadelphia.

1728

- Danish explorer Vitus Jonassen Bering sails through the Bering Strait, proving that Asia and America are separate land masses.
- Cotton Mather dies.

1729

- Frenchman Chaussegros de Léry explores the Allegheny and Ohio Rivers.

1730

- Philadelphian Thomas Godfrey improves the mariner's quadrant for determining latitude at sea.

1732

- Benjamin Franklin publishes the first *Poor Richard's Almanack.*
- Englishman Mark Catesby publishes the first edition of *Natural History of Carolina, Florida, and the Bahama Islands.*

1733

- English agriculturist Jethro Tull publishes *Horse-Hoeing Husbandry,* advocating the use of the plow to keep fields fertile.

- An experimental garden is established near Savannah, Georgia, for testing the horticulture of such items as coffee and tea.

1734

- Virginia physician John Tennent publishes the popular medical guide *Everyman His Own Doctor: Or, the Poor Planter's Physician.*

1736

- The Medical Society of Boston is founded.

1738

- The Frenchman Sieur de La Verendrye explores North Dakota.

- A smallpox epidemic starts in South Carolina.

1739

- Pierre and Paul Mallet reach the foothills of the Rocky Mountains in present-day Colorado and New Mexico.

1742

- Benjamin Franklin invents the Franklin stove.

1744

- Benjamin Franklin organizes the American Philosophical Society "for promoting useful knowledge."

1745

- Isaac Greenwood, the first Harvard Hollis Professor and a mathematician and physicist of note, dies.

1747

- Benjamin Franklin coins the terms *positive* and *negative* to refer to electrical charges.

- New England physician William Douglass publishes *A Summary, Historical and Political, of the . . . British Settlements in North America.*

1748

- Peter Kalm arrives in America as the scientific emissary of Swedish botanist Carolus Linnaeus.

1750

- Dr. Timothy Walker crosses the Appalachian Mountains and reaches the Cumberland Gap.
- Parliament restricts colonial iron production in the Iron Act.

1751

- Christopher Gist of Maryland crosses the Appalachian Mountains into Kentucky.
- American naturalist John Bartram publishes his natural history of upstate Pennsylvania and New York.
- English patron of science Peter Collinson publishes Benjamin Franklin's letters to him about electricity as *Experiments and Observations on Electricity, Made at Philadelphia in America, by Mr. Benjamin Franklin.*
- Franklin writes *Observations Concerning the Increase of Mankind.*
- Philadelphia scientist and patron of science James Logan dies.

1752

- Benjamin Franklin's kite experiment proves that lightning is electricity.
- Franklin proposes the use of the lightning rod on buildings.
- The American colonies adopt the New Style, or Gregorian, Calendar, making 1 January the first day of the year; in the Old Style, or Julian, Calendar the year started on 25 March.
- William Douglass, Boston physician and participant in the smallpox inoculation controversy, dies.
- The Pennsylvania Hospital, the first permanent American hospital, opens its doors at Philadelphia.

1753

- Americans attempt to observe the transit of Mercury across the disk of the sun.

1754

- Philippe Buache's map of Louisiana appears.
- Benjamin Franklin publishes *Some Account of the Pennsylvania Hospital.*

OVERVIEW

Science in the Wilderness. The first scientists in America were explorers. Adventurers, sailors, traders, missionaries, and soldiers such as Capt. John Smith and Samuel de Champlain observed, mapped, and wrote about the New World. Science and invention assisted Europeans in surviving the American wilderness. The landscape and natural resources of America, more than European discoveries and theories, influenced colonial science. Europeans were the leading scientists and inventors of the seventeenth and eighteenth centuries. No American scientist could compare with Sir Isaac Newton; few could comprehend his genius. Colonial Americans contributed to science and technology according to their own needs in response to the environment. In fact, American inventions were less original than useful. Benjamin Franklin's experiments in electricity resulted in the lightning rod and reduced the number of fires in Philadelphia. Franklin's American Philosophical Society, founded in 1744, existed to uncover and apply useful knowledge. American craftsmen, farmers, and inventors responded to immediate practical needs rather than to abstract theories and utopian notions about benefiting humankind.

An Elite Club. Science and technology in the thirteen colonies lagged behind European developments in physics, astronomy, medicine, and agriculture. Although America's greatest scientist, Franklin lacked the skills and knowledge of his European counterparts. American physicians rarely had adequate medical training, and those who did had degrees from European schools. Americans borrowed European ideas in art, politics, literature, and music as well as in science and technology. Europeans condescended to correspond with and employ colonial scientists simply to receive the hitherto unknown specimens of New World flora and fauna. Some individuals like John Winthrop Jr., who accommodated requests for knowledge and specimens, were allowed to join the Royal Society of London. Theorists of the Royal Society thought up the projects that courageous explorers such as the Pennsylvania naturalist John Bartram accomplished by hiking the American wilderness.

Journeys into Nature. The most notable American scientists were naturalists, students of plant and animal life. John Josselyn and Bartram climbed mountains to ac-quire specimens. Some, such as John Lawson, lost their lives in the pursuit of knowledge. John Smith sailed and mapped the coastal waters of the Atlantic Ocean while René-Robert Cavelier de La Salle explored the Ohio and Mississippi Rivers. These men looked upon prairies, mountains, and lakes never before known to Europeans. To be a scientist in early America required not only intellect but also stamina and bravery.

Mapping America. The first European focus of scientific study in America was geography. The extent of the New World, its river systems, inhabitants, and flora and fauna intrigued the royal courts of Europe. The unknown character of the shoreline and interior forced explorers to become geographers and mapmakers. The first scientific treatises on America often accompanied detailed maps of a region. Smith, for example, created some of the best early maps of the Chesapeake Bay and New England coast. Along with the maps he published an extensive descriptive commentary on these wilderness regions. It took centuries for Europeans and Americans to trace the varied topography of North America. The line of settlement moved west across the continent in the wake of explorers who opened up the wilderness with maps and narrative descriptions. William Byrd, John Carver, Jacques Marquette, Samuel de Champlain, and a host of others made the map one of the premier tools of early American science.

Local Goods. Before 1754 American society had towns and villages but few large cities. Americans on the frontier often, through necessity, made most of their own goods, including cider, beer, flour, salt, soap, candles, bricks, clapboards, wool, flax thread, rope, and leather goods. Rich plantation owners often had skilled slaves perform such tasks. Most settlers, however, lived in or near towns with blacksmiths, tanners, wheelwrights, brewers, tailors, and stores. Farm families could buy goods (in kind or in coin) that they could not make themselves, although many farmers were also part-time artisans such as blacksmiths and shoemakers. Larger towns had more workers and skilled craftsmen, including metalworkers. Manufacturing on a large scale was rare, though a few communities such as Saugus in Massachusetts boasted extensive iron-producing operations.

"Unscientific" Farmers. Observers of American farming practices such as the Connecticut clergyman Jared Eliot lamented that few colonials used advanced agricultural techniques. The agricultural revolution sweeping England during the 1700s barely nicked the thirteen colonies. Often farmers employed Native American farming practices such as girdling trees. Some farmers avoided using plows, being content to use hoes to make holes into which to drop seeds. Many farmers used fertilizers (such as manure) and rotated crops, but just as many did not. Americans never developed "professional" farm practices because of the extent of the wilderness. One could afford to be wasteful when more of the same existed wherever one looked. Americans often found it easier to exhaust the soil and move on rather than to experiment with soil-saving and -replenishing methods. Even so, there were significant exceptions to American amateurism. Agricultural scientists established experimental gardens in South Carolina in 1669 and near Savannah, Georgia, in 1733. Generally, however, experimentation and agriculture were rarely complementary in colonial America.

Itinerant Physicians. American amateurism affected the practice of medicine to the detriment of the sick. Not until the mid eighteenth century did students take courses in medicine at American colleges. Nor were there any medical societies or other professional organizations for physicians until the 1730s. Skilled physicians, like medical books, had to be imported from Europe, especially England and Scotland. Notwithstanding claims that the New World environment was so healthy as to preclude disease, Americans suffered from yellow fever, smallpox, malaria, and hookworms. Newly arrived immigrants to the southern colonies in the 1600s often did not survive the time of "seasoning," the adjustment to the climate and disease environment of America. At the same time only one in ten Native Americans survived the diseases brought by Europeans. Those who practiced "physick" often traveled from town to town selling their limited knowledge and suspect cures. Apothecaries sold homemade remedies, and midwives assisted in the birth of babies. When no physician was available, which was often, the most learned person in the community, usually the clergyman, stepped in to render aid. Even among physicians remedies were often based on fable and folklore. The discovery of the role of microorganisms in the spread of disease was still centuries in the future. Colonial Americans and Europeans still believed in the ancient notion that disease was caused when the four "humours" of the body—blood, phlegm, black bile, and yellow bile—were out of balance. Many remedies involved trying to restore balance to the body, and patients were bled, given purgatives, or subjected to the torture of "blistering" the skin. If at a loss of what else to do, many turned to an almanac or the Bible for assistance.

The "Hard" Sciences. Even though most American scientists were naturalists, botanists, and geographers, there were a few scientists devoted to physics, astronomy, and mathematics. James Logan of Philadelphia, for example, was one of the few Americans who could fully understand Sir Isaac Newton's theories. Logan was interested in physics and taught himself mathematics. He studied astronomy and natural science and patronized such scientists as the botanist John Bartram. Other American students of mathematics, physics, and astronomy during the 1600s and 1700s included the Harvard professors Charles Morton, Isaac Greenwood, John Winthrop Jr., and John Winthrop IV.

Scientists for God. Logan, Winthrop IV, Franklin, and other mathematicians, astronomers, and experimental scientists were the exception. Lack of specialization more often characterized early American science. The leaders of American science and medicine were often simply those with the most complete education—the clergymen. The curricula of colonial colleges before 1750 focused on training young men for the ministry. While studying Christian writers, Greek and Roman classics, and languages, students at Harvard and Yale took courses in science. One of the best courses was John Winthrop IV's class on experimental philosophy offered at Harvard. One of the greatest American scientists, the Bostonian Cotton Mather, was a cleric. His most significant contribution to American science was his advocacy of inoculation to provide immunity to smallpox. His counterpart in Virginia, the Reverend John Clayton, was one of the finest naturalists in the South. Greenwood was a minister who became the first Hollis Professor at Harvard, teaching math and physics. The French naturalists Louis Hennepin and Jacques Marquette were Catholic priests, as were Eusebio Francisco Kino and Silvestre de Velez de Escalante, explorers of the American Southwest.

Multicultural Character. The pursuit of scientific knowledge in America was open to all, no matter one's religious beliefs, ethnic and cultural background, economic and social status, or gender. The American wilderness did not discriminate. Spanish naturalists explored the American Southwest from their base of New Spain. French naturalists sailed up the Saint Lawrence and explored the Great Lakes and eventually the Mississippi River. Because the British American colonies were more settled than the French and Spanish settlements in North America, Anglo-American achievements in science were more noteworthy. But west of the Appalachian Mountains, in the Ohio, Mississippi, and Missouri River valleys, the Great Plains, and the Rocky Mountains, the wilderness made all outsiders equal. The greatest achievements in early American science were made by the diverse naturalists-explorers of varying cultural backgrounds who had the courage to penetrate the American unknown.

TOPICS IN THE NEWS

ALMANACS

Guidebooks. Before 1700 early Americans got their news about the world from random and inconstant sources: the neighbor next door, the clergyman on Sunday mornings, the stranger on the road. But one consistent source of information was the annual almanac. It was a potpourri of news and information. Aside from predicting the weather and the date of the harvest moon, almanacs listed recipes, court dates and locations, and the routes and mileages of local roads. They provided chronologies of events and became the most important vehicle for spreading scientific knowledge in early America.

Astrology and Astronomy. Alongside the most recent European discoveries, the reader of an almanac found astrological tables and diagrams. Benjamin Franklin, more out of playfulness than seriousness, included astrology and prophecies in his first edition of *Poor Richard's Almanack* (1732). But clearly early Americans expected astrological tables and symbols in their almanacs. There was still a pervasive belief in the influence of the planets on human affairs. Perhaps because almanac publishers were less credulous and more rational, they countered astrology with astronomy. The first edition of *Poor Richard's Almanack* also included the dates of two lunar and two solar eclipses. Three years later the almanac had a full "description of the planets" in which Franklin provided a detailed guide for the amateur astronomer. As the years passed and Franklin's own knowledge increased, he included tables on planetary motions, descriptions and diagrams of eclipses, and information on such astronomical events as the transit of Mercury across the disk of the sun. *Poor Richard's Almanack* for 1753 and 1754 included extensive analyses on the distance, appearance, and orbits of planets; an inquiry into the nature of comets; and a discussion of Sir Isaac Newton's ideas on planetary astronomy.

New Science. Few almanac publishers were original thinkers. They borrowed their ideas from Europeans and then communicated them to the American reading public. The almanac was something of a textbook of the new ideas of Copernicus, Galileo, Johannes Kepler, and Newton. In the 1600s most people in America thought that the sun literally rose and set in its orbit around the

NOR'EASTERS

The daily weather fascinated early American scientists. They kept track of wind direction, changes in temperature, and types of precipitation. Rarely were they able to form valid explanations for weather patterns, much less make accurate predictions. Even so, almanac publishers spent a great deal of print and paper making predictions. Benjamin Franklin's *Poor Richard's Almanack* did its share of weather forecasting from 1732 to 1757. Yet Franklin set himself apart from others with his ability to observe and to analyze weather patterns. In October 1743 a storm prevented Franklin from observing a lunar eclipse. The storm was what New Englanders call a Nor'easter, named for the strong winds from the Northeast. Franklin discovered that Bostonians (living to the Northeast of Philadelphians) observed the eclipse before the storm hit. If the winds blew in from the Northeast, why did the storm hit Philadelphia before Boston? Franklin explained it by thinking about how a fireplace moves air. The fire heats air that rises up the chimney. "The air next [to] the chimney," Franklin explained in a letter, "flows in to supply its place . . . ; and in consequence the rest of the air successively, quite back to the door." Likewise, low-pressure rain- or snowstorms that develop along the southeast Atlantic coast move northeast, displacing air. These storms are also called cyclones because they cause winds to move counterclockwise. Franklin realized that as the storm moved up the coast, it paradoxically caused winds to blow from the Northeast when common sense told him they should blow from the Southwest, the direction from which the storm came.

Sources: Benjamin Franklin, *The Complete Poor Richard Almanacks*, 2 volumes (Barre, Mass.: Imprint Society, 1970);
Carl Van Doren, *Benjamin Franklin* (New York: Viking, 1938).

```
Poor RICHARD improved:

BEING AN
ALMANACK
AND
EPHEMERIS
OF THE
MOTIONS of the SUN and MOON;
THE TRUE
PLACES and ASPECTS of the PLANETS;
THE
RISING and SETTING of the SUN;
AND THE
Rising, Setting and Southing of the Moon,
FOR THE
YEAR of our LORD 1753:
Being the First after LEAP-YEAR.

Containing also,
The Lunations, Conjunctions, Eclipses, Judg-
ment of the Weather, Rising and Setting of the
Planets, Length of Days and Nights, Fairs, Courts,
Roads, &c. Together with useful Tables, chro-
nological Observations, and entertaining Remarks.

Fitted to the Latitude of Forty Degrees, and a Meridian of near
five Hours West from London; but may, without sensible Error,
serve all the NORTHERN COLONIES.

By RICHARD SAUNDERS, Philom.

PHILADELPHIA:
Printed and Sold by B. FRANKLIN, and D. HALL.
```

Title page for one of Benjamin Franklin's almanacs, which
made "Poor Richard" a household name in
colonial America

earth. By the mid eighteenth century more Americans realized that the ancient idea of an earth-centered universe was wrong. Almanacs did their part in teaching this new conception of the universe. In 1659 the first almanac produced in America, Zechariah Brigden's *A Brief Explication and Proof of the Philolaick Systeme*, presented a formal attack on the Ptolemaic (geocentric) universe. A 1674 almanac discussed Kepler's theory of the elliptical trajectory of planets. A few years later the almanac of John Foster discarded the ancient idea of the "fixed stars" in favor of Galileo's idea of an infinite universe. During the eighteenth century almanacs carried information on Newton's laws of motion. Often it was in the annual almanac that colonists first read about Deism, a philosophy that maintained the universe worked without divine intervention. *Poor Richard's Almanack* frequently discussed deist ideas.

Sources:
George Daniels, *Science in American Society: A Social History* (New York: Knopf, 1971);

Benjamin Franklin, *The Complete Poor Richard Almanacks*, 2 volumes (Barre, Mass.: Imprint Society, 1970).

ASTRONOMY

An Old Science. For almost two thousand years the greatest European thinkers agreed with the Greek scientist Aristotle's conception of the universe. Aristotle believed that the Earth was at the center of the universe, surrounded by the Moon, the Sun, the planets, and the stars. Each heavenly body orbited the Earth in a perfect circular motion. There was only one Moon in the universe. The Sun's orbit around Earth was between the spheres of Venus and Mars. The realm of fixed stars was at the outer edge of a small, finite, limited universe. Copernicus, Johannes Kepler, Galileo, and Sir Isaac Newton had different views. During the same decades that Columbus discovered America, Jacques Cartier discovered the Saint Lawrence River, and John Smith founded Jamestown, Europeans were restructuring the universe. They believed that the Sun, not the Earth, was the center. Moreover, the Sun was the center not of the universe but of one solar system in one galaxy in a possibly infinite universe. The Earth was one of several planets orbiting the Sun in an elliptical path. Other planets besides the Earth had moons. The universe operated according to precise forces, such as gravity, which made the universe logical and predictable. The observations of astronomers helped humans understand the fundamental laws of the universe.

Colonials. Beginning in the 1650s the ideas of the new science began to cross the Atlantic to America. The first colonial astronomer of note was John Winthrop Jr., son of the founder of Massachusetts Bay. Winthrop owned two telescopes, which he used to observe comets and planets. In 1672, he donated a three-and-one-half-foot telescope to Harvard College. In 1680 Thomas Brattle used it to make precise observations of Newton's Comet. By this time Harvard had established itself as the leader of scientific observation in the colonies. In ensuing decades Isaac Greenwood, Charles Morton, and other professors taught the theories of Copernicus and Newton. Graduates such as Increase Mather, Samuel Sewall, and Thomas Robie observed the aurora borealis (northern lights), comets, eclipses, and planetary motions. Robie, a Harvard teacher and physician, calculated the distances of the planets to the Sun, observed the solar eclipse of November 1722 and the transit of Mercury in 1723, and tried to explain the aurora borealis. James Logan of Philadelphia and Cadwallader Colden of New York also made significant astronomic observations. Although few in number, these colonial Americans turned their attention from the practical affairs of everyday life to observe the motions of the heavens.

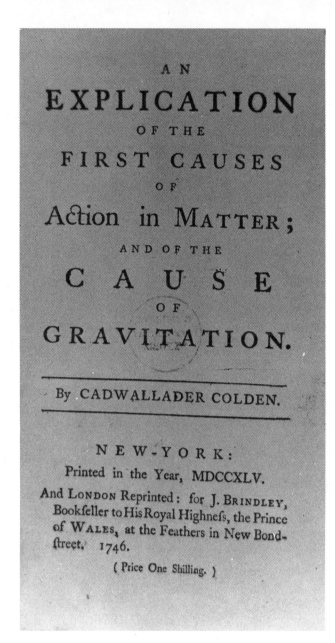

AN EXPLICATION OF THE FIRST CAUSES OF Action in Matter; AND OF THE CAUSE OF GRAVITATION.

By CADWALLADER COLDEN.

NEW-YORK:
Printed in the Year, MDCCXLV.
And LONDON Reprinted: for J. BRINDLEY, Bookseller to His Royal Highness, the Prince of WALES, at the Feathers in New Bond-street. 1746.

(Price One Shilling.)

Title page for a treatise on theoretical physics

Other Planets. Since antiquity humans have speculated on the possibility of life on other planets within and beyond the solar system. Scientists fueled these speculations by showing that the Earth was not unique but like the other planets in that it orbited the Sun. And if the Earth orbited a star (the Sun), why should there not be in the universe other stars with other planets capable of supporting life? There was no better example of the impact of the new science on Americans than the growing concerns about extraterrestrial life. Cotton Mather so believed in the efficiency of the universe and the Creator that he assumed some of the stars in the universe must support life. Benjamin Franklin speculated on extraterrestrial life in the course of his lengthy discussion on astronomy in *Poor Richard's Almanack* for 1753 and 1754. After discussing the tremendous heat of Mercury,

Franklin observed that "it does not follow, that *Mercury* is therefore uninhabitable; since it can be no Difficulty for the Divine Power and Wisdom to accomodate the Inhabitants to the place they are to inhabit; as the Cold we see Frogs and Fishes bear very well, would soon deprive any of our Species of Life." Franklin put himself in the place of possible inhabitants of Mars and wondered what they would see. "The Earth and Moon will appear to them, thro' Telescopes if they have any such Instruments, like two Moons, a larger and a smaller, sometimes horned, sometimes Half or three Quarters illuminated, but never full." Franklin was not willing to deny the possibility of life on the Moon, Jupiter, Saturn, and even comets. "If there are any Inhabitants in the Comets, they must live a Life wholly inconceivable to us." Franklin closed his discourse in astronomy speculating on the vast numbers of stars, the planets orbiting them, and the variety of life that must exist on those planets in the universe.

Sources:

George Daniels, *Science in American Society: A Social History* (New York: Knopf, 1971);

Benjamin Franklin, *The Complete Poor Richard Almanacks,* 2 volumes (Barre, Mass.: Imprint Society, 1970);

Raymond Stearns, *Science in the British Colonies of North America* (Urbana: University of Illinois Press, 1970).

CRAFTSMEN

Shipbuilding. The first European settlers in America founded towns along navigable rivers and next to deep Atlantic harbors. Waterways were the bases of transportation, communication, and travel. Necessity impelled colonists to use boats as their principal means of travel and trade as well as to ensure their future survival and wealth. The shipbuilding industry was of central importance to the New England economy from 1600 to 1754. Colonial shipyards during the 1600s produced five different classes of vessels: the shallop, a small, single-masted boat without a deck; the bark and the ketch, both of which had decks and two masts; the pinnace, a larger vessel used for coastal trading and exploration; and the ship, the largest vessel, having a cargo capacity of well over one hundred tons. During the 1700s the types of vessels changed, and four new classes of vessels appeared. The sloop was a coastal vessel in widespread use but was not as popular as the schooner, a more maneuverable boat. The brigantine was much larger than the schooner, and the snow larger than the brigantine. Colonial vessels usually had square sails in the fore and main masts (front and center of vessel) and a lateen (triangular) sail on the mizzenmast (at the stern). Locally grown hemp was used as cordage in rigging. Larger vessels often had several decks, and for stability sand or stone ballast filled the holds.

Shipwrights. Master shipwrights drew up the plans and then directed the building of colonial vessels. Noise and activity filled colonial shipyards. Dozens of craftsmen worked over the space of a year to build one vessel. It was built next to the water, and an elaborate oak scaf-

COLONIAL IRONWORKS

America was the perfect place to produce iron. The colonies had iron-ore deposits in bogs and plentiful forests to produce charcoal for heating the ore. Colliers were craftsmen who felled timber and then built elaborate pits in which to burn the wood to form charcoal. Ironmasters put charcoal, iron ore, and limestone into a furnace. Large bellows, often powered by waterwheels, maintained the high temperatures of the furnace. Molten iron ran from the furnace to clay molds to form pig iron. Blacksmiths working at forges hammered and shaped pig iron into wrought iron for use in the kitchen, on the farm, or on sailing vessels. Colonial iron was usually for domestic, not foreign, use; whatever amount that was exported went directly to Britain, where it was processed into steel. Most ironworks were small affairs, and few were financial successes. One of the more famous ironworks was at Saugus in Massachusetts. Opened in 1648, the Saugus Ironworks smelted about a ton of iron a day. Even with such production the Saugus Ironworks went bankrupt in 1652.

Sources: George Daniels, *Science in American Society: A Social History* (New York: Knopf, 1971);

Alan Marcus and Howard Segal, *Technology in America: A Brief History* (New York: Harcourt Brace Jovanovich, 1989).

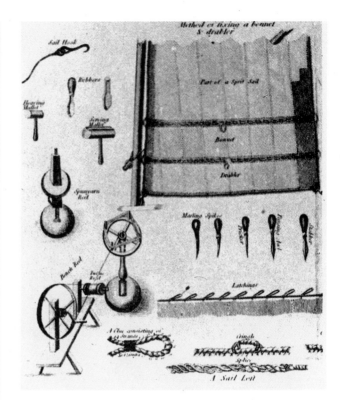

Tools used by sailmakers, circa 1750

folding supported the boat during the construction process. The oak keel formed the backbone of the vessel, running fore and aft (bow to stern). Shipwrights fitted oak ribs (the frame) to the keel. Builders attached ribs to a beam, upon which the deck was built. Shipwrights preferred pine for the deck and outside planking. Locust pegs joined the keel to ribs and ribs to beam. Sawyers sawed the wood for the boat; joiners did much of the interior carpentry; and caulkers used oakum, made from hemp, to fill all seams. Pitch and tar from New England forests made the boat watertight.

Apprentices. Workers in the colonial shipyard included journeymen, apprentices, indentured servants, and slaves. The journeyman was a former apprentice who worked for the shipwright learning the master's craft. Apprenticeship was a widespread colonial program of providing vocational education for boys under age twenty-one. Parents bound their sons to a master craftsman in return for room and board, the rudiments of liberal education, and sometimes a small wage. The boy who worked for the master shipwright did odd jobs and various chores around the shipyard, slowly learning the craft until the contract ended. Servants worked for no pay up to seven years. English convicts transported to the colonies worked up to fourteen years. Southern shipyards frequently used black slaves for manual labor. Some slaves (and indentured servants) were skilled workmen. One Maryland merchant in 1754 used slave shipwrights to design and construct his ship. Other slaves were apprenticed to master craftsmen (but without the hope of ultimate freedom).

Other Trades. At one time or another colonial vessels used or carried the vast and diverse productions of American craftsmen. Each city had a ropewalk on the harbor where rope and cable were made that eventually formed the boat's rigging. Blacksmiths forged the iron anchor as well as the heads of tools such as the adze, so important in woodwork. Coppersmiths made bolts used in shipbuilding, the copper sheaths that often covered the hull, and bronze for the compass and sextant. Boston, New York, Philadelphia, and other cities had specialized craftsmen such as glassblowers, pewter makers, silversmiths, wheelwrights, cobblers, weavers, wainwrights, gunsmiths, tanners, millers, and coopers who supplied goods for domestic and foreign trade as well as for the use of the captains, mates, and sailors of America's sailing ships.

Sources:
Joseph Goldenberg, *Shipbuilding in Colonial America* (Charlottesville: University Press of Virginia, 1976);

Alan Marcus and Howard Segal, *Technology in America: A Brief History* (New York: Harcourt Brace Jovanovich, 1989);

Samuel Eliot Morison, *The Great Explorers: The European Discovery of America* (New York: Oxford University Press, 1978);

Edwin Tunis, *Colonial Craftsmen and the Beginnings of American Industry* (Cleveland: World, 1965).

An oak chest made by Thomas Dennis of Ipswich, Massachusetts, in 1678 (The Henry Francis du Pont Winterthur Museum, Winterthur, Delaware)

EXPLORERS

Jamestown. John Smith never pretended to be a scientist. When the Englishman arrived at the James River in April 1607, Smith and the other 120 colonists were intent on finding a likely spot to camp, build a fort, and begin to trade with the native inhabitants. Some of the English hunted for gold. They soon discovered that a powerful Indian confederation surrounded them. During the first nine months sixty-seven settlers died. They were entirely dependent on the Indians for food. In this increasingly desperate situation, John Smith decided to go exploring.

Journeys. Smith sailed up the James River in search of food. In the process he began to realize the plenty, and potential, of the American wilderness. Smith was one of the first Englishmen to see that success in America would not result from concentrating on discovering gold or a waterway through the continent to China. Smith felt that colonies should be established to cultivate and to harvest the vast resources of the continent: the crops yielded from the land, the fish caught from the sea, and the timber cut from the forests. Determined to discover the true riches of America, he journeyed north by boat to the Chesapeake Bay, where he talked and traded with the Indians, recorded his observations of plant and animal life, took note of regional topography, and made compass readings. Smith took a scientific approach to the New World; knowledge, not ships, guns, or gold, was the key to success in America.

New England. When Smith returned to England in 1608, he began to write. His first publication was *A Map of Virginia,* a narrative description of the region accompanied by an accurate map of the Chesapeake Bay. Six years later, in 1614, Smith returned to America, this time voyaging along the New England coast. Once again he took accurate compass readings to produce a map. His *Description of New England,* published in 1616, provided a wealth of concrete data on harbors, islands, bays, and rivers. Smith described animal life, such as the "Moos, a beast bigger than a Stagge." He described the abundant and various types of fish found in the sea and rivers. He discussed the eagle, "diverse sorts of Hawkes," and other birds. He wrote about soil, vegetation, and the "most pure" waters "proceeding from the intrals of rockie mountaines." His description of Native American customs showed he had a gift for ethnography.

Scientists by Default. Smith was neither the first nor the last explorer who would find himself becoming a geographer, cartographer, naturalist, geologist, and ethnographer. Samuel de Champlain was the French counterpart to Smith, fully the Englishman's equal in his explorations, success at colonizing, and talent for describing the natural history of the New World, especially the Saint Lawrence River valley. Others who explored Virginia and wrote of their travels included John Brereton

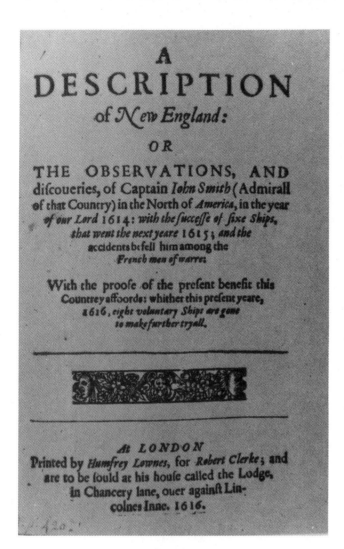

Title page for John Smith's account of his exploration of the
New England coast

WATER MILLS

Successful living in early America depended on harnessing the environment to one's benefit. A necessity in the colonial community for grinding grain or cutting wood was the water mill. Wind powered some early mills, but the most efficient mills were driven by the force of a falling stream or river. Some colonists built horizontal mills, where the waterwheel lay parallel to the water. This was a quick and inexpensive way to build a mill. More efficient were mills where the waterwheel was perpendicular to the water. Undershot waterwheels rotated clockwise as water rushed onto the blades; overshot waterwheels rotated counterclockwise as water fell from above, hitting the blades and turning the wheel. As the wheel turned, it transferred power to a shaft that rotated gears connected to another shaft that rotated the millstone. Since the water rarely ceased, the mill could operate indefinitely, except during prolonged drought. Farmers from the surrounding region brought their grain or lumber to the mill. There they talked to neighbors and turned the produce of the land into flour for baking bread or boards for building shelters.

Sources: Alan Marcus and Howard Segal, *Technology in America: A Brief History* (New York: Harcourt Brace Jovanovich, 1989);

Edwin Tunis, *Colonial Craftsmen and the Beginnings of American Industry* (Cleveland: World, 1965).

(1602), James Rosier (1605), and William Strachey (1609). All of these men were explorers, colonists, and—in their ability to observe, analyze, and record the natural history of America—scientists.

Sources:

D. W. Meinig, *The Shaping of America: Atlantic America, 1492–1800* (New Haven: Yale University Press, 1986);

David B. Quinn, *North America from Earliest Discovery to First Settlements: The Norse Voyages to 1612* (New York: Harper & Row, 1977);

John Smith, *The Generall Historie of Virginia, New-England, and the Summer Isles . . .* (London: Printed by I. D. & I. H. for Michael Sparks, 1624).

FARM LIFE

A New World. Beginning with the first English settlements at Jamestown and Plymouth, settlers relied on the natives for food and knowledge of agricultural methods. The Pilgrims learned to fertilize the soil with small fish. The land was so plentiful, however, that many farmers did not bother to fertilize; when the soil gave out, they would clear more land. The first colonists did not use plows, but hoes, spades, and sturdy sticks. After 1650 more farmers used wooden plows with an iron plowshare, a blade that cut deep into the soil. Plowing depended on the soil and surrounding vegetation. Hard and stony soil where the white oak grew required plowing. Land dominated by beech, maple, and birch denoted a rich soil that would grow corn without plowing. Pine grew in a sandy soil that, though often not needing the plow, lost its fertility within a few years. Plowed soil required a harrow (a large tree branch dragged by a team of horses or oxen) to break up clods of dirt. Colonists used iron sickles to harvest crops.

Girdling. Before one could farm, trees had to be removed. Some farmers chose to cut them down during June after the planting was done. Later in the summer the farmer burned the dead branches. Stump and root removal required the combined effort of animal and human strength. The easiest method of clearing trees was girdling, which colonists learned from the Indians. The prospective farmer could girdle dozens of trees in one day. All that he required was a sharp knife or ax. The farmer cut a deep incision that penetrated the bark into the wood. The incision encircled the trunk near the base. In time the vegetation of the tree died, and its branches

A diorama of Chippewa Indians making maple sugar in early spring, circa 1750 (American Museum of Natural History)

became brittle. Eventually the tree would fall in a windstorm. Girdling was best on land that did not need plowing. The farmer walked in and about the dead trees, digging small holes into which he dropped corn seeds. What had been a forest became a cornfield.

Sap to Syrup. It was rare in early America to find a farmer not wearing a homespun item of clothing, using an ax handle that was not carved from local ash, eating a dinner that was not the product of one's own land, or living in a house not made of wood cut into boards at a local sawmill. The colonist relied on neighbors as much as possible, but often farm life required self-sufficiency. In some cases what was homemade was superior to products imported from anywhere in the world. Early each year New England farmers placed wooden troughs around the maple trees of the forest. Farmers made these troughs by hand, using an ax; an experienced individual could make three dozen troughs in a day. In March, when the winter nights were cold but the days were sometimes mild, the farmer cut a circular incision an inch or two in diameter in the maple tree to allow the sap to drip into the trough. Some maples gave two to three gallons of sap per day. After the farmer collected the sap in barrels, he brought it to a large outdoor fire over which hung large kettles. Women tended the kettles and boiled the liquid to a heavy maple syrup; repeated boiling produced sugar for candies and cakes.

Sources:

Jeremy Belknap, *The History of New-Hampshire* (Boston: Belknap & Young, 1792);

Alan Marcus and Howard Segal, *Technology in America: A Brief History* (New York: Harcourt Brace Jovanovich, 1989).

FRANKLIN'S EXPERIMENTS

Electricity. What to us is an everyday phenomenon with which we heat our homes, start our cars, light our rooms, and operate our appliances was to colonial Americans a mysterious, unknown force. For centuries Europeans had known about the static charge that results when two objects rub together. Scientists invented a primitive generator in the 1600s and a battery, the Leiden jar, in the next century. But what kind of force was electricity and to what use could it be put were unanswered questions. During the eighteenth century in Europe electricity became the most popular scientific study, the source of entertainment at royal palaces, and the means by which seemingly magical tricks could be performed. Benjamin Franklin's interest in electricity originated when he saw an itinerant scientific lecturer, Archibald Spencer, perform an "electricity show" in Boston. Soon Franklin acquired enough glass tubes, iron rods, silk, cork, and chains to perform his own experiments. By the late 1740s Franklin spent most of his time performing experiments in electricity and recording his results in various letters to American and European correspondents.

The Kite. Franklin made several important discoveries about electricity. Contemporary European theories suggested that electricity consisted of two fluids, but Franklin found it to be a single force. He realized that this force was present in nature in varying amounts, that its "particles" subtly penetrated matter, and that a net increase of electric charge in one body corresponded with a net decrease of electric charge in another. His most famous discovery confirmed what Europeans had long suspected, that lightning was an electrical phenomenon. In June 1752 Franklin constructed a silk kite with a metal wire protruding from its top. He flew the kite in a thunderstorm while standing in a shed for protection. In his hand he held twine tied to the kite. He tied a silk ribbon to the twine near his hand and attached a key as well. A bolt of lightning never struck the kite. Rather the kite conducted the electric charge of the clouds along the twine to the key. When Franklin moved his hand to the

Various plows used in eighteenth-century America

key, he felt a sharp electric spark. Franklin concluded in a letter to Peter Collinson, "from Electric Fire thus obtained, . . . all the Other Electrical Experiments [may] be performed, which are usually done by the help of a rubbed Glass Globe or Tube, & thereby the Sameness of the Electric Matter with that of Lightning compleatly demonstrated."

Lightning Rod. Having shown that an object in a storm attracted an electric charge from clouds, Franklin advocated the use of iron rods to protect buildings and even ships from lightning strikes. Indeed, in September 1752 Franklin installed a lightning rod on his own house in Philadelphia. Franklin believed in grounded lightning rods to conduct the electricity from clouds through the rod to the ground. Franklin's lightning rod rose nine feet above his chimney. The thin metal rod extended from the chimney through the staircase to his study, where it split into two rods, each with a bell at the end. Between the two bells hung a metal ball attached to a silk thread. When the lightning rod conducted an electric charge from a storm, the charge forced the ball to ring the bells. "One night," Franklin wrote to a friend, "I was . . . awaked by loud cracks on the staircase." He found not ringing bells but an intense electric charge of white light going from bell to bell, illuminating the entire staircase. Benjamin Franklin was the first in world history to use a

THE FRANKLIN STOVE

When the venerable Franklin stove is mentioned, one invariably thinks of a large cast-iron stove with a simmering kettle. But the Franklin stove of popular imagination is quite different from the one of history. Franklin described and advertised his invention in a 1744 pamphlet, *An Account of the New Invented Pennsylvanian Fire-Places*. The purpose of the fireplace, or stove, was to warm cool air efficiently and displace it into a room while safely forcing smoke out of a flue. Franklin's pamphlet included a diagram of the fireplace, which was made entirely of iron. Cool air entered through a hole in the bottom plate. The cool air warmed in the air box, which was heated by wood burning in the fireplace. Heated air entered the room by means of ventilated side plates. Smoke had to descend below the stove before rising in the flue, situated behind the stove.

Franklin was a great inventor, but his Pennsylvania Fireplace had a serious flaw: the problem was the smoke. According to Franklin's design, smoke had to descend by means of a passageway cut through the floor before ascending in the flue. But smoke could not descend unless the floor was comparatively warm, which would provide the necessary draft. A cool floor meant that the smoke backed up into the stove and hence into the room.

Source: I. Bernard Cohen, *Benjamin Franklin's Science* (Cambridge, Mass.: Harvard University Press, 1990).

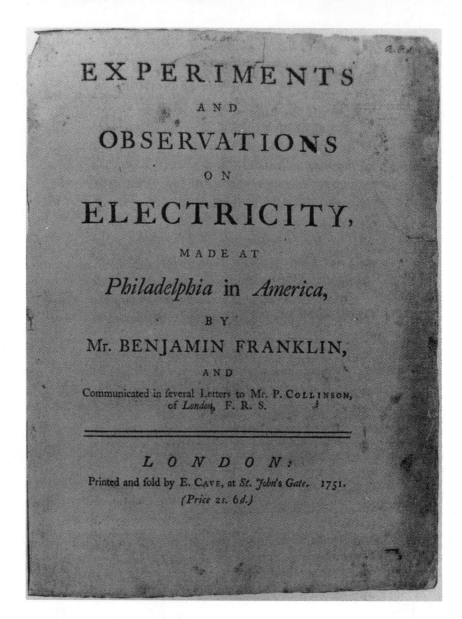

Title page for a landmark scientific study

grounded lightning rod to protect a public or private building.

Sources:
I. Bernard Cohen, *Benjamin Franklin's Science* (Cambridge, Mass.: Harvard University Press, 1990);

Cohen, *Science and the Founding Fathers* (New York: Norton, 1995);

Carl Van Doren, *Benjamin Franklin* (New York: Viking, 1938);

Mitchell Wilson, *American Science and Invention: A Pictorial History* (New York: Simon & Schuster, 1954).

GEOGRAPHY: THE FIRST AMERICAN SCIENCE

Open-Air Laboratory. America was a virtual scientific laboratory for Europeans. The astonishing and hitherto unsuspected presence of North and South America became the measure by which scientists tested ancient theories of the size and shape of the Earth, the extent of oceans, and the nature of the world's peoples. In 1590 the Spaniard José de Acosta speculated on the origins of the Native Americans in *The Naturall and Morall Historie of the East and West Indies*. The gigantic laboratory of America allowed extensive fieldwork in search of data about mountains, rivers, lakes, and bays. Explorers turned geographers and cartographers fanned out across the continent in a seemingly endless process of hypothesis and analysis.

Endless Mountains. John Farrer's *Mapp of Virginia* in 1651 revealed that the exact nature of the North American continent was still largely unknown. His map showed the Pacific Ocean at the western foothills of the Appalachian Mountains. Soon after, in 1671, Thomas Batts and Robert Fallam saw from the Appalachians a vast country, not a sea, extending to the West. A more rational speculation about the extent of the continent began with John Lederer's account of his own journey to the Appalachians. Lederer reached the eastern edge of the Appalachians, the Blue Ridge, and from there realized the error of the assumption that the continent was a narrow band separating the Atlantic and Pacific oceans. Over the course of the next century British colonists became aware of French exploration of the Mississippi River valley and lands even farther west. The Appalachians became not a barrier to another sea but rather a barrier to the settlement of the rich lands to the West. Dr. Thomas Walker in 1750 discovered the Cumberland Gap, one of the many passes through the mountains to Kentucky and other fertile lands. When in 1785 Thomas Jefferson, in his *Notes on Virginia,* penned a description of what the Native Americans had called the "endless mountains," there were few Appalachian locales not known to Americans or featured on maps.

Louisiana. The French led the way into the Mississippi River valley, which they dubbed Louisiana in honor of their king. Explorers who became naturalists, such as Father Jacques Marquette and Father Louis Hennepin, descended the Mississippi River, explored its tributaries, described its topography, and wrote about its native peoples. Hennepin's *Description de la Louisiane* (1683) is a masterful discussion of adventure, geography, and ethnography. In 1718 Guillaume Delisle published a map of Louisiana that would guide explorers for the next halfcentury. Meanwhile, French and Spanish explorers competed over, mapped, and familiarized themselves with the American coastline of the Gulf of Mexico. From 1738 to 1743 the Frenchman Sieur de La Vérendrye and his two sons explored and described the Dakotas. From knowledge of their expedition Philippe Buache drew a detailed map of Louisiana and the Great Lakes in 1754.

To the Sea. During their journey from the Missouri River to Santa Fe in 1739–1740, the brothers Pierre and Paul Mallet spotted unnamed mountains to the West. Jonathan Carver several decades later christened them the "Shining Mountains." But the Rocky Mountains

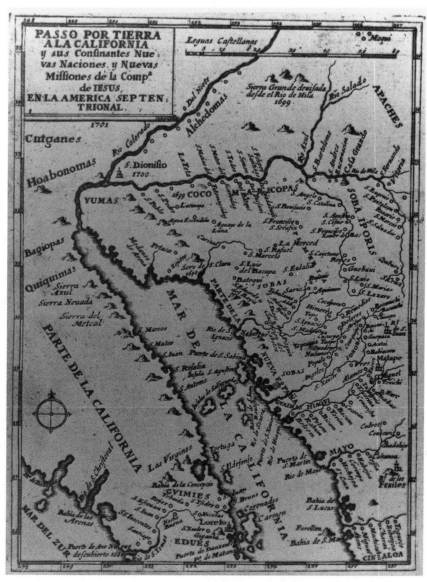

Father Eusebio Kino's 1701 map showing Baja California as a peninsula rather than an island

eluded exact exploration and description until after the American Revolution. Spanish explorers penetrated the wilderness west and south of the Rockies. Father Eusebio Kino explored and described the southwest region and California. His 1701 map showed California to be not an island, as cartographer Henry Briggs had thought in 1625, but a part of the mainland. Further Spanish narrative descriptions and maps of the West and Southwest, including the Rockies, were produced toward the close of the eighteenth century.

Sources:

William Goetzmann and Glyndwr Williams, *The Atlas of North American Exploration* (New York: Prentice Hall, 1992);

Louis Hennepin, *Description of Louisiana* (Minneapolis: University of Minnesota Press, 1938);

Thomas Jefferson, *Notes on the State of Virginia . . .* (Paris: Privately printed, 1785);

Raymond Stearns, *Science in the British Colonies of North America* (Urbana: University of Illinois Press, 1970).

THE INOCULATION CONTROVERSY

Colonial Plague. Smallpox was the dread disease of the eighteenth century. Highly contagious, it was marked by fever, vomiting, and the formation of pustules that scarred the body. It often reached epidemic propor-

tions, especially in cities. Although known in Europe for centuries, smallpox was unknown in America until Europeans arrived. Smallpox and other infectious diseases raged through Native American populations. In early American towns the disease was a less frequent visitor than in European towns, hence in America it was more terrifying. Americans were sometimes hesitant about sailing to Europe simply because of their fear of the disease. As a result wealthy Americans who would otherwise send their sons to Edinburgh or London to be educated sent them instead to Harvard, Yale, or William and Mary.

Boston. In April 1721 a ship that carried smallpox among its crew entered Boston Harbor. Upon the appearance of the disease Boston authorities quarantined the sick and infected houses, but the epidemic spread. Clergyman Cotton Mather had heard about the use of inoculation from his slave Onesimus. Described by Mather as "pretty intelligent," Onesimus informed his master that in Africa he had been inoculated for the smallpox and had never caught the disease. Asians and Africans had used this process for centuries. The physi-

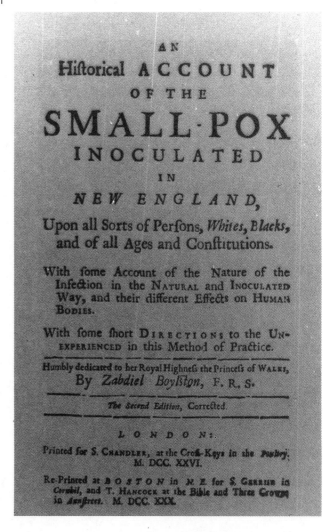

Title page for a 1730 pamphlet that proposes several
preventive measures against smallpox

cian drew pus from a pustule of an infected person who had a mild case and inserted the same pus into a healthy person. Nine times out of ten the healthy person developed a mild case of the disease that was not life-threatening. Once the disease ran its course the person was immune to smallpox. Mather publicly called upon local physicians to inoculate Bostonians. Dr. Zabdiel Boylston responded by inoculating his six-year-old son and two slaves. During subsequent months Boylston inoculated over 150 more patients. Other doctors contributed as well, so that by the following year when the epidemic was over, almost three hundred people had been inoculated. Only six died, or 2 percent of the infected. Of the five thousand Bostonians who caught the disease but who had not been inoculated, about 18 percent died. Clearly inoculation worked.

Opposition. The only physician in Boston with a European medical degree, William Douglass, opposed inoculation from the outset. He organized most Boston physicians in opposition to the practice. Douglass argued that widespread inoculation without careful planning and execution could actually spread the disease. The opposition argued as well that Mather and Boylston were interfering in divine matters. If God chose certain people to become sick, what human should dare to oppose God's will? Surprisingly, Boston clergymen came out on the side of Mather. Attacks and counterattacks occurred in the newspapers, but time and the obvious success of inoculation won the argument. Eventually Douglass himself came around to inoculation and became a lifelong advocate.

Sources:

Isaac Asimov, *Asimov's Chronology of Science and Discovery* (New York: Harper & Row, 1989);

Otho Beall and Richard Shryock, *Cotton Mather: First Significant Figure in American Medicine* (Baltimore: Johns Hopkins University Press, 1954);

Daniel Boorsin, *The Americans: The Colonial Experience* (New York: Random House, 1958);

James Cassedy, *Medicine in America: A Short History* (Baltimore: Johns Hopkins University Press, 1991);

Raymond Stearns, *Science in the British Colonies of North America* (Urbana: University of Illinois Press, 1970).

NATURAL THEOLOGY

Faith and Reason. The rise of modern science spawned such controversies as the debate over whether or not the universe was the result of divine creation or natural evolution. Intellectuals regarded science as rational and objective rather than intuitive and subjective. The empirical scientific method implied that the scientist understood and controlled the forces of nature. Nothing was mystical, magical, or divine in the laboratory. But at the beginning of the scientific revolution when America was first explored and colonized, faith and reason seemed complementary. Nicholas Copernicus was a Catholic clergyman. Christopher Columbus thought God directed his voyages to America. Carolus

Linnaeus believed that God had created an unchanging Chain of Being neither subject to evolution nor to extinction. Cotton Mather was a physician and scientist but also a leading Puritan clergyman. The Protestant leader John Calvin welcomed the discoveries of science. The Quaker William Penn believed that the study of science revealed the laws of nature and their Creator.

Elder Scripture. The most religious and devout Christians in America, the New England Puritans, ironically welcomed the new science. The discoveries of Copernicus, Johannes Kepler, and Sir Isaac Newton led to greater reverence for God. Knowing that the Earth was not the center of a possibly infinite universe was for Puritans proof of God's power and benevolence. Indeed, Puritans perceived science as complementing faith. God revealed himself to humans by means of the Old and New Testaments as well as through his works. God's creation, nature, was considered to be "elder scripture." The scientific study of nature led to knowledge of God, resulting in wonder and praise. In more simple terms, science strengthened faith.

Deism. During the eighteenth century in Europe and America some scientists and philosophers began to reach conclusions different from those of the Puritans. The new science implied a universe that ran like a machine. This natural machine operated according to laws that never changed. God appeared to deists as the Creator who made a universe that always operated the same way. Franklin, for example, wrote that the "supreme Being" acts "in and upon the Machine of the World." The scientist, using experimentation, reason, and mathematics, discovered the predictable laws of the universe. God obeyed his own laws and was passive. He set the universe in motion and then sat back to watch, never intervening or performing miracles. God was a craftsman, and the universe was his invention. Deists were not atheists, but they were not Christians either. The idea of Christ's resurrection contradicted natural law. The deist believed that faith, prayer, and worship of God were meaningless activities. Throughout the 1700s the deists and Puritans debated God's role in the universe. Although both sides believed in the validity and methods of the new science, they reached vastly different conclusions.

Sources:

Jeremy Belknap, *The History of New-Hampshire* (Boston: Belknap & Young, 1792);

George H. Daniels, *Science in American Society: A Social History* (New York: Knopf, 1971);

Benjamin Franklin, *The Complete Poor Richard Almanacks*, 2 volumes (Barre, Mass.: Imprint Society, 1970);

Frederick Tolles, *Meeting House and Counting House: The Quaker Merchants of Colonial Philadelphia, 1682–1763* (New York: Norton, 1948);

Conrad Wright, *The Beginnings of Unitarianism in America* (Boston: Starr King Press, 1955);

Louis B. Wright, *Cultural Life of the American Colonies* (New York: Harper, 1957).

PHYSICIANS

The Frontier. Medicine in early America was random, diverse, and unspecialized. University-trained medical practitioners were rare in the colonies. Most doctors were surgeons, apothecaries, or barbers educated under the apprenticeship system. They could prescribe herbal remedies, pull teeth, lance a boil, and bleed or purge a patient. But they were helpless when faced with serious illnesses such as typhoid fever, smallpox, or dysentery. Often both doctor and patient relied on home remedies learned from Indians. The feverish patient seeking relief sometimes followed the Indian example of steam baths. Louis Hennepin treated one of his fellow priests with a potion made of the herb hyacinth. He noted that the Native Americans cured the fever of malaria with a medicine contrived by boiling cinchona bark, which contained quinine. He approved of the European practice of sometimes bleeding patients to relieve pain.

House Calls. Historian William Smith in 1757 claimed that in regard to the quality and quantity of physicians in America, "Quacks abound like locusts in Egypt." Indeed, for a young society colonial America had a high percentage of doctors. In one Virginia town in 1730 there was one physician for every 135 people. Even farmers living in rural areas could find treatment for illnesses. John Mitchell of Virginia was one of many itinerant physicians who traveled throughout the colonies earning a living. The abundance of untrained physicians and the lack of a colonial licensing system led to the widespread views that most doctors were quacks and that the sick might as well treat themselves. Clergymen often doubled as physicians because of their education. There were so many virulent diseases in America that it

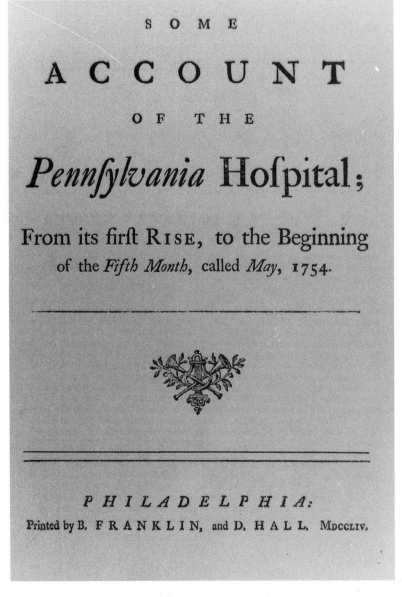

Title page for Benjamin Franklin's 1754 book promoting the medical facility
with the highest sanitary standards in the colonies

THE PENNSYLVANIA HOSPITAL

Benjamin Franklin involved himself in just about every aspect of colonial science and public concern, including the establishment of the Pennsylvania Hospital. Conceived in 1751 and opened the next year, the Pennsylvania Hospital was the first modern hospital in America. Before the hospital the sick and poor of Pennsylvania received what care they could from almshouses, workhouses, and houses of correction. For the first time in Pennsylvania they received free care from trained physicians. The hospital also cared for mentally ill patients. Perhaps because the hospital accepted wealthy patients, their medical standards and facilities were the best of the time on both sides of the Atlantic. Indeed, the mortality rate of Pennsylvania Hospital patients was 10 percent, half that of comparable European institutions. Franklin advertised the success of the hospital in *Some Account of the Pennsylvania Hospital,* published in 1754. Years later in his *Autobiography* (1868) Franklin wrote: "A convenient and handsome building was soon erected; the institution has by constant experience been found useful, and flourishes to this day."

Sources: *Autobiography of Benjamin Franklin,* first complete edition, edited by John Bigelow (Philadelphia: Lippincott, 1868);

I. Bernard Cohen, *Benjamin Franklin's Science* (Cambridge, Mass.: Harvard University Press, 1990).

formed the first autopsy in America. His contemporary, John Lining of Charleston, South Carolina, graduated from the University of Edinburgh. Concerned with the high mortality rate of the South, Lining kept statistics on the correlation of disease with changes in the weather. He even observed and kept precise records on his own personal health. Another great physician of the early eighteenth century was the Bostonian William Douglass. Initially opposed to proponents of smallpox inoculation such as Cotton Mather, Douglass later contributed to the vast evidence showing that inoculation worked. Douglass was a leader in the formation of the short-lived Boston Medical Society. There were other medical organizations, such as at Charlestown, Massachusetts, but most did not last long. Their lack of longevity showed on the one hand the primitive nature of American medicine, but on the other hand the attempt to form such societies illustrated the birth pangs of the organized medical profession in America.

Sources:

James Cassedy, *Medicine in America: A Short History* (Baltimore: Johns Hopkins University Press, 1991);

Louis Hennepin, *Description of Louisiana* (Paris: Chez la veuve Sebastien Hure, 1683);

Richard Shryock, *Medicine and Society in Early America, 1660–1860* (New York: New York University Press, 1960);

Raymond Stearns, *Science in the British Colonies of North America* (Urbana: University of Illinois Press, 1970);

Frederick Tolles, *Meeting House and Counting House: The Quaker Merchants of Colonial Philadelphia, 1682–1763* (New York: Norton, 1948);

Patricia A. Watson, *The Angelical Conjunction: The Preacher-Physicians of Colonial New England* (Knoxville: University of Tennessee Press, 1991).

was convenient that the man who treated the sick could also pray for them and perform last rites. Particularly in the southern colonies mortality rates were high due to yellow fever, malaria, and hookworm, all of African origin. Diseases of European origin such as mumps, measles, and smallpox thrived in America as well, especially in the cities.

Disease Control. There was no truly organized medical profession in America until the end of the colonial period. Communities did, however, develop techniques to prevent and to combat disease. Cities such as Boston set aside places to quarantine the sick who had communicable diseases. (In the case of Boston an island in the harbor was used.) These were the infamous pest houses. The temporary residents of the pest houses were frequently inoculated for the smallpox. In some cases towns tried to improve community sanitation and clean-water standards.

Medical Community. The prevalence of homespun medicine and itinerant doctors began to change with the emergence of a class of physicians trained in European medical schools. The Philadelphia physician Thomas Cadwalader, for example, studied in London and then taught medical techniques at Philadelphia. He per-

WOMEN

Responsibilities. The confrontation with the wilderness in colonial America involved females as well as males. Women were as apt as men to use the common-sense, practical approach to knowledge so necessary for life in early America. Women practiced crafts and manufactured goods to feed and clothe the family. Early Americans wore clothing made or mended with wool or flax thread produced by a woman's work at the spinning wheel. Variety at mealtime depended on the farmwife's ability as a horticulturist in the family garden. The farmwife was simultaneously a butcher, baker, candlestick maker, cook, seamstress, and gardener. Baking bread, for example, was something of a science, requiring the perfect temperature in the fireplace and the right quantities of yeast, water, and grain. Acquiring yeast itself was a chore. The housewife used yeast from old dough or, in the words of one historian, "from the foamy 'barm' found on top of fermenting ale or beer." Cheesemaking was also a long and tiresome process. The housewife combined milk with rennet (taken from the stomach lining of a farm animal), heated the mixture, scraped off the coagulating curds, dried and pressed them, wrapped the curds in cloth, and let them dry and age in the basement. When the husband was ill or away, the wife took over managing all affairs of the farm. Some colonial women ran their own shops and produced their own crafts. There were female gunsmiths, blacksmiths, tanners, shipwrights, milliners, dressmakers, millers, printers, and tailors. Often these craftswomen inherited the business from their deceased husbands. Each large town had a selection of several women entrepreneurs.

Medicine. An important job of the colonial wife was "family physick," or doctor. Women who owned *The Compleat Housewife; or Accomplished Gentlewoman's Companion* (1742) could find information on a host of homemade remedies for illnesses, pains, and injuries. Perhaps because of their caring for family illnesses, many women became practicing physicians and apothecaries. Cotton Mather trained his daughter Katherine in "knowledge in Physic, and the Preparation, and the Dispensation of noble Medicines." The most common practitioner of medicine in early America was the midwife. Obstetrics was the domain of women, not men. Midwives rarely had formal medical training. Their knowledge simply came from experience and a great deal of folklore. They used garden herbs to relieve pain and fresh churned butter as a lubricant. Often the midwife helped the mother stand, kneel, or squat to give birth. Midwives were assistants and helpers rather than crucial participants. In the case of an emergency they were helpless to save the mother or the child. Even so, midwives had remarkable success delivering healthy babies.

Naturalists. A few colonial women had the abilities and courage to challenge the male scientific establishment. Hannah Pemberton of Philadelphia questioned the typical explanation of earthquakes as signs of God's wrath. She was familiar with the *Transactions* of the Royal Society of London, using them as a source for her rational, scientific explanation of earthquakes. Hannah Williams of South Carolina was a great collector of reptiles and insects, especially butterflies. Eliza Lucas Pinckney was a planter who engaged in agricultural experiments on her South Carolina plantation. She kept notes on how various plants grew at different seasons. She experimented with growing figs and indigo, a plant that produces rich blue dye. Perhaps the greatest female naturalist was Jane Colden of New York. Trained by her scientist father Cadwallader Colden, Jane became proficient in the Linnaean system of plant classification. She became a published author and corresponded with leading European and American scientists. Jane Colden's example showed that with proper education and training American women could make significant contributions to science.

Sources:
Otho Beall and Richard Shryock, *Cotton Mather: First Significant Figure in American Medicine* (Baltimore: Johns Hopkins University Press, 1954);

Richard Middleton, *Colonial America: A History, 1585–1776,* second edition (Oxford: Blackwell, 1996);

Marilyn Bailey Ogilvie, *Women in Science: Antiquity through the Nineteenth Century* (Cambridge, Mass.: MIT Press, 1986);

Julia Spruill, *Women's Life and Work in the Southern Colonies* (New York: Norton, 1972);

Frederick Tolles, *Meeting House and Counting House: The Quaker Merchants of Colonial Philadelphia, 1682–1763* (New York: Norton, 1948);

Laurel Thatcher Ulrich, *Good Wives: Image and Reality in the Lives of Women in Northern New England, 1650–1750* (New York: Oxford University Press, 1980);

Ulrich, *A Midwife's Tale: The Life of Martha Ballard. Based on Her Diary, 1785–1812* (New York: Knopf, 1990).

A WOODEN WORLD

Axmen. European immigrants quickly realized that their lifestyles did not always prepare them for the wilderness. They had to adapt to the new environment in order to survive. The basic rudiments of life and society had to be constructed out of the materials of the wilderness. The ax was the most important tool for the first settlers and those who, as time passed, moved with the frontier. Made of iron fitted to a hickory or ash handle, the ax cleared the forest for planting, cut rails for fencing, split logs for the fireplace, and cleared the way for roads. Road building was often nothing more than cutting a path through the forest. In time it involved the use of surveying instruments, teams of oxen to drag away fallen trees, gunpowder to split boulders, and crushed rock to lay a roadbed. In low-lying areas logs lashed together with hemp formed causeways over bogs and bridges over streams.

Native Knowledge. Road builders often followed paths used for centuries by the Indians. In fact settlers learned a great deal from their predecessors. Trappers without proper iron traps could still catch beaver, martins, and mink using the culheag, or log trap. The trapper made the culheag out of two logs joined at one end but open at the other, one propped on top in scissorlike fashion. The top log was propped up with a stick that rested on another rounded stick that lay perpendicular to it. The trapper attached bait of raw meat to the rounded

North Carolina Indians making a canoe, circa 1585 (engraving by Theodor de Bry after a drawing by John White)

THE BIRCH-BARK CANOE

The first explorers of the rivers of North America discovered early that the quickest way to get around was by canoe. The natives were experts at making these small, durable vessels. Some made canoes by alternately burning and scraping logs to form a buoyant shell in which two or three people could sit. But the best canoes by far were made of bark from the white birch. The white birch grows in northern climates. Its bark is like paper, can be peeled in long sheets, and is tough but flexible; one can even write on it. The skilled canoe builder felled the tree and then cut through the bark to the wood along the length of the tree. The bark easily peeled off, especially in summer months. The builder fit the bark around a frame made of cedar, spruce, or maple. Indian women used black spruce roots as thread to sew the bark onto the frame. The frame itself was wood bent into position after being softened in hot water. Thin strips of wood formed the internal floors and sides of the canoe. Gum from spruce trees mixed with animal fat and charcoal made a paste that, when applied generously, produced a watertight seal at the seams. Birch canoes were extremely light and fast in the water. Yet some canoes were over twenty feet in length, built to hold up to two dozen passengers.

Source: George Fichter, *How to Build an Indian Canoe* (New York: McKay, 1977).

stick. The animal tugged at the bait on the rounded stick, which collapsed the raised log, thus crushing the animal's head. Colonists learned from the natives that the softest leather came from soaking deerskin in a mixture of animal brains and fat. Indians taught the settlers fishing, farming, and medical techniques. Hunters rarely got lost in northern forests once they learned from Indians that moss grows on the north side of trees away from direct sunlight. Cooks learned how to make hominy, succotash, and upaquontop, a stew made from hominy and fish heads. Farmers learned to plant maize. The easiest way to travel in early America was by water. Explorers of New England and New France learned from Indians how to build light but sturdy bark canoes and pettiaugers, made by burning and scraping out logs to form buoyant shells. During winter, when rivers were frozen and the snow was deep, snowshoes were a means of quickly traversing the landscape.

Forest of Bounty. The most used resource in early America was wood. Forests of elm, oak, pine, maple, cherry, birch, walnut, and ash provided the basic materials needed for shelter, warmth, transportation, and trade. Colonists used oak to produce staves for barrels to store and ship dry and wet goods. Black oak made excellent keels for ships. Some oaks produced an ingredient used to make writing ink. Carpenters fashioned elm into chairs and wagon wheels, walnut into gunstocks, and hemlock into floors. Ship carpenters used locust for trunnels (wooden pegs) and yellow pine for ship decks. Pine was the best source of naval stores (tar and turpentine). White pines, the tallest trees in the eastern forest, were cut, dragged to rivers, and then floated to shipyards where shipwrights used them to make masts for ships. Ash was the favorite wood for kitchen utensils and fence rails. Some families made beer from the black spruce. Colonists joined the Indians in preferring birch bark to the bark of other trees in the making of durable canoes.

Sources:

Jeremy Belknap, *History of New-Hampshire* (Boston: Belknap & Young, 1792);

Brooke Hindle, ed., *America's Wooden Age: Aspects of Its Early Technology* (Tarrytown, N.Y.: Sleepy Hollow Restorations, 1975);

Edwin Tunis, *Colonial Craftsmen and the Beginnings of American Industry* (Cleveland: World, 1965).

HEADLINE MAKERS

JOHN BARTRAM

1699-1777
BOTANIST

Philadelphia. John Bartram was a farmer who, because of his interests in botany and his tireless fieldwork, became one of America's finest naturalists. Bartram was a simple Quaker who lived at the outskirts of Philadelphia, the scientific center of the middle colonies. Open to new ideas, he allowed some of the greatest minds of the eighteenth century to guide his scientific research. He was friends with the Philadelphia scientists Benjamin Franklin and Joseph Breintnall. James Logan, one of the most influential Philadelphia sponsors of science, introduced Bartram to Latin, the medium of scientific correspondence. Logan loaned science books to Bartram, helped him master the microscope, and turned his attention to the great Swedish botanist Carolus Linnaeus. Bartram was never a great thinker but rather was an active fieldworker who traveled thousands of miles throughout America collecting specimens of plant life.

Journeys. There were few regions of colonial British America that John Bartram did not visit. In 1738 he journeyed eleven hundred miles through Maryland and Virginia and crossed the Blue Ridge Mountains. Four years later he journeyed up the Hudson River to the Catskill Mountains, paralleled the Schuylkill and Susquehanna Rivers of Pennsylvania, and crossed the Allegheny Mountains to upstate New York and Lake Ontario. He took note of the topography of the land and described Native American customs. His account of the journeys was subsequently published in London as *Observations on the Inhabitants, Climate, Soil, Rivers, Productions, Animals, and Other Matters Worthy of Notice* (1751). Beginning in 1754 Bartram took his son William, the future naturalist and ornithologist, on his travels. They journeyed to Florida in 1765 and ascended the Saint John's River to its source. In the same year King George III made John Bartram the Royal Botanist of America.

Correspondence. Bartram's journeys often occurred at the instigation of his correspondents. Beginning in the 1730s and continuing to his death forty years later, Bar-

tram received requests for plant and animal specimens from English and European scientists. Bartram and the Englishman Peter Collinson were lifelong friends, though they never met. Collinson heard about Bartram's abilities and, being a collector, initiated a correspondence with the American. Bartram fulfilled Collinson's endless requests for specimens of sarsaparilla, hellebore, cypress, white cedar, laurel, locusts, and butterflies. Bartram was so accommodating that Collinson found other patrons for his activities: Mark Catesby, Linnaeus, Sir Hans Sloane, Dr. John Fothergill, J. F. Gronovius, and other leading European scientists. Bartram often received payment for his work, making him the first professional scientist in America. He also received seeds from the gardens of his correspondents, which he added to his own five-acre botanical garden at Kingsessing, near Philadelphia. Bartram's garden was so exotic and varied it was the talk of the colonial American scientific community.

Sources:

Edmund and Dorothy Smith Berkeley, *The Life and Travels of John Bartram* (Tallahassee: University Presses of Florida, 1982);

Helen Cruickshank, ed., *John and William Bartram's America* (New York: Devin-Adair, 1957).

JANE COLDEN

1724-1766
SCIENTIST

Father's Footsteps. Jane Colden's interest in botany derived from her father, Cadwallader Colden. The Scotsman Colden immigrated to New York in 1710. A trained physician, his universal interests led him to study, experiment, and write on ethnography, physics, medicine, and government. Colden generally had a haughty, limited view toward women and science. He felt that most women were incapable of true scientific study. Ironically, however, he trained his daughter Jane in the systematic study of botany. He believed women could become adept students of plant life because of their innate ability to recognize beautiful things. Women were also naturally sympathetic and nurturing; hence they were able to contribute to the study and practice of medicine, which at this time continued to be heavily influenced by botanical research. Colden apparently saw scientific study as a worthwhile "amusement" to keep his daughter's mind occupied and productive.

Accomplishments. Jane Colden's abilities to observe, research, catalogue, and understand botany surprised her father and surpassed his narrow expectations. She was the first scientist to describe the gardenia. Although she had to read the works of Carolus Linnaeus in translation, she mastered the Linnaean system of plant classification perfectly. She catalogued, described, and sketched at least four hundred plants. She was active—as were so many other American and European botanists—in exchanging seeds and specimens of New World flora. Jane Colden was America's first great woman scientist.

International Reputation. Jane Colden married Dr. William Farquhar in 1759, and until her death in 1766 she was involved in housekeeping and child-rearing. But her reputation as a great botanist had been established years before in the mid 1750s. Peter Collinson wrote Linnaeus that Jane Colden "is perhaps the first lady that has so perfectly studied your system. She deserves to be celebrated." The South Carolina scientist Dr. Alexander Garden wrote that Jane Colden "is greatly master of the Linnaean method, and cultivates it with assiduity." Her work on plant classification was eventually published in a Scottish scientific journal in 1770.

Sources:

Marilyn Bailey Ogilvie, *Women in Science: Antiquity Through the Nineteenth Century* (Cambridge, Mass.: MIT Press, 1986);

Joan Hoff Wilson, "Dancing Dogs of the Colonial Period: Women Scientists," *Early American Literature,* 7 (1973): 225–235.

BENJAMIN FRANKLIN

1706-1790
SCIENTIST AND INVENTOR

The American. The life of Benjamin Franklin best represents the American scientific character. He was a self-made man who was not against making money from his scientific achievements. A native Bostonian, Franklin as a teenager ran away to Philadelphia and started his own printing business. He retired a rich man in 1748. Franklin's scientific interests were universal. His annual *Poor Richard's Almanack* was a cornucopia of astronomical data, advice about medicine, rhymes and anecdotes to teach morals, and meteorological predictions. Franklin was the most famous American scientist of his time because of his experiments with electricity. Yet he remained an amateur, a tinkerer rather than a theorist. He respected but could not completely comprehend Sir Isaac Newton's *Philosophiae Naturalis Principia Mathematica* (1687). Franklin's

interests tended toward applied science: how knowledge of natural phenomena could yield useful technology. To this end, in 1744 he began the American Philosophical Society, the first scientific society in America. Franklin modeled it in part on the Royal Society of London, of which he became a fellow in 1757.

Approach to Life. The best source of information for the life of Benjamin Franklin is his *Autobiography,* first published in 1868. In the *Autobiography* Franklin discussed his scientific interests and inventions. The book also reveals how Franklin's scientific thinking pervaded all aspects of his life. Franklin wrote that as a young man "I conceiv'd of the bold and arduous project of arriving at moral perfection." He listed thirteen virtues to which he aspired: temperance, silence, order, resolution, frugality, industry, sincerity, justice, moderation, cleanliness, tranquillity, chastity, and humility. He drew up a chart that listed all virtues according to the days of the week. At the end of each day he contemplated his behavior; if he failed to accomplish one or more virtues, he made a star in the appropriate column. By charting his behavior Franklin recorded the data of his faults, systematically studied the trends of vice over time, and worked to correct his behavior. He had a scientific approach to morality. Franklin also made a daily schedule that fitted all of his activities to the time of day. Each day he set out in an orderly fashion to accomplish the daily goal. He planned his meals and entertainment and thought that six hours of sleep would be sufficient. From the application of science to his own life, Franklin hoped to prepare himself for more public scientific pursuits.

Universal Thinker. All branches of science interested Benjamin Franklin. His fame rested on his experiments in electricity, which he undertook in the 1740s and 1750s. Franklin's description of his experiments in letters to Peter Collinson, published in 1751, made his name known all over Europe. Franklin also studied astronomy, being particularly fascinated with solar and lunar eclipses. He made preparations to observe the transit of Mercury across the disk of the sun in 1753, but a cloudy sky intervened. He speculated on the cause and character of comets and wondered whether or not they were inhabited. *Poor Richard's Almanack* was Franklin's chief medium to spread his interest in astronomy. Likewise he used his almanac to inform his readers about remedies for illnesses. In the 1737 almanac Franklin included a long description of a so-called Rattle-snake Herb, an antidote to rattlesnake venom. Reputedly Native Americans chewed the herb, boiled it, and either drank the resulting concoction or bound wounds with it. The 1740 almanac contained "Dr. Tennent's Infallible Cure for the Pleurisy." The cure involved bleeding as well as heavy doses of "Rattle-snake Root." In the 1742 almanac Franklin discussed his "Rules of Health and long Life, and to Preserve from Malignant Fevers, and Sickness in general." The theme of the treatise was that moderation in eating and drinking prevented illness and resulted in long life.

Inventions. Franklin used science as a means to acquire useful knowledge; gaining it for its own sake was less important. Franklin applied his knowledge of medicine to create technology that could help humans live longer, happier lives. He invented a urinary catheter as well as bifocal lenses for glasses. He studied the effects of electricity on the human body and experimented with electric-shock therapy. A visitor of the aged Franklin found the old man, afflicted with rheumatism and other ailments, sitting in a shoelike bathtub of his own design. Franklin built the tub for his own comfort. A platform attached to the tub extending over the water allowed the scientist to read his favorite book while he soaked in hot water. A result of Franklin's studies of heat was the Franklin stove, which was an ingenious iron fireplace that warmed and circulated air while disposing of smoke. The practical side of Franklin's experiments in electricity was the invention of the grounded lightning rod. In response to one critic of his experiments and inventions, Franklin reputedly asked, "Of what use is a new-born babe?" Franklin's mind was always working, thinking about current problems and future solutions.

Sources:

I. Bernard Cohen, *Benjamin Franklin's Science* (Cambridge, Mass.: Harvard University Press, 1990);

William and Julia Cutler, eds., *Life, Journals, and Correspondence of Rev. Manasseh Cutler, LL.D.*, 2 volumes (Cincinnati: R. Clerke, 1888);

George Daniels, *Science in American Society: A Social History* (New York: Knopf, 1971);

Benjamin Franklin, *Autobiography* (New York: Macmillan, 1962);

Franklin, *The Complete Poor Richard Almanacks*, 2 volumes (Barre, Mass.: Imprint Society, 1970).

LOUIS HENNEPIN

1640-1701?
FRENCH EXPLORER AND NATURALIST

Background. Louis Hennepin's fame rested on a journey into the wilderness of the upper Mississippi River valley and his subsequent narrative of his adventures, the *Description de la Louisiane* (1683). The story of his life in Europe remains obscure. He was born in Belgium, and when he was about twenty, he joined the Roman Catholic religious order of Franciscans. He served as a priest and military chaplain until 1675 when he immigrated to New France to become a missionary to the Native American tribes of the Saint Lawrence River, Great Lakes, and Mississippi River.

Explorer for God. There were many Jesuit and Franciscan priests in New France who devoted their lives to missionary work. They lived sparingly and dressed simply. The natives called them "bare feet." In 1678 Hennepin set out from Quebec "in a little bark canoe with [a] portable altar, a blanket, and a rush matting which served as a mattress." Under the leadership of René-Robert Caëelier de La Salle, Hennepin journeyed from Lake Ontario to Niagara Falls to Lake Erie, then on to Lake Huron, Lake Michigan, and the Saint Joseph River, which flows into the southeastern corner of Lake Michigan. From the Saint Joseph, La Salle, Hennepin, and their men descended the Illinois River. At Fort Crèvecoeur on the Illinois River La Salle ordered two boatmen and Hennepin to go down the river to reconnoiter the route to the Mississippi. But once they reached the Mississippi, Sioux warriors captured them and forced Hennepin and his companions to journey up the Mississippi to their villages in Minnesota. The ascent was long and difficult. The natives expected the French to paddle upstream for hours at a time with little rest and food. They remained prisoners of the Sioux, living in tepees and joining their hunts, for four months. Finally the Sioux released the priest upon the intervention of the Sieur Du Luth, a French colonist whom the natives respected. In 1682 Hennepin returned to France.

Geography of Louisiana. The French conceived of Louisiana as the entire region of the Mississippi River and its tributaries. Hennepin initially saw Louisiana as a place for the extension of French power and as fertile ground to make Christian converts. But after his journeys and harrowing experiences he began to see the territory from the perspective of a scientist. Notwithstanding Hennepin's lack of formal scientific training, he penned a geographic description of Upper Louisiana. He described in detail the extent and character of the Great Lakes. Niagara Falls deeply impressed him: the rapid current of the river approaching the falls, the terrifying sight of the falls accompanied by the thundering of the water, the high banks from which it was "frightening to look down." He detailed as well the flora and fauna of the lakes and rivers, especially in respect to food sources. Fascinated by the buffalo, Hennepin discussed the animal's physical characteristics and behavior. He reported on Indian hunting techniques and uses of the buffalo for food, clothing, and shelter. He informed his readers about river sources, lengths, direction of descent, and currents as well as the fertility of the soil.

Ethnographer. During the course of the narrative of his adventures and in a lengthy appendix to the book, Hennepin described in detail the society and customs of native tribes such as the Iroquois, Miami, and Sioux. Although Hennepin suffered abusive treatment from the Sioux, his comments were generally mild and objective. His biggest criticism of the natives was their lack of table manners and cleanliness. But he was clearly fascinated by their ability to survive in the wilderness. Even so, Hennepin realized these people often flirted with starvation.

He was impressed by their dignity and bearing and wondered whether or not they were one of the lost tribes of Israel. He praised the skills and endurance of female natives, noting they were stronger than European males. Hennepin described women who give birth at night "without making the slightest disturbance and in the morning [act] . . . as if nothing had happened." He recorded their stories told around the campfire, marriage rituals, child-rearing practices, and celebrations. He wrote with approval of the calumet, or peace pipe, which was a "sort of safe-conduct" for the traveler going from tribe to tribe. Notwithstanding Hennepin's sensitive portrait of Native American life, he concluded that Indians needed to give up their beliefs and culture and accept European civilization and Christianity.

Source:
Louis Hennepin, *Description of Louisiana* (Minneapolis: University of Minnesota Press, 1938).

John Josselyn

1608?-1675?
Physician and Mountaineer

Voyages. The English physician John Josselyn voyaged to New England twice during the seventeenth century. His first voyage lasted several months during the summer of 1638. His second, much longer visit to America lasted from 1663 to 1671. Not much is known about Josselyn's life. He was born and he died in England. His brother Henry lived in Maine, and John visited America partly to see him. No doubt Henry had told John of the wonders of America, and that compelled him to see them firsthand. He traveled up and down the New England coast, explored rivers, and journeyed into the mountainous interior of New Hampshire. He recorded his observations in two books: *New-Englands Rarities Discovered* (1672) and *An Account of Two Voyages to New-England* (1674). Josselyn described the landscape and native peoples, but his main interest was botany.

Wilderness. Josselyn practiced medicine at a time when cures and remedies lay within a bed of wildflowers or the bark of trees. Josselyn was not an empirical scientist; he was a collector. He acquired scientific information not in the laboratory but by exploring the countryside, recording observations, and taking samples. As an active scientist he used his newfound knowledge prescribing remedies for ailing New Englanders. Josselyn discovered that for a toothache one should place the powder of the root of the white hellebore in the tooth cavity. In *An Account of Two Voyages to New-England* he prescribed tobacco for colds, coughs, influenza, indigestion, gout, toothache, and lice—but only if chewed or smoked in moderation. Josselyn based much of his medical knowledge on common sense, but he also relied on hearsay and folklore. He learned a great deal of questionable home remedies from Native Americans and colonial housewives. He believed, for example, that codfish had a stomach stone that if removed, ground, and drank with wine would cure kidney stones. If one had indigestion Josselyn prescribed drinking a mixture of wine and wolf dung. The heart of a rattlesnake, dried and mixed with wine, was an antidote to rattlesnake venom. Even if Josselyn was uncritical of his information, his account of New England plant life was the most complete discussion for over one hundred years.

Mount Washington. Josselyn went to great lengths (and heights) to discover the medicinal value of plants. At some point around 1663 he journeyed to the White Mountains of New Hampshire and ascended the tallest peak of New England, Mount Washington (6,288 feet). Josselyn was the first scientific mountaineer in American history. Mount Washington is not the tallest mountain in America, but it proved to be a challenge to the colonial adventurer with its strong winds and alpine environment. In *New-Englands Rarities Discovered* Josselyn recorded his exhausting journey, the snow he found on the peak, the topography of the mountain, and his observations of the surrounding landscape. He described as "daunting terrible" the wilderness north of the White Mountains—a region scarcely seen by Europeans before Josselyn.

Sources:
John Josselyn, *An Account of Two Voyages to New-England* (London: Printed for G. Widdows, 1674);

Josselyn, *New-Englands Rarities Discovered* (London: Printed for G. Widdowes, 1672);

Raymond Stearns, *Science in the British Colonies of North America* (Urbana: University of Illinois Press, 1970).

Cotton Mather

1663-1728
Clergyman and Physician

Mather Family. Cotton Mather was born at a time when Boston was the capital of American science. Cotton's father, Increase Mather, was a leader of the scientific community. A historian of note and leading Boston clergyman, Increase Mather adopted the new scientific ideas coming from Europe in the 1600s. Influenced by Francis Bacon and Robert Hooke, Increase Mather incorporated scientific ideas into his Sunday sermons. He tried to counter superstition with realistic explanations about comets and the nature of the universe. Newton's Comet of 1680 in particular inspired Increase Mather's interest in astronomy. Acting upon his scientific interests, Mather organized the Philosophical Club of Boston in 1683. One of the members was twenty-year-old Cotton Mather.

Christian Philosopher. Cotton Mather's life and work illustrate two sides of early American science. As a Congregational clergyman and a firm believer in divine revelation and miracles, Mather accepted some very unscientific notions, such as the power of witchcraft. His first publication was an analysis of the validity of the story of Noah's Ark. Mather firmly believed in the literal truth of the Bible and in God's constant providence at work in world affairs. At the same time, Mather was one of the leading American scientists of the early eighteenth century. He became a fellow of the Royal Society of London in 1713. He read and praised the work of such European scientists as Robert Boyle and Isaac Newton. Mather believed that the study of science could teach humans about God. Natural phenomena were "second causes" to God, the First Cause. "There is not a Fly," Mather wrote in 1690, "but what would confute an *Atheist*." In 1721 Mather's philosophy about religion and science appeared in *The Christian Philosopher*. Mather argued that everything in the universe had a reason and a purpose. The universe glorified the wisdom of its Creator, who with perfect thrift and economy created only necessary things. Everything in God's kingdom was essential.

Medical Knowledge. Mather had broad scientific interests. He wrote on fossils, astronomy, mathematics, zoology, entomology, ornithology, and botany. Medicine particularly interested him. Like other clergymen, Mather studied and practiced medicine as an amateur. He was the foremost advocate of smallpox inoculation in America. His interest was perhaps due to the terrible toll the disease had wrought on his own life: two of his children and his wife succumbed to it. Indeed, only two of Mather's fifteen children survived him. In his autobiography Mather explained his attraction to medicine as owing to hypochondria. As a teenager he read widely in medical literature, which spurred his mind into imagining upon himself the symptoms of dread diseases. As the years passed, Mather became interested in the causes and cures of mental illness, measles, scurvy, fevers, and of course smallpox.

Angel of Bethesda. In 1724 Mather wrote a learned medical treatise, *The Angel of Bethesda*. In this book Mather argued that disease resulted from sin: there was a clear connection between the mind and the body. He provided a sympathetic appraisal of mental illness and discussed techniques of psychotherapy. He prescribed prayer as a means of combating illness. Otherwise the book was an extensive clinical description of diseases, modes of prevention, and cures. Mather also discussed in detail the theory, then debated in Europe but not well known in America, that microorganisms (germs) were causal agents in disease. Notwithstanding his religious views, Cotton Mather was clearly one of the great scientists of colonial America.

Sources:

Otho Beall and Richard Shryock, *Cotton Mather: First Significant Figure in American Medicine* (Baltimore: Johns Hopkins University Press, 1954);

George Daniels, *Science in American Society: A Social History* (New York: Knopf, 1971).

PUBLICATIONS

José de Acosta, *The Naturall and Morall Historie of the East and West Indies* (London: Printed by V. Sims for E. Blount & W. Aspley, 1604)—a natural history based on New World discoveries;

John Bartram, *Observations on the Inhabitants, Climate, Soil, Rivers, Productions, Animals, and Other Matters Worthy of Notice* (London: Whiston & White, 1751)—one of Bartram's most important works and a significant source of information on the natural history and native inhabitants of early America, especially in the northern colonies;

Robert Beverley, *The History and Present State of Virginia, in Four Parts* (London: R. Parker, 1705)—includes an assessment of natural resources and an ethnographic discussion of Native Americans;

William Brattle, *An Ephemeris of Coelestral Motions, Aspects, Eclipses* . . . (Cambridge, Mass.: Printed by S. Green, 1682)—an astronomy text with information on eclipses and astrology;

Thomas Cadwalader, *Essay on the West-India Dry-Gripes* (Philadelphia: B. Franklin, 1745)— a medical treatise discussing lead poisoning;

Mark Catesby, *The Natural History of Carolina, Florida, and the Bahama Islands* (London: Printed for C. Marsh, 1754)—a natural history by an Englishman who stayed in America for eleven years;

Cadwallader Colden, *An Explication of the First Causes of Action in Matter* (New York: Printed by J. Parker, 1745)—a treatise on theoretical physics;

Colden, *The History of the Five Indian Nations Depending on the Province of New York* (New York: Printed and sold by William Bradford, 1727)—a major ethnohistorical discussion of the Iroquois tribes;

William Douglass, *A Summary, Historical and Political, of the . . . British Settlements in North-America* (Boston: Rogers & Fowle, 1747–1752)—an historical work that includes a discussion of inoculation;

Benjamin Franklin, *An Account of the New Invented Pennsylvania Fire-Places . . .* (Philadelphia: Printed and sold by B. Franklin, 1744)—Franklin's account of his fireplace, or stove;

Franklin, *Experiments and Observations on Electricity, made at Philadelphia in America . . .* (London: Printed and sold by E. Cave, 1751)—a collection of letters from Franklin to Peter Collinson describing the former's research;

Franklin, *Observations Concerning the Increase of Mankind* (Philadelphia: Printed & sold by B. Franklin & D. Hall, 1755)—the first colonial American treatise on population;

Isaac Greenwood, *A Philosophical Discourse Concerning the Mutability and Changes of the Material World* (Boston: Printed for S. Gerrish, 1731);

Louis Hennepin, *Description de la Louisiane* (Paris: Chez la veuve Sebastien Hure, 1683)—a natural history of the Great Lakes and upper Mississippi River;

John Josselyn, *An Account of Two Voyages to New-England* (London: Printed for G. Widdows, 1674);

Josselyn, *New-Englands Rarities Discovered* (London: Printed for G. Widdowes, 1672);

John Lawson, *A New Voyage to Carolina: Containing the Exact Description and Natural History of That Country . . .* (London: J. Knapton, 1708)—the author served as surveyor general of the colony and helped found New Bern;

Cotton Mather, *The Christian Philosopher* (London: E. Matthews, 1721)—illustrates the compatibility of Puritanism and science;

John Smith, *A Description of New England* (London: Printed by Humfrey Lownes for Robert Clerke, 1616)—accounts of Smith's experiences interspersed with natural history and ethnological descriptions;

Smith, *The Generall Historie of Virginia, New-England, and the Summer Isles . . .* (London: Printed by I. D. & I. H. for Michael Sparks, 1624);

William Strachey, *The Historie of Travaile into Virginia Britannia* (London: Printed for W. Burre, 1612);

John Tennent, *An Epistle to Dr. Richard Mead, Concerning the Epidemical Diseases of Virginia . . .* (Edinburgh: Printed by P. Matthie, 1738)—a discussion of the Seneca rattlesnake root, the cure for such ailments as pleurisy, gout, rheumatism, and dropsy;

William Wood, *New Englands Prospect* (London: Printed by Tho. Cotes, 1635).

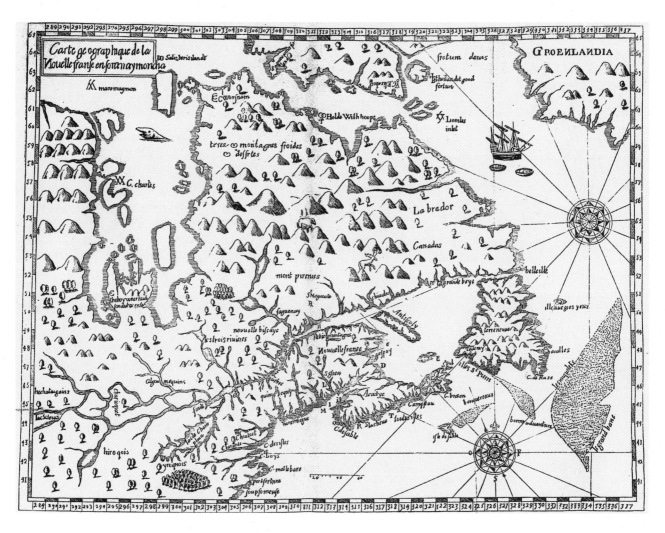

Samuel de Champlain's 1612 map of New France

SPORTS AND RECREATION

by JESSICA KROSS

CONTENTS

Sidebars and tables are listed in italics.

1618
- James I issues what becomes known as the Book of Sports, which allows various sports and recreations after church on Sundays; this ruling infuriates English Puritans.

1619
- Virginia passes laws prohibiting dice and cards.

1621
- Gov. William Bradford of Plymouth confiscates the sports equipment of settlers found playing on Christmas Day instead of working.

1631
- Massachusetts passes a law outlawing card playing.

1650
- Kolven, a popular game in the Netherlands somewhat akin to golf and hockey, is played at Rensselaerswyck.

1654
- By this year bowling greens are established at Fort Orange (Albany, New York) and New Amsterdam (New York City).

1656
- A New Netherland Sabbatarian law prohibits "idle and forbidden exercises and plays" on Sunday.

1665
- Gov. Richard Nicolls of New York establishes the first organized horse race on Hempstead Plain, Long Island.

1668
- Gov. Richard Nicolls awards the winners of the horse races at Hempstead Plain a silver, engraved porringer—the first sports trophy in British North America.

1680
- Throwing the cock, a game which involves tossing a stick at a cock tied to a stake, becomes popular in New England.

1682

- Pennsylvania adopts William Penn's Body of Laws, which forbids recreation on the Sabbath as well as the "rude and riotous sports" of animal fighting, cards, and dice.

1686

- A game similar to football is played at Rowley, Massachusetts.

1700

- Pennsylvania officials pass new laws against "Riotous Sports, Plays and Games"; Queen Anne, however, "disallows" the statutes, making them null and void.

1706

- Pennsylvania passes another series of laws against sports, but Queen Anne again disallows the statutes.

1711

- For the third time Pennsylvania attempts to enforce laws against sports and recreation, but they are again revoked by royal authorities.

1715

- Horse racing is advertised in the *Boston News-Letter*.

1730

- Bulle-Rocke arrives in North America, the first blooded horse to be imported from England for stud purposes.

1732

- New York City's Common Council leases land for a public bowling green.
- The Colony in Schuylkill, an elite fishing club, is organized in Philadelphia.

1735

- The first jockey club in America is organized in South Carolina.

1739

- The first mile track is laid out in Williamsburg, Virginia, for horse races.

1752

- The stallion Janus is brought to America.

OVERVIEW

Old World Models. Throughout history all societies have had sports of some kind. The Native Americans had a long history of both team games and individual contests. Some of the team sports were also played by women, and many of these contests had ties to religion. Early accounts of Native American sports were positive and contrasted the cheating and foul behavior that marred some European games. Africans also had a long history of games. The skill that most impressed Europeans was swimming, which for Africans (and Native Americans) was tied to a personal cleanliness that Europeans lacked.

Gender. Europeans, more than either Native Americans or Africans, confined most sports to males. Women rarely competed in games of skill. Females fished but did not hunt, and they did not race on land, sea, or ice although they often were spectators. Women played billiards and gambled at cards and dice games, but in private homes, not taverns. Indeed, respectable women only entered taverns while traveling.

Animal Sports. Many colonial sports involved animals. These could be hunted or fished. They could be raced either at impromptu pick-up races along the street or on more-formalized race courses. By 1754 there were several race tracks in the colonies, and the first jockey club had been organized. Colonists also enjoyed some animal sports that modern Americans would consider cruel. The most famous of these was baiting, in which a large, potentially dangerous animal such as a bull, bear, or wolf was tied down so it could not escape and was then set upon by dogs. Eventually the larger animal was killed, although it could also kill or maim its tormentors in the process. Wild animals were also allowed to turn on one another in arenas or pits. Cockfighting, in which spurred cocks were set in an enclosed ring to fight to the death, was popular throughout the colonies. Men rather than women attended blood sports.

Individual v. Team Sports. In their original homelands colonists might have indulged in team sports. Various "football" games pitted one town against another. The Native Americans played on teams. But settlers in America seem to have left these practices behind. Except in New England, most people came from different coun-

tries and so had differing local traditions. There was also a lack of the old European calendar year, which specified when people would take time off and celebrate. For whatever reason, in America team sports did not last. Instead, individuals competed against individuals, thus honing a personal identity and prowess at the expense of a more collective, cooperative sense of identity.

Gambling. Just as sport is found in all cultures, so is the gambling which often accompanies it. Native Americans, Africans, and Europeans all knew about gambling before they encountered one another. Both men and women could bet. Races and blood sports lent themselves to betting, as did the various card, board, table, and dice games that colonists played. Taverns and coffeehouses provided the main setting for men getting together to play games. In addition men and women played together, for money, in private homes.

Recreation. Sports and various outdoor activities were considered healthy in the colonial period. Fresh air was often considered a tonic, especially for those who through illness or work had been kept indoors. Men and women enjoyed walking and riding either on horseback or in carriages or sleighs. Fishing and hunting were often recreational rather than necessary. The countryside offered opportunities to take in the beauties of nature, and the colonists showed a sentimental, romantic attachment to lovely views, meandering creeks, and majestic waterfalls.

Limitations. While colonists in this period enjoyed various sports, the day of a real sporting scene was yet to come. Aside from horse racing there was little organized sport. Philadelphia's elite organized a few fishing clubs, which allowed them to gather together on the banks of the Schuylkill River. The fellowship, eating, and drinking was probably as large a draw as the fishing. No major sports figures emerged from this period. Given the lack of organized sport, there were no professional athletes. Isolated individuals probably excelled at one thing or another, but their exploits were only known locally. The wealthy were businessmen or planters, busy with other things and so unable to devote themselves entirely to recreational pastimes. The day of the sportsman was yet to come.

TOPICS IN THE NEWS

BALL SPORTS

Background. Ball games were part of English village life. Local custom dictated the rules, and there were various ways games could be played. Even football, which evolved into three distinct games—rugby, soccer, and American football—had no set format, rules, number of players, or standardized playing field. In some places the ball was kicked; in others it was carried or thrown. Games could be impromptu or highly ritualized. Teams could have ten players or, in a big match pitting one town against another, more than a hundred. The playing area could be a field, and the goal could be as far as a mile away. Football was a sport for ordinary people. Cricket, on the other hand, was an elite sport from the eighteenth century onward, although others might occasionally play it. Cricket had rules and a defined field of play. Part of its popularity was the opportunity to place bets.

Teams. Ball sports on the team level did not arrive in the New World until relatively late in the colonial era. There are a few descriptions of football in the seventeenth century. In 1686 at Rowley, Massachusetts, clothiers played some of the neighboring villagers. The game took place on a sandy shore, and the players went barefoot. But this must have been one of the few examples of football, played by those who knew about the game from England. Cricket was never popular in America, although there are a few references to the game. In 1708 William Byrd II played what he called cricket while in

Theodor de Bry's 1591 engraving of Native American youths at play

Williamsburg, Virginia, but each team had only two men. At other times he played with four on a side. Europeans who settled in America were not willing or perhaps able to maintain the team sports that they knew in the Old World. Those who did play a team sport were the Native Americans, who had various kinds of ball games. Among the Southern Indians was a form of basketball. Northern Indians had a version of what today is called lacrosse, played with a basket on the end of a stick. A kind of football seems to have been part of Eastern Woodlands culture, stretching from New England to Virginia. In Virginia it was played by women and young boys. European observers were all impressed with how civil the game was, how fair the Indians played, and how little violence was indulged in by the players.

Kolven. Colonists seemed more at home with contests that pitted individuals against individuals, not teams against teams. Two ball sports which did this were kolven and bowling. Both kolven and bowling were sports enjoyed by Europeans. Kolven originated in Holland and is played either on the ground or ice. The game is a cross between golf and hockey. It is played with a club that looks like a golf club, but the object is to move a ball across a court and strike a post. Kolven was probably the game translated as *golf* that was played at Rensselaerswyck, near Albany, New York, in 1650. Golf as we know it originated in Scotland, and records suggest that from 1502 to 1688 the Stuart monarchs played the game. There are no references to this form of the sport actually being played in America before the Revolutionary War. Kolven must have remained a Dutch sport, as there is no mention of the English playing it.

Bowling. Another individual sport, well known in Europe and brought to America by both the English and the Dutch, was bowling. The most popular version was ninepins, played outdoors on a track or green some twenty or thirty feet long, where bowlers tried to knock down three sets of three pins with a wooden or stone ball. Bowling appears in the earliest accounts of Jamestown, Virginia, as those sent to labor instead went searching for gold or bowled in the streets. In 1636 a herdsman was punished for leaving his cows to play ninepins. By 1654 there were bowling greens in both Fort Orange (Albany, New York) and New Amsterdam (New York City). These were often owned by tavern keepers and formed part of the recreational opportunities provided by inns and taverns. In 1732 the Common Council of New York leased property fronting the fort to some of the colony's elite so they could "make a Bowling-Green with Walks therein, for the Beauty and ornament of said street, as well as for Recreation." Charging only a token rent, the Council obviously intended this facility to be open to the public. Two years later it was finished, fenced, and "Very Pretty, . . . with a handsome Walk of trees Raild and Painted." The eighteenth century also saw Southern planters and Northern merchants lay out private bowling greens on their estates.

Sources:

Robert Browning, *A History of Golf: The Royal and Ancient Game* (London: A & C Black, 1990);

George Eisen, "Early European Attitudes toward Native American Sports and Pastimes," in *Ethnicity and Sport in North American History and Culture*, by George Eisen and David K. Wiggins (Westport, Conn.: Greenwood Press, 1994), pp. 1–18;

Leo Hershkowitz and Isidore S. Meyer, eds., *Letters of the Franks Family (1733–1748)* (Waltham, Mass.: American Jewish Historical Society, 1968);

Robert W. Malcolmson, *Popular Recreations in English Society 1700–1850* (Cambridge: Cambridge University Press, 1973);

Nancy L. Struna, *People of Prowess: Sport, Leisure, and Labor in Early Anglo-America* (Urbana: University of Illinois Press, 1996);

A. J. F. van Laer, ed. and trans., *Minutes of the Court of Rensselaerswyck 1648–1652* (Albany: University of the State of New York, 1922);

Louis B. Wright and Marion Tinling, eds., *The Great American Gentleman: The Secret Diary of William Byrd of Westover 1709–1712* (New York: Capricorn Books, 1963).

BLOOD SPORTS

Old World. Sports which resulted in the death or injury of animals were part of European recreational life. Bulls, badgers, and bears were tethered so they could not escape and then set upon by dogs. Men on horseback chased foxes with the aid of dogs who tore the foxes apart once the animals were caught. In Spain unarmed men ran in the streets with bulls, and in the end the animals were slaughtered.

Animal Baits. Europeans brought many of their blood sports with them. Bull baits apparently were confined to the New England and Middle Colonies. Bull baiting was one of the sports that taverns sponsored since it was relatively easy to clear a space for the bull and the dogs. These contests, which catered to the lower classes, took place in the evening hours when workingmen and apprentices could get away from their employers and masters. In Virginia at least one tavern offered bear baiting as a recreational alternative. An early Massachusetts account describes a wolf bait in which hunters trapped a wolf, tied it down, and then set their dogs on it.

Fox Hunting. While the evidence is fuller for fox hunting after 1754 (George Washington was an avid fox hunter), the wealthy in the Middle Colonies seemed to have enjoyed this activity during the early colonial period. Outside of Philadelphia an individual simply known as Butler was the hounds keeper for the town's elite. By the mid 1750s an expansion in population and the size of the town had forced Philadelphia's gentlemen hunters to move to New Jersey.

Cock Sports. Cock throwing formed a diversion in England on Shrove Tuesday, the day before Ash Wednesday and the beginning of Lent. It involved throwing a stick or a cudgel at a cock tied to a stake. Throwing the cock appeared after 1680 in New England. As in England it marked Shrove Tuesday. But like many other European sports, this one died out. In the Netherlands villagers "pulled the goose," during which a goose was tied to a pole and its neck greased. Whoever could snatch the goose (thus beheading it) kept the bird. In New Netherland, Dutch authorities tried to prevent this activity, arguing not that it was cruel or dangerous but "unprofitable, heathenish and Popish." Later petitions to the director general and council to allow the sport were refused on the grounds that the custom was being outlawed in Holland. In New Netherland those going after the goose were mounted on horseback.

Gamecocks. Cockfighting was a contest between two roosters, often armed with metal spurs, called gaffs, on their feet. Money and honor rode on the cocks, and breeders of good birds gained reputation just as breeders of good horses did. Unlike horses, however, the losers of a cockfight did not live to run another day since the pur-

pose of a fight was for one cock to kill another.

Cities. Cockfighting, with its use of an enclosed space or cockpit, lent itself to city life. Cockpits were often associated with taverns and drew men of varied social backgrounds. In 1711 the chaplain to the fort guarding New York harbor, Rev. John Sharpe, spent several February evenings "at ye fighting cocks." In 1741 the shoemaker John Romme and his wife also ran a tavern which catered to slaves. There "a negro (the father of Mr. Philipse's Cuffee) kept game-fowls . . . and used to come there to bring them victuals." Cocks appealed to high and low, rich and poor, ignorant and well educated. The Philadelphia physician William Shippen wrote to a friend in 1735, "I have sent you a young game cock, to be de-

A tavern brawl provoked by an overindulgence in alcoholic beverages (drawing by Dr. Alexander Hamilton of Annapolis, between 1712 and 1756; Maryland Historical Society)

Frontispiece for the 1680 edition of Charles Cotton's *The Compleat Gamester*
(1674), which describes popular tavern amusements such as billiards, backgammon, hazzard, cockfights, and card games

pended upon—which I would advise you to put to a walk by himself with the hen I sent you before—I have not sent an old cock—our young cockers have contrived to kill and steal all I had."

Countryside. In the more rural areas cockpits were often associated with taverns and other places where men gathered. In the South, beginning in the 1750s, these were sometimes advertised in the newspapers, and people might come from as far away as forty miles for a day of cockfighting which might include up to sixty birds. All classes of men attended a cockfight, from the highest gentry to the lowest white farmer. Slaves also had their own cockfights, in makeshift rings easily set up and taken down. Betting on various cocks was an essential part of the sport. In the 1760s Robert Wormeley Carter confided to his diary that he had lost over £21 at a large "main" with many birds. This sum was more than all the property that an average poor man owned.

Sources:

Berthold Fernow, *The Records of New Amsterdam from 1653 to 1674* (Baltimore: Genealogical Publishing, 1976);

Daniel Horsmanden, *The New York Conspiracy* (Boston: Beacon, 1971);

Rhys Isaac, *The Transformation of Virginia 1740–1790* (Chapel Hill: University of North Carolina Press for the Institute of Early American History and Culture, 1982);

"Journal of Rev. John Sharpe," *Pennsylvania Magazine of History and Biography*, 40 (1916): 257–297;

Nancy L. Struna, *People of Prowess: Sport, Leisure, and Labor in Early Anglo-America* (Urbana: University of Illinois Press, 1996);

John F. Watson, *Annals of Philadelphia and Pennsylvania, in the Olden Time*, volume 1 (Philadelphia: Carey & Hart, 1845).

CONTESTS AND FIGHTS

Foot Races. Foot racing is among the oldest of human sports. It requires no equipment or paved track. All European, African, and Native American nations undoubtedly pitted the speed of one person against another. In England there were also women's races, which were more like sack races than actual feats of speed. In the colonies racing was popular throughout the period of 1600 to 1754. On muster days militiamen in the Chesapeake often engaged in races and wrestling. Gov. Francis Nicholson celebrated St. George's Day in New York by sponsoring prizes for various sports, including foot racing. William Byrd II mentions several impromptu foot races in his diary, although he himself did not run. Perhaps in his midthirties he felt himself too old, or he might have viewed it beneath his station to engage in such an activity.

Boxing. Pugilism was a popular sport in England, where it pitted two men against each other with their bare fists; in America the same form applied. Boxing was apparently a lower-class sport and one in which one or both parties could be badly hurt. It was the kind of sport that gentlemen wagered on but did not participate in. Boxing was one of the spectator sports that drew men to taverns, where they would watch and bet.

Cudgels. Another type of man-to-man fight was cudgels, in which the participants each held a long, heavy stick with both hands. Using the stick both to attack and parry, each fighter tried to wear down the other. The man left standing won the match. Cudgels matches occurred frequently on muster days or during certain celebrations. They could also be sponsored by various taverns. Contests featuring man-to-man combat were also popular in the backcountry, especially among the Scots, whose major migration to America would be after 1754.

Sources:

Kym S. Rice, *Early American Taverns: For the Entertainment of Friends and Strangers* (Chicago: Regnery Gateway, 1983);

Nancy L. Struna, *People of Prowess: Sport, Leisure, and Labor in Early Anglo-America* (Urbana: University of Illinois Press, 1996);

Louis B. Wright and Marion Tinling, eds., *The Great American Gentleman: The Secret Diary of William Byrd of Westover 1709–1712* (New York: Capricorn Books, 1963).

FISHING

Unorganized Recreation. Even the earliest commentators recognized that America's lakes, rivers, and streams were overflowing with fish and shellfish. Since early settlements and all colonial cities were built near water, few people lived far from a fishing spot. Fishing was relatively easy since all one needed was a line, a pole, and some bait. Both blacks and whites also seemed to find small boats or canoes from which to fish. In the early 1730s the indentured servant William Moraley and a friend fished the Delaware River near Philadelphia and in twenty minutes "caught between us 140 Perch and Roach." They sold some sixty of them for "Rum and Sugar" and used the rest to serve a fish dinner, complete with drink, to four friends. Men and women went fishing together, one of the few recreations that saw the genders mingle. The great marshes of the Carolinas were ecological niches similar to those of many parts of the West African coast, so slaves there were even better suited to exploit these resources than the Europeans. In their free time they fished and collected shellfish for themselves and for sale to their masters or others.

Fishing Companies. Philadelphia's position between two rivers lent itself to more-organized water sports. Wealthy male Philadelphians created clubs dedicated to the pastime. These included the Colony in Schuylkill, the Fishing Company of Fort St. David's, and the Mount Regale Fishing Company, all housed along the waterfront. Perhaps the oldest social organization in America, the Colony in Schuylkill was founded in 1732 to serve as a social club where each member in turn served a dinner the first Thursday of the month at "the Castle." Fort St. David was a summer pavilion decorated with Indian artifacts owned by its attendant fishing company. There the members either fished themselves or feasted on fish they hired others to catch for them. The Mount Regale Fishing Company, composed of Philadelphia's gentlemen elite, met at Robinson's Tavern every other week in the summer.

Sources:

W. A. Newman Dorland, "The Second Troop Philadelphia City Cavalry," *Pennsylvania Magazine of History and Biography*, 46 (1922): 57–77;

Susan E. Klepp and Billy G. Smith, eds., *The Infortunate: The Voyage and Adventures of William Moraley, an Indentured Servant* (University Park: Pennsylvania State University Press, 1992);

John F. Watson, *Annals of Philadelphia and Pennsylvania, in the Olden Time*, volume 1 (Philadelphia: Carey & Hart, 1845);

Peter H. Wood, *Black Majority: Negroes in Colonial South Carolina from 1670 through the Stono Rebellion* (New York: Norton, 1974).

GAMBLING

Background. Colonists knew many board, card, and gambling games that were popular in Europe. For the most part these were inside activities played in taverns or private homes. Often they were played for money and rewarded both luck and skill. Men and women played various kinds of games with each other. Heavy gambling was a male vice since women did not have access to the taverns and private clubs where much of this play occurred. During the eighteenth century taverns became larger, offering more rooms and thus a greater variety of games and diversions. While the law attempted to limit such recreation right from the beginning, especially on the Sabbath, it was not successful. People wanted to play and used even Sunday time to do it.

Backgammon. Among the oldest games known to humans is backgammon. Ancient Egypt, Rome, Greece, Ja-

English-pattern playing cards: jacks of spades and clubs, circa 1750

pan, China, and the Near East all have versions of a game played on a board using dice and pieces moved along the board. By the Middle Ages all European nations had a form of backgammon, also called trictrac. The Spanish, French, Dutch, and English all brought it with them to their colonies. As early as 1656 New Netherland listed "backgammon or ticktack" among a host of other "idle and forbidden exercises and plays" which were banned on Sunday. Like so many other games, backgammon was portable and required little equipment. It could be played on a table with the points inlaid into it or on a portable game board or box. Taverns and coffeehouses often had multiple games going at once, each making the characteristic click of the pieces being laid down.

Billiards. Played on a special table with a cue and balls, billiards was known to the many European nationalities that settled in America. Because the average billiard table was twelve feet long, it was played in public houses, taverns, or the homes of the wealthy. Southern plantation owners were drawn to billiards for a variety of reasons. The table itself made a statement about wealth, and the game required only two people. William Byrd II outfitted Westover, his plantation on the James River, with many diversions, including a billiard table. In 1711 he confided to his diary that "Mr. Mumford and I played at billiards till dinner. . . . In the afternoon we played at billiards again and I lost two bits." Byrd also on occasion played with his wife.

Cards. Playing cards, like backgammon, is an old recreation and is known through many parts of the world. By the eve of colonization all European nations had playing cards, often of great beauty. These were standardized into four suits, although different games called for different numbers of playing cards. Card playing came to the New World with the earliest colonists and was recognized as a great seducer of people's time. The Dutch tried to regulate card playing on the Sabbath. Early Virginia, not usually thought of as being overly restrictive, was

faced with so many problems that the government there passed harsh laws against idleness, which included card and dice games. A Massachusetts law directed ordinary citizens to get rid of their playing cards in 1631. William Penn's "Great Law" of 1682 prohibited playing and placed a fine or five days in jail on all lawbreakers. None of this worked, and by the end of the seventeenth century card playing was a normal part of tavern life everywhere.

Colonial Games. Three colonial card games were whist, euchre, and piquet. Whist, also called whisk, came into its own in the eighteenth century. It is a game of fifty-two cards played by two pairs of partners who try to win tricks; it is an ancestor of modern bridge. Euchre was a French game and possibly came into America through French Louisiana. It uses a thirty-two-card deck, ace through seven. It is also played by four players, two to a team, and has one suit as trump. Piquet was originally a French game that spread to other parts of Europe. It could be played by two people, so it was suitable for home entertainment. Piquet required a deck like euchre. In piquet both sides declare what they hold, thus providing room to lie. William Byrd and his wife, Lucy Parke, played piquet during quiet afternoons or evenings at Westover, but as Byrd recorded in his secret diary, his wife could get annoyed with him when she found him cheating.

Lower-Order Games. All males in colonial America had opportunities to play games and to gamble on their outcome. In the New York City of the 1740s male slaves had the leisure and the wherewithal to play and gamble as whites did. At the alehouse of John Hughson they gambled at cards. As children they played with marbles. They played for pennies, threw dice, and played a game called papa. Taverns catered to slaves and to lower-class

---

A SMALL LOSS

William Byrd II kept a diary in which he recorded his daily activities. As a member of Virginia's Royal Council he spent some time in the capital, Williamsburg. This entry from Williamsburg is dated 17 April 1712:

After dinner [lunch] I went to Mrs. Whaley's where I saw my sister Custis and my brother who is just returned. Here we drank some tea till the evening and then I took leave and went to the coffeehouse, where I played at cards and won 40 shillings [£2] but afterwards I played at dice and lost almost £10. This gave me a resolution to play no more at dice and so I went to my lodgings where I said a short prayer and had good health, good thoughts, and good humor, thank God Almighty.

An unskilled laborer in Virginia at this time would get ten pounds for ten weeks' worth of work.

Source: Louis B. Wright and Marion Tinling, eds., *The Great American Gentleman: The Secret Diary of William Byrd of Westover 1709–1712* (New York: Capricorn Books, 1963).

THE KINGS
MAIESTIES
Declaration to His
Subiects,

CONCERNING
lawfull Sports to
be vsed.

LONDON
Printed by BONHAM NORTON,
and IOHN BILL, Deputie Printers
for the Kings most Excellent
Maiestie.

M.DC.XVIII.

James I's list of sports and recreations that were permitted on Sundays

whites, offering them an outlet for competitive urges and a place away from the eyes of masters and spouses.

Sources:

Berthold Fernow, *The Records of New Amsterdam from 1653 to 1674* (Baltimore: Genealogical Publishing, 1976);

Daniel Horsmanden, *The New York Conspiracy* (Boston: Beacon, 1971);

Louis B. Wright and Marion Tinling, eds., *The Great American Gentleman: The Secret Diary of William Byrd of Westover 1709–1712* (New York: Capricorn Books, 1963);

Oswald Jacoby and John R. Crawford, *The Backgammon Book* (New York: Viking Press, 1970);

J. Thomas Joble, "Sport, Amusements, and Pennsylvania Blue Laws, 1682–1973," dissertation, Pennsylvania State University, 1974;

Kym S. Rice, *Early American Taverns: For the Entertainment of Friends and Strangers* (Chicago: Regnery Gateway, 1983);

Nancy L. Struna, *People of Prowess: Sport, Leisure, and Labor in Early Anglo-America* (Urbana: University of Illinois Press, 1996).

HEALTHFUL RECREATIONS

Walking. Perhaps the earliest New Englanders were afraid of the wilderness, but during most of the colonial period settlers, especially in the older, established areas, enjoyed getting out into the open air and walking. Some did it just because they liked being there, while others considered walking healthy. They went to visit sights such as Cohoes Falls outside of Albany or Passaic Falls in New Jersey. Especially in the eighteenth century they enjoyed going to streams or pretty woods and climbing hills to look at the vistas. Abigail Franks of New York City wrote to her son in London that "you'll be Surprised that I have taken a ramble for a day twice this Summer." The Lutheran minister Henry Melchior Muhlenberg "wanted a little exercise and some fresh air, so with out friends we climbed three miles up to the highest peak of the great mountain from which we were able to see about thirty miles in all directions." William Byrd of Virginia rambled the grounds of his plantation most days, often with his wife and other company. During the eighteenth century both Northern and Southern elites laid out gardens which they walked themselves and invited other people, sometimes perfect strangers, to enjoy.

Riding. Horseback, carriage, and sleigh riding were also considered pleasant, healthy ways to spend discretionary time. Both men and women rode on horseback, but while women rode in carriages and sleighs, it does not seem that they learned how to drive them. When Muhlenberg's congregation wanted to show their appreciation of his efforts by giving him a gift, they gave him some money to buy a horse so that he could ride for his own recreation. Carriage rides were also a way to get away from the city, or home, and be refreshed. Muhlenberg, ministering to the congregation in New York City and therefore away from his more usual rural haunts, noted, "In the afternoon, Captain Hartel, an upright man and steadfast confessor of our religion, took me outside city in his chaise to an estate where his brother-in-law, whose wife is a member of our congregation, lives, in order to preserve my health. I had suddenly been taken away from the vigorous exercise to which I had been accustomed for years and away from the fresh country air of Providence." In the winter sleighs replaced chaises. Snow, oddly perhaps, made traveling easier. Madame Sarah Kemble Knight, in New York City on business in the winter of 1704, fondly remembered being taken out to a farmhouse in a sleigh. Rev. John Sharpe, chaplain to the fort guarding New York harbor, loved all sorts of outdoor recreations, including fishing and hunting. On 6

March 1710 he recorded in his diary, "I rid out in my Slae with &c, the day was unprofitably spent Lord pardon me & give me grace to redeem my time!" But he did not get rid of the sleigh. All ages and both genders enjoyed the exhilaration of riding out on a cold day. The poor, unable to either own the equipment or rent it, would not have had this winter sport available to them.

Swimming. European and African males and both genders among Native Americans enjoyed swimming. The Indians were excellent swimmers, and Africans, many of whom came from the rivers and coasts of West Africa, also were good swimmers. In the Carolinas slaves swam and dived and even showed their skills in the water by hunting sharks armed only with a knife. Europeans swam both as a recreation and as a means of bathing in an era before bathtubs and showers. Men swam in ponds, creeks, and rivers in all the colonies. William Byrd II noted one warm June evening in 1711 that he "took a walk about the plantation and then swam in the river to wash and refresh myself."

Sources:

Leo Hershkowitz and Isidore S. Meyer, eds., *Letters of the Franks Family (1733–1748)* (Waltham, Mass.: American Jewish Historical Society, 1968);

Madame Sarah Kemble Knight, *The Journal of Madame Knight* (Boston: David R. Godine, 1972);

Henry Melchior Muhlenberg, *The Journals of Henry Melchior Muhlenberg*, volume 1, translated by Theodore G. Tappert and John W. Doberstein (Philadelphia: Muhlenberg Press, 1942);

"Journal of Rev. John Sharpe," *Pennsylvania Magazine of History and Biography*, 40 (1916): 257–297;

Nancy L. Struna, *People of Prowess: Sport, Leisure, and Labor in Early Anglo-America* (Urbana: University of Illinois Press, 1996);

Louis B. Wright and Marion Tinling, eds., *The Great American Gentleman: The Secret Diary of William Byrd of Westover 1709–1712* (New York: Capricorn Books, 1963).

HORSE RACING

Old World Models. Horse racing probably began as soon as humans domesticated horses. In England modern racing, as opposed to other types of competitive horsemanship like dressage, was first organized during the reign of Henry VIII. Cities sponsored races during festivals as just one of the many available entertainments. By 1600 there were a dozen or more English towns sponsoring races. In time silver trophies for first, second, and third places became commonplace, and towns built grandstands and marked off courses for the events. Spectators watched for free and betted on the outcome. Races were as long as four miles and were run in several heats, which rewarded stamina as well as speed. The first specialized racecourse was developed by James I at Newmarket by 1622. While some members of the royal court raced, others watched them from permanent stands. Newmarket became so identified with dissipated court life that when the Puritans came to power during the civil war, they demolished the stands and plowed up the course. The Restoration in 1660 brought to power Charles II, a fine, competitive rider who established

The Godolphin Arabian, the sire of all great American racing horses in the colonial era (engraving by John Faber, 1753)

an annual race, the Plate, which he himself later won. Under him Newmarket became the fashion center of the nation. Other courses developed later. Queen Anne founded the famous races at Ascot and also established the breeding lines known as "thoroughbred" using horses of Arabian stock. These pedigrees would become formalized, and some of this stock would find its way to America.

America's Newmarket. Informal races between riders on horseback undoubtedly occurred everywhere that there were horses. Formal horse racing was introduced to the colonies by New York's governor, Richard Nicolls, in 1668 when he sponsored an annual race at Hempstead Plain on Long Island. This oval course of two miles was named Newmarket after its English model. Races were run in the spring and fall, with the winners taking home an engraved silver porringer. The popularity of horse racing gave New York a second racetrack closer to the city by the 1730s when Church Farm was developed on Manhattan Island. In 1744 Peter De Lancey and the Honorable William Montague raced their horses, Ragged Kate and Monk, respectively, for a prize of £200, more than five times what a laborer might make in a year. Other tracks also opened in New York in the years before the Revolution.

Other Northern Courses. Puritan and Quaker disapproval of time-wasting entertainments such as horse racing meant that formal courses were slower in developing in New England and Pennsylvania. During the eighteenth century both Boston and Philadelphia held races. By 1720 horses ran at Cambridge and Rumney Marsh outside of Boston for money prizes. Race Street in Philadelphia led to the racecourse, and before 1726 Sassafras Street served as a straight racetrack. By 1761 races in Philadelphia were advertised in colonial newspapers, suggesting that those who wished to contain such sports had lost the battle.

The Chesapeake. Horse racing was one of the most popular sports in the South, and the Chesapeake (Maryland and Virginia) developed both the quarter race and the quarter horse. Races were run on a straight quarter-mile track rather than an oval course. The horses that ran this quarter mile were known for stamina and the ability to put on quick bursts of speed. These events operated under a variety of rules, agreed to before the race, which specified any handicap one horse might have and the

An eighteenth-century painting of a Virginia fox hunt (Garbisch Collection, National Gallery of Art, Washington, D.C.)

weight of the riders. Growing colonial wealth and a disposition toward competition and gambling led to better breeding and the importation of English blooded stock. The first recorded stallion was Bulle-Rock, sired by the Darley Arabian and sent to Virginia in 1730. The most famous imported horse was Janus, a grandson of the Godolphin Arabian, brought over in 1752. These imported horses were bred to local mares, producing a fast horse that could also go the distance. Their speed and stamina led to the same kind of course racing as in England and the Northern colonies.

The Lower South. Charleston was the center of horse racing in the Lower South. By 1734 racing was a semi-

public sport advertised in the *South Carolina Gazette*. That year the prize was a saddle and bridle. The next year a jockey club organized. In their races horses ran one mile for prizes worth £100 at the York course. By 1743 there were monthly races there and a new course opened at Goose Creek. In 1754 a third racecourse opened on the Neck outside of Charleston. Prizes included not only money and trophies but also watches and, in 1744, a finely embroidered jacket.

Sources:

Carl Bridenbaugh, *Cities in the Wilderness: Urban Life in America 1625–1742* (New York: Capricorn Books, 1964);

Thomas S. Henricks, *Disputed Pleasures: Sport and Society in Preindustrial England* (New York: Greenwood Press, 1991);

John B. Irving, *The South Carolina Jockey Club* (Spartanburg, S.C.: Reprint Co., 1975);

Nancy L. Struna, *People of Prowess: Sport, Leisure, and Labor in Early Anglo-America* (Urbana: University of Illinois Press, 1996).

HUNTING

Europe. On the surface hunting might seem to have been a natural sport for almost everybody in pre-industrial Europe, but such was not the case. City dwellers did not have much opportunity for hunting. In England the woods were progressively reserved for the nobility and the gentry. Ordinary people were prohibited from taking the birds, deer, and rabbits from these reserves, and while some poached, others never even tried their hands. Guns were also much less accurate and much more difficult and time-consuming to operate. The rifled bore, which gives the rifle its name, was used in the eighteenth century, but even by 1800 there were still smoothbore muskets sitting on people's mantles. John Winthrop, the first governor of Massachusetts, loved bird hunting as a young man but eventually gave it up for a series of reasons which suggest why ordinary Englishmen were not hunters: it was against the law as well as too expensive, strenuous, dangerous, and just plain difficult. Winthrop noted, "I have ever binne crossed in usinge it, for when I have gone about it not without some woundes of conscience, and have taken much paynes and hazarded my healthe, I have gotten sometimes a verye little but most commonly nothinge at all towards my cost and labour." Africans and Native Americans probably did better. Hunting was an integral part of male work in their cultures, and they were trained to use spears or bows and arrows from a young age.

New World. Even as game was denied to most of those living in Europe, promotional literature for the colonies noted the immense herds and flocks of animals suitable for hunting. Initially colonists bought wild game from the Native Americans rather than kill it themselves. In time, however, some colonists became good marksmen. Various colonies offered bounties on "vermin"—crows, foxes, squirrels, and wolves—animals which destroyed crops or killed domesticated animals. New England farmers hunted with one or two other men. In the South hunting parties were organized which sometimes utilized Native Americans. Men hunted on foot and on horseback, with dogs or without. In South Carolina men hunted alligators from boats. By the eighteenth century there was leisure time for hunting, but except perhaps on the frontier most colonists never relied upon their own skill to put meat on their tables. On the other hand, while settlement pushed out larger animals such as deer, birds and especially pigeons were plentiful, even in the cities. As late as 1720 Philadelphia passed laws against shooting pigeons, doves, partridges, or other birds in the streets and orchards within the city limits.

TRUE TO THE MARK

Caesar Rodeney of Delaware kept a diary in which he recorded his everyday activities. Among these were recreational marksmanship:

1727. December 23. We went to Shooting for 7 yds of Drugt. [Drugget, a kind of cloth] which I had Set up to be Shot for it wass woun by John Willson.

1728. January 13. after brakt [breakfast] Met Nowell at the Gum trees In order to *Shote for five Pounds* Which he wan[.] My Parte wass 20 Shilling [one pound.]

January 20. I Set up a hat to be Shot for Bro Danil Woun it[.] We Shot In ye Woods.

February 3. I went to John Willsons to a Shooting Match for a fidel: John Hart & I Woun it between us[.] I gave him my Part for Paying my Shot—

February 9. Shot 2 or 3 Guns at Marks[.]

Source: "'Fare Weather and Good Helth': The Journal of Caesar Rodeney, 1727–1729," edited by Harold B. Hancock, *Delaware History*, 10 (1962): 33–70.

Ducks and other fowl were still available in the marshes close to all port cities.

Sources:

Edmund S. Morgan, *The Puritan Dilemma: The Story of John Winthrop* (Boston: Little, Brown, 1958);

Nancy L. Struna, *People of Prowess: Sport, Leisure, and Labor in Early Anglo-America* (Urbana: University of Illinois Press, 1996);

John F. Watson, *Annals of Philadelphia and Pennsylvania, in the Olden Time*, volume 1 (Philadelphia: Carey & Hart, 1845).

MARKSMANSHIP

"Shooting the Parrot." In the Netherlands the militia units often engaged in personal games of skill, one of which was called shooting the parrot. Either a live bird or a wooden one was set on top of a pole, and the men had to shoot it. This particular exercise came with the Dutch to New Netherland. In 1655 Fort Orange magistrates granted a tavern keeper permission to have the burgher guard shoot the parrot on the third day of Pentecost, "provided he keeps good order and takes care that no accidents occur or result therefrom."

Contests. By the eighteenth century the English held contests in which men target shot for prizes. Caesar Rodeney of Delaware, father of the Caesar Rodney who signed the Declaration of Independence, helped organize several turkey shoots where people competed for various goods. These meets were advertised, and at a certain time and place marksmen gathered. Rodeney, who was somewhat better off than the average colonist, had time to practice and the money to buy ammunition. He was apparently a fair shot and competed for cloth, money, a hat, and a fiddle, which he also played.

A CLOSE CALL

Racing with sleds on frozen lakes or rivers could be dangerous. Sleds could upset or run into each other, while horses could stumble or slip on the ice. In 1659 the young administrator of the Rensselaerswyck patroonship was not about to let his life become all work and no play. The Hudson River had frozen, and he was out on the ice. He wrote to his brother in the Netherlands:

As to news, I have not much to write, except that it has been a severe winter, so that we could have all the racing with the sleigh that we wanted. but I have been again in trouble, for my sleigh turned over with me on the river, or was upset by another sleigh, so that I severely hurt my left hand, from which I suffered much pain, but now it is again nearly all right.

Source: *Correspondence of Jeremias van Rensselaer: 1651–1674*, translated and edited by A. J. F. van Laer (Albany: University of the State of New York, 1932).

Personal Skill. Men were proud of their abilities and sometimes took the time to shoot just for the joy of the sport and the chance to hone their skills. Anthony Klincken, who lived in Germantown outside of Philadelphia, always brought his gun when he came to the city. "He also used to speak with wonder of seeing hundreds of rats in the flats among the spatterdocks at Pool's bridge, and that he was in the habit of killing them for amusement as fast as he could load." William Byrd II shot targets with a bow and arrow, sometimes just for fun, but sometimes in a contest with others.

Sources:

"'Fare Weather and Good Helth': The Journal of Caesar Rodeney, 1727–1729," edited by Harold B. Hancock, *Delaware History*, 10 (1962): 33–70;

Charles T. Gehring, ed. and trans., *Fort Orange Court Minutes 1652–1660* (Syracuse, N.Y.: Syracuse University Press, 1990);

Simon Schama, *The Embarrassment of Riches: An Interpretation of Dutch Culture in the Golden Age* (New York: Knopf, 1987);

John F. Watson, *Annals of Philadelphia and Pennsylvania, in the Olden Time*, volume 1 (Philadelphia: Carey & Hart, 1845).

WINTER SPORTS

Sleigh Racing. Winter sports were especially popular among the Dutch and Swedish settlers who came to the Middle Colonies (New York, Pennsylvania, New Jersey, and Delaware). Frozen lakes and rivers provided not only easier access to neighbors since they could be walked over but also provided raceways for sleighs pulled by horses. In 1663 Jeremias van Rensselaer, living near Albany, New York, wrote to his brother in the Netherlands that the Hudson River froze for fourteen straight days, "so hard as within the memory of Christians it has ever done, so that with the sleigh one could use the river everywhere, without danger for the races, in which [the sport of racing] we now indulge [a good deal]." Colonists did not need rivers on which to race but could use roads or fields—any place where two or more sleighs could compete.

Ice Skating. Another recreation of northern Europe was ice skating. Skates were tied onto shoes or boots and were made of horn, wood, or metal. In America skating extended as far south as Virginia when winters permitted ice to form on lakes and ponds. In the Netherlands everybody skated, men and women, old and young. Charles Wolley, a military chaplain in New York at the end of the seventeenth century, was captivated by this sport and the freedom it brought both men and women since English women did not skate. In time, as English customs overcame Dutch ones, women left the ice, but men of all classes and conditions enjoyed the sport. Philadelphia Quaker John Smith rode out one cold February day with his friends Abel James, James Pemberton, and others to skate on the Schuylkill River. The ice being rough they left to try again more successfully about two weeks later. While a few dedicated souls in the colonies became "High Dutch" figure skaters, others became speed skaters, including some of Philadelphia's blacks.

Sources:

Correspondence of Jeremias van Rensselaer: 1651–1674, translated and edited by A. J. F. van Laer (Albany: University of the State of New York, 1932);

John Smith, *Hannah Logan's Courtship*, edited by Albert Cook Myers (Philadelphia: Ferris & Leach, 1904);

John F. Watson, *Annals of Philadelphia and Pennsylvania*, volume 1 (Philadelphia: Carey & Hart, 1845);

Charles Wolley, *Two Years Journal in New York, and Part of its Territories in America*, edited by E. B. O'Callaghan (New York: William Gowans, 1860).

HEADLINE MAKER

JAMES DE LANCEY

1732-1800
NEW YORK LANDOWNER

Family Responsibility. Like William Byrd II, James De Lancey was the English-educated son of a prominent colonist. His father, James De Lancey, was arguably the most important political figure in mid–eighteenth century New York. Son James was educated at Eton and Cambridge, after which he joined the British army. Also like William Byrd II, he was called home upon the death of his father to take responsibility for the family estates. In 1760 De Lancey moved back to America and brought with him a profound love of sports.

"Sportsman." De Lancey came as close as one could to being a sportsman in the years before the American Revolution. Shortly after his return he brought the first thoroughbreds to New York and established one of the finest stud farms and stables in the colonies. His horses raced not only in New York but also Philadelphia, Annapolis, and Virginia. De Lancey owned not only fine horses but fighting cocks as well. On 6 March 1770 "the most famous main of the period" pitted the cocks of James De Lancey against those of Timothy Matlack of Philadelphia, at Richardson's Tavern on the Germantown Road outside of Philadelphia. De Lancey's role in sports ended with the American Revolution. He and his family were Loyalists. Unable to take up arms against the Crown, De Lancey sold his horses, farms, and stables and left America when war seemed imminent. He died in England.

Source:
Carl Bridenbaugh, *Cities in Revolt: Urban Life in America 1743–1776* (Oxford: Oxford University Press, 1955).

PUBLICATIONS

Charles Cotton, *The Compleat Gamester* (London: Printed by A. M. for R. Cutler, sold by Henry Brome, 1674) — a description of billiards, bowls, chess, and other popular tavern games;

Cotton, Izaak Walton, and Col. Robert Venables, *The Universal Angler, Made So, By Three Books of Fishing* (London: Printed for Richard Marriott, 1676);

The Kings Maiesties Declaration to His Subjects, Concerning Lawfull Sports to be Used (London: Bonham Norton & John Bill, 1618) — King James I's list of sports that people can play on the Sabbath.

Woodcut of a seventeeth-century coffeehouse from "A Broadside against Coffee," circa 1672

GENERAL REFERENCES

GENERAL

Bernard Bailyn, *The Peopling of British North America: An Introduction* (New York: Knopf, 1986);

Daniel Boorstin, *The Americans: The Colonial Experience* (New York: Random House, 1958);

Jacob Ernest Cooke, ed., *Encyclopedia of the North American Colonies,* 3 volumes (New York: Scribners, 1993);

Jack P. Greene and J. R. Pole, eds., *Colonial British America: Essays in the New History of the Early Modern Era* (Baltimore: Johns Hopkins University Press, 1984);

Richard Middleton, *Colonial America: A History, 1585–1776,* second edition (Oxford: Blackwell, 1996);

Jerome R. Reich, *Colonial America,* third edition (Englewood Cliffs, N.J.: Prentice Hall, 1994);

Harry M. Ward, *Colonial America, 1607–1763* (Englewood Cliffs, N.J.: Prentice Hall, 1991).

THE ARTS

Richard L. Bushman, *The Refinement of America: Persons, Houses, Cities* (New York: Knopf, 1992);

Gilbert Chase, *America's Music, from the Pilgrims to the Present,* third edition, revised (Urbana: University of Illinois Press, 1987);

Wayne Craven, *Colonial American Portraiture* (Cambridge, London & New York: Cambridge University Press, 1986);

Craven, *Sculpture in America* (New York: Crowell, 1968);

Diana Fane, ed., *Converging Cultures: Art and Identity in Spanish America* (New York: Abrams, 1996);

Bernard Hewitt, *Theatre U.S.A., 1668 to 1957* (New York, Toronto & London: McGraw-Hill, 1959);

Harold S. Jantz, *The First Century of New England Verse* (Worcester, Mass.: American Antiquarian Society, 1944);

Walter J. Meserve, *An Emerging Entertainment: The Drama of the American People to 1828* (Bloomington & London: Indiana University Press, 1977);

Kenneth Silverman, ed., *Colonial American Poetry* (New York & London: Hafner, 1968);

Marcus Whiffen and Frederick Koeper, *American Architecture, 1607–1976* (Cambridge, Mass.: MIT Press, 1981);

John Wilmerding, *American Art* (Harmondsworth, U.K. & New York: Penguin, 1976);

Louis B. Wright, George B. Tatum, John W. McCoubrey, and Robert C. Smith, *The Arts in America: The Colonial Period* (New York: Scribners, 1966).

BUSINESS AND COMMUNICATIONS

Carl Bridenbaugh, *Myths and Realities: Societies of the Colonial South* (New York: Atheneum, 1976);

Peter A. Coclanis, *The Shadow of a Dream: Economic Life and Death in the South Carolina Low Country, 1670–1920* (New York: Oxford University Press, 1989);

William Cronon, *Changes in the Land: Indians, Colonists, and the Ecology of New England* (New York: Hill & Wang, 1983);

Ralph Davies, *The Rise of the Atlantic Economies* (Ithaca, N.Y.: Cornell University Press, 1973);

David Galenson, *White Servitude in Colonial American: An Economic Analysis* (Cambridge: Cambridge University Press, 1981);

Carol Groneman and Mary Beth Norton, eds., *"To Toil the Livelong Day:" America's Women at Work, 1780–1980* (Ithaca, N.Y.: Cornell University Press, 1987);

Stephen Innes, ed., *Work and Labor in Early America* (Chapel Hill: University of North Carolina Press, 1988);

Alice Hanson Jones, *Wealth of a Nation to Be: The American Colonies on the Eve of the Revolution* (New York: Columbia University Press, 1980);

Winthrop Jordan, *White Over Black: American Attitudes Toward the Negro, 1550–1812* (New York: Norton, 1977);

Alice Kessler-Harris, *Women Have Always Worked: A Historical Overview* (Old Westbury, N.Y.: Feminist Press, 1981);

Sung Bok Kim, *Landlord and Tenant in Colonial New York: Manorial Society, 1664–1775* (Chapel Hill: University of North Carolina Press, 1978);

Peter Kolchin, *American Slavery, 1619–1877* (New York: Hill & Wang, 1995);

Allan Kulikoff, *Tobacco and Slaves: The Development of Southern Cultures in the Chesapeake, 1680–1800* (Chapel Hill: University of North Carolina Press, 1986);

James T. Lemon, *The Best Poor Man's Country: A Geographical Study of Early Southeastern Pennsylvania* (Baltimore: Johns Hopkins University Press, 1972);

John J. McCusker and Russell R. Menard, *The Economy of British America, 1607–1789* (Chapel Hill: University of North Carolina Press, 1985);

Menard, "Financing the Lowcountry Export Boom: Capital and Growth in Early South Carolina," *William and Mary Quarterly*, 51 (October 1994): 659–676;

Edmund Morgan, *American Slavery, American Freedom* (New York: Norton, 1975);

Samuel Eliot Morison, *The Maritime History of Massachusetts, 1783–1860* (Boston: Houghton Mifflin, 1961);

Elise Pinckney, *The Letterbook of Eliza Lucas Pinckney, 1739–1762* (Chapel Hill: University of North Carolina Press, 1972);

Marcus Rediker, *Between the Devil and the Deep Blue Sea: Merchant Seamen, Pirates, and the Anglo-American Maritime World, 1700–1750* (Cambridge: Cambridge University Press, 1987);

Carole Shammas, "How Self-Sufficient Was Early America?," *Journal of Interdisciplinary History*, 13 (Autumn 1982): 247–272;

Billy G. Smith, "The Material Lives of Laboring Philadelphians, 1750–1800," *William and Mary Quarterly*, 38 (1981): 163–202;

Laurel Thatcher Ulrich, "'A Friendly Neighbor': Social Dimensions of Daily Work in Northern Colonial New England," *Feminist Studies*, 6 (1980): 398–405.

COLONIAL AMERICANS

Ian Adams and Meredyth Somerville, *Cargoes of Despair and Hope: Scottish Emigration to North America 1603–1803* (Edinburgh: John Donald, 1993);

Bernard Bailyn, *Voyagers to the West: A Passage in the Peopling of America on the Eve of the Revolution* (New York: Vintage, 1986);

Bailyn and Philip D. Morgan, eds., *Strangers within the Realm: Cultural Margins of the First British Empire* (Chapel Hill: University of North Carolina Press, 1991);

John Francis Bannon, *The Spanish Borderlands Frontier, 1513–1821* (New York: Holt, Rinehart & Winston, 1970);

Hugh Barbour and J. William Frost, *The Quakers* (New York: Greenwood Press, 1988);

Winstanley Briggs, "Le Pays des Illinois," *William and Mary Quarterly*, 47 (1990): 30–56;

Thomas E. Burke Jr., *Mohawk Frontier: The Dutch Community of Schenectady, New York, 1661–1710* (Ithaca, N.Y.: Cornell University Press, 1991);

Jon Butler, *The Huguenots in America: A Refugee People in New World Society* (Cambridge, Mass.: Harvard University Press, 1983);

Kenneth Coleman, *Colonial Georgia: A History* (Millwood, N.Y.: KTO Press, 1989);

Philip D. Curtin, *The Atlantic Slave Trade* (Madison: University of Wisconsin Press, 1969);

Bruce Daniels, *Dissent and Conformity on Narragansett Bay* (Middletown, Conn.: Wesleyan University Press, 1984);

John Demos, *Remarkable Providences: Readings in Early America History*, revised edition (Boston: Northeastern University Press, 1991);

David De Sola Pool, *Portraits Etched in Stone: Early Jewish Settlers 1682–1831* (New York: Columbia University Press, 1952);

W. J. Eccles, *France in America*, revised edition (Markham, Ontario: Fitzhenry & Whiteside, 1990);

Aaron Spencer Fogelman, *Hopeful Journeys: German Immigration, Settlement, and Political Culture in Colonial America, 1717–1775* (Philadelphia: University of Pennsylvania Press, 1996);

Adelaide L. Fries, *The Road to Salem* (Chapel Hill: University of North Carolina Press, 1972);

Gillian Lindt Gollin, *Moravians in Two Worlds: A Study of Changing Communities* (New York: Columbia University Press, 1967);

Joyce D. Goodfriend, *Before the Melting Pot: Society and Culture in Colonial New York City, 1664–1730* (Princeton: Princeton University Press, 1992);

Ian Charles Cargill Graham, *Colonists from Scotland: Emigration to North America, 1707–1783* (Ithaca, N.Y.: Cornell University Press, 1956);

Evarts B. Greene and Virginia D. Harrington, *American Population before the Federal Census of 1790* (Gloucester, Mass.: Peter Smith, 1966);

David G. Hackett, *The Rude Hand of Innovation: Religion and Social Order in Albany, New York 1652–1836* (New York: Oxford University Press, 1991);

James William Hagy, *This Happy Land: The Jews of Colonial and Antebellum Charleston* (Tuscaloosa: University of Alabama Press, 1993);

Gwendolyn Midlo Hall, *Africans in Colonial Louisiana: The Development of Afro-Creole Culture in the Eighteenth Century* (Baton Rouge: Louisiana State University Press, 1992);

Joseph Illick, *Colonial Pennsylvania: A History* (New York: Scribners, 1976);

Carlton Jackson, *A Social History of the Scotch-Irish* (Lanham: Madison Books, 1992);

Michael Kammen, *Colonial New York: A History* (New York: Oxford University Press, 1975);

Benjamin W. Labaree, *Colonial Massachusetts: A History* (Millwood, N.Y.: KTO Press, 1979);

Aubrey C. Land, *Colonial Maryland: A History* (Millwood, N.Y.: KTO Press), 1981;

Ned Landsman, *Scotland and Its First American Colony, 1683–1765* (Princeton: Princeton University Press, 1985);

George D. Langdon Jr., *Pilgrim Colony: A History of New Plymouth 1620–1691* (New Haven, Conn.: Yale University Press, 1966);

Hugh Talmage Lefler and Albert Ray Newsome, *The History of a Southern State: North Carolina* (Chapel Hill: University of North Carolina Press, 1973);

Charles H. Lesser, *South Carolina Begins: The Records of a Proprietary Colony, 1663–1721* (Columbia: South Carolina Department of Archives and History, 1995);

James G. Leyburn, *The Scotch-Irish: A Social History* (Chapel Hill: University of North Carolina Press, 1962);

Jacob R. Marcus, *The Colonial American Jew: 1492–1776* (Detroit: Wayne State University Press, 1970);

Duane Meyer, *The Highland Scots of North Carolina 1732–1776* (Chapel Hill: University of North Carolina Press, 1957);

Richard L. Morton, *Colonial Virginia* (Chapel Hill: University of North Carolina Press for the Virginia Historical Society, 1960);

William D. Pierson, *Black Yankees: The Development of an Afro-American Subculture in Eighteenth-Century New England* (Amherst: University of Massachusetts Press, 1988);

William S. Powell, *North Carolina: A Bicentennial History* (New York: Norton, 1977);

Carl O. Sauer, *Seventeenth Century North America* (Berkeley, Cal.: Turtle Island Foundation, 1980);

Sally Schwartz, *"A Mixed Multitude": The Struggle for Toleration in Colonial Pennsylvania* (New York: New York University Press, 1987);

Thad W. Tate and David L. Ammerman, eds., *The Chesapeake in the Seventeenth-Century: Essays on Anglo-American Society* (Chapel Hill: University of North Carolina Press, 1979);

Robert J. Taylor, *Colonial Connecticut: A History* (Millwood, N.Y.: KTO Press, 1979);

John Thornton, *Africa and Africans in the Making of the Atlantic World, 1400–1680* (New York: Cambridge University Press, 1992);

Daniel H. Usner, *Indians, Settlers, & Slaves in a Frontier Exchange Economy* (Chapel Hill: University of North Carolina Press, 1992);

Joseph I. Waring, *The First Voyage and Settlement at Charles Town 1670–1680* (Columbia: Tricentennial Commission by the University of South Carolina Press, 1970);

Jean Parker Waterbury, ed., *The Oldest City: St. Augustine Saga of Survival* (Saint Augustine, Fla.: Saint Augustine Historical Society, 1983);

David J. Weber, *The Spanish Frontier in North America* (New Haven, Conn.: Yale University Press, 1992);

Robert M. Weir, *Colonial South Carolina: A History* (Millwood, N.Y.: KTO Press, 1983);

Peter Wood, *Black Majority: Negroes in Colonial South Carolina from 1670 through the Stono Rebellion* (New York: Norton, 1974).

EDUCATION

James Axtell, *The School upon a Hill: Education and Society in Colonial New England* (New Haven, Conn.: Yale University Press, 1974);

Henry Warner Bowden, *American Indians and Christian Missions: Studies in Cultural Conflict* (Chicago: University of Chicago Press, 1981);

John Calam, *Parsons and Pedagogues: The S.P.G. Adventure in American Education* (New York: Columbia University Press, 1971);

Sheldon Cohen, *A History of Colonial Education, 1607–1776* (New York: Wiley, 1974);

Lawrence A. Cremin, *American Education: The Colonial Experience, 1607–1783* (New York: Harper & Row, 1970);

Margaret Gay Davies, *The Enforcement of English Apprenticeship: A Study in Applied Mercantilism* (Cambridge, Mass.: Harvard University Press, 1956);

Richard Beale Davis, *A Colonial Southern Bookshelf: Reading in the Eighteenth Century* (Athens: University of Georgia Press, 1979);

Marcus Wilson Jernegan, *Laboring and Dependent Classes in Colonial America, 1607–1783* (Chicago: University of Chicago Press, 1931);

William H. Kilpatrick, *The Dutch Schools of New Netherland and Colonial New York* (Washington, D.C.: U.S. Government Printing Office, 1912);

Kenneth Lockridge, *Literacy in Colonial New England* (New York: Norton, 1974);

Robert Middlekauff, *Ancients and Axioms: Secondary Education in Eighteenth-Century New England* (New Haven, Conn.: Yale University Press, 1963);

Howard Miller, *The Revolutionary College: American Presbyterian Higher Education: 1707–1837* (New York: New York University Press, 1976);

Samuel Eliot Morison, *The Founding of Harvard College* (Cambridge, Mass.: Harvard University Press, 1935);

Robert F. Seybolt, *The Evening Schools of Colonial New York City* (Albany: University of the State of New York, 1921);

Seybolt, *The Public Schools of Colonial Boston* (Cambridge, Mass.: Harvard University Press, 1935);

Margaret C. Szasz, *Indian Education in the American Colonies, 1607–1763* (Albuquerque: University of New Mexico Press, 1988).

GOVERNMENT AND POLITICS

Charles M. Andrews, *The Colonial Period of American History,* 4 volumes (New Haven, Conn.: Yale University Press, 1938);

George Louis Beer, *The Origins of the British Colonial System, 1578–1660* (New York: Peter Smith, 1933);

Ralph Paul Bieber, *The Lords of Trade and Plantations, 1675–1696* (Allentown, Pa.: H. Ray Haas, 1919);

Beverley W. Bond, *The Quit-Rent System in the American Colonies* (New Haven, Conn.: Yale University Press, 1919);

Patricia U. Bonomi, *A Factious People: Politics and Society in Colonial New York* (New York: Columbia University Press, 1971);

Timothy Breen, "Looking Out for Number One: Conflicting Cultural Values in Early Seventeenth-Century Virginia," *South Atlantic Quarterly,* 78 (1979): 342–360;

Bradley Chapin, *Criminal Justice in Colonial America, 1606–1660* (Athens: University of Georgia Press, 1983);

John J. Clarke, *A History of Local Government of the United Kingdom* (London: Jenkins, 1955);

George Dargo, *Roots of the Republic: A New Perspective on Early American Constitutionalism* (New York: Praeger, 1974);

John Demos, ed., *Remarkable Providences: Readings on Early American History,* revised edition (Boston: Northeastern University Press, 1991);

Robert J. Dinkin, *Voting in Provincial America: A Study of Elections in the Thirteen Colonies, 1689–1776* (Westport, Conn.: Greenwood Press, 1977);

Mary Maples Dunn, *William Penn: Politics and Conscience* (Princeton: Princeton University Press, 1967);

Douglas Greenberg, *Crime and Law Enforcement in the Colony of New York, 1691–1776* (Ithaca, N.Y.: Cornell University Press, 1976);

Greenberg, "Crime, Law Enforcement, and Social Control in Colonial America," *American Journal of Legal History,* 26 (1982): 293–325;

Greenberg, "Middle Colonies in Recent American Historiography," *William and Mary Quarterly,* 36 (1979): 396–427;

Jack P. Greene, *Negotiated Authorities: Essays in Colonial Political and Constitutional History* (Charlottesville: University Press of Virginia, 1994);

Greene, *Peripheries and Center: Constitutional Development in the Extended Polities of the British Empire and the United States, 1607–1788* (New York: Norton, 1990);

Greene, *The Quest for Power: The Lower Houses of Assembly in the Southern Royal Colonies, 1689–1776* (Chapel Hill: University of North Carolina Press, 1963);

Helen Kohn Hennig, *Great South Carolinians From Colonial Days to the Confederate War* (Chapel Hill: University of North Carolina Press, 1940);

Don Higginbotham, *War and Society in Revolutionary America: The Wider Dimensions of Conflict* (Columbia: University of South Carolina Press, 1988);

Charles J. Hoadly, ed., *The Public Records of the Colony of Connecticut,* volume 6 (Hartford: Press of Case, Lockwood & Brainard, 1872);

Dan M. Hockman, "Commissary William Dawson and the Anglican Church in Virginia, 1743–1752," *Historical Magazine of the Protestant Episcopal Church,* 54 (June 1985): 125–149;

Hockman, "William Dawson: Master and Second President of the College of William and Mary," *Historical Magazine of the Protestant Episcopal Church,* 52 (September 1983): 199–214;

Peter Charles Hoffer, *Law and People in Colonial America* (Baltimore: Johns Hopkins University Press, 1992);

Joseph E. Illick, *Colonial Pennsylvania: A History* (New York: Scribners, 1976);

Michael Kammen, *Colonial New York: A History* (New York: Scribners, 1975);

Stanley N. Katz, ed., *Colonial America: Essays in Politics and Social Development* (Boston: Little, Brown, 1976);

Jessica Kross, *The Evolution of an American Town: Newtown, New York, 1642–1775* (Philadelphia: Temple University Press, 1983);

Jon Kukla, "Order and Chaos in Early America: Politics and Social Stability in Pre-Restoration Virginia," *American Historical Review,* 90 (April 1985): 275–298;

Leonard Woods Labaree, *Royal Government in America: A Study of the British Colonial System Before 1783* (New York: Ungar, 1958);

Aubrey C. Land, *Colonial Maryland: A History* (Millwood, N.Y.: KTO Press, 1981);

Samuel Lucas, ed., *Charters of the Old English Colonies in America* (London: John W. Parker, 1850);

Frederic William Maitland, *Township and Borough* (Cambridge: Cambridge University Press, 1898);

Louis Morton, "The Origins of American Military Policy," *Military Affairs,* 22 (1958): 75–82;

Gary B. Nash, "The Framing of Government in Pennsylvania: Ideas in Contact with Reality," *William and Mary Quarterly,* 23 (1966): 183–209;

Curtis P. Nettels, *The Roots of American Civilization: A History of American Colonial Life* (New York: F. S. Crofts, 1945);

Edwin Powers, *Crime and Punishment in Early Massachusetts, 1620–1692: A Documentary History* (Boston: Beacon, 1966);

Richard P. Sherman, *Robert Johnson: Proprietary & Royal Governor of South Carolina* (Columbia: University of South Carolina Press, 1966);

John Shy, *A People Numerous and Armed: Reflections on the Military Struggle for American Independence* (London: Oxford University Press, 1976);

M. Eugene Sirmans, *Colonial South Carolina: A Political History, 1663–1763* (Chapel Hill: University of North Carolina Press, 1966);

Alan Tully, *William Penn's Legacy: Politics and Social Structure in Provincial Pennsylvania, 1726–1755* (Baltimore: Johns Hopkins University Press, 1977);

Carl Ubbelohde, *The American Colonies and the British Empire, 1607–1763* (New York: Crowell, 1968);

David William Voorhees, "The 'fervent Zeal' of Jacob Leisler," *William and Mary Quarterly,* 51 (July 1994): 447–472;

Robert M. Weir, *Colonial South Carolina: A History* (Millwood, N.Y.: KTO Press, 1983);

Weir, "'The Harmony We Were Famous For': An Interpretation of Pre-Revolutionary South Carolina Politics," *William and Mary Quarterly,* 26 (1969): 473–501.

LAW AND JUSTICE

Daniel J. Boorstin, *The Mysterious Science of the Law* (Boston: Beacon, 1958);

Paul Boyer and Stephen Nissenbaum, *Salem Possessed: The Social Origins of Witchcraft* (Cambridge, Mass.: Harvard University Press, 1974);

Thomas Buckley, *Church and State in Revolutionary Virginia, 1776–1787* (Charlottesville: University Press of Virginia, 1977);

Anton-Hermann Chroust, *The Rise of the Legal Profession in America, Volume I: The Colonial Experience* (Norman: University of Oklahoma Press, 1965);

Thomas Curry, *The First Freedoms: Church and State in America to the Passage of the First Amendment* (New York: Oxford University Press, 1986)

W. J. Eccles, *France in America* (New York: Harper & Row, 1972);

Charles Gibson, *Spain in America* (New York: Harper & Row, 1966);

David D. Hall, *The Antinomian Controversy, 1636–1638: A Documentary History* (Middletown, Conn.: Wesleyan University Press, 1968);

Kermit Hall, William Wiecek, and Paul Finkelman, *American Legal History: Cases and Materials* (New York: Oxford University Press, 1991);

Peter Charles Hoffer, *Law and People in Colonial America* (Baltimore: Johns Hopkins University Press, 1992);

Carol F. Karlson, *The Devil in the Shape of a Woman: Witchcraft in Colonial New England* (New York: Random House, 1987);

Alfred Hinsey Kelly, *The American Constitution: Its Origins and Development,* seventh edition (New York: Norton, 1991);

David Thomas Konig, *Law and Society in Puritan Massachusetts: Essex County, 1629–1692* (Chapel Hill: University of North Carolina Press, 1979);

Leonard W. Levy, ed., *Freedom of the Press from Zenger to Jefferson* (Indianapolis: Bobbs-Merrill, 1966);

Edgar J. McManus, *Law and Liberty in Early New England: Criminal Justice and Due Process, 1620–1692* (Amherst: University of Massachusetts Press, 1993);

Richard B. Morris, *Government and Labor in Early America* (New York: Harper & Row, 1946);

David E. Narrett, *Inheritance and Family Life in Colonial New York City* (Ithaca, N.Y.: Cornell University Press, 1992);

Edwin J. Perkins, *The Economy of Colonial America* (New York: Columbia University Press, 1980);

Marylynn Salmon, *Women and the Law of Property in Early America* (Chapel Hill: University of North Carolina Press, 1986);

Bernard Schwartz, *The Law in America* (New York: McGraw-Hill, 1974);

Alan Watson, *Slave Law in the Americas* (Athens: University of Georgia Press, 1989);

David J. Weber, *The Spanish Frontier in North America* (New Haven: Yale University Press, 1992);

Robert A. Williams Jr., *The American Indian In Western Legal Thought: The Discourses of Conquest* (New York: Oxford University Press, 1990).

LIFESTYLES, SOCIAL TRENDS, AND FASHION

Carol Berkin, *First Generations: Women in Colonial America* (New York: Hill & Wang, 1996);

Richard D. Brown, *Knowledge is Power: The Diffusion of Information in Early America* (New York: Oxford University Press, 1989);

Richard L. Bushman, *King and People in Provincial Massachusetts* (Chapel Hill: University of North Carolina Press, 1985);

Bushman, *The Refinement of America: Persons, Houses, Cities* (New York: Knopf, 1992);

William Byrd, *William Byrd's Histories of the Dividing Line Betwixt Virginia and North Carolina,* edited by Percy G. Adams (New York: Dover, 1967);

Ann Cameron, *The Kidnapped Prince: The Life of Olaudah Equiano* (New York: Knopf, 1995);

Cary Carson, Ronald Hoffman, and Peter J. Albert, eds., *Of Consuming Interests: The Style of Life in the Eighteenth Century* (Charlottesville: University Press of Virginia, 1994);

Jack Cassin-Scott, *Costume and Fashion in Colour, 1550–1760* (Poole, U.K.: Blandford, 1975);

Christopher Clark, *The Public Prints: The Newspaper in Anglo-American Culture, 1665–1740* (New York: Oxford University Press, 1994);

Hennig Cohen and Tristramm Potter Coffin, eds., *The Folklore of American Holidays* (Detroit: Gale Research, 1988);

Bruce Daniels, *Puritans at Play: Leisure and Recreation in Colonial New England* (New York: St. Martin's Press, 1995);

Natalie Zemon Davis, *Women on the Margins: Three Seventeenth-Century Lives* (Cambridge, Mass.: Harvard University Press, 1995);

Alice Morse Earle, *Costume of Colonial Times* (Detroit: Gale Research, 1974);

David Hackett Fischer, *Albion's Seed: Four British Folkways in America* (New York: Oxford University Press, 1989);

Benjamin Franklin, *The Autobiography of Benjamin Franklin,* edited by Louis P. Masur (Boston: Bedford Books, 1993);

Ramón Gutiérrez and Geneviève Fabre, *Feasts and Celebrations in North American Ethnic Communities* (Albuquerque: University of New Mexico Press, 1995);

Gutiérrez, *When Jesus Came, the Corn Mothers Went Away: Marriage, Sexuality, and Power in New Mexico, 1500–1846* (Stanford, Cal.: Stanford University Press, 1991);

David Freeman Hawke, *Everyday Life in Early America* (New York: Harper & Row, 1988);

Rhys Isaac, *The Transformation of Virginia, 1740–1790* (Chapel Hill: University of North Carolina Press, 1982);

Barry Levy, *Quakers and the American Family: British Settlement in the Delaware Valley* (New York: Oxford University Press, 1988);

Kenneth Lockridge, *The Diary, and Life, of William Byrd II of Virginia, 1674–1744* (New York: Norton, 1987);

Gerald F. Moran, *Religion, Family, and the Life Course: Exploration in the Social History of Early America* (Ann Arbor: University of Michigan Press, 1992);

Mechal Sobel, *The World They Made Together: Black and White Values in Eighteenth-Century Virginia* (Princeton: Princeton University Press, 1987);

Ann Stanford, *Anne Bradstreet: The Worldly Puritan* (New York: Burt Franklin, 1974);

Susan Struna, *People of Prowess: Sport, Leisure, and Labor in Early Anglo-America* (Urbana: University of Illinois Press, 1996);

Myron Tassin and Gaspar Stahl, *Mardi Gras and Bacchus: Something Old, Something New* (Gretna, La.: Pelican, 1984);

Dell Upton, *Common Places: Readings in American Vernacular Architecture* (Athens: University of Georgia Press, 1986);

Esmond Wright, *Franklin of Philadelphia* (Cambridge, Mass.: Belknap Press, 1986);

Louis B. Wright, *The Cultural Life of the American Colonies* (New York: Harper & Row, 1957).

NATIVE AMERICANS

Kathryn E. Holland Braund, *Deerskins and Duffels: The Creek Indian Trade with Anglo-America, 1685–1815* (Lincoln: University of Nebraska Press, 1993);

John Demos, *The Unredeemed Captive: A Family Story from Early America* (New York: Knopf, 1994);

Gregory Evans Dowd, *A Spirited Resistance: The North American Indian Struggle for Unity, 1745–1815* (Baltimore: Johns Hopkins University Press, 1992);

R. David Edmunds, *American Indian Leaders: Studies in Diversity* (Lincoln: University of Nebraska Press, 1980);

Jack D. Forbes, *Black Africans and Native Americans: Color, Race, and Caste in the Evolution of Red-Black Peoples* (London: Blackwell, 1988);

Michael D. Green, *The Politics of Indian Removal: Creek Government and Society in Crisis* (Lincoln: University of Nebraska Press, 1982);

John H. Hann, *Apalachee: The Land Between the Rivers* (Gainesville: University Presses of Florida, 1988);

Thomas Hatley, *The Dividing Paths: Cherokees and South Carolinians Through the Era of Revolution* (New York: Oxford University Press, 1993);

Charles Hudson, *The Southeastern Indians* (Knoxville: University of Tennessee Press, 1987);

Hudson and Carmen Chaves Tesser, eds., *The Forgotten Centuries: Indians and Europeans in the American South, 1521–1704* (Athens: University of Georgia Press, 1994);

Francis Jennings, *The Ambiguous Iroquois Empire: The Covenant Chain Confederation of Indian Tribes with English Colonies from its Beginnings to the Lancaster Treaty of 1744* (New York: Norton, 1984);

Jennings, *Empire of Fortune: Crowns, Colonies, and Tribes in the Seven Years' War in America* (New York: Norton, 1988);

Jennings, *The Invasion of America: Indians, Colonialism and the Cant of Conquest* (New York: Norton, 1976);

James Merrell, *The Indians' New World: Catawbas and Their Neighbors from European Contact Through the Era of Removal* (Chapel Hill: University of North Carolina Press, 1989);

Gary B. Nash, *Red, White, and Black: The Peoples of Early America,* second edition (Englewood Cliffs, N.J.: Prentice-Hall, 1982);

Daniel K. Richter, *The Ordeal of the Longhouse: The Peoples of the Iroquois League in the Era of European Colonization* (Chapel Hill: University of North Carolina Press, 1992);

Neal Salisbury, *Manitou and Providence: Indians, Europeans, and the Making of New England, 1500–1643* (Oxford: Oxford University Press, 1982);

Richard Slotkin and James K. Folson, eds., *So Dreadful a Judgment: Puritan Responses to King Philip's War, 1676–1677* (Middletown, Conn.: Wesleyan University Press, 1978);

Daniel H. Usner, *Indians, Settlers, and Slaves in a Frontier Exchange Economy: The Lower Mississippi Valley before 1783* (Chapel Hill: University of North Carolina Press, 1992);

Richard White, *The Middle Ground: Indians, Empires, and Republics in the Great Lakes Region, 1650–1815* (Cambridge: Cambridge University Press, 1991);

J. Leitch Wright, *The Only Land They Knew: The Tragic Story of the American Indians in the Old South* (New York: Free Press, 1981).

RELIGION

Sidney Ahlstron, *A Religious History of the American People,* 2 volumes (New Haven: Yale University Press, 1972);

Patricia U. Bonomi, *Under the Cope of Heaven: Religion, Society, and Politics in Colonial America* (New York: Oxford University Press, 1986);

Francis J. Bremer, *The Puritan Experiment: New England Society from Bradford to Edwards,* revised edition (Hanover, N.H.: University Press of New England, 1995);

Jon Butler, *Awash in a Sea of Faith: Christianizing the American People* (Cambridge, Mass.: Harvard University Press, 1990);

Robert G. Horbert, *A History of the Baptists* (Philadelphia: Judson Press, 1950);

James Jones, *The Shattered Synthesis: New England Puritanism Before the Great Awakening* (New Haven, Conn.: Yale University Press, 1973);

Norman H. Maring, *Baptists in New Jersey: A Study in Transition* (Valley Forge, Pa.: Judson Press, 1964);

William McLoughlin, *New England Dissent, 1630–1833: The Baptists and Separation of Church and State* (Cambridge, Mass.: Harvard University Press, 1991);

Albert J. Raboteau, *Slave Religion: The "Invisible Institution" in the Antebellum South* (New York: Oxford University Press, 1975);

Neil Salisbury, *Manitou and Providence: Indians, Europeans, and the Making of New England, 1500–1763* (New York: Oxford University Press, 1982);

Dell Upton, *Things Holy and Profane: Anglican Parish Churches in Colonial Virginia* (Cambridge, Mass.: Harvard University Press, 1987);

Alden T. Vaughan, *New England Frontier: Puritans and Indians, 1620–1676,* second edition (New York: Norton, 1979);

John F. Woolverton, *Colonial Anglicanism in North America* (Detroit: Wayne State Press, 1984);

J. William T. Youngs Jr., *God's Messengers: Religious Leadership in Colonial New England, 1700–1750* (Baltimore: Johns Hopkins University Press, 1976).

SCIENCE AND MEDICINE

Isaac Asimov, *Asimov's Chronology of Science and Discovery* (New York: Harper & Row, 1989);

Martha J. Bailey, *American Women in Science: A Biographical Dictionary* (Denver: ABC-Clio, 1994);

Otho T. Beall and Richard H. Shryock, *Cotton Mather: First Significant Figure in American Medicine* (Baltimore: Johns Hopkins University Press, 1954);

Edmund Berkeley and Dorothy Smith Berkeley, *The Life and Travels of John Bartram: From Lake Ontario to the River St. John* (Tallahassee: University Presses of Florida, 1982);

Daniel Boorstin, *The Discoverers: A History of Man's Search to Know His World and Himself* (New York: Random House, 1983);

Carl Bridenbaugh, *Cities in the Wilderness: The First Century of Urban Life in America, 1625–1742* (New York: Oxford University Press, 1938);

James H. Cassedy, *Medicine in America: A Short History* (Baltimore: Johns Hopkins University Press, 1991);

I. Bernard Cohen, *Benjamin Franklin's Science* (Cambridge, Mass.: Harvard University Press, 1990);

Cohen, *Birth of a New Physics* (New York: Norton, 1985);

Cohen, *Science and the Founding Fathers* (New York: Norton, 1995);

Helen Gere Cruickshank, ed., *John and William Bartram's America: Selections from the Writings of the Philadelphia Naturalists* (New York: Devin-Adair, 1957);

George H. Daniels, *Science in American Society: A Social History* (New York: Knopf, 1971);

George S. Fichter, *How to Build an Indian Canoe* (New York: McKay, 1977);

William H. Goetzmann and Glyndwr Williams, *The Atlas of North American Exploration* (Englewood Cliffs, N.J.: Prentice Hall, 1992);

Joseph A. Goldenberg, *Shipbuilding in Colonial America.* (Charlottesville: University Press of Virginia, 1976);

James Henretta, *The Evolution of American Society, 1700–1815* (Lexington, Mass.: D. C. Heath, 1973);

Brooke Hindle, ed., *America's Wooden Age: Aspects of its Early Technology* (Tarrytown, N.Y.: Sleepy Hollow Restorations, 1975);

Hindle, *The Pursuit of Science in Revolutionary America, 1735–1789* (Chapel Hill: University of North Carolina Press, 1956);

Thomas S. Kuhn, *The Copernican Revolution: Planetary Astronomy in the Development of Western Thought* (Cambridge, Mass.: Harvard University Press, 1957);

Paul J. Lindholdt, ed., *John Josselyn: Colonial Traveler: A Critical Edition of Two Voyages to New-England* (Hanover, N.H.: University Press of New England, 1988);

Alan I. Marcus and Howard P. Segal, *Technology in America: A Brief History* (New York: Harcourt Brace Jovanovich, 1989);

Samuel Eliot Morison, *The Great Explorers: The European Discovery of America* (New York: Oxford University Press, 1978);

Marilyn Bailey Ogilvie, *Women in Science: Antiquity through the Nineteenth Century* (Cambridge, Mass.: MIT Press, 1993);

Margaret W. Rossiter, *Women Scientists in America: Struggles and Strategies to 1940* (Baltimore: Johns Hopkins University Press, 1982);

Richard H. Shryock, *Medicine and Society in Early America, 1660–1860* (New York: New York University Press, 1960);

Julia C. Spruill, *Women's Life and Work in the Southern Colonies* (New York: Norton, 1972);

Raymond P. Stearns, *Science in the British Colonies of North America* (Urbana: University of Illinois Press, 1970);

Ian K. Steele, *The English Atlantic, 1675–1740: An Exploration of Communication and Community* (New York: Oxford University Press, 1986);

Frederick B. Tolles, *Meeting House and Counting House: The Quaker Merchants of Colonial Philadelphia, 1682–1763* (New York: Norton, 1948);

Edwin Tunis, *Colonial Craftsmen and the Beginnings of American Industry* (Cleveland: World, 1965);

Laurel Thatcher Ulrich, *Good Wives: Image and Reality in the Lives of Women in Northern New England, 1650–1750* (New York: Oxford University Press, 1980);

Ulrich, *A Midwife's Tale: The Life of Martha Ballard. Based on Her Diary, 1785–1812* (New York: Knopf, 1990);

Carl Van Doren, *Benjamin Franklin* (New York: Viking Press, 1938);

Joan Hoff Wilson, "Dancing Dogs of the Colonial Period: Women Scientists," *Early American Literature,* 7 (1973): 225–235;

Mitchell Wilson, *American Science and Invention: A Pictorial History* (New York: Simon & Schuster, 1954).

SPORTS AND RECREATION

Carl Bridenbaugh, *Cities in Revolt: Urban Life in America, 1743–1776* (New York: Knopf, 1955);

Bridenbaugh, *Cities in the Wilderness: The First Century of Urban Life in America, 1625–1742* (New York: Oxford University Press, 1971);

Bruce C. Daniels, *Puritans at Play: Leisure and Recreation in Colonial New England* (New York: St. Martin's Press, 1995);

Nancy L. Struna, *People of Prowess: Sport, Leisure, and Labor in Early Anglo-America* (Urbana: University of Illinois Press, 1996).

Contributors

THE ARTS

KAREN L. ROOD
Manly, Inc.

TIMOTHY D. HALL
Central Michigan University

BUSINESS & COMMUNICATIONS

ELIZABETH PRUDEN
Wilmington College

TIMOTHY D. HALL
Central Michigan University

COLONIAL AMERICANS

JESSICA KROSS
University of South Carolina

EDUCATION

RONALD HOWARD
Mississippi College

GOVERNMENT & POLITICS

SAMUEL C. SMITH
University of South Carolina

LAW & JUSTICE

THOMAS T. TAYLOR
Wittenberg University

LIFESTYLES, SOCIAL TRENDS,
& FASHION

TIMOTHY D. HALL
Central Michigan University

NATIVE AMERICANS

PATRICK RIORDAN
University of South Florida

RELIGION   ELIZABETH NYBAKKEN
                                        Mississippi State University

SCIENCE & MEDICINE   RUSSELL LAWSON
                                        Oklahoma School of Science and Mathematics

SPORTS & RECREATION   JESSICA KROSS
                                        University of South Carolina

GENERAL INDEX

A

Abenaki tribe   312, 316
L'Academie Royale des Sciences de Paris
   186
Academy and Charitable School of
   Philadelphia   168. 365
The Accomplished Singer (Mather)   44
*An Account of the New Invented
   Pennsylvanian Fire-Places* (Franklin)
   391
An Account of Two Voyages to New-England
   (Josselyn)   377, 403
Acoma tribe   313, 329
Acosta, José de   374, 392
Act of Religious Toleration in Maryland
   (1649)   208, 250, 362
Act of Union (1707)   114, 149
Adams, John   221
Addison, Joseph   48, 74, 186
Admiral Vernon Tavern, Boston, Mass.
   63
Admiralty Court   158, 218, 245
Advancement of Learning (Bacon)   187
Aeneid (Virgil)   65, 200
Aesop   200
African American music   71
African American oral tradition   67
African Americans   50, 67, 71, 89, 114,
   142, 145, 175, 251–252, 282, 285, 293,
   322–323
African religions   338–339, 352
Agriculture   312, 382–383, 398
Albany Congress of 1754   311
Albany, N.Y.   53, 58, 93, 105, 109,
   142–143, 161–162, 175, 194–195, 226,
   301, 308, 311, 328, 412, 417, 422
Alcoholic beverages   93–94, 101, 132, 239,
   263, 276, 281–282, 320, 322, 325, 362,
   382, 397, 399
Alexander, David, sixth Earl of Stirling
   271
Alexander, James   261–262, 271, 273
Algonquian Bible (Eliot)   39, 192–193,
   343
Algonquian language   192, 317
Algonquian tribes   98, 170, 283, 305, 313,
   375
Alice Mason (portrait)   40
Alison, Francis   336, 348, 365

Allen, Arthur   55
Allis, John   63
Allouez, Claude-Jean   377
Allyón, Lucas Vásquez de   127–128
Almanacs   50, 58, 186, 384–385, 401
Alsop, George   40, 67
Altamirano, Bishop Juan de las Cabezas
   128
"Amazing Grace" (Newton)   202
American Company   74
American Lutheran Church   368
American Philosophical Society   168, 184,
   187, 271, 379–380, 382, 401
American Revolution   114, 135, 137, 146,
   150, 159, 175, 203, 253, 255, 267, 312,
   322, 324, 327, 349, 394, 423
American Weekly Mercury   89
Ames, William   181
Amish sect   294, 354, 355
Anabaptists   143–144, 146, 294, 300
Anderson, Hugh   46, 68
Andrews, William   194–195
Androboros (Hunter)   43, 73
Andros, Sir Edmund   211, 215, 230, 236,
   245, 251
The Angel of Bethesda (Mather)   404
Anglican Church. *See* Church of England.
Anglo-Palladian style of Architecture. *See*
   Georgian architecture.
Annapolis, Md.   42, 64, 137, 179, 187, 423
Anne of England   149–150, 194, 419
Anti-itinerant legislation   336
Antinomianism   207, 254, 320, 332, 367
Apache tribe   152, 189–190, 329–330
Apalachee tribe   111, 114, 129, 188, 314,
   317
Apothecaries   383, 396, 398
Appalachian Mountains   72, 295,
   376–377, 381, 383, 392
Appeals courts   265
Apprenticeship   176–179, 193, 196–197,
   298, 387, 396
Arbella (ship)   163
Architecture   51–57
The Architecture of A. Palladio (Leoni)   57
Argall, Samuel   276, 329
Aristo, Ludovico   185
Aristotle   385
Ark (ship)   137
Arminianism   141, 183, 367–368
Art   57–64

Articles of Agreement for Springfield, Mass.
   (1636)   140
Artisans   89, 94, 125–126, 137, 145, 176,
   262, 281, 284, 286–287, 291, 301
Ascot race course   419
Ashkenazic Jews   135
Aston, Anthony   73
Astrology   351, 384
Astronomy   382–386, 401, 403–404
Auchmuty, Samuel   175
Audiencias   265
Augsburg Confession of 1530   346
Augustus Adolphus of Sweden   110
Aupaumut, Hendrick   203
Autobiography (Franklin)   397, 401
*Autos de la conquista de la Provincia de
   Coahuila* (Laiors, Bosque)   41
Avilés, Pedro Menéndez de   123, 127–128,
   228
Ayllón, Lucas Vásquez de   322
Aztecs   151, 188

B

Bacchanale (Hesselius)   61
Bacchus and Ariadne (Hesselius)   61
Backerus, Domine Johannes   171, 195
Backus, Isaac   342
Bacon, Francis   169, 186–187, 403
Bacon, Nathaniel   55, 215, 238
Bacon's Castle, Surry County, Va.   55
Bacon's Rebellion of 1676   55, 210, 215,
   238, 321
Badger, Joseph   61
Baeza, Diego de   184
Baffin, William   375
Bahamas   123, 125, 158, 188
Baja California   157
Baker, Richard   304
Bakers   92, 95, 140, 263, 305, 397
Bambara tribe   121, 131
Banjars (or Banjers)   71
Banjos   71
Baptism   174, 188–189, 300–339, 341,
   355, 358–359, 361, 371
Baptists   86, 126, 137, 155, 183, 198, 202,
   221, 253, 255, 292, 332, 337–339,
   341–342, 345, 348–349, 354, 359,
   370–371

Foster, John 40, 58, 62, 385
Fothergill, Dr. John 400
Fowle, Isaac 63
Fowler, Mary 202
Fox, George 145, 159, 362, 371
Fox hunting 412
Fox tribe 310, 312–314
Frame of Government (Penn) 211, 250, 362
Franciscans 71, 128–129, 151–152, 170, 172, 188–190, 265, 361, 364, 402
Franklin, Benjamin 44, 47, 49–50, 83, 89, 91, 146, 167–168, 183–184, 186–187, 281, 284, 347, 370, 379–384, 386, 390–391, 394–395, 397, 400–402
Franklin, James 58
Franklin College 369
Franklin stove 380, 391, 402
Franks, Abigail 417
Free will 341, 359, 366
Freedom of conscience 124, 334
Freedom of religion 118, 208, 332, 333, 338
Freedom of speech 259, 261
Freedom of the press 261–262
"Freedom of the Will" (Edwards) 336
Freeholders 210, 232, 239, 250, 284
Freeman, Bernardus 194
Freemasons 70, 279
Frelinghuysen, Theodorus 357, 360
French colonial architecture 51–53
French colonial literature 66–67
French colonial theater 73
French and Indian War (1754–1763) 128, 136, 188, 194, 311, 317
French and Indian Wars. *See* King William's War, Queen Anne's War, War of Jenkins' Ear, *and* King George's War.
French colonial law 290
French Company of the Indies 133
French Huguenots 85–86, 96, 108, 112, 118, 123, 126–127, 134–135, 144, 175, 188, 241, 245, 273, 279, 334, 338
French West Indies 174
Freneau, Philip 70
Frethorne, Richard 155
Fundamental Constitutions of Carolina 124, 135, 210–211, 250
Fundamental Orders of Connecticut 140, 208
Funerals 282, 300
Fur trade 80–81, 83, 85, 86, 93, 99–102, 105, 117, 125, 142, 148–149, 161, 171, 177, 186, 190, 192, 196, 226, 264, 267, 285–286, 303, 312–313, 315–316, 324–325, 343, 362, 398
Furnaces 94, 387
A Further Account of the Province of Pennsylvania (Penn) 41

G

Gaines, Hugh 48
Gale, Christopher 230
Galileo 169, 181, 384–385
Gambling 279, 410, 415, 420
Garden, Dr. Alexander 401
Garden, Reverend Alexander 336

Gardening 144, 418
—experimental 380, 383
Gardent, Alexander 175
Gates, Thomas 206
General Baptists 341, 345
The Generall Historie of Virginia, New England, and the Summer Isles (Smith) 160, 375
Geneva University 245
Geography 382–383, 388, 392–393
Geology 388
George I of England 43, 57, 72, 105
George II of England 168, 240
George III of England 369, 400
Georgia 83–84, 97, 104, 113, 115–117, 128–129, 131–132, 134, 136, 155, 172–173, 175, 178, 188, 193, 198, 202, 212–213, 221, 233, 235–236, 244, 251, 255, 262, 285, 289, 304, 322–323, 347, 355, 370
Georgian style architecture 57, 292
German Reformed Church 50, 115, 198, 335, 338, 354, 360, 369
Gibbs family 59
Gibson, Bishop Edmund 240
Gifford, Andrew 202
Gilbert, Claudius 68
Gist, Christopher 381
Giton, Pierre 135
Glass products 99, 287, 312, 323
Glassblowers 387
Glassworks 83, 94
Gloria Dei Church, Wicaco, Pa. 349
Godfrey, Thomas 74, 379
Godin, Benjamin 135
Godolphin Arabian (horse) 420
Gold 85, 99, 101, 117–118, 276, 312–313, 329, 388
Golf 408, 412
Gooch, Gov. William 150, 241
Good Order Established in Pennsilvania & New-Jersey (Budd) 41, 68
Gookin, Daniel 68
Gordon, Patrick 239
Gordon, Thomas 261
Gorges, Sir Ferdinando 211, 233
Gorton, Samuel 110, 141
Gosnold, Bartholomew 108, 147, 160, 374
Gothic architecture 62
Governor's Palace, Santa Fe, N.M. 38, 51
Grace Abounding to the Chief of Sinners (Bunyan) 45
Gracia Real de Santa Teresa de Mose 116, 128, 158
The Grammarian's Funeral (Tompson) 42
The Grave (Blair) 48
Gravestones 62
Gray's Inn, London 162, 272–273
Great Awakening 50, 90, 173, 183, 194–195, 202, 255, 335–336, 338–343, 347–348, 354, 356–357, 363, 365–367, 369
The Great Christian Doctrine of Original Sin Defended (Edwards) 367

Great Fire of London (1666) 57
Great Lakes tribes 325
Great Migration 110, 139, 332
Great Wagon Road 104, 119, 126, 155
Green, Joseph 45, 47, 70, 300
Green, Samuel 41, 50
Greenwood, Isaac 167–168, 379–380, 383, 385
Greenwood, John 61, 76
Gregorian Calendar 381
Grenville, Sir Richard 67
Greven, Philip 180
Griffin, Charles 193
Grimston, Edward 374
Gronovius, J. F. 400
The Grounds and Rules of Musick Explained (Walter) 44, 72
Guast, Pierre du, Comte de Monts 80, 108
Guilds 176, 177, 262
Gunpowder 286, 325, 398
Gunpowder Plot of 1605 302
Guns 316, 325, 388, 399
Gunsmiths 378, 387, 398
Gustavus Vasa (play) 73
Guy Fawkes Day 302
Gyles, John 65, 66

H

Hairstyles 280
Half Moon (ship) 108, 142
Half-Way Covenant 333, 342, 358–359, 366
Hallam, Lewis 74
Hallam, William 74
Halley's Comet 378
Hamilton, Alexander 146, 287, 292
Hamilton, Andrew 242, 261–262, 271, 273
Hammon, Jupiter 67, 70
Hammond, John 39, 67
Hancock, John 105
Hancock, Rev. John 104
Hancock, Thomas 94, 104–105
Hancock family 57
Handel, George Frideric 72
Harriot, Thomas 67
Harris, Benjamin 82, 89
Hart family 135
Hartford Colony 110, 140, 198, 249, 319
Harvard, John 181, 186
Harvard College 50, 73, 166–168, 181–183, 332, 335, 348, 359, 376–378, 380, 383, 385, 394
Hat Act of 1731 83, 99, 267
Hawley, Gideon 194
Hawthorne, Nathaniel 40, 55, 63, 72
The Sovereignty & Goodness of God (Rowlandson) 41, 43
Heaten, John 59
Heath, Sir Robert 123
Heidelberg Catechism 195
Heidelberg Reform Group 360
Henchman, Lydia 104
Hennepin, Father Louis 65, 378, 383, 393, 396, 402

Jonson, Ben 187
Josselyn, Henry 403
Josselyn, John 40, 377, 382, 403
The Journal of Major George Washington 48
"A Journey from Patapsco to Annapolis" (Lewis) 45, 70
Judges 224, 252, 260–261, 272
Judicial systems 264
Julian Calendar 381
The Junto 50, 187, 281, 379
Justices of the peace 222, 278, 298
Juvenal 200

K

Kalm, Peter 381
Kasihta 314
Kaskaskia, Ill. 113–114, 226, 130
Kay, John 325
Kay, William 241
Kean, Thomas 74
Keith, George 334, 341, 363
Kelpius, Johannes 133, 351
Kendall, George 248
Kentucky 381, 393
Kepler, Johannes 169, 384–385, 395
Kidney stones 403
Kieft, Willem 276
King, Robert 304
King George's War (1744–1748) 242, 311, 317
King Philip's War (1675–1676) 66, 68, 192, 210, 308, 318, 328, 343
King William's School, Annapolis, Md. 197
King William's War (1689–1697) 194, 309, 316
King's Chapel, Boston, Mass. 43, 62, 71–72
King's College, New York 168, 183–184, 271
Kinnersley, Ebenezer 348, 394
Kino, Father Eusebio Francisco 113, 157, 189, 378, 383, 394
Kirke, Lewis 109
Kirke, Thomas 109
Kirkland, Samuel 195
Klemm, Johann Gottlob 45–46
Klincken, Anthony 422
Kneeling to God, at Parting with Friends (Danforth) 42
Kneller, Sir Godfrey 60, 61, 76
Knight, Sarah Kemble 418
Knives 313, 317, 325
Knott, Francis 157
Knox, John 344
Kolven 408, 412
The Koran 339, 352
Kort en Klaer Ontwerp (Plockhoy) 67
Kraft, Valentine 369
Kühn, Justus Engelhardt 42, 60
Kukla, John 229

L

L'Anglois, Philip 135

La Barre, Joseph-Antoine Le Febvre de 309
Laborers 140, 146, 149, 153, 263, 284
Laclede Liguestor, Pierre de 185
Lacrosse 412
Lady Day 137
La Harpe, Bénard de 379
Lahontan, Louis-Armand de Lom d'Arce de 66
Laiors, Juan 41
Lakota tribe 170, 191
Lalemand, Charles 190
La Mothe-Fénelon, François de Salignac de 185
Land grants 109, 115, 124, 137, 150, 259, 271, 284
Land speculation 144
Langlade, Charles 311
La Peltrie, Madeline de 305
La Salle, René-Robert Cavelier, Sieur de 51, 112, 129, 152, 309, 377, 382, 402
Las Casas, Bartolomeo de 257, 265
Last Supper (Hesselius) 61
Latin 175, 369, 400
Latin grammar schools 200
Laud, William, Archbishop of Canterbury 75, 216, 344
La Vérendrye, Sieur de 380, 393
Law and justice 247–273
Lawson, John 67, 378, 382
Lawyers 252, 260–261, 263–264, 271–272
Laydon, John 276
Lead shot 286
Leah and Rachel, or The two fruitfull sisters Virginia and Mary-land (Hammond) 39, 67
Leather Apron Club 281
Leather goods 94, 298, 382, 399
Leck, IIreland 365
Lederer, John 377, 392
Lee family 57, 238, 284
Leeth, Robert 201
Leiden jar 390
Leisler, Jacob 211–212, 230–231, 244–245, 251, 265–266
Leisler, Jacob Victorian 245
Leisler's Rebellion 215, 224, 231, 259, 265. 338
Le Jeune, Paul 65–66
Le Moyne, Pierre, sieur d'Iberville 113, 227
Lenni Lenape tribe 86
Lent 301
Leoni, Giacomo 57
Léry, Chaussegros de 379
Les Voyages de la Nouvelle-France occidentale dicte Canada (Champlain) 38
Lescarbot, Marc 66, 73, 185, 375
Levy, Barry 172
Lewis, Richard 45, 70
Libel laws 261
Libraries 64, 126
Library Company of Philadelphia 64, 167, 187
Licensing Act 89
Life expectancy 138
Lighthouse, Little Brewster Island, Boston Harbor 83

Lightning 390, 394
Lightning rods 381, 382, 391, 394, 402
Lily, William 200
Limners 57–58
l'Incarnation, Marie de 305
Lining, Dr. John 397
Lining out 71
Linnaean system of plant classification 398, 401
Linnaeus, Carolus 381, 395, 400–401
Literacy rates 64, 166, 168
Literature 64–71
"Little Admiral" statue 63
Livingston, John 105
Livingston, Robert 98, 105
Livingston, William 47, 70, 184
Locke, John 90, 124, 135, 169, 180, 182, 184, 186, 210, 261, 366–367
Loe, Thomas 159
Log cabins 53, 292
Log College 357, 365
Logan, James 46, 70, 187, 273, 381, 383, 385, 400
London Company 147, 206, 233
Long Island, N.Y. 53–54, 110, 143–144, 172, 194, 202, 280, 287
Long Island Presbytery 202
Longer and Shorter Catechism 333, 345
Loockermans, Anna 161
Lopez, Moses 135
Lords of Trade. *See* Board of Trade.
Lotteries 281
Louis XIV of France 112, 134, 174, 227, 241, 245, 264, 334, 338
Louisiana Territory 51, 66–67, 71, 73, 84, 115, 118, 120–121, 129–130, 152, 172, 174, 188, 196, 226–227, 310, 325, 379, 381, 393, 402, 416
Lovick, John 230
Lucas, Eliza 103, 105, 106
Lucas, Lt. Col. George 105
Lumber 101, 119, 125, 133, 267, 285–286, 291, 389
Luna y Arellano, Tristán de 127
Luther, Martin 169, 186, 346, 349
Lutherans 50, 86, 115, 133, 134, 143, 146, 198, 254, 334, 336, 338, 346, 349, 353–354, 368–369
Lucyck, Aegidius 186, 196

M

M. T. Cicero's Cato Major (Logan) 46, 70
Machiavelli, Niccolò 160
Madagascar 144
Magic 350, 352–353
Magistrates 222, 226, 288, 370
Magistri 244–245
Magna Carta 229
Magnalia Christi Americana (Mather) 42, 68
Mahican (Mohican) tribe 203, 308, 312
Maine 72, 110, 118, 140, 147, 208, 210–211, 233, 325, 374, 403
Maize 86, 102, 296, 312, 324, 399
Makemie, Francis 335, 356

Malaguetta (Pepper) Coast   121
Malaria   155, 296, 383, 396–397
La Malinche   291
Mallet, Paul   380, 393
Mallet, Pierre   380, 393
Maltravers, Henry, Lord   123
Mance, Jeanne   110
Mandingo tribe   121
Manhattan Island   80, 109, 142–143, 170, 419
Manorial courts   259
Manorial system   221–222
Manufactured goods   94, 286
A Map of Virginia (Smith)   375, 388
Maple syrup   389–390, 399
Mapp of Virginia (Farrer)   376, 392
Maps   117, 160, 381–382, 393–394
Marbury, Francis   367
Marcus Aurelius   160
Mariner's quadrant   379
Marquette, Jacques   65, 112, 129, 191, 361, 377, 382–383, 393
Marriage   255, 278–281, 290, 292, 296–298, 403
Marshall, John   264
Martial law   155, 206
Martin, Claude   305
Maryland   70–71, 80–81, 97–98, 102, 110, 118–119, 131–132, 136–137, 144, 146, 155–156, 159, 170–172, 178, 197, 201, 207–208, 214–215, 221, 233–234, 237, 248, 254, 260, 263–264, 269, 271–273, 280, 283, 294–295, 298, 321, 332–333, 337–338, 340–341, 361, 381, 400, 419
The Maryland Muse (Cook)   45
Mason, Capt. John   193, 207, 320
Masons   95, 125, 281. *See also* Freemasons.
Massachusetts Bay   50, 55, 67–68, 72, 75, 81, 85, 89, 94, 100, 110, 112, 114, 118–119, 131–132, 139–141, 149, 153, 163, 166, 171–172, 178, 181, 187, 192–193, 197–198, 200, 207–208, 210–211, 214–218, 225–226, 235–236, 239, 245, 249, 253–255, 258–260, 262–263, 265, 268–270, 276–280, 282–283, 285–286, 288–289, 294, 300–301, 319–320, 328, 332–333, 337, 341–342, 345, 348, 358–359, 370–371, 374–375, 385, 408, 412, 416, 421
Massachusetts Bay Company   97, 109, 138, 162, 207, 233, 260
Massachusetts Body of Liberties   208
Massachusetts General Court   81, 138, 166, 197, 207–208, 249, 254, 276–277, 282, 368
Massasoit   148, 328
Masse, Ennemond   190
Masts   267, 399
Masyck, Isaac   135
Mathematics   395, 404
Mather, Cotton   41–44, 50, 58, 68, 70–71, 90, 166, 175, 187, 193, 289, 352, 378–379, 383, 386, 394–395, 397–398, 403–404
Mather, Increase   40–41, 58, 66, 68, 166–167, 378, 385, 403
Mather, Katherine   398
Mather, Nathaniel   378

Mather, Richard   40, 58–59, 68–69
Matlack, Timothy   423
May, Cornelis Jacobsen   226
May Day   301–302
Mayflower   138, 148, 160, 206, 248, 345
Mayflower Compact   148, 206, 222, 248, 260
Mayhew, Thomas   192, 343
Measles   86, 308, 325, 397, 404
Meat Out of the Eater (Wigglesworth)   40–44, 69
Medical Society of Boston   380
Medicine   382–383, 396–404
Meetinghouses   55, 300, 363
Megapolensis, Johannes   192
Memeskia   327, 328
Memoirs of Odd Adventures, Strange Deliverances, etc., in the Captivity of John Gyles, Esq. (Gyles)   66
Memorable Providences, Relating to Witchcrafts and Possessions (Mather)   41
Men's Musical Society of Boston   45, 72
Mendizabal, Bernardo Lopez de   184
Mendoza Grajales, Francisco López de   129
Menéndez, Francisco   128, 158
Mennonites   113, 118, 143, 146, 294, 354–355
Merchants   80, 82, 89–90, 94, 100–101, 105, 117, 135, 145, 230, 238, 244–245, 254, 263–264, 281, 285, 342, 412
Mestizos   170, 176, 197, 269, 288
Metacom (King Philip)   192, 210, 308, 318–319, 320, 328, 343
Metal products   286-287, 312–313, 315, 324, 343
Metamorphoses (Ovid)   70, 200
Metaphysical poets   70
Methodists   146, 304, 339, 370
Mettawan, John   194
Mexico   65, 117, 119, 123, 128, 151, 157, 170, 172, 176, 189, 309, 312–313, 316, 323, 364, 374
Mexico City   104, 126, 151, 157, 170, 176, 180, 185, 227
Mezzotint engravings   44, 58
Miami tribe   311, 313, 327, 328, 402
Michaelius, Johannes   171, 192
Mickva Israel synagogue, Savannah, Ga.   136
Micmac tribe   311–312
Middle passage   100, 122
Midwives   92, 291–292, 368, 383, 398
Milborne, Jacob   266
Mills, Mary   156
Mills   94, 375, 387–389, 390, 398,

Milner, Solomon   62
Milton, John   169, 182, 186, 261
Mingo tribe   324
Mint, Simsbury, Conn.   83
Minuit, Peter   80
Mission de la Sainte Famille, Cahokia, Ill.   113
Missionaries   46, 49, 51, 65, 71, 84, 96, 118, 128–129, 131, 151–152, 157, 175, 188–189, 190, 194–195, 202, 227, 244, 257, 305, 313–314, 322, 327–328, 334, 339, 341, 343, 349, 353, 402

Missions   110, 113–114, 128–129, 151–152, 157, 188, 190, 192–193, 292, 313, 361
Mitchell, Dr. John   396
Mithridate (Racine)   181
"A Modell of Christian Charity" (Winthrop)   163
Mohawk Book of Common Prayer   195, 327
Mohawk Gospel of Mark   327
Mohawk tribe   66, 192, 194–195, 313, 317, 319, 327
Mohegan tribe   193, 202–203, 320, 327
Molasses   83, 94, 104–105, 267, 286
Molasses Act (1733)   83
Molière   185
Monat, William   282
Montagnais tribe   190, 313
Montague, Dr. Johannes de la   186
Montague, William   419
Montaigne, Michel Eyquem de   185
Montauk tribe   194, 202-203
Montero, Father Sebastian   129
Montesinos, Friar Antonio de   257
Montiano, Manuel de   128, 158
Montigny, Bishop François Laval de   196
Montigny, Dumont de   67
A Monumental Memorial of Marine Mercy (Steere)   41
Moor, Joshua   198
Moore, James   114, 128, 129, 314
Moore, Thoroughgood   194
Moor's Charity School   194
Moraley, William   415
Moravians   43, 72, 115–116, 118, 133–134, 146, 175, 193–194, 198, 262, 336, 348, 350, 354–355, 369
More, Col. Joshua   194
More, Samuel   63
Moros y Cristianos (drama)   73
Mortality rates   85, 95, 100, 140, 153, 155, 397
Morton, Charles   378, 383, 385
Morton, Nathaniel   40, 68
Morton, Thomas   38, 72, 302
Mosaic Decalogue (Ten Commandments)   208
Mosaic Law   140
Mose Creek   128
Moses, His Judicials (Cotton)   249
Moslems   117, 119, 121, 256
Mount Regale Fishing Company   415
Mount Washington, N.H.   376–377, 403
Mr John Freake (portrait)   40
Mrs Elizabeth Freake and Baby Mary (portrait)   40
Muhlenberg, Henry Melchior   198, 336, 350, 368–369, 417–418
Mulattoes   170, 176, 197, 269
Mumford, Samuel   287
Munday, Richard   57
Murray, Walter   74
Musgrove, Mary   132
Musgrove, Robert   132
Music   39, 43–48, 50, 71–73
Muskogean tribes   191
Muskogean language   317

N

Index of Photographs